Thinking
About
Schools

Thinking
About
Schools

A FOUNDATIONS OF
EDUCATION READER

EDITED BY

ELEANOR BLAIR HILTY

**WESTVIEW
PRESS**

A Member of the Perseus Books Group

Westview Press was founded in 1975 in Boulder, Colorado, by notable publisher and intellectual Fred Praeger. Westview Press continues to publish scholarly titles and high-quality undergraduate- and graduate-level textbooks in core social science disciplines. With books developed, written, and edited with the needs of serious nonfiction readers, professors, and students in mind, Westview Press honors its long history of publishing books that matter.

Find us on the World Wide Web at www.westviewpress.com.

Every effort has been made to secure required permissions to use all text and art included in this volume.

Westview Press books are available at special discounts for bulk purchases in the United States by corporations, institutions, and other organizations. For more information, please contact the Special Markets Department at the Perseus Books Group, 2300 Chestnut Street, Suite 200, Philadelphia, PA 19103, or call (800) 810-4145, ext. 5000, or e-mail special.markets@perseusbooks.com.

Designed by Trish Wilkinson
Set in 10.5 point Adobe Garamond Pro

A CIP Catalog record is available from the Library of Congress.
ISBN: 978-0-8133-4490-4
E-book ISBN: 978-0-8133-4519-2

10 9 8 7 6 5 4 3 2 1

To Taylor and Leonard—
the greatest loves of my life. Your loyalty and support have
sustained me through many storms.

And, to Richard Wisneiwski and Clinton B. Allison—
my greatest teachers.
Your influence on my "thinking about schools"
is immeasurable. Thank you.

 Contents

Preface   *xi*

Introduction: The Questions That Guide Our Practice   *xiii*
    Eleanor Blair Hilty

PART I
WHAT ARE THE AIMS AND PURPOSES OF EDUCATION?

Part I Introduction   3

  1 **Carl F. Kaestle**   7
    Conflict and Consensus Revisited:
    Notes Toward a Reinterpretation of American Educational History

  2 **Donald R. Warren**   13
    A Past for the Present: History, Education, and Public Policy

  3 **E. D. Hirsch, Jr.**   29
    Intellectual Capital: A Civil Right

  4 **Larry Cuban and David Tyack**   59
    Learning from the Past

  5 **John I. Goodlad**   69
    We Want It All

Part I Additional Resources
  Discussion Questions   93
  Guide to Further Reading   93
  Related Resources   94

PART II
WHAT SHOULD BE THE CONTENT OF THE CURRICULUM?

Part II Introduction   97

  6 **William Ayers**   99
    The Shifting Ground of Curriculum Thought and Everyday Practice

7 **Gloria Ladson-Billings**   107
But That's Just Good Teaching!
The Case for Culturally Relevant Pedagogy

8 **Paulo Freire**   117
The Banking Concept of Education

9 **Michael W. Apple**   129
Markets, Standards, God, and Inequality

10 **Lisa D. Delpit**   157
The Silenced Dialogue:
Power and Pedagogy in Educating Other People's Children

Part II Additional Resources
Discussion Questions   177
Guide to Further Reading   177
Related Resources   178

PART III
WHAT ARE THE ROLES AND RESPONSIBILITIES OF TEACHER LEADERS?

Part III Introduction   181

11 **Henry A. Giroux**   183
Teachers as Transformative Intellectuals

12 **Phillip C. Schlechty**   191
On the Frontier of School Reform with
Trailblazers, Pioneers, and Settlers

13 **Linda Lambert**   201
How to Build Leadership Capacity

14 **Marilyn Cochran-Smith**   205
Against the Grain

15 **Joe L. Kincheloe**   227
What Are We Doing Here? Building a Framework for Teaching

Part III Additional Resources
Discussion Questions   249
Guide to Further Reading   249
Related Resources   250

PART IV
WHAT ARE THE ROLES AND RESPONSIBILITIES OF STUDENTS?

Part IV Introduction   253

16   Harry F. Wolcott   255
Adequate Schools and Inadequate Education:
The Life History of a Sneaky Kid

17   James T. Sears   283
Educators, Homosexuality, and Homosexual Students:
Are Personal Feelings Related to Professional Beliefs?

18   Barry M. Franklin   323
At-Risk Children and the Common School Ideal

19   Michelle Fine   337
Silencing and Nurturing Voice in an Improbable Context:
Urban Adolescents in Public School

20   George Wood   357
Standing for Students, Standing for Change

Part IV Additional Resources
Discussion Questions   361
Guide to Further Reading   361
Related Resources   362

PART V
WHAT ARE THE ISSUES THAT IMPACT TWENTY-FIRST-CENTURY SCHOOLS?

Part V Introduction   365

21   K. B. Rogers   367
Grouping the Gifted and Talented: Questions and Answers

22   Frank Smith   379
Let's Declare Education a Disaster and Get On with Our Lives

23   Eleanor Blair Hilty   389
The Professionally Challenged Teacher:
Teachers Talk About School Failure

24   Linda McNeil   411
The Educational Costs of Standardization

25 **Linda Darling-Hammond**   419
    From "Separate but Equal" to "No Child Left Behind":
    The Collision of New Standards and Old Inequalities

26 **Carol Corbett Burris and Kevin G. Welner**   439
    Closing the Achievement Gap by Detracking

27 **Jonathan Kozol**   445
    Still Separate, Still Unequal: America's Educational Apartheid

28 **Beverly Daniel Tatum**   465
    Talking About Race, Learning About Racism:
    The Application of Racial Identity Development
    Theory in the Classroom

29 **Mary Jean Ronan Herzog**   491
    Come and Listen to a Story:
    Understanding the Appalachian Hillbilly in Popular Culture

30 **Allan Collins and Richard Halverson**   503
    Rethinking Education in a Technological World

Part V Additional Resources
    Discussion Questions   519
    Guide to Further Reading   519
    Related Resources   520

About the Editor and Contributors   *521*
Credits   *527*
Index   *531*

 Preface

I started school in 1960. I attended a typical large, urban school in Memphis, Tennessee. The school, Sherwood Elementary, was a concrete fortress that resembled a prison more than a place for young children to come to be educated. One of my earliest memories of school has to do with a comment on the back of my first grade report card; I still have that report card in a frame in my office. My teacher wrote the following: "Eleanor Jane never smiles." When my parents questioned me about this phenomenon, I replied that "there is nothing to smile about at school." Through the years, my sentiments about school did not change. I found schools to be generally unchallenging, boring, and staffed with people who seemed more intent on enforcing rules than actually teaching. Of course there were exceptions, but those wonderful people stood out as different from the others, not the norm. I hated school; my grades were mediocre, and I dreamed of the day when I would finally be free from the shackles of schooling and education.

Of course there is a bit of irony in the fact that I have spent the larger part of my life in schools: working in schools; talking about schools; and, yes, thinking about schools every day for most of my adult life. I often talk to students about why they want to become teachers. There always seem to be two groups of individuals in my classes: those who loved school and want to be just like the teachers who inspired them, and those who hated school and believe they can do a better job of creating schools that are filled with joy and excitement about teaching and learning. Interestingly, throughout both of these groups are poignant stories of good and bad teachers who will never be forgotten. The preceding exercise, I hope, helps students begin to think about how prior experiences influence their values and beliefs about teaching and learning in powerful ways. Do we attempt to imitate and become the teachers whom we loved and admired? Or do we counter unfortunate experiences by becoming the exact opposite of those teachers whom we despised? Challenging students to consider where they have been educationally and where they want to go in the future is an important part, I believe, of making the successful transition from student "behind the desk" to teacher "in front of the classroom," a transition that must be filled with critical inquiry, dialogue, and a consideration of teaching and learning from multiple perspectives. In the final analysis, however, it is up to each individual to think about who he or she will be as a teacher and what experiences will one day be woven into the rich tapestry of her or his professional life.

So here I am trying to change the world by teaching teachers. I have never regretted going into education; I am just as passionate now about schools and learning as I was thirty years ago when I began teaching. The only difference today is my unwavering commitment to equity and justice in schools and classrooms, a commitment to what I believe is not negotiable but rather, the only right and moral thing to do. Teachers do change lives. I believe that under the right circumstances, schools can be exciting places in which a love of learning can be nurtured and minds can be opened to possibilities never before imagined. But I am painfully aware that schools can also be places in which children are denied access to opportunities, knowledge, and resources that are prerequisite to even basic notions regarding a good education. I believe that teachers do have the power to change the world, one student at a time, and I am hopeful that some of the ideas in this book will help students to better understand where we have been and where we must go in the future if we are to achieve our goals for better teachers and schools in America.

—*Eleanor Blair Hilty*

Introduction
The Questions That Guide Our Practice

One of the problems plaguing our efforts to reform or re-vision schools and education is the fact that everyone is an "expert" on education. Most people have spent significant amounts of time sitting in classrooms and participating in educational efforts; thus, they believe that they are qualified to make suggestions and judgments about what constitutes a good education. Few people would suggest to a doctor that he or she should do things the way they used to be done ten or twenty years ago; however, I frequently hear the suggestion that schools should revert to the practices of an earlier generation. Defining good education within the context of past practices fails to acknowledge a contemporary reality that is quite different from previous eras. We live in a global, multicultural world in which students are exposed to ideas that extend beyond the traditional classroom in a typical school. It is imperative that we spend more time defining the problems of today before we begin to articulate and propose solutions that will have a lasting impact on contemporary students. If we don't ask the right questions, we won't get the right answers, and we won't ever ask the right questions if we don't spend significant amounts of time participating in attempts to understand and define the problems that we face from multiple perspectives. There are no easy answers, no easy solutions to the problems that plague our schools.

George and Louise Spindler (2000), educational anthropologists, suggested many years ago that it was important for us "to make the familiar strange, and the strange familiar." Too often our thinking about the schools is blurred by the familiarity that we all bring to school settings. American schools are unique in many ways, but we seldom step out of our comfort zones to examine how strange some of our practices may be when compared with those of schools in other parts of the world. By the same token, we often look at nontraditional or alternative educational approaches as too strange or not appropriate for American schools that are based on earlier models of good schools and good teaching. The chasm created by these misguided perceptions prevents us from considering multiple models of teaching and learning that might better meet the needs of a rapidly changing student population, a group that increasingly doesn't look or act in a way that is familiar to traditional educators.

Most of today's educators would agree that traditional approaches to teaching and learning are not working for a large number of twenty-first-century students. Communities, families, and students have changed, and we are not meeting their most basic educational needs. Rather than simply defining our problems as student problems, we need to acknowledge that many of the issues that we face today are school problems associated with the organization and delivery of educational programs that are ineffective in meeting student needs. Schools must respond to the needs of the students we serve. If we are not meeting student needs, we are not doing our jobs! A static model of schooling that isn't responsive to changing societal norms will not endure. Educators must be prepared to look at fluid, dynamic models of schooling that challenge us "to make the familiar strange, and the strange familiar." Schools need to be places in which both students and teachers are encouraged "to think outside the box" when thinking about teaching and learning. I hope the ideas presented in this book will generate sufficient "cognitive dissonance" to cause students to begin the process of asking hard questions about schools and refusing to accept easy answers.

Over the years, as I have talked to preservice and in-service teachers, I have asked them to consider that the questions we ask about teaching and learning revolve around basic concerns regarding how and why we do the things that we do in schools. For all teachers, but particularly novice teachers, a consideration of these basic questions is essential to thinking about schools in new and innovative ways and shaping practices that are consistent with the values and beliefs that we bring to schools and classrooms. This book is organized around four basic questions:

1. What are the aims and purposes of education?
2. What should be the content of the curriculum?
3. What are the roles and responsibilities of teacher leaders?
4. What are the roles and responsibilities of students?
5. What are the issues that impact twenty-first-century schools?

Notions about effective schools will depend on how we answer these questions. By necessity, the answers will vary by individual because they reflect the personal values, beliefs, and experiences that shape how a person views schools and classrooms and, most importantly, the needs of children. However, many teachers will feel that their answers to these questions are also often shaped by the rules and regulations of the school districts where they work. Either way, it is important that each of us have a vision of where we want to go before we can begin to formulate a "map" that will guide our progress. Paulo Freire (2007) wrote in *Pedagogy of the Oppressed*, "Education either functions as an instrument which is used to facilitate integration of the younger generation into the logic of the present system and bring about conformity or it becomes the practice of freedom, the means by which men and women deal critically and creatively with reality and discover how to participate in the transformation of their world." The consistency between each person's answers to my four questions and her or his educational practices is paramount in importance. Educators must strive to create a vision of good schools that will inform their professional practices in new and innovative ways. The readings selected for each section of this book will challenge students to consider the ways in which they answer each of the four questions that guide the book's organization. There are no right or wrong answers, but it is important that we consider the values and beliefs that are reflected in the responses to each of these questions, and ultimately, the long-term consequences of these answers for the schools and classrooms in which teachers do their work.

REFERENCES

Freire, P. 2007. *Pedagogy of the Oppressed*, 3rd ed. New York: The Continuum International Publishing Group.

Spindler, G., and L. Spindler. 2000. *Fifty Years of Anthropology and Education: 1950–2000: A Spindler Anthology*. New York: Routledge.

Part I

WHAT ARE THE AIMS AND PURPOSES OF EDUCATION?

Introduction

When considering the aims and purposes of education, we have to ask ourselves to think about our beliefs regarding the reasons that we have schools. Most educational philosophers would argue that educational purposes fall into four major categories:

1. Intellectual
2. Economic
3. Social
4. Political

Through the years I have regularly asked students to rank these purposes by level or degree of importance. Over a period of twenty years, attempts by students to rank these purposes have shifted according to the sociopolitical forces that shape notions about the aims and purposes of education. For example during the 1980s, everyone talked about teaching "the basics"; we were never clear about identifying who wanted only the basics in education, but it seemed that teaching a basic education, or focusing on "core knowledge," would be the answer to what we perceived as the shortcomings of our educational system. Of course, simultaneously, we were also concerned with preparing students for economic survival, and job preparation was quietly accepted as a responsibility of successful schools. The increased reliance on standardized tests facilitated the role of the schools in the "tracking" and "sorting" of students into ready-made programs that catered to the "special" needs of various groups of students. In the 1990s, high-stakes testing became "the great equalizer," a political tool used to propagate the fantasy that low test scores were the real problems in the schools and that resources needed to be marshaled for the purpose of increasing test scores for *all* children. This kind of solution, however, ignored the more complex reasons that students fail to succeed in school; for those willing to ask the hard questions, it became more difficult to focus on substantive issues and problems that would not be solved with a quick fix, or "Band-Aid" solution.

Increasingly, we have to ask ourselves what we really know about the skills and knowledge needed by all students. Is it really possible to predict the destiny of every student? What constitutes a basic education? And, finally, is a basic education good enough for everyone? Few parents ask for only the minimum when thinking about the education that they desire for their children, yet only a few privileged parents have the opportunity to select a program that includes much more than a basic education guided by standardized test scores.

Important among educational purposes are the social purposes of education—the amelioration of social problems. Public schools have always played a role in solving the issues that are perceived as threats to the order and progress of society. In the latter part of the twentieth century, we saw schools take responsibility for addressing a variety of social ills. Didn't we try to address inequity and racism through the desegregation of schools? Weren't many of our early-childhood education programs designed to meet the needs of children from less advantaged homes? Didn't our concern with equality of educational opportunity lead us to consider the "special" education needs of "exceptional" children? How many college students today remember a time when the schools didn't have free breakfast and lunch programs and after-school activities as a regular part of the school day? Twentieth-century schools were expected to change in response to the needs of society, the needs of changing communities and families. However, twenty-first-century schools have brought into the picture a new set of problems.

Once again, the schools will be the site where social issues and concerns intersect with educational aims and purposes. Finally, schools are political. In fact, teachers are political. Teaching and learning inevitably favor some students and leave others struggling to find their way. In earlier times, we were quite explicit that schools were founded to support the needs of a democratic nation. We needed an educated citizenry to understand the issues and participate in the political process that would elect officials who would represent the voice of the largest number of American people. Have we lost sight of these lofty goals? How many truly under-stand that we have already debated and attempted to resolve the issues concerning whose best interests are served by making sure that *all* students are educated?

Our future as a country is dependent on the support of public schools in which access to knowledge is *not* differentiated and affected by one's membership in a particular group. The race of life should not begin at birth; rather, there is a moral imperative for educators to ensure that the circumstances of one's birth should not be the largest factor influencing one's opportunities to successfully learn and eventually have choices regarding future roles and responsibilities in life. In this book, I refer to ideas associated with a commitment to the ideals of social justice. Oakes and Lipton (2006) define a socially just education as follows: "It considers the values and politics that pervade education, as well as the more technical issues of teaching and organizing schools; it asks critical questions about how conventional thinking and practice came to be, and who in society benefits from them; and it pays particular attention to inequalities associated with race, social class, language, gender, and other social categories, and looks for alternatives to the inequalities." These ideas emphasize the social and political aims and purposes of education and also highlight the importance of ongoing dialogue and debate about the appropriate roles and responsibilities of schools in a democratic nation.

So yes, questions regarding aims and purposes are critical to a consideration of American schools. The reconciliation of the American dream with reality is an ongoing effort. In Part I of this book, five authors consider how American public education came to be the way it is today.

Education students often shun discussions about the history of education, yet I continue to believe that we must understand the thinking about why we have public schools before we can begin to consider how to make them function the way in which we intended them to work. Chapter 1 by Carl Kaestle and Chapter 2 by Donald Warren deliver a "painless" consideration of the history of American schools. Chapters 3–5 by E. D. Hirsch, Jr.; Larry Cuban and David Tyack; and John Goodlad encourage readers to think about the intersection of knowledge, history, and school reform within the context of discussions regarding the aims and purposes of education. After reading these chapters, students will have a better sense of how the past informs the present and how questions regarding who is served best by the schools tell us everything about the goals and aspirations of present-day schools in America.

—————

Carl F. Kaestle

CHAPTER 1

Conflict and Consensus Revisited

Notes Toward a Reinterpretation
of American Educational History

Ellwood P. Cubberley was the most fa-mous educational historian of the lauda-tory tradition that prevailed in America until the 1950s. According to Cubberley, the American public school emerged from seven great battles in the early nineteenth century. The war for public schooling fea-tured "the battle for tax support," "the battle to establish state supervision," "the battle to eliminate sectarianism," and oth-ers.[1] The "bitter discussion of a public question forced an alignment of the people for or against" public schools. Aligned with the Good Guys were "philanthropists and humanitarians," "the intelligent working-men in cities," "Calvinists," and "New En-gland men." Obstructing Providence were "the old aristocratic class," "Lutherans and Quakers," "Southern men," "the non-English-speaking classes," and other oppo-nents of public schools.[2] In Cubberley's view, dubbed "Whiggish" by recent critics, historical conflict consisted of the progres-sive victories of the forces of democracy and modernity, whose eventual triumph over self-interested, mean-spirited, or mis-led opponents was inevitable.

Within this framework, Cubberley con-structed much good institutional history. The framework itself, however, far out-lived its usefulness. Increasingly it ap-peared to fit neither the available evidence nor historians' understanding of America's ideological development.[3] The recent his-toriography of American education has witnessed two attempts to end the celebra-tion of school reformers as triumphant gladiators; both address the role of social conflict in the creation of public schools.

The first group of historians, relying on the insights of the so-called consensus historians of the 1950s, argued that the conflict was chimerical, that most Ameri-cans were not divided on the issue of free public education, and that "die-hard con-servatives" were impotent in the American context. Reacting against this consensus view, some recent historians have reasserted conflict, this time the conflict between an anxious and self-serving elite attempting to ensure social stability and the working class upon whom public schooling was im-posed. This account turns Cubberley's nor-mative world upon its head. These two attempted revisions have established the terms for much current debate about our educational history.

Asserting that America had never known any true radicals or classical conservatives, the consensus historians pointed out the conservatism of the Jeffersonians, the republicanism of the Federalists, the nostalgia of the Jacksonians, and the egalitarianism of the Whigs.[4] Applying this theory of liberal consensus to educational development, Rush Welter charted the democratization of educational theory in America. Welter portrayed American educators as opting for "anarchy with a schoolmaster," for schools that would create harmony and unity in an otherwise loosely governed nation. "In spite of obvious disagreements, workingmen and Democrats, Whigs and educational reformers established universal public education as the indispensable institution of the American democracy."[5] Similarly, Jonathan Messerli noted the lack of controversy in local Massachusetts school reports and claimed that they reflected not "class conflict, but something closer to collective confusion, . . . a plurality of interests and a mixture of loyalties, institutionalized in an open society through compromise and experimentation."[6] By "collective confusion" Messerli seems to have meant that problems concerning local schooling were pragmatic, not principled, and that the solutions were short-term adjustments arranged in the context of a widely shared perception of the legitimacy and necessity of an increased role for schooling in antebellum Massachusetts. It is "the story of groups and individuals devising provisional solutions for immediate and commonplace problems. . . . The element of controversy is almost totally absent."[7]

Even at the time of its inception, the consensus view was criticized as partial and normatively conservative.[8] By the end of the turbulent 1960s, many historians found little appeal in the concepts of American pragmatism, consensus, and an open soci-

ety. Criticizing Messerli and others, Michael Katz wrote that the "consensus viewpoint applied to education is no more satisfactory than the older conflict version." For Katz, "the estrangement between the culture of the school and the working-class community" became the central focus of educational history:[9] school reformers, in the interest of the middle class and a stable industrial society, imposed public education upon an ill-served and often reluctant working class.

Both the consensus and the class-conflict interpretations of educational history are reductionist. They each assert as the essence of educational development only one aspect of a complex process. Moreover, each version misses evidence that would bolster its particular emphasis. For example, the consensus view not only underemphasizes conflict but also, in my view, neglects evidence that would illustrate more precisely what elements of consensus about the desirability of schooling did exist. Likewise, the class-conflict interpretation not only underestimates consensus but also, I believe, fails to provide a complete enough view of different types of conflict over the control and content of schooling. Brief examples will illustrate these criticisms.

Messerli, focusing on the lack of conflict in the Massachusetts local school reports, was not very critical of his sources. Local reports were written not by parents or by district school committees but by town-wide committees. Because these committees tended to act and speak as the local agents of centralization and modernization, their reports often mimicked the statements of Horace Mann and his successor. Historians who want to find evidence of political and economic conflict over common schooling should seek additional sources.

Messerli explained school reform as being impelled by a virtually unanimous sense of impending social disruption due to the failure of parental socialization and low school attendance. This argument now appears wrong on two counts, one related to the existence of conflict and one to the breadth of consensus. First, parents did not acquiesce in the verdict of their own failure. Even in the school-committee reports there is much evidence of conflict between parents and the schools, and this conflict is apparent—though downplayed—in Messerli's essay. In fact, the relationship between family and school seems to have been fraught with conflict, centering largely on control. The reports abound in complaints about parents who sided with their children against teachers and failed to defer to the school's authority.[10] Second, school attendance was not "low"; recent research shows high enrollment rates prior to the reforms of the 1840s, particularly in rural areas.[11]

The consensus theme is appropriate to the creation of public school systems in two different ways. First, among American elites (except in the South), there was almost no opposition to the provision of mass education.[12] Second, at the popular level, parents during the early nineteenth century voted with their children's feet to demonstrate their commitment to school attendance. But as schooling became more state-supported and state-regulated, more centralized and standardized, with more types and levels of schools added, conflicts erupted in many directions, belying the rosy consensus version. Katz seized upon these conflicts, viewing them through the lens of class structure. One

weakness of his *Irony of Early School Reform* is that it ignores the pervasive elements of consensus I have just cited. Another is that it interprets all conflict as class conflict. Indeed, Katz's case studies of Beverly and Groton (particularly the latter) are more plausibly explained as examples of conflicts between sections of the towns (near-far, new-old) than as examples of clashes between occupational groups. The data presented make only an equivocal case for class conflict. This is true even though the Beverly and Groton debates were about high schools, which, because their clients were disproportionately middle-class, most logically should have elicited controversy along class lines.

Despite the obvious importance of socioeconomic status as one variable in educational development, the evidence I have seen suggests that historians have been involved in a Procrustean effort to view as class-based conflicts that are ethnic, religious, geographical, generational, and institutional—all of which may or may not be related to class. We will open up our history to a richness of conflict interpretations when we stop worrying so much about whether each instance bolsters a class theorem. The work of Ralf Dahrendorf is suggestive on this point. He described as "pluralistic" a society in which conflict on some matters—for example, church-state matters—does not coincide very strongly with conflict on other matters, such as disagreements between managers and employers. The opposite situation, "superimposition," means that the participants are aligned similarly in different types of conflicts. To the extent that conflict is pluralistic, societies are more stable.[13] The issue, in other words, is not whether conflict existed but whether the emphasis on class has led us to underestimate the independent importance of other forms of conflict and to miss the complex interaction between them. In a related theory Lee Benson proposed that "the wider the area of agreement on political fundamentals" and "the more heterogeneous the society, . . . then the greater the number and variety of factors that operate as determinants of voting behavior."[14] Applying their theory to antebellum New York State, Benson found broad consensus on political economy and both diverse and intense conflict on matters of religion and cultural preferences.

Because there is abundant evidence of both pervasive consensus and pervasive conflict in America's educational development, I believe historians' disposition in future research should be to (1) define more precisely what relationship we are looking at when we assert consensus or conflict, (2) eschew an interpretive framework which sees either as the essence of development, and (3) find a more elegant way to relate the two. In my view the notion of "elegance" should denote for historians the effort to construct—without lapsing into mere eclecticism—an interpretation that will help explain a greater bulk of the conflicting evidence than do existing interpretations. We need to emulate and improve upon sociologists who, in the wake of criticism of the Parsons equilibrium formulation, attempted to produce social-change theories that would incorporate—indeed emphasize—conflict without making economic class the sole focus.[15]

One more complex way to relate conflict and consensus (the verdict of elegance awaits the performance) would be to think of conflict not simply between groups but within groups and even within individuals lives. We all know that conflict takes place at these levels, but it has escaped us in the recent historiography of American education. For example, the history of immigrant education is not just the history of imposition by natives on dubious but powerless newcomers; it is also the story of a running battle between cultural conservatives and Americanizing moderns within various ethnic groups. At the individual level, prime examples of internal conflict are William Whyte's ambivalent Italian youth and E. Franklin Frazier's black bourgeoisie.[16] Again, Dahrendorf's definition of pluralism—that of a set of overlapping and non-overlapping identities—is more sophisticated than the commonplace notion of coexisting but distinct groups.

From this perspective, school attendance can often be seen as a set of trade-offs (not happy adjustments, for sometimes the bargain is a hard one). Imagine the trade-offs if you are a rural New England Calvinist in 1845: you are ambivalent about creeping centralization, the teacher's assertion of authority, and rules against religious instruction in public schools, but you value rudimentary education and your children need to go someplace on boring winter days, so you send them to school. Or suppose you are a teen-aged textile worker in 1840: you believe you might get ahead if you finished grammar school, but you dislike school and your family needs your income as a hedge against hard times, so you work. Or an urban immigrant in 1890: the public school attacks your culture and alienates your children from you, but you believe school is their entrée to American society, so you send them.

Although I have emphasized school attendance, the same logic of trade-offs could be applied to the motives and behavior of educational reformers or teachers. The result of all these trade-offs has been an ever-expanding system of public education, basically but not totally supportive of the majoritarian ethic and the evolving economic system. Is it illustrative of consensus or conflict? Both, obviously. However, a more interesting answer will require not only continuing research into the social history of education but some model building as well. I have suggested here that the new models will have to accommodate competing identities, intragroup as well as intergroup conflict, and a pluralism of conflicts in different dimensions of life. I have also suggested that what appears to be American consensus on education is to some extent the result of ambivalence, muted conflict, and trade-offs. The American public school is a gigantic standardized compromise most of us have learned to live with.

NOTES

1. Ellwood P. Cubberley, *Public Education in the United States*, rev. ed. (Boston: Houghton Mifflin, 1934), p. 177.

2. Cubberley, pp. 164–65.

3. See Bernard Bailyn, *Education in the Forming of American Society: Needs and Opportunities for Study* (Chapel Hill, N.C.: Univ. of North Carolina Press, 1960); and Lawrence A. Cremin, *The Wonderful World of Ellwood Patterson Cubberley: An Essay on the Historiography of American Education* (New York: Teachers College Press, 1965).

4. Louis B. Hartz, *The Liberal Tradition in America* (New York: Harcourt Brace, 1955); Richard Hofstadter, *The American Political Tradition* (New York: Knopf, 1948); and Marvin Meyers, *The Jacksonian Persuasion: Politics and Belief* (Stanford, Calif.: Stanford Univ. Press, 1957).

5. Rush Welter, *Popular Education and Democratic Thought in America* (New York: Columbia Univ. Press, 1962), pp. 4, 103.

6. Jonathan C. Messerli, "Controversy and Consensus in Common School Reform," *Teachers College Record*, 66 (1964–65), 759. See also his *Horace Mann: A Biography* (New York: Knopf, 1971).

7. Messerli, "Controversy and Consensus," pp. 750, 754.

8. See John Higham, "The Cult of the 'American Consensus': Homogenizing Our History," *Commentary*, Feb. 1959, pp. 93–100; and Dwight W. Hoover, "Some Comments on Recent United States Historiography," *American Quarterly*, 17 (1965), 299–318.

9. Michael B. Katz, *The Irony of Early School Reform: Educational Innovation in Mid-Nineteenth Century Massachusetts* (Cambridge, Mass.: Harvard Univ. Press, 1968), pp. 1–2. A different class-conflict interpretation is found in Samuel Bowles and Herbert Gintis, *Schooling in Capitalist America: Educational Reform and the Contradictions of Economic Life* (New York: Basic Books, 1975), ch. 6.

10. See Carl F. Kaestle and Maris A. Vinovskis, "From Apron Strings to ABC's: The Transition from Family to School in Nineteenth-Century New England," *American Journal of Sociology* 84 (1978), 539.

11. See Albert Fishlow, "The American Common School Revival: Fact or Fancy?" in *Industrialization in Two Systems: Essays in Honor of Alexander Gerschenkron*, ed. Henry Rosovsky (New York: Wiley, 1966), pp. 40–67; and Carl F. Kaestle and Maris A. Vinovskis, "From One Room to One System: The Impact of Urbanization on Schooling in Nineteenth-Century Massachusetts," unpublished paper, March 1976.

12. See Carl F. Kaestle, "'Between the Scylla of Brutal Ignorance and the Charybdis of a Literary Education': Elite Attitudes Toward Mass Schooling in Early Industrial England and America," in *Schooling and Society*, ed. Lawrence Stone (Baltimore: Johns Hopkins Univ. Press, 1976).

13. Ralf Dahrendorf, *Class and Class Conflict in Industrial Society*, rev. English ed. (Stanford, Calif.: Stanford Univ. Press, 1959), ch. 6.

14. Lee Benson, *The Concept of Jacksonian Democracy: New York as a Test Case* (Princeton, N.J.: Princeton Univ. Press, 1961), p. 276.

15. The literature is too vast to summarize here. A now-classical critique of functionalism is Kingsley Davis, "The Myth of Functional Analysis as a Special Method in Sociology and Anthropology," *American Sociological Review*, 24 (1959), 757–72. An important recent contribution is Anthony D. Smith, *The Concept of Social Change: A Critique of the Functionalist Theory of Social Change* (London: Routledge & Kegan Paul, 1973). Attempts to incorporate conflict into theories of social change are also legion; see, for example, Gideon Sjoberg, "Contradictory Functional Requirements and Social Systems," *Journal of Conflict Resolution*, 4 (1960), 198–208; and the much more thoroughgoing effort of Dahrendorf cited above. Also relevant are the literature on contradictory demands of democracy, such as Bernard Berelson, Paul F. Lazarsfeld, and William N. McPhee, *Voting* (Chicago: Univ. of Chicago Press, 1954), pp. 313–23; and sociological studies of contradictory directions in organizational life, for example, Donald R. Cressy, "Contradictory Directives in Complex Organizations: The Case of the Prison," *Administrative Science Quarterly*, 4 (1959), 1–19.

16. William F. Whyte, *Street Corner Society: The Social Structure of an Italian Slum* (Chicago: Univ. of Chicago Press, 1943); and E. Franklin Frazier, *Black Bourgeoisie* (New York: Free Press, 1957).

Donald R. Warren

A Past for the Present
History, Education, and Public Policy

In few periods prior to the past two decades have historians of American education enjoyed their quarrels more or, conversely, taken them more seriously. Nor have their research productivity and its relevance to public policy been higher. Of recent developments in the field, revisionism easily ranks among the most widely and hotly debated, and not merely among educational historians. In the process, the traditional story of American education and the historians who wrote it have been challenged fundamentally. The familiar accounts depicted unqualified success: the construction, despite strenuous opposition, of a well-intentioned public school system to which American children of whatever race, sex, or social class eventually gained access. Revisionists tend to view the educational past differently. First, they see it as encompassing more than schools. Second, when they focus on schools, they provide more critical accounts of institutional openness and the school's record in promoting educational opportunity. They present evidence suggesting that schools have exhibited a greater concern with moral training than education and that the goals of those who have controlled schools have been ambivalent at best relative to the education of minorities and working-class people. Equally pointed criticisms have

been leveled against earlier generations of educational historians. Viewed as a Whiggish cadre given to the retelling of distorted tales, they are charged with sharing unfounded assumptions about the value of schools, erring collectively in equating education and schooling, and producing pietistic histories of formal education.[1]

Intrinsically valuable in most instances, debate over these criticisms has also drawn attention to recent significant gains in American educational history and historiography. A closer kinship with general history is being established. Comparative and interdisciplinary approaches provide concepts and resources for assessing educational development in the United States. There is also a discernible trend away from survey history in favor of basic research and case study. A wealth of new literature has appeared that utilizes new sources and techniques, employs fresh critical perspectives, and, in turn, generates new research questions. That conflicting interpretations of the American educational past have surfaced is on the whole a healthy sign. More significant, however, are advances in the sophistication and subtlety by which complex educational phenomena are analyzed and explained.

The infusion of vitality and self-esteem may be the most striking development of all. Over the past two decades, the *History of Educational Quarterly* has grown in stature as a quality research journal. The worth and volume of historical research in education have earned increasing recognition among academic scholars generally and other historians in particular. As annual meetings of the History of Education Society make clear, no new consensus history has yet emerged; nor does there appear to be much urgency to force one. Instead, one finds conflict, controversy, and general confidence that significant findings are being unearthed and important issues confronted.

History and Education

Common to the field of history generally are problems of method, source, and perspective. These problems reflect triangular approaches to interpreting historical developments and ideas. Recovering the past is literally impossible. The sources, being partial records in more than one meaning of the term, do not permit it. Documents that survive do not, by that fact alone, shed clear, unassailable light on the past. They were, after all, written by someone with a particular perspective. Empirical data contain limits and possible flaws of their own. They lend themselves to sophisticated statistical analyses, but require context and corroboration before they become intelligible. And they are incapable of penetrating all aspects of the past. Valuable and tough-minded, quantitative history risks being unreadable and enigmatic. The weaknesses of documentary history run in the opposite direction toward subjectivity and imprecision. Each can produce similar results: accounts cleansed of human content.

Even if all the puzzle pieces come to light, the "oceans of facts," to use Alfred North Whitehead's phrase, there remain the difficulties of identifying, analyzing, and articulating their interactions and relations, including the complex, usually unrecorded feelings, hopes, and desperations of another age. As time-bound people, historians open windows onto a past which, in the final analysis, remains elusive because it, too, is finite. They use perspective to illuminate a past, and, in the end, what they produce is perspective. That limitation, however, is not a license. Historical interpretation is a bounded field. There is evidence to be obtained and context to be protected. Reflecting its reliance on both the humanities and the social sciences, history is a science of perspective.

As a general guideline, that observation has limited utility. In the history of education as in other branches of the parent discipline, disagreements inevitably arise over which poles of the interpretive task deserve the greatest emphasis: data gleaned from the sources, analytic techniques intended to transform data into evidence, or the historian's developed intuition. Alone, each poses difficulties. History as mere technique relinquishes descriptive power. Attempts to write histories that permit the educational past to speak for itself from within its own setting stumble finally over the limitations of the sources and of historians themselves. On the other hand, reconstructing the past as a reflection of the present, or, more restrictive still, forcing it to serve political ideologies, produces superficial history and, ultimately, fantasy or propaganda. Writing what Carl Kaestle might term "elegant" history is not simply a matter of balancing the poles of the interpretive task.[2] It follows, rather, from the historian's discipline: knowing that sufficient reliable sources have been consulted, that the context is clearly retained, that the mode of analysis can explain the data, and that the historian's perspective has not imposed alien forms on the past. No historian avoids tangling with this dilemma. Nor are there formulas at hand to ease its resolution. With that in mind, Arthur Schlesinger, Jr., cautioned an audience of his peers against misplaced arrogance. "All any of us can do," he advised, "is descry a figure in the carpet—realizing as we do that contemporary preoccupations define our own definitions."[3] "That is all right," he added, "so long as we recognize what we are doing." M. I. Finley has put the matter more bluntly: "The study and writing of history, in short, is a form of ideology."[4] He is not sanctioning "crude, politically motivated distortions, falsifications, and suppressions" in history, but, rather he employs the term in its more neutral sense, as defined in the *Shorter Oxford English Dictionary*: "a system of ideas concerning phenomena, esp. those of social life; the manner of thinking characteristic of a class or an individual." History, therefore, has a temporal quality. Heartfelt denials notwithstanding, all history, even or perhaps most especially the dry, textbook variety, is interpretation.

The interpretive task may be completed with authority and grace, but portions of it are bound to be repeated. Out-of-print books are not readily available. New sources come to light. Other historians arrange the parts to form a different whole. A new story will be told. The history of education, like history generally, is a labor of Sisyphus.

It does not follow that all history contains revisionist elements or that historical revision is akin to a natural process. At a crude level, historical revision occurs, as

M. I. Finley observes, because historians are inevitably ignorant of the future.[5] Revision itself, however, is not so much inevitable as problematic. Such is the case particularly when it challenges fundamental assumptions in accepted accounts. Like uninspected memories, the latter tend to acquire lives of their own and devoted defenders. Quarrels among historians over revisionist interpretations thus can assume political proportions, with vested interests forming on all sides. The heat of battle, and the argument can reach that level of intensity, is sometimes necessary to ascertain soundness of interpretation, that is, adequacy relative to sources, technique, and perspective. But it is equally important not to suppress or lose sight of fresh questions and perspectives, however inadequately pursued, which carry the potential for significant additions to the body of historical knowledge.

Revision in the history of the American Reconstruction period, which has been gathering momentum since the early 1960s, illustrates the range and dimension of conflicts that can arise among historians representing traditional and antitraditional perspectives.[6] The American Reconstruction represents an authentic episode in social problem solving. There has been general agreement as to what the problems were. At issue were national purpose, constitutional questions, economic recovery, political stability, the role and status of black Americans, and, in general, the easing of regional hostilities. Other questions have proved far more provocative in historical reanalysis. What solutions were attempted? With what results? Were the problems susceptible to the ministries of special programs, such as those of the Freedmen's Bureau, or to the long-range amelioration promised through public schools? Could they be eased and finally resolved through rational debate and negotiation? Or were they systemic and national, thus requiring, in addition to moderate strategies, a redistribution of political and economic power and an extension of the franchise to black people nation-wide? Not surprisingly, historians' answers have proved to be almost as controversial as the original issues. The debate has forced reconsideration of ground once thought settled: Who did or attempted to do what to whom? When and for how long? Why? To what effect? Documentary and quantitative sources and techniques have been employed, with stunning achievements and pratfalls scored on all sides. Final results are not in, but a richer understanding of a complex and pivotal period of the American past is evident.

Substantial revision in the history of American education has occurred during the same period. Educational revisionists, like their counterparts among Reconstruction historians, represent a diverse group. Beyond the necessity of expanding the scope of their field, they recognize the importance of social and cultural factors in examining educational phenomena. Beneath this general consensus, there are differences over assumptions, techniques, and sources. It is not a simple matter to identify the revisionists or to date precisely the beginning of their efforts. Not all historians grouped as revisionists accept the label, and, indeed, some are not even historians.[7] Nor is there convincing evidence that revisionists are more susceptible to unfounded assertion than their peers, as some critics have charged. One difficulty is that, since the late 1950s, there have been two distinct, if nonetheless related,

revisionist trends in educational history.[8] The earlier one, represented most strongly in the work of Lawrence Cremin, expanded the field by adopting a broad definition of education, sought new and more rigorous research methodologies, and drew educational history closer to general history, particularly intellectual and political history. So much controversy has centered around a more recent and more radical revisionist trend, however, that the term is frequently applied solely to those historians designated in some quarters and occasionally by themselves as "radical."

Historical revision seldom constitutes an unprecedented, complete break with past interpretations. That is at least true in educational history. The work of Michael B. Katz, who has been instrumental in initiating radical revisionism, includes a thorough critique of the origins of American public schools.[9] He views them as detrimental to the working class, racist, and sexist. They were intended to suppress and pacify marginal groups—goals shared with such other nineteenth-century educational agencies as reformatories. He judges them successful, not as vehicles for educational opportunity but as barriers to hope and liberation. Freeman Butts, the dean of American educational historians, accepts none of these conclusions. For him, the American public school represents a "great idea."[10] It is not a romantic notion. His research over the past forty years touches on persistent themes: patterns of educational exclusion, church-state conflicts, violations of civil rights, and struggles to advance educational opportunity for minorities.

Public schools have not always succeeded in matching their promise, Butts finds, and they have been guilty of exclusion and unequal treatment of particular groups. But, on balance and in the long run, they have provided learning opportunities for Americans. Fundamentally, it is the continuation of the idea of public education within the American "experiment" that Butts explores and seeks to defend.

In large measure, these two positions are irreconcilable; their assumptions and perspectives are worlds apart. There are also threads of continuity and differences in emphasis and opinion. Both, for example, tend to focus the history of education on schools and related issues. Merle Curti's critiques of American school reformers even more strikingly illustrate the connections between past and current research in the field.[11] The point is that there are antecedents to the radical critique. Themes evident in earlier works are developed with a vengeance in the more recent revisionist ones.

But substantive and methodological departures have also occurred, and these constitute major contributions to the history of education. The later revisionists tend to treat the goals, policies, organization, and outcomes of schooling more as issues to be examined than as portions of a chronology. Their research emphasizes developments in selected periods or cities, the rise of school bureaucracy, and the impact of organizational forms of education on learning. Of special interest have been differences in educational opportunity and achievement for females, racial minorities, immigrants, and working-class people generally. The methodologies of the later revisionists encourage case study and the use of new sources, quantitative data, interdisciplinary approaches, and explicitly stated perspectives in examining educational outcomes from the client's point of view.

It is not yet clear where, for example, social-class analyses of American educational history will lead. That there have been social-class differences in the delivery and outcomes of American public schooling can hardly be debated. Far more telling is research that seeks to establish when, where, and under what circumstances the differences occurred. And, of course, there must be some reason why the public schools attracted working-class children, which they increasingly did throughout the nineteenth century. In pursuing such questions, Marxism and anarchism have proved to have little more utility than liberalism, if only because such metatheories tend to encourage historians of limited ability and insight to precategorize and simplify educational and social-class phenomena. Quantification offers limited assistance. It represents one among several possible approaches to rigorous historical analysis of social-class variables.[12] Qualitative data from documentary sources or literature also may be needed to account for apparent connections between cultural and social-class characteristics of educational outcomes. There remains the often repeated, but not necessarily lame, conclusion familiar among scholars: more research is needed. What is essential, however, is the realization that social-class analyses are undoubtedly legitimate in the attempt to understand educational development in a nation where equal opportunity enjoys a rich oral and written tradition, if not a very strong history.

Education and Public Policy

Historians of education cannot proceed very far without an understanding of how and through what kinds of agencies and experiences people learn. They cannot proceed at all without marking the boundaries of their specialization. What is education? In his multivolume history, *American Education*, Lawrence Cremin views it "as the deliberate, systematic, and sustained effort to transmit or evoke knowledge, attitudes, values, skills, and sensibilities, a process that is more limited than what the anthropologist would term enculturation or the sociologist socialization, though obviously inclusive of some of the same elements."[13] That definition, or some version of it, now dominates the history of American education. As employed by Cremin, it enables investigation of the formal and informal agencies that "have shaped American thought, character, and sensibility over the years and . . . the relationships between these agencies and the society that has sustained them."[14] Hypothetically, a range of variables is limitless. Nor should one be put off by such qualifiers as "deliberate, systematic, and sustained." As Cremin sees them, such educational agencies as families and television follow curricula and assess their results.[15]

When education is defined as both institution and process, its history becomes more encompassing and complex. Intellectual, political, and cultural factors emerge as necessary resources for full-bodied chronicles. Indeed, during the years since the late 1950s, historians of education have produced a richly varied research literature utilizing perspectives and analytic tools borrowed from literature and the arts, social change theory, theology, church history, demography, economics, and psychoanalytic theory.[16] Although some have been used with greater frequency and confidence than others, the list of potential sources is far from complete. Maxine Greene has argued persuasively that poetry, drama, film, and novels remain largely untapped as sources in the history of education.[17] On the other hand, among historians in various specialties, including education, there is enormous interest in cultural phenomena and ethnicity within the American context.[18]

Expanding the concept of education, however, has not solved one basic dilemma of historians. It has, on the contrary, become more acute. Learning theories abound, and, while the state of knowledge is not so fluid that one can be selected by tossing a coin, historians of education have inevitably assumed positions on the nature and value of education. With equal necessity, they have adopted criteria for locating and assessing its outcomes. Openly, covertly, or indirectly, their work displays attitudes and philosophical assumptions of education. If learning is perceived as essentially cognitive development, its history differs from chronicles that start by assuming that education involves feelings and behavior to significant degrees. The surest course touches all bases: cognition, affect, skill, and morality—in short, the phenomena necessary for creating flesh-and-blood histories. That, of course, only restates the problem. Balanced, presumably neutral, approaches risk offering little more than dull comfort. Identifying and sifting the sources remain the historian's essential labors. But while these tasks can possibly be begun, they cannot be completed without the aid of a point of view. Granted, examples of incompetent, witless history can still be found.

It is more accurate to admit that the educational point of view colors and shapes historical research on education from the outset. If the latter has integrity, the former is altered and honed in the process. Without that dialectic, some fairly dreadful history appears in print. Consider two examples. What constitutes the history of American Indian education? Without at least crude knowledge of the characteristics distinguishing the various tribes and nations of Native Americans, historians blunder at the outset. A general history is possible, although none has yet been published, but only if built on analyses of relatively discrete elements of culture and tradition.[19] Such precision remains necessary even if historians limit their focus to the forms of education imposed on Indians by white people. Educational policies, programs, and practices intended for Indians, whether devised at federal or state levels, varied over time and often by locality. There were, in short, several histories in the making—a point that raises a more profound question for historians of education. Is the history of Native American education solely or even primarily the story of white attempts to school, train, or acculturate Indian peoples? Here is a legitimate area of research. When done well, important contributions to knowledge follow. But they constitute a partial account, resting possibly on the assumption that education only occurs in forms and processes familiar within Western European traditions. Vast segments of the story are omitted: the forms, processes, and traditions of learning indigenous to the various tribes and nations. Admittedly, a history from that perspective is a difficult achievement, written primary sources being almost nonexistent, but the effort brings us closer to telling the whole story. Furthermore, it may shed light on American Indians' astonishing capacity for cultural survival.[20]

The history of Native American education helps to illustrate other general problems in educational historiography. Analyzing the points of cultural conflict and imposition encourages one to move beyond mere description to weigh the gains and losses. Simplistic notions of progress or failure become difficult to defend. Without the aid of narrow provincialisms, one cannot conclude that white people civilized Indians, or failed to do so. Even assuming that the effort issued from humane and pious intentions, and quite often it did not, the ultimate result was altered civilization. Native Americans had civilizations of their own well before the white invasion. And in those instances of relative assimilation or even acculturation, the effective forces may not have been white education or the attraction of European culture but technological progress and insurmountable economic and military power. That hypothesis points to the history of American Indian education as a possible testing ground for assumptions about education as a principal agent of social development and reform. Although much research remains to be done, what appears to be emerging as the history of Native American education is a tale rife with ambiguity and anguish, few heroes, and an ending not yet in sight—in other words, history on a human scale.

Attempts to write the history of education from learners' perspectives further illustrate the complex relation between the historian's point of view and historical research. Note that Cremin's definition of education encourages such attempts. The goal is to transcend the intentions of teachers and other educators, and perhaps the institutional boundaries of education as well, in order to assess learning outcomes and give voice to "the inarticulate." Despite apparent difficulties, there have been impressive gains in historical research on child-rearing practices, the family, the life of the college student, inmates of reformatories, and the effects of pedagogy and teacher attitudes.[21] Through census data, biographical research, street directories, and such sources as municipal voter registries and school records, historians can on occasion reconstruct literacy levels and mobility patterns and assess their correlations with identifiable educational experiences. They can make judgments about the forms and extent of practical intelligence in a particular time or place by examining the kinds of work people performed, the content of popular literature, and the dominant modes of social interaction.[22]

The fundamental difficulty in such research is locating valid sources that speak from within the learner's world. Short of that, there are risks that an elitist history of education will be supplanted by a new determinism wherein learners are viewed, if only tacitly, as passive recipients. Entering the learner's world through sources and records reflecting their own experiences not only helps assess actual educational practices and outcomes; it also presents fresh perspectives on the learning process. Education, after all, is more than imposition, that is, something done to someone. At some point and by a chemistry not always clear, learners may join the process as active participants, singularly altering it. Perhaps in education, as in voting behavior, people can act in what they perceive to be their own interests.[23] A history of education that avoids depicting learners as mere victims or consumers can include careful analyses of the politics of education, that is, who controls or influences it and to what extent, who is accountable for its outcomes, and who can

change or redirect it. Required, too, is consideration of qualitative data on the relation of education to the ways people experience and express meaning, hope, and failure. Biographical research can be of assistance, and, as Maxine Greene has argued, among the most readily available and instructive sources are literature and the arts.[24]

Whatever educational theory or philosophy historians adopt, they find themselves contending with education's elusiveness. It attaches to some experiences but not others. Not all schools prove to be educational, and some are miseducative. There are agencies that intend to promote specified learning, but do not; others enable education accidentally. As idea or intellectual vision, education remains larger and more complex than any single agency or institutional form. It would seem, therefore, that education cannot be reduced to schooling, training, or the accumulation of credentials. Strictly speaking, educational theory or philosophy does not educate. That assignment falls to particular historical forms and processes that can offer actual, rather than hypothetical or illusory, educational opportunities. Greene suggests that these complexities constitute education's paradox, its essential power. They also point to its fundamental connection with policy. As process or institution, education takes particular forms. It acquires goals, rationales, participants, and something akin to evaluation criteria—matters mediated through formal or informal policy.

In the American context, the relation of education to policy is more precise. By the end of the eighteenth century, formal education had been identified as a nation-building strategy. Its possible intrinsic value received little attention relative to the social benefits expected to accrue from the education of citizens. The benefits contained contradictory elements. On one hand, there was talk about education as a means of preparing people for self-government and of freeing them from European attachments and sectional loyalties. On the other hand, there were suggestions that education represented a way to pacify the masses. Both points of view acknowledged that education was needed to promote the national welfare. This double-minded vision—education for public liberation and public control—constitutes a continuing thread in the nation's history. It accounts for the fact that, in the United States, education, at least in part, is a matter of public policy.

Public Policy and History

David Tyack illustrates the relation between American education and public policy in *The One Best System*.[25] A major contribution, this book synthesizes a wealth of research literature, brings to bear the panoply of urban-related variables in analyzing the history of city schools, and offers a framework for comparing school systems that maintains intact their unique features. Tyack characterizes the book as "an interpretive history," thus serving notice of its critical content and perspective. Actually, it encompasses several perspectives, most notably those not typically found in traditional histories of American education: female teachers, black parents and students, ethnic school administrators, and immigrant parents and their offspring. This history is not peopled with caricatures of heroes and villains, controllers and victims, and it is not inspirational. Without apology, Tyack focuses intentionally on public schools. In an institutionalized so-

ciety such as the United States, he argues, schools offer reference points in analyzing the interactions of institutions and in marking social development, and, in this country, the latter involves accounting for urbanization. More fundamentally, Tyack insists on characterizing public schools as educational. Despite failure, inadequacy, and even bad faith, they represent a vast delivery system for learning opportunity. Because no other American institution holds that potential, the goals, organization, accessibility, and outcomes of schools represent both educational phenomena and public policy issues.

The One Best System also illustrates intentionally the relation of public policy and history, a relatively new but widely shared emphasis among historians of education. The recent works of such historians as Freeman Butts, Lawrence Cremin, Carl Kaestle, and Michael B. Katz indicate the depth of their interest in policy.[26] On one level, the focus is substantive, as revealed in research on the history of various educational policies. In addition, the relevance of historical research to contemporary policymaking is endorsed explicitly. Concern with policy issues is evident in earlier works by Butts, Cremin, and Tyack, and, indeed, in the research and writings of some nineteenth- and early twentieth-century historians of education as well. The shift is primarily one of emphasis and reflects growing appreciation for the structural character and connections of social and educational problems.

The major issues in American society and in American education during the past two decades can be traced to similar sources: racial injustice, cold war colonialism, war protest, urban decay, poverty, scarcity of resources, misuse of authority and law, unemployment, and inflation. The list should be longer, but these examples serve to indicate the range and depth of the social dysfunctions and controversies that marked the 1960s and 1970s. Some clearly were more fundamental than others. In addition, significant changes were witness in the rising expectations of minorities and working-class people, the heightened consciousness of purpose and meaning among women and racial and ethnic groups, the structure of the family, sexual mores, urban demography, technology, and the pervasiveness of communications media. Again, the list is illustrative only. The controversies and changes have proved to be unresponsive to piecemeal or programmatic approaches, suggesting the necessity of more fundamental alterations in the goals and structure of society. Confidence in that insight, which is neither radical nor conservative in origin, can be detected throughout the political spectrum, for it has given rise to the search for policy solutions to social and educational problems. Widespread interest in policy and policy-making is evident among academic scholars, particularly social scientists. Among historians of American education, it stems both from concern with current issues and the expanded research field within which they work. In the 1970s, if not before, no fancy footwork is required for educational historians to be socially relevant. It comes with the territory.

Involvement in policy research reflects and strengthens the expanded field of educational history. It invites inquiry into not only the history of selected policies, for example, compulsory school attendance, but also the history of agencies which operate at some distance from educational institutions but nonetheless influence programs and policies to varying degrees. State departments of education, the U.S. Office of Education, and the National Institute of Education represent obvious examples. The effects on educational practice of professional organizations, accreditation agencies, national testing services, large corporations, and labor unions further illustrate the potential for policy-oriented research in educational history.

Such research rarely can proceed along traditional lines. It is rigorously interdisciplinary. Narrative may be subsumed within a topical analysis. Goals and intentions are weighed against results that in turn can be taken as bases for speculation about unpublished objectives. Policy statements issued by an agency are examined in the context of the agency's organization and budget in order to determine the extent to which public pronouncements disclose or conceal actual priorities. Policies can be formal or informal, manifest or latent, and careful detection may be required to characterize them accurately. Measured in terms of their effects, formal policy may prove to be less potent than informal policy. One of the tasks of policy research is to ascertain whether that is indeed the case. Quantitative analysis is clearly useful in assessing policy outcomes, but couching results in human terms is likely to require documentary and oral sources as well. For example, reconstructing the intent of educational enactments involves analysis of legislative voting patterns, which can be quantified in the case of recorded votes. But there are other matters to be examined: preceding debates, voice votes, party affiliation, cloakroom compromises, and legislators' relations with their constituents. All of these may be stages in the process leading to the passage of a bill. The most influential determinants of legislative intent may not be immediately obvious or clearly susceptible to quantification. Other examples come to mind. Policy research typically requires penetrating the inner reaches of a bureaucracy. That alone may constitute an insurmountable barrier. If accomplished, other difficulties arise. Middle-echelon career bureaucrats tend to play instrumental roles in formal and informal policymaking, but they may not be highly visible within the organization. How is the historian to locate such significant actors and assess their influence? Research on bureaucratic personnel, including biographical study, would seem to be required, but sources may be scarce, examination of data tedious, and the story, in terms of interest value, underwhelming. Of greater historical significance, although equally difficult to produce, are assessments of the effects of federal educational policies and programs on communities and individuals in the late nineteenth and early twentieth centuries. Such research requires bringing multiple focuses to bear on relevant actions in Congress, presidential initiatives, court decisions, and the work of several federal agencies, including some no longer in operation. Yet none of these sources speaks directly to the question of local effect. For research in that direction, the sources are scattered and the empirical data not always reliable, both of which hamper the important task of comparing policy outcomes in various settings and among different segments of the population.

In one noteworthy respect policy research in educational history departs from recent trends in the field. Inquiry tends to be particularized and typically employs the case study method, but, as in the case of federal or state policy, it may not be focused on local educational practices and programs. On the contrary, historians who adopt a policy orientation confront the possibility that rigorous analysis of public education in Chicago might, for example, require devoting considerable attention to distant agencies and influences. In other respects, policy research in the history of education builds on the revisionist tradition developed over the past two decades. It ranges far beyond schools, utilizes quantitative and nonquantitive methods and sources, and necessarily adopts a critical posture in analyzing the educational past. It may also seek to influence contemporary policy.

Short of possible effects on policymaking, history contributes directly to the study of educational policy. Best characterized as a developing interdiscipline, the policy sciences in general remain conceptually parochial. Analytic models that allow systematic comparisons across national and cultural boundaries are rare.[27] As a rule, usable theory is borrowed from one or more of the social sciences, which adds yet another dimension to the parochialism of policy research. Thus, one finds American welfare policy and British social policy, which, as the late Richard Titmuss lamented, is distinct from British economic policy.[28] Finally, there is the matter of limited objectivity in the policy sciences. Far from being ideologically free, policy research proceeds from value commitments. Such bias, in combination with rigorous analysis of policy objectives and outcomes, represented for Titmuss a major strength, "providing us with an ideological framework which may stimulate us to ask the significant questions and expose the significant choices."[29] An innovative theorist who taught at the London School of Economics,

Titmuss viewed the policy sciences as an applied research field. Its aim was not merely to study policy but to promote social change through policy formation. The policy sciences contribute to the process directly by clarifying and extending the range of choices. That expectation optimistically assumes at least a consultative relation between policymakers and policy scientists.

Similar optimism can be detected when David Tyack discusses the relevance of educational history to policy:

> We stand at a point in time when we need to examine those educational institutions and values we have taken for granted. We need to turn facts into puzzles in order to perceive alternatives both in the past and in the present. The way we understand that past profoundly shapes how we make choices today.[30]

In short, the contributions of history to educational policy must be presumed and insisted upon.

There is, first and obviously, the introduction of a longitudinal dimension that facilitates the assessment of policy outcomes. Linear studies of particular policy issues hold some interest but a more significant contribution is the analysis of such developments within broader social and cultural contexts. The range of policy options at selected points in the past can be reconstructed and grounds established for speculating about the outcomes of rejected possibilities. As a related resource, research literature on the history of education in various national and cultural settings enables comparative policy studies. Finally, and perhaps least susceptible to fine measurement, there is the contribution of educational history—a humanities-related field—to policy study—a research area dominated by the social and behavioral sciences. Supplementing empirical data with qualitative assessments, history can bring to policy research the humanizing resources available in memory, ideas, values, and traditions that join with grander economic, social, and political developments in shaping educational policies and determining their effects on people. History also can be useful in understanding the extent to which policy and policymaking are influenced by inertia, the weight of established practice, familiar ideas, and traditional approaches to problem solving. Within an interdisciplinary approach, history can liberate policy study from presentism.

But it is futile to claim too much. There is a noticeable gap separating policy research from policymaking.[31] Isolated from each other, the former is blunted by lack of import, while the latter, at least from the standpoint of scholars, falls prey to special interests. The fact is that policy represents an effective response to systemic social problems only under certain conditions. It may, as Titmuss argued, promote social change and even structural redistributions of power and resources. Depending on who makes it and their objectives, it may also move in opposite directions. Policy can serve as a façade for the status quo as easily as an instrument for change. And policymaking can become a routine and ritualistic reaffirmation of established goals and values and acceptable responses to social dysfunctions. Such potentialities explain in part Cremin's characterization of the policy orientation as Whiggish.[32] History enters policy study and policymaking with similar limitations. Perceptions of the past, which provide negligible leverage within the political process, may reflect nothing more resourceful than self-serving rationales for business as usual.

These general considerations have direct application to educational policy and its relation to history and historiography. The Whiggish and anti-Whiggish strands in the history of American education offer two general but starkly distinct perceptions of the past.[33] One lays a foundation for the ratification of established educational goals and institutions and the values they reflect. The other encourages critical reassessment and fresh policy departures. Alone or in combination, each can be appropriate and useful in policy study, depending upon the issue being confronted and its context. In either case, the contributions to policy-making remain at best indirect. The potential for history may take subtly complex forms, as historian David Donald has observed to his colleagues, a warning that applies with particular force to historians of American education.[34] The nation's present, he finds, is so radically different from previous eras that its people may be well advised to sever connections. The proposed role for history becomes, ironically, helping people to appreciate the irrelevance of the past, the need to reconceptualize their problems, and the likelihood that solutions will come slowly. It is a limited assignment serving to remind historians that the quality and persuasiveness of their work hold consequences for others and extend into the future.

NOTES

1. Among the first and most scholarly treatments of such criticisms is Lawrence A. Cremin, *The Wonderful World of Ellwood Patterson Cubberley: An Essay on the Historiography of American Education* (New York: Bureau of Publications, Teachers College, Columbia University, 1965). See also Richard J. Storr, "The Role of Education in American History: A Memorandum," *Harvard Educational Review* 46 (August 1976): 331–354.

2. Carl F. Kaestle, "Conflict and Consensus Revisited: Notes toward a Reinterpretation of American Educational History," *Harvard Educational Review* 46 (August 1976): 390–396.

3. Arthur Schlesinger, Jr., "America: Experiment or Destiny?" *American Historical Review* 82 (June 1977): 505.

4. M. I. Finley, "'Progress' in Historiography," *Daedalus* 106 (Summer 1977): 132.

5. *Ibid.*, 126.

6. See, e.g., Bernard A. Weisberger, "The Dark and Bloody Ground of Reconstruction Historiography," *Journal of Southern History* 25 (November 1959): 427–447; David H. Donald, *The Politics of Reconstruction, 1863–1867* (Baton Rouge: Louisiana State University Press, 1965); and Robert Kelley, "Ideology and Political Culture from Jefferson to Nixon," *American Historical Review* 82 (June 1977): 531–562, esp. 544–547 and notes. See also responses to Kelley's paper by Ronald P. Formisano and Willie Lee Rose in "Comments," *ibid.*, 568–582.

7. The most thoroughly documented critical assessment of radical revisionist historiography, including historical interpretations by several nonhistorians, is Diane Ravitch, "The Revisionists Revised: Studies in the Historiography of American Education," *Proceedings of the National Academy of Education* 4 (1977): 1–84. Also, Charles A. Tesconi, Jr., "Review of *Reason and Rhetoric*," *Teachers College Record* 78 (February 1977): 383–391.

8. Ravitch, "The Revisionists Revised," 2–5; and Sol Cohen, "The History of the History of American Education, 1900–1976: The Uses of the Past," *Harvard Educational Review* 46 (August 1976): 298–330. For recent comment by Cremin, see Lawrence A. Cremin, *Traditions of American Education* (New York: Basic Books, 1977), 131–134.

9. See esp. Michael B. Katz, *Class, Bureaucracy, and Schools: The Illusion of Educational Change in America*, expanded ed. (New York: Praeger Publishers, 1975). Cremin dates the beginning of the later revisionism with the publication of Michael B. Katz, *The Irony of Early School Reform: Educational Innovation in Mid-Nineteenth Century Massachusetts* (Cambridge, Mass.: Harvard University Press, 1968). See Cremin, *Traditions of American Education*, 131.

10. R. Freeman Butts, "The Public School: Assaults on a Great Idea," *Nation* (April 30, 1973): 553–560.

11. See *id., Public Education in the United States: From Revolution to Reform, 1776–1976* (New York: Holt, Rinehart and Winston, Inc., 1978); Cremin, *Traditions of American Education*, 132; and Merle Curti, *The Social Ideas of American Educators* (New York: Charles Scribner's Sons, 1935).

12. Katz discusses the limited utility of metatheories and quantitative analysis in interdisciplinary approaches to the history of higher education in Michael B. Katz, "Review of *The University in Society: I, Oxford and Cambridge from the Fourteenth to the Early Nineteenth Century; II, Europe, Scotland, and the United States from the Sixteenth to the Twentieth Century*," *Journal of Interdisciplinary History* 7 (Autumn 1976): 319–322.

13. Lawrence A. Cremin, *American Education: The Colonial Experience, 1607–1783* (New York: Harper and Row, 1970), xiii.

14. *Ibid.*, xi.

15. Lawrence A. Cremin, "Public Education and the Education of the Public," *Teachers College Record* 77 (September 1975). For an elaboration of his 1975 John Dewey Lecture, see *id., Public Education* (New York: Basic Books, 1976).

16. See the bibliographic essay in Cremin, *Traditions of American Education*, 131–163. A thorough survey of recent work in the field, with an excellent bibliography, is Geraldine Joncich Clifford, "Education: Its History and Historiography," *Review of Research in Education* 4 (1976): 210–267.

17. See esp. Maxine Greene, "Identities and Contours: An Approach to Educational History," *Educational Researcher* 3 (April 1973).

18. Kelley, "Ideology and Political Culture from Jefferson to Nixon," 531–562. Also, responses to Kelley's paper by Geoffrey Blodgett and Formisano in "Comments," *American Historical Review* 82 (June 1977): 563–577.

19. A general history of twentieth-century developments is Margaret Szasz, *Education and the American Indian: The Road to Self-Determination, 1928–1973* (Albuquerque: University of New Mexico Press, 1974). Cremin cautions historians to note Indians' educational contributions to white settlers, especially during the colonial period, and the education available to both general groups through "the experience of culture contact." See Cremin, *Traditions of American Education*, 4–5. For a brief, provocative survey of white efforts to "educate" Native Americans, see Diane Ravitch, "On the History of Minority Group Education in the United States," *Teachers College Record* 78 (December 1976).

20. A deliberately "overenthusiastic" study of indigenous Indian education, using anthropological tools and resources, is George A. Pettitt, "Primitive Education in North America," *University of California Publications in American Archeology and Ethnography* 43 (No. 1, 1946): 1–182. For a fictionalized depiction of indigenous Indian education and culture contact, see Edwin Corle, *Fig Tree John* (New York: Pocket Books, 1972; originally published in 1935).

21. Clifford, "Education: Its History and Historiography," 219–243.

22. See, for example, Daniel Calhoun, *The Intelligence of a People* (Princeton, N.J.: Princeton University Press, 1973); and esp. Cremin, *Traditions of American Education*, 134–163.

23. For observations on "a new determinism" in analyses of ethnic voting patterns, see Rose, "Comments," *American Historical Review* 82 (June 1977): 580.

24. See, for example, Greene, "Identities and Contours."

25. David B. Tyack, *The One Best System: A History of American Urban Education* (Cambridge, Mass.: Harvard University Press, 1974).

26. See, for example, Butts, *Public Education in the United States*; Cremin, *Public Education*; Carl F. Kaestle, *The Evolution of an Urban School System: New York City, 1750–1850* (Cambridge, Mass.: Harvard University Press, 1973); and Katz, *Class, Bureaucracy, and Schools*.

27. For an analysis of one aspect of the policy field, see Richard M. Titmuss, *Social Policy: An Introduction* (New York: Pantheon Books, 1974). See also Philip W. Semas, "How Influential Is Sociology?" *Chronicle of Higher Education* (September 19, 1977): 4.

28. Titmuss, *Social Policy*, 20, 60–74.

29. *Ibid.*, 136.

30. Tyack, *The One Best System*, 4.

31. Semas, "How Influential Is Sociology?" 4.

32. Cremin, *Traditions in American Education*, 132.

33. *Ibid.*, and Clifford, "Education: Its History and Historiography," 215–218.

34. David Herbert Donald, "Personal View: The Past Is Irrelevant," *Chicago Daily News* (September 19, 1977): 15.

E. D. Hirsch, Jr.

Intellectual Capital
A Civil Right

Shared Knowledge in Democracies

The need in a democracy to teach children a shared body of knowledge was explained many years ago by Thomas Jefferson when he described his bill "to diffuse knowledge more generally through the mass of the people." A common grade-school education would create a literate and independent citizenry as well as a nesting ground for future leaders. It would be a place where every talent would be given an equal chance to excel, where "every fibre would be eradicated of ancient and future aristocracy; and a foundation laid for a government truly republican."[1] Despite his distrust of central authority, Jefferson encouraged the devising of a common curriculum in order that "the great mass of the people" should be taught not just the elements of reading, writing, and arithmetic, but also that "their memories may here be stored with the most useful facts from Grecian, Roman, European, and American history," as well as "the first elements of morality."

Of the views of this [education] law, none is more important, none more legitimate, than of rendering the people the safe, as they are the ultimate, guardians of their own liberty. For this purpose, the reading in the first stage [of schooling] where [many] will receive their whole education, is proposed to be chiefly historical. History by apprizing them of the past will enable them to judge of the future. It will avail them of the experience of other times and other nations; it will qualify them as judges of the actions and designs of men; it will enable them to know ambition under every disguise it may assume; and knowing it to defeat its views. In every government on earth is some trace of human weakness, some germ of corruption and degeneracy, which cunning will discover, and wickedness insensibly open, cultivate, and improve. Every government degenerates when trusted to the rulers of the people alone. The people themselves therefore are its only safe depositories. And to render even them safe, their minds must be improved to a certain degree.[2]

Jefferson's conception was later seconded by Horace Mann, who argued that democracy required a "common school" to provide all children equally with the knowledge and skills that would keep them economically independent and free. Other early prophets of democratic education, such as Louis-Michel Le Peletier, François Guizot, and Jules Ferry in France, propounded similarly inspiring principles of commonality in early education. In the early years of this century, John Dewey (who said many, sometimes inconsistent things about education) reaffirmed the connections between such common learnings and the goals of community and democracy in *Democracy and Education:*

> Beings who are born not only unaware of but quite indifferent to the aims and habits of the social group have to be rendered cognizant of them and actively interested. Education, and education alone, spans the gap. . . . Men live in a community in virtue of the things which they have in common; and communication is the way in which they come to possess things in common. What they must have in common are aims, beliefs, aspirations, knowledge—a common understanding.[3]

And from William C. Bagley, a colleague of Dewey's at Columbia University and a profound scholar of education: "A most important function of formal education, especially in a democracy, is to insure as high a level of common culture as possible."[4]

More recently, in 1994, the dependency of the democratic vision on commonly shared knowledge was brought up to date and ratified unanimously by the Parliament of Norway:

> It is a central tenet of popular enlightenment that shared frames of reference must be the common property of all the people—indeed must be an integral part of general education—to escape avoidable differences in competence that can result in social inequality and be abused by undemocratic forces. Those who do not share the background information taken for granted in public discourse will

often overlook the point or miss the meaning. Newcomers to a country who are not immersed in its frames of reference often remain outsiders because others cannot take for granted what they know and can do; they are in constant need of extra explanations. Common background knowledge is thus at the core of a national network of communication between members of a democratic community. It makes it possible to fathom complex messages, and to interpret new ideas, situations and challenges. Education plays a leading role in passing on this common background information—the culture everybody must be familiar with if society is to remain democratic and its citizens sovereign.[5]

In the late industrial era, the need for common learnings has acquired a more than political urgency. The purely economic need for a high level of shared knowledge among workers has led to an unforeseen strengthening of democratic political principles in previously non-democratic regimes. When the Soviet Union collapsed, the experienced Soviet hand George Kennan was asked in a TV interview whether the new Russian revolution would prove as durable as the former one of 1917. Without hesitation, Kennan predicted that the democratic revolution would prove more lasting than its predecessor: the Soviet state had been forced by economic imperatives to make its people literate, whereas the revolution of 1917 had been carried out by uneducated and therefore malleable peasants.

Because economic imperatives have now been added to political ones, the need to provide effective schooling to all has become more pressing than in any previous era. Politically, citizens must still be educated in order to be protected from their rulers, and, as Jefferson indicated, from themselves. Economically, citizens now require an especially strong schooling to sustain themselves in the workplace. To express the socioeconomic implications of education in the modern world, sociologists have devised the useful concept of "intellectual capital."

"Intellectual capital" has been described by Secretary of Labor Robert Reich as the key to American competitiveness and prosperity. In the popular press, the phrase has been used to denote the knowledge that makes the workers of one country or company more effective than those of another. But the implications of the concept transcend purely economic consequences. And the widening gap between rich and poor is not the only injustice that results from an inequitable distribution of intellectual capital. Sociologists have shown that intellectual capital (i.e., knowledge) operates in almost every sphere of modern society to determine social class, success or failure in school, and even psychological and physical health. The French scholar Pierre Bourdieu has shown that those who possess a larger share of "cultural capital" tend to acquire much more wealth and status, and to gain more abilities, than those who start out with very little of this precious resource.[6]

Just as it takes money to make money, it takes knowledge to make knowledge. Underlying the implied analogy between money capital and intellectual capital lodges an ancient Biblical paradox (Matthew 13:12): "For whosoever hath, to him shall be given, and he shall have more abundance: but whosoever hath not, from him shall be taken away even that he hath."

The paradox holds more inexorably for intellectual than for money capital. Those who are well educated can make money without inherited wealth, but those who lack intellectual capital are left poor indeed. The paradox of Matthew is powerfully at work in the American educational system.[7] Those children who possess intellectual capital when they first arrive at school have the mental scaffolding and Velcro to catch hold of what is going on, and they can turn that new knowledge into still more mental Velcro to gain still more knowledge. But those children who arrive at school lacking the relevant experience and vocabulary— they see not, neither do they understand. They fall further and further behind. The relentless humiliations they experience continue to deplete their energy and motivation to learn. Lack of stimulation has depressed their IQs.[8] The ever-increasing differential in acquired intellectual capital that occurs during the early years ends up creating a permanent gap in such children's acquired abilities, particularly in their abilities to communicate in speech and writing, to learn new things, and to adapt to new challenges. In short, an early inequity in the distribution of intellectual capital may be the single most important source of avoidable injustice in a free society.

Despite claims to the contrary, we know that the initial knowledge deficits of children can be remedied in the early years of preschool and primary school, and that their subsequent learning can be made to proceed at a rate that could guarantee a literate and relatively just society. Other nations in the modern world have shown that this educational achievement is possible even for heterogeneous societies like the United States.[9] One practical advantage in the idea of intellectual capital, therefore, is the direction it gives to educational theory and policy. The implied analogy with money capital suggests the commonsense truth that a child's accumulation of wide-ranging foundational *knowledge* is the key to educational achievement.

The money analogy also suggests a further truth: not just any knowledge will work—only that knowledge which constitutes the shared intellectual currency of the society. Selectivity is critical. To be useful to children, their intellectual capital needs to be broadly shared with others, to enable them to communicate and learn effectively. Confederate or Monopoly money won't work. As democratic theorists from Jefferson to Gudmund Hernes (author of the recent Norwegian Education Act) have argued, the intellectual currency has to be the widely useful and negotiable coin of the realm.[10]

Unfortunately, for several decades the American educational community has operated under a guiding metaphor very different from "intellectual capital." American educational theory has held that the child needs to be given the all-purpose *tools* that are needed for him or her to continue learning and adapting. The particular content used to develop those tools need not be specified. The claim that all-purpose intellectual competencies are independent of the matter out of which they have been formed, if it corresponded to reality, would indeed be an attractive educational idea. For conveniently, in that case, it wouldn't matter greatly what particular things a child learned. The chief aims of education would simply be to ensure that children acquired "love of learning" and gained "critical-thinking" techniques for acquiring and using whatever they would need later—the pliers and wrenches that would

permit them to set up shop even on a desert island. But when this tool metaphor has been taken apart and examined for its literal content, its highly exaggerated claims have been powerfully contradicted by research, and after six decades, it has shown itself to be ineffective.

The tool metaphor, with its encouragement of an indifference to specific knowledge, has resulted in social consequences of tragic proportions. It is probably not an exaggeration to say that the broad sway of this theoretical mistake has all but nullified the bright promise of school integration and the civil rights movement. The role that education under a more adequate theory could have played in consolidating social justice after the *Brown* decision can be suggested by two studies—one from 1925, before a process orientation began to dominate in our schools; the other from 1966, after the ascendancy of the tool theory.

In 1966, the Coleman Report found that under the current American educational system the home is, except in the case of extremely good or extremely bad schools, the decisive influence on academic outcomes; our schools on average do little to improve the economic chances of disadvantaged children.[11] Coleman's finding is highly consistent with the idea of the importance of intellectual capital, since under the current process-dominated theory it is the home, by default, and not the school that supplies most of the intellectual capital which enables children to acquire more. When the home is the dominant influence in education, it follows that economically and educationally depressed groups will not be greatly advanced by schooling. This pattern of social determinism found by Coleman in 1966 still persists in the schools of the 1990s.[12]

But history has contributed some very telling contrary results that complement and qualify the research of Coleman and his associates. A 1925 study published by Professor William C. Bagley of Teachers College, Columbia University, powerfully illustrates that researches into the social outcomes of schooling and into the relative influence of the home greatly depend on the educational context in which those researches are conducted. Bagley's *Determinism in Education* analyzed results of the Army Alpha tests given in World War I to some 1,700,000 soldiers.[13] Bagley was interested in correlating the IQ scores of large groups with the states they came from. Some states, such as Oregon and Massachusetts, had good systems of elementary education; others, such as Mississippi, had poor systems. Previously, based on various objective criteria, L. P. Ayres had formed a ranking of the various states according to the quality of their school systems.[14] Bagley wanted to determine whether IQ and competency tests on this vast scale (which tend to balance out innate differences) would correlate with the general quality of schooling as rated independently by Ayres.

Bagley found a high correlation, .72, between the mean IQ of soldiers and the educational quality of their native states during the period when the soldiers would have been in grade school. Interestingly, African-American soldiers from educationally high-ranking states had higher IQs than white soldiers from low-ranking states. Thus, during an era when American schools operated on traditional rather than progressivist principles, excellent schools, even more than the home or the family income (family income of African-Americans in 1900 was not high), made a decisive difference in average IQ and general competence. This striking observation, which is just the reverse of the 1966 findings, supports the theory of intellectual capital over the theory of abstract intellectual tools as the foundation of intellectual competence. Indeed, as I shall be concerned to show in Chapter 5, intellectual capital is *itself* the great all-purpose tool of adaptation in the modern world.

Dependency of Learning upon Shared Knowledge

Why is shared knowledge among students essential to an effective classroom? Anyone who has ever taught a class knows that explaining a new subject will induce smiles of recognition in some students but looks of puzzlement in others. Every teacher who reads exams has said or thought, "Well, I *taught* them that, even if some of them didn't *learn* it." What makes the click of understanding occur in some students but not in others?

Psychological research has shown that the ability to learn something new depends on an ability to accommodate the new thing to the already known. When the automobile first came on the scene, people called it a "horseless carriage," thus accommodating the new to the old. When a teacher tells a class that electrons go around the nucleus of an atom as the planets go around the sun, that analogy may be helpful for students who already know about the solar system, but not for students who don't. Relevant background knowledge can be conceived as a stock of potential analogies that enable new ideas to be assimilated. Experts in any field learn new things faster than novices do, because their rich, highly accessible background knowledge gives them a greater variety of means for capturing the new ideas. This enabling function of relevant prior knowledge is essential at every stage of learning.

When a child "gets" what is being offered in a classroom, it is like someone getting a joke. A click occurs. People with the requisite background knowledge will get the joke, but those who lack it will be puzzled until somebody explains the background knowledge that was assumed in telling the joke. A classroom of twenty-five to thirty children cannot move forward as a group until all students have gained the taken-for-granted knowledge necessary for "getting" the next step in learning. If the class must pause too often while its lagging members are given background knowledge they should have gained in earlier grades, the progress of the class is bound to be excruciatingly slow for better-prepared students. If, on the other hand, instead of slowing down the class for laggards, the teacher presses ahead, the less-prepared students are bound to be left further and further behind. In the American context, this familiar problem is not adequately overcome by placing students in different "ability" tracks, because the basic structural problem has little to do with ability. Even smart people don't always get jokes.

That all first graders should enter school "ready to learn" was the number one principle enunciated by President Bush and forty-nine governors at the education summit of 1989, and confirmed by Congress in 1993. Implicit in the ready-to-learn principle is the (true) assumption that children cannot keep up in first grade unless they arrive there with the knowledge and vocabulary that will enable them to participate actively in the class. They must be able to talk to the teacher and to other children, and they must in turn be able to understand what the teacher and other children are saying to them. In short, being "ready to learn" means, at a minimum, sharing critical skills, elements of knowledge, and vocabulary with other members of the first-grade community.

This special focus on first graders is understandable if one assumes that an initial readiness to learn will provide the momentum necessary to carry the child through subsequent grades. Otherwise, it would be hard to justify such preferential emphasis on first graders. But since the underlying assumption of continued momentum for all is demonstrably false in our current educational system, logical consistency would require that we extend the readiness-to-learn principle to second graders and third graders, and so on. For it is a fundamental requirement of democratic education that every student who enters a class at the beginning of the year should be vouchsafed the academic preparation needed to gain the knowledge and skills to be taught in that year. The readiness-to-learn principle cries out for generalization: In a democracy, all students should enter a grade ready to learn. True, the requisite skills, background knowledge, and vocabulary for such readiness are very unequally provided by the children's home environments. But precisely for that reason, it is the duty of schools to provide each child with the knowledge and skills requisite for academic progress—regardless of home background.

For effective classroom learning to take place, class members need to share enough common reference points to enable all students to learn steadily, albeit at differing rates and in response to varied approaches. Harold Stevenson and James Stigler in their important book, *The Learning Gap*, show that when this requisite commonality of preparation is lacking, as it is in most American classrooms today, the progress of learning will be slow compared with that of educational systems which do achieve commonality of academic preparation within the classroom. It is arguable that this structural difference between American classrooms and those of more effective systems is an important cause of the poor showing of American students in international comparisons. Stevenson and Stigler make the following shrewd observation about the "error" of attributing our classroom incoherence to the much-discussed "diversity" of American students as compared with that of children in more "homogeneous" nations:

The error . . . is the assumption that it is the diversity in children's social and cultural backgrounds that poses the greatest problem for teaching. In fact, a far greater problem is variability in children's educational background, and thus in their levels of preparation for learning the academic curriculum.[15]

The learning gap that Stevenson and Stigler describe is a gap in academic performance between American and Asian students. Subsequent work by Stevenson and his colleagues has shown that this gap grows wider over time, putting American students much further behind their Asian peers by eleventh grade than they were in sixth.[16] The funnel shape of this widening international gap has an eerie similarity to the funnel shape of the widening gap *inside* American schools between advantaged and disadvantaged students as they progress through the grades. A plausible explanation for the widening in both cases is that a lack of academic commonality in

the American classroom not only slows down the class as a whole, thus making us lag behind other countries, but also creates an increasing discrepancy between students who are lucky enough to have gained the needed background knowledge at home and those who have to depend mainly on what they get sporadically in school. The learning of luckier students snowballs upon their initial advantage, while that of the less fortunate ones, dependent on what the incoherent American school offers, never even begins to gather momentum. The lack of shared knowledge among American students not only holds back their average progress, creating a national excellence gap, but, more drastically, holds back disadvantaged students, thus creating a fairness gap as well.

These gaps in excellence and fairness explain why the most consistent problems of misbehavior occur among students at the top and at the bottom of the academic range, the one group antagonized by boredom, the other by boredom compounded with humiliation—emotions that are induced and exacerbated by lack of shared knowledge in the classroom. Constance Jones has found that when American grade-schoolers are offered schooling that provides them with needed background preparation, there is a sharp decline in absenteeism and disciplinary problems.[17] In Britain, research by Dennis O'Keeffe has similarly concluded that if students are "equipped with the requisite intellectual tools, levels of truancy are less." He concludes that "the pathology is mostly in the intellectual transmission and not in the children."[18]

Reduction of truancy and misbehavior is just one advantage that accrues when all students are made ready to learn. More positively, giving young children enabling knowledge is inherently motivational; it liberates their natural eagerness to learn. Steven Pinker has shown that children are born with a "language instinct."[19] It is arguable, and indeed it has been argued since Aristotle, that the language instinct is part of a more general instinct to learn, which impels youngsters toward becoming members of the adult community. A human child is biologically so helpless and vulnerable in its early years, so dependent upon the wider community for survival, that in the course of human evolution, children who lacked the learning instinct would not have been likely to survive.[20] Their natural curiosity and eagerness are inborn instincts that have to be systematically *thwarted* in order to make the children bored or indifferent.

The positive effects of giving children enabling knowledge thus accomplishes a lot more than just making them better behaved. They are better behaved mainly because they are absorbed in learning. In the first year during which a coherent, content-oriented curriculum is introduced into an American elementary school, library use rises typically by 70 percent. This suggests that the "Velcro hooks" image of enabling knowledge is inadequate to describe the phenomenon. The metaphor explains the click effect of enabling knowledge, but it doesn't convey the active curiosity that it encourages in young children. "Velcro hooks" make learning seem a passive occupation, like waiting to hook a fish. But a child's intellectual fishing is highly active, as the increase in library use indicates. Giving children enabling knowledge gives them not just passive hooks but also active tentacles. I owe this image to the distinguished child psychologist Sandra Scarr, who provided the following example. A child walks into the school library and sees a book called *Exploring the Nile*. She says to herself, "I've already learned something about the Nile. Let's see what this book has to say." By contrast, a child who doesn't know anything about the Nile, not even the name, will often just pass the book by. Among advantaged children, wide knowledge nourishes an active curiosity to learn still more, and more, so that the ever-active tentacles create still more tentacles. There is no insuperable reason why American schools cannot make all children more advantaged in this respect.

The Myth of the Existing Curriculum

The curricular chaos of the American elementary school is a feature of our public education that few people are even remotely aware of. We know, of course, that there exists no national curriculum, but we assume, quite reasonably, that agreement has been reached locally regarding what shall be taught to children at each grade level—if not within the whole district, then certainly within an individual school. After all, the stated reason for preserving the principle of local control of education is that the *localities* ought to determine what our children shall learn. But despite the democratic virtue of that principle, the idea that there exists a coherent plan for teaching content within the local district, or even within the individual school, is a gravely misleading myth.

That the idea is a myth is not a darkly kept secret. Rather, the idea that there is a local curriculum is accepted as truth by experts within the school system. Recently, a district superintendent told me that for twenty years he had mistakenly assumed each of his schools was determining what would be taught to children at each grade level, but was shocked to find that assumption entirely false; he discovered that no principal in his district could tell him what minimal content each child in a grade was expected to learn. He was not surprised when I told him I had received a letter from a distraught mother of identical twins in which she complained that her children had been placed in different classes at the same school and were learning totally different things. Anyone who wishes to conduct an experiment to confirm the proposition that the existence of the local curriculum is a myth can easily do so. Simply ask the principal of your nearest elementary school for a description of the minimal specific content that all children at a grade level are supposed to learn. Those who have tried this experiment have come away empty-handed.

Perhaps "empty-handed" is the wrong word. The principal might hand you a big sheaf of papers. Many states and local districts have produced thick documents called "curriculum guides," which, for all their thickness, do not answer the simple question "What specific content are all children at a grade level required to learn?" Or, in addition to the guidelines, your principal might hand you a list of textbooks that each teacher at a grade level is supposed to use. But a list of textbooks does not provide an answer to the question about minimal content any more than does a thick pile of district guidelines. Consider the following research regarding textbook use in American schools:

Daunted by the length of most textbooks and knowing that the children's future teachers will be likely to return to the material, American teachers often omit some topics. Different topics are omitted by different teachers, thereby making it impossible for the children's later teachers to know what has been covered at earlier grades—they cannot be sure what their students know and do not know.[21]

Four years ago, I had a vivid confirmation of the mythical nature of the local curriculum. A Core Knowledge school had started up the year before, which meant its teachers at each grade level had agreed to teach content far more specifically defined than that in official district "curricula." Now the school was announcing a big rise in test scores and a decline in discipline problems. A *Wall Street Journal* reporter, preparing an article about the school, asked the principal, "What has the school given up from the old curriculum to adopt the new one?" The principal kept replying that the school had not given up anything; the teachers were still following the same district guidelines. The skeptical reporter insistently repeated the question; he could not understand how two different curricula could occupy the same space at the same time. But of course the principal was right. The district guidelines were so vague that they and the more specific curriculum could both be followed at the same time.

Such lack of specificity in district guidelines explains why principals cannot state with confidence what children in a grade are learning within their schools. In fact, the children are learning quite different things. I emphasize in this context the importance of defining content for a particular grade level, since the school year is the critical unit for curricular planning. The normal pattern is: a new year, a new teacher. Guidelines developed in multi-year units are ineffective in practice because students change teachers in successive years. Value, multiyear goals make neither the student nor the teacher responsible for gaps; a gap is always something that should have been filled in some other year! Close monitoring becomes impossible. Accountability cannot be maintained for either students or teachers.

It might be wondered how it is possible for states and localities to produce lengthy curricular guides that, for all their bulk, fail to define specific knowledge for specific grade levels. Here are some typical instructions (they pertain to first-grade social studies): "The child shall be able to identify and explain the significance of national symbols, major holidays, historical figures and events. Identify beliefs and value systems of specific groups. Recognize the effects of science and technology on yesterday's and today's societies."

These words disclose a characteristic reluctance on the part of district guides to impinge upon the teachers' prerogatives—in this case, by not stating *which* national symbols, major holidays, historical figures, and historical events the local curriculum makers have in view. But, in the absence of specifics, is there any reason to believe that different teachers will respond to these directions in similar ways? When children from diverse first-grade classes that follow these instructions enter second grade, what shared knowledge can the second-grade teacher take for granted among them? What are the "specific" groups the students became acquainted with in studying the "beliefs and value systems of specific groups"? The word "specific" in such a context carries an unintended irony.

I have found a tiny number of district curricula that are much more specific than the typical guidelines just quoted—particularly in science and social studies. Let me therefore examine the very best one I have found so far, since it will, with fairness, illustrate the sort of problem that leads even in the best of cases to our curricular incoherence. The first-grade science instructions in this superior local guide admirably state that the child shall "use the term 'decay' to describe the breakdown of organic material." In social studies, the guide states (again admirably) that the child shall "locate North and South Poles, the Equator and oceans bordering North America on map/globe." That is exactly the sort of guidance such documents ought to provide.

But even in this best of guides there is grave unevenness in specificity and coherence. Take, for example, the subject of plants and seeds in the science section:

- Grade one: "Describe seeds and grow plants from seeds. State three requirements for seed germination and plant growth."
- Grade two: "Arrange illustrations of plants in various stages of development in order from seed to adult."
- Grade four: "Plant seeds and identify and determine the environmental factors responsible for the success and failure of plant development."
- Grade five: "Identify and plot the growth of the seed parts and infer that the cotyledon is food for the living embryo."

The theory behind this sort of repetition is one of deepening through "spiraling." But it is universally experienced by students as boring repetition, as in the oft-heard complaint from those who have been made to read *Charlotte's Web* three times in six grades.

The spiraling method of forming local curriculum frameworks proceeds as follows: One first defines a few highly general "objectives," and one then carries them through several grades. In this particular local district, science in each grade follows general objectives such as: "Illustrate interrelationships of organisms and their interaction with the environment." Since this "objective" or "strand" is one of the four main principles for science through the first five elementary grades, it is not surprising that the district curriculum repeats themes grade after grade. In this case, the repetition is seeds. But here's another of the four science objectives: "Describe the interactions of physical features and their effects on planet Earth." Given that objective, it isn't surprising that we find units on the *sun* repeated in grades one, two, four, and five; units on the *Earth* repeated in grades one, two, and four; units on the *moon* repeated in grades one, two, three, and four.

If repetition and boredom are dangers in the "strand" approach, a corollary danger is the creation of *gaps* that open up in the spaces between the strands. Frequent repetitions and gaps are the besetting weaknesses of local curricula, and they are made inevitable when the strand approach is compounded with vagueness. Huge gaps are bound to arise. There was no indication even in this topflight local curriculum that children were to be introduced to the basic character of photosynthesis, nor that they were to be made

aware of simple tools and how they work, nor that they would know how to measure physical things in inches, feet, pounds, kilograms, grams, quarts, pints, and cubic centimeters. It might be assumed that the individual teacher would fill in these gaps. But experience has shown this to be an unwarranted assumption. Major gaps in the local guidelines become major gaps in students' minds.

How did we achieve this degree of curricular ineptitude, unique in the developed world? Beginning in the 1930s as part of the advance of progressive education in the public schools and the colleges of education, there were curriculum-revision movements across the land.[22] Over the past six decades, such vague, gap-ridden "conceptual" curricula have been developed as a reaction to earlier, content-oriented approaches to forming a curriculum. The new curricula have attempted to get beyond the "rote learning" of "mere facts," and to gain unity and conceptual depth by following broad and deep instructional aims. But the examples just cited illustrate the kinds of defects that result from curricula which rely primarily on processes, "objectives," and "strands." Even the best local guides of this type have fundamental weaknesses.

The first inherent weakness is the arbitrariness of the large-scale conceptual schemes and classifications that make up all such curricular "strands" or "objectives." Such schemes may appear to be deep and comprehensive, but most of them are indeed quite arbitrary. The conceptual objectives in each district tend to be different from one another, with each district preferring its own. Equally striking is the arbitrariness of the various conceptual schemes recently produced by curricular experts for the American Association for the Advancement of Science, the National Council of Teachers of Science, and the National Academy of Sciences. These documents all follow different conceptual schemes.

There is another inherent shortcoming in the overreliance on large-scale abstract objectives (as opposed to "mere" content) as a means of determining a curriculum. These general objectives do not compel either a definite or a coherent sequence of instruction. That is because the large conceptual scheme and its concrete expressions (through particular contents) have a very tenuous and uncertain relationship to each other. A big scheme is just too general to guide the teacher in the selection of particulars. For instance, one multigrade science objective in our superior local district states, "Understand interactions of matter and energy." This is operationally equivalent to saying, "Understand physics, chemistry, and biology." The teachers who must decide what to include under such "objectives" are given little practical help.

Apart from a misplaced reliance in local curricula on arbitrary conceptual schemes, the main source of their repetitions and gaps continues to be their lack of content specificity. At first glance, my superior district is something of a puzzle in this respect. Its social science guide is splendidly specific in places. First graders must "distinguish between a globe, political, and relief maps." Second graders must "label a compass rose correctly" and "tell the meaning of 'the stars and stripes.'" By the time students get to grade six, they are to identify the Hwang, Yangtze, and Hsi rivers; the Himalaya Mountains, the Tlin Ling Mountains, the Central Mountains

of Japan, and Mount Fuji; the Gobi Desert, the East China Plains, and the Manchurian Plain; Hong Kong, Taiwan, and Yokohama; the Pacific Ocean, the Sea of Japan, and the Yellow Sea. There are similarly explicit geographical specifications for Southeast Asia, India, and Africa! One is surprised and happy to see this untypical focus on concrete geographical knowledge, and this useful guidance to the teacher regarding which of the innumerable geographical features are the essential ones to know.

How, then, may we explain the absence of similar specific guidance to the most important geographical features of the United States? No rivers, not the Mississippi, the Missouri, the Snake, the Rio Grande, or the James; no mountains, not the Alleghenies, the Rockies, or the Cascades; no mention of the Great Plains or the Great Lakes; no city (except that in the school district itself) and no state (except for that of the district). Yet all the foregoing geographical detail about Asia and Africa is presented as essential knowledge. Does the teacher need no guidance about key elements of U.S. geography that should be learned in the early grades? The textbooks themselves contain far too much detail to be useful in that regard. Why is there no specific decision about the essential elements of U.S. geography when there are such definite decisions about the Mekong, the Irrawaddy, and the Salween?

Let me offer an explanation for this highly typical omission which may help explain the unevenness in American curricular specificity. To select Asian geographical features is a noncontroversial activity. To select geographical features within the United States may be considered a highly controversial act. What cities shall *not* be mentioned? Akron, Ohio? But that city is very important for rubber manufacture; shouldn't kids know that tires come from Akron? Heavens! Once you start down that road, where will you stop? There are ninety U.S. cities as big as or bigger than Akron. Are we going to make kids learn ninety cities? And who is to determine the cutoff for U.S. rivers? Hadn't we better leave the whole question of specific U.S. geographical features alone? Such decisions are best left up to the individual teacher. Except for decisions about Asia and Africa, which no one will challenge, we'll just explain how to use an atlas and read a map.

Nowhere is this unhelpful vagueness more apparent than in language arts curricula throughout the United States. While the specificity of some district curricula in science and social studies may be admirable in places, the same cannot be said for any local language arts framework I know of. The only specific book, story, or poem I could find in the district curriculum I have been describing was in grade seven: *The Reader's Guide to Periodical Literature.*

The following is the first broad "objective" to be found in the district's language arts curriculum, and like the other language arts objectives, it spirals through each of the first six grades:

- Grade one: "Develop and apply a word attack system independently using appropriate contextual, phonetic, structural and reference clues."
- Grade two: "Develop and apply a word attack system independently using appropriate contextual, phonetic, structural and reference clues."

- Grade three: "Develop and apply a word attack system independently using appropriate contextual, phonetic, structural and reference clues."
- Grade four: "Develop and apply a word attack system independently using appropriate contextual, phonetic, structural and reference clues."
- Grade five: "Develop and apply a word attack system independently using appropriate contextual, phonetic, structural and reference clues."
- Grade six: "Develop and apply a word attack system independently using appropriate contextual, phonetic, structural and reference clues."

Then, through all six grades, the teacher is instructed to engage the students in formal operations that are subsumed under "contextual clues," "phonetic clues," "structural clues," "reference clues."

While these elements of literacy do need to be taught, this purely formal approach to teaching them, lacking as it does any guidance to specific writings through which they might be taught, is psychologically unsound, according to the research community.[23] It seems almost calculated to be repetitive, deadening, and boring. Its sharp focus on process, as well as its neglect of particular books, stories, and essays as means of teaching literacy skills, not only fails to guide teachers but misses an opportunity to teach both skills and important traditional knowledge simultaneously to children. It is precisely the sort of vague framework that leads to multiple readings of *Charlotte's Web*, and to disadvantaged children's lack of acquaintance with knowledge that advantaged children pick up at home.

Adequately detailed guidelines help teachers by discriminating between knowledge that is required and knowledge that is merely desirable. The selection of particular important facts actually reduces the total amount of specific information that a teacher needs to consider essential. Such guidelines encourage greater depth and coherence in teaching. It's true that they also tend to generate disagreement—which partly explains why our school districts continue to issue vague guidelines: why be specific when vagueness will avoid controversy? On the other hand, without specifics, disadvantaged students and their teachers play a Kafkaesque game whose rules are never clearly defined. Soon the unlucky are consigned to slow tracks and never enter the mainstream of learning and society.

Our Migrant Children

What chiefly makes our schools unfair, then, even for children who remain in the same school year after year, is that some students are learning less than others not because of their innate lack of academic ability or their lack of willingness to learn but because of inherent shortcomings in curricular organization. A systemic failure to teach all children the knowledge they need in order to understand what the next grade has to offer is *the* major source of avoidable injustice in our schools. It is impossible for a teacher to reach all children when some of them lack the necessary building blocks of learning. Under these circumstances, the most important single task of an individual school is to ensure that all children within that school gain the prior knowledge they will need at the next grade level. Since our system currently leaves that supremely important

task to the vagaries of individual classrooms, the result is a systemically imposed unfairness even for students who remain in the same school. Such inherent unfairness is greatly exacerbated for children who must change schools, sometimes in the middle of the year.

Consider the plight of Jane, who enters second grade in a new school. Her former first-grade teacher deferred all world history to a later grade, but in her new school many first graders have already learned about ancient Egypt. The new teacher's references to the Nile River, the Pyramids, and hieroglyphics simply mystify Jane, and fail to convey to her the new information that the allusions were meant to impart. Multiply that incomprehension by many others in Jane's new environment, and then multiply those by further comprehension failures which accrue because of the initial failures of uptake, and we begin to see why Jane is not flourishing academically in her new school. Add to these academic handicaps the emotional devastation of not understanding what other children are understanding, and add to avoidable academic problems the *un*avoidable ones of adjusting to a new group, and it is not hard to understand why newcomers fail to flourish in American schools. Then add to all of these drawbacks the fact that the social group with the greatest percentage of school changers is made up of low-income families who move for economic reasons, and one understands more fully why disadvantaged children suffer disproportionately from the curricular incoherence of the American educational system.

It is often said that we are a nation of immigrants. We are also a people that continues to migrate within the nation's borders. According to the United States General Accounting Office, about one-fifth of all Americans relocate every year: "The United States has one of the highest mobility rates of all developed countries; annually, about one-fifth of all Americans move. Elementary school children who move frequently face disruption to their lives, including their schooling."[24] Few young families are able to time their moves to coincide with the beginning and end of the school year.[25] In a typical community, the average rate at which students transfer in and out of schools during the school year is nearly one-third: "The average rate for Milwaukee public elementary schools is around 30 percent."[26] And among the parents who move, it is those in the lowest income brackets who move most frequently—much more often than middle- and high-income families.[27] This high mobility among low-income parents guarantees that the disadvantaged children who will be most severely affected by the educational handicaps of changing schools are the very ones who move most often. In a typical inner-city school, only about half the students who start in September are still there in May.[28] The myth of the local curriculum can be matched by the myth of the local school—if one means by that term not just a building and a staff but also the students who attend it during the year.

Like most Americans, I was ignorant of the huge dimensions of this little-publicized problem. Student mobility is rarely mentioned in discussions of school reform—which says more about the self-imposed restrictions on our educational thinking than about the urgencies of our educational problems. Any challenge to the principle of an autonomous local curriculum is considered taboo. Hence all the problems exacerbated by that taboo, including the deleterious effects of student mobility, receive far less public attention than they deserve. I was first alerted to the magnitude of the mobility problem in 1992 when I began receiving official reports from Core Knowledge Schools. The first one I saw was from Public School No. 179, in San Antonio, Texas, the Hawthorne School. On the first page of the report, under the rubric "Students," was a box with the following data:

TABLE 3.1

Grade levels served:	PK–5
Membership:	522
Ethnicity: Asian	2.5%
Black	4.8%
Hispanic	83.2%
White	9.5%
Transfers: In	108
Out	176
Percent of membership transferred:	54.4%

The term of art for the percentages of transferred students is "mobility rate." The average mobility rates for the inner city lie routinely between 45 and 80 percent, with many suburban rates between 25 and 40 percent. Some inner-city schools in New York City and elsewhere have mobility rates of over 100 percent. That is to say, the total number of students moving in and out during the year exceeds the total number of students attending the school. "In some of the nation's most transient districts where some slots turn over several times, schools have mobility rates of more than 100 percent."[29]

A recent report from the General Accounting Office stated that one-sixth of all third graders attend at least three schools between first and third grade. A quarter of low-income third graders have attended at least three different schools, a figure that rises to over a third among those with limited English proficiency.[30] The adverse effects of these moves on educational achievement contribute significantly to the low achievement of our system as a whole. The General Accounting Office found that many more migrating third graders were reading below grade level, compared with those who had not yet changed schools.[31] Given the curricular incoherence faced even by those who stay at the same school, the fragmentation of the education provided to frequently moving students approaches the unthinkable.

The adverse effects of such social and academic incoherence are powerful even among nonpoverty students, and are greatly intensified when parents have low educational levels and when compensatory education is not available in the home. Dr. David Wood and his associates have analyzed the effects of mobility on 9,915 children. With this large group, the researchers were able to factor out the influences of poverty, race, single-parent households, and lack of parental education in order to isolate just the effects of school changing alone. Even with these adverse influences factored out, children who changed school often were much more likely to exhibit behavioral problems and to fail a grade—which is difficult to do in current American schools. In an interview, Dr. Wood summarized his findings by saying that mobility alone "is as potent a predictor [of poor school performance] as

having parents who are not well educated, or parents who are poor."[32]

It is important, however, not to regard these authoritative findings as inevitable consequences of student mobility. The findings describe, rather, the consequences of mobility within the American system as it is currently constituted. Just as with the 1966 Coleman Report, which disclosed the decisive importance of the home, the Wood results of 1993 should be placed in their particular historical, cultural, and educational contexts rather than conceived of as timeless and inevitable. There is strong evidence that the adverse educational effects of student mobility are much greater in the United States than in countries that use a nationwide core curriculum. In a summary of research, Herbert Walberg, citing the work of Bruce C. Straits, states that "common learning goals, curriculum, and assessment within states (or within an entire nation), moreover, also alleviate the grave learning disabilities faced by children, especially poorly achieving children who move from one district to another with different curricula, assessment, and goals."[33]

Before I learned the extent of the student-mobility problem in the United States, I already suspected that the issue had been inadequately dealt with for children of migrant farmworkers, who must change schools several times in the course of the year as their parents move northward to gather crops. The adverse consequences of this degree of curricular instability are easily imagined. One would have thought, therefore, that at least in this special case a core curriculum could be devised in order to provide for more educational coherence and stability. Indeed, in 1989 a group of educational researchers ventured to suggest that perhaps a nationwide core curriculum (confined of course to migrant children) might be desirable. The November 29, 1989, issue of *Education Week* contained an article about this study and reactions to it:

> In an interview last week, Mr. Trotter, one of the authors, elaborated on two of the boldest suggestions to emerge from the study: the establishment of a national curriculum and diploma tailored to the needs of migrant children. "In talking to the kids there were incredible levels of frustration," he said. "They almost were being pushed out of school by the whip-lash effect of changing curriculum as they changed schools." . . . Officials at the Pennsylvania and U.S. Education Departments have already distanced themselves from those recommendations. Mr. Ledebur, who oversees the state's education programs for migrant workers, last week stressed that all the recommendations represent the views of the authors, and not the state. . . . "Even though there are serious problems regarding the education of migrant children," he said, "a [migrant] national curriculum may not be the best way to deal with those problems." . . . And Francis V. Corrigan, acting director of migrant education for the federal department, said, . . . "In spite of their merits in terms of the needs of migrant students, we also have some state and local responsibilities to consider here."

Though the problem of high mobility rates has grown more pressing and acute, it is hardly a new problem in the United States. In the 1930s, William Bagley, with his customary courage, had this to say:

> The notion that each community must have a curriculum all its own is not only silly, but tragic. It neglects two important needs. The first, as we have already seen, is the need of a democracy for many common elements in the culture of all the people, to the end that the people may discuss collective problems in terms that will convey common meanings. The second need is extremely practical. It is the need of recognizing the fact that American people simply will not "stay put." They are the most mobile people in the world. . . . Under these conditions, failure to have a goodly measure of uniformity in school subjects and grade placement is a gross injustice to at least ten million school children at the present time.[34]

While few would be likely to follow Bagley in courageously calling the principle of the local curriculum "silly," many researchers would agree that Bagley was right to call its consequences "tragic." Even those experts who hold strongly to the principle of local control of curriculum might well concede the need for a voluntary agreement about a common sequence in the curriculum—at least in those areas like math and science and the basic facts of history and geography, which, unlike sex education, are not and should not be subjects of controversy. The principle of the local curriculum is desirable in a democracy, so long as schooling is effective and fair. But against the principle of local autonomy must be weighed the paramount principles of educational excellence and social fairness. Democratic principles sometimes conflict with one another; none is absolute. In any case, a strong majority of the American public shares Bagley's view. According to a 1991 Gallup Poll, that majority clearly recognizes the desirability of curricular coherence and commonality as a necessary precondition of excellence and fairness in education, and favors it by a very wide margin.[35] How long before the clear will of the majority is accepted by the ruling experts, who continue to view curricular particularism as an absolute and inviolable principle?

International Research on Shared Knowledge

In view of the strong theoretical and practical reasons for providing common intellectual capital in early grades, one would predict that the advantages of a core curriculum would show up in comparisons between national systems which do and those which do not use core curricula. Such comparisons ought to be especially informative with subjects, like math and science, for which similar achievement goals are set in all national systems. I am not making the argument that a core curriculum alone is necessary and sufficient to produce uniformly good results but, rather, that it is a *necessary* condition for producing them, to which must be added other factors like strong support in the general culture. The prediction that a core curriculum is necessary to produce greater excellence and fairness is strongly confirmed by analyzing such comparisons. The following graph traces student math achievement in a core system (Japan) and in a noncore system (United States). In conducting this cross-national comparison, Harold Stevenson and his colleagues made sure that the test accurately reflected the knowledge and skills which eleventh graders in both nations were mandated to

learn, and that the socioeconomic sampling of students was exactly comparable. Other factors, such as the time of the school year when the data were collected and the conditions under which the tests were taken, were carefully controlled.

The graph shows that much larger percentages of U.S. students are performing at very low levels. If we assume that innate math ability is normally distributed, outcomes under a fair educational system should reflect that normal distribution. Children with high math abilities should be enabled to realize their talents, while the far greater number of children with middling abilities should achieve at a respectable level, and children with low abilities should be brought to an acceptable minimal competence. That pattern of equity and excellence is precisely the pattern illustrated in the Japanese results. By contrast, the U.S. curve is abnormally populous on the left, low side of the scores, showing that large percentages of students who began with a normal diversity of math abilities have been hindered from achieving their potentials; a percentage of students, presumably with low abilities, made scores of zero and slightly above, while top students did not perform as well as their foreign counterparts. The U.S. system produces an inequitable distribution of scores, a low average performance, and a large amount of mathematical incompetence.

Such contrasts are so dramatic that every conceivable mode of defense has been deployed to call them in question and explain them away. Comparative international research can always be challenged on the ground that apples and oranges are being compared. Such a defense falls on sympathetic ears in the United States. A long tradition of American exceptionalism assumes

FIGURE 3.1

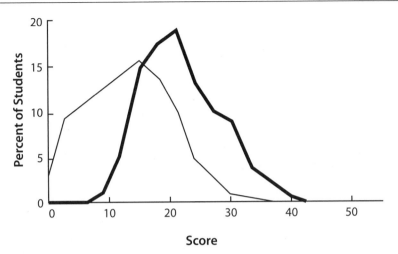

Score

Eleventh graders' scores on the mathematics test: Japan, heavy line; United States, light line. Mean ± 1 standard deviation: 21.72 ± 6.59 and 13.39 ± 7.06, respectively. Sample sizes: 1120 and 1197.

Source: H. Stevenson, C. Chaunsheng, and L. Shin-Ling, "Mathematics Achievement of Chinese, Japanese, and American Children: Ten Years Later," *Science* 259 (January 1, 1993): 51–58.

that the United States will always be an apple, while other nations will always be oranges. But there are two considerations (besides common sense) that tell against the peremptory dismissal of the growing number of international comparisons that show unfavorable results for the United States. The first is the evidence of an absolute educational decline in the United States in the period 1966–80 using U.S. data alone. The second is the evidence of a relative decline vis-à-vis other nations during that same period using identical modes of comparison over time.

It is often stated that the reason for the sharp decline in verbal SAT scores in the United States between 1966 and 1980 was the democratization of the test-taking population. But, as I documented in 1987, this defense does not explain the 64 per-

cent decline in the *absolute number* of high-achieving students—those who had formerly been scoring above 600 on the verbal SAT.[36] No one believes or argues that the population from which this group comes—that is, the absolute number of top students taking the SAT—has declined. From the decline at the top, and the large drop in the overall mean, one can reasonably infer a decline in the educational quality of the system for all students, including those at the top.

As to the apples-vs.-oranges objection to international studies, it might apply to a single-shot comparison but not to identical comparisons over time. Whatever apple-orange inappropriatenesses existed in the first study would also exist in the second, making the *direction* of results highly informative. If a comparison done in 1985 (and published in 1988) showed a relative decline from a similar one done in 1970, the change would reliably indicate the direction of American educational quality as compared to that of other nations. In the 1970s, the International Association for the Evaluation of Educational Achievement (IEA) conducted a multinational study of science achievement, and then in the 1980s repeated the study. In the 1970 study, the United States ranked seventh out of seventeen countries; in the 1980s it ranked fifteenth out of seventeen—third from the bottom, a drop that was considered worthy of special mention in the executive summary of the 1988 IEA report.[37]

In contemplating such results from the IEA and other sources, it's important to keep in mind why they carry so much weight. Every modern nation educates over 98 percent of its children in the early grades, so the data are not unfairly slanted against a country like the United States, which "educates everybody." Also, because the comparative data are derived from the entire range of abilities in the population, they indicate the *inherent* effectiveness of the systems producing the results. The special value of large-scale comparative research is that it washes out many of the variables which cannot be controlled for in the small scale. International comparisons take large, representative samples from educational systems which have been operating for many years with millions of children and whose average results can be known. Hence, the conclusions derived from these large populations of students in diverse cultural contexts are far more reliable than the results, however dramatic, of more confined research that cannot factor out cultural and historical variables. Only when an educational arrangement suc-

ceeds on a large scale over a long period in diverse contexts can one confidently accept its claim to general application.

It is true that most educational programs, national and local, including those performing badly, are based on genuine, if sometimes partial, insights into the nature of children and learning. Few school reforms have been tried that haven't worked reasonably well on a small scale. Yet the primary cause of an initial success may not have been the innovation itself but other factors, such as the enthusiasm of the participants. This false positive is known among sociologists as the "Hawthorne effect," and its workings are often invoked when a school reform that one *doesn't* like appears to be successful. Education is such a slow-moving and multifaceted enterprise that no innovation can be securely evaluated right away, any more than a new drug can be confidently evaluated on the basis of small clinical trials. The efficacy of either new drugs or new educational policies may not be known until they have been used over many years by many thousands of people—as both the thalidomide affair and U.S. education since the late 1960s have dramatically illustrated.

In determining the relative efficacy of core-curriculum policies, the decade-long separation of the two IEA studies allows us to observe that between the 1970s and the 1980s the rank order of science achievement in core-curriculum nations rose or stayed stable, while the rank order in noncore countries declined. What counts here is relative movement. One would expect the core countries to stay stable with respect to one another and—since most countries in the sample do use core curricula—not to shift much in rankings. One would expect the noncore countries to show a relative decline. That is what happened. Among the three noncore countries, England dropped from ninth to eleventh, Australia from third to tenth, and the United States from seventh to fifteenth. Among the core nations, Sweden remained at sixth, Finland rose from seventh to fifth (the United States having vacated seventh place), while Japan and Hungary traded second and first place.[38]

Another effect of using core curricula shows up in the IEA comparisons. The 1988 report evaluated national systems according to the equality of educational opportunity they provided children—a fairness rating for each system. This was a measure of the extent to which a nation educates children at all schools to an appropriate average level of achievement, regardless of location or social class. Strikingly, the systems that ranked high in fairness also ranked high in excellence; the best-performing systems were also the most equitable ones. For instance, among Finnish schools, only 2 percent of schools showed below-standard average achievement; in Japan, it was 1 percent; in Korea, 5 percent; in Sweden, 1 percent; and in Hungary, 0 percent. Among the noncore countries, the percentages of schools below par were Australia, 8 percent; the Netherlands, 16 percent; England, 19 percent; and the United States, 30 percent.[39]

One fairness score was anomalous—that of the Netherlands. Whereas Holland placed third of seventeen in average science achievement, its fairness score (16 percent of schools below par) was a distant last among the countries of northern continental Europe. Britain did even worse, with 19 percent of schools below par. One cause of these results was probably that Holland and Britain, in contrast to their European neighbors, lacked a common core curriculum. When the results were analyzed, the British had not yet adopted their national curriculum. Any private school in the Netherlands that met certain basic standards for plant and faculty was eligible to receive public funding. That 16 percent of Dutch schools fell below par was probably owing to the fact that in the Netherlands there are many schools doing their own thing—a theory strongly supported by the similar results from Britain, the other noncore-curriculum nation of Northern Europe.

A country that lacks nationwide curricular standards can produce high average results when each of its schools has a good common curriculum and when mobility rates between schools are low, keeping the student body stable, so that each child receives a coherent education. Switzerland, for example, which did not participate in the IEA study but which has top scores for excellence and fairness according to other studies, uses a different core curriculum within each small canton. But since the Swiss do not move very often, the result is a coherent curriculum for each child.[40] If the students at good Dutch schools performed superbly, that would explain how average achievement could remain high even though scores were low at 16 percent of Dutch schools. All the more reason to conclude that, in the Dutch context, students at these inferior schools were being cheated. In the Netherlands, the absence of a core curriculum has permitted spots of unfairness even within a generally excellent system. The Dutch result is very useful, therefore, as an apparent exception that confirms the rule.

Support for this generalization about core curricula comes from France, which did not participate in the 1988 IEA study. The French have been keeping educational data on a national scale for many decades and can justly pride themselves on having greatly diminished the socially induced learning gap between advantaged and disadvantaged children. Remarkably, in France the initial gap between advantaged and disadvantaged students, instead of widening steadily as in the United States, decreases with each school grade. By the end of seventh grade, the child of a North African immigrant who has attended two years of French preschool (*école maternelle*) will on average have narrowed the socially induced learning gap.[41] Such success in achieving fairness is explained at least in part by the fact that national systems which have core curricula are able to provide a school-based education which relies relatively less on the undependable home curriculum to supply the prior knowledge needed for learning in each grade.

The New Civil Rights Frontier

In the 1960s and '70s, when the legal foundations of social justice were getting firmer, public schools across the United States were getting worse. Bad schools hold back disadvantaged children disproportionately because disadvantaged homes are typically less able than advantaged ones to compensate for the knowledge gaps left by the schools. An overall decline in the quality of schooling will thus have an uneven social effect. All children, including those of the middle class, will be poorly educated, but the negative effects will be strongest among the least privileged. As they go through the grades, disadvantaged students will accumulate relatively less intellectual capital than they would have

under a more demanding system. Educational injustice will grow—whether or not the schools are racially integrated. Since inferior education is today the primary cause of social and economic injustice, the struggle for equality of educational opportunity is in effect the new civil rights frontier.[42] This new struggle is more subtle and complex than the earlier one of sit-ins and freedom rides. In this struggle, it is harder to tell good from evil, true from false.

The basic explanation for the strong correlation between equality of educational opportunity and use of a core curriculum has been given. A core curriculum induces grade readiness for all children and thus enables all members of a classroom to learn. When all children possess the prior knowledge they need for understanding new material, the teacher will spend far less time in boring reviews and in special coaching of those who are behind. Everybody will be more stimulated, more accountable, and will learn more. In the preceding section, I showed that all national systems rated fair by the IEA standard use this core-curriculum approach, and I showed, moreover, that *no* noncore system cited in the report has managed to achieve fairness.[43]

Since some children are apter and harder-working than others, equality of educational opportunity does not mean that all students will make very high test scores. Yet overall school scores are indicative. It is of course true that good schools in the inner city can never *entirely* equalize educational opportunity compared with schools in the suburbs, because the home is also a school, where students spend more time than in the official one. Other things being equal, students from good-home schools will always have an educational advantage over students from less-good-home schools. Nonetheless, basic gaps in knowledge can be compensated for in the classroom, as the international data prove. It follows that a moderately high average achievement in all schools is a roughly accurate index to national educational fairness, whether the schools are in the inner city or the suburbs.

In the United States, our schools' inequitable distribution of intellectual capital causes the gap between academic haves and have-nots to grow wider in each successive early grade until, by fourth grade, it is usually unbridgeable. This tragic process currently seems inexorable. The longitudinal researches of Walter Loban in the 1960s tracked the acquired learning abilities of disadvantaged and advantaged students as they moved from grade one to grade four and beyond, with results that the following graph vividly indicates. Note that some crucial data are not directly represented, namely, that one group showed low, oral skills in kindergarten, the other high oral skills before either group learned to read.

FIGURE 3.2

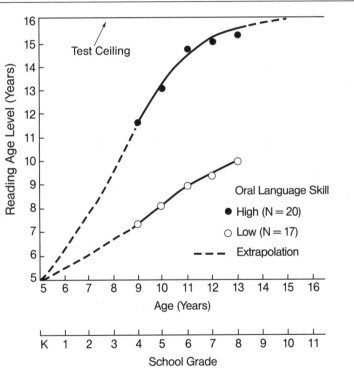

Relationship between chronological-age/school-age level and median reading ability for students rated high or low in oral language skills in kindergarten.

Source: Constructed by T. G. Sticht et al., *Auding and Reading: A Developmental Model* (Alexandria, Va.: Human Resources Organization, 1974), from data presented in W. Loban, *Language Ability: Grades Seven, Eight, and Nine* (Berkeley: University of California, 1964), Table 16, page 117.

Later researches by Jeanne Chall duplicated this result, as did the Coleman Report of 1966. One observation by Coleman and his colleagues has important implications for explaining and overcoming the widening gap. It is the finding that good schools have stronger positive effects and poor schools stronger negative ones on disadvantaged students. This may be denominated "Coleman's Law."[44] Since our public school system as a whole is not very good, a small educational disadvantage in kindergarten normally widens to a big learning gap by grade four—a result that unfortunately applies even to graduates of Head Start.

Head Start is politically popular as a tool for achieving equal educational opportunity. Many believe that the program should be extended to all disadvantaged children. Despite occasional political setbacks and temporary damage to its reputation by research impugning its efficacy, Head Start has managed to emerge as a Great Society program that still enjoys the protection of both political parties. But just how complex the search for equal educational opportunity has become may be gauged from the fact that Head Start does not achieve educational *improvement*, much less educational equity.

That is the well-documented conclusion of the Department of Health and Human Services, which in 1985 published a review of all existing research on the effects of Head Start. It stated that "in the long run, cognitive and socioemotional test scores of former Head Start students do not remain superior to those of disadvantaged students who did not attend Head Start."[45] Why does this astonishing fade-out occur? Edward Zigler, Sterling Professor of Psychology at Yale and one of the founders of Head Start, gives an unintended clue in an anecdote about his time as director of the Office of Child Development. He was presiding at a meeting of

> the department's power structure, including the HEW [Department of Health Education and Welfare] deputy secretary. They were impressed with "Sesame Street" and dwelled on the fact that it was so inexpensive. "We can get 'Sesame Street' to reach poor kids by spending sixty-five cents per child," they said. "Why should we spend over a thousand dollars per child on Head Start?" . . . Finally, as they kept pressing I said I would give Head Start money to "Sesame Street" if they could answer this question: How long would a poor child have to watch "Sesame Street" to get his or her teeth filled? When nobody could answer, that was the end of the meeting.[46]

From its inception in the 1960s, Zigler and his cofounders conceived of Head Start as much more than an educational program. The health, nutrition, motivation, and self-confidence of poor children were deemed to be at least as important to their future well-being as their academic learning. Another feature present from the beginning was Head Start's rule that parents be involved in running each local program. A rationale for that principle: building parents' self-esteem would help develop their children's. In short, Head Start has not been primarily an *academic* program. Though momentary academic benefits have sometimes been measured, they are not securely fixed and they quickly fade.

Researchers have sought further explanations for this academic fade-out. The team of scientists who wrote the 1985 review of Head Start research offered the following: "The educational environment in elementary schools does not support and stimulate the children as effectively as Head Start did. This suggests that more innovative arrangements designed to sustain the early developmental benefits of Head Start would be desirable."[47] The researchers imply that while Head Start may have yielded momentary benefits, later schooling erases them. Children fortunate enough to attend Head Start must enter a public school system that is incoherent and fragmented. But this explanation of fade-out is only half the story. Head Start is not a single, academically describable program. Its academics vary greatly from place to place. While it is usually beneficial for a time, it tends to lack academic coherence and is rarely accountable for specific academic outcomes. When its graduates subsequently enter a program that also lacks academic coherence and is also unaccountable for specific academic outcomes, the children have left the frying pan for the fire. This is implicitly an argument for extending Head Start while at the same time improving its academic rigor and that of the schooling which follows.

Preschool programs elsewhere in the world *do* achieve long-term academic benefits for disadvantaged students. In France, early schooling permanently boosts educational achievements of children of low-paid workers and immigrants

from North Africa.[48] What, then, makes the academic benefits of early education endure in some countries but fade in our own? A few contrasts: Head Start lasts three hours, is staffed by nonprofessionals, and is nonacademic. The *école maternelle* (attended by over 90 percent of French three- and four-year-olds) lasts all day and goes twelve months a year, is staffed by professionals, and has well-defined academic goals. Children then enter a grade-school system that also has a well-defined academic and cognitive core.

American experts have developed astonishingly resourceful techniques for denying the desirability of an academic core curriculum. In effect, they say:

- We have educated children reasonably well in the past without using a core of universal content standards.
- We already have an informal core-knowledge system in the United States, determined by the widespread use of just a few textbooks.
- We do not need to emphasize particular content; knowledge is changing and increasing so rapidly that the best approach is to teach children *how* to learn.
- There is a danger that standardization of content would be imposed by the federal government and would open the way to federal control of education.
- It is illegitimate to compare the United States with other countries, which are in every case far less diverse than we are.
- A canned, lockstep curriculum would obliterate the distinctive characteristics

of American localities and make schools into cookie cutters that turn out the same product everywhere.

In the preceding pages, I have tried to expose these stand-pat positions for the evasions they are. Indeed, if the foregoing analyses are right, a diverse, nomadic nation like ours has a greater need for a grade-by-grade core curriculum than do countries that are less migratory and diverse, just as a nomadic, disadvantaged child has a greater need for academic coherence than does an advantaged child. Head Start, especially, needs an agreed-on cognitive core of basic knowledge and vocabulary. Extreme localism, coupled with vagueness, seems increasingly outmoded at a time when children must change schools a lot and when the educational needs of young children have become very much the same throughout the world.

It is a fundamental injustice that what American children are enabled to learn in school should be determined by what their homes have already given them. Although this chapter has focused on this injustice, nothing said here should be construed to imply that our *advantaged* children are on the whole receiving an adequate education. They are not. The public schools of a democracy have a duty to educate all students to their potential. A child's initial lack of intellectual capital is not an immutable given that our schools are powerless to change; rather, it is a challenge that schools can meet by overcoming their academic incoherence. Throughout the world, just one way has been devised to meet the double challenge of educational excellence and fairness: to teach definite skills and a solid core of content appropriate in an effective man-

ner in each year of preschool and grade-school education.

REFERENCES

Ayres, L. P. *An Index Number for State School Systems.* New York: Warwick and York, 1922.

Bagley, W. C. *Determinism in Education.* Baltimore: Warwick & York, 1925; 2nd printing with corrections, 1928.

———. *Education and Emergent Man: A Theory of Education with Particular Application to Public Education in the United States.* New York: Nelson, 1934.

Boulot, S., and Boyzon-Fradet, D. *Les Immigrés et l'école: une course d'obstacles.* Paris: L'Harmattan, 1988.

Bourdieu, P. "Le Capital social: notes provisoires." *Actes de la recherché en sciences socials* 3 (1980): 2–3.

Centre for Educational Research and Innovation. *Immigrants' Children at School.* Paris: Organisation for Economic Co-operation and Development, 1987.

Chall, J. S. *Families and Literacy: Final Report to the National Institute of Education.* Washington, D.C., 1982.

Chall, J. S., Jacobs, V. A., and Baldwin, L. E. *The Reading Crisis: Why Poor Children Fall Behind.* Cambridge, Mass.: Harvard University Press, 1990.

Cohen, D. "Moving Images." *Education Week,* August 3, 1994, 32–39.

———. "Frequent Moves Said to Boost Risk of School Problems." *Education Week,* September 22, 1994, 15.

Coleman, J. S. *Equality of Educational Opportunity.* Washington, D.C.: U.S. Department of Health, Education, and Welfare, Office of Education, 1966.

College Board. *College-Bound Seniors: Eleven Years of National Data from the College Board's Admission Testing Program, 1973–83.* New York, 1984.

Dewey, J. *Democracy and Education: An Introduction to the Philosophy of Education.*

New York: The Free Press/Macmillan, 1916, 1944.

Elam, S., Rose, L., and Gallup, A. "The 23rd Annual Gallup Poll of the Public's Attitudes Toward the Public Schools." *Phi Delta Kappan*, September 1991, 41–47.

Ferguson, R. F. "Shifting Challenges: Fifty Years of Economic Change Towards Black-White Earnings Equality." *Daedalus* 124 (Winter 1995): 1, 37–76.

Geary, D. "Reflections of Evolution and Culture in Children's Cognition." *American Psychologist*, January 1995, 24–36.

General Accounting Office. *Elementary School Children: Many Change School Frequently, Harming Their Education.* GAO/HEHS-94-45. Washington, D.C., 1994.

Hernes, G. *Core Curriculum for Primary, Secondary, and Adult Education in Norway.* Oslo: Royal Ministry of Church, Education, and Research, 1994.

Ingersoll, G. M., Scamman, J. P., and Eckerling, W. D. "Geographic Mobility and Student Achievement in an Urban Setting" [Denver public schools]. *Educational Evaluation & Policy Analysis* (Summer 1989): 143–49.

International Association for the Evaluation of Educational Achievement. *Science Achievement in Seventeen Countries: A Preliminary Report.* Elmsford, N.Y.: Pergamon Press, 1988.

Jefferson, T. "Notes on Virginia." In *The Life and Selected Writings of Thomas Jefferson*, ed. A. Koch and W. Peden. New York: Random House, 1944.

———. *The Life and Selected Writings of Thomas Jefferson*, ed. A. Koch and W. Peden. New York: Random House, 1944.

Johnson, R. A., and Lindblad, A. H. "Effect of Mobility on Academic Performance of Sixth Grade Students." *Perceptual and Motor Skills* 72 (April 1991): 547–52.

Jones, Constance. *Quality and Equity of Education Outcomes: The Effects of School-Wide Content Specificity*, Ph.D. diss., University of South Florida, Tampa, 1993.

Lapointe, A. E., Mead, N. A., and Askew, J. M. *Learning Mathematics.* Princeton, N.J.: International Assessment of Educational Progress and the Educational Testing Service, 1992.

———. *Learning Science.* Princeton, N.J.: International Assessment of Educational Progress and the Educational Testing Service, 1992.

National Academy of Education, Commission on Reading. *Becoming a Nation of Readers: The Report of the Commission on Reading.* Pittsburgh, Pa., 1985.

O'Keeffe, D. J. *Truancy in English Secondary Schools.* London: Her Majesty's Stationery Office, 1994.

Pinker, S. *The Language Instinct.* New York: William Morrow, 1994.

Ravitch, D. *The Troubled Crusade: American Education, 1945–1980.* New York: Basic Books, 1983.

Stevenson, H., Chuansheng, C., and Shin-Ying, L. "Mathematics Achievement of Chinese, Japanese, and American Children: Ten Years Later." *Science* 259 (January 1, 1993): 51–58.

Stevenson, H., and Stigler, J. *The Learning Gap: Why Our Schools Are Failing and What We Can Learn from Japanese and Chinese Education.* New York: Summit Books, 1992.

Thompson, R. F. *The Brain: A Neuroscience Primer.* New York: W. H. Freeman, 1993.

U.S. Department of Health and Human Services. *The Impact of Head Start on Children, Families and Communities: Final Report of the Head Start Evaluation, Synthesis and Utilization Project, Executive Summary.* Washington, D.C., 1985.

Walberg, H. J. "Improving Local Control and Learning." Typescript, 1994. Walberg cites: Straits, B. C. "Residence, Migration, and School Progress." *Sociology of Education* 60 (1987): 34–43.

Walberg, H. J., and Tsai, S. "Matthew Effects in Education." *American Educational Research Journal* 20 (Fall 1983): 359–73.

Wood, D., Halfon, N., and Scarlata, D. "Impact of Family Relocation on Children's Growth, Development, School Function, and Behavior." *Journal of the American Medical Association* 270 (September 15, 1993): 1334–38.

Zigler, E., and Muenchow, S. *Head Start: The Inside Story of America's Most Successful Educational Experiment.* New York: HarperCollins/Basic Books, 1992.

NOTES

1. Jefferson, *The Life and Selected Writings of Thomas Jefferson*, 51.

2. Ibid., 265.

3. Dewey, *Democracy and Education*, 3–4.

4. Bagley, *Education and Emergent Man*, 139.

5. Hernes, *Core Curriculum for Primary, Secondary, and Adult Education in Norway*, 26.

6. Bourdieu, "Le Capital social: notes provisoires," 2–3. See also Coleman, *Parental Involvement in Education*.

7. Walberg and Tsai, "Matthew Effects in Education," 359–73.

8. Thompson, *The Brain*, 299–333. See also Husen, *Talent, Equality, and Meritocracy*.

9. Statistical data on Belgium, France, Germany, Luxembourg, the Netherlands, Sweden, and Switzerland may be found in Centre for Educational Research and Innovation, *Immigrants' Children at School*, 178–259. The French studies have been the fullest. They show that, when all other factors are accounted for, the difference in performance between Third World immigrant students and French students "decreased more or less markedly, although they did not disappear completely." For further details, see Boulot and Boyzon-Fradet, *Les Immigrés et l'école*, 54–58.

10. Hernes, *Core Curriculum for Primary, Secondary, and Adult Education in Norway*, 26.

11. Coleman, *Equality of Educational Opportunity*.

12. See Chall, *Families and Literacy*; and especially, Chall, Jacobs, and Baldwin, *The Reading Crisis*.

13. Bagley, *Determinism in Education*.

14. Ayres, *An Index Number for State School Systems*.

15. Stevenson and Stigler, *The Learning Gap*, 196.

16. Stevenson, Chuansheng, and Shin-Ying, "Mathematics Achievement of Chinese, Japanese, and American Children," 51–58.

17. Jones, *Quality and Equity of Education Outcomes*.

18. O'Keeffe, *Truancy in English Secondary Schools*.

19. Pinker, *The Language Instinct*.

20. Geary, "Reflections of Evolution and Culture in Children's Cognition," 24–36.

21. Stevenson and Stigler, *The Learning Gap*, 140.

22. Ravitch, *The Troubled Crusade*, 52–55.

23. National Academy of Education, *Becoming a Nation of Readers*.

24. General Accounting Office, *Elementary School Children*, 1.

25. Ibid, 32.

26. Cohen, "Moving Images," 32–39.

27. Wood, Halfon, and Scarlata, "Impact of Family Relocation on Children's Growth, Development, School Function, and Behavior," 1334–38.

28. Cohen, "Moving Images," 32–39.

29. Ibid.

30. General Accounting Office, *Elementary School Children*, 5.

31. Ibid., 6.

32. Quoted in Cohen, "Frequent Moves Said to Boost Risk of School Problems," 15. See also Wood, Halfon, and Scarlata, "Impact of Family Relocation on Children's Growth, Development, School Function, and Behavior," 1334–38. For further confirmation on adverse effects of changing schools, see Johnson and Lindblad, "Effect of Mobility on Academic Performance of Sixth Grade Students," 547–52; and Ingersoll, Scamman, and Eckerling, "Geographic

Mobility and Student Achievement in an Urban Setting," 143–49.

33. Walberg, "Improving Local Control and Learning." Walberg cites Straits, "Residence, Migration, and School Progress," 34–43.

34. Bagley, *Education and Emergent Man*, 145.

35. Elam, Rose, and Gallup, "The 23rd Annual Gallup Poll of the Public's Attitudes Toward the Public Schools," 41–47. In response to the question "Would you favor or oppose requiring the public schools in this community to use a standardized [*sic!*] national curriculum?", the response was 68 percent in favor, 24 percent opposed, and 8 percent undecided. The majority was even greater when the tendentious term "standardized" was omitted, as in this question: "Would you favor or oppose requiring the public schools in this community to conform to national achievement standards and goals?" Here the response was 81 percent in favor, 12 percent opposed, and 7 percent undecided.

36. College Board, *College-Bound Seniors*. The College Board sent me further details showing the breakdown of scores over 600 between 1972 and 1984. With a constant number of about one million students taking the test, the percentage of students who scored over 600 was 7.3 percent in 1984 and 11.4 percent in 1972. The percentage scoring over 650 was 3.0 percent in 1984 and 5.29 percent in 1972. See also Hirsch, *Cultural Literacy*, 4, 5, 217. Still firmer numbers: "In 1972 over 116,000 students scored above 600 on the verbal S.A.T. In 1982 fewer than 71,000 scored that high even though a similar number took the exam" (from an article by David Barulich in *Education Week*, February 15, 1995, page 31).

37. International Association for the Evaluation of Educational Achievement, *Science Achievement in Seventeen Countries*.

38. Ibid., 100.

39. Ibid., 42.

40. The superb Swiss results are found in two highly informative comparative studies: Lapointe, Mead, and Askew, *Learning Mathematics* and *Learning Science*.

41. Data from Boulot and Boyzon-Fradet, *Les Immigrés et l'école*, 54–58; and Centre for Educational Research and Innovation, *Immigrants' Children at School*, 178–259.

42. Ferguson, "Shifting Challenges," 37–76.

43. International Association for the Evaluation of Educational Achievement, *Science Achievement in Seventeen Countries*, 42.

44. Coleman, *Equality of Educational Opportunity*; for strongest effects of poor schools and teachers on disadvantaged children, see pages 22, 316–18. See also Chall, *Families and Literacy*; and especially, Chall, Jacobs, and Baldwin, *The Reading Crisis*.

45. U.S. Department of Health and Human Services, *The Impact of Head Start on Children, Families and Communities*, 1.

46. Zigler and Muenchow, *Head Start*, 145.

47. U.S. Department of Health and Human Services, *The Impact of Head Start*, 2.

48. Statistical data on Belgium, France, Germany, Luxembourg, the Netherlands, Sweden, and Switzerland may be found in Centre for Educational Research and Innovation, *Immigrants' Children at School*, 178–259. The French studies have been the fullest. They show that, when all other factors are accounted for, the difference in performance between Third World immigrant students and French students "decreased more or less markedly, although they did not disappear completely." For further details, see Boulot and Boyzon-Fradet, *Les Immigrés et l'école*, 54–58.

Larry Cuban and David Tyack

Learning from the Past

For over a century citizens have sought to perfect the future by debating how to improve the young through education. Actual reforms in schools have rarely matched such aspirations, however. The words "utopia" and "tinkering" each have positive and negative connotations. Utopian thinking can be dismissed as pie-in-the-sky or valued as visionary; tinkering can be condemned as mere incrementalism or praised as a commonsense remedy for everyday problems. Both positive and negative examples of tinkering and utopian thinking abound in the record of educational reform. At the heart of that history lies the complex interplay between the purposes and processes of institutional change.[1]

Reforming the public schools has long been a favorite way of improving not just education but society. In the 1840s Horace Mann took his audience to the edge of the precipice to see the social hell that lay before them if they did not achieve salvation through the common school. In 1983 a presidential commission produced another fire-and-brimstone sermon about education, *A Nation at Risk*, though its definition of damnation (economic decline) differed from Mann's (moral dissolution). For over a century and a half, Americans have translated their cultural anxieties and hopes into dramatic demands for educational reform.[2]

Utopian thinking about education has been a tapestry woven of many strands. One was political. The new nation declared on its national seal the aim of becoming "The New Order of the Ages." From the Revolution onward, educational theorists have self-consciously used schooling to construct the citizens of that new order. A Protestant-republican ideology of making the United States literally God's country inspired the promoters of the public school movement of the nineteenth century.[3]

The political theorist Hannah Arendt argued that in the United States education has played a "different and, politically, incomparably more important role" than elsewhere, in large part because of "the role that continuous immigration plays in the country's political consciousness and frame of mind." Educational leaders have tried to transform immigrant newcomers and other "outsiders" into individuals who matched their idealized image of what an "American" should be. But the newcomers and "outsiders," of course, were not simply wax figures on which dominant groups impressed their values. Many groups have contested with one another to define and create model citizens through schooling, and this political debate has shaped the course of public education.[4]

Millennial thinking about schooling has also been a favored solution to social and economic problems. In the early twentieth century, educational elites saw themselves as expert social engineers who could perfect the nation by consciously directing the evolution of society. When Lyndon B. Johnson sought to build the "Great Society" and declared war on poverty in the 1960s, he asserted that "the answer to all our national problems comes down to a single word: education."[5]

Americans have thought it easier to instruct the young than to coerce the adult. Debates over how to create perfect citizens through schooling long antedated Miss Manners's *Guide to Raising Perfect Children*. In theory, if the child was properly educated, the adult would need no reform. But if adults did prove wayward—ending up in traffic court, for example—taking a course might set things straight. In 1990, when state legislators in California faced charges of corruption, they passed a law requiring all lobbyists to enroll in a class on ethics.[6]

Repeatedly, Americans have followed a common pattern in devising educational prescriptions for specific social or economic ills. Once they had discovered a problem, they labeled it and taught a course on the subject: alcohol or drug instruction to fight addictions; sex education to combat syphilis or AIDS; home economics to lower the divorce rate; driver education to eliminate carnage on the highway; and vocational training or courses in computer literacy to keep the United States economically competitive.[7]

Faith in the power of education has had both positive and negative consequences. It has helped to persuade citizens to create the most comprehensive system of public schooling in the world. Americans have used discourse about education to articulate and instill a sense of the common good. But overpromising has often led to disillusionment and to blaming the schools for not solving problems beyond their reach. More important, the utopian tradition of social reform through schooling has often diverted attention from more costly, politically controversial, and difficult societal reforms. It's easier to provide vocational education than to remedy inequities in employment and gross disparities in wealth and income.

When we speak of educational reforms, we mean planned efforts to change schools in order to correct perceived social and educational problems. Sometimes broad social crises triggered school reforms, and sometimes reforms were internal improvements initiated by professionals. Diagnoses of problems and proposed solutions changed over time. But whatever the reform, it usually entailed a long and complex set of steps: discovering problems, devising remedies, adopting new policies, and bringing about institutional change.[8]

Americans celebrate innovation. In education this penchant for the new has produced, time and again, criticism that educators are mossbacks who resist change. In his studies of educational reforms, Paul Mort concluded that about half a century elapsed between the introduction of a new practice and its widespread implementation; he called the latecomers "laggards."[9]

While some lament that educational reform is an institutional Bermuda Triangle into which intrepid change agents sail, never to appear again, others argue that public education is too trendy, that entirely too many foolish notions circulate through the system at high velocity. Are schools too resistant to change or too faddish? Viewed over the course of history, they may seem to be both. Educators have often paid lip service to demands for reform to signify their alertness to the public will. But their symbolic responses often protected school people from basic challenges to their core practices.[10]

In the last generation reforms have come thick and fast, as educators can testify. Since the value of change is in the eye of the beholder, one set of innovators may seek to undo the results of previous reforms. At one time reformers thought that the graded school—which groups children by age and proficiency—greatly enhanced educational efficiency; later critics sought to create ungraded schools as a way to break the lockstep of fixed grades. Curriculum designers succeeded in substituting easy texts for classic works in English classes for "slow learners," only to find the new curriculum condemned as the educational equivalent of junk food.[11]

Focusing only on change runs the danger of ignoring continuity in the basic practices of schools. The film *Hope and Glory*, about London during the Blitz in World War II, vividly portrays the persistence of familiar routines under the most trying conditions. Crowded in a bomb shelter during an air raid, schoolchildren sit in rows under the stern eye of their instructor as they recite their multiplication tables through their gas masks.

We want to probe the meaning of continuity in schooling as well as to understand change. Change, we believe, is not synonymous with progress. Sometimes preserving good practices in the face of challenges is a major achievement, and sometimes teachers have been wise to re-sist reforms that violated their professional judgment.

Although policy talk about reform has had a utopian ring, actual reforms have typically been gradual and incremental—tinkering with the system. It may be fashionable to decry such change as piecemeal and inadequate, but over long periods of time such revisions of practice, adapted to local contexts, can substantially improve schools. Rather than seeing the hybridizing of reform ideas as a fault, we suggest it can be a virtue. Tinkering is one way of preserving what is valuable and reworking what is not.

Integrating our own research with the work of many colleagues, we explore some broad interpretive questions about the character of school reform. Typically we pose a puzzle, explore its dimensions and meanings through historical evidence and case studies, and then reflect on the issue in the light of the contemporary situation in education. Here we address some questions about reform that have intrigued us for years:[12]

Why have Americans believed in progress in education for over a century but have come to doubt it in recent years?

How accurate is the common notion that educational reforms come in cycles? Can this be reconciled with the notion of progress?

What is the relation between policy talk, policy action, and institutional trends?

How have schools changed reforms, as opposed to reforms changing schools?

What constitutes "success" in school reform? Why have some "successes" become invisible?

Why has the "grammar of schooling"— the organizational forms that govern instruction—persisted, while challenges to it have mostly been evanescent?

Why have outsiders' attempts to reinvent schooling—break-the-mold strategies—generally been short-lived shooting stars?

We hope that this book, which takes a century as its time span, will contribute to the broader conversation about educational reform today, for improving public schools is everybody's business. And it is a special concern of parents and students, activists and scholars, school board members and federal and state officials, and the millions of educators who work daily in the schools.

———————

Why, given the urgency of educational problems today, should anyone be concerned about the history of educational reform? To judge from the ahistorical character of most current policy talk about reform, innovators may consider amnesia a virtue. And in those rare occasions when reformers do discuss the history of schooling, they often portray the past in politicized, stylized ways as a golden age to be restored or a dismal legacy to be repudiated.

Anyone who would improve schooling is a captive of history in two ways. All people and institutions are the product of history (defined as past events). And whether they are aware of it or not, all people use history (defined as an interpretation of past events) when they make choices about the present and future. The issue is not whether people use a sense of the past in shaping

their lives but how accurate and appropriate are their historical maps: Are their inferences attentive to context and complexity: Are their analogies plausible? And how might alternative understandings of the past produce different visions of the future?[13]

History provides a whole storehouse of experiments on dead people. Studying such experiments is cheap (no small matter when funds are short); and it does not use people (often the poor) as live guinea pigs. Many educational problems have deep roots in the past, and many solutions have been tried before. If some "new" ideas have already been tried, and many have, why not see how they fared in the past?

Studies of past reforms confer the benefits of psychological distance on issues obscured by the passions of the present. Consider controversies over providing day care for young children. Generation after generation of Americans have rediscovered that working mothers need help in caring for their children, but they have tended to make patchwork day-care arrangements, assuming that the problem of minding the children would wither away when the family regained its rightful status. Once people recognize that the need for day care is not a new or temporary problem, they might conclude that its permanence is best understood as the result of long-term trends in families and public institutions.[14]

Finally, history provides a generous time frame for appraising reforms. It is not driven by the short-term needs of election cycles, budgets, foundation grants, media attention, or the reputations of professional reformers. Certain reforms may look successful when judged soon after adoption, but in fact they may turn out to be fireflies, flickering brightly but soon fading; the recurrent desire to employ technology as a teacher-proof form of instruction is a case in point. Other reforms may seem of questionable benefit in the short run but effective in the long run. The positive effects of the Head Start program become more obvious when the participants are young adults than when they were in the primary grades. When reforms aim at basic institutional changes or the eradication of deep social injustices, the appropriate period for evaluation may be a generation or more.[15]

———————

Our interpretation of school reform blends political and institutional analysis. A political perspective shows how groups become mobilized to publicize problems, devise remedies, and secure the adoption of policies by school boards and legislatures. Understanding actual implementation of reforms in schools—or lack of implementation—requires insight into the distinctive institutional character of schools.

Not all reforms are born equal; some enjoy strong political sponsors while others are political orphans. But even reforms with strong supporters do not always become embedded in the schools. Outside forces shape the course of school reform, but schools are also in some respects autonomous, buffered institutions. Educators have variously welcomed, improved, deflected, coopted, modified, and sabotaged outside efforts at reform.

Over long periods of time schools have remained basically similar in their core operation, so much so that these regularities have imprinted themselves on students, educators, and the public as the essential features of a "real school." Resistance to

change is sometimes dismissed as the result of popular ignorance or institutional inertia, but that oversimplifies. Often teachers have had well-founded reasons for resisting change, as have parents. If reformers have had their plans for schools, people in schools and local communities have had their own ways of dealing with reforms.[16]

The disparities evident in the political economy of the nation have strongly constricted or enhanced what people thought possible or desirable in educational policy and practice. These inequalities have been apparent in regional differences of wealth and economic power; sharp contrasts of life in rural and urban communities; racial, class, and gender discrimination; the honoring of some cultures and the ignoring or dismissing of others; and the great disparities in political power between groups. Life at the bottom of the social system has been far different from life at the top. Many people who claimed that the educational system has been marching up the ladder of progress paid scant attention to what was happening to the students on the lower rungs.[17]

Educational reforms are intrinsically political in origin. Groups organize and contest with other groups in the politics of education to express their values and to secure their interests in the public school. Conflicts in education have arisen over ethnic, religious, racial, gender, and class differences. Controversies over language policies—English only or bilingual instruction—have recurred for over a century, as did contests over racial or gender segregation or the use of the Bible and prayer in schools.[18]

Although many groups have entered school politics, especially in the protest movements of the last half-century, this apparent pluralism is misleading. The politics of education has not been conducted on a level playing field. Policy elites—people who managed the economy, who had privileged access to the media and to political officials, who controlled foundations, who were educational leaders in the universities and in city and state superintendencies, and who redesigned and led organizations of many kinds—gained a disproportionate authority over educational reform, especially during the first half of the twentieth century. These leaders inside and outside education generally shared a common vision of scientific management and a similar blueprint for reorganizing the educational system.[19]

Policy elites often claimed to be "taking the schools out of politics." They sought to do this by centralizing control of schools and delegating decisions about education, wherever possible, to "experts." In the process they did not, of course, eliminate politics, but they acquired formidable powers: to set the agenda of reform, to diagnose problems, to prescribe solutions, and often to influence what should *not* be on the agenda of reform. Their template for structural change in education set the dominant pattern of school reform during the period from 1900 to 1950.

During the last century, there has been much continuity in the structures, rules, and practices that organize the work of instruction. These organizational regularities, the grammar of schooling include such familiar practices as the age-grading of students, the division of knowledge into separate subjects, and the self-contained classroom with one teacher. At the core of the school—in classroom instruction—change was slow. Reforms took place, but

they were largely accretions around that core. To understand why, consider how different institutions maintain their distinctiveness. One way is by developing specific rules and cultures to channel the behavior of people within them. People act in different ways in armies, churches, and schools because these institutions socialize individuals to their different organizational norms. People who move from one institution to another come to take these differences for granted: children know that they should raise their hands in class to get the teacher's attention but not during a sermon in church; a rookie in boot camp does not expect his sergeant to treat him the way his first-grade teacher did.[20]

Most Americans have been to school and know what a "real school" is like. Congruence with that cultural template has helped maintain the legitimacy of the institution in the minds of the public. But when schooling departed too much from the consensus model of a "real school," failed to match the grammar of schooling, trouble often ensued. If teachers did not maintain strict discipline and consistently supervise students in class, if traditional subjects were neglected, if pupils did not bring report cards home, reforms might be suspect.[21]

For their part, teachers also have had an investment in the familiar institutional practices of the school. They learned these as students, and as they moved to the other side of the desk, they often took traditional patterns of organization for granted as just the way things were. It was one thing to add on a popular innovation at the border of the school—say a new vocational wing or dental examinations—and quite another to ask teachers, faced with the job of controlling and instructing a large number of students, to make fundamental changes in their daily routines. Such alterations in basic practices have increased teachers' workloads, often without compensatory time or resources. Because teachers retained a fair degree of autonomy once the classroom door was closed, they could, if they chose, comply only symbolically or fitfully or not at all with the mandates for change pressed on them by platoons of outside reformers. Or teachers could respond to reforms by hybridizing them, blending the old and the new by selecting those parts that made their job more efficient or satisfying.

The institutional character of the school, then, influenced the chances that a particular reform would be incorporated in the educational system, how it would be implemented, and how the public and teachers would view the results. Both general beliefs in the broader culture about what a "real school" was and the hold of standard operating procedures on staff and students put a brake on innovators who sought basic changes in classroom instruction.

Local educational leaders faced a potential Catch-22 if political demands for innovation conflicted with institutional conservatism. As a public enterprise, the schools might be expected to respond to innovations advocated by politically organized groups. Superintendents who wanted to keep their jobs needed to convince their school boards and policy elites that they were ready to adopt improvements. Among their peers, too, they felt the pressure to be up to date lest they be branded laggards. If the reforms they adopted were add-ons, such as kindergartens or classes in commercial education, few citizens or teachers would complain (except, perhaps, about expense). But if re-

forms reached into regular classrooms and departed too much from consensual notions of a "real school," protests or foot-dragging might ensue.

———

Change where it counts the most—in the daily interactions of teachers and students—is the hardest to achieve and the most important, but we are not pessimistic about improving the public schools. We think it difficult and essential, above all for the educationally dispossessed. To do this requires not only political will and commitment but also an accurate understanding of schools as institutions.

We favor attempts to bring about such improvements by working from the inside out, especially by enlisting the support and skills of teachers as key actors in reform. This might be seen as a positive kind of tinkering, adapting knowledgeably to local needs and circumstances, preserving what is valuable and correcting what is not. But teachers cannot do the job alone. They need resources of time and money, practical designs for change, and collegial support. And they can succeed best if they do their work in partnership with parents.

Policy talk about educational reform has been replete with extravagant claims for innovations that flickered and faded. This is a pie-in-the-sky brand of utopianism, and it has often led to disillusionment among teachers and to public cynicism. Exaggeration has pervaded these public rituals of dismay and promise.

There is, however, a different kind of utopianism—a vision of a just democracy— that has marked the best discourse about educational purpose over the past century. We believe that debate over educational and social goals has become radically restricted in the past generation. An essential political task today is to renegotiate a pluralistic conception of the public good, a sense of trusteeship that preserves the best of the past while building a generous conception of a common future.

NOTES

1. On the dramaturgic quality of debate over education, see David K. Cohen and Bella H. Rosenberg, "Functions and Fantasies: Understanding Schools in Capitalist America," *History of Education Quarterly* 17 (1977): 113–137.

2. Horace Mann, *Life and Works* (Boston: Walker, Fuller, and Co., 1865–1868), vol. 4, pp. 345, 354, 364–365; Robert H. Wiebe, "The Social Functions of American Education," *American Quarterly* 21 (Summer 1969): 147–164; National Commission on Excellence in Education, *A Nation at Risk: The Imperative for Educational Reform* (Washington, D.C.: GPO, 1983); Thomas S. Popkewitz, "Educational Reform: Rhetoric, Ritual, and Social Interest," *Educational Theory* 38 (Winter 1988): 77–93.

3. Michael Sadler, "Impressions of American Education," *Educational Review* 25 (March 1903): 219; David Tyack, "Forming the National Character: Paradox in the Educational Thought of the Revolutionary Generation," *Harvard Educational Review* 35 (Winter 1966): 29–41.

4. Hannah Arendt, "The Crisis in Education," *Partisan Review* 25 (Fall 1958): 493–513; Bernard J. Weiss, ed., *American Education and the European Immigrant, 1840–1940* (Urbana: University of Illinois Press, 1982); Paula Fass, *Outside In: Minorities and the Transformation of American Education* (New York: Oxford University Press, 1989).

5. Johnson is quoted in Henry Perkinson, *The Imperfect Panacea: American Faith in Ed-ucation, 1865–1965* (New York: Random House, 1979), frontispiece.

6. Richard C. Paddock, "Lobbyists Greet Class in Ethics with Yawns," *Los Angeles Times*, December 6, 1990, p. A3.

7. Jesse K. Flanders, *Legislative Control of the Elementary Curriculum* (New York: Teachers College Press, 1925); Jane Bernard Powers, *The "Girl Question" in Education: Vocational Education for Young Women in the Progressive Era* (Washington, D.C.: Falmer Press, 1992), ch. 2; David Tyack, Thomas James, and Aaron Benavot, *Law and the Shaping of Public Education, 1785–1954* (Madison: University of Wisconsin Press, 1987), ch. 6.

8. Paul R. Mort and Francis G. Cornell, *American Schools in Transition: How Our Schools Adapt Their Practices to Changing Needs* (New York: Teachers College Press, 1941), chs. 1–3.

9. Mort and Cornell, *American Schools in Transition*, p. 53; Paul R. Mort, "Studies in Educational Innovation from the Institute of Administrative Research: An Overview," in Matthew B. Miles, ed., *Innovation in Education* (New York: Bureau of Publications, Teachers College, Columbia University, 1964) pp. 317–328.

10. On the attack on "fads and frills" in the Great Depression, see George Strayer, "Educational Economy and Frontier Needs," in Department of Superintendence, *Official Report*, 1933 (Washington, D.C.: NEA, 1933), pp. 138–146; David Tyack, Michael Kirst, and Elisabeth Hansot, "Educational Reform: Retrospect and Prospect," *Teachers College Record* 81 (Spring 1980): 253–269.

11. Diane Ravitch, *The Troubled Crusade: American Education, 1945–1980* (New York: Basic Books, 1983).

12. There are many valuable ways to examine educational reforms historically. Scholars have analyzed, for example, individual reforms such as vocational education or individual reformers such as John Dewey. They have linked transformations in the political economy to changes in the schools. They

have assessed the impact on schools of movements such as progressive education or broad social and political reforms such as civil rights. They have written illuminating monographs on reform in one school district or even one school. While we have benefited from all these types of research, we have written this book as a broad interpretive work aimed at a variety of readers rather than as a monograph primarily for specialists.

13. As Richard E. Neustadt and Ernest R. May observe, "the future has no place to come from but the past, hence the past has predictive value." See *Thinking in Time: The Uses of History for Decision Makers* (New York: The Free Press, 1986), p. 251.

14. Margaret O'Brien Steinfels, *Who's Minding the Children? The History and Politics of Child Care in America* (New York: Simon and Schuster, 1973).

15. Harold Silver and Pamela Silver, *An Educational War on Poverty: American and British Policy-Making* (Cambridge: Cambridge University Press, 1991), pp. 119, 266–268.

16. On the concept of a "real school" and cultural constructions of schooling, see Mary Hayward Metz, "Real School: A Universal Drama amid Disparate Experience," in Douglas E. Mitchell and Margaret E. Goertz, eds., *Education Politics for the New Century* (New York: Falmer Press, 1990), pp. 75–91; John W. Meyer and Brian Rowan, "Institutionalized Organizations: Formal Structure as Myth and Ceremony," *American Journal of Sociology* 83 (September 1977): 340–363; John W. Meyer and Brian Rowan, "The Structure of Educational Organizations," in Marshall W. Meyer, ed., *Environments and Organizations* (San Francisco: Jossey-Bass, 1978), pp. 78–109.

17. Ira Katznelson and Margaret Weir, *Schooling for All: Class, Race, and the Decline of the Democratic Ideal* (New York: Basic Books, 1985); W. Lloyd Warner, Robert J. Havighurst, and Martin B. Loeb, *Who Shall Be Educated? The Challenge of Unequal Opportunities* (New York: Harper and Brothers, 1944).

18. Diane Ravitch, *The Great School Wars: New York City, 1805–1973* (New York: Basic Books, 1974); Herbert M. Kliebard, *The Struggle for the American Curriculum, 1893–1958* (New York: Routledge & Kegan Paul, 1987); Michael W. Apple, *Ideology and Curriculum* (London: Routledge & Kegan Paul, 1979); David Tyack, "Constructing Difference: Historical Reflections on Schooling and Social Diversity," *Teachers College Record* 95 (Fall 1993): 9–34.

19. *Public Schools and Their Administration: Addresses Delivered at the Fifty-Ninth Meeting of the Merchants' Club of Chicago, Saturday, December 8, 1906* (Chicago: The Merchants' Club, 1906); Corinne Gilb, *Hidden Hierarchies: The Professions and Government* (New York: Harper & Row, 1966); David Tyack and Elisabeth Hansot, *Managers of Virtue: Public School Leadership in America, 1820–1980* (New York: Basic Books, 1982), pt. 2.

20. Willard Waller, *The Sociology of Teaching* (New York: Russell and Russell, 1961).

21. Metz, "Real School"; Meyer and Rowan, "Institutionalized Organizations."

We Want It All

At the White House Conference on Education of 1965, Vice President Hubert Humphrey said that our country would go down in history for having used its educational system to overcome problems of illiteracy, unemployment, crime and violence, urban decay, and even war among nations. However, just a few years later some citizens were asking if our schools were capable of teaching our young to read, write, and spell. The press picked up this theme vigorously, reflecting an impression that parents as well as other adults generally favored returning to a time of more limited expectations for schools. "Back to basics" became a popular slogan. Many school board members and school administrators responded as though this were a mandate from the people.

I was skeptical. For a nation that had given its schools a broad role and placed them at the heart of its well-being—perhaps overgenerously—to shift position as abruptly as the changing rhetoric suggested appeared unreasonable. Was not this rhetoric in part a reaction to overly grandiose expectations of the preceding decade? Such reactions have occurred in the past. But it does not appear to me that the school system in our society moves purposefully, swiftly, and distinctively in the direction of the prevailing rhetoric of criticism, whatever it is. Rather, it expands

or contracts a little around the edges while continuing to play its traditional role—a sign that society doesn't want that role drastically changed.

Specifically, I was skeptical of two assumptions that were questioned rarely during the 1970s. The first was that parents were highly dissatisfied with the schools their children attended. It is one thing to be critical of schooling, especially when one reads or hears regularly that the schools are doing a poor job. It is quite another to think similarly about "my child's school." Word of declining test scores nationwide is a piece of news ranking low in significance compared with whether one's own child enjoys school, is safe and attended to there, and appears to be doing reasonably well. Policymakers worry about statistics; parents worry about their children.

The second assumption I questioned was that parents wanted a more limited kind of schooling for their children. It seemed reasonable to assume that most parents want for their children the kind of education that equips them for work, citizenship, and a measure of personal well-being—which to me suggests a broad, general education grounded in the 3 Rs but involving much more.

The central theme of this chapter is what we do in fact want and expect of our schools. It is explored from both a historical and a contemporary perspective. The data gathered to enlighten this theme include state and school district directives, as well as the responses of more than 8,000 parents to questions we asked of them.

These data tend to support my belief that the trends of the 1970s, many of them continuing into the 1980s, do not signal an abrupt turning away from the comprehensive expectations for education that have characterized this country historically. But it would be a serious mistake to assume that it will be business as usual in the future for our system of public schooling. As I suggested earlier, the unraveling of certain major features of this system that has been proceeding for some time accelerated during the 1970s. One feature in decline is the coalition of legislators, educators, parents, and others that held the system together and expanded it.[1] Another is the configuration of home, school, and church that traditionally did the educating. If these components are not, in the future, what they were in the past, the school too will not be what it was in the past. The context of schooling is changing dramatically in other ways too. For example, recordings, radio, and television pervade every resting place, be it home or resort, and accompany us all from birth to death. Consequently, the electronic media and the schools now must be viewed side by side as major educating agencies—which again means that the place of schools in educating will change.

Our expectations for schools are both idealistic and grandiose, representing a synthesis of what many diverse segments of our population want. This is one of the problems of schools; there are so many expectations for them. Some of these are met through private schools, some through specialized academic or vocational public schools. But central to our traditions is the idea and ideal of a free public school, available to all, commonly educating—the common school. At the turn of the century an eight-grade elementary school (frequently called the grade school) was the typical common school. Then completion of a relatively common secondary school became the expectation of many parents for their children. Today, a twelve-grade school is generally expected to play a relatively distinct and distinguishable role in a configuration of institutions that educate. It does not exist, however, nor can it be understood, as an institution apart.

Accordingly, the effort to address the question of what our schools are expected to do must go beyond the data from "A Study of Schooling" [printed in vol. 6, *Phi Delta Kappan*]. The Study is of schools only—a small number of schools and only nonspecialized public schools. Therefore the following discussion is not confined to our Study data; rather, my interpretations of these data are placed within a larger body of source materials and personal experiences regarding the educational scene in the United States. While the focus is on schooling, the context is a shifting ecology of educating institutions.

Parents View Their Children's Schools

The data we gathered tended to support my doubts that in the 1970s parents were highly dissatisfied with their children's schools and held narrow, more limited educational expectations for schools than had prevailed in the past. It is important to remember that these data were obtained during the second half of the decade, when the so-called back-to-basics movement was at its height. The decline in test scores was being widely publicized, and the public schools were experiencing widespread criticism in the daily press and popular weekly magazines.

We surveyed 8,624 parents—1,724 elementary, 2,688 junior high, and 4,212 at the senior high level. They varied considerably in age, income, race/ethnicity, and education. Regrettably, it proved exceedingly difficult to reach the adult clients of the schools studies. Only 31% of the total parent population of these schools responded, and we believe the sample to somewhat overrepresent the more educated and affluent. However, these probably are the parents likely to be most aware of polls and most publicly critical of the quality of education being provided. The response rate to the questionnaires varied widely from school to school, from a meager 16% at one to a more gratifying 57% at another.

We asked parents, as well as students and teachers, to grade their schools—A, B, C, D, or F (Fail)—and then we averaged the marks. None of our schools received an average D or F—not from students, teachers, or parents. About 10% of the parents clearly were dissatisfied; about 7%

gave their school a mark of D, and another 3% gave a grade of F. But notice in Table 5.1 that average grades even as low as C were received from the parent group by only 7 of the 38 schools. Of these, 4 were senior high schools.

Clearly, the predominantly B ratings of elementary and middle schools convey rather substantial satisfaction. Although B and C grades suggest a falling off in satisfaction at the high school level, the absence of average D and F grades tends to deflect the notion that schools are perceived as an unmitigated disaster. The data on high schools in particular suggest reservations and concern, but somewhat more among students and teachers than among parents. Interestingly, parents were more generous than either teachers or students in grading both the junior and senior high schools attended by their children. Overall, the data do not convey the deep parental dissatisfaction with their schools that supposedly has prevailed widely. Nor do they lead to the conclusion that parents have a perception of all being well with the schools their children attend.

There almost always are several levels of perception regarding schools, depending

TABLE 5.1 Distribution of Schools Receiving Average Grades of A, B, or C from Students, Teachers, and Parents

	High Schools			Jr. High/Middle Schools			Elementary Schools		
	A	B	C	A	B	C	A	B	C
STUDENTS	0	5	8	0	7	5	1	12	0
TEACHERS	0	7	6	0	9	3	1	11	1
PARENTS	0	9	4	0	11	1	0	11	2
TOTAL	0	21	18	0	27	9	2	34	3

NOTE: No schools received an average grade below C. Because one junior high functioned as one school with a senior high, the number of junior highs graded as such was reduced from 13 to 12.

in large part on the nature of our experience with them. We are easily persuaded by polls on matters extending beyond our direct experience. The quality of schools and schooling is not very good, but the school down the street to which our own children go isn't bad—in fact, it's quite good. At least this kind of mixed vision is what is suggested by some Gallup Polls of the late 1970s and supported by the responses of the parents in our sample.

Now what of parents' expectations for schools? Our nation's overall goals for education can be informative here. At the beginning of "A Study of Schooling," several colleagues and I examined a vast array of documents reporting the ongoing effort to define, over a period of more than three hundred years, the goals of education and schooling in this country. Education and schooling usually are not differentiated in these documents, which in itself is significant. It commonly is assumed that the aims of education and the goals of schools coincide exactly. We concluded that four broad areas of goals for the schools have emerged. They are the following: (1) academic, embracing all intellectual skills and domains of knowledge; (2) vocational, geared to developing readiness for productive work and economic responsibility; (3) social and civic, related to preparing for socialization into a complex society; and (4) personal, emphasizing the development of individual responsibility, talent, and free expression. They are reiterated, somewhere, in the official documents of most states. These goals presumably frame the educational function of schools.

McIntire adapted these goal categories in a study of parents' educational expectations in a medium-sized school district. He found a high level of support for all of them.[2] In "A Study of Schooling," we used these same categories in questioning parents about what they expected of their children's schools. On the questionnaire we spoke of social development as involving instruction which helps students learn to get along with other students and adults, prepares students for social and civic effectiveness, and develops their awareness and appreciation of our own and other cultures. Intellectual development involves instruction in basic skills in mathematics, reading, and written and verbal communication, and in critical thinking and problem-solving abilities. Personal development calls for instruction which builds self-confidence, creativity, ability to think independently, and self-discipline. Vocational development involves instruction which prepares students for the expectations of the workplace, develops skills necessary for getting a job, and fosters awareness of career alternatives. These statements imply a good deal more than what one conjures up mentally when the words "back to basics" are used. We asked respondents to rate each goal area on a scale ranging from "very unimportant" to "very important."

It is probably not surprising that parents, on the average, gave "very important" ratings to all four areas, with the vocational dropping toward the "somewhat important" rating for parents of elementary school children. Approximately 90% of the parents sampled at all three levels rated intellectual goals as "very important." Personal goals approached this percentage among elementary school parents and dropped only to 80% at junior and senior high school levels. Vocational goals were rated only slightly lower by high school parents and somewhat lower by junior high parents. Social goals were rated "very important" by 73% of the elementary school parents, with the percentage dropping only to 66% and 64% at junior and senior high levels, respectively.

We also asked teachers and secondary students in our sample of schools to rate the goal areas. Like parents, both of these other groups thought all four goal areas "very important," with the vocational sagging a bit toward the "somewhat important" category for elementary school teachers. The relative importance that all three groups attach to the several goal areas is seen in Table 5.2. Note especially the similarity between teachers' and parents' ratings.

One could argue that there was no hard choice here. There is virtue in all these goal areas, as in God, motherhood, and apple pie. We forced the issue a bit with a second question, asking each group (now including elementary students) to make a single most preferred choice among the four. In Table 5.3 the responses are summarized. Roughly half of the parents and nearly half of the teachers chose the intellectual category. But the fact that the other half distributed this preferential choice across the social, personal, and vocational goals implies that a substantial number of these parents and teachers would be unhappy to have such goals eliminated. Apparently even more students feel strongly about the importance of each of these goals. They spread their preferences more evenly across all four categories.

The message here, it seems to me, is that those closest to schools—parents, teachers, and students—see as important all four of those goal areas which have emerged over the centuries and which had become well established in the rhetoric of educational expectations for schools decades before the 1970s.

Our data thus show no withering in goal commitments by the parent group we

TABLE 5.2 Relative Importance of Goals for Students, Teachers, and Parents

	High Schools	*Jr. High/Middle Schools*	*Elementary Schools*
STUDENTS	Vocational	Intellectual	
	Intellectual	Vocational	
	Personal	Personal	
	Social	Social	
TEACHERS	Intellectual	Intellectual	Intellectual
	Personal	Personal	Personal
	Social	Social	Social
	Vocational	Vocational	Vocational
PARENTS	Intellectual	Intellectual	Intellectual
	Personal	Personal	Personal
	Vocational	Social	Social
	Social	Vocational	Vocational

NOTE: Elementary school students were not asked for these ratings.

TABLE 5.3 Goal Preferences of Students, Teachers, and Parents (in percent)

	Social	Intellectual	Personal	Vocational	N
STUDENTS					
High Schools	15.9	27.3	25.6	31.1	6,670
Jr. High/Middle Schools	13.4	38.0	18.3	30.3	4,733
Elementary Schools	13.8	47.1	17.3	21.8	1,567
TEACHERS					
High Schools	9.9	45.6	29.7	14.8	656
Jr. High/Middle Schools	13.9	46.7	29.3	10.1	396
Elementary Schools	14.0	48.9	33.5	3.5	278
PARENTS					
High Schools	8.7	46.5	19.3	25.5	4,065
Jr. High/Middle Schools	9.5	51.1	21.1	18.2	2,605
Elementary Schools	9.3	57.6	24.5	8.6	1,681

sampled, and indeed I do not know of serious studies that come up with a narrow list of parental expectations for schools. When it comes to education, it appears that most parents want their children to have it all. I believe, then, that many policymakers have been misinterpreting parents' expectations for schools and then overreacting to this misinterpretation.

A Changing Configuration of Educating Institutions

It should not surprise us for parents to want comprehensive educations for their children. Indeed, it would be strange to discover the opposite. And it should not surprise us to learn that parents want a major part of the educating to be done in schools. For most parents today, life is very demanding. As I noted earlier, over half of the mothers with school-age children are now working. There is little time for recreation with one's children, let alone time to provide for their formal edu-

cation. Schools today do not only educate. Together with television they also provide a babysitting service for parents who go off to work early and are not yet at home when their children return from school. Of course this was not always so. Indeed, the change in just a single generation has been dramatic. And until relatively recent times, things were profoundly different.

The early colonists transplanted to the New World, as best the circumstances permitted, the towns and villages they had known at home. They also transplanted, as best they could, "an educational configuration of household, church and school, each standing in time-honored relation to the others. . . . The configuration taught, in different combinations for different orders of the society, the values and substance of piety, civility, and learning."[3]

Of the three institutions, the school was the most marginal. Many of the immigrants had not gone to school at all. Those who had gone had attended a dame school for a year or two of instruction in writing and reading. A few had attended a grammar school where they studied more exotic things such as Latin and Greek. In the New World, schools—where they existed—provided merely an add-on to what was learned through household and church. The household mediated all learning acquired outside of it; the household modeled most of what was required for living beyond it. It turned to the church for teaching the larger meaning of life; it joined with the church in teaching piety. The shadows of both institutions fell over the schools. All three institutions buttressed each other in the rearing and educating of the young.

Increasingly, the press joined this trio in producing by the time of the Revolution a level of literacy among whites approaching that of the homeland. Although half of the child population attended no schools, reading was a significant part of the culture. There were books, almanacs, newspapers, the Bible, letters to be read and to be written. School was not the only place for learning to read. Older brothers and sisters, uncles, aunts, and parents nurtured all aspects of life. And this educating by the household was reinforced by other households in the community. Of course, there were many without this kind of nurturing. Some families were small and isolated and had little time for all that was to be done. Blacks had been rudely torn from households in Africa; the Native Americans were a people apart. As today, many generalizations about "the people" two hundred years ago simply did not apply to various groups in our culture.

Nevertheless, enough people learned to read to create a demand for things to read. The role of the press in the American educational scene has been underestimated, of-

ten ignored. It did much more than contribute to literacy. Printed materials opened up new vistas, presented alternatives, stimulated criticism, and helped communicate the idea of revolution. Certainly the press helped foment the American Revolution.

Following the Revolution, it was no longer appropriate to inculcate European ways. A new national character was in the making. It had to be taught even while it was being created—and transmitted to waves of immigrants. Parents were ill-equipped to do the teaching required. Schools assumed this responsibility as one of their functions.

The locus of work shifted from the household to factory and shop. The workplace became a shaper of values and outlook and, to a considerable degree, a place to discuss what one read in the press. The size of families declined, and families moved, separating relatives from children they had helped. There were fewer in the household to do the educating. And there were new perspectives to be acquired. The America emerging was not the homeland left behind.

As a result, though the traditional relationships among home, church, and school persisted, the relative educational influence of school and press grew rapidly. The institutional mix broadened as organized work expanded, commercial entities proliferated, government enlarged, custodial institutions grew, and specialized educational institutions came into being. The need for an American form of education to transmit these developments, articulated by eloquent spokesmen and extolled in the newspapers, together with unprecedented immigration into the second half of the nineteenth century, increasingly defined and enlarged the place of the school.

The shift in the balance between home and school as educators that took place in the nineteenth century accelerated in the twentieth. Increasingly the school took over, teaching smatterings of subject matter to which parents had not been privy and which they assumed their children needed to know. With business and industry wanting the vocational preparation that schools were providing and colleges more interested in the precollegiate preparation of their students, the school's mediating influence took on greater independence from the home. The emergence of an educational system, with its inevitable bureaucratization, and the professionalization of teachers and administrators differentiated and separated the educational roles of home and school. The advent of counseling in schools professionalized a client relationship different from the traditional joint nurturing relationship of home and school.

Nonetheless, the relationship between the two remained, in general, a productive, supportive one for decades into the present century. In the democratic society emerging, a home stressing ethnicity, family origins, and the significance of the individual within the household and a school emphasizing common learnings relative to a larger, dynamic world together came close to providing the desired educational balance.[4]

Yet we have never quite achieved the desired balance between the home teaching individuality and the school teaching commonality. Some would say that we have not come close. When the home was perceived not to be doing its nurturing, the school was asked to do more. When the school was asked to do more for more people, specifically since the 1950s, the range of values it inevitably embraced

tended to broaden. And as a consequence, it was seen as less desirable by many of the kinds of people who had profited most from it in previous decades.

Paralleling these changes, the growth of schools as a daily gathering place for almost all youths helped create a powerful new educational force—the peer group. As the age of entering the workforce went up, the length of attendance at school increased, and peer-group socializing took up the additional time that otherwise would have been spent at home with the family. The systematization of schooling created considerable segmenting by age and necessitated socialization into an age group, even as families moved about. A child in grade five in a school in Ohio entered a fifth-grade class on moving to Oregon. Peer-group mores became increasingly powerful. Teachers and even parents began to decline in significance as role models.

During the 1960s and 1970s, the electronic media moved in on this increasingly cohesive young group, catering to its interests, providing it a passing array of larger-than-life role models, creating its tastes, molding its habits of consumption, teaching it strategies to use with parents—educating while selling and entertaining. The teen-oriented television program *Making It* well exemplified how the medium can not only entertain but also introduce and reinforce attitudes toward home, school, and work. In several half-hour programs that I recall, all three were treated with essentially the same slightly patronizing, supercilious banter—wittily, irreverently, and clearly as of secondary importance to the basics in life for the targeted adolescent audience. Those basics, presented with verve to the beat of rock music, were the skills of risqué dialogue, moving in on one of the opposite sex, and dating—skills requisite to "making it" in the teenage culture, all modeled by beautiful young women and handsome young men. The message I received in several fast-moving half-hour segments was that these activities and the values behind them represented all that was important. This message was punctuated by that of the advertisers, joining the television network to mutual advantage. How could dull old work, school, and home compete? At best, presumably, they could provide money, a place of assured associations, and the rudiments of nutrition, all of which, probably in that order of importance, might be useful in making it.

Have the electronic media replaced home and school and started to "mediate" the life experience of the young? Has television become the common school? If so, what is left for the public school? Presumably, this should be what is not readily done by other institutions: fostering that learning which requires deliberate, systematic attention sustained over a period of years. Television does not effectively perform such educating.

Today, we function as individuals within a complex array of educating institutions and agencies. For this educational ecosystem to be healthy, it is essential for each educating organism to perform a needed function somewhat self-consciously, to be aware of the others, and in fact to portray the others empathetically. The television program *Making It* was a caricature of the worst in that medium. But it serves to remind us of what can happen when an institution increasingly becomes educative without also becoming conscious of its new role.

Evolving Educational Expectations for Schools

Our school system grew phenomenally from soon after the middle of the nineteenth century to beyond the midpoint of the twentieth—in size, complexity, and even confidence. And as the school's role enlarged, the role of the other institutions in the traditional configuration declined and the school stood more and more alone. The beneficent, supporting shadow of home and church reached it less and less. The school's enlarged role resulted, however, not just from its assuming more of what homes and churches once did but also from society's increased educational expectations.

The first colonial schools were expected to take account of a child's need to read sufficiently well to comprehend religious concepts and the laws of the land. The teachings were to be conducted in an atmosphere of piety and respect for authority. Infringements were known about almost immediately in the home. Much of the teaching was tutorial; pupils often were taught individually in a group setting.

Three kinds of learnings proceeded in the classroom. There were the academics, steadily expanding. Simultaneously, there were moral learnings, including the work ethic, ratified by home and church and embedded in the school's custodial role. Then there was the social and personal learning to be derived from expectations for individual performance in the group settings of classrooms. All three remained part and parcel of schooling. The whole was pervaded by concepts of individual opportunity and responsibility. This relatively simple charge remained unchanged for two hundred years—into the second half of the nineteenth century.

Industrialization, accelerating immigration, and urbanization then changed these expectations rapidly. Parents were unable to teach the young many kinds of learning they appeared to require. Schools increasingly taught not just good work habits but also about the world of work; they even began to prepare deliberately for specific vocations. They were called upon not just to reinforce the values and attitudes of home and community, but to teach the ideas and ideals of political democracy. Many of the concepts to be learned were quite abstract. The subjects of the curriculum expanded. New kinds of textbooks were required for their teaching. The amount of schooling gained by the young steadily surpassed that of their parents. Each generation became more schooled than the previous one.

One development peculiar to the twentieth century was the idea that education in schools should develop individuals for their own sake. Cremin succinctly paraphrases John Dewey's formulation of this intent "as a way of saying that the aim of education is not merely to make citizens, or workers, or fathers, or mothers, but ultimately to make human beings who will live life to the fullest."[5] For more than fifty years, goal statements for American education have testified to the importance of this kind of development of the individual. During the 1960s, in particular, various impressions of the concept appeared on the banners of those seeking free, open, or alternative schools. To the perhaps uniquely American ideas of unlimited geographic and economic frontiers for exploration and development was added the idea of unlimited individual frontiers.

The academic, vocational, and civic goals constituting the mandate to schools at the beginning of this century were to be achieved in the common school. The curriculum was common for all, except that the boys usually studied some form of manual training while the girls pursued courses that later became known as home economics. Only about one student in ten went on to secondary school, and a large proportion of these went on to college. It was assumed that these high school students required college-educated teachers. The state of California set a requirement of five years of higher education for secondary school teachers early in the century.

Well into the twentieth century, teachers in high schools had to concern themselves primarily with providing quality education for only a fraction of the students completing the usually eight-grade common school. But the Great Depression of the '30s removed job opportunities for youth. At the same time there was a growing belief that an eighth-grade education was insufficient to educate our increasingly heterogeneous population for participation in a democratic society. The legal age for leaving school moved up to 16 in most states. The diversity of the student population entering secondary schools began to increase. Pressure to provide educationally for this changing enrollment spurred the development of vocational education in many schools and the creation of trade and technical schools for students not planning for college-level academic studies.

The Supreme Court decision of 1954 ruled out race as a barrier to attending any school. The subsequent movement toward desegregated schools diversified school enrollments dramatically, even though change came slowly in suburban school districts. The issue initially was whether schools can be segregated and at the same time offer equal educational opportunity for all. The issue that had emerged for many people by the 1980s was whether schools can be integrated successfully and simultaneously provide quality education for all—particularly if this means diversifying the student population of local schools through busing.

The charge to public schools emerging from these complex, connected developments is formidable. First, they are to provide free elementary and secondary education in a "common" school embracing grades one through twelve or, in many states, kindergarten through grade twelve. Second, they are to utilize every possible means to assure optimum access to this expanded common school for an increasingly diverse student population. Third, each school is to both provide a reasonably comprehensive program of studies and assure a balance of academic, vocational, social, and personal instruction for each student. Fourth, each school is to provide such special instructional provisions as are needed to assure that individual differences, particularly those stemming from economic and racial or ethnic circumstances, will interfere minimally with access to such a program.[6] Equality and quality are the name of the game. These two concepts will frame dialogue, policy, and practice regarding schooling for years to come.

The charge to provide quality and equality simultaneously is formidable under the best of circumstances. Given present circumstances, we must address seriously the question of whether our system of schooling is up to it. It seems before one challenge can be met, another emerges. Currently, the traditional financial support of schools through local property taxes is crumbling and has been challenged in the courts. The message of the Supreme Court of 1954 has been obfuscated at state and local levels and by the Supreme Court itself. Rapidly changing demographics in most large cities are outrunning any possibility of desegregating schools, short of extensive busing and consolidation of urban and suburban school districts. As we shall see in later discussion, there is not at any level of the system even minimal provision for renewing curricula and reconstructing schools to meet changing needs. With expanding career options for women, the pool of prospective female teachers is declining markedly. And there are millions of children and youths coming along who require unusual stimuli and support for their learning if they are to complete successfully a common school of 12 or 13 years.

Two prerequisites stand out as essential for schools to have even a modicum of success. First, the central charge to them must be clearly understood at all levels of the system and by those persons schools serve. Second, a new coalition comparable to the one that developed and sustained the present system of schooling must emerge. But this coalition must support more than schools. It must embrace new configurations for education in the community that include not only home, school, and church but also business, industry, television, our new means of information processing and all the rest of the emerging new technology of communications, and those cultural resources not yet drawn on for their educational potential. Education is too important and too all encompassing to be left only to schools.

Clarifying and Articulating the Mandate

Unfortunately, the mandate to schools has not been made clear. The Constitution of the United States does not give the federal government responsibility for education and schooling. Further, there is no federal policy with respect to the nature or quality of educational goals and programs. But federal agencies have entered actively into formulating policies and funding programs in harmony with their interpretation of equality of educational opportunity. Consequently, even though responsibility and authority must be assumed at state and local levels, state and local school systems have been nudged—and shoved—this way and that because of federal laws, interests, and funds. Indeed, many state departments of education are organized so as to be effective conduits of these federal interventions in school policy and practice.[7]

It is difficult to determine just how much the federal interest in schooling in recent years has detracted from the authority and especially the clarification of responsibility for education on the part of states and school districts. At any rate, the state and district documents we examined in "A Study of Schooling" reflect much less than a clear mandate for schools. One would think that the states would articulate very clearly where they now stand with respect to the expectations for education and schooling that have emerged out of three hundred years of growth and change. They do not.

More than three decades ago Ralph W. Tyler, one of our most eminent educational statesmen, proposed that principals and teachers should have available to them a set of a dozen or so educational goals to guide program development and teaching in their schools.[8] These were not to be narrowly and prescriptively stated for separate subjects or grades. Rather, they were to provide a common set of purposes for everyone to strive toward. Elementary as well as secondary teachers, teachers of English as well as of social studies, science, and mathematics were to address themselves to how they might help students learn to think rationally, master fundamental processes of learning, develop positive attitudes toward work, and much more. Within this broad framework of common, general goals for education, they might then go on to clarify the particular contribution to be made by their own teaching of specific subjects.

Tyler recommended that such goals should suggest both the kind of behavior students were to develop and the domains of knowledge and human experience likely to be most relevant and vital in their learning. Further reduction and refinement of these goals was to be left to teachers, with whatever local help they could get. There was not to be further specification by states and school districts for fear of stultifying dialogue in the local school and usurping teachers' prerogatives.

We looked to state and district guidelines for the kinds of goals Tyler recommended. State superintendents of public instruction responded generously to our requests for documents in which expectations for schools might be found. We examined materials from all 50 states. Those from the seven states in which we studied schools were analyzed in greater depth, as were comparable documents from our 13 school districts. Because of the comprehensive coverage of states, we can formulate generalizations about this extensive body of material with some confidence. We must be much more constrained in generalizing from the sample of documents from the school districts.

The documents produced by states to guide education in local schools are not markedly different in what they contain and how they present their messages. Usually there is a philosophic preamble extolling the virtues of education. Almost always there is emphasis on the individual and the kinds of traits to be developed through education. The cultivation of cognitive abilities is paramount. States were quite consistent in stating their concern for mastery of basic skills and fundamental learning processes, often even using similar language in expressing their concern. Frequently missing were goals directed specifically to multicultural understanding and appreciation and to aesthetic development. These two goal areas, the first of which would include global understanding, must be thought of as emerging rather than established in states' articulated expectations. In comparing these documents with earlier ones, a major conclusion emerges: state guidelines have remained relatively consistent over the past fifty years in their commitment to the intellectual, social and civic, vocational, and personal development of students, with greatest emphasis on the first.

What is most disappointing in these documents, with some exceptions, is the rather disordered array of topics and form of presentation. There is something for everyone in the materials prepared by states. But because the documents range over such a variety of topics—goals, activities, instructional resources, suggestions for evaluation, and so on—one gets little sense of what is essential and what is secondary. It all reads as though teachers might ignore any or all of it. There is no clear mandate.

Should not all states make a clear commitment to schooling and back it with a statement of the support they intend to give? There is disagreement over the kinds of mandates that are most useful. In an earlier, informal inquiry into state mandates, I found a rather consistent reluctance on the part of state education officials to admit to any precise requirements for local districts or schools. The irony is that most states do intervene very directly through financial specifications, textbook adoptions, testing, specifying topics to be taught (such as drug abuse), and various aspects of instruction—elements which appear to be more controlling and yet perhaps less constructively guiding than a broad, legislated mandate would be. The nature and quantity of bills pertaining to schooling introduced into state legislatures—often several hundred in a year—boggle the mind. It has been common, for example, for the California Legislature to introduce in a single year over 500 bills related to public education and to pass a fifth of these. The California Education Code in effect in 1980 required 42 pages to set forth all the mandates related to bilingual education. It used only two pages to list the subjects to be taught in elementary and secondary classrooms. No doubt the volume and variety of state legislative activity have contributed to obfuscating the central educational charge not only to local school districts but to the states' own departments of education as well.

My major conclusion from perusing most state guides to education in schools is that this entire area is a conceptual swamp. We have assumed since ratifying the Constitution that the states share with local communities responsibility for providing, regulating, and guiding public schools. Nevertheless, there remains enormous ambiguity regarding the states' responsibility for leadership and execution. Are Machiavellian tendencies at work here? There are some advantages, from a politician's point of view, in keeping undefined those areas of policy which can be argued readily and alternatively from many persuasions. Schooling is one of these. The net result is, however, that the schools suffer from lack of a clearly articulated mandate and so are peculiarly susceptible to fads and fashions. These, in turn, become matters for legislative attention, which too often produces just more emergency splints, each holding in place a joint thought to be malfunctioning.

The district guides for local schools we examined were less philosophical and more directly oriented to the classroom than the state documents. Goals were more in number and more specific. Although goals paralleled state emphases, including the dominant commitment to cognition and subject matter, they appeared not to be derived from the state's commitment. Like state guides, district guides covered a smattering of many things—objectives, topics of instruction, suggested materials, hints for teaching, and on occasion, suggestions for time allocation. And like state guides, district directives were not organized, on the whole, in a comprehensive, orderly fashion. Even the goals often were a combination of behaviors desired in students, purposes for teachers, and admonitions to schools (e.g., "Improve articulation of programs between the elementary school, middle school, and high school").

When both states and local districts departed from *general* expectations in the form of total school programs and turned to curriculum and instruction in the subject fields, however, the nature of the documents changed. Three of our seven states, for example, produced subject-oriented guides intended to be helpful not just to local districts but to individual teachers. Indeed, some of these could be used, with very little modification or extra effort, as frameworks for entire courses. However, there were no trends in our data to suggest that teachers in the 18 schools we studied in these three states, more than teachers in the other 20 schools, perceived their curriculum guides as useful. Overall, teachers in our sample viewed state and local curriculum guides as of little or moderate usefulness in guiding their teaching.

The foregoing does not necessarily lead to the conclusion that there is nothing helpful that states and local districts can do to guide school programs and classroom instruction. But my observation is that the documents produced at both levels do not command attention. Commitments and expectations are there, if one digs for them, but lack precision, clarity, and a ring of authority. Neither state nor district officials come out loud and clear as to what our schools are for and how they intend to fulfill these commitments. It is easier or more appealing, presumably, to list expectations and requirements for teachers and students and hold both accountable.

The states must do better. Two of the theses running through this volume are that those working at all levels of the educational system must be accountable and that better schools will come about through multiple actions, no one of them sufficient in itself. "Accountable" is a good word. *Webster's Third* defines it as both "capable of being accounted for" and "subject to giving an account." In the second sense, state legislators and policymakers, including those at the district level, have been diligent in seeking to make others educationally accountable but have been restrained with respect to their own responsibility for articulating priorities based on careful studies of need and sound educational concepts.

If it is a message that educators and others are looking for, let that message be couched in the most compelling terms and have the highest professional appeal. The time has come, past come, for the 50 states to articulate as basic policy a commitment to a broad array of educational goals in the four areas that have emerged in this country over more than three hundred years.

These goals should be revised as needed and endorsed by each successive governor and legislature. Each local district should then reiterate the state's commitment and assume responsibility for assuring every child and youth a sequential, balanced program of academic, civic and social, vocational, and personal studies.

We have been told frequently in recent years that people want to go back to an earlier, simpler time in our history when the 3 Rs were the sole expectation for schools. If the preceding review of our educational history is reasonably correct, there was never such a time. I doubt that this time has now come.

Goals for Schools

As much of the above suggests, what has been happening in recent years at both state and local district levels is a far cry from what Tyler had in mind. Comprehensive lists of goals are hard to find. Instead, one finds long lists of goals and objectives for the separate subject fields and, recently in

many states and districts, lists of proficiencies students are to acquire for high school graduation or grade-to-grade promotion. And in my own visits to many schools, I find little evidence of goals consciously shared by the teachers and precious little dialogue about what their schools are for.

Some people would argue that there is not and cannot be agreement on a set of educational goals for schools. If not, how is it that we seem to know what specific proficiencies we want students to acquire and what tests to use in determining their competence? Clearly, there is inconsistency here. Others say that general goals are too vague and mean different things to different people. Of course; that is their virtue. They provide a common sense of direction but also some room for interpretation and adaptation to meet varying local circumstances.

In the spirit of Tyler's recommendation and the need for states to provide districts and schools with a guiding framework for curriculum planning and teaching, I offer below a set of goals derived from two inquiries conducted as part of "A Study of Schooling." The first was the historical review of goals for schooling conducted at the very beginning of the Study. The second was the analysis of state documents just described, conducted toward the end of the Study. Although statements of goals were hard to find, often accompanying philosophical discussions or buried within recommendations for policy or practice, we were able to put together a list representing those most commonly appearing in the documents examined.

The list is presented here to guide school board members, parents, students, and teachers in the needed effort to achieve a common sense of direction for their schools and to build programs of teaching and learning related to these goals. They might very well serve as a beginning point in the dialogue about education and what schools are for that should be underway in this nation. There is no need to begin from scratch, as though we have no goals for schooling. Rather, we should be addressing ourselves to such questions as the significance and meaning of these goals, whether or not they are adequately comprehensive, their implications for educational policy and practice, and whether or not we intend to carry out what they imply for teaching and learning.

Goals for Schooling in the U.S.

A. Academic Goals

1. Mastery of basic skills and fundamental processes
   1.1 Learn to read, write, and handle basic arithmetical operations.
   1.2 Learn to acquire ideas through reading and listening.
   1.3 Learn to communicate ideas through writing and speaking.
   1.4 Learn to utilize mathematical concepts.
   1.5 Develop the ability to utilize available sources of information.

In our technological civilization, an individual's ability to participate in the activities of society depends on mastery of these skills and processes and ability to utilize them in the varied functions of life. With few exceptions, those who are deficient in them will be severely limited in their ability to function effectively in our society.

2. Intellectual development
   2.1 Develop the ability to think rationally, including problem-solving skills, application of principles of logic, and skill in using different modes of inquiry.
   2.2 Develop the ability to use and evaluate knowledge, i.e., critical and independent thinking that enables one to make judgments and decisions in a wide variety of life roles—citizen, consumer, worker, etc.—as well as in intellectual activities.
   2.3 Accumulate a general fund of knowledge, including information and concepts in mathematics, literature, natural science, and social science.
   2.4 Develop positive attitudes toward intellectual activity, including curiosity and a desire for further learning.
   2.5 Develop an understanding of change in society.

As civilization has become increasingly complex, people have had to rely more heavily on their rational abilities. Also, today's society needs the full intellectual development of each member. This process includes not only the acquisition of a fund of basic knowledge but also the development of basic thinking skills.

B. Vocational Goals

3. Career education–vocational education:
   3.1 Learn how to select an occupation that will be personally satisfying and suitable to one's skills and interests.
   3.2 Learn to make decisions based on an awareness and knowledge of career options.

3.3 Develop salable skills and specialized knowledge that will prepare one to become economically independent.

3.4 Develop habits and attitudes, such as pride in good workmanship, that will make one a productive participant in economic life.

3.5 Develop positive attitudes toward work, including acceptance of the necessity of making a living and an appreciation of the social value and dignity of work.

In our society, people spend a large amount of their time working. Therefore, an individual's personal satisfaction will be significantly related to satisfaction with his or her job. In order to make an intelligent career decision, one needs to know one's own aptitudes and interests as they relate to career possibilities. Next, one must be able to obtain whatever specialized training is necessary to pursue the vocation selected and to develop attitudes that will help one succeed in a field. This goal is important also for the continued growth and development of society.

C. Social, Civic, and Cultural Goals

4. Interpersonal understandings

4.1 Develop a knowledge of opposing value systems and their influence on the individual and society.

4.2 Develop an understanding of how members of a family function under different family patterns as well as within one's own family.

4.3 Develop skill in communicating effectively in groups.

4.4 Develop the ability to identify with and advance the goals and concerns of others.

4.5 Learn to form productive and satisfying relations with others based on respect, trust, cooperation, consideration, and caring.

4.6 Develop a concern for humanity and an understanding of international relations.

4.7 Develop an understanding and appreciation of cultures different from one's own.

In our complex, interdependent world, mental health is closely related to the larger social structure—to one's interpersonal relations. No one goes unaffected by the actions of other people. Whoever pursues a mindless, self-indulgent course offends the sensibilities, endangers the health, or even threatens the lives of others. Understanding oneself is not enough—one must transcend self to become aware of and understand other people and their institutions, other nations and their relations, other cultures and civilizations past and present. Schools should help children to understand, appreciate, and value persons belonging to social, cultural, and ethnic groups different from their own and thus to increase affiliation and decrease alienation.

5. Citizenship participation

5.1 Develop historical perspective.

5.2 Develop knowledge of the basic workings of the government.

5.3 Develop a willingness to participate in the political life of the nation and the community.

5.4 Develop a commitment to the values of liberty, government by consent of the governed, representational government, and one's responsibility for the welfare of all.

5.5 Develop an understanding of the interrelationships among complex organizations and agencies in a modern society, and learn to act in accordance with it.

5.6 Exercise the democratic right to dissent in accordance with personal conscience.

5.7 Develop economic and consumer skills necessary for making informed choices that enhance one's quality of life.

5.8 Develop an understanding of the basic interdependence of the biological and physical resources of the environment.

5.9 Develop the ability to act in light of this understanding of interdependence.

More than ever before, humankind is confronted with confusion regarding the nature of man, conflicting value systems, ambiguous ethical, moral, and spiritual beliefs, and questions about his own role in society. There is a major struggle over the issue of whether man is for government or government is for man. The question is not whether there should be some form of government, but what should be its roles, functions, and structures, and what are its controls? Young people now are becoming involved earlier in politics and national life, and minorities are demanding greater access to power in our country. A democracy can survive only by the participation of its members. Schools are expected to generate such participation.

6. Enculturation

6.1 Develop insight into the values and characteristics, including language, of the civilization of which one is a member.

6.2 Develop an awareness and understanding of one's cultural heritage and become familiar with the achievements of the past that have inspired and influenced humanity.

6.3 Develop understanding of the manner in which traditions from the past are operative today and influence the direction and values of society.

6.4 Understand and adopt the norms, values, and traditions of the groups of which one is a member.

6.5 Learn how to apply the basic principles and concepts of the fine arts and humanities to the appreciation of the aesthetic contributions of other cultures.

A study of traditions that illuminate our relationship with the past can yield insight into our present society and its values. Moreover, one's sense of belonging to a society is strengthened through an understanding of one's place in its tradition, and its record of human aspiration may suggest direction for one's own life. All these perceptions will contribute to the development of a person's sense of identity.

7. Moral and ethical character

7.1 Develop the judgment to evaluate events and phenomena as good or evil.

7.2 Develop a commitment to truth and values.

7.3 Learn to utilize values in making choices.

7.4 Develop moral integrity.

7.5 Develop an understanding of the necessity for moral conduct.

Society, religion, and philosophy provide guideposts for moral conduct. The individual is expected to control personal behavior according to one or several systems of values. Models for some of these values are implicit in other persons' behavior (parents, teachers, state leaders), and other values are manifested in the form of a moral code. Schools are expected to teach the young how to discern the values inherent in human behavior.

D. Personal Goals

8. Emotional and physical well-being

8.1 Develop the willingness to receive emotional impressions and to expand one's affective sensitivity.

8.2 Develop the competence and skills for continuous adjustment and emotional stability, including coping with social change.

8.3 Develop a knowledge of one's own body and adopt health practices that support and sustain it, including avoiding the consumption of harmful or addictive substances.

8.4 Learn to use leisure time effectively.

8.5 Develop physical fitness and recreational skills.

8.6 Develop the ability to engage in constructive self-criticism.

The emotional stability and the physical fitness of the student are perceived in state goals as necessary conditions for attaining the other objectives. But physical well-being, emotional sensitivity, and realistic acceptance of self and others also are ends in themselves.

9. Creativity and aesthetic expression

9.1 Develop the ability to deal with problems in original ways.

9.2 Develop the ability to be tolerant of new ideas.

9.3 Develop the ability to be flexible and to consider different points of view.

9.4 Develop the ability to experience and enjoy different forms of creative expression.

9.5 Develop the ability to evaluate various forms of aesthetic expression.

9.6 Develop the willingness and ability to communicate through creative work in an active way.

9.7 Seek to contribute to cultural and social life through one's artistic, vocational, and avocational interests.

The ability to create new and meaningful things and the ability to appreciate the creations of other human beings help one toward personal self-realization and benefit human society. Schools have a role to play in cultivating such appreciation and creativity.

10. Self-realization

10.1 Learn to search for meaning in one's activities, and develop a philosophy of life.

10.2 Develop the self-confidence necessary for knowing and confronting one's self.

10.3 Learn to assess realistically and live with one's limitations and strengths.

10.4 Recognize that one's self-concept is developed in interaction with other people.

10.5 Develop skill in making decisions with purpose.

10.6 Learn to plan and organize the environment in order to realize one's goals.

10.7 Develop willingness to accept responsibility for one's own decisions and their consequences.

10.8 Develop skill in selecting some personal, lifelong learning goals and the means to attain them.

The ideal of self-realization is based on the idea that there is more than one way of being a human being and that efforts to develop a better self contribute to the development of a better society. Schools which do not produce self-directed citizens have failed both society and the individual. Adults unable to regulate and guide their own conduct are a liability to society and themselves. As a society becomes more complex, more relative, more ambiguous, and less structured, demands upon the individual multiply. We have created a world in which there no longer is a common body of information that everyone must or can learn. The only hope for meeting the demands of the future is the development of people who are capable of assuming responsibility for their own needs. Schools should help

every child to prepare for a world of rapid changes and unforeseeable demands in which continuing education throughout adult life should be a normal expectation.

These goals, or their approximations, appeared with sufficient frequency to suggest considerable national agreement, on a state-by-state basis. We are not without goals for schooling. But we are lacking an articulation of them and commitment to them.

Conclusions and Implications

What parents, teachers, and students expect of schools is an important but insufficient criterion for determining what our schools should seek to do. To say that schools belong to their communities means little until we define community. It is the responsibility of the state, presumably, to raise expectations for schools beyond only those of local significance so that they encompass national and, indeed, global awareness and understanding.[9]

The picture emerging for me is one of substantial concurrence between what client groups expect of their schools and what official state and district documents say our schools are for but fail to articulate clearly. Not surprisingly, this concurrence is greater among the adults—parents and teachers—than the students. Presumably, state and local directives are written with adults, not children and youths, in mind.

What I find missing in the state and local pronouncements is a definition and clarification of what I call the education gap: "The distance between man's most noble visions of what he might become and present levels of functioning."[10] The clear and widely disseminated articulation of this gap would define educational needs and motivate large numbers of people to participate in change and reform. If this articulation fails to come from the state, from where might we expect to receive it?

My analysis suggests timidity on the part of the several states—a general failure to grasp the opportunity for leadership in a realm where the role of the federal government is ambiguous at best. Perhaps this results from an overdesire, for reasons of political expediency, to reflect the wishes of local constituencies. Whatever the reasons, the unfortunate consequence is the lack of a long-term agenda generated at the state level to guide educational effort at the district level. This lack, in turn, is conducive to galvanic and frequently insensitive responses to perceived but usually not carefully diagnosed problems.

I sense a degree of cynicism in the general absence of a definitive, forthright, idealistic commitment to education and schooling. There is on the part of many legislators with whom I have talked an understandable frustration about how to improve schools. This frustration is accompanied by considerable naivete regarding schooling and a belief that school people (particularly administrators) are inordinately resistant to new ideas—specifically the ideas of these legislators. Also, it is widely believed that teachers have an easy time of it, with a short work day and a long summer vacation. There follows a tendency to overlook the broad focus of reform and the awesome task of hammering out state policy, and to zero in on school and classroom—not to listen and learn, but to change things quickly. As Atkin puts it, government is in the classroom and in all probability will stay there.[11] But so long as those in state capi-

tals concentrate almost exclusively on the accountability of administrators, teachers, and students, the state commitments we need will not be forthcoming. The message from those responsible for formulating state policy will continue to be punitive rather than inspirational. And those who legislate will continue to wonder why their "perfectly rational" solutions to obvious problems produce such bland and unsatisfying results.[12]

Many state officials will disagree with the foregoing. They will send me documents to disprove my generalization. Some of their protests will be well taken. Nonetheless, I am convinced that most, perhaps all, of the states are groping for rather than striding toward a definition of their authority and responsibility. When members of state boards of education tell me that they have no long-term agenda, that what happens from meeting to meeting depends on the items brought by members, I grow uneasy. When local superintendents desiring to effect change grow fearful of state restraints, my uneasiness increases. When textbook publishers tell me how difficult it is to get adoption of books and materials not clearly oriented to "the basics," I worry about what students are doing in the schools. And when I see how much time and energy are going into the development and use of proficiency tests for students—at the highest levels of policy making as well as at all other levels of the system—I wonder whether we have the right priorities.

The more I look at schools and our data from "A Study of Schooling," the more convinced I am that we lack educational agendas for the several levels of the system. Further, we have not yet installed the mechanisms by which to get the data necessary to determine these agendas. And the needed data go far beyond the measures of student achievement on which we now largely depend for determining the quality of our schools.

Segments of these agendas emerge from the foregoing. As stated earlier, the first priority for each state is to articulate as basic policy a commitment to the four broad areas of educational goals that have steadily emerged in this nation.

A second priority for each state is to make clear that simply offering curricula in all four goal areas by each school is not sufficient. Each student must secure this balance in the course of his or her total precollegiate education. It becomes the responsibility of each school district, with the assistance of the state (e.g., through county offices or regional service centers), to develop a means of gathering data to continually assess each student's individual program and a means of guiding his or her curricular selections.

Third, states must use representative samples of these data to determine areas of overall imbalance and the kind of effort needed to correct this imbalance. For example, students with stated intentions of becoming physicians or engineers could be prematurely and excessively emphasizing science and mathematics. It might be necessary to enlist deans and professors of university schools of medicine and engineering in seeking to discourage this trend by altering their entrance requirements and selection processes.

Fourth, states should take the lead in emphasizing the limitations of schools' ability to fulfill society's educational functions, let alone do the other things schools are called upon to do. It should not surprise us that parents' concept of educa-

tional development for their children embraces all aspects of education. But it no longer is reasonable to assume that schools can or should do all or perhaps even most of the educating. It may be necessary to recognize that the school will continue to be a viable, appreciated institution only if we define its mission more precisely, including only those things educational which the rest of society cannot do well. Parents might accept a leaner role for the local school if they were aware of and had confidence in the educative possibilities of other institutions.

The state should be in the lead in planning and promoting alternative configurations of agencies and institutions for educational purposes. But it often constrains. For example, the formulas used for distributing resources often make it difficult for schools to enrich their programs by using the resources even of other parts of the system, e.g., for secondary schools to draw on the programs of nearby community colleges. But states need to go beyond the eliminating of restraints and deliberately experiment with a variety of collaborative educational delivery systems. They should vigorously and forthrightly endorse communitywide education and be alert in the search for ways to help local communities implement the concept.[13] This will not occur so long as states remain overwhelmingly and disproportionately school-based in their educational commitment.

The states need to gather and be sensitive to data pertaining to the total system of education. What is business now doing, and what might this sector do most effectively in the future? For what segments of the population is school attendance increasing and declining? What are nonattenders doing? What proportion of those registered in schools is not in daily attendance? What is the significance of these data? What is the impact of state policies and actions? Do they facilitate or inhibit local initiative and creativity? Do states gather the right kinds of data? Literally dozens of such questions having profound implications for the welfare of young people and our nation are begging for attention. But questions of this kind usually are not asked, in part because of our preoccupation with what schools are doing and our tendency to equate schooling and education. Offices adjacent to departments of education in state capitals frequently gather, for other purposes, large amounts of data relevant to education and schooling. But sharing information across departmental lines is not characteristic of bureaucracies—more because of unawareness and custom than unwillingness.

Preceding pages suggest the appropriate leadership role of states. The suggested agenda is intended to remind elected and appointed state officials of their leadership role at the very highest level of constitutional authority for education and schooling. They must not be timid in exercising this leadership. Only to develop regulations for holding educators accountable is to sidestep state responsibility.

Ironically, as states have gained power, especially because of their role in financing schools, the use of state prerogatives in seeking to get schools to do what legislators and other officials want them to do has not been markedly successful. In fact, it soon may be perceived as one of our major social failures. And with this increased power, states appear to have become less mindful of their role in setting a tone of challenge and stimulation. Instead, they

often have been more punitive than supportive in the legislation enacted. Let the states send a strong message of guidance, challenge, and hope for education and accompany it with clearly articulated expectations for education in schools.

This is not the message that people closest to schools generally have been hearing in recent years. It is, I believe, a message they are ready to hear.

NOTES

1. For a discussion of the decline of this coalition and its effects, see Stephen K. Bailey, "Political Coalitions for Public Education," *Daedalus* (Summer 1981), pp. 27–43.

2. Ronald G. McIntire, "The Development of a Conceptual Model for Selection of Optional Educational Programs in an Elementary School," unpublished doctoral dissertation, University of California, Los Angeles, 1976.

3. Lawrence A. Cremin, *Traditions of American Education*, p. 12. New York: Basic Books, 1977. For elaboration of this configuration and the component parts, see Lawrence A. Cremin, *American Education: The Colonial Experience.* New York: Harper and Row, 1970.

4. Joseph J. Schwab, "Education and the State: Learning Community," *The Great Ideas Today*, pp. 234–271. Chicago: Encyclopaedia Britannica Inc., 1976.

5. Lawrence A. Cremin, *The Transformation of the School*, pp. 122–123. New York: Alfred A. Knopf, 1961.

6. For purposes of comparing these concepts with those that guided provisions for free public schooling throughout the second half of the nineteenth century and well into the twentieth, see James S. Coleman, "The Concept of Equality of Educational Opportunity," *Harvard Educational Review*, Vol. 28, (1968), p. 11.

7. For further analysis, see Ernest R. House, *The Politics of Educational Innovation.* Berkeley, Calif.: McCutchan Publishing Co., 1974.

8. Ralph W. Tyler, *Basic Principles of Curriculum and Instruction.* Chicago: University of Chicago Press, 1949.

9. For an intriguing glimpse into what a global education program in schools might look like, see Lee and Charlotte Anderson, "A Visit to Middleton's World-Centered Schools: A Scenario," in *Schooling for a Global Age* (ed. James M. Becker). New York: McGraw-Hill, 1979.

10. John I. Goodlad, *What Schools Are For*, p. 16. Bloomington, Ind.: Phi Delta Kappa Educational Foundation, 1979.

11. Myron J. Atkin, "The Government in the Classroom," *Daedalus*, Vol. 109, No. 3 (Summer 1980), pp. 85–97.

12. For a compelling analysis of bureaucratic rationality applied to the improvement of educational practice, see Arthur E. Wise, *Legislated Learning.* Berkeley: University of California Press, 1979.

13. For a comprehensive discussion of what is required, see Don Davis (ed.), *Communities and Their Schools.* New York: McGraw-Hill, 1980.

Part I Additional Resources

Discussion Questions

Students should carefully read each question and support each response with examples and specific references to the readings that are being considered.

1. Think about the aims and purposes of education. Create a chart with columns for the past few decades. For each decade, identify four things: (a) societal trends and issues, (b) the dominant educational philosophy, (c) key curricular emphases, and (d) examples of school practices. In small groups, discuss how the aims and purposes of education shifted for each decade as a response to societal influences.

2. After reading about the history of American education and considering multiple views on the aims and purposes of public schools, attempt to answer the following questions: Who "owns" the public schools, and who benefits from the work that is being done in them? Who determines what knowledge will be included in the school curriculum? How are debates and differences regarding the answers to these questions reconciled in both public and private domains? If public schools are not successfully educating all children, whom should be held accountable? How do the answers to these questions tell us something about the larger aims and purposes of education?

3. Who should determine the primary goals of public schools? Should the primary goals of public education be based upon larger sociopolitical purposes, or should they reflect local community beliefs and values? How might these goals differ?

4. Schools are frequently blamed for social and political problems. Should schools be responsive to solving larger social and political problems, for example, racism, poverty, and teenaged pregnancy? How does the answer to this question affect the ways in which we view the aims and purposes of public education?

5. The aims and purposes of education do not always coincide with the goals of business. Are business leaders major stakeholders in education and schooling? Should the corporate world have a voice in discussions regarding the goals and purposes of public schools? Why or why not?

Guide to Further Reading

Cremin, Lawrence A., ed. 1957. *The Republic and the School: Horace Mann and the Education of Free Men*. New York: Teachers College Press.

Dewey, John. 1916. *Democracy and Education: An Introduction to the Philosophy of Education*. New York: Macmillan.

Katz, Michael. 1968. *The Irony of Early School Reform: Educational Innovation in Mid–Nineteenth Century Massachusetts*. Boston: Beacon Press.

Oakes, Jeannie, and Martin Lipton. 2006. *Teaching to Change the World*. New York: McGraw-Hill.

Ravitch, Diane. 2010. *The Death and Life of the Great American School System: How Testing and Choice Are Undermining Education*. New York: Basic Books.

Spring, Joel. 1998. *Education and the Rise of the Global Economy*. Mahway, NJ: Lawrence Erlbaum Associates, Inc.

Tyack, David. 1974. *The One Best System: A History of American Urban Education*. Cambridge, MA: Harvard University Press.

Whitehead, Alfred North. 1929. *The Aims of Education and Other Essays*. New York: Macmillan.

Related Resources

http://www.americanpromise.com
   The American Promise
http://www.edweek.org
   Education Week
http://ericir.syr.edu
   The Educator's Reference Desk: Resource Guides
http://www.newhorizons.org
   New Horizons for Learning
http://www.ed.gov
   U.S. Department of Education

Part II

WHAT SHOULD BE THE CONTENT OF THE CURRICULUM?

INTRODUCTION

Access to knowledge is a key issue in discussions of equity and social justice. It is one thing to talk about an equal education but another thing to decide who gets to learn what. Does the future president of the United States need a depth and breadth of knowledge that is not required by the plumber in our community? Most people would answer that question easily by saying that there must be differences; however, who decides what the future vocational needs of students might be? How do we go about identifying future presidents or chief executive officers? How do we know who our blue-collar workers will be? Can we successfully identify those who will drop out of school? Statistics, of course, guide our preconceptions, but are they always correct? Of course not. Through the years, I have entertained my students with stories of my working class background. Neither of my parents went to college; my father dropped out of high school, and although my mother graduated from high school, she went to work immediately thereafter. Both of my parents had blue-collar, semiskilled positions at the Veterans' Hospital in Memphis, Tennessee. I was a mediocre student with mediocre grades; my parents knew nothing about college and thus did not encourage me to enter a world that was foreign to them. It is probably not surprising that in my senior year, when I approached a guidance counselor for assistance with college applications, she told me I wasn't college material and suggested that I look at technical schools that might be better suited to my needs. At this point in the story, I always smile and suggest that clearly this guidance counselor didn't know me because no one should ever tell me I can't do something. It is almost perverse that despite my dislike of school, I continued my education until I was thirty-two years old. I left high school and graduated from college with honors four years later, and then I continued to attend school until I subsequently received my master's degree and Ph.D. I tell this story not simply to pat myself on the back; more important, I tell it to emphasize that we really have no idea where our students are going or who they will become. We cannot look in their eyes at the age of five, ten, or even sixteen and know what they are capable of doing, yet we frequently attempt to test and sort and guide them toward futures that we really know nothing about.

Step back and think about how we determine the content of the curriculum. What is really the *best* education for *all* students regardless of who and what they will become one day? This section of the book is, perhaps, the most thought-provoking.

The different perspectives of William Ayers, Gloria Ladson-Billings, Paulo Freire, Michael Apple, and Lisa Delpit in Chapters 6–10 challenge us to think about how we define and articulate the curriculum and how our interpretation of basic knowledge is shaped by our understanding of the relationship between the aims and purposes of education, access to knowledge, and issues of equity and social justice. Each of these scholars is a prolific writer in the field of education, and the work presented here has had a significant influence on contemporary thinking about curriculum; however, these ideas are also controversial. Students may not agree with them all, but familiarity with this work is essential to thoughtful discussions about how, what, and why we teach in twenty-first-century schools.

William Ayers

The Shifting Ground of Curriculum Thought and Everyday Practice

I spend a lot of time in Chicago public schools.[1] It is a world I live in, and this is some of what I see:

- Visiting a fourth-grade class, I was greeted by the teacher. "Welcome to our class," she said. "I'm on page 307 of the math text, exactly where I'm supposed to be according to board guidelines."

  There was not much going on—two students were asleep, several were looking out the window, a few were reading their math books. I discovered later that virtually every student in the class was failing math. But this teacher was doing her job, moving through the set curriculum, dutifully delivering the material, passing out the grades. If the students did not learn math, that was not her responsibility.

- Attending a local school council meeting, I listened as people debated how to spend funds designated to help poor students achieve. Some wanted to buy specific curriculum materials, others to hire two part-time classroom aides. In the end the money went to buy metal detectors to keep weapons out of the school,

and to hire a guard to monitor the entrance.

- Working together, a group of progressive public school teachers devised a set of more learner-centered and teacher-friendly alternatives to the standard report cards to parents, and struggled to get them accepted as options in several schools. It was an uphill battle, but they succeeded in some instances. One teacher told the group, "I'm so exhausted from this one fight at my school that I've caved in on a hundred other fights that I could have had and should have had."

We need to look at the world as it is, to attend to its variety and complexity, its idiosyncrasy and its particularity. Each of the examples above contains a contradiction. The math teacher is oppressive and oppressed, the school council is wise and limited, the progressive teachers are daring and conventional.

Schools and school systems turn teachers into clerks. Curriculum is the product of someone else's thought, knowledge, experience, and imagination. It becomes the package developed somewhere out there. The teacher takes the package and hands it on to the students. Everyone is passive, everyone a consumer, everyone deficient and dependent.

A teacher told me recently a tiny tale of liberation. Her second-grade class was supposed to do a two-week unit on rocks. She walked with her class to a pond to collect some samples, but the children's imaginations were captured by their frequent sightings of minnows and carp: "There's one!" "Where did it go?" "What do they eat?" "When do they sleep?"

Throwing caution to the wind, and following the lead of her students, this teacher built a project of inquiry around fish: fish pictures, fish prints, fish observations, fish in history, the life cycles of fish. . . . "But you know," she told me, "The whole time we were doing fish I felt guilty about the rocks."

Her concern was only partly that she would be discovered. She was also worried that she was somehow doing a disservice to the students. Was she cheating them out of information they needed? Would they be ready for third-grade science? Of course this whole approach to curriculum assumes that knowledge is finite and knowing passive—never mind that people get Ph.D.s in rocks as well as fish—the scope and sequence and plan are in control. Some academic, state bureaucrat, researcher, or publisher must know that the second grade needs rocks and not fish, or fish and rocks and not stamps.

The curriculum is the stuff that is taught in urban, public schools. The curriculum is a thing, something bought and sold, packaged and delivered. The teachers are the clerks, the line employees doing their jobs. There is virtually no talk among school people of the curriculum as interactive or constructed, of teachers as transformative intellectuals or moral agents.

Talk of school improvement generally means buying a different package and inserting it into the existing structures, cultures, and realities. Ideas that are potentially transforming—for example "whole language," "cooperative learning," or "Afro-centric curriculum"—become thus reduced to fit into mindless, airless spaces: "We have a critical thinking unit first thing in the morning," or "We do character ed. just before lunch." The name remains, but the larger reality has overwhelmed whatever might have been hopeful there.

It is not simply the expensive, command-style central office that is killing city schools. Teaching itself is a victim of bureaucratization. It is the acceptance of the model, the reduction of teaching, for example, to a set of regulations to be spelled out as a result of negotiated conflict, and the re-creation of bureaucracy (with its focus on procedure and function and interchangeable parts) into the classroom itself, that distorts teaching and destroys teachers and students alike.

Critical Questions

Schubert (1986) describes the kinds of questions that concern critical theorists, for example:

- How is knowledge reproduced by schools?
- How do students and teachers resist or contest that which is conveyed through lived experience in schools?
- Whose interests are served by outlooks and skills fostered by schooling?
- When served, do these interests move more in the direction of eman-

cipation, equity, and social justice, or do they move in the opposite direction?

- How can students be empowered to attain greater liberation, equity, and social justice through schooling? (p. 315)

If taken seriously and pursued vigorously, questions such as these go to the very heart of the crisis in urban education today. Of course, the questions are not new, they were raised powerfully through the stories of Herb Kohl (1967), Jonathan Kozol (1967), and other teacher-authors in the 1960s and 1970s, and they were addressed, as well, in the work of Caroline Pratt (1948), Lucy Sprague Mitchell (1950), and other progressives in the 1920s and 1930s.

The critical theorists of today stand on these shoulders, of course, and trace their roots directly to the work of John Dewey, the "original critical theorist," according to Schubert (1986, p. 331). Schubert argues that Dewey's philosophy of education is a "thorough basis for praxis," and that Dewey as philosopher, social critic, sensitive practitioner, and social activist understood that a "philosophy of education is never complete except as developed and refined in the continuous flow of experience" (p. 331).

It is a commonplace for academics to be dismissed by schoolteachers as being impractical, theoretical, philosophical—"That sounds very fine, but this is the real world." Equally common (but less discussed at the university) is a practically universal condescension and patronization toward teachers, toward the practical. Their experiences are not particularly worthwhile, it is assumed, since they are deficient, lacking knowledge or correct curriculum, and in need of our interventions and ministrations. Academics barely see them and rarely hear them—they are silent shadows in our consciousness. This is as true for critical theorists as for empirical analytical academics.

In fact, the entire reward structure at most colleges of education pulls faculty away from any direct contact with schools or schoolteachers. Younger and newer faculty, graduate students, and adjuncts interface with schools; their more senior colleagues disappear into research and writing.

It is a neat split—if an old one—this mind/body duality. Education fractures along lines of thinking and doing, venues and concerns divide, everyone's vision and capacity narrows. We become Butch Cassidy and the Sundance Kid—the classic macho male relationship—either all brains or all body in a sick symbiosis. The tragic consequences of this dualism for teaching are as predictable as the movie's bloody ending.

The questions Schubert enumerates are significant. The problem is that unlike the "critical theorists" of the 1920s or the 1960s, those who profess critical theory today are most likely to do so in a language that is arid and arcane, and from the relative safety of academe. Critical theorists espouse praxis, a complex integration of political action with intellectual inquiry, but tend to be heavy on the latter and light on the former. Where are the voices of classroom teachers struggling with these questions? Where are the insurgent alternative schools? What role do critical theorists have in making any of this happen?

People involved in changing schools have taken an important first step, a step away from the taken-for-granted, a step into the unknown. They are searching for new ways of thinking and doing, and they are moving with courage and hope. In this context I have found that no question is too radical, none too provocative. In fact, I have consistently been pushed by parents, students, and teachers to see the workings of politics and power in schools in much greater detail. I often ask school people whose interests are being served here, and I consistently find a complex grasp of the subtleties of control embodied in the lunchroom and the playground as well as the classroom.

Empowering

In a sense all education is about power—its goal is for people to become more skilled, more able, more dynamic, more vital. Teaching is about strengthening, invigorating, and empowering others. People may not agree about how to get there, but there is general accord that good teaching enables and strengthens learners.

While education is about empowering people, the machinery of schooling is on another mission altogether. Schooling is most often about obedience and conformity; it is about crowd control, competition, hierarchy, and one's place in it. It is rule-bound and procedure-driven. Schooling fosters dependence, passivity, and dullness. In fact, many normal, discerning students, wondering what kind of intelligence will be rewarded in school, conclude that being quiet, dull, and invisible is the dominant expectation, and act accordingly.

In the first year of the Chicago school reform, the dramatic decentralization of the city schools, the parent-led local school councils were free to seek "train-

ing" and education from any source they chose. At the end of the year, many council members had two complaints: (a) They had inadequate knowledge and training to do the job; and (b) they had been worked to the bone and trained to death.

This paradox can be understood, I believe, by looking at the nature of the training experience and the expectations of the participants. There was a strong sense that some piece of skill or knowledge was out there that should be given to council members. In fact, however, no training would have been adequate prior to the actual doing of the job. That is, being a council member was itself the only true training for being a council member. Where specific knowledge or skills were needed (e.g., making a budget or writing a funding proposal), specific experts could always be brought in. This was not, in the main, what happened.

Typically councils were offered packages—a curriculum on hiring the principal, a curriculum on law, a curriculum on budgeting—and these were built on the top-down, either-or, we-know-you-don't-know, theory-practice paradigm. Even the more enlightened curriculum on school improvement planning suffered this orientation. The hidden curriculum in these instances is invariably powerlessness.

If we want to participate fully in the revitalization of teaching and curriculum, we will need to conceive of ourselves and our work in new ways. We will have to move beyond brilliance, beyond living in our heads, beyond an exclusive focus on correct ideas. We will have to address all the destructive dualisms, the either-ors, that obscure our vision. We will have to create a holistic language, a language both clear enough and complex enough to capture the realities and possibilities of teaching. We will have to reinvent our profession if we hope to help reinvent schools.

Theory *is* important. Theory helps us to organize the world, to sort out the details, to make some coherent sense out of a kaleidoscope of sensations. Without theory we would collapse exhausted from our encounter with experience, and this is precisely what describes some forms of mental disease. From the toddler playing peek-a-boo and struggling to understand her vanishing and reappearing mother to the physicist imagining that high energy particles are invested with "charm"— making theory is simply what human beings do.

Living in the world is also what we do (and all our worlds are real worlds—even the world of the college classroom, even the world of our imaginations). Our theories are neither a reflection of the world nor a logical rendering of it. Einstein, in fact, once pointed out that theory-building requires intuition and a sympathetic understanding of lived experience, for there is no absolute, logical, theoretical bridge between phenomena and theory (Pilsig, 1974, p. 99). Theories, then, adjust, change, and shift in relation to our feeling for living—or they do not. And here is part of the problem. Too much adjusting, changing, and shifting and we have no framework of sense-making; too little and we are descending into dogmatism.

For example, we often find ourselves not much different from the apocalyptic Christians standing in the Indiana cornfield waiting for the world to end. Our ideologies—whether well-defended by a blizzard of inaccessible theoretical and statistical data, or revealed truth, or simple common sense (which can be as dogmatic and totalizing as any religion or political affiliation)—hide the truth. They cut us off from the very detail that could be our true salvation. They become an obstacle.

We should be reminded (as the women's movement so powerfully taught) that the personal is political, that we embody a stance and a social statement in our experiences, our choices, our daily lives. We should also know that there is no politics without people, that what we do or do not do matters in its detail. We can, then, stop waiting for the big moment when we can be strong, courageous, and correct, and get on with the business of living as if it made a difference.

We can resist the notion that ideas flow from thinkers to doers. Again, the modern women's movement is a case in point. Although feminist thought, literature, and theory is extensive, the movement arose largely from the meeting of women's daily lives with the increased political activity around civil rights and peace. Women did not bring the feminist thinking of intellectuals into their daily lives in a one-directional way.

We should resist dogma—theory as a closed, justifying framework that hides reality. We should stay alive to questions, to contradiction, to ambiguity, to the next utterance in the dialogue. And, yes, to spontaneity. We should be for intellect, for a continual desire to see more, to know more. And we should be for a morality linked to action.

Beinfield and Korngold (1991) remind us that "by choosing between mutually exclusive either-or options, we splinter our world into winners and losers, masters and slaves, superiors and inferiors, haves and have-nots. Such hierarchical divisions are reinforced by a self-serving morality" (p. 381).

We can fight for a stance of interconnection, commitment, struggle, and continuity. We can integrate an understanding that the people with the problems are also the people with the solutions, and that experience (our own as well as others') is a powerful teacher if we will only wake up and pay attention.

Doing It—Collaboratively

All of this leads me to think that there is no proper way to ground curriculum thought in school practice outside of the doing of it. That is, we need to reorganize and restructure and rethink the entire educational enterprise, top to bottom, if we are to make a real difference. Instead of university faculty and school staff as fragmented parts of a whole, for example, we can think of teachers as working now at the university, now in a public school.

Magdalene Lampert (1985) at Michigan State, whose scholarship is based on her ongoing practical work as a fifth-grade math teacher and whose teaching is informed by her continuing scholarly inquiry, perhaps provides an incipient model to examine. Or, perhaps educational resources can begin to be reorganized to provide for teacher-researchers rather than the currently constituted cadre of researchers above the army of teachers. Good teaching is always in pursuit of improvement, after all; teacher-researchers inquiring into the improvement of teaching may be a sensible goal.

Some are searching for ways to build a collaborative process of inquiry, one that explicitly serves the needs of teachers and students rather than the more self-absorbed goal of "knowledge production" disembodied from conduct (Schubert & Ayers, 1991). They are dissatisfied with knowledge as industry, or as top-down and objective, or as something to be divided up. They are interested in linking inquiry and action, thought and conduct, theory and practice. They want to participate in a process in which people define both the questions and seek the solutions for themselves.

Noddings (1986) argues that researchers "have perhaps too often made *persons* (teachers and students) the objects of research. An alternative is to choose *problems* that interest and concern researchers, students, and teachers. . . . Such research would be genuine research *for* teaching instead of simply research *on* teaching" (p. 394). Paley (1979), to begin, may be a helpful example of this integration. Paley is a classroom teacher whose inquiry into her own teaching has resulted in a steady stream of compelling ethnographies. In any case, academics and researchers can stop hiding behind their sanctified methods, their exclusive resources, their impenetrable rhetoric. They can give it all away now.

In the current upheaval in the Chicago schools, I have mainly run to keep up. I have attended every meeting, rushed from place to place, observed, recorded, and written down all that I have seen. Still something was incomplete. Somewhere I shook loose, and an idea planted in my head by a group of teachers took root and grew. The idea was to become a principal, to gather a group of progressive teachers together, to create a model of a dramatically different, learner-centered, and successful school for urban kids.

Five years ago, the idea would not have found fertile soil—a principalship was my idea of hell. But in the reconstituted context of Chicago schools and in the company of these teachers it seemed doable, possible, and then right. So far it is just an idea, but we have written down our thoughts on schools and I have dragged myself through the tedious and wacky world of certification. And now I am late for an interview with a local school council. I've got to go.

REFERENCES

Beinfield, H., & Korngold, E. (1991). *Between heaven and earth*. New York: Ballantine Books.

Kohl, H. (1967). *36 children*. New York: Knopf.

Kozol, J. (1967). *Death at an early age*. New York: New American Library.

Lampert, M. (1985). How do teachers manage to teach? *Harvard Educational Review, 55*(2), 178–194.

Mitchell, L. S. (1950). *Our children and our schools*. New York: Simon & Schuster.

Noddings, N. (1986). Fidelity in teaching, teacher education, and research for teaching. *Harvard Educational Review, 56*(4), 384–389.

Paley, V. (1979). *White teacher*. Cambridge, MA: Harvard University Press.

Pilsig, R. M. (1974). *Zen and the art of motorcycle maintenance*. New York: Bantam.

Pratt, C. (1948). *I learn from children*. New York: Cornerstone.

Schubert, W. H. (1986). *Curriculum: Perspective, paradigm, and possibility*. New York: Macmillan.

Schubert, W. H., & Ayers, W. C. (1991). *Teacher lore: Learning from our own experience*. New York: Longman.

NOTE

1. On December 12, 1988, Illinois Governor James Thompson signed Public Act 85-1418, and the most far-reaching mandate to restructure a big-city school system in American history became law. The Chicago School Reform Act called for the creation of strong local school councils made up of parents, teachers, citizens, and principals at each schoolhouse. Each council consists of six parents, two teachers, two community representatives, and the principal. Council members are elected by their constituent group (that is, parents of children attending the school elect parent representatives, and so on) except the principal, who is hired by the local school council.

The intent of the law was crystal clear: Power was to shift from a large central office to each local school site, and a bureaucratic, command-oriented system was to yield to a decentralized and democratic model. The traditional pyramid-shaped organizational structure was to be inverted. It was widely acknowledged that this shift would be complex and difficult under any circumstances. In a situation of wildly divergent interpretations, long-standing political rivalries, and deeply entrenched patronage and power relationships, the contention was certain to be fierce, and the resulting upheaval dramatic.

The author has been an active participant in the Chicago school upheaval for many years. He has written widely about Chicago schools, and from September 1989 to June 1990, he served as assistant deputy mayor for education in Chicago, responsible for educational activities for local school councils. He is currently chair of an activist coalition, the Alliance for Better Chicago Schools (ABC's).

Gloria Ladson-Billings

But That's Just Good Teaching!
The Case for Culturally Relevant Pedagogy

For the past 6 years I have been engaged in research with excellent teachers of African American students (see, for example, Ladson-Billings, 1990, 1992b, 1992c, 1994). Given the dismal academic performance of many African American students (The College Board, 1985), I am not surprised that various administrators, teachers, and teacher educators have asked me to share and discuss my findings so that they might incorporate them in their work. One usual response to what I share is the comment around which I have based this article, "But, that's just good teaching!" Instead of some "magic bullet" or intricate formula and steps for instruction, some members of my audience are shocked to hear what seems to them like some rather routine teaching strategies that are a part of good teaching. My response is to affirm that, indeed, I am describing good teaching, and to question why so little of it seems to be occurring in the classrooms populated by African American students.

The pedagogical excellence I have studied is good teaching, but it is much more than that. This article is an attempt to describe a pedagogy I have come to identify as "culturally relevant" (Ladson-Billings, 1992a) and to argue for its centrality in the academic success of African American and other children who have not been well served by our nation's public schools. First, I provide some background information about other attempts to look at linkages between school and culture. Next, I discuss the theoretical grounding of culturally relevant teaching in the context of a 3-year study of successful teachers of African American students. I conclude this discussion with further examples of this pedagogy in action.

Linking Schooling and Culture

Native American educator Cornel Pewewardy (1993) asserts that one of the reasons Indian children experience difficulty in schools is that educators traditionally have attempted to insert culture into the education, instead of inserting education into the culture. This notion is, in all probability, true for many students who are not a part of the White, middle-class mainstream. For almost 15 years, anthropologists have looked at ways to develop a closer fit between students' home culture and the school. This work has had a variety of labels including "culturally appropriate" (Au & Jordan, 1981), "culturally congruent" (Mohatt & Erickson, 1981), "culturally responsive" (Cazden & Leggett, 1981; Erickson & Mohatt, 1982), and "culturally compatible" (Jordan 1985; Vogt, Jordan,

& Tharp, 1987). It has attempted to locate the problem of discontinuity between what students experience at home and what they experience at school in the speech and language interactions of teachers and students. These sociolinguists have suggested that if students' home language is incorporated into the classroom, students are more likely to experience academic success.

Villegas (1988), however, has argued that these micro-ethnographic studies fail to deal adequately with the macro social context in which student failure takes place. A concern I have voiced about studies situated in speech and language interactions is that, in general, few have considered the needs of African American students.[1]

Irvine (1990) dealt with the lack of what she termed "cultural synchronization" between teachers and African American students. Her analysis included the micro-level classroom interactions, the "mid-level" institutional context (i.e., school practices and policies such as tracking and disciplinary practices), and the macro-level societal context. More recently Perry's (1993) analysis has included the historical context of the African American's educational struggle. All of this work—micro through macro level—has contributed to my conception of culturally relevant pedagogy.

What Is Culturally Relevant Pedagogy?

In the current attempts to improve pedagogy, several scholars have advanced well-conceived conceptions of pedagogy. Notable among these scholars are Shulman (1987), whose work conceptualizes pedagogy as consisting of subject matter knowledge, pedagogical knowledge, and pedagogical content knowledge, and Berliner (1988), who doubts the ability of expert pedagogues to relate their expertise to novice practitioners. More recently, Bartolome (1994) has decried the search for the "right" teaching strategies and argued for a "humanizing pedagogy that respects and uses the reality, history, and perspectives of students as an integral part of educational practice" (p. 173).

I have defined culturally relevant teaching as a pedagogy of opposition (1992c) not unlike critical pedagogy but specifically committed to collective, not merely individual, empowerment. Culturally relevant pedagogy rests on three criteria or propositions: (a) Students must experience academic success; (b) students must develop and/or maintain cultural competence; and (c) students must develop a critical consciousness through which they challenge the status quo of the current social order.

Academic Success

Despite the current social inequities and hostile classroom environments, students must develop their academic skills. The way those skills are developed may vary, but all students need literacy, numeracy, technological, social, and political skills in order to be active participants in a democracy. During the 1960s when African Americans were fighting for civil rights, one of the primary battlefronts was the classroom (Morris, 1984). Despite the federal government's failed attempts at adult literacy in the South, civil rights workers such as Septima Clark and Esau Jenkins (Brown, 1990) were able to teach successfully those same adults by ensuring that the students learned that which was most meaningful to them. This approach is similar to that advocated by noted critical pedagogue Paulo Freire (1970).

While much has been written about the need to improve the self-esteem of African American students (see for example, Banks & Grambs, 1972; Branch & Newcombe, 1986; Crooks, 1970), at base, students must demonstrate academic competence. This was a clear message given by the eight teachers who participated in my study.[2] All of the teachers demanded, reinforced, and produced academic excellence in their students. Thus, culturally relevant teaching requires that teachers attend to students' academic needs, not merely make them "feel good." The trick of culturally relevant teaching is to get students to "choose" academic excellence.

In one of the classrooms I studied, the teacher, Ann Lewis,[3] focused a great deal of positive attention on the African American boys (who were the numerical majority in her class). Lewis, a White woman, recognized that the African American boys possessed social power. Rather than allow that power to influence their peers in negative ways, Lewis challenged the boys to demonstrate academic power by drawing on issues and ideas they found meaningful. As the boys began to take on academic leadership, other students saw this as a positive trait and developed similar behaviors. Instead of entering into an antagonistic relationship with the boys, Lewis found ways to value their skills and abilities and channel them in academically important ways.

Cultural Competence

Culturally relevant teaching requires that students maintain some cultural integrity as well as academic excellence. In their widely cited article, Fordham and Ogbu (1986) point to a phenomenon called "acting White," where African American students fear being ostracized by their peers for demonstrating interest in and succeeding in academic and other school related tasks. Other scholars (Hollins, 1994; King, 1994) have provided alternate explanations of this behavior.[4] They suggest that for too many African American students, the school remains an alien and hostile place. This hostility is manifest in the "styling" and "posturing" (Majors & Billson, 1992) that the school rejects. Thus, the African American student wearing a hat in class or baggy pants may be sanctioned for clothing choices rather than specific behaviors. School is perceived as a place where African American students cannot "be themselves."

Culturally relevant teachers utilize students' culture as a vehicle for learning. Patricia Hilliard's love of poetry was shared with her students through their own love of rap music. Hilliard is an African American woman who had taught in a variety of schools, both public and private for about 12 years. She came into teaching after having stayed at home for many years to care for her family. The mother of a teenaged son, Hilliard was familiar with the music that permeates African American youth culture. Instead of railing against the supposed evils of rap music, Hilliard allowed her second grade students to bring in samples of lyrics from what both she and the students determined to be non-offensive rap songs.[5] Students were encouraged to perform the songs, and the teacher reproduced them on an overhead so that they could discuss literal and figurative meanings as well as technical aspects of poetry such as rhyme scheme, alliteration, and onomatopoeia.

Thus, while the students were comfortable using their music, the teacher used it as a bridge to school learning. Their understanding of poetry far exceeded what either the state department of education or the local school district required. Hilliard's work is an example of how academic achievement and cultural competence can be merged.

Another way teachers can support cultural competence was demonstrated by Gertrude Winston, a White woman who has taught school for 40 years.[6] Winston worked hard to involve parents in her classroom. She created an "artist or craftsperson-in-residence" program so that the students could both learn from each other's parents and affirm cultural knowledge. Winston developed a rapport with parents and invited them to come into the classroom for 1 or 2 hours at a time for a period of 2–4 days. The parents, in consultation with Winston, demonstrated skills upon which Winston later built.

For example, a parent who was known in the community for her delicious sweet potato pies did a 2-day residency in Winston's fifth grade classroom. On the first day, she taught a group of students[7] how to make the pie crust. Winston provided supplies for the pie baking and the students tried their hands at making the crusts. They placed them in the refrigerator overnight and made the filling the following day. The finished pies were served to the entire class.

The students who participated in the "seminar" were required to conduct additional research on various aspects of what they learned. Students from the pie baking seminar did reports on George Washington Carver and his sweet potato research, conducted taste tests, devised a marketing plan for selling pies, and researched the culinary arts to find out what kind of preparation they needed to become cooks and chefs. Everyone in Winston's class was required to write a detailed thank you note to the artist/craftsperson.

Other residencies were done by a carpenter, a former professional basketball player, a licensed practical nurse, and a church musician. All of Winston's guests were parents or relatives of her students. She did not "import" role models with whom the students did not have first-hand experience. She was deliberate, in reinforcing that the parents were a knowledgeable and capable resource. Her students came to understand the constructed nature of things such as "art," "excellence," and "knowledge." They also learned that what they had and where they came from were of value.

A third example of maintaining cultural competence was demonstrated by Ann Lewis, a White woman whom I have described as "culturally Black" (Ladson-Billings, 1992b; 1992c). In her sixth grade classroom, Lewis encouraged the students to use their home language while they acquired the secondary discourse (Gee, 1989) of "standard" English. Thus, her students were permitted to express themselves in language (in speaking and writing) with which they were knowledgeable and comfortable. They were then required to "translate" to the standard form. By the end of the year, the students were not only facile at this "code-switching" (Smitherman, 1981) but could better use both languages.

Critical Consciousness

Culturally relevant teaching does not imply that it is enough for students to choose academic excellence and remain culturally grounded if those skills and abilities represent only an individual achievement. Beyond those individual characteristics of academic achievement and cultural competence, students must develop a broader sociopolitical consciousness that allows them to critique the cultural norms, values, mores, and institutions that produce and maintain social inequities. If school is about preparing students for active citizenship, what better citizenship tool than the ability to critically analyze the society?

Freire brought forth the notion of "conscientization," which is "a process that invites learners to engage the world and others critically" (McLaren, 1989, p. 195). However, Freire's work in Brazil was not radically different from work that was being done in the southern United States (Chilcoat & Ligon, 1994) to educate and empower African Americans who were disenfranchised.

In the classrooms of culturally relevant teachers, students are expected to "engage the world and others critically." Rather than merely bemoan the fact that their textbooks were out of date, several of the teachers in the study, in conjunction with their students, critiqued the knowledge represented in the textbooks, and the system of inequitable funding that allowed middle-class students to have newer texts. They wrote letters to the editor of the local newspaper to inform the community of the situation. The teachers also brought in articles and papers that represented counterknowledge to help the students develop multiple perspectives on a variety of social and historical phenomena.

Another example of this kind of teaching was reported in a Dallas newspaper (Robinson, 1993). A group of African American middle school students were involved in what they termed "community problem solving" (see Tate, *Theory into Practice*, Summer 1995). The kind of social action curriculum in which the students participated is similar to that advocated by scholars who argue that students need to be "centered" (Asante, 1991; Tate, 1994) on the *subjects* rather than the objects of study.

Culturally Relevant Teaching in Action

As previously mentioned, this article and its theoretical undergirding come from a 3-year study of successful teachers of African American students. The teachers who participated in the study were initially selected by African American parents who believed them to be exceptional. Some of the parents' reasons for selecting the teachers were the enthusiasm their children showed in school and learning while in their classrooms, the consistent level of respect they received from the teachers, and their perception that the teachers understood the need for the students to operate in the dual worlds of their home community and the White community.

In addition to the parents' recommendations, I solicited principals' recommendations. Principals' reasons for recommended teachers were the low number of discipline referrals, the high attendance rates, and standardized test scores.[8] Teachers whose names appeared as both parents' and principals' recommendations were asked to participate in the study. Of the nine teachers' names who appeared on both lists, eight were willing to participate. Their participation required an in-depth ethnographic interview (Spradley, 1979), unannounced classroom visitations, videotaping of their teaching, and participation in a research collective with the other teachers in the study. This study was funded for 2 years. In a third year I did a follow-up study of two of the teachers to investigate their literacy teaching (Ladson-Billings, 1992b; 1992c).

Initially, as I observed the teachers I could not see patterns or similarities in their teaching. Some seemed very structured and regimented, using daily routines and activities. Others seemed more open or unstructured. Learning seemed to emerge from student initiation and suggestions. Still others seemed eclectic—very structured for certain activities and unstructured for others. It seemed to be a researcher's nightmare—no common threads to pull their practice together in order to relate it to others. The thought of their pedagogy as merely idiosyncratic, a product of their personalities and individual perspectives, left me both frustrated and dismayed. However, when I was able to go back over their interviews and later when we met together as a group to discuss their practice, I could see that in order to understand their practice it was necessary to go beyond the surface features of teaching "strategies" (Bartolome, 1994). The philosophical and ideological underpinnings of their practice, i.e., how they thought about themselves as teachers and how they thought about others (their students, the students' parents, and other community members), how they structured social relations within and outside of the classroom, and how they conceived of knowledge, revealed their similarities and points of congruence.[9]

All of the teachers identified strongly with teaching. They were not ashamed or embarrassed about their profession. Each had chosen to teach and, more important, had chosen to teach in this low-income, largely African American school district. The teachers saw themselves as a part of the community and teaching as a way to give back to the community. They encouraged their students to do the same. They believed their work was artistry, not a technical task that could be accomplished in a recipe-like fashion. Fundamental to their beliefs about teaching was that all of the students could and must succeed. Consequently, they saw their responsibility as working to guarantee the success of each student. The students who seemed furthest behind received plenty of individual attention and encouragement.

The teachers kept the relations between themselves and their students fluid and equitable. They encouraged the students to act as teachers, and they, themselves, often functioned as learners in the classroom. These fluid relationships extended beyond the classroom and into the community. Thus, it was common for the teachers to be seen attending community functions (i.e., churches, students' sports events) and using community services (e.g., beauty parlors, stores). The teachers attempted to create a bond with all of the students, rather than an idiosyncratic, individualistic connection that might foster an unhealthy competitiveness. This bond was nurtured by the teachers' insistence on creating a community of learners as a priority. They encouraged the students to learn collaboratively, teach each other, and be responsible for each other's learning.

As teachers in the same district, the teachers in this study were responsible for meeting the same state and local curriculum guidelines.[10] However, the way they met and challenged those guidelines helped to define them as culturally relevant teachers. For these teachers, knowledge is continuously re-created, recycled, and shared by the teachers and the students. Thus, they were not dependent on state curriculum frameworks or textbooks to decide what and how to teach.

For example, if the state curriculum framework called for teaching about the "age of exploration," they used this as an opportunity to examine conventional interpretations and introduce alternate ones. The content of the curriculum was always open to critical analysis.

The teachers exhibited a passion about what they were teaching—showing enthusiasm and vitality about what was being taught and learned. When students came to them with skill deficiencies, the teachers worked to help the students build bridges or scaffolding so that they could be proficient in the more challenging work they experienced in these classrooms.

For example, in Margaret Rossi's sixth grade class, all of the students were expected to learn algebra. For those who did not know basic number facts, Rossi provided calculators. She believed that by using particular skills in context (e.g., multiplication and division in the context of solving equations), the students would become more proficient at those skills while acquiring new learning.

Implications for Further Study

I believe this work has implications for both the research and practice communities. For researchers, I suggest that this kind of study must be replicated again and again. We need to know much more about the practice of successful teachers

for African American and other students who have been poorly served by our schools. We need to have an opportunity to explore alternate research paradigms that include the voices of parents and communities in non-exploitative ways.[11]

For practitioners, this research reinforces the fact that the place to find out about classroom practices is the naturalistic setting of the classroom and from the lived experiences of teachers. Teachers need not shy away from conducting their own research about their practice (Zeichner & Tabachnick, 1991). Their unique perspectives and personal investment in good practice must not be overlooked. For both groups—researchers and practitioners alike—this work is designed to challenge us to reconsider what we mean by "good" teaching, to look for it in some unlikely places, and to challenge those who suggest it cannot be made available to all children.

REFERENCES

Asante, M. K. (1991). The Afrocentric idea in education. *Journal of Negro Education, 60*, 170–180.

Au, K., & Jordan, C. (1981). Teaching reading to Hawaiian children: Finding a culturally appropriate solution. In H. Trueba, G. Guthrie, & K. Au (Eds.), *Culture and the bilingual classroom: Studies in classroom ethnography* (pp. 69–86). Rowley, MA: Newbury House.

Banks, J., & Grambs, J. (Eds.). (1972). *Black self-concept: Implications for educational and social sciences.* New York: McGraw-Hill.

Bartolome, L. (1994). Beyond the methods fetish: Toward a humanizing pedagogy. *Harvard Educational Review, 64*, 173–194.

Berliner, D. (1988, October). Implications of studies of expertise in pedagogy for teacher education and evaluation. In *New directions for teacher assessment* (Invitational conference proceedings). New York: Educational Testing Service.

Branch, C., & Newcombe, N. (1986). Racial attitudes among young Black children as a function of parental attitudes: A longitudinal and cross-sectional study. *Child Development, 57*, 712–721.

Brown, C. S. (Ed.). (1990). *Ready from within: A first person narrative.* Trenton, NJ: Africa World Press.

Cazden, C., & Leggett, E. (1981). Culturally responsive education: Recommendations for achieving Lau remedies II. In H. Trueba, G. Guthrie, & K. Au (Eds.), *Culture and the bilingual classroom: Studies in classroom ethnography* (pp. 69–86). Rowley, MA: Newbury House.

Chilcoat, G. W., & Ligon, J. A. (1994). Developing democratic citizens: The Mississippi Freedom Schools as a model for social studies instruction. *Theory and Research in Social Education, 22*, 128–175.

The College Board. (1985). *Equality and excellence: The educational status of Black Americans.* New York: Author.

Crooks, R. (1970). The effects of an interracial preschool program upon racial preference, knowledge of racial differences, and racial identification. *Journal of Social Issues, 26*, 137–148.

Edwards, P. A. (1991). Fostering early literacy through parent coaching. In E. Hiebert (Ed.), *Literacy for a diverse society: Perspectives, programs, and policies* (pp. 199–213). New York: Teachers College Press.

Erickson, F., & Mohatt, C. (1982). Cultural organization and participation structures in two classrooms of Indian students. In G. Spindler, (Ed.), *Doing the ethnography of schooling* (pp. 131–174). New York: Holt, Rinehart & Winston.

Fordham, S., & Ogbu, J. (1986). Black students' success: Coping with the burden of "acting White." *Urban Review, 18*, 1–31.

Freire, P. (1970). *Pedagogy of the oppressed.* New York: Herder & Herder.

Gee, J. P. (1989). Literacy, discourse, and linguistics: Introduction. *Journal of Education, 171*, 5–17.

Hale-Benson, J. (1990). Achieving equal educational outcomes for Black children. In A. Baron & E. E. Garcia (Eds.), *Children at risk: Poverty, minority status, and other issues in educational equity* (pp. 201–215). Washington, DC: National Association of School Psychologists.

Heath, S. B. (1983). *Ways with words.* Cambridge, UK: Cambridge University Press.

Hollins, E. R. (1994, April). *The burden of acting White revisited: Planning school success rather than explaining school failure.* Paper presented at the annual meeting of the American Educational Research Association, New Orleans.

Irvine, J. J. (1990). *Black students and school failure.* Westport, CT: Greenwood Press.

Jordan, C. (1985). Translating culture: From ethnographic information to educational program. *Anthropology and Education Quarterly, 16*, 105–123.

King, J. (1994). *The burden of acting White re-examined: Towards a critical genealogy of acting Black.* Paper presented at the annual meeting of the American Educational Research Association, New Orleans.

Ladson-Billings, G. (1990). Like lightning in a bottle: Attempting to capture the pedagogical excellence of successful teachers of Black students. *International Journal of Qualitative Studies in Education, 3*, 335–344.

Ladson-Billings, G. (1992a). Culturally relevant teaching: The key to making multicultural education work. In C. A. Grant (Ed.), *Research and multicultural education* (pp. 106–121). London: Falmer Press.

Ladson-Billings, G. (1992b). Liberatory consequences of literacy: A case of culturally relevant instruction for African-American students. *Journal of Negro Education, 61*, 378–391.

Ladson-Billings, G. (1992c). Reading between the lines and beyond the pages: A culturally relevant approach to literacy teaching. *Theory Into Practice, 31*, 312–320.

Ladson-Billings, G. (1994). *The dreamkeepers: Successful teaching for African-American students*. San Francisco: Jossey-Bass.

Majors, R., & Billson, J. (1992). *Cool pose: The dilemmas of Black manhood in America*. New York: Lexington Books.

McLaren, P. (1989). *Life in schools*. White Plains, NY: Longman.

Mohatt, G., & Erickson, F. (1981). Cultural differences in teaching styles in an Odawa school: A sociolinguistic approach. In H. Trueba, G. Guthrie, & K. Au (Eds.), *Culture and the bilingual classroom: Studies in classroom ethnography* (pp. 105–119). Rowley, MA: Newbury House.

Morris, A. (1984). *The origins of the civil rights movement: Black communities organizing for change*. New York: The Free Press.

Perry, T. (1993). *Toward a theory of African-American student achievement*. Report No. 16. Boston, MA: Center on Families, Communities, Schools and Children's Learning, Wheelock College.

Pewewardy, C. (1993). Culturally responsible pedagogy in action: An American Indian magnet school. In E. Hollins, J. King, & W. Hayman (Eds.), *Teaching diverse populations: Formulating a knowledge base* (pp. 77–92). Albany: State University of New York Press.

Robinson, R. (1993, Feb. 25). P. C. Anderson students try hand at problem-solving. *The Dallas Examiner*, pp. 1, 8.

Shulman, L. (1987). Knowledge and teaching: Foundations of the new reform. *Harvard Educational Review, 57*, 1–22.

Smitherman, G. (1981). *Black English and the education of Black children and youth*. Detroit: Center for Black Studies, Wayne State University.

Spradley, J. (1979). *The ethnographic interview*. New York: Holt, Rinehart & Winston.

Tate, W. F. (1994). Race, retrenchment, and reform of school mathematics. *Phi Delta Kappan, 75*, 477–484.

Villegas, A. (1988). School failure and cultural mismatch: Another view. *The Urban Review, 20*, 253–265.

Vogt, L., Jordan, C., & Tharp, R. (1987). Explaining school failure, producing school success: Two cases. *Anthropology and Education Quarterly, 18*, 276–286.

Zeichner, K. M., & Tabachnick, B. R. (1991). Reflections on reflective teaching. In B. R. Tabachnick & K. M. Zeichner (Eds.), *Inquiry-oriented practices in teacher education* (pp. 1–21). London: Falmer Press.

NOTES

1. Some notable exceptions to this failure to consider achievement strategies for African American students are *Ways With Words* (Heath, 1983); "Fostering Early Literacy Through Parent Coaching" (Edwards, 1991); and "Achieving Equal Educational Outcomes for Black Children" (Hale-Benson, 1990).

2. I have written extensively about this study, its methodology, findings, and results elsewhere. For a full discussion of the study, see Ladson-Billings (1994).

3. All study participants' names are pseudonyms.

4. At the 1994 annual meeting of the American Educational Research Association, King and Hollins presented a symposium entitled, "The Burden of Acting White Revisited."

5. The teacher acknowledged the racism, misogyny, and explicit sexuality that is a part of the lyrics of some rap songs. Thus, the students were directed to use only those songs they felt they could "sing to their parents."

6. Winston retired after the first year of the study but continued to participate in the research collaborative throughout the study.

7. Because the residency is more than a demonstration and requires students to work intensely with the artist or craftsperson, students must sign up for a particular artist. The typical group size was 5–6 students.

8. Standardized test scores throughout this district were very low. However, the teachers

in the study distinguished themselves because students in their classrooms consistently produced higher test scores than their grade level colleagues.

9. As I describe the teachers I do not mean to suggest that they had no individual personalities or practices. However, what I was looking for in this study were ways to describe the commonalities of their practice. Thus, while this discussion of culturally relevant teaching may appear to infer an essentialized notion of teaching practice, none is intended. Speaking in this categorical manner is a heuristic for research purposes.

10. The eight teachers were spread across four schools in the district and were subjected to the specific administrative styles of four different principals.

11. Two sessions at the 1994 annual meeting of the American Educational Research Association in New Orleans, entitled "Private Lives in Public Conversations: Ethics of Research Across Communities of Color," dealt with concerns for the ethical standards of research in non-White communities.

CHAPTER 8

Paulo Freire

The Banking Concept of Education

A careful analysis of the teacher-student relationship at any level, inside or outside the school, reveals its fundamentally *narrative* character. This relationship involves a narrating subject (the teacher) and patient, listening objects (the students). The contents, whether values or empirical dimensions of reality, tend in the process of being narrated to become lifeless and petrified. Education is suffering from narration sickness.

The teacher talks about reality as if it were motionless, static, compartmentalized, and predictable. Or else he expounds on a topic completely alien to the existential experience of the students. His task is to "fill" the students with the contents of his narration—contents which are detached from reality, disconnected from the totality that engendered them and could give them significance. Words are emptied of their concreteness and become a hollow, alienated, and alienating verbosity.

The outstanding characteristic of this narrative education, then, is the sonority of words, not their transforming power. "Four times four is sixteen; the capital of Pará is Belém." The student records, memorizes, and repeats these phrases without perceiving what four times four really means, or realizing the true significance of "capital" in the affirmation "the capital of Pará is Belém," that is, what Belém means for Pará and what Pará means for Brazil.

Narration (with the teacher as narrator) leads the students to memorize mechanically the narrated content. Worse yet, it turns them into "containers," into "receptacles" to be "filled" by the teacher. The more completely she fills the receptacles, the better a teacher she is. The more meekly the receptacles permit themselves to be filled, the better students they are.

Education thus becomes an act of depositing, in which the students are the depositories and the teacher is the depositor. Instead of communicating, the teacher issues communiqués and makes deposits which the students patiently receive, memorize, and repeat. This is the "banking" concept of education, in which the scope of action allowed to the students extends only as far as receiving, filing, and storing the deposits. They do, it is true, have the opportunity to become collectors or cataloguers of the things they store. But in the last analysis, it is the people themselves who are filed away through the lack of creativity, transformation, and knowledge in this (at best) misguided system. For apart from inquiry, apart from the praxis, individuals cannot be truly human. Knowledge emerges only through invention and re-invention, through the restless, impatient, continuing, hopeful inquiry human beings pursue in the world, with the world, and with each other.

In the banking concept of education, knowledge is a gift bestowed by those who consider themselves knowledgeable upon those whom they consider to know nothing. Projecting an absolute ignorance onto others, a characteristic of the ideology of oppression, negates education and knowledge as processes of inquiry. The teacher presents himself to his students as their necessary opposite; by considering their ignorance absolute, he justifies his own existence. The students, alienated like the slave in the Hegelian dialectic, accept their ignorance as justifying the teacher's existence—but, unlike the slave, they never discover that they educate the teacher.

The raison d'être of libertarian education, on the other hand, lies in its drive toward reconciliation. Education must begin with the solution of the teacher-student contradiction, by reconciling the poles of the contradiction so that both are simultaneously teachers *and* students.

This solution is not (nor can it be) found in the banking concept. On the contrary, banking education maintains and even stimulates the contradiction through the following attitudes and practices, which mirror oppressive society as a whole:

(a) the teacher teaches and the students are taught;

(b) the teacher knows everything and the students know nothing;

(c) the teacher thinks and the students are thought about;

(d) the teacher talks and the students listen—meekly;

(e) the teacher disciplines and the students are disciplined;

(f) the teacher chooses and enforces his choice, and the students comply;

(g) the teacher acts and the students have the illusion of acting through the action of the teacher;

(h) the teacher chooses the program content, and the students (who were not consulted) adapt to it;

(i) the teacher confuses the authority of knowledge with his or her own professional authority, which she or he sets in opposition to the freedom of the students;

(j) the teacher is the subject of the learning process, while the pupils are mere objects.

It is not surprising that the banking concept of education regards men as adaptable, manageable beings. The more students work at storing the deposits entrusted to them, the less they develop the critical consciousness which would result from their intervention in the world as transformers of that world. The more completely they accept the passive role imposed on them, the more they tend simply to adapt to the world as it is and to the fragmented view of reality deposited in them.

The capability of banking education to minimize or annul the students' creative power and to stimulate their credulity serves the interests of the oppressors, who care neither to have the world revealed nor to see it transformed. The oppressors use their "humanitarianism" to preserve a profitable situation. Thus they react almost instinctively against any experiment in education which stimulates the critical faculties and is not content with a partial view of reality but always seeks out the ties which link one point to another and one problem to another.

Indeed, the interests of the oppressors lie in "changing the consciousness of the oppressed, not the situation which oppresses them";[1] for the more the oppressed can be led to adapt to that situation, the more easily they can be dominated. To achieve this end, the oppressors use the banking concept of education in conjunction with a paternalistic social action apparatus, within which the oppressed receive the euphemistic title of "welfare recipients." They are treated as individual cases, as marginal persons who deviate from the general configuration of a "good, organized, and just" society. The oppressed are regarded as the pathology of the healthy society, which must therefore adjust these "incompetent and lazy" folk to its own patterns by changing their mentality. These marginals need to be "integrated," "incorporated" into the healthy society that they have "forsaken."

The truth is, however, that the oppressed are not "marginals," are not people living "outside" society. They have always been "inside"—inside the structure which made them "beings for others." The solution is not to "integrate" them into the structure of oppression, but to transform that structure so that they can become "beings for themselves." Such transformation, of course, would undermine the oppressors' purposes; hence their utilization of the banking concept of education to avoid the threat of student *conscientização*.

The banking approach to adult education, for example, will never propose to students that they critically consider reality. It will deal instead with such vital questions as whether Roger gave green grass to the goat, and insist upon the importance of learning that, on the contrary, *Roger gave green grass to the rabbit*. The "humanism" of the banking approach masks the effort to turn women and men into automatons—the very negation of their ontological vocation to be more fully human.

Those who use the banking approach, knowingly or unknowingly (for there are innumerable well-intentioned bank-clerk teachers who do not realize that they are serving only to dehumanize), fail to perceive that the deposits themselves contain contradictions about reality. But, sooner or later, these contradictions may lead formerly passive students to turn against their domestication and the attempt to domesticate reality. They may discover through existential experience that their present way of life is irreconcilable with their vocation to become fully human. They may perceive through their relations with reality that reality is really a *process*, undergoing constant transformation. If men and women are searchers and their ontological vocation is humanization, sooner or later they may perceive the contradiction in which banking education seeks to maintain them, and then engage themselves in the struggle for their liberation.

But the humanist, revolutionary educator cannot wait for this possibility to materialize. From the outset, her efforts must coincide with those of the students to engage in critical thinking and the quest for mutual humanization. His efforts must be imbued with a profound trust in people and their creative power. To achieve this, they must be partners of the students in their relations with them.

The banking concept does not admit to such partnership—and necessarily so. To resolve the teacher-student contradiction, to exchange the role of depositor, prescriber, domesticator, for the role of student among students would be to undermine the power of oppression and serve the cause of liberation.

Implicit in the banking concept is the assumption of a dichotomy between human beings and the world: a person is merely *in* the world, not *with* the world or with others; the individual is spectator, not re-creator. In this view, the person is not a conscious being (*corpo consciente*); he or she is rather the possessor of *a* consciousness: an empty "mind" passively open to the reception of deposits of reality from the world outside. For example, my desk, my books, my coffee cup, all the objects before me—as bits of the world which surround me—would be "inside" me, exactly as I am inside my study right now. This view makes no distinction between being accessible to consciousness and entering consciousness. The distinction, however, is essential: the objects which surround me are simply accessible to my consciousness, not located within it. I am aware of them, but they are not inside me.

It follows logically from the banking notion of consciousness that the educator's role is to regulate the way the world "enters into" the students. The teacher's task is to organize a process which already occurs spontaneously, to "fill" the students by making deposits of information which he or she considers to constitute true knowledge.[2] And since people "receive" the world as passive entities, education should make them more passive still, and adapt them to the world. The educated individual is the adapted person, because she or he is better "fit" for the world. Translated into practice, this concept is well suited to the purposes of the oppressors, whose tranquility rests on how well people fit the world the oppres-

sors have created, and how little they question it.

The more completely the majority adapt to the purposes which the dominant minority prescribe for them (thereby depriving them of the right to their own purposes), the more easily the minority can continue to prescribe. The theory and practice of banking education serve this end quite efficiently. Verbalistic lessons, reading requirements,[3] the methods for evaluating "knowledge," the distance between the teacher and the taught, the criteria for promotion: everything in this ready-to-wear approach serves to obviate thinking.

The bank-clerk educator does not realize that there is no true security in his hypertrophied role, that one must seek to live *with* others in solidarity. One cannot impose oneself, nor even merely coexist with one's students. Solidarity requires true communication, and the concept by which such an educator is guided fears and proscribes communication.

Yet only through communication can human life hold meaning. The teacher's thinking is authenticated only by the authenticity of the students' thinking. The teacher cannot think for her students, nor can she impose her thought on them. Authentic thinking, thinking that is concerned about *reality*, does not take place in ivory tower isolation, but only in communication. If it is true that thought has meaning only when generated by action upon the world, the subordination of students to teachers becomes impossible.

Because banking education begins with a false understanding of men and women as objects, it cannot promote the development of what Fromm calls "biophily," but instead produces its opposite: "necrophily."

While life is characterized by growth in a structured, functional manner, the necrophilous person loves all that does not grow, all that is mechanical. The necrophilous person is driven by the desire to transform the organic into the inorganic, to approach life mechanically, as if all living persons were things. . . . Memory, rather than experience; having, rather than being, is what counts. The necrophilous person can relate to an object—a flower or a person—only if he possesses it; hence a threat to his possession is a threat to himself; if he loses possession he loses contact with the world. . . . He loves control, and in the act of controlling he kills life.[4]

Oppression—overwhelming control—is necrophilic; it is nourished by love of death, not life. The banking concept of education, which serves the interests of oppression, is also necrophilic. Based on a mechanistic, static, naturalistic, spatialized view of consciousness, it transforms students into receiving objects. It attempts to control thinking and action, leads women and men to adjust to the world, and inhibits their creative power.

When their efforts to act responsibly are frustrated, when they find themselves unable to use their faculties, people suffer. "This suffering due to impotence is rooted in the very fact that the human equilibrium has been disturbed."[5] But the inability to act which causes people's anguish also causes them to reject their impotence, by attempting

to restore [their] capacity to act. But can [they], and how? One way is to submit to and identify with a person or group having power. By this symbolic partici-

pation in another person's life, [men have] the illusion of acting, when in reality [they] only submit to and become a part of those who act.[6]

Populist manifestations perhaps best exemplify this type of behavior by the oppressed, who, by identifying with charismatic leaders, come to feel that they themselves are active and effective. The rebellion they express as they emerge in the historical process is motivated by that desire to act effectively. The dominant elites consider the remedy to be more domination and repression, carried out in the name of freedom, order, and social peace (that is, the peace of the elites). Thus they can condemn—logically, from their point of view—"the violence of a strike by workers and [can] call upon the state in the same breath to use violence in putting down the strike."[7]

Education as the exercise of domination stimulates the credulity of students, with the ideological intent (often not perceived by educators) of indoctrinating them to adapt to the world of oppression. This accusation is not made in the naïve hope that the dominant elites will thereby simply abandon the practice. Its objective is to call the attention of true humanists to the fact that they cannot use banking educational methods in the pursuit of liberation, for they would only negate that very pursuit. Nor may a revolutionary society inherit these methods from an oppressor society. The revolutionary society which practices banking education is either misguided or mistrusting of people. In either event, it is threatened by the specter of reaction.

Unfortunately, those who espouse the cause of liberation are themselves surrounded and influenced by the climate which generates the banking concept, and often do not perceive its true significance or its dehumanizing power. Paradoxically, then, they utilize this same instrument of alienation in what they consider an effort to liberate. Indeed, some "revolutionaries" brand as "innocents," "dreamers," or even "reactionaries" those who would challenge this educational practice. But one does not liberate people by alienating them. Authentic liberation—the process of humanization—is not another deposit to be made in men. Liberation is a praxis: the action and reflection of men and women upon their world in order to transform it. Those truly committed to the cause of liberation can accept neither the mechanistic concept of consciousness as an empty vessel to be filled, nor the use of banking methods of domination (propaganda, slogans—deposits) in the name of liberation.

Those truly committed to liberation must reject the banking concept in its entirety, adopting instead a concept of women and men as conscious beings, and consciousness as consciousness intent upon the world. They must abandon the educational goal of deposit-making and replace it with the posing of the problems of human beings in their relations with the world. "Problem-posing" education, responding to the essence of consciousness—*intentionality*—rejects communiqués and embodies communication. It epitomizes the special characteristic of consciousness: being *conscious of*, not only as intent on objects but as turned in upon itself in a Jasperian "split"—consciousness as consciousness *of* consciousness.

Liberating education consists in acts of cognition, not transferrals of information.

It is a learning situation in which the cognizable object (far from being the end of the cognitive act) intermediates the cognitive actors—teacher on the one hand and students on the other. Accordingly, the practice of problem-posing education entails at the outset that the teacher-student contradiction be resolved. Dialogical relations—indispensable to the capacity of cognitive actors to cooperate in perceiving the same cognizable object—are otherwise impossible.

Indeed, problem-posing education, which breaks with the vertical patterns characteristic of banking education, can fulfill its function as the practice of freedom only if it can overcome the above contradiction. Through dialogue, the teacher-of-the-students and the students-of-the-teacher cease to exist and a new term emerges: teacher-student with students-teachers. The teacher is no longer merely the-one-who-teaches, but one who is himself taught in dialogue with the students, who in turn while being taught also teach. They become jointly responsible for a process in which all grow. In this process, arguments based on "authority" are no longer valid; in order to function, authority must be *on the side of* freedom, not *against* it. Here, no one teaches another, nor is anyone self-taught. People teach each other, mediated by the world, by the cognizable objects which in banking education are "owned" by the teacher.

The banking concept (with its tendency to dichotomize everything) distinguishes two stages in the action of the educator. During the first, he cognizes a cognizable object while he prepares his lessons in his study or his laboratory; during the second, he expounds to his students about that object. The students are not called upon to know, but to memorize the contents narrated by the teacher. Nor do the students practice any act of cognition, since the object toward which that act should be directed is the property of the teacher rather than a medium evoking the critical reflection of both teacher and students. Hence in the name of the "preservation of culture and knowledge" we have a system which achieves neither true knowledge nor true culture.

The problem-posing method does not dichotomize the activity of the teacher-student: she is not "cognitive" at one point and "narrative" at another. She is always "cognitive," whether preparing a project or engaging in dialogue with the students. He does not regard cognizable objects as his private property, but as the object of reflection by himself and the students. In this way, the problem-posing educator constantly re-forms his reflections in the reflection of the students. The students—no longer docile listeners—are now critical coinvestigators in dialogue with the teacher. The teacher presents the material to the students for their consideration, and reconsiders her earlier considerations as the students express their own. The role of the problem-posing educator is to create; together with the students, the conditions under which knowledge at the level of the *doxa* is superseded by true knowledge, is at the level of the *logos*.

Whereas banking education anesthetizes and inhibits creative power, problem-posing education involves a constant unveiling of reality. The former attempts to maintain the *submersion* of consciousness; the latter strives for the *emergence* of consciousness and *critical intervention* in reality.

Students, as they are increasingly posed with problems relating to themselves in the world and with the world, will feel increasingly challenged and obliged to respond to that challenge. Because they apprehend the challenge as interrelated to other problems within a total context, not as a theoretical question, the resulting comprehension tends to be increasingly critical and thus constantly less alienated. Their response to the challenge evokes new challenges, followed by new understandings; and gradually the students come to regard themselves as committed.

Education as the practice of freedom—as opposed to education as the practice of domination—denies that man is abstract, isolated, independent, and unattached to the world; it also denies that the world exists as a reality apart from people. Authentic reflection considers neither abstract man nor the world without people, but people in their relations with the world. In these relations consciousness and world are simultaneous: consciousness neither precedes the world nor follows it.

La conscience et le monde sont donnés d'un meme coup: extérieur par essence à la conscience, le monde est, par essence relative à elle.[8]

In one of our culture circles in Chile, the group was discussing (based on a codification[9]) the anthropological concept of culture. In the midst of the discussion, a peasant who by banking standards was completely ignorant said: "Now I see that without man there is not world." When the educator responded: "Let's say, for the sake of argument, that all the men on earth were to die, but that the earth itself remained, together with trees, birds, animals, rivers, seas, the stars . . . wouldn't all this be a world?" "Oh no," the peasant replied emphatically. "There would be no one to say: 'This is a world'."

The peasant wished to express the idea that there would be lacking the consciousness of the world which necessarily implies the world of consciousness. *I* cannot exist without a *non-I*. In turn, the *not-I* depends on that existence. The world which brings consciousness into existence becomes the world *of* that consciousness. Hence, the previously cited affirmation of Sartre: *"La conscience et le monde sont donnés d'un même coup."*

As women and men, simultaneously reflecting on themselves and on the world, increase the scope of their perception, they begin to direct their observations towards previously inconspicuous phenomena:

> In perception properly so-called, as an explicit awareness [*Gewahren*], I am turned towards the object, to the paper, for instance. I apprehend it as being this here and now. The apprehension is a singling out, every object having a background in experience. Around and about the paper lie books, pencils, inkwell, and so forth, and these in a certain sense are also "perceived", perceptually there, in the "field of intuition"; but whilst I was turned towards the paper there was no turning in their direction, nor any apprehending of them, not even in a secondary sense. They appeared and yet were not singled out, were not posited on their own account. Every perception of a thing has such a zone of background intuitions or background awareness, if "intuiting" already includes the state of being turned towards, and this also is a "conscious experience", or more briefly a "consciousness of" all indeed that in point of fact lies in the co-perceived objective background.[10]

That which had existed objectively but had not been perceived in its deeper implications (if indeed it was perceived at all) begins to "stand out," assuming the character of a problem and therefore of challenge. Thus, men and women begin to single out elements from their "background awareness" and to reflect upon them. These elements are now objects of their consideration, and, as such, objects of their action and cognition.

In problem-posing education, people develop their power to perceive critically *the way they exist* in the world *with which* and *in which* they find themselves; they come to see the world not as a static reality, but as a reality in process, in transformation. Although the dialectical relations of women and men with the world exist independently of how these relations are perceived (or whether or not they are perceived at all), it is also true that the form of action they adopt is to a large extent a function of how they perceive themselves in the world. Hence, the teacher-student and the students-teachers reflect simultaneously on themselves and the world without dichotomizing this reflection from action, and thus establish an authentic form of thought and action.

Once again, the two educational concepts and practices under analysis come into conflict. Banking education (for obvious reasons) attempts, by mythicizing reality, to conceal certain facts which explain the way human beings exist in the world; problem-posing education sets itself the task of demythologizing. Banking education resists dialogue; problem-posing education regards dialogue as indispensable to the act of cognition which unveils reality. Banking education treats students as objects of assistance; problem-posing education makes them critical thinkers. Banking education inhibits creativity and domesticates (although it cannot completely destroy) the *intentionality* of consciousness by isolating consciousness from the world, thereby denying people their ontological and historical vocation of becoming more fully human. Problem-posing education bases itself on creativity and stimulates true reflection and action upon reality, thereby responding to the vocation of persons as beings who are authentic only when engaged in inquiry and creative transformation. In sum: banking theory and practice, as immobilizing and fixating forces, fail to acknowledge men and women as historical beings; problem-posing theory and practice take the people's historicity as their starting point.

Problem-posing education affirms men and women as beings in the process of *becoming*—as unfinished, uncompleted beings in and with a likewise unfinished reality. Indeed, in contrast to other animals who are unfinished, but not historical, people know themselves to be unfinished; they are aware of their incompletion. In this incompletion and this awareness lie the very roots of education as an exclusively human manifestation. The unfinished character of human beings and the transformation character of reality necessitate that education be an ongoing activity.

Education is thus constantly remade in the praxis. In order to *be*, it must *become*. Its "duration" (in the Bergsonian meaning of the word) is found in the interplay

of the opposites *permanence* and *change*. The banking method emphasizes permanence and becomes reactionary; problem-posing education—which accepts neither a "well-behaved" present nor a predetermined future—roots itself in the dynamic present and becomes revolutionary.

Problem-posing education is revolutionary futurity. Hence it is prophetic (and, as such, hopeful). Hence, it corresponds to the historical nature of humankind. Hence, it affirms women and men as beings who transcend themselves, who move forward and look ahead, for whom immobility represents a fatal threat, for whom looking at the past must only be a means of understanding more clearly what and who they are so that they can more wisely build the future. Hence, it identifies with the movement which engages people as being aware of their incompletion—a historical movement which has its point of departure, its subjects and its objective.

The point of departure of the movement lies in the people themselves. But since people do not exist apart from the world, apart from reality, the movement must begin with the human-world relationship. Accordingly the point of departure must always be with men and women in the "here and now," which constitutes the situation within which they are submerged, from which they emerge, and in which they intervene. Only by starting from this situation—which determines their perception of it—can they begin to move. To do this authentically they must perceive their state not as fated and unalterable, but merely as limiting—and therefore challenging.

Whereas the banking method directly or indirectly reinforces men's fatalistic perception of their situation, the problem-posing method presents this very situation to them as a problem. As the situation becomes the object of their cognition, the naïve or magical perception which produced their fatalism gives way to perception which is able to perceive itself even as it perceives reality, and can thus be critically objective about that reality.

A deepened consciousness of their situation leads people to apprehend that situation as a historical reality susceptible of transformation. Resignation gives way to the drive for transformation and inquiry, over which men feel themselves to be in control. If people, as historical beings necessarily engaged with other people in a movement of inquiry, did not control that movement, it would be (and is) a violation of their humanity. Any situation in which some individuals prevent others from engaging in the process of inquiry is one of violence. The means used are not important; to alienate human beings from their own decision-making is to change them into objects.

This movement of inquiry must be directed toward humanization—the people's historical vocation. The pursuit of full humanity, however, cannot be carried out in isolation or individualism, but only in fellowship and solidarity; therefore it cannot unfold in the antagonistic relations between oppressors and oppressed. No one can be authentically human while he prevents others from being so. Attempting *to be more* human, individualistically, leads to *having more*, egotistically, a form of dehumanization. Not that it is not fundamental *to have* in order *to be* human. Precisely because it *is* necessary, some men's *having* must not be allowed to constitute an obstacle to others' *having*, must not consolidate the power of the former to crush the latter.

Problem-posing education, as a humanist and liberating praxis, posits as fundamental that the people subjected to domination must fight for their emancipation. To that end, it enables teachers and students to become subjects of the educational process by overcoming authoritarianism and an alienating intellectualism; it also enables people to overcome their false perception of reality. The world—no longer something to be described with deceptive words—becomes the object of that transforming action by men and women which results in their humanization.

Problem-posing education does not and cannot serve the interests of the oppressor. No oppressive order could permit the oppressed to begin to question: Why? While only a revolutionary society can carry out this education in systematic terms, the revolutionary leaders need not take full power before they can employ the method. In the revolutionary process, the leaders cannot utilize the banking method as an interim measure, justified on grounds of expedience, with the intention of *later* behaving in a genuinely revolutionary fashion. They must be revolutionary—that is to say, dialogical—from the outset.

NOTES

1. Simone de Beauvoir, *La Pensée de Droite, Aujord'hui* (Paris); ST, *El Pensamiento político de la Derecha* (Buenos Aires, 1963), p. 34.

2. This concept corresponds to what Sartre calls the "digestive" or "nutritive" concept of education, in which knowledge is "fed" by the teacher to the students to "fill them out." See Jean-Paul Sartre, "Une idée fundamentale de la phenomenology de Husserl: L'intentionalité," *Situations I* (Paris, 1947).

3. For example, some professors specify in their reading lists that a book should be read from pages 10 to 15—and do this to "help" their students!

4. Fromm, *op. cit.*, p. 41.

5. *Ibid.*, p. 31.

6. *Ibid.*

7. Reinhold Niebuhr, *Moral Man and Immoral Society* (New York, 1960), p. 130.

8. Sartre; *op. cit.*, p. 32.

9. Translator's note.

10. Edmund Husserl, *Ideas—General Introduction to Pure Phenomenology* (London, 1969), pp. 105–106.

Michael W. Apple

CHAPTER 9

Markets, Standards, God, and Inequality

Open season on education continues. The media, candidates for public office, conservative pundits, corporate leaders, nearly everyone it seems, has an opinion on what's wrong with schools. I have mixed emotions about all this attention. On the one hand, what could be wrong with placing issues of what education does and should do front and center? As someone deeply involved in thinking about and acting upon schools, it's rather pleasing to see that conversations about teaching, curricula, evaluation, funding, and so much more are not seen as the logical equivalent of conversations about the weather. The fact that these discussions often are heated is also something to be welcomed. After all, what our children are to know and the values this should embody is serious business.

On the other hand, all of this attention creates some disquietude. One word in the last sentence of the previous paragraph explains one reason for this—business. For all too many of the pundits, politicians, corporate leaders, and others, education is a business and should be treated no differently than any other business. The fact that this position is now becoming increasingly widespread is evidence of some worrisome tendencies. Of the many voices now talking about education, only the most powerful tend to be heard. Although there is no one unitary position that organizes those with political, economic, and cultural power, the central tendencies around which they are found tend to be more conservative than not.

What are these voices saying? Over the past decades, conservative groups in particular have been pressing for public funding for private and religious schools. Voucher plans have been at the forefront of this movement. In the eyes of voucher proponents, only by forcing schools onto a competitive market will there be any improvement. These pressures are complemented by other kinds of attacks, such as the following argument. "Facts" are missing in the curriculum. Traditional content and methods have been jettisoned as our schools move toward trendy (and overly multicultural) subjects that ignore the knowledge that made us such a great nation. Raise standards. Get more tests in schools, based on "real" knowledge. Raise the stakes for teachers and students who fail them. This will guarantee that our schools return to time-honored content and more traditional methods. If tests are not enough, mandate and legislate traditional methods and content at a state level.

Vouchers are in the air—and in the courts. High stakes testing is also in the air—and in news reports that document the damaging bureaucratic and technical problems that have occurred when such tests were instituted all too quickly in a number of cities and states. Other evidence for some of the latter pressures on traditional content and methods is not hard to find either. In several states, hotly contested bills have been introduced, and in some instances passed, that mandate the use of phonics in literacy instruction. Indeed, the federal government has now put its imprimatur—and its funding—behind such "scientific" models of literacy instruction, and labeled other approaches as basically not worthy of our attention. The stereotype that what are called "whole-language" methods—that is, methods that are grounded in the lived experience of students' actual language and literacy use—have totally replaced phonics is widespread. There is actually little evidence that this is the case, since most teachers seem to use a "bricolage" of multiple approaches depending on the needs that have to be met.[1] However, this has not interrupted the agenda of those who are deeply committed to the politics of conservative restoration in education. The same groups sponsoring legislative mandates of this type also often stand behind the attacks on the teaching of evolution and the supposed loss of God's guiding word in schools.

All these movements are swirling around simultaneously. Every time one begins to understand one set of pressures, another one enters from a different direction. Each has "the" answer, if only we would become true believers and follow them. Each and every one of these pressures is situated within larger dynamics. I want to stop the swirl for a little while in order to make sense of them both in education and in their relation to larger ideological and economic forces in societies like our own. Because these pressures and forces are complicated, let me begin this sense-making process in a straightforward way—with a story about a child, a teacher, and a school in a particular community.

Joseph's Story

Joseph sobbed at my desk. He was a tough kid, a hard case, someone who often made life difficult for his teachers. He was all of nine years old and here he was sobbing, holding on to me in public. He had been in my fourth-grade class all year, a classroom situated in a decaying building in an East Coast city that was among the most impoverished in the nation. At times I wondered, seriously, whether I would make it through that year. There were many Josephs in that classroom, and I was constantly drained by the demands, the bureaucratic rules, the daily lessons that bounced off the kids' armor. Yet somehow that year was satisfying, compelling, and important, even though the prescribed curriculum and the textbooks that were meant to teach it were often beside the point. They were boring to the kids and boring to me.

I should have realized the first day what it would be like when I opened that city's "Getting Started" suggested lessons for the first few days and it began with the suggestion that "as a new teacher" I should circle the students' desks and have them introduce each other and tell something about themselves. It's not that I was against this activity; it's just that I didn't have enough unbroken desks (or even chairs) for all the students. A number of the kids had nowhere to sit. This was my first lesson—but certainly not my last—in understanding that the curriculum and those who planned it lived in an unreal world, a world *fundamentally* disconnected from my life with those children in that inner-city classroom.

But here's Joseph. He's still crying. I've worked extremely hard with him all year long. We've eaten lunch together; we've read stories; we've gotten to know each other. There are times when he drives me to despair and other times when I find him to be among the most sensitive children in my class. I just can't give up on this kid. He's just received his report card and it says that he is to repeat fourth grade. The school system has a policy that states that failure in any two subjects (including the "behavior" side of the report card) requires that the student be left back. Joseph was failing "gym" and arithmetic. Even though he had shown improvement, he had trouble staying awake during arithmetic, had done poorly on the mandatory citywide tests, and hated gym. One of his parents worked a late shift and Joseph would often stay up, hoping to spend some time with her. And the things that students were asked to do in gym were, to him, "lame."

The thing is, he had made real progress during the year. But I was instructed to keep him back. I knew that things would be worse next year. There would still not be enough desks. The poverty in that community would still be horrible, and health care and sufficient funding for job training and other services would be diminished. I knew that the available jobs in this former mill town paid deplorable wages and that even with both of his par-

ents working for pay, Joseph's family income was simply insufficient. I also knew that, given all that I already had to do each day in that classroom and each night at home in preparation for the next day, it would be nearly impossible for me to work any harder than I had already done with Joseph. And there were another five children in that class whom I was supposed to leave back.

So Joseph sobbed. Both he and I understood what this meant. There would be no additional help for me—or for children such as Joseph—next year. The promises would remain simply rhetorical. Words would be thrown at the problems. Teachers and parents and children would be blamed. But the school system would look like it believed in and enforced higher standards. The structuring of economic and political power in that community and that state would again go on as "business as usual."

The next year Joseph basically stopped trying. The last time I heard anything about him was that he was in prison.

This story is not apocryphal. Although the incident took place a while ago, the conditions in that community and that school are much worse today. And the intense pressure that teachers, administrators, and local communities are under is equally worse. It reminds me of why I mistrust our incessant focus on standards, increased testing, marketization and vouchers, and other kinds of educational "reforms" that may sound good in the abstract but often work in exactly the opposite way when they reach the classroom level. It is exactly this sensibility of the contradictions between proposals for reform and the realities and complexities of education on the ground that provides the impetus for this chapter.

We face what I call *conservative modernization*. This is a powerful, yet odd, combination of forces that is in play in education, a combination that many educators, community activists, critical researchers, and others believe poses substantial threats to the vitality of our nation, our schools, our teachers, and our children. As I noted, we are told to "free" our schools by placing them into the competitive market, restore "our" traditional common culture and stress discipline and character, return God to our classrooms as a guide to all our conduct inside and outside the school, and tighten central control through more rigorous and tough-minded standards and tests. This is all supposed to be done at the same time. It also is all supposed to guarantee an education that benefits everyone. Well, maybe not.

Education is too often thought of as simply the delivery of neutral knowledge to students. In this discourse, the fundamental role of schooling is to fill students with the knowledge that is necessary to compete in today's rapidly changing world. To this is often added an additional caveat: Do it as cost-effectively and as efficiently as possible. The ultimate arbiter of whether we have been successful at this is students' mean gains on achievement tests. A neutral curriculum is linked to a neutral system of accountability, which in turn is linked to a system of school finance. Supposedly, when it works well, these linkages guarantee rewards for merit. "Good" students will learn "good" knowledge and will get "good" jobs.

This construction of good schooling, good management, and good results suffers from more than a few defects. Its foundational claims about neutral knowledge are simply wrong. If we have learned anything from the intense and continuing conflicts over what and whose knowledge should be declared "official" that have raged throughout the history of the curriculum in so many nations, it should have been one lesson. There is an intricate set of connections between knowledge and power.[2] Questions of whose knowledge, who chooses, how this is justified—these are *constitutive* issues, not "add-ons" that have the status of afterthoughts. This construction of good education not only marginalizes the politics of knowledge but also offers little agency to students, teachers, and community members. In some ways, it represents what Stephen Ball has characterized as "the curriculum of the dead."[3]

Furthermore, it is unfortunate but true that most of our existing models of education tend to ratify or at least not actively interrupt many of the inequalities that so deeply characterize this society. Much of this has to do with the relations between schooling and the economy, with gender, class, and race divisions in the larger society, with the intricate politics of popular culture, and with the ways we finance and support (or don't) education.[4] The connections between schooling and good jobs are weakened even more when we closely examine what the paid labor market actually looks like. Rosy statistics of stock market gains and wealth creation obscure the fact that in the real existing economy, all too many jobs require low levels of skills and low levels of formal education. A decided mismatch exists between the promises of schooling and actual job creation in our supposedly glorious free market economy, a mismatch that is distinctly related to the exacerbation of race, gender, and class divisions in this society.[5]

Of course, there are those who see a much different connection between the market and education, one that is much more positive. For them, markets may offer hope for children, but even more so for the entrepreneurs who invest in marketized schooling. In their minds, the $700 billion education sector in the United States is ripe for transformation. It is seen as the "next health care"—that is, as a sphere that can be mined for huge profits. The goal is to transform large portions of publicly controlled nonprofit educational institutions into a "consolidated, professionally managed, money-making set of businesses that include all levels of education."[6] Even though comparatively little money is being made now, for-profit companies are establishing law schools; creating or managing elementary, middle, and secondary schools; and engaging in education on factory floors and in businesses. Billions of dollars from corporations, investment funds, and even your pension funds (if you are lucky enough to have one) are pouring into for-profit educational ventures. In essence, in the words of Arthur Levine, the president of Teachers College at Columbia University, capital has said, "You guys are in trouble and we're going to eat your lunch."[7] The motives of the private companies involved are clear. At the same time as they will eliminate the waste that putatively always comes from public schooling, they will turn education into "an efficiently run and profitable machine—using investors' money instead of tax dollars."[8] I wonder what Joseph would say as he sits in his perhaps soon-to-be for-profit prison, having come from a city whose economic base was destroyed as owners and investors closed the factories there and moved them to nonunionized areas so that they wouldn't have to pay a livable wage, or for decent schooling, health care, or pensions.

Conservative Agendas

From my comments so far, you may have guessed that this chapter is situated in a specific place on the political/educational spectrum. Although there may occasionally be problems with the traditional categories of "left" and "right" in sorting through the complexities of politics on the ground in all of our nations, I consciously and without apology position myself on the left. In my mind, the United States remains a vast experiment, one in which both right and left argue about what it is an experiment *in*. The debate over this is vital and undoubtedly will continue. Indeed, it is part of the political lifeblood of the nation. However, like Richard Rorty, I also believe that it is the left that keeps it going.

> For the Right never thinks that anything much needs to be changed: it thinks the country is basically in good shape, and may well have been in better shape in the past. It sees the Left's struggle for social justice as mere trouble making, as utopian foolishness. [Yet] the Left, by definition is the party of hope. It insists that our nation remains unachieved.[9]

Rorty is insightful about the role of progressive criticism in keeping this nation moving. After all, almost all of the social programs that many of us now take as "natural"—social security, for example—came about because of progressive mobilizations against the denial of basic human rights. However, Rorty is on less secure grounds when he claims that "the Right never thinks anything much needs to be changed," for a good deal of the right is very much involved in radical transformations. Over the past two to three decades, the right has mounted a concerted attack on what many of us took as natural. The entire public sphere has been brought into question. Although these attacks on public institutions are broader than education, educational institutions have been centrally located in rightist criticisms. For this very reason, I want to devote this chapter to an analysis of rightist educational beliefs, proposals, and programs—and to their effects in the real world.

My reason for doing this is grounded in a particular political claim. Not only are rightist social movements exceptionally powerful now, but one of the most important elements of learning how to interrupt them is to understand what they did and do. Rightist movements have engaged in a vast social and ideological project. Examining how this has worked and why it has been successful can tell those of us who oppose it how it might best be countered. In my mind, if you want to stop the right, it is absolutely crucial to study what it did. This is what this chapter is about.

We need to be careful about essentializing here. The right is not a unitary movement. It is a coalition of forces with many different emphases; some overlap and others conflict with each other. Thus, my goal is to examine the contradictions within this movement, demonstrating how these tensions are creatively solved so that this society *does* in fact change—but in particular directions. In none of these directions, however, will children such as Joseph be helped in the long run. Yet it is important to realize that although I dis-

agree profoundly with many of the conservative proposals for education, it would be foolish to mindlessly support schools as they exist today. One of the reasons some people listen carefully to rightist criticisms is because there *are* problems in these institutions. Indeed, this is one of the reasons behind the popularity as well of a number of more critical and democratic school reforms.[10] Recognizing problems, however, does not mean that conservative "solutions" are correct.

One of the most important objects of the rightist agendas is changing our common sense, altering the meanings of the most basic categories, the key words, we employ to understand the social and educational world and our place in it. In many ways, a core aspect of these agendas is about what has been called identity politics. The task is to radically alter who we think we are and how our major institutions are to respond to this changed identity. Let me say more about this, especially since who we are and how we think about our institutions are closely connected to who has the power to produce and circulate new ways of understanding our identities. Both the politics of education and of the construction of common sense have played large parts here.

Mapping the Right

The concepts we use to try to understand and act on the world in which we live do not by themselves determine the answers we may find. Answers are not determined by words but by the power relations that impose their interpretations of these concepts.[11] Yet there are key words that continually surface in the debates over education. These key words have complicated histories, histories that are connected to the social movements out of which they arose and in which they are struggled over today.[12] These words have their own histories, but they are increasingly interrelated. The concepts are simple to list: markets, standards, God, and inequality. Behind each of these topics is an assemblage of other words that have an emotional valence and that provide the support for the ways in which differential power works in our daily lives. These concepts include democracy, freedom, choice, morality, family, culture, and a number of other key concepts. And each of these in turn is intertextual. Each and every one of these is connected to an entire set of assumptions about "appropriate" institutions, values, social relationships, and policies.

Think of this situation as something of a road map. Using one key word—*markets*—sends you onto a highway that is going in one direction and that has exits in some places but not others. If you are on a highway labeled market, your general direction is toward a section of the country named *the economy*. You take the exit named *individualism* that goes by way of another road called *consumer choice*. Exits with words such as *unions, collective freedom, the common good, politics*, and similar destinations are to be avoided if they are on the map at all. The first road is a simple route with one goal—deciding where one wants to go without a lot of time-wasting discussion and getting there by the fastest and cheapest method possible. There is a second route, however, and this one involves a good deal of collective deliberation about where we might want to go. It assumes that there may be some continuing deliberation about not only the goal, but even the route itself. Its

exits are the ones that were avoided on the first route.

As we shall see, powerful interests have created the road map and the roads. Some want only the road labeled market, because this supposedly leads to individual choice. Others will go down that road, but only if the exits are those that have a long history of "real culture" and "real knowledge." Still others will take the market road because for them God has said that this is "his" road. And finally, another group will sign on to this tour because they have skills in mapmaking and in determining how far we are from our goal. There's some discussion and some compromise—and perhaps even some lingering tension—among these various groups about which exits will ultimately be stopped at, but by and large they all head off in that direction.

This exercise in storytelling maps onto reality in important ways. Although I develop this in much greater detail in my book *Educating the "Right" Way*, the first group is what I call *neoliberals*. They are deeply committed to markets and to freedom as "individual choice." The second group, *neoconservatives*, has a vision of an Edenic past and wants a return to discipline and traditional knowledge. The third is what I call *authoritarian populists*—religious fundamentalists and conservative evangelicals who want a return to (their) God in all of our institutions. And finally, the mapmakers and experts on whether we got there are members of a particular fraction of the managerial and professional *new middle class*.

In analyzing this complex configuration of interests on the right, I want to act in a way similar to what Eric Hobsbawm described as the historian's and social critic's duty. For Hobsbawm (and for me), the task is to be the "professional remembrancers of what [our] fellow citizens wish to forget."[13] That is, I want to detail the absent presences, the "there that is not there," in most rightist policies in education. How does their language work to highlight certain things as "real" problems while marginalizing others? What are the effects of the policies that they have promoted? How do the seemingly contradictory policies that have emerged from the various fractions of the right—such as the marketization of education through voucher plans, the pressure to "return" to the Western tradition and to a supposedly common culture, the commitment to get God back into the schools and classrooms of America, and the growth of national and state curriculum and national and state (and often "high stakes") testing—actually get put together in creative ways to push many of the aspects of these rightist agendas forward?

Contested Freedom

One of the key concepts that is at stake in the discussions over who we are and how our institutions should respond to us is the idea of freedom. Many of the ideological positions that are currently embattled in the arena of education have different presuppositions about this key word. Some of the history of the dominant uses of this concept may be useful here, as these varied uses surface continually in the current debates over education.

Some of our earliest intuitions about the meaning of freedom are religious. For example, Christianity had an ideal of freedom. However, by and large it was not a worldly one but a spiritual one. Ever since "the Fall," "man has been prone to suc-

cumb to his lusts and passions."[14] Freedom has a specific meaning here, one involving abandoning this life of sin and in turn embracing the teachings of Christ in all of one's activities. This definition of freedom can seem contradictory since in essence freedom and servitude exist side by side. Yet these are seen as mutually reinforcing. Those who accept the teachings of Christ are at the very same time "free from sin" and "servants of God."[15] This spiritual definition of freedom was planted early on in the history of the United States by the Puritan settlers of Massachusetts. It is clearly in evidence in the distinction between "natural liberty" and "moral liberty" made in 1645 by John Winthrop, the Puritan governor of the Massachusetts Colony. The former was "a liberty to do evil," whereas the latter was "a liberty to do only what is good." The distinction itself has an interesting history of effects.

> This definition of freedom as flowing from self-denial and moral choice was quite compatible with severe restraints on freedom of speech, religion, movement, and personal behavior. Individual desires must give way to the needs of the community, and "Christian liberty" meant submission not only to the will of God but to secular authority as well, to a well-understood set of interconnected responsibilities and duties, a submission no less complete for being voluntary. The most common civil offense in the courts of colonial New England was "contempt of authority."[16]

Religious definitions of freedom were partly countered and sometimes supplanted by what might be called "republican" visions. Here, the citizen reached his (and it was quite gender specific) highest fulfillment in pursuing the common good rather than private self-interest. This too had contradictory elements. It could be embodied as a form of "thick" democracy by valorizing the common rights of an entire community. Yet such republicanism could embody a distinctly class-based vision when it was applied to the real world. This is visible in its assumption that only those who owned property "possessed the quality known as virtue."[17] Ordinary men were clearly not virtuous.

The religious and republican visions of freedom were not alone. The freedom of living with God and the freedom of living in a state bound by the consent of the governed through a common will were joined by a particular theory of liberty, which was essentially private and individual, enshrined in eighteenth-century liberalism. For classical liberals, only by shielding the realm of private life and personal concerns (the family, religion, and above all economic activity) from the state's interference could freedom be guaranteed. "The public good was less an ideal to be consciously pursued by government than the outcome of free individuals' pursuit of their myriad private ambitions."[18]

There were positive moments here. It needs to be recognized that such classical liberalism did call into question an entire array of hierarchical privileges and arrangements that made individual advancement extremely difficult. It established rights both of chartered corporations independent of the aristocracy and of religious tolerance. Furthermore, there can be no doubt that its grounding in a belief that "mankind" had natural rights that govern-

ment could not legitimately violate enabled disenfranchised women, paid workers, and slaves to challenge the social and educational barriers they constantly faced. Yet, having said this, it is equally important to note that both republicanism and classical liberalism were also themselves grounded in a belief that only certain kinds of persons were actually capable of exercising the rights of freedom. "Dependents lacked a will of their own and thus were unable to participate in public affairs." Given the central place that self-direction and self-government held in these ideas of freedom, those who were not able to control their own lives should not be given a voice in governance. In this way, economic independence became a defining element in political freedom. Freedom and property became intertwined, and economic independence became the identificatory sign of being worthy.[19]

It is not too difficult to see how this connects with the dynamics of class, gender, and race. Any definition of freedom based on economic independence must by its very nature draw a line between those classes of people who have it (economic independence) and those who do not. The definition is also rooted in gender relations, since this ideal of autonomy has historically been defined as a masculine trait, with woman being seen as dependent.[20] Furthermore, slaves and people of color in general were usually seen as either animalistic or childlike. Freedom cannot be extended to those who by their very nature are dependent, especially since "they are not people, but property."

In opposition to these ways of understanding the meaning of freedom, progressive movements took certain elements of the classical liberal understanding of personal freedom, radicalized them, and mobilized around them. By organizing around issues of free speech, labor rights, economic security, women's rights, birth control and the control of one's body, a socially conscious national and regional state, racial justice, the right to a truly equal education, and many other struggles for social justice, a much more expansive positive definition of freedom has been fought for both inside and outside of education. Because of the long history of sacrifices extending beyond even this extensive list to include the struggles by environmental, gay and lesbian, and disability rights activist groups, major elements of this more expensive definition of freedom have been institutionalized within both the state and civil society. Our very idea of freedom has been deepened and transformed, and extended into realms well beyond the more limited positions I described earlier in this section.[21] However, this more expansive ideal of freedom, and each and every one of the gains associated with it, now under threat.

For example, as consumer culture has grown, the measure of freedom's success has moved away from issues involving, say, the social relations surrounding paid and unpaid labor and has moved toward the gratification of market desires.[22] Although this does have its roots in the notions of personal freedom associated with classical definitions of liberalism, freedom means, as a number of commentators have reminded us, more than satisfying one's market desires and more than doing what one pleases. It requires real chances to "formulate the available choices," something many of our fellow citizens are effectively denied.[23] Educational questions enter here in powerful ways, as we shall see.

The turn to freedom as the market is registered in the influential writings of Friedrich von Hayek, in many ways the intellectual progenitor of the neoclassical economist Milton Friedman, who delights in voucher plans as the solution to educational problems. For von Hayek, the problem of freedom is related to the fact that conservatives supposedly have let the left both define the concept and mobilize it in debates over what our institutions should do. Instead of apologizing for capitalism, libertarian conservatives influenced by von Hayek and others pressed forward the case that "real" freedom can only come from a combination of decentralized political power, extremely limited government, and unregulated markets. Only in this way can conservatives reclaim the idea of freedom and win the consent of the public. To win this kind of freedom, this meant instilling a belief in what are truly radical policies. The public had to be convinced that the unregulated marketplace of the neoliberals was not only the truest expression of individual freedom, but the marketplace must be expanded into every sphere of life. Only through market competition can "people [get] what they want."[24] Why should a marketized society keep schools out of such a market? They must be "freed" as well.

Yet the idea of freedom as a market was too libertarian for some conservatives. It placed individual choice as the arbiter of freedom. This ignored the need for "transcendental" values, for absolute truths. Only in reasserting a definition of freedom grounded in "tradition" and in the primacy of a return to Christian moral values and the values and traditions of the "West" could "virtue" be restored. For without virtue, there could be no freedom. For them, von Hayek's and Friedman's vision of freedom did not lay the foundation for a moral community whose members shared a common heritage. Naked self-interest, in Marx's apposite phrase, was hardly an appropriate starting point for the defense of "timeless" values. The bottom-line individualism of neoliberals conflicts with the organic society united by the strong moral authority of tradition envisioned by neoconservatives such as William Bennett, who decries the loss of virtues, character, and "real" knowledge in schools.[25] This is one of the defining tensions of conservative movements today, a tension that must be resolved if conservative movements are to move society in the directions they ardently desire to go.[26] How this tension is resolved in practice in education is important.

Part of the problem of moving a society in conservative directions has been the association of neoconservative arguments with elitism. How could people be won to a position that seemed so committed to abstract ideas of truth and virtue? Some of this was accomplished through the development of an antigovernment populism, a stress on law and order, on the evils of welfare and on the breakdown of morality and the family, and on the sanctity of property. Virtue was being lost because of government interference not only into the market, but also into one's home and schools. Morality was lost when government entered, especially liberal government. As Thomas Frank has shown, rightist groups often cynically manipulated such cultural issues to win support for neoliberal economic policies; but cynical or not, they were—and continue to be—very effective strategies.[27]

Part of this dilemma was also solved through the growth, and then integration within the larger conservative cause, of conservative evangelical movements. Estranged from a culture "that seemed to trivialize religion and exalt immorality," conservative Christians embraced not only the free market but also the need for strong moral authority. Freedom here was the combination of capitalism and what they perceived as the moral life as ordained by God.[28] Authoritarian populist religious conservatives had found a home under the conservative umbrella.

As we shall see later on, much of this movement was and is organized around both conscious and unconscious racial dynamics.[29] It has at its basis as well specific histories and dynamics surrounding gender relations. It also occurred at exactly the same time as the transfer of wealth upward in the United States and from the "Third World" to the "First World" reached almost obscene levels. And it was successful in part because the concept of freedom that became dominant, and that looked forward both to a modernized economy of stimulating desire and giving individual choice, was itself combined with a set of backward-looking visions that brought us closer to supposedly traditional Western values and to the God that established them. Let me say somewhat more about each of these visions.

Marketizing the World

If we were to point to one specific defining political/economic paradigm of the age in which we live, it would be neoliberalism. This term may be less visible in the United States, but it is definitely known throughout the rest of the world. Although we here in the United States may be less familiar with the term itself, we are not unfamiliar with its tendencies and effects. Robert McChesney defines it in the following way:

> Neoliberal initiatives are characterized as free market policies that encourage private enterprise and consumer choice, reward personal responsibility and entrepreneurial initiative, and undermine the dead hand of the incompetent, bureaucratic and parasitic government, that can never do good even if well intended, which it rarely is.[30]

Such policies almost never require justification any more. They have become the common sense of an emerging international consensus. Indeed, even with the recent powerful and one would hope lasting protests in Seattle, in Washington, D.C., in Prague, in Genoa and elsewhere against the arrogant policies of the World Trade Organization, neoliberal policies still have something of a sacred aura now, especially since we are repeatedly told that there are *no* alternatives worth considering. It may be imperfect, but it is the only system that is even feasible in a world governed by global markets and intense competition. Although we are constantly told that nothing else is possible, it is important to realize that neoliberalism is in essence "capitalism with the gloves off."[31]

As I have argued elsewhere, neoliberalism transforms our very idea of democracy, making it only an economic concept, not a political one.[32] One of its effects is the destruction of what might best be seen as "thick democracy," substituting a much "thinner" version of possessive individual-

ism. Once again, McChesney puts it well in his usual biting way:

> To be effective, democracy requires that people feel a connection to their fellow citizens, and that this connection manifests itself through a variety of nonmarket organizations and institutions. A vibrant political culture needs community groups, libraries, public schools, neighborhood organizations, cooperatives, public meeting places, voluntary associations, and trade unions to provide ways for citizens to meet, communicate, and interact with their fellow citizens. Neoliberal democracy, with its notion of the market *uber alles*, takes dead aim at this sector. Instead of communities, it produces shopping malls. The net result is an atomized society of disengaged individuals who feel demoralized and socially powerless.[33]

Even with these effects, it is still possible to argue on the grounds of efficiency that corporate models should dominate our societies. After all, they do allow for choice. Yet to valorize this vision of democracy as the correct one is to neglect one simple but crucial point. Most major corporations are anything but democratic. In many ways, they are more totalitarian than is admitted openly. Thus, jobs are cut ruthlessly. Profits are much more important than the lives, hopes, and well-being of employees who have given their working lives to these organizations. In general, no level of profit ever makes these jobs secure; profit must be constantly increased, no matter what the cost to families and employees. One must question if this is the ethic we should be introducing as *the* model for our public institutions and our children.

Although the marketizers and privatizers feel free to hearken back to Adam Smith for justification of their policies, they are being more than a little selective. Yes, Smith sang the praises of the division of labor. But he also was more than a little clear in his denunciation of many of its inhuman effects. Government action was to be constantly promoted to overcome the destructive effects of the "invisible hand." For Smith, government "regulation in favour of the workmen is always just and equitable," but not "when in favour of the masters." Indeed, underpinning much of his argument was a call for equality of outcome, a position that was at the heart of his argument for markets.[34] It is easy to forget that it was not Karl Marx but Adam Smith who recognized that for every one rich person there must be five hundred poor ones.[35]

Of course, there are multiple ways of understanding this: Grasping what this means is made harder in daily life for all of us because of the dominant forms of interpretation that are now made available or *not* made easily available in education and in the media. As I note earlier, the very concepts we employ to make sense out of the social relations that organize our lives not only reflect these relations but produce them. For example, our system of economic production and exchange can be understood within very different ideological frameworks using very different systems of representation. The discourse of the "market" brings distinctly different visions front and center than, say, the discourse of production. The language of "consumer" creates a reality that is not the same as the language of worker, capitalist, owner, or producer. Each term posits one of those road maps I discussed earlier; each term situates us as social actors in particular relations in economic and social processes. Each has attached to it an identity that positions us in relation to the account of the process as depicted in the discourse itself. In the words of Stuart Hall:

> The worker who relates to his or her condition of existence in the capitalist process as "consumer" . . . participates in the process by way of a different practice from those who are inscribed in the system as "skilled laborer"—or not inscribed in it at all as "housewife." All of these inscriptions have effects which are real. They make a material difference, since how we act in certain situations depends on what our definitions of the situation are.[36]

For these very reasons, I displace our usual understanding of concepts such as the "consumer" and the "market" in which we see these things as good. I place them in a different and much more socially critical framework, one that interrogates their actual functioning in the real world of education. Unless this is done, the use of market categories and concepts prevents us from seeing the process as a whole.[37] Looking at education as part of a mechanism of market exchange makes crucial aspects literally invisible, thereby preventing critique before it even starts.[38] There are no exits to such a critique on its map.

Restoring Cultural Order

The economic focus on flexible accumulation, economic insecurity, and the marketization of social life does not stand alone. An ideology of market freedom and equality based on "choice" is not sufficient to deal with the contradictions and conditions that emerge from such economic, social, and educational policies. Impoverishment, the loss of job security and benefits, racial and gender disparities in the ways "fast capitalism" trickles down to those on the bottom, and so much more—all of these also require a much stronger state to complement the weak state supposedly favored by neoliberals. This smaller strong state, however, is often a repressive one. It is involved in rigorously policing the population of those left out by the economy. Thus, in state after state, a huge amount of money is being spent on prison construction and maintenance. In many states, this is even more than similar expenditures on higher education. As I have argued in *Cultural Politics and Education*, the United States has found a way to deal with many of the effects of poverty; we jail poor people, and especially poor persons of color.[39]

However, as I hinted at before, these things are also accompanied by other ideological movements that are connected, but not reducible, to neoliberal economic policies and their associated small but strong state. It should come as no surprise that in times of insecurity and fragmentation, there is a concomitant rise in longings for social and cultural stability and an increased emphasis on the authority of basic institutions. Against the fears of moral decay and social and cultural disintegration, there is a sense of a need for a "return." In conditions such as these, a romantic past is often constructed, a past that glorifies (particular versions of) family and tradition, patriotism, Victorian values, hard work, and the maintenance of cultural order.[40] Barbarians are at the gates. And unless we restore "our" knowledge, values, and traditions to the central place they once had, civilization will be lost. It should not be surprising that here, too, schools and the curricula, teaching, and testing that are found or not found in them become prime areas of attack. That the United States did suffer a murderous attack in September 11, 2001, adds more steam to this ideological project and makes it seem as if "civilization" is indeed under attack—even when the understandings of Islam that may underpin some people's fear may be more than a little ahistorical and incorrect.[41]

Again, we should not be too surprised by the rather checkered history these concerns have had both inside and outside of education. Let me give an example.

The manufacturing baron Abram Hewitt said it best when, in the latter part of the nineteenth century, he claimed that the task of social science and education was to find ways of making "men who are equal in liberty [content with the] inequality in distribution inevitable in modern society."[42] Not only the rich, but the middle class in general as well, believed that one's inability to advance in society was simply evidence of a lack of "character." A failure to advance bespoke a moral incapacity, the absence of those characteristics that guaranteed mobility—self-reliance and perseverance. Unions were not the answer, nor was government help. The only way to advance was to demonstrate the force of character to do it oneself, "to practice personal economy, keep out of debt, and educate their children in the principles of the marketplace."[43]

Thus, the suturing together of the needs and norms of the market and conservative views of appropriate character has a long history. Fears of economic decline, of the loss of "genteel" culture, of the loss of a common language and culture have constantly surfaced, often in times of market crisis and surges in immigration. Hybrid cultures are in essence bad cultures. They exacerbate our fears of cultural decline and economic uncertainty. The nature of this is indicated in the invention of (compulsory) common rituals. As Foner writes:

> Wracked by fears that the economic and ethnic unity of American society were in danger of disintegrating, government and private organizations in the 1890s promoted a unifying, coercive patriotism. These were the years when rituals like the Pledge of Allegiance and the practice of standing for the playing of "The Star-Spangled Banner" came into existence, Americans had long honored the Stars and Stripes, but the "cult of the flag," including an official Flag Day, dates to the 1890s.[44]

The current emphasis on "character education," on patriotism, and on restoring "our" culture must be understood in relation to this history. It is not an accident that it has occurred at this time. Nor is it a mere coincidence that those who promote these educational and social answers are also less than critical about both this history and the ways in which dominant economic dynamics may produce the ideological conditions they so lament—although we should remember that the truly tragic events of September 11 also brought out feelings of patriotism in a very

wide swath of our population.[45] The fact that widespread sympathy for the United States internationally in the wake of the murders of so many people unfortunately has been squandered by the current administration is too often forgotten.

Church and State

Markets and the restoration of character and "real" knowledge in education do not stand alone today. For a rapidly growing segment of the conservative population, God's message to all of us is to turn to both capitalism and tradition. Hence, in a tense but still complementary way, much of this emphasis on a "return" is supported by major elements of the Christian right currently. They believe that only by turning one's entire life over to *their* particular religious beliefs will this society and its schools be saved. Because of this, I shall need to pay a good deal of attention to them in this volume.

As odd as it seems, given my own political and educational beliefs, let me state that the Christian right is correct to the extent that in much of the colonial United States there was no firm separation between church and state. Although they would see this positively, as ratification of the status of the United States as a Christian nation, the reality was often rather less positive. In Pennsylvania, while offering "Christian Liberty" to all of those who acknowledged "one Almighty God," all officeholders had to swear to an oath affirming their belief in Jesus Christ. Discrimination against Catholics, Jews, and even dissenting Protestants was rife.[46] Indeed, up until the Revolutionary War, those Baptists who refused to pay taxes to support Congregational ministers were jailed in Massachusetts.[47]

The drive to separate church and state, to build a "wall of separation" as the deist Thomas Jefferson would say, was based on an attempt both by people such as Jefferson and others to free politics and "reason" from theological control and by a number of evangelical movements that wanted to protect religion from the "corrupting embrace of government." Only through such toleration would people be able to lead "truly Christian lives." In the process, many powerful churches lost their supply of public revenue and their special privileges. Yet, in many states, church and state were still closely wedded. Non-Christians were barred from public office; blasphemy and breaches of the Sabbath were rigorously prosecuted.[48] Anyone who believes that the United States is and was a Christian nation also needs to be reminded that this is what it means to be a Christian nation as well.

In saying this and in pursuing my arguments, I do not wish to imply that religion has no place in schools. I have some sympathy with Warren Nord's position when he argues on secular and liberal grounds that "all students should receive a liberal education that takes seriously a variety of ways of making sense of the world, religious ways included, if they are to be informed, reasonable, and responsible individuals."[49] For Nord, America's public schools are illiberal in their refusal to take religion seriously enough. In the world of elite academic and educational life, religious sensibilities play little or no role. In the process, educational institutions have "disenfranchised large segments of the American people."[50] Nord may be overstating his case a bit here, but clearly religion plays a central role in the lives of a considerable number of people—and they do feel disenfranchised by the absence of religion in schools. Of course, for many of them it is not the study of religion as one of the aforementioned multiple perspectives that they wish to promote. Rather, it is a particular vision of religious truth, of biblical authority in all realms of life, that guides them.[51] And there is a world of difference here.

Economics and Religion

There is nothing new about movements that try to put all of these elements—capitalist markets, a romantic cultural past, and God—together. Take Christianity and its historical connection to capitalism as an example.

The great economist John Maynard Keynes, the author of one of the "dangerous" books on the *Human Events* list, once wrote that modern capitalism is "absolutely irreligious." The love of money, and the accumulation of capital, had led to the steady decay of religion. Religion had lost its moral significance because it did not touch on matters economic, except in the most tangential ways. The "creative destructiveness" of capitalism and the marketization of all aspects of our lives disrupted families, communities, traditions, paid and unpaid work, the "natural rhythms" of daily life, indeed all of our life.[52] In what is perhaps one of the most famous quotes about this process of creative destruction, Marx and Engels wrote that all "ancient and venerable prejudices and opinions are swept away, all new-formed ones become antiquated before they can ossify. All that is solid melts into air, all that is sacred is profaned."[53]

Yet there has been a powerful sociological and historical tradition that, although admitting the profaning of the sacred under capitalism, argues that capitalism and, say, particular forms of Protestantism have formed a symbiotic relation, each informing and shaping the other. The emphasis in Calvinism on hard work, saving, and asceticism, for example, closely paralleled the needs of an emerging capitalist economy.[54]

This set of tensions—capitalism destroys traditional religions and uproots any sense of tradition, on the one hand, and capitalism and particular religions form a couplet that support each other, on the other—is creatively solved in the conservative evangelical movement. Capitalism is "God's economy." "Economic freedom" and market economies in education and the larger society are given biblical warrant. As we shall see, this is done quite creatively in schools and the larger society in such a way that the individual choice to be "born again" is mirrored in a market that allows for personal accumulation of wealth and choice.

Yet choice has its limits. For conservative evangelicals, one cannot choose without firm and foundational knowledge of what is right. And there is but one way, one place, to find this out. That is the Bible—and the Bible says what it means and means what it says. This inerrantist position is best exemplified and codified in the Chicago Statement on Biblical Inerrancy. "Holy Scripture, being God's own Word, written by men prepared and superintended by His Spirit, is of infallible divine authority in all matters upon which it touches. . . . Being wholly and verbally God-given, Scripture is without error or fault in its teaching."[55] The Bible, then, is not "man's truth" but God's truth. Its truth does not change; it was given *fully* in biblical times.[56]

Such "truth" is not new to education, by any means. Even a brief examination would show the ways in which biblical forms were powerfully influential in early schooling in the United States. Take as one example the ways in which children were to be instructed in literacy in the New England colonies. The most commonly used schoolbook in the later part of the seventeenth century, the *New England Primer*, instructed children in the alphabet in the following way:

A wise son makes a glad Father, but a foolish son is the heaviness of his mother.

B etter is little with the fear of the Lord, than great treasure and trouble therewith.

C ome unto Christ all ye that labour and are heavy laden, and He will give you rest.[57]

The *Primer* did not stop there. Lessons followed on "The Dutiful Child's Promises" in which one vowed that "I will fear GOD, and honour the KING." It included the Lord's Prayer, the Apostle's Creed, and a listing of the books of the Bible. Numbers were to be learned in order to "serve for the ready finding of any Chapter, Psalm, and Verse in the Bible." It ended with the Westminster Assembly's Shorter Catechism, including questions such as "What is the chief end of Man?" The answer is "Man's chief end is to glorify God, and to enjoy him forever." Another question asks, "What rule hath God given to direct us how we may glorify and enjoy him?" This is answered by, "The word of God which is contained in the Scriptures of the Old and New Testament, is the only rule to direct us how we may glorify and enjoy him."[58] Thus, there is no doubt that religion was central to the founding of schooling in America.

Later texts showed this continued influence. The McGuffey Readers, of which over 120 million were printed and used in the nineteenth and early twentieth centuries, read as much like a text in theology as in literacy. God was omnipresent within it, just but stern. The truths of the Bible were unquestioned; nor did one question their relevance to everyday life. Life was "God-conscious and God-centered." Students are to "live for salvation." All elements of the natural world can only be understood as "the expression of God's order." Indeed, as Nord reminds us, there are more references to God in the *Annotated McGuffey* than any other subject. Interestingly, the subject of death has the second largest number.[59]

These are not the only possibilities of understanding religion and its relations to the larger society, of course. The ways we think socially about religion have been varied. For some commentators, religion symbolizes the "felt whole" of a society and involves the deployment of symbols of social identity. Thus, religious meanings and institutions provide integrative forms that keep societies together and promote harmony. For others, such as Emile Durkheim, religion's very action in dividing the sacred from the profane is a positive response that celebrates sociality. It "sacralizes the fact and manner of human bonding as a prerequisite of any particular form of society."[60] For still others, such as some versions of Marx and Engels, religion played a less positive symbolic and material role. Beliefs in the supernatural

and in divine powers represented ways in which social relations and inequalities were masked. Their social function was to obscure or distort the prevailing distribution of power and wealth and the social relations that supported them.[61] For those such as Weber and Simmel, religion is a vast symbolic resource in which meanings are able to be produced, transmitted, and contested. It is separated from other symbolic resources by the fact that it provides a warrant for claims to ultimate significance, but it could be adapted to suit the interests of particular sections of the society.[62] Thus, for Weber, there were close connections between particular kinds of Protestantism and the rationalization of the modern world.

Closer in time to us, those observers such as Peter Berger argue that religion plays another crucial role in "modern" societies. It keeps the existential nightmare away. For him, culture today is unstable, as are people's identities. Religious beliefs enable one to better withstand the corrosive effects of bureaucratic rationality and the development of *homo economicus*, the person who is defined only by her or his place as an economic being.[63] Finally, Michel Foucault traces out the ways in which the "pastoral power" that had been fostered by the major Christian churches spread out throughout society. It was assimilated into the state and used as an "individualizing tactic which characterized a series of powers: those of the family, medicine, psychiatry, education, and employers."[64] Yet, no matter what the differences in each of these perspectives on religion, each sees religion fundamentally *socially*, not as apart from society in some other-worldly realm but as integral to society. It has power—individually and collectively, positively and negatively. This is exactly what I explore in my book *Educating the "Right" Way* when I discuss the growing influence of authoritarian populist religious conservatism on education as well.

However, I want to do this in a particular way. Following the leadership of Antonio Gramsci, I believe that the social meaning of religion has to be decoded in terms of the real-life experiences of people at particular times and places. He urged us to examine the ways in which churches worked to prevent a gap from forming between its formalized institutions and rituals and "the people"—that is, how at specific times and places religion connected to popular culture and the meanings of daily life. Gramsci's interest was in making organic connections between working-class and poor people and progressive movements for social justice.[65] My own interest is grounded in a similar politics; but I want to explore how organic connections are now made between people's daily lives and *conservative* religious movements, as these are the one's increasingly dominant today and these are the ones that seem to be exceptionally powerful in polarizing our beliefs about schooling currently. At the same time, I want to show connections that have been made between such religious tendencies and the growing belief that only through markets and a return to an Edenic past can schools, our children, and our nation itself be "saved." In doing this, I again want to be absolutely clear that I am not taking a position that religious meanings and institutions must by their very nature be conservative. Popular religious meanings, movements, and institutions are not a priori radical or conservative. Much depends on the uses to which they are put

and on the balance of social and ideological forces at a given time.[66] (Actually, from my own personal experiences working outside the United States, I tend to believe that in many nations it would be impossible to develop larger liberatory movements without religious mediations as one of the major dynamics. I take this position not only for empirical reasons— that is, because of the power of religion in these nations—but because I believe that utopian hopes are important for envisioning a better future. And religious yearnings often embody such dreams and must be treated with the respect they deserve.)

Managerialism

The three previous elements of the radical restructuring of education and other institutions that I've just described— neoliberalism, neoconservatism, and authoritarian populism—do not cover all of the tendencies currently in motion on the conservative side of the spectrum. A final one concerns the impulses driving the restructuring of the role of government and the ways in which a relatively autonomous fraction of the managerial and professional middle class has taken on even more power in directing social and educational policies in directions that actually give this particular group of people more power and new identities as well. I pointed out earlier that the role of the state has been altered along the lines of a radical redefinition of the boundaries between public and private. We can think of this as involving three strategic transformations. First, many public assets have been privatized. Public utilities are sold off to the highest bidder; schools are given to corporations to run. Second, rigorous competition between institutions is sponsored so that public institutions are constantly compared with supposedly more efficient private ones. Hence, even if schools and other institutions are still state funded, their internal procedures increasingly mirror those of the corporate sector. Third, public responsibilities have been shifted onto the informal sector, under the argument that the government can no longer afford the expense of such services. In practice this has meant that a good deal of child care, caring for the elderly and the infirm, and so much more has been "dumped" onto the local community and the family. This is one of the reasons that it is crucial to realize that behind a good deal of the new managerialism and the importation of business models into the state is a specifically patriarchal set of assumptions and effects, as it is largely the unpaid labor of women in the family and in local communities that will be exploited to deal with the state's shedding of its previous responsibilities.[67] At the same time, although some aspects of the state are indeed dumped onto local communities, other aspects of state control are enhanced and made even stronger, especially its control over knowledge and values in schools and over the mechanisms of evaluating institutional success or failure in such cultural reproduction. One of the most powerful examples of this process in the United States is the legislation commonly called "No Child Left Behind." Underneath its rhetoric of helping those children who have not been well-served by existing schooling (and this clearly *cannot* be denied), its characteristics include a massive centralization of control, a loss of local autonomy, and a redefinition of what counts as good or bad education that is simply reduced to

scores on problematic tests of achievement. As we shall see, it can actually create even more inequalities than before.

However, managerialism is not only about altering what the state does and how much power it has. It also offers new and powerful roles for the individuals and groups who occupy positions within the state. In technical terms, we might say that managerial discourse provides "subject positions" through which people can imagine themselves and their institutions in different ways. Thus, one of the key characteristics of managerial discourse is in the positions it offers to managers. They are not passive, but active agents—mobilizers of change, dynamic entrepreneurs, shapers of their own destinies.[68] No longer are the organizations they inhabit ploddingly bureaucratic and subjected to old-fashioned statism. Instead, they and the people who run them are dynamic, efficient, productive, "lean and mean."[69]

By importing business models and tighter systems of accountability into education and other forms of public services, managerialism doesn't just offer state managers new ways of thinking about their lives and their organizations. Aside from giving new meaning to the lives of managers within the new middle class, it promises—in the words of new managerialism—transparency, at the same time as it supposedly empowers the individual consumer. It is an ideal project, merging the language of empowerment, rational choice, efficient organization, and new roles for managers all at the same time. Although the "spartan language" of efficiency does have its attractiveness to certain business groups, it has only limited appeal to many others. By reappropriating the discourse of antipaternalism and user-centeredness, it offers metaphors for a range of people to see their place in the new more responsive future. One can modernize the machinery of schools and of the government in general, be an efficient and business-like manager, and help people by ensuring "quality" at the same time.[70] What could be wrong with that? As I show later, however, this is not the rolling back of state power, nor is it really "empowering" for either the least-advantaged members of our communities or people who work in those institutions now subject to managerialism's demands. Furthermore, its vision of managers organized around an efficient and revitalized professionalism in the service of consumers is partly a fiction. Active professionals are free to follow their entrepreneurial urges—as long as they "do the right thing."[71] As we shall see, Foucault's panopticon is everywhere.

Analyzing Conservative Modernization

In my book *Educating the "Right" Way*, I provide a picture of how the odd combination of markets, return to lost traditions and values, a godly education, and the managerialism of tightened standards and guaranteeing "quality" are pulled together. In the process, I want to demonstrate which groups of people will wind up winning and losing as this constellation of "reforms" goes forward. In pursuit of this, I must bring to the attention of people in the United States not only research and arguments about what is happening here, but also evidence of similar reforms that have appeared in other nations. There are several reasons for approaching these issues with an international perspective. All too many discussions of education in the United States are characterized by a partic-

ular form of arrogance. "We" have nothing to learn from other nations. Or such discussions are unaware that many of the things in which we are engaged here have a history elsewhere, a history whose effects should make us rather cautious about engaging in the same policies. Or, finally, there is an assumption that our motives are pure and our traditions democratic. Hence, whatever has occurred in educational reforms in other nations (say, an increase in social inequalities in education when a particular change is instituted) simply couldn't happen here. It can and it is.

In my book, Chapter 2 goes into more detail about the assumptions that underpin the forces of conservative modernization specifically in education today and gives a clearer sense of the tensions and contradictions in the conservative movements. Chapter 3 deals with the actual effects that "reforms" such as establishing a competitive market in schooling, national and state curricula, ever-rising standards, and the increasing mandates of testing have had in schools in a number of countries. Its focus is on the neoliberal and neoconservative proposals that are having such a profound effect on educational policy and practice. This chapter also critically examines the ways in which the supposed alternative to these proposals—that is, ones that center around the literature on "critical pedagogy"—are weak in crucial ways, and thus will have a hard time interrupting rightist transformations. (This is a difficult issue for me, since I have long been associated with this tradition.) Chapter 4 is new to this edition and specifically focuses on the processes and effects of such reforms as No Child Left Behind and their attempts at recasting education along the logics of what I call "audit cultures."

In the process, the complicated roles that class and race dynamics play in this logic and in various groups' reactions to it are highlighted.

Chapters 5 and 6 deal directly with the growing power of conservative religious groups in debates over the ends and means of schooling. Chapter 5 discusses some of their recent effects and traces out the history of such movements, whereas Chapter 6 critically illuminates the ways in which their beliefs about curricula and pedagogy cohere with their larger positions on the economy, government, the family, gender relations, and the politics of class and race. Chapter 7 examines the ways in which the home schooling movement provides a mechanism for many of these emphases to come together. Chapter 8 goes further into the home schooling movement, both into its status as a social movement and into the ways in which it is carried out. As will be evident here as in other chapters, understanding the ways in which gender politics works is absolutely crucial if we are to also understand the actual practices of teaching and learning in home schooling. In Chapter 9, I assess the possibilities of interrupting the movement toward the right and suggest some strategies for doing so.

A good deal of time is spent on conservative religious critics of schooling in the later sections of my book. I do this for a number of reasons. First, although it is crucial to pay close attention to the criticism of markets, standards, and testing (and I do), too often the creative ways in which many other groups have been brought under the umbrella of neoliberal leadership have been largely ignored. Second, such religious groups have been very powerful in putting pressure on schools in

states and municipalities throughout the country, often making educators think twice (or three or four times) about what they will and will not teach and how they will and will not teach it. These groups have also been growing rapidly in influence so that many more people now consider themselves to be conservative evangelicals and are willing to take a public position on education based on this identification than ever before in recent history. Third, perhaps unlike many other people on the left, as I've noted I believe that there are elements of insight in the position of the populist religious critics and that they have been stereotyped and ignored. Not only do I think that this is intellectually suspect, but it is also dangerous strategically if we do wish to counter the rightist turn in education in serious ways.

Because of this, although I am deeply concerned about what their implications are, I also want to be fair to the concerns they express—many of which cannot be easily dismissed. Thus, I will be at pains to show the elements of "good sense" as well as "bad sense" in their criticisms of some aspects of formal education.

These are the complicated tendencies I focus on in *Educating the "Right" Way*. I wish that it could be simpler. That certainly would make the story I need to tell much easier. However, when reality itself is complex and contradictory, so too must be our critical analyses. Throughout the book I combine the theoretical and the empirical. I must admit to being deeply worried that we have played the theoretical card so often at such a level of abstraction that we have vacated the empirical space and left it open for neoliberals and neoconservatives to occupy—which they predictably have done. Yet at times we positively *need* the distance that theory gives us in order to think through difficult issues.

Because of this, I fully recognize that there are tensions in what I do here. I criticize the kinds of theories and assumptions that underpin many of the current educational reforms; and sometimes I do this theoretically as well as empirically. However, having done this I tend to take the position that "the only theory worth having is that which you fight off, not that which you speak with profound fluency."[72] This is a bit of an overstatement of course, since we do need to be "fluent" in any theory we propose to use. But it does point out that one's theoretical success should not be measured by whether there is an exact "fit." Rather, the efficacy of our theories needs to be measured by our ability to work productively with theories that are almost always inadequate in some ways but push us "further down the road" and enable us to see things that were hidden before.[73] The road I want us to travel on has exits that are not visible on the maps about education, culture, government, and the economy provided to us by dominant groups. Let us now look at these maps in more detail.

REFERENCES

Apple, Michael W., ed. *Teachers and Texts: A Political Economy of Class and Gender Relations in Education.* New York: Routledge, 1988.

———. *Ideology and Curriculum*, 2d ed. New York: Routledge, 1990.

———. *Cultural Politics and Education.* New York: Teachers College Press, 1996.

———. *Official Knowledge: Democratic Education in a Conservative Age*, 2d ed. New York: Routledge, 2000.

Apple, Michael W., and James A. Beane, eds. *Democratic Schools.* Alexandria, Va.: Association for Supervision and Curriculum Development, 1995.

———. *Democratic Schools: Lessons from the Chalk Face.* Buckingham, England: Open University Press, 1999.

Apple, Michael W., Jane Kenway, and Michael Singh, eds. *Globalizing Education.* New York: Peter Lang, 2005.

Ball, Stephen. *Education Reform: A Critical and Post-Structural Approach.* Buckingham, England: Open University Press, 1994.

Beckford, James A. *Religion and Advanced Industrial Society.* New York: Routledge, 1989.

Bennett, William, Chester E. Finn Jr., and John T. E. Cribb Jr. *The Educated Child.* New York: Free Press, 1999.

Chomsky, Noam. *Profit Over People: Neoliberalism and the Global Order.* New York: Seven Stories Press, 1999.

Clarke, John, and Janet Newman. *The Managerial State.* Thousand Oaks, Calif.: Sage, 1997.

Coles, Gerald. *Reading Lessons: The Debate Over Literacy.* New York: Hill & Wang, 1998.

Foner, Eric. *The Story of American Freedom.* New York: Norton, 1998.

Foucault, Michel. "The Subject and Power." In *Michel Foucault: Beyond Structuralism and Hermeneutics*, ed. Herbert Dreyfus and Paul Rabinow, 208–26. Chicago: University of Chicago Press, 1982.

Frank, Thomas. *What's the Matter with Kansas: How Conservatives Won the Heart of America.* New York: Metropolitan Books, 2004.

Fraser, Nancy, and Linda Gordon. "A Genealogy of Dependency." *Signs* 19 (Winter 1994): 309–36.

Gee, James P., Glynda Hull, and Colin Lankshear. *The New Work Order: Behind the Language of the New Capitalism*. Boulder, Colo.: Westview Press, 1996.

Hall, Stuart. "The Problem of Ideology: Marxism Without Guarantees." In *Stuart Hall: Critical Dialogues in Cultural Studies*, ed. David Morley and Kuan-Hsing Chen, 25–46. New York: Routledge, 1996.

Hall, Stuart, and Lawrence Grossberg. "On Postmodernism and Articulation: An Interview with Stuart Hall." In *Stuart Hall: Critical Dialogues in Cultural Studies*, ed. David Morley and Kuan-Hsing Chen, 131–50. New York: Routledge, 1996.

Hobsbawm, Eric. *The Age of Extremes: A History of the World, 1914–1991*. New York: Pantheon, 1994.

Kao, Grace, Marta Tienda, and Barbara Schneider. "Racial and Ethnic Variation in Academic Performance." In *Research in Sociology of Education and Socialization, Volume 11*, ed. Aaron Pallas, 263–97. Greenwich, Conn.: JAI Press, 1996.

Kepel, Gilles. *Allah in the West: Islamic Movements in America and Europe*. Stanford, Calif.: Stanford University Press, 1997.

———. *Jihad: The Trial of Political Islam*. Cambridge, Mass.: Belknap Press of Harvard University Press, 2002.

Loewen, James W. *Lies My Teacher Told Me: Everything Your American History Textbook Got Wrong*. New York: New Press, 1995.

Marx, Karl, and Friedrich Engels. "Manifesto of the Communist Party." In *Marx and Engels: Basic Writings on Politics and Philosophy*, ed. Lewis S. Feuer, 1–41. New York: Anchor Books, 1959.

Mills, Charles W. *The Racial Contract*. Ithaca, N.Y.: Cornell University Press, 1997.

Nord, Warren A. *Religion and American Education: Rethinking a National Dilemma*. Chapel Hill: University of North Carolina Press, 1995.

Rorty, Richard. *Achieving Our Country: Leftist Thought in Twentieth-Century America*.

Cambridge, Mass.: Harvard University Press, 1998.

Slack, Jennifer D. "The Theory and Method of Articulation in Cultural Studies." In *Stuart Hall: Critical Dialogues in Cultural Studies*, ed. David Morley and Kuan-Hsing Chen, 112–127. New York: Routledge, 1996.

Smith, Adam. *The Wealth of Nations*. Oxford: Clarendon Press, 1976.

Williams, Raymond. *Keywords: A Vocabulary of Culture and Society*. New York: Oxford University Press, 1985.

Wyatt, Edward. "Investors See Room for Profit in the Demand for Education." *New York Times*, November 4, 1999, A1.

NOTES

1. For a discussion of this and of the problems of using this dichotomy between phonics and whole language, see Gerald Coles, *Reading Lessons* (New York: Hill & Wang, 1998).

2. I have demonstrated these connections in a number of places. See, for example, Michael W. Apple, *Ideology and Curriculum*, 3rd ed. (New York: RoutledgeFalmer, 2004); Michael W. Apple, *Education and Power*, 2d ed. (New York: Routledge, 1995); Michael W. Apple, *Teachers and Texts* (New York: Routledge, 1988); and Michael W. Apple, *Official Knowledge*, 2d ed. (New York: Routledge, 2000). See also James Loewen, *Lies My Teacher Told Me* (New York: The New Press, 1995).

3. See Stephen Ball, *Education Reform: A Critical and Post-Structural Approach* (Buckingham, England: Open University Press, 1994).

4. An articulate and thoughtful analysis of these relations is Jean Anyon's *Ghetto Schooling: A Political Economy of Urban Educational Reform* (New York: Teachers College Press, 1997). See also Grace Kao, Marta Tienda, and Barbara Schneider, "Race and Ethnic Variation in Academic Performance," in *Research in Sociology of Education and Socialization, Vol-*

ume 11, ed. Aaron Pallas (Greenwich, Conn.: JAI Press, 1996), 263–97.

5. This is described in considerably more detail in Michael W. Apple, *Cultural Politics and Education* (New York: Teachers College Press, 1996), 68–90.

6. Edward Wyatt, "Investors See Room for Profit in the Demand for Education," *New York Times*, November 4, 1999, A1.

7. Ibid.

8. Ibid.

9. Richard Rorty, *Achieving Our Country: Leftist Thought in Twentieth-Century America* (Cambridge, Mass.: Harvard University Press, 1998), 14.

10. See, for example, Michael W. Apple and James A. Beane, eds., *Democratic Schools* (Alexandria, Va.: Association for Supervision and Curriculum Development, 1995) and Michael W. Apple and James A. Beane, eds., *Democratic Schools: Lessons from the Chalk Face* (Buckingham, England: Open University Press, 1999).

11. Noam Chomsky, *Profits Over People: Neoliberalism and the Global Order* (New York: Seven Stories Press, 1999), 145.

12. See, for example, Raymond Williams, *Keywords: A Vocabulary of Culture and Society* (New York: Oxford University Press, 1983).

13. Eric Hobsbawm, *The Age of Extremes: A History of the World, 1914–1991* (New York: Pantheon, 1994), 3.

14. Eric Foner, *The Story of American Freedom* (New York: W. W. Norton, 1998), 4.

15. Ibid.

16. Ibid.

17. Ibid., 7–8.

18. Ibid., 8.

19. Ibid., 9. See also Nancy Fraser and Linda Gordon, "A Genealogy of Dependency," *Signs* 19 (Winter 1994): 309–36.

20. Foner, *Story of American Freedom*, 10.

21. Ibid., xx. Foner's book is absolutely essential for anyone interested in the continuing struggle over what freedom means and how it has been embodied in our daily life.

22. Ibid., 264.

23. Ibid., 269.

24. Ibid., 308–9.

25. William Bennett, Chester E. Finn Jr., and John T. E. Cribb Jr., *The Educated Child* (New York: The Free Press, 1999) and William Bennett, *Our Children and Our Country* (New York: Simon & Schuster, 1988).

26. Foner, *Story of American Freedom*, 310–11.

27. Thomas Frank, *What's the Matter With Kansas: How Conservatives Won the Heart of America* (New York: Metropolitan Books, 2004).

28. Foner, *Story of American Freedom*, 317–18.

29. Charles W. Mills argues insightfully that nearly all of our economic, political, and cultural/educational institutions in the past and today are undergirded by what he calls "the racial contract" that marginalizes people of color. See Charles W. Mills, *The Racial Contract* (Ithaca, N.Y.: Cornell University Press, 1997).

30. Robert McChesney, "Introduction" to Noam Chomsky, *Profit Over People: Neoliberalism and the Global Order* (New York: Seven Stories Press, 1999), 7.

31. Ibid., 8.

32. Apple, *Cultural Politics and Education*.

33. McChesney, "Introduction," 11.

34. Chomsky, *Profit Over People*, 39.

35. Adam Smith, *The Wealth of Nations* (Oxford: Clarendon Press, 1976), 709–10.

36. Stuart Hall, "The Problem of Ideology: Marxism without Guarantees," in *Stuart Hall: Critical Dialogues in Cultural Studies*, ed. David Morley and Kuan-Hsing Chen (New York: Routledge, 1996), 40.

37. For more on this, see Michael W. Apple, Jane Kenway, and Michael Singh, eds., *Globalizing Education: Policies, Pedagogies, and Politics* (New York: Peter Lang, 2005).

38. Hall, "The Problem of Ideology," 37.

39. Apple, *Cultural Politics and Education*; see especially 68–90.

40. Jorge Larrain, "Stuart Hall and the Marxist Concept of Ideology," in *Stuart Hall: Critical Dialogues in Cultural Studies*, ed. David Morley and Kuan-Hsing Chen (New York: Routledge, 1996), 68.

41. See Gilles Kepel, *Jihad: The Trial of Political Islam* (Cambridge, Mass.: Belknap Press of Harvard University Press, 2002) and Gilles Kepel, *Allah in the West: Islamic Movements in America and Europe* (Stanford, Calif.: Stanford University Press, 1997) for a more complicated sense of the United States' role in supporting a number of the movements that we now see as "threats to civilization" and for a better sense of the various Islamic tendencies in the West.

42. Foner, *Story of American Freedom*, 119.

43. Ibid., 121.

44. Ibid., 134.

45. I have discussed this at greater length in Michael W. Apple, *Ideology and Curriculum*, 3rd ed. (New York: RoutledgeFalmer, 2004).

46. Such forced allegiance had a long history in Europe as well of course. See, for example, Janet Liebman Jacobs, *Hidden Heritage: The Legacy of the Crypto-Jews* (Berkeley: University of California Press, 2002).

47. Foner, *Story of American Freedom*, 26.

48. Ibid., 26–27.

49. Warren A. Nord, *Religion and American Education: Rethinking a National Dilemma* (Chapel Hill: University of North Carolina Press, 1995), 8.

50. Ibid.

51. See Steven Vryhoff, *Between Memory and Vision: The Case for Faith-Based Schooling* (Grand Rapids, Mich.: William B. Eerdmans Publishing Co., 2004) for further discussion of this from the point of view of one of the advocates of faith-based schooling.

52. Nord, *Religion and American Education*, 32.

53. Karl Marx and Friedrich Engels, *Manifesto of the Communist Party*, in *Marx and Engels: Basic Writings on Politics and Philosophy*, ed. Lewis S. Feuer (New York: Anchor Books, 1959), 10. For a more personal account of what this meant to Marx, see Francis Wheen, *Karl Marx: A Life* (New York: W. W. Norton, 1999).

54. The writings on this issue are vast and filled with a good deal of empirical and theoretical debate. For a brief overview, see, for example, James A. Beckford, *Religion and Advanced Industrial Society* (New York: Routledge, 1989).

55. Nord, *Religion and American Education*, 50.

56. Ibid., 51.

57. Ibid., 65.

58. Ibid.

59. Ibid., 67.

60. Beckford, *Religion and Advanced Industrial Society*, 25.

61. Ibid., 18.

62. Ibid., 6–7.

63. Ibid., 89–105.

64. Michel Foucault, "The Subject and Power," in *Michel Foucault: Beyond Structuralism and Hermeneutics*, ed. Herbert Dreyfus and Paul Rabinow (Chicago: University of Chicago Press, 1982), 215.

65. Beckford, *Religion and Industrial Society*, 132–33.

66. Ibid., 142. See also Stuart Hall and Lawrence Grossberg, "On Postmodernism and Articulation: An Interview with Stuart Hall," in *Stuart Hall: Critical Dialogues in Cultural Studies*, ed. David Morley and Kuan-Hsing Chen (New York: Routledge, 1996), 142.

67. John Clarke and Janet Newman, *The Managerial State* (Thousand Oaks, Calif.: Sage, 1997), 27–28.

68. Ibid., 93.

69. See the analysis of managerial discourse in James Paul Gee, Glynda Hull, and Colin Lankshear, *The New Work Order: Behind the Language of the New Capitalism* (Boulder, Colo.: Westview Press, 1996).

70. Clarke and Newman, *The Managerial State*, 76. Clarke and Newman argue that corporate missions have moved from the bare pursuit of efficiency to the pursuit of "excellence" and the achievement of continuous improve-

ment. In their words, there has been an "epidemic of quality." There is of course nothing necessarily wrong with pursuing quality, but much of this represents the colonization of professional discourse by corporate models whose ultimate concern is not quality, but profit.

71. Ibid., 30.

72. Jennifer Daryl Slack, "The Theory and Method of Articulation in Cultural Studies," in *Stuart Hall: Critical Dialogues in Cultural Studies*, ed. David Morley and Kuan-Hsing Chen (New York: Routledge, 1996), 113.

73. Ibid.

Lisa D. Delpit

The Silenced Dialogue
Power and Pedagogy in Educating Other People's Children

A Black male graduate student who is also a special education teacher in a predominantly Black community is talking about his experiences in predominantly White university classes:

> There comes a moment in each class where we have to discuss "The Black Issue" and what's appropriate education for Black children. I tell you, I'm tired of arguing with those White people, because they won't listen. Well, I don't know if they really don't listen or if they just don't believe you. It seems like if you can't quote Vygotsky or something, then you don't have any validity to speak about your *own* kids. Anyway, I'm not bothering with it anymore, now I'm just in it for a grade.

A Black woman teacher in a multicultural urban elementary school is talking about her experiences in discussions with her predominantly White fellow teachers about how they should organize reading instruction to best serve students of color:

> When you're talking to White people they still want it to be their way. You can try to talk to them and give them examples, but they're so headstrong, they think they know what's best for *everybody*, for *everybody's* children. They won't listen, White folks are going to do what they want to do *anyway*.
>
> It's really hard. They just don't listen well. No, they listen, but they don't *hear*— you know how your mama used to say you listen to the radio, but you *hear* your mother? Well they don't *hear* me.
>
> So I just try to shut them out so I can hold my temper. You can only beat your head against a brick wall for so long before you draw blood. If I try to stop arguing with them I can't help myself from getting angry. Then I end up walking around praying all day "Please Lord, remove the bile I feel for these people so I can sleep tonight." It's funny, but it can become a cancer, a sore.
>
> So, I shut them out. I go back to my own little cubby, my classroom, and I try to teach the way I know will work, no matter what those folk say. And when I get Black kids, I just try to undo the damage they did.
>
> I'm not going to let any man, woman, or child drive me crazy—White folks will try to do that to you if you let them. You just have to stop talking to them,

that's what I do. I just keep smiling, but I won't talk to them.

A soft-spoken Native Alaskan woman in her forties is a student in the Education Department of the University of Alaska. One day she storms into a Black professor's office and very uncharacteristically slams the door. She plops down in a chair and, still fuming, says, "Please tell those people, just don't help us anymore! I give up. I won't talk to them again!"

And finally, a Black woman principal who is also a doctoral student at a well-known university on the West Coast is talking about her university experiences, particularly about when a professor lectures on issues concerning educating Black children:

> If you try to suggest that that's not quite the way it is, they get defensive, then you get defensive, then they'll start reciting research.
>
> I try to give them my experiences, to explain. They just look and nod. The more I try to explain, they just look and nod, just keep looking and nodding. They don't really hear me.
>
> Then, when it's time for class to be over, the professor tells me to come to his office to talk more. So I go. He asks for more examples of what I'm talking about, and he looks and nods while I give them. Then he says that that's just my experiences. It doesn't really apply to most Black people.
>
> It becomes futile because they think they know everything about everybody. What you have to say about your life, your children, doesn't mean anything. They don't really want to hear what you have to say. They wear blinders and earplugs. They only want to go on research they've read that other White people have written.
>
> It just doesn't make any sense to keep talking to them.

Thus was the first half of the title of this text born—"The Silenced Dialogue." One of the tragedies in the field of education is that scenarios such as these are enacted daily around the country. The saddest element is that the individuals that the Black and Native American educators speak of in these statements are seldom aware that the dialogue *has* been silenced. Most likely the White educators believe that their colleagues of color did, in the end, agree with their logic. After all, they stopped disagreeing, didn't they?

I have collected these statements since completing a recently published article (Delpit, 1986). In this somewhat autobiographical account, entitled "Skills and Other Dilemmas of a Progressive Black Educator," I discussed my perspective as a product of a skills-oriented approach to writing and as a teacher of process-oriented approaches. I described the estrangement that I and many teachers of color feel from the progressive movement when writing-process advocates dismiss us as too "skills oriented." I ended the article suggesting that it was incumbent upon writing-process advocates—or indeed, advocates of any progressive movement—to enter into dialogue with teachers of color, who may not share their enthusiasm about so-called new, liberal, or progressive ideas.

In response to this article, which presented no research data and did not even cite a reference, I received numerous calls and letters from teachers, professors, and even state school personnel from around the country, both Black and White. All of the White respondents, except one, have wished to talk more about the question of skills versus process approaches—to support or reject what they perceive to be my position. On the other hand, *all* of the non-White respondents have spoken passionately on being left out of the dialogue about how best to educate children of color.

How can such complete communication blocks exist when both parties truly believe they have the same aims? How can the bitterness and resentment expressed by the educators of color be drained so that the sores can heal? What can be done?

I believe the answer to these questions lies in ethnographic analysis, that is, in identifying and giving voice to alternative worldviews. Thus, I will attempt to address the concerns raised by White and Black respondents to my article "Skills and Other Dilemmas" (Delpit, 1986). My charge here is not to determine the best instructional methodology; I believe that the actual practice of good teachers of all colors typically incorporates a range of pedagogical orientations. Rather, I suggest that the differing perspectives on the debate over "skills" versus "process" approaches can lead to an understanding of the alienation and miscommunication, and thereby to an understanding of the "silenced dialogue."

In thinking through these issues, I have found what I believe to be a connecting and complex theme: what I have come to call "the culture of power." There are five aspects of power I would like to propose as given for this presentation:

1. Issues of power are enacted in classrooms.
2. There are codes or rules for participating in power; that is, there is a "culture of power."
3. The rules of the culture of power are a reflection of the rules of the culture of those who have power.
4. If you are not already a participant in the culture of power, being told explicitly the rules of that culture makes acquiring power easier.
5. Those with power are frequently least aware of—or least willing to acknowledge—its existence. Those with less power are often most aware of its existence.

The first three are by now basic tenets in the literature of the sociology of education, but the last two have seldom been addressed. The following discussion will explicate these aspects of power and their relevance to the schism between liberal educational movements and that of non-White, non-middle-class teachers and communities.[1]

1. *Issues of power are enacted in classrooms.*

These issues include: the power of the teacher over the students; the power of the publishers of textbooks and of the developers of the curriculum to determine the view of the world presented; the power of the state in enforcing compulsory schooling; and the power of an individual or group to determine another's intelligence or "normalcy." Finally, if schooling prepares people for jobs, and the kind of job a person has determines her or his economic status and, therefore, power, then schooling is intimately related to that power.

2. *There are codes or rules for participating in power; that is, there is a "culture of power."*

The codes or rules I'm speaking of relate to linguistic forms, communicative strategies, and presentation of self; that is, ways of talking, ways of writing, ways of dressing, and ways of interacting.

3. *The rules of the culture of power are a reflection of the rules of the culture of those who have power.*

This means that success in institutions—schools, workplaces, and so on—is predicated upon acquisition of the culture of those who are in power. Children from middle-class homes tend to do better in school than those from non-middle-class homes because the culture of the school is based on the culture of the upper and middle classes—of those in power. The upper and middle classes send their children to school with all the accoutrements of the culture of power; children from other kinds of families operate within perfectly wonderful and viable cultures but not cultures that carry the codes or rules of power.

4. *If you are not already a participant in the culture of power, being told explicitly the rules of that culture makes acquiring power easier.*

In my work within and between diverse cultures, I have come to conclude that members of any culture transmit information implicitly to comembers. However,

when implicit codes are attempted across cultures, communication frequently breaks down. Each cultural group is left saying, "Why don't those people say what they mean?" as well as, "What's wrong with them, why don't they understand?"

Anyone who has had to enter new cultures, especially to accomplish a specific task, will know of what I speak. When I lived in several Papua New Guinea villages for extended periods to collect data, and when I go to Alaskan villages for work with Alaskan Native communities, I have found it unquestionably easier—psychologically and pragmatically—when some kind soul has directly informed me about such matters as appropriate dress, interactional styles, embedded meanings, and taboo words or actions. I contend that it is much the same for anyone seeking to learn the rules of the culture of power. Unless one has the leisure of a lifetime of "immersion" to learn them, explicit presentation makes learning immeasurably easier.

And now, to the fifth and last premise:

5. *Those with power are frequently least aware of—or least willing to acknowledge—its existence. Those with less power are often most aware of its existence.*

For many who consider themselves members of liberal or radical camps, acknowledging personal power and admitting participation in the culture of power is distinctly uncomfortable. On the other hand, those who are less powerful in any situation are most likely to recognize the power variable most acutely. My guess is that the White colleagues and instructors of those previously quoted did not perceive themselves to have power over the non-White speakers. However, either by virtue of their position, their numbers, or their access to that particular code of power of calling upon research to validate one's position, the White educators had the authority to establish what was to be considered "truth" regardless of the opinions of the people of color, and the latter were well aware of that fact.

A related phenomenon is that liberals (and here I am using the term "liberal" to refer to those whose beliefs include striving for a society based upon maximum individual freedom and autonomy) seem to act under the assumption that to make any rules or expectations explicit is to act against liberal principles, to limit the freedom and autonomy of those subjected to the explicitness.

I thank Fred Erickson for a comment that led me to look again at a tape by John Gumperz[2] on cultural dissonance in cross-cultural interactions. One of the episodes showed an East Indian interviewing for a job with an all-White committee. The interview was a complete failure, even though several of the interviewers appeared to really want to help the applicant. As the interview rolled steadily downhill, these "helpers" became more and more indirect in their questioning, which exacerbated the problems the applicant had in performing appropriately. Operating from a different cultural perspective, he got fewer and fewer clear clues as to what was expected of him, which ultimately resulted in his failure to secure the position.

I contend that as the applicant showed less and less aptitude for handling the interview, the power differential became ever more evident to the interviewers. The "helpful" interviewers, unwilling to acknowledge themselves as having power over the applicant, became more and more un-

comfortable. Their indirectness was an attempt to lessen the power differential and their discomfort by lessening the power-revealing explicitness of their questions and comments.

When acknowledging and expressing power, one tends towards explicitness (as in yelling to your 10-year-old, "Turn that radio down!"). When de-emphasizing power, there is a move toward indirect communication. Therefore, in the interview setting, those who sought to help, to express their egalitarianism with the East Indian applicant, became more and more indirect—and less and less helpful—in their questions and comments.

In literacy instruction, explicitness might be equated with direct instruction. Perhaps the ultimate expression of explicitness and direct instruction in the primary classroom is Distar. This reading program is based on a behaviorist model in which reading is taught through the direct instruction of phonics generalizations and blending. The teacher's role is to maintain the full attention of the group by continuous questioning, eye contact, finger snaps, hand claps, and other gestures, and by eliciting choral responses and initiating some sort of award system.

When the program was introduced, it arrived with a flurry of research data that "proved" that all children—even those who were "culturally deprived"—could learn to read using this method. Soon there was a strong response, first from academics and later from many classroom teachers, stating that the program was terrible. What I find particularly interesting, however, is that the primary issue of the conflict over Distar has not been over its instructional efficacy—usually the students did learn to read—but the expression of explicit power in the classroom. The liberal educators opposed the methods—the direct instruction, the explicit control exhibited by the teacher. As a matter of fact, it was not unusual (even now) to hear of the program spoken of as "fascist."

I am not an advocate of Distar, but I will return to some of the issues that the program—and direct instruction in general—raises in understanding the differences between progressive White educators and educators of color.

To explore those differences, I would like to present several statements typical of those made with the best of intentions by middle-class liberal educators. To the surprise of the speakers, it is not unusual for such content to be met by vocal opposition or stony silence from people of color. My attempt here is to examine the underlying assumptions of both camps.

"I want the same thing for everyone else's children as I want for mine."

To provide schooling for everyone's children that reflects liberal, middle-class values and aspirations is to ensure the maintenance of the status quo, to ensure that power, the culture of power, remains in the hands of those who already have it. Some children come to school with more accoutrements of the culture of power already in place—"cultural capital," as some critical theorists refer to it (for example, Apple, 1979)—some with less. Many liberal educators hold that the primary goal for education is for children to become autonomous, to develop fully who they are in the classroom setting without having arbitrary, outside standards forced upon them. This is a very reasonable goal for people whose children are already participants in the culture of power and who have already internalized its codes.

But parents who don't function within that culture often want something else. It's not that they disagree with the former aim, it's just that they want something more. They want to ensure that the school provides their children with discourse patterns, interactional styles, and spoken and written language codes that will allow them success in the larger society.

It was the lack of attention to this concern that created such a negative outcry in the Black community when well-intentioned White liberal educators introduced "dialect readers." These were seen as a plot to prevent the schools from teaching the linguistic aspects of the culture of power, thus dooming Black children to a permanent outsider caste. As one parent demanded, "My kids know how to be Black—you all teach them how to be successful in the White man's world."

Several Black teachers have said to me recently that as much as they'd like to believe otherwise, they cannot help but conclude that many of the "progressive" educational strategies imposed by liberals upon Black and poor children could only be based on a desire to ensure that the liberals' children get sole access to the dwindling pool of American jobs. Some have added that the liberal educators believe themselves to be operating with good intentions, but that these good intentions are only conscious delusions about their unconscious true motives. One of Black anthropologist John Gwaltney's (1980) informants reflects this perspective with her tongue-in-cheek observation that the biggest difference between Black folks and White folks is that Black folks *know* when they're lying!

Let me try to clarify how this might work in literacy instruction. A few years ago I worked on an analysis of two popular reading programs, Distar and a progressive program that focused on higher-level critical thinking skills. In one of the first lessons of the progressive program, the children are introduced to the names of the letter *m* and *e*. In the same lesson they are then taught the sound made by each of the letters, how to write each of the letters, and that when the two are blended together they produce the word *me*.

As an experienced first-grade teacher, I am convinced that a child needs to be familiar with a significant number of these concepts to be able to assimilate so much new knowledge in one sitting. By contrast, Distar presents the same information in about forty lessons.

I would not argue for the pace of the Distar lessons; such a slow pace would only bore most kids—but what happened in the other lesson is that it merely provided an opportunity for those who already knew the content to exhibit that they knew it, or at most perhaps to build one new concept onto what was already known. This meant that the child who did not come to school already primed with what was to be presented would be labeled as needing "remedial" instruction from day one; indeed, this determination would be made before he or she was ever taught. In fact, Distar was "successful" because it actually *taught* new information to children who had not already acquired it at home. Although the more progressive system was ideal for some children, for others it was a disaster.

I do not advocate a simplistic "basic skills" approach for children outside of the culture of power. It would be (and

has been) tragic to operate as if these children were incapable of critical and higher-order thinking and reasoning. Rather, I suggest that schools must provide these children the content that other families from a different cultural orientation provide at home. This does not mean separating children according to family background, but instead, ensuring that each classroom incorporate strategies appropriate for all the children in its confines.

And I do advocate that it is the school's job to attempt to change the homes of poor and non-White children to match the homes of those in the culture of power. That may indeed be a form of cultural genocide. I have frequently heard schools call poor parents "uncaring" when parents respond to the school's urging, that they change their home life in order to facilitate their children's learning, by saying, "But that's the school's job." What the school personnel fail to understand is that if the parents were members of the culture of power and lived by its rules and codes, then they would transmit those codes to their children. In fact, they transmit another culture that children must learn at home in order to survive in their communities.

"Child-centered, whole language, and process approaches are needed in order to allow a democratic state of free, autonomous, empowered adults, and because research has shown that children learn best through these methods."

People of color are, in general, skeptical of research as a determiner of our fates. Academic research has, after all, found us genetically inferior, culturally deprived, and verbally deficient. But beyond that general caveat, and despite my or others' personal preferences, there is little research data supporting the major tenets of process approaches over other forms of literacy instruction, and virtually no evidence that such approaches are more efficacious for children of color (Siddle, 1986).

Although the problem is not necessarily inherent in the method, in some instances adherents of process approaches to writing create situations in which students ultimately find themselves held accountable for knowing a set of rules about which no one has ever directly informed them. Teachers do students no service to suggest, even implicitly, that "product" is not important. In this country, students will be judged on their product regardless of the process they utilized to achieve it. And that product, based as it is on the specific codes of a particular culture, is more readily produced when the directives of how to produce it are made explicit.

If such explicitness is not provided to students, what it feels like to people who are old enough to judge is that there are secrets being kept, that time is being wasted, that the teacher is abdicating his or her duty to teach. A doctoral student in my acquaintance was assigned to a writing class to hone his writing skills. The student was placed in the section led by a White professor who utilized a process approach, consisting primarily of having the students write essays and then assemble into groups to edit each others' papers. That procedure infuriated this particular student. He had many angry encounters with the teacher about what she was doing. In his words:

I didn't feel she was teaching us anything. She wanted us to correct each others' papers and we were there to learn from her. She didn't teach anything, absolutely nothing.

Maybe they're trying to learn what Black folks knew all the time. We understand how to improvise, how to express ourselves creatively. When I'm in a classroom, I'm not looking for that, I'm looking for structure, the more formal language.

Now my buddy was in [a] Black teacher's class. And that lady was very good. She went through and explained and defined each part of the structure. This [White] teacher didn't get along with that Black teacher. She said that she didn't agree with her methods. But *I* don't think that White teacher *had* any methods.

When I told this gentleman that what the teacher was doing was called a process method of teaching writing, his response was, "Well, at least now I know that she *thought* she was doing *something*. I thought she was just a fool who couldn't teach and didn't want to try."

This sense of being cheated can be so strong that the student may be completely turned off to the educational system. Amanda Branscombe, an accomplished White teacher, recently wrote a letter discussing her work with working-class Black and White students at a community college in Alabama. She had given these students my "Skills and Other Dilemmas" article (Delpit, 1986) to read and discuss, and wrote that her students really understood and identified with what I was saying. To quote her letter:

One young man said that he had dropped out of high school because he failed the exit exam. He noted that he had then passed the GED without a problem after three weeks of prep. He said that his high school English teacher claimed to use a process approach, but what she really did was hide behind fancy words to give herself permission to do nothing in the classroom.

The students I have spoken of seem to be saying that the teacher has denied them access to herself as the source of knowledge necessary to learn the forms they need to succeed. Again, I tentatively attribute the problem to teachers' resistance to exhibiting power in the classroom. Somehow, to exhibit one's personal power as expert source is viewed as disempowering one's students.

Two qualifiers are necessary, however. The teacher cannot be the only expert in the classroom. To deny students their own expert knowledge *is* to disempower them. Amanda Branscombe, when she was working with Black high school students classified as "slow learners," had the students analyze RAP songs to discover their underlying patterns. The students became the experts in explaining to the teacher the rules for creating a new RAP song. The teacher then used the patterns the students identified as a base to begin an explanation of the structure of grammar, and then of Shakespeare's plays. Both student and teacher are expert at what they know best.

The second qualifier is that merely adopting direct instruction is not the answer. Actual writing for real audiences and real purposes is a vital element in helping

students to understand that they have an important voice in their own learning processes. Siddle (1988) examines the results of various kinds of interventions in a primarily process-oriented writing class for Black students. Based on readers' blind assessments, she found that the intervention that produced the most positive changes in the students' writing was a "mini-lesson" consisting of direct instruction about some standard writing convention. But what produced the *second* highest number of positive changes was a subsequent student-centered conference with the teacher. (Peer conferencing in this group of Black students who were not members of the culture of power produced the least number of changes in students' writing. However, the classroom teacher maintained—and I concur—that such activities are necessary to introduce the elements of "real audience" into the task, along with more teacher-directed strategies.)

"It's really a shame but she (that Black teacher upstairs) seems to be so authoritarian, so focused on skills and so teacher directed. Those poor kids never seem to be allowed to really express their creativity. (And she even yells at them.)"

This statement directly concerns the display of power and authority in the classroom. One way to understand the difference in perspective between Black teachers and their progressive colleagues on this issue is to explore culturally influenced oral interactions.

In *Ways With Words*, Shirley Brice Heath (1983) quotes the verbal directives given by the middle-class "townspeople" teachers (p. 280):

- "Is this where the scissors belong?"
- "You want to do your best work today."

By contrast, many Black teachers are more likely to say:

- "Put those scissors on that shelf."
- "Put your name on the papers and make sure to get the right answer for each question."

Is one oral style more authoritarian than another?

Other researchers have identified differences in middle-class and working-class speech to children. Snow et al. (1976), for example, report that working-class mothers use more directives to their children than do middle- and upper-class parents. Middle-class parents are likely to give the directive to a child to take his bath as, "Isn't it time for your bath?" Even though the utterance is couched as a question, both child and adult understand it as a directive. The child may respond with "Aw Mom, can't I wait until . . . ," but whether or not negotiation is attempted, both conversant understand the intent of the utterance.

By contrast, a Black mother, in whose house I was recently a guest, said to her eight-year-old son, "Boy, get your rusty behind in that bathtub." Now I happen to know that this woman loves her son as much as any mother, but she would never have posed the directive to her son to take a bath in the form of a question. Were she to ask, "Would you like to take your bath now?" she would not have been issuing a directive but offering a true alternative. Consequently, as Heath suggests, "upon entering school the child from such a fam-

ily may not understand the indirect statement of the teacher as a direct command. Both White and Black working-class children in the communities Heath studied had difficulty interpreting these indirect requests for adherence to an unstated set of rules" (p. 280).

But those veiled commands are commands nonetheless, representing true power, and with true consequences for disobedience. If veiled commands are ignored, the child will be labeled a behavior problem and possibly officially classified as behavior disordered. In other words, the attempt by the teacher to reduce an exhibition of power by expressing herself in indirect terms may remove the very explicitness that the child needs to understand the rules of the new classroom culture.

A Black elementary school principal in Fairbanks, Alaska, reported to me that she has a lot of difficulty with Black children who are placed in some White teachers' classrooms. The teachers often send the children to the office for disobeying teacher directives. Their parents are frequently called in for conferences. The parents' response to the teacher is usually the same: "They do what I say; if you just *tell* them what to do, they'll do it. I tell them at home that they have to listen to what you say." And so, does not the power still exist? Its veiled nature only makes it more difficult for some children to respond appropriately, but that in no way mitigates its existence.

I don't mean to imply, however, that the only time the Black child disobeys the teacher is when he or she misunderstands the request for certain behavior. There are other factors that may produce such behavior. Black children expect an authority figure to act with authority. When the teacher instead acts as a "chum," the message sent is that this adult has no authority, and the children react accordingly. One reason this is so is that Black people often view issues of power and authority differently than people from mainstream middle-class backgrounds.[3] Many people of color expect authority to be earned by personal efforts and exhibited by personal characteristics. In other words, "the authoritative person gets to be a teacher because she is authoritative." Some members of middle-class cultures, by contrast, expect one to achieve authority by the acquisition of an authoritative role. That is, "the teacher is the authority because she is the teacher."

In the first instance, because authority is earned, the teacher must consistently prove the characteristics that give her authority. These characteristics may vary across cultures, but in the Black community they tend to cluster around several abilities. The authoritative teacher can control the class through exhibition of personal power; establishes meaningful interpersonal relationships that garner student respect; exhibits a strong belief that all students can learn; establishes a standard of achievement and "pushes" the students to achieve that standard; and holds the attention of the students by incorporating interactional features of Black communicative style in his or her teaching.

By contrast, the teacher whose authority is vested in the role has many more options of behavior at her disposal. For instance, she does not need to express any sense of personal power because her authority does not come from anything she herself does or says. Hence, the power she actually holds may be veiled in such questions/commands as "Would you like to sit down now?" If the children in her class understand authority as she does, it is mutually agreed upon that they are to obey her no matter how indirect, soft-spoken, or unassuming she may be. Her indirectness and soft-spokenness may indeed be, as I suggested earlier, an attempt to reduce the implication of overt power in order to establish a more egalitarian and non-authoritarian classroom atmosphere.

If the children operate under another notion of authority, however, then there is trouble. The Black child may perceive the middle-class teacher as weak, ineffectual, and incapable of taking on the role of being the teacher; therefore, there is no need to follow her directives. In her dissertation, Michelle Foster (1987) quotes one young Black man describing such a teacher:

> She is boring, bo::ring.[4] She could do something creative. Instead she just stands there. She can't control the class, doesn't know how to control the class. She asked me what she was doing wrong. I told her she just stands there like she's meditating. I told her she could be meditating for all I know. She says that we're supposed to know what to do. I told her I don't know nothin' unless she tells me. She just can't control the class. I hope we don't have her next semester. (pp. 67–68)

But of course the teacher may not view the problem as residing in herself but in the student, and the child may once again become the behavior-disordered Black boy in special education.

What characteristics do Black students attribute to the good teacher? Again, Foster's dissertation provides a quotation that supports my experience with Black students. A young Black man is discussing a former teacher with a group of friends:

> We had fun in her class, but she was mean. I can remember she used to say, "Tell me what's in the story, Wayne." She pushed, she used to get on me and push me to know. She made us learn. We had to get in the books. There was this tall guy and he tried to take her on, but she was in charge of that class and she didn't let anyone run her. I still have this book we used in her class. It's a bunch of stories in it. I just read one on Coca-Cola again the other day (p. 68).

To clarify, this student was *proud* of the teacher's "meanness," an attribute he seemed to describe as the ability to run the class and pushing and expecting students to learn. Now, does the liberal perspective of the negatively authoritarian Black teacher really hold up? I suggest that although all "explicit" Black teachers are not also good teachers, there are different attitudes in different cultural groups about which characteristics make for a good teacher. Thus, it is impossible to create a model for the good teacher without taking issues of culture and community context into account.

And now to the final comment I present for examination:

"Children have the right to their own language, their own culture. We must fight cultural hegemony and fight the system by insisting that children be allowed to express themselves in their own language style. It is not they, the children, who must change, but the schools. To push children to do anything else is repressive and reactionary."

A statement such as this originally inspired me to write the "Skills and Other Dilemmas" article. It was first written as a letter to a colleague in response to a situation that had developed in our department. I was teaching a senior-level teacher education course. Students were asked to prepare a written autobiographical document for the class that would also be shared with their placement school prior to their student teaching.

One student, a talented young Native American woman, submitted a paper in which the ideas were lost because of technical problems—from spelling to sentence structure to paragraph structure. Removing her name, I duplicated the paper for a discussion with some faculty members. I had hoped to initiate a discussion about what we could do to ensure that our students did not reach the senior level without getting assistance in technical writing skills when they needed them.

I was amazed at the response. Some faculty implied that the student should never have been allowed into the teacher education program. Others, some of the more progressive minded, suggested that I was attempting to function as gatekeeper by raising the issue and had internalized repressive and disempowering forces of the power elite to suggest that something was wrong with a Native American student just because she had another style of writing. With few exceptions, I found myself alone in arguing against both camps.

No, this student should not have been denied entry to the program. To deny her entry under the notion of upholding standards is to blame the victim for the crime. We cannot justifiably enlist exclusionary standards when the reason this student lacked the skills demanded was poor teaching at best and institutionalized racism at worst.

However, to bring this student into the program and pass her through without attending to obvious deficits in the codes needed for her to function effectively as a teacher is equally criminal—for though we may assuage our own consciences for not participating in victim blaming, she will surely be accused and convicted as soon as she leaves the university. As Native Alaskans were quick to tell me, and as I understood through my own experience in the Black community, not only would she not be hired as a teacher, but those who did not hire her would make the (false) assumption that the university was putting out only incompetent Natives and that they should stop looking seriously at any Native applicants. A White applicant who exhibits problems is an individual with problems. A person of color who exhibits problems immediately becomes a representative of her cultural group.

No, either stance is criminal. The answer is to *accept* students but also to take responsibility to *teach* them. I decided to talk to the student and found out she had recognized that she needed some assistance in the technical aspects of writing soon after she entered the university as a freshman. She had gone to various members of the education faculty and received the same two kinds of responses I met with four years later: faculty members told her either that she should not even attempt to be a teacher, or that it didn't matter and that she shouldn't worry about such trivial issues. In her desperation, she had found a helpful professor in the English Department, but he left the university when she was in her sophomore year.

We sat down together, worked out a plan for attending to specific areas of writing competence, and set up regular meetings. I stressed to her the need to use her own learning process as insight into how best to teach her future students those "skills" that her own schooling had failed to teach her. I gave her some explicit rules to follow in some areas; for others, we devised various kinds of journals that, along with readings about the structure of the language, allowed her to find her own insights into how the language worked. All that happened two years ago, and the young woman is now successfully teaching. What the experience led me to understand is that pretending that gatekeeping points don't exist is to ensure that many students will not pass through them.

Now you may have inferred that I believe that because there is a culture of power, everyone should learn the codes to participate in it, and that is how the world should be. Actually, nothing could be further from the truth. I believe in a diversity of style, and I believe the world will be diminished if cultural diversity is ever obliterated. Further, I believe strongly, as do my liberal colleagues, that each cultural group should have the right to maintain its own language style. When I speak, therefore, of the culture of power, I don't speak of how I wish things to be but of how they are.

I further believe that to act as if power does not exist is to ensure that the power status quo remains the same. To imply to children or adults (but of course the adults won't believe you anyway) that it doesn't matter how you talk or how you write is to ensure their ultimate failure. I prefer to be honest with my students. Tell them that their language and cultural style is unique and wonderful but that there is a political power game that is also being played, and if they want to be in on that game there are certain games that they too must play.

But don't think that I let the onus of change rest entirely with the students. I am also involved in political work both inside and outside of the educational system, and that political work demands that I place myself to influence as many gatekeeping points as possible. And it is there that I agitate for change—pushing gatekeepers to open their doors to a variety of styles and codes. What I'm saying, however, is that I do not believe that political change toward diversity can be effected from the bottom up, as do some of my colleagues. They seem to believe that if we accept and encourage diversity within classrooms of children, then diversity will automatically be accepted at gatekeeping points.

I believe that will never happen. What will happen is that the students who reach the gatekeeping points—like Amanda Branscombe's student who dropped out of high school because he failed his exit exam—will understand that they have been lied to and will react accordingly. No, I am certain that if we are truly to effect societal change, we cannot do so from the bottom up, but we must push and agitate from the top down. And in the meantime, we must take the responsibility to *teach*, to provide for students who do not already possess them, the additional codes of power.[5]

But I also do not believe that we should teach students to passively adopt an alternate code. They must be encouraged to understand the value of the code they already possess as well as to understand the power realities in this country. Otherwise they will be unable to work to change these realities. And how does one do that?

Martha Demientieff, a masterly Native Alaskan teacher of Athabaskan Indian students, tells me that her students, who live in a small, isolated, rural village of less than two hundred people, are not aware that there are different codes of English. She takes their writing and analyzes it for features of what has been referred to by Alaskan linguists as "Village English," and then covers half a bulletin board with words or phrases from the students' writing, which she labels "Our Heritage Language." On the other half of the bulletin board she puts the equivalent statements in "standard English," which she labels "Formal English."

She and the students spend a long time on the "Heritage English" section, savoring the words, discussing the nuances. She tells the students, "That's the way we say things. Doesn't it feel good? Isn't it the absolute best way of getting that idea across?" Then she turns to the other side of the board. She tells the students that there are people, not like those in their village, who judge others by the way they talk or write.

We listen to the way people talk, not to judge them, but to tell what part of the river they come from. These other people are not like that. They think everybody needs to talk like them. Unlike us, they have a hard time hearing what people say if they don't talk exactly like them. Their way of talking and writing is called "Formal English."

We have to feel a little sorry for them because they have only one way to talk. We're going to learn two ways to say things. Isn't that better? One way will be our Heritage way. The other will be Formal English. Then, when we go to get jobs, we'll be able to talk like those people who only know and can only really listen to one way. Maybe after we get the jobs we can help them to learn how it feels to have another language, like ours, that feels so good. We'll talk like them when we have to, but we'll always know our way is best.

Martha then does all sorts of activities with the notions of Formal and Heritage or informal English. She tells the students,

In the village, everyone speaks informally most of the time unless there's a potlatch or something. You don't think about it, you don't worry about following any rules—it's sort of like how you eat food at a picnic—nobody pays attention to whether you use your fingers or a fork, and it feels *so* good. Now, Formal English is more like a formal dinner. There are rules to follow about where the knife and fork belong, about where people sit, about how you eat. That can be really nice, too, because it's nice to dress up sometimes.

The students then prepare a formal dinner in the class, for which they dress up and set a big table with fancy tablecloths, china, and silverware. They speak only Formal English at this meal. Then they prepare a picnic where only informal English is allowed.

She also contrasts the "wordy" academic way of saying things with the metaphoric style of Athabaskan. The students discuss how book language always uses more words, but in Heritage language,

the shorter way of saying something is always better. Students then write papers in the academic way, discussing with Martha and with each other whether they believe they've said enough to sound like a book. Next, they take those papers and try to reduce the meaning to a few sentences. Finally, students further reduce the message to a "saying" brief enough to go on the front of a T-shirt, and the sayings are put on little paper T-shirts that the student cut out and hang throughout the room. Sometimes the students reduce other authors' wordy texts to their essential meanings as well.

The following transcript provides another example. It is from a conversation between a Black teacher and a Southern Black high school student named Joey, who is a speaker of Black English. The teacher believes it very important to discuss openly and honestly the issues of language diversity and power. She has begun the discussion by giving the student a children's book written in Black English to read.

Teacher: What do you think about that book?
Joey: I think it's nice.
Teacher: Why?
Joey: I don't know. It just told about a Black family, that's all.
Teacher: Was it difficult to read?
Joey: No.
Teacher: Was the text different from what you've seen in other books?
Joey: Yeah. The writing was.
Teacher: How?
Joey: It use more of a southern-like accent in this book.
Teacher: Uhm-hmm. Do you think that's good or bad?

Joey: Well, uh, I don't think it's good for people down this a way, cause that's the way they grow up talking anyway. They ought to get the right way to talk.

Teacher: Oh. So you think it's wrong to talk like that?

Joey: Well . . . [*Laughs*]

Teacher: Hard question, huh?

Joey: Uhm-hmm, that's a hard question. But I think they shouldn't make books like that.

Teacher: Why?

Joey: Because they not using the right way to talk and in school they take off for that and li'l chirren grow up talking like that and reading like that so they might think that's right and all the time they getting bad grades in school, talking like that and writing like that.

Teacher: Do you think they should be getting bad grades for talking like that?

Joey: [*Pauses, answers very slowly*] No . . . No.

Teacher: So you don't think that it matters whether you talk one way or another?

Joey: No, not long as you understood.

Teacher: Uhm-hmm. Well, that's a hard question for me to answer, too. It's, ah, that's a question that's come up in a lot of schools now as to whether they should correct children who speak the way we speak all the time. Cause when we're talking to each other we talk like that even though we might not talk like that when we get into other situations, and who's to say whether it's—

Joey: [*Interrupting*] Right or wrong.

Teacher: Yeah.

Joey: Maybe they ought to come up with another kind of . . . maybe Black English or something. A course in Black English. Maybe Black folks would be good in that cause people talk, I mean Black

people talk like that, so . . . but I guess there's a right way and wrong way to talk, you know, not regarding what race. I don't know.

Teacher: But who decided what's right or wrong?

Joey: Well that's true . . . I guess White people did.

[*Laughter. End of tape.*]

Notice how throughout the conversation Joey's consciousness has been raised by thinking about codes of language. This teacher further advocates having students interview various personnel officers in actual workplaces about their attitudes toward divergent styles in oral and written language. Students begin to understand how arbitrary language standards are, but also how politically charged they are. They compare various pieces written in different styles, discuss the impact of different styles on the message by making translations and back translations across styles, and discuss the history, apparent purpose, and contextual appropriateness of each of the technical writing rules presented by their teacher. *And* they practice writing different forms to different audiences based on rules appropriate for each audience. Such a program not only "teaches" standard linguistic forms, but also explores aspects of power as exhibited through linguistic forms.

Tony Burgess, in a study of secondary writing in England by Britton, Burgess, Martin, McLeod, and Rosen (1975/1977), suggests that we should not teach "iron conventions . . . imposed without rationale or grounding in communicative intent," but "critical and ultimately cultural awarenesses" (p. 54). Courtney Cazden (1987) calls for a two-pronged approach:

1. Continuous opportunities for writers to participate in some authentic bit of the unending conversation . . . thereby becoming part of a vital community of talkers and writers in a particular domain, and

2. Periodic, temporary focus on conventions of form, taught as cultural conventions expected in a particular community. (p. 20)

Just so that there is no confusion about what Cazden means by a focus on conventions of form, or about what I mean by "skills," let me stress that neither of us is speaking of page after page of "skill sheets" creating compound words or identifying nouns and adverbs, but rather about helping students gain a useful knowledge of the conventions of print while engaging in real and useful communicative activities. Kay Rowe Grubis, a junior high school teacher in a multicultural school, makes lists of certain technical rules for her eighth graders' review and then gives them papers from a third grade to "correct." The students not only have to correct other students' work, but also tell them why they have changed or questioned aspects of the writing.

A village teacher, Howard Cloud, teaches his high school students the conventions of formal letter writing and the formulation of careful questions in the context of issues surrounding the amendment of the Alaska Land Claims Settlement Act. Native Alaskan leaders hold differing views on this issue, critical to the future of local sovereignty and land rights. The students compose letters to leaders who reside in different areas of the state seeking their perspectives, set up audioconference calls for interview/debate ses-sions, and, finally, develop a videotape to present the different views.

To summarize, I suggest that students must be *taught* the codes needed to participate fully in the mainstream of American life, not by being forced to attend to hollow, inane, decontextualized subskills, but rather within the context of meaningful communicative endeavors; that they must be allowed the resource of the teacher's expert knowledge, while being helped to acknowledge their own "expertness" as well; and that even while students are assisted in learning the culture of power, they must also be helped to learn about the arbitrariness of those codes and about the power relationships they represent.

I am also suggesting that appropriate education for poor children and children of color can only be devised in consultation with adults who share their culture. Black parents, teachers of color, and members of poor communities must be allowed to participate fully in the discussion of what kind of instruction is in their children's best interest. Good liberal intentions are not enough. In an insightful study entitled "Racism without Racists: Institutional Racism in Urban Schools," Massey, Scott, and Dornbusch (1975) found that under the pressures of teaching, and with all intentions of "being nice," teachers had essentially stopped attempting to teach Black children. In their words: "We have shown that oppression can arise out of warmth, friendliness, and concern. Paternalism and a lack of challenging standards are creating a distorted system of evaluation in the schools" (p. 10). Educators must open themselves to, and allow themselves to be affected by, these alternative voices.

In conclusion, I am proposing a resolution for the skills/process debate. In short, the debate is fallacious; the dichotomy is false. The issue is really an illusion created initially not by teachers but by academics whose world view demands the creation of categorical divisions—not for the purpose of better teaching, but for the goal of easier analysis. As I have been reminded by many teachers since the publication of my article, those who are most skillful at educating Black and poor children do not allow themselves to be placed in "skills" or "process" boxes. They understand the need for both approaches, the need to help students to establish their own voices, but to coach those voices to produce notes that will be heard clearly in the larger society.

The dilemma is not really in the debate over instructional methodology, but rather in communicating across cultures and in addressing the more fundamental issue of power, of whose voice gets to be heard in determining what is best for poor children and children of color. Will Black teachers and parents continue to be silenced by the very forces that claim to "give voice" to our children? Such an outcome would be tragic, for both groups truly have something to say to one another. As a result of careful listening to alternative points of view, I have myself come to a viable synthesis of perspectives. But both sides do need to be able to listen, and I contend that it is those with the most power, those in the majority, who must take the greater responsibility for initiating the process.

To do so takes a very special kind of listening, listening that requires not only open eyes and ears, but open hearts and minds. We do not really see through our eyes or hear through our ears, but through our beliefs. To put our beliefs on hold is to cease to exist as ourselves for a moment—

and that is not easy. It is painful as well, because it means turning yourself inside out, giving up your own sense of who you are, and being willing to see yourself in the unflattering light of another's angry gaze. It is not easy, but it is the only way to learn what it might feel like to be someone else and the only way to start the dialogue.

There are several guidelines. We must keep the perspective that people are experts on their own lives. There are certainly aspects of the outside world of which they may not be aware, but they can be the only authentic chroniclers of their own experience. We must not be too quick to deny their interpretations, or accuse them of "false consciousness." We must believe that people are rational beings, and therefore always act rationally. We may not understand their rationales, but that in no way militates against the existence of these rationales or reduces our responsibility to attempt to apprehend them. And finally, we must learn to be vulnerable enough to allow our world to turn upside down in order to allow the realities of others to edge themselves into our consciousness. In other words, we must become ethnographers in the true sense.

Teachers are in an ideal position to play this role, to attempt to get all of the issues on the table in order to initiate true dialogue. This can only be done, however, by seeking out those whose perspectives may differ most, by learning to give their words complete attention, by understanding one's own power, even if that power stems merely from being in the majority, by being unafraid to raise questions about discrimination and voicelessness with people of color, and to listen, no, to *hear* what they say. I suggest that the results of such interactions may be the most powerful and empowering coalescence yet seen in the educational realm—for *all* teachers and for *all* the students they teach.

REFERENCES

Apple, M. W. (1979). *Ideology and curriculum*. Boston: Routledge & Kegan Paul.

Bernstein, B. (1975). Class and pedagogies: Visible and invisible. In B. Bernstein, *Class, codes, and control* (Vol. 3). Boston: Routledge & Kegan Paul.

Britton, J., Burgess, T., Martin, N., McLeod, A., & Rosen, H. (1975/1977). *The development of writing abilities*. London: Macmillan Education for the Schools Council, and Urbana, IL: National Council of Teachers of English.

Cazden, C. (1987, January). *The myth of autonomous text*. Paper presented at the Third International Conference on Thinking, Hawaii.

Delpit, L. D. (1986). Skills and other dilemmas of a progressive Black educator. *Harvard Educational Review, 56* (4), 379–385.

Foster, M. (1987). *"It's cookin' now": An ethnographic study of the teaching style of a successful Black teacher in an urban community college*. Unpublished doctoral dissertation, Harvard University.

Gwaltney, J. (1980). *Drylongso*. New York: Vintage Books.

Heath, S. B. (1983). *Ways with words*. Cambridge: Cambridge University Press.

Massey, G. C., Scott, M. V., & Dornbusch, S. M. (1975). Racism without racists: Institutional racism in urban schools. *The Black Scholar, 7* (3), 2–11.

Siddle, E. V. (1986). *A critical assessment of the natural process approach to teaching writing*. Unpublished qualifying paper, Harvard University.

Siddle, E. V. (1988). *The effect of intervention strategies on the revisions ninth graders make in a narrative essay*. Unpublished doctoral dissertation, Harvard University.

Snow, C. E., Arlman-Rup, A., Hassing, Y., Josbe, J., Joosten, J., & Vorster, J. (1976). Mother's speech in three social classes. *Journal of Psycholinguistic Research, 5,* 1–20.

NOTES

1. Such a discussion, limited as it is by space constraints, must treat the intersection of class and race somewhat simplistically. For the sake of clarity, however, let me define a few terms: "Black" is used herein to refer to those who share some or all aspects of "core black culture" (Gwaltney, 1980, p. xxiii), that is, the mainstream of Black America—neither those who have entered the ranks of the bourgeoisie nor those who are participants in the disenfranchised underworld. "Middle-class" is used broadly to refer to the predominantly White American "mainstream." There are, of course, non-White people who also fit into this category; at issue is their cultural identification, not necessarily the color of their skin. (I must add that there are other non-White people, as well as poor White people, who have indicated to me that their perspectives are similar to those attributed herein to Black people.)

2. *Multicultural Britain: "Crosstalk,"* National Centre of Industrial Language Training, Commission for Racial Equality, London, England, John Twitchin, Producer.

3. I would like to thank Michelle Foster, who is presently planning a more in-depth treatment of the subject, for her astute clarification of the ideas.

4. *Editor's note:* The colons [::] refer to elongated vowels.

5. Bernstein (1975) makes a similar point when he proposes that different educational frames cannot be successfully institutionalized in the lower levels of education until there are fundamental changes at the post-secondary levels.

Part II Additional Resources

Discussion Questions

Students should carefully read each question and support each response with examples and specific references to the readings that are being considered.

1. Choose a subject and/or grade level and go to your state's department of public instruction web site. Examine the state standards for that subject and/or grade level, and consider the strengths and weakness of having standards to guide the work of teachers. What are the struggles that teachers face when trying to implement these standards in diverse classrooms? Do standards prevent teachers from being creative and innovative in their classrooms? Why or why not?

2. Discuss the controversy regarding a national curriculum. What are the pros and cons of a national curriculum? How would a national curriculum differ from a state-mandated curriculum? How do local needs intersect with national- and/or state-level concerns and issues?

3. The curriculum typically reflects the values and beliefs of the dominant group in society. Is it possible to create a school environment that addresses the discrimination and bias that may be present in the curriculum? Defend your answer.

4. Many education questions are also sociopolitical questions. Discussion of these kinds of issues appears daily in local and national newspapers and magazines. Keep a file for a several weeks and pay attention to the relationship between various sociopolitical issues and perceptions about schools and learning. Attempt to summarize and discuss the relevance of this information to our thinking about twenty-first-century schools and the curriculum.

5. Identify and discuss educational practices that you believe may limit educational opportunities. Do these practices have anything to do with the characteristics of particular students, for example, race, social class, gender, sexual orientation, or disability? Is it possible to modify these practices in ways that would facilitate equality of educational opportunity? Why or why not?

Guide to Further Reading

Adler, M. 1984. *The Paideia Program: An Educational Syllabus.* New York: Macmillan.

Apple, Michael. 1990. *Ideology and Curriculum.* New York: Routledge.

Howard, Gary. 2006. *We Can't Teach What We Don't Know: White Teachers, Multiracial Schools*, 2nd ed. New York: Teachers College Press.

Lieberman, Ann, and Lynne Miller. 1999. *Teachers—Transforming Their World and Their Work.* New York: Teachers College Press.

Tyler, Ralph W. 1949. *Basic Principles of Curriculum and Instruction.* Chicago: University of Chicago Press.

Related Resources

http://mingo.info-science.uiowa.edu/~stevens/critped
  Critical Pedagogy on the Web
http://www.edgateway.net/er101/curr.html
  Curriculum in Education Reform
http://www.education-world.com/standards
  Education World: The Educator's Best Friend,
  State and National Standards
http://www.freireproject.org
  The Freire Project: The Paulo and Nita Freire International Project
  for Critical Pedagogy
http://www.nameorg.org
  National Association for Multicultural Education:
  Advocates for Educational Equity and Social Justice
http://www.tcrecord.org
  Teacher's College Record: The Voice of Scholarship in Education
http://www.ed.gov
  U.S. Department of Education

Part III

WHAT ARE THE ROLES AND RESPONSIBILITIES OF TEACHER LEADERS?

INTRODUCTION

Teacher leadership cannot exist in a vacuum; expanded roles and responsibilities for teachers inevitably have an impact on all aspects of teachers' lives. A "new" focus on teacher leadership is one of the most exciting trends in education today. In the position of teacher leader, teachers are given opportunities to assume roles of responsibility and leadership in schools and classrooms. Furthermore, a focus on leadership capacity building places teachers at the center of attempts to increase student achievement (and school effectiveness) through broad-based participation in the leadership of schools by a variety of stakeholders.

This movement is critical for teachers to gain the power that is needed to move the profession toward higher professional status; however, I also believe that we can't change the profession without laying the foundation for change within the bureaucratic and institutional structure of the schools. We must create school communities that are receptive and supportive of changing roles for teachers. Teachers *and* administrators *and* students *and* parents must understand the gain that will occur when teachers are provided with an arena for the knowledge and expertise that they bring to schools. Consideration of these ideas is essential if teachers are to work in schools in which they will have the opportunity to embrace opportunities to assume new roles and responsibilities. Thus, the readings in Chapters 11–15 by Henry A. Giroux, Phillip C. Schlechty, Linda Lambert, Marilyn Cochran-Smith, and Joe L. Kincheloe provide a foundation for thinking about the roles and responsibilities of teacher leaders. Each of these writers views the recognition of teachers as intellectuals and capable leaders as essential to school reform. Simultaneously, there is also acknowledgment that teacher leadership is multifaceted and that there is no "one size fits all" recipe for teacher leadership. Guiding the work of each teacher are the unique values, beliefs, and interests that will also shape the roles and responsibilities that he or she will assume as a teacher leader. These readings provide a variety of perspectives on the work of teacher leaders.

Henry A. Giroux

CHAPTER

11

Teachers as Transformative Intellectuals

The call for educational reform has gained the status of a recurring national event, much like the annual Boston Marathon. There have been more than 30 national reports since the beginning of the 20th century, and more than 300 task forces have been developed by the various states to discover how public schools can improve educational quality in the United States.[1] But unlike many past educational reform movements, the present call for educational change presents both a threat and challenge to public school teachers that appears unprecedented in our nation's history. The threat comes in the form of a series of educational reforms that display little confidence in the ability of public school teachers to provide intellectual and moral leadership for our nation's youth. For instance, many of the recommendations that have emerged in the current debate either ignore the role teachers play in preparing learners to be active and critical citizens, or they suggest reforms that ignore the intelligence, judgment, and experience that teachers might offer in such a debate. Where teachers do enter the debate, they are the object of educational reforms that reduce them to the status of high-level technicians carrying out dictates and objectives decided by "experts" far removed

from the everyday realities of classroom life.[2] The message appears to be that teachers do not count when it comes to critically examining the nature and process of educational reform.

The political and ideological climate does not look favorable for teachers at the moment. But it does offer them the challenge to join in a public debate with their critics as well as the opportunity to engage in a much-needed self-critique regarding the nature and purpose of teacher preparation, in-service teacher programs, and the dominant forms of classroom teaching. Similarly, the debate provides teachers with the opportunity to organize collectively so as to struggle to improve the conditions under which they work and to demonstrate to the public the central role that teachers must play in any viable attempt to reform the public schools.

In order for teachers and others to engage in such a debate, it is necessary that a theoretical perspective be developed that redefines the nature of the educational crisis while simultaneously providing the basis for an alternative view of teacher training and work. In short, recognizing that the current crisis in education largely has to do with the developing trend toward the disempowerment of teachers at all levels of education is a necessary theoretical precondition in order for teachers to organize effectively and establish a collective voice in the current debate. Moreover, such a recognition will have to come to grips not only with a growing loss of power among teachers around the basic conditions of their work, but also with a changing public perception of their role as reflective practitioners.

I want to make a small theoretical contribution to this debate and the challenge it calls forth by examining two major problems that need to be addressed in the interest of improving the quality of teacher work, which includes all the clerical tasks and extra assignments as well as classroom instruction. First, I think it is imperative to examine the ideological and material forces that have contributed to what I want to call the proletarianization of teacher work; that is, the tendency to reduce teachers to the status of specialized technicians within the school bureaucracy, whose function then becomes one of managing and implementing curricula programs rather than developing or critically appropriating curricula to fit specific pedagogical concerns. Second, there is a need to defend schools as institutions essential to maintaining and developing a critical democracy and also to defending teachers as transformative intellectuals who combine scholarly reflection and practice in the service of educating students to be thoughtful, active citizens. In the remainder of this essay, I will develop these points and conclude by examining their implications for providing an alternative view of teacher work.

Toward a Devaluing and Deskilling of Teacher Work

One of the major threats facing prospective and existing teachers with the public

schools is the increasing development of instrumental ideologies that emphasize a technocratic approach to both teacher preparation and classroom pedagogy. At the core of the current emphasis on instrumental and pragmatic factors in school life are a number of important pedagogical assumptions. These include: a call for the separation of conception from execution; the standardization of school knowledge in the interest of managing and controlling it; and the devaluation of critical, intellectual work on the part of teachers and students for the primary of practical considerations.[3]

This type of instrumental rationality finds one of its strongest expressions historically in the training of prospective teachers. That teacher training programs in the United States have long been dominated by a behavioristic orientation and emphasis on mastering subject areas and methods of teaching is well documented.[4] The implications of this approach, made clear by Zeichner, are worth repeating:

Underlying this orientation to teacher education is a metaphor of "production," a view of teaching as an "applied science" and a view of the teacher as primarily an "executor" of the laws and principles of effective teaching. Prospective teachers may or may not proceed through the curriculum at their own pace and may participate in varied or standardized learning activities, but that which they are to master is limited in scope (e.g., to a body of professional content knowledge and teaching skills) and is fully determined in advance by others often on the basis of research on teacher effectiveness. The prospective teacher is viewed primarily as a passive recipient of this professional knowledge and plays little part in determining the substance and direction of his or her preparation program.[5]

The problems with this approach are evident in John Dewey's argument that teacher training programs that emphasize only technical expertise do a disservice both to the nature of teaching and to their students.[6] Instead of learning to reflect upon the principles that structure classroom life and practice, prospective teachers are taught methodologies that appear to deny the very need for critical thinking. The point is that teacher education programs often lose sight of the need to educate students to examine the underlying nature of school problems. Further, these programs need to substitute for the language of management and efficiency a critical analysis of the less obvious conditions that structure the ideological and material practices of schooling.

Instead of learning to raise questions about the principles underlying different classroom methods, research techniques, and theories of education, students are often preoccupied with learning the "how to," with "what works," or with mastering the best way to teach a *given* body of knowledge. For example, the mandatory field-practice seminars often consist of students sharing with each other the techniques they have used in managing and controlling classroom discipline, organizing a day's activities and learning how to work within specific timetables. Examining one such program, Jesse Goodman raises some important questions about the incapacitating silences it embodies. He writes:

There was no questioning of feelings, assumptions, or definitions in this discus-

sion. For example, the "need" for external rewards and punishments to "make kids learn" was taken for granted; the educational and ethical implications were not addressed. There was no display of concern for stimulating or nurturing a child's intrinsic desire to learn. Definitions of *good kids* as *"quiet kids," workbook work* as "reading," *on task time* as "learning," and *getting through the material on time* as "the goal of teaching"—all went unchallenged. Feelings of pressure and possible guilt about not keeping to time schedules also went unexplored. The real concern in this discussion was that everyone "shared."[7]

Technocratic and instrumental rationalities are also at work within the teaching field itself, and they play an increasing role in reducing teacher autonomy with respect to the development and planning of curricula and the judging and implementation of instruction. This is most evident in the proliferation of what has been called "teacher-proof" curriculum packages.[8] The underlying rationale in many of these packages reserves for teachers the role of simply carrying out predetermined content and instructional procedures. The method and aim of such packages is to legitimate what I call management pedagogies. That is, knowledge is broken down into discrete parts, standardized for easier management and consumption, and measured through predefined forms of assessment. Curricula approaches of this sort are management pedagogies because the central questions regarding learning are reduced to the problem of management, i.e., "how to allocate resources (teachers, students and materials) to produce the maximum number of certified . . . students within a designated time."[9] The underlying theoretical assumption that guides this type of pedagogy is that the behavior of teachers needs to be controlled and made consistent and predictable across different schools and student populations.

What is clear in this approach is that it organizes school life around curricular, instructional, and evaluation experts who do the thinking while teachers are reduced to doing the implementing. The effect is not only to deskill teachers, to remove them from the processes of deliberation and reflection, but also to routinize the nature of learning and classroom pedagogy. Needless to say, the principles underlying management pedagogies are at odds with the premise that teachers should be actively involved in producing curricula materials suited to the cultural and social contexts in which they teach. More specifically, the narrowing of curricula choices to a back-to-basics format, and the introduction of lock-step, time-on-task pedagogies operate from the theoretically erroneous assumption that all students can learn from the same materials, classroom instructional techniques, and modes of evaluation. The notion that students come from different histories and embody different experiences, linguistic practices, cultures, and talents is strategically ignored within the logic and accountability of management pedagogy theory.

Teachers as Transformative Intellectuals

In what follows, I want to argue that one way to rethink and restructure the nature of teacher work is to view teachers as transformative intellectuals. The category of intellectual is helpful in a number of ways. First, it provides a theoretical basis for examining teacher work as a form of intellectual labor, as opposed to defining it

in purely instrumental or technical terms. Second, it clarifies the kinds of ideological and practical conditions necessary for teachers to function as intellectuals. Third, it helps to make clear the role teachers play in producing and legitimating various political, economic and social interests through the pedagogies they endorse and utilize.

By viewing teachers as intellectuals, we can illuminate the important idea that all human activity involves some form of thinking. In other words, no activity, regardless of how routinized it might become, can be abstracted from the functioning of the mind in some capacity. This is a crucial issue because by arguing that the use of the mind is a general part of all human activity we dignify the human capacity for integrating thinking and practice, and in doing so highlight the core of what it means to view teachers as reflective practitioners. Within this discourse, teachers can be seen not merely as "performers professionally equipped to realize effectively any goals that may be set for them. Rather [they should] be viewed as free men and women with a special dedication to the values of the intellect and the enhancement of the critical powers of the young."[10]

Viewing teachers as intellectuals also provides a strong theoretical critique of technocratic and instrumental ideologies underlying an educational theory that separates the conceptualization, planning, and design of curricula from the processes of implementation and execution. It is important to stress that teachers must take active responsibility for raising various questions about what they teach, how they are to teach, and what the larger goals are for which they are striving. This means that they must take a responsible role in shaping the purposes and conditions of schooling. Such a task is impossible within a division of labor in which teachers have little influence over the ideological and economic conditions of their work. This point has a normative and political dimension that seems especially relevant for teachers. If we believe that the role of teaching cannot be reduced to merely training in the practical skills, but involves, instead, the education of a class of intellectuals vital to the development of a free society, then the category of intellectual becomes a way of linking the purpose of teacher education, public schooling, and inservice training to the very principles necessary for developing a democratic order and society.

I have argued that by viewing teachers as intellectuals those persons concerned with education can begin to rethink and reform the traditions and conditions that have prevented schools and teachers from assuming their full potential as active, reflective scholars and practitioners. It is imperative that I qualify this point and extend it further. I believe that it is important not only to view teachers as intellectuals, but also to contextualize in political and normative terms the concrete social functions that teachers perform. In this way, we can be more specific about the different relations that teachers have both to their work and to the dominant society.

A fundamental starting point for interrogating the social function of teachers as intellectuals is to view schools as economic, cultural, and social sites that are inextricably tied to the issues of power and control. This means that schools do more than pass on in an objective fashion a common set of values and knowledge. On the contrary, schools are places that represent forms of knowledge, language practices, social relations, and values that are representative of a particular selection and exclusion from the wider culture. As such, schools serve to introduce and legitimate *particular* forms of social life. Rather than being objective institutions removed from the dynamics of politics and power, schools actually are contested spheres that embody and express a struggle over what forms of authority, types of knowledge, forms of moral regulation, and versions of the past and future should be legitimated and transmitted to students. This struggle is most visible in the demands, for example, of right-wing religious groups currently trying to institute school prayer, remove certain books from the school library, and include certain forms of religious teachings in the science curricula. Of course, different demands are made by feminists, ecologists, minorities, and other interest groups who believe that the schools should teach women's studies, courses on the environment, or black history. In short, schools are not neutral sites, and teachers cannot assume the posture of being neutral either.

In the broadest sense, teachers as intellectuals have to be seen in terms of the ideological and political interests that structure the nature of the discourse, classroom social relations, and values that they legitimate in their teaching. With this perspective in mind, I want to conclude that teachers should become transformative intellectuals if they are to subscribe to a view of pedagogy that believes in educating students to be active, critical citizens.

Central to the category of transformative intellectual is the necessity of making the pedagogical more political and the political more pedagogical. Making the pedagogical more political means inserting schooling directly into the political sphere by arguing that schooling represents both a struggle to define meaning and a struggle over power relations. Within this perspective, critical reflection and action become part of a fundamental social project to help students develop a deep and abiding faith in the struggle to overcome economic, political, and social injustices, and to further humanize themselves as part of this struggle. In this case, knowledge and power are inextricably linked to the presupposition that to choose life, to recognize the necessity of improving its democratic and qualitative character for all people, is to understand the preconditions necessary to struggle for it.

Making the political more pedagogical means utilizing forms of pedagogy that embody political interests that are emancipatory in nature; that is, using forms of pedagogy that treat students as critical agents; make knowledge problematic; utilize critical and affirming dialogue; and make the case for struggling for a qualitatively better world for all people. In part, this suggests that transformative intellectuals take seriously the need to give students an active voice in their learning experiences. It also means developing a critical vernacular that is attentive to problems experienced at the level of everyday life, particularly as they are related to pedagogical experiences connected to classroom practice. As such, the pedagogical starting point for such intellectuals is not the isolated student but individuals and groups in their various cultural, class, racial, historical, and gender settings, along with the particularity of their diverse problems, hopes, and dreams.

Transformative intellectuals need to develop a discourse that unites the language of critique with the language of possibility, so that social educators recognize that they can make changes. In doing so, they must speak out against economic, political, and social injustices both within and outside of schools. At the same time, they must work to create the conditions that give students the opportunity to become citizens who have the knowledge and courage to struggle in order to make despair unconvincing and hope practical. As difficult as this tack may seem to social educators, it is a struggle worth waging. To do otherwise is to deny social educators the opportunity to assume the role of transformative intellectuals.

NOTES

1. K. Patricia Cross, "The Rising Tide of School Reform Reports," *Phi Delta Kappan*, 66:3 (November 1984), p. 167.

2. For a more detailed critique of the reforms, see my book with Stanley Aronowitz, *Education Under Siege* (South Hadley, MA: Bergin and Garvey Publishers, 1985); also see the incisive comments on the impositional nature of the various reports in Charles A. Tesconi, Jr., "Additive Reforms and the Retreat from Purpose," *Educational Studies* 15:1 (Spring 1984), pp. 1–11; Terrence E. Deal, "Searching for the Wizard: The Quest for Excellence in Education," *Issues in Education* 2:1 (Summer 1984), pp. 56–67; Svi Shapiro, "Choosing Our Educational Legacy: Disempowerment or Emancipation?" *Issues in Education* 2:1 (Summer 1984), pp. 11–22.

3. For an exceptional commentary on the need to educate teachers to be intellectuals, see John Dewey, "The Relation of Theory to Practice," in John Dewey, *The Middle Words, 1899–1924*, edited by Jo Ann Boydston (Carbondale, IL: Southern Illinois University Press, 1977) [originally published in 1904]. See also Israel Scheffler, "University Scholarship and the Education of Teachers," *Teachers College Record* 70:1 (1968), pp. 1–12; Henry

A. Giroux, *Ideology, Culture, and the Process of Schooling* (Philadelphia: Temple University Press, 1981).

4. See for instance, Herbert Kliebard, "The Question of Teacher Education," in D. McCarty (ed.), *New Perspectives on Teacher Education* (San Francisco: Jossey-Bass, 1973).

5. Kenneth M. Zeichner, "Alternative Paradigms on Teacher Education," *Journal of Teacher Education* 34:3 (May–June 1983), p. 4.

6. Dewey, op. cit.

7. Jesse Goodman, "Reflection and Teacher Education: A Case Study and Theoretical Analysis," *Interchange* 15:3 (1984), p. 15.

8. Michael Apple, *Education and Power* (Boston: Routledge & Kegan Paul, 1982).

9. Patrick Shannon, "Mastery Learning in Reading and the Control of Teachers and Students," *Language Arts* 61:5 (September 1984), p. 488.

10. Scheffler, op. cit., p. 11.

Phillip C. Schlechty

CHAPTER 12

On the Frontier of School Reform with Trailblazers, Pioneers, and Settlers

Improvement focuses on doing the same things better with the intent of changing and enhancing the performance of individuals within existing systems. Restructuring is aimed at changing systems so that new types of performances will be possible and encouraged and new or different outcomes can be produced.

Educational leaders and those in charge of training and development activities in schools have had much more experience in trying to improve things than in trying to restructure. As a result, the training and support which is provided to encourage and facilitate restructuring is often inappropriate.

Distinctions between improvement and restructuring are significant and have implications for those who lead restructuring efforts and for those who provide training and support to participants in the restructuring process. Unfortunately, too few educational leaders and staff developers seem to appreciate the significance of the distinction. In this article, I share some of the lessons I have learned about providing training and support to those who are trying to restructure schools.

Differences That Make a Difference

Staff development which is aimed at improvement is typically based on prior experience and research. This is seldom the case with staff development aimed at encouraging or supporting restructuring. Restructuring creates new conditions which neither the staff developer nor the participants have experienced. Restructuring, therefore, always requires one to be willing to act beyond the data and without benefit of guidance from empirical research. Creating new systems, which is what restructuring is about, calls for faith, logic, wisdom, and intuition, at least to the degree that it calls for disciplining action with facts.

Most staff developers have been taught to place experience and research at the center of their agenda. They are often not prepared to proceed in areas where faith and a new vision, more than research and prior experience, must serve as a guide to action. Yet, this is what they must do if staff development is to be relevant for the restructuring effort.

Four Key Questions

Four key questions must be answered if the process of restructuring is to move forward effectively. These questions suggest four different types of "lessons" that must be taught by leaders and need to be learned by all if the restructuring process is to be properly directed. The content and structure differs for each of the four lessons.

1. What is the new circumstance or system that we are trying to create? This question asks that a vision, direction, or intention be clearly articulated. It must be articulated in a way that the person asking the question understands the answer and in a way that is appealing and compels action. This requires a *concept development* lesson.

Those who are best at concept development often seem to rely heavily on Socratic dialogue, focused discussion, and pointed questions, combined with the use of metaphors and counterexamples intended to distinguish the concept of concern from other notions with which it might be confused. (For example, I began this discussion with a distinction between improvement and restructuring, and now I am using that distinction as an example of another concept—the concept of a concept development lesson.)

2. Can it be done? This question is a request for real-life, hands-on experience or testimony from those who have had such experience. This requires a *demonstration* lesson.

Demonstration lessons require models and exemplars which are real or contrived, empirically demonstrable, or theoretically described. Those who ask the question "Can it be done?" seek assurance that what they are being called on to do is possible and that, if they commit effort to the task, it is likely that they can do what the concept or vision calls them to do.

Modeling and illustrating are techniques associated with demonstration lessons. Where real life situations do not yet exist, simulating actions based on theoretically derived models are often used.

3. Should we do it? This question calls for the analysis of values, beliefs, commitments, context, studies of the past, and anticipation of the future. This requires a *values clarification* lesson.

Value clarification lessons, like concept development lessons, rely heavily on dialogue, discussion, and logical analysis. Such lessons require detailed attention to the values which participants bring to the discussion, the values which the proposed change promises to enhance or serve, and the values which the change is likely to threaten. For example, the value of security is most likely to be threatened by any radical change. Thus, those who promote restructuring must be carefully attuned to the significance various actors give to security, for it is in protecting this value that some of the greatest resistance to change can occur.

4. How do we do it? The last question is a request for assistance in developing the skills and habits required to do the job. This requires a *skill development* lesson.

Skill development lessons, like demonstration lessons, usually rely heavily on modeling and simulation. But skill development lessons are more likely to be active and involve opportunities to practice, coaching, experimental efforts, and corrective feedback. Demonstration lessons are intended to be persuasive, to show that things can be done. Skill development lessons are intended to develop understandings, skills, attitudes, and habits of mind that permit one to do with confidence and ease that which is at first exceedingly difficult, awkward, and, perhaps, even threatening and frightening.

Five Types of Roles

There are five types of roles that become activated in the restructuring process. Each of these role types requires support from staff developers and other school leaders. Some of these roles are more prominent at some stages of restructuring than at others. Further, those who play these roles have vastly different training and support needs related to the lessons for the four key questions previously posed. It is, therefore, critical that staff developers understand who they are addressing at distinct stages in the process, for the needs of different actors will be different from time to time.

1. Trailblazers. Paradigm-breaking journeys are not for the timid, and one should not expect everyone to volunteer to undertake such a journey. Those who take the first steps in restructuring are trailblazers, for they are willing to go—in terms understood by *Star Trek* fans—without maps to places where no person has gone before them, without the benefit of empirically based models, and with little to guide them except belief in themselves, a desire for novelty, the freedom to try, and a vision that motivates and guides them.

The most important requirement for trailblazers is a clear guiding vision. Trailblazers want to know that there is someplace to go that is different; they are motivated by novelty and excited by risks. Once trailblazers have found a vision in which they believe, all they want and need is encouragement and support for that pursuit. Most of all, they want to be recognized for their unique brand of courage, and they want to be celebrated, recognized, praised, and honored—at least most of them do. Staff developers and school leaders must, therefore, find ways to celebrate the trailblazers among them.

Trailblazers are not egomaniacs, but they are often monomaniacs with a mission. They know where they are going, even if they are not quite sure how they are going to get there or what obstacles they will confront on the way. When they confront obstacles, they are likely to view them in highly personal terms, for the vision of the trailblazer is a personal vision, and anything that stands in the way of the pursuit of that vision is a personal threat. Thus, trailblazers need much personal and personalized support.

Staff developers and other school leaders should be sensitive to the fact that trailblazers need to be constantly reinforced that the vision they are pursuing is worth the quest and that others, especially powerful others, see that what they are about is important. It is important enough, in fact, that the trailblazers should receive unusual latitude and unconventional forms of support (e.g., noncategorical funding, flexible schedules, and special access to the human and physical resources of the system).

Equally important, trailblazers need to be constantly reminded that it is a community quest they are on, not a private venture. Because the vision the trailblazer pursues is a private vision, it is up to other leaders in the system to link it to a larger shared vision. For example, Lewis and

Clark were motivated by the excitement of exploring new frontiers, and Thomas Jefferson linked their quest to a vision of America that spread from shore to shore. Teachers who become enthusiastic about one curriculum innovation or another also often need leaders to help them see the linkage between their private adventures and the common good.

Since trailblazers lead the way into a new world, whether that world is a physical frontier or the creation of a new way of doing business, they do not have access to a body of research and experience to guide them. What then do trailblazers use as guides?

First, they use experiences they and others have gained in circumstances that are analogous to those they are about to confront. For instance, it is not coincidental, I think, that the language of space travel is laced with language which refers to early explorers who took voyages on the ocean, just as spaceships now take voyages to the moon. And names of spacecraft often refer to explorers in other times.

Trailblazers need the opportunity to read about and visit with trailblazers from other fields (e.g., business, the military, medical services, and so on). They also need time to discuss and assimilate what they learn from these encounters. It is from such experiences that relevant analogies are discovered and come to be understood. I have found that leaders whose language is rich with metaphors and who argue by analogy are particularly good at inspiring and directing trailblazers.

A second source of guidance for trailblazers is the experiences of other trailblazers who are moving in roughly the same direction and over the same terrain. The rendezvous was one of the ways early

trailblazers on America's frontier got information from other trailblazers. Today, we refer to such rendezvous as "networks" where people who are moving in a common direction develop mechanisms to ensure regular interactions. Providing opportunities for such networking is one of the primary contributions staff developers can make to the continuing growth and development of trailblazers.

It is important to understand that networks and rendezvous do much more than provide opportunities for the sharing of information. Such networking provides opportunities for self-affirmation and more than a bit of bragging and storytelling. Networking turns lonely ordeals into shared ordeals. Lonely ordeals debilitate; shared ordeals inspire and motivate.

Alert staff developers and trainers who listen to these stories can learn much that will be of value to pioneers (the second type of role). Furthermore, if staff developers watch carefully, they can get some insight concerning which of the trailblazers have the temperament and the style to be guides as well as trailblazers. After all, the pioneers and settlers who come later will need guides as well.

Leaders and staff developers need to create conditions so that what is learned by the trailblazers is not lost. Trailblazers tell stories. Unfortunately, they seldom turn the stories into lessons for others. It is up to the staff developers, therefore, to turn the stories of trailblazers into lessons that can serve as sources of guidance for those who would follow. This is much like the mapmakers of the early fourteenth century who translated the tales and reports of the early explorers into crude maps which in turn were rendered more accurate and refined with further exploration.

Trailblazers need public acknowledgment for their efforts. They need the opportunity to tell others about places they have been and about what they have done. Such storytelling not only serves as a source of information for others, but it also serves as a continuing source of motivation for the trailblazers. Furthermore, telling stories also gives one the opportunity to listen to the stories of others and thus to learn from others as well, especially from other trailblazers.

Staff development budgets that do not make provision for sending trailblazers to conferences where they can brag a bit are not adequate budgets. And staff developers are not doing their job if they do not seek every opportunity to put local trailblazers out in front, including helping them write proposals that will get support for their work and that will permit the trailblazers to share their work at conferences.

2. Pioneers. Closely following the trailblazers are the pioneers. Like the trailblazers, pioneers are an adventurous and hardy lot and are willing to take considerable risks.

Pioneers have many of the same needs as trailblazers. Like trailblazers, concept development lessons (i.e., the development of a vision that links a personal quest to a larger agenda) are the most important lessons they must learn. But the pioneers also have considerable need for assurance that the trip upon which they will embark is worthwhile. More than the trailblazers, pioneers need demonstrations to provide assurances that the journey can, in fact, be made. But pioneers understand that there are really few people who can teach them "how to do it" since only the trailblazers have gone to the frontiers which they are set to explore.

Thus, pioneers need concept development lessons, value clarification lessons, and demonstration lessons. They do not need skill development lessons, and staff developers would be ill-advised to try to provide them.

What does all of this mean in practical terms? First, it means that when staff developers approach pioneers, or are attempting to recruit them, their best allies are those who write about trailblazers (e.g., Fiske, 1991, *Smart Kids, Smart Schools*; Sizer, 1992, *Horace's School*). Such writings do not provide research data, but they do provide anecdotal accounts, reports, and stories. Such stories can inspire prospective pioneers to take the journey. These stories contain some possible lessons regarding what one must know and be able to do to survive the rigors of the journey.

Trailblazers can help motivate pioneers, especially if they are colorful and good storytellers. Davy Crockett did much more to inspire pioneers than he did as a true trailblazer. Indeed, one could argue that Davy Crockett was a staff developer rather than a trailblazer since he often took the stories of others and embellished them a bit, making himself the hero. He used the stories to inspire others to act. Thus, an effective trailblazer may provide needed assurances to encourage pioneers.

I have found that trailblazer teachers and administrators are invaluable sources of inspiration and direction for pioneers, and even for settlers (which are discussed next). But a caution is in order. Too often staff development specialists, in their quest for authenticity, remove trailblazers from their natural habitat on the "frontier" and move them into the central office, or worse to the university campus, in the hope that the stories they will tell will reach a wider audience.

Sometimes this works, but more frequently it is a bad experience for both the trailblazer and for those with whom they work. The teamwork that it takes to "build community," which is what pioneers must do, requires a different style than does the early explorations of new frontiers.

Monomaniacs with a mission can quickly come to appear to others to be egomaniacs whose only mission is to advance themselves. Trailblazers are needed, but they are not easy to live with in the more sedate environments of committee meetings and seminar rooms.

3. Settlers. After the trailblazers and pioneers come the settlers. Settlers need to know what is expected of them and where they are going to go. They need much more detail and more carefully drawn maps than do those who have gone before them. Settlers are bold, but they are not adventurers. They need to be persuaded that the venture upon which they are being asked to embark is worthwhile. Thus, staff developers must provide value clarification lessons that help the settlers understand why the change is needed.

Settlers also want assurance that the task can be accomplished and that they are not set on a fool's mission. Thus, settlers have considerable need for demonstration lessons (e.g., site visits where pioneering work is already under way, conversations with pioneers and trailblazers, testimonials from those who have tried, books and articles that provide rich descriptions of what can be expected, and so on).

Much more than either pioneers or trailblazers, settlers want skill development lessons. They want to be sure they know how to do what will be required of them. Indeed, many potential settlers will not move until they have assurance that the requisite knowledge and support are available to them.

School leaders and staff developers who support them must, therefore, give attention to providing systematic training which is supported by coaching, opportunities for feedback and critique, and, above all, protection from negative consequences for failed efforts.

Perhaps the most critical thing to remember about settlers is that they need strong, constant, and reassuring leadership that inspires them to keep going when they are tempted to turn back. Change of the sort envisioned in an honest restructuring agenda is likely to create uncertainty, doubt, and confusion. The new practices called for are likely to be frightening and demanding, and the results may be no better—at least in the short run—than doing things the "old way."

Fullan's (Fullan with Stiegelbauer, 1991) notion of the "implementation dip" comes to mind here; he assumes that a natural part of the change process is short-term deterioration in performance capacity. This occurs because the new way is unfamiliar and requires learning and practice. While the old way of doing things may not be as good as the new way, at least it is familiar and people know how to do it.

Without persistent leadership by people who have been there and without encouragement from others who are going there (settlers traveled in wagon trains and were not isolated travelers), it is unlikely that settlers will stay the course. Thus, it is critical that staff developers and leaders understand the terrain well enough that they can point out progress when settlers become discouraged.

Benchmarks of progress and feedback regarding progress toward these benchmarks are essential. To this extent, assessment and constant monitoring, coupled with public appraisals of progress toward restructuring goals (as opposed to the goals of restructuring), are important. For example, a restructuring goal might be to have teachers and building administrators become more systematic in the use of data regarding student performance as a means of evaluating the merit and worth of decisions the administrators and teachers make. But, informed student performance would be a goal of restructuring.

Helping settlers learn how to use evidence of progress is a necessary antecedent to answering the question "Does restructuring improve student performance?" Until restructuring has occurred, this question cannot be answered. Therefore, the first-order assessment question is "What evidence is there that we (those who are engaged in restructuring) are, in fact, doing our business differently today than we did business yesterday, and why do we think the new way of doing business will improve our results?" Settlers need the answers to such questions to keep them going and also to provide assurance that where they are going is worth the effort.

4. Stay-at-Homes. There are two conditions that motivate change. First, present conditions are so intolerable or dangerous to one's interests and values that the only alternative is to do something. The Separatists who left England to settle in America were driven by such motives. Second, there is a new and compelling vision—one that so inspires hope of a new day, a better life, or a fuller realization of existing values—that causes risks to seem tolerable when measured against rewards. The Utopian settlements on the American frontier are examples of such vision-driven change.

However, as the Declaration of Independence states so eloquently, fundamental changes are not lightly undertaken, and people will tolerate a great deal rather than give up what is known. Furthermore, intolerable or threatening conditions, which can serve as an initial impetus for change, cannot sustain change. In fact, negative forces are seldom adequate to motivate fundamental change and are almost never adequate to sustain it.

The Mayflower Separatists—who had among them some trailblazers, some pioneers, and a substantial number of reluctant and frightened settlers—may have left England because of oppression, but it did not take their leaders long to recognize that a new and compelling vision would be required to sustain them. This new vision, expressed first in the Mayflower Compact and reinforced by visions based in religious symbols, was as important to the settlement of the new world as were the oppressive conditions that started the movement to that world.

Stay-at-homes are not bad people. Indeed, in the long view of history, they are inconsequential people, for no one remembers the stay-at-homes after the change has occurred. How many Tory supporters of King George are American students expected to recall?

At the time a change is being contemplated, however, stay-at-homes receive a great deal—I think too much—of attention. This is because most leaders need approval from those they want to lead, which is usually everybody in their sphere of influence. Thus, those who do not respond enthusiastically—or at least compliantly—with the desires of change leaders are often viewed as problems.

Effective leaders seem to understand that early in the change process it is probably not wise to spend too much energy trying to convince the stay-at-homes that they, too, need to move to the frontier. These leaders accept the fact that some will never come along, and those who do change will only do so after the pioneers and settlers have done their work very well. Of course, some will only come to the new land for a visit.

One of the greatest dangers when dealing with stay-at-homes in the restructuring process is that the strategies used to entice them to change may backfire and thus may convert these relatively benign actors into supporters of the saboteurs discussed below. Saboteurs' favorite strategy is to sow distrust through rumors and disinformation, and they will destroy even the best organized wagon train if they can gain enough followers. The most likely source of recruits for the saboteurs are the stay-at-homes and the more timid settles who feel pressured to move before they have the assurances they need and before they have identified leaders they trust.

I have found the best strategy to use with stay-at-homes, at least in the early stages of the restructuring process, is benign neglect coupled with as much generosity of spirit as is possible. One must remember that those who do not particularly want to change are not necessarily opposed to others changing if they choose to do so. Many stay-at-homes stay at home because they truly love the place. As John

Dewey has observed, "Familiarity breeds contempt, but it also breeds something like affection. We get used to the chains we wear, and through custom we finally embrace what at first wore a hideous mien."

And there are, of course, those who are simply too timid to go to unfamiliar places. Such persons are not likely to be encouraged to move by direct assaults on what they currently value or by threats to what little security they now enjoy.

5. Saboteurs. Saboteurs are actively committed to stopping change. Not only do they refuse to take the trip, but they do not want others to go either.

Many of those who take on the role of saboteurs do so because they receive benefits from this role which are not provided if they were to support change. I have also been struck by the fact that some of the most effective saboteurs have many qualities and needs which are similar to trailblazers.

Saboteurs are often lone rangers. They are not afraid of taking risks. The difference is that while the trailblazers will go to places that others fear to go, saboteurs are likely to remain in place when others are beginning to feel afraid to stay. Loneliness does not have the same meaning to them as it has to the settlers, and isolation often inspires the saboteur to even greater effort. To be persecuted, it seems, is to be appreciated, and, in a perverse way, to be isolated or excluded is to be honored.

Saboteurs can cause trouble, no matter where they are. But I have found that the best place to have them is on the inside where they can be watched rather than on the outside where they can cause trouble without its being detected until the effects are felt. Certainly, saboteurs can be disruptive, and some will not cooperate even enough to communicate their concerns.

If, however, change leaders continue to reach out to saboteurs and critics and try hard to hear what they are saying, sometimes there is much to be learned. It might be learned that some saboteurs were once trailblazers and pioneers who at some time in the past had the misfortune to follow leaders who did not give them the support they needed and abandoned them at the first sign of trouble.

A Concluding Comment

Creating commitment to change is not the same thing as overcoming resistance to change. To create commitment, one must understand motives. Trailblazers are motivated by novelty, excitement, and sometimes by the possibility of fame and glory. Pioneers sometimes begin their journey because of intolerable conditions, but they will stay the course only if they become convinced that the new world is really better.

Settlers need to know, almost for certain, that the world they are being asked to move to is better than the one they are leaving and that the way to get there is known. And, most of all, they need to know that they are not taking the trip alone.

Stay-at-homes will only move when all—or nearly all—of their friends and neighbors have deserted them or when they muster the courage to "come for a visit" and find that they prefer it.

Some saboteurs will never come along, and if they do, they will make the trip as difficult as possible. Saboteurs, however, are people who in some prior movement to another frontier behaved as trailblazers and pioneers, but were betrayed by their leaders. As a result, they became cynical about the prospects of change. Most of all, they want to be assured that those who are sounding the latest call to move to a new frontier will stay the course rather than turn around and go back.

Whether the present demand that our schools be restructured will be responded to positively remains to be seen. But of one thing I am confident: Without leaders who will stay the course and without staff developers who understand what draws men and women to the frontier and what these people need to keep on going, all our efforts to reform schools will fail.

REFERENCES

Fiske, E. (1991). *Smart schools, smart kids.* New York: Simon & Schuster.

Fullan, M. with Stiegelbauer, S. (1991). *The new meaning of educational change* (2nd ed.). New York: Teachers College Press.

Sizer, T. (1992). *Horace's school.* New York: Houghton Mifflin.

Linda Lambert

How to Build Leadership Capacity

Several years ago, I had a conversation with a man considered to be an outstanding principal. I asked, "What happened at the school where you were last principal? Are the reforms still in place?"

"That has been a real disappointment for me," he lamented. "You see, conditions and programs at the school soon returned to the way they were before I got there."

Over the intervening years, I've held several similar conversations. "Returning to normal" is the usual story. It is not surprising that schools do not maintain their improvements. New principals and superintendents often come to a school or district with their own agendas. Or they respond to a charge from the superintendent or board to "turn this school around," "get us back on an even keel," "undo what the incumbent did," or "move us into the future." Such sweeping mandates ignore the history, passions, and qualities of an incumbent staff, choosing instead to import reforms that are both generic and popular.

Less often do new administrators hear, "This is a good school that is getting better. Structures are in place to continue the work. Teacher and parent leadership is strong. We need a principal who can co-lead this school in the direction it is already going."

Most schools cannot yet be described in these glowing terms—they have yet to reach the capacity to sustain improvements on their own. Whether the school is advanced or a beginner in reform, what it does not need is to start over. Each time a school is forced to start over, its staff and community lose some of their personal energy and commitment.

If we are to sustain our improvements and build on the strength and commitment of educators, we need to address the capacity of schools to lead themselves. We need to rethink both leadership and capacity building.

Rethinking Leadership

When we think about leadership, we are accustomed to picturing people in roles with formal authority, such as principals, vice-principals, directors, or superintendents. But we can view *leadership* as a verb, rather than a noun, by considering the processes, activities, and relationships in which people engage, rather than as the individual in a specific role.

Let's define *leadership* as the reciprocal learning processes that enable participants in a community to construct meaning toward a shared purpose. This definition is known as "constructivist leadership" (Lambert et al. 1995). Leadership in this context means learning among adults in a community that shares goals and visions. Leadership as learning involves these assumptions:

- *Leadership is not a trait; leadership and leader are not the same.* A leader is anyone who engages in the work of leadership.
- *Leadership is about learning that leads to constructive change.*
- *Everyone has the potential and right to work as a leader.*
- *Leading is a shared endeavor,* the foundation for the democratization of schools.
- *Leadership requires the redistribution of power and authority.* To encourage shared learning, superintendents and principals need to explicitly release authority, and staff need to learn how to enhance personal and collective power and informal authority (Lambert in press).

If leadership is everyone's work, it does not require extraordinary charismatic qualities and uses of authority. If teachers perceive the work as a natural outgrowth of their roles as professional educator, they are less likely to opt out, insisting, "I'm not a leader." Teachers have long attended to the learning of students and themselves; leadership asks that they attend to the learning of their colleagues as well. The skills and dispositions of effective leaders include convening and facilitating dialogue, posing inquiry questions, coaching one another, mentoring a new teacher, and inviting others to become engaged with a new idea. This kind of leadership is naturally engaging and leads to broad-based participation.

Framing Leadership

Building capacity in schools includes developing a new understanding of *leadership capacity*—broad-based, skillful participation in the work of leadership. Leadership capacity can be seen as a complex, interactive framework, with four types of schools and school communities. A caveat is needed here. Frameworks, matrixes, or scales somewhat artificially categorize human behavior. Individuals—and schools—have unique characteristics.

- *School 1: Low Participation, Low Skillfulness.* Here, the principal often exercises autocratic leadership. Parents and community members tend to have limited participation. Information flows from the principal to the staff (often originating with the district office), yet is rarely a two-way process. This information often includes rules that govern behavior and practices. Staff often attribute problems to children, family, and the community rather than instructional practices. Collegial work is rare. Staff members—and parents and students—often express resistance by being absent from meetings or school. Teachers rarely initiate new practices, although they may comply with mandates temporarily. Although students may initially show some improvement in achievement when staff members implement mandates, they rarely sustain these gains.

- *School 2: High Participation, Low Skillfulness.* The principal's style is often unpredictable or predictably disengaged. He or she may make unilateral or surprising decisions, often depending on who is asking the question or requesting the action. Information tends to be sparse. Faculty meetings are often composed of "sit and git" sound bites without dialogue. No schoolwide focus on teaching and learning is evident; thus, both excellent and poor classrooms may exist. Many staff work with individual grants, projects, or partnerships that are disconnected from each other. Staff members may not concern themselves with nonachieving classrooms; referrals, attendance, and achievement differ across the school. Roles and responsibilities are unclear. Overall student achievement is often static, with higher achievement for students in particular socioeconomic and gender groups. The range of achievement from high to low is as broad as the range of quality.

- *School 3: High Skillfulness, Low Participation.* This school tends to make concentrated efforts to provide for skillful leadership work for a few teachers and the principal, perhaps as a leadership team. These people may have had opportunities for training through a reform-oriented center, network, or coalition. There may be growing polarization among the staff, who may strengthen their resistance as they see favored colleagues leading a change effort. Teams have learned to accumulate and use data to make school decisions, although the data may raise objections or denials from other staff members. Staff caught in the middle (neither thoroughly involved nor disengaged) are often thoughtful allies but relatively unskilled in resolving conflicts. These teachers are unclear what role to play as tension increases between the "haves" and "have nots." Pockets of

strong innovation and excellent classrooms tend to exist, but focus on student learning is not schoolwide. Student achievement may show only slight gains.

- *School 4: High Skillfulness, High Participation.* This school tends to have high leadership capacity and broad-based participation. The principal and other leaders make concentrated efforts to include all staff in leadership development and decision making. Staff members have gathered evidence from existing sources or through action research and tend to base decisions on these data. The school has a clear purpose, focusing on student and adult learning. Information loops keep staff, parents, and students informed, with opportunities to discuss, clarify, and refine ideas as they are being formed—long before a final decision is made. Roles and responsibilities are shared and blended, but clear. The school community tends to assume collective responsibility for the work of leadership and learning. Staff members consider themselves to be part of a professional community in which innovation is the norm. Student achievement is high across the student population and within each subgroup as well.

A School on Its Way

New Century High School (a pseudonym) is moving up on the scale of leadership capacity. The school joined a reform network and developed an effective leadership team. The team led in many improvements, including the use of student data to inform decisions. Yet the harder they worked, the more they seemed to alienate some teachers.

"There are some missing pieces here," reflected one team member. "We may have to slow down to speed up." The team then focused on involving more staff, students, and parents in the leadership process. Team members began to converse with staff—to really listen and to engage everyone in schoolwide inquiry.

Six months later, New Century's professional culture is changing. Faculty meetings are devoted to dialogue about teaching and learning. The majority of the staff are involved in the reform effort. People feel that their voices are heard. There are fewer student referrals and failing grades. School-wide improvement now seems possible.

Encouraging Leadership

Schools and districts need to create the following conditions if they are to build leadership capacity:

1. Hire personnel with the proven capacity to do leadership work, and develop veteran staff to become skillful leaders.
2. Get to know one another; build trusting relationships.
3. Assess staff and school capacity for leadership. Do you have a shared purpose? Do you work collaboratively? Is there a schoolwide focus on student achievement and adult learning?[1]
4. Develop a culture of inquiry that includes a continuous cycle of reflecting, questioning, gathering evidence, and planning for improvement.
5. Organize for leadership work by establishing inclusive governance structures and collaborative inquiry processes.
6. Implement plans for building leadership capacity—and anticipate role changes and professional development needs.
7. Develop district policies and practices that support leadership capacity building. These practices include district-school relationships built on high engagement but few rules and regulations, as well as shared decision making and site-based school management. Districts should model the processes of a learning organization.

Sustaining the momentum of our work in schools is essential if we are going to stay the course with program improvements long enough to know whether they succeed. We must institutionalize the processes of collaboration and collective responsibility. Building leadership capacity is not the next innovation, but the foundation for sustaining school and district improvements.

REFERENCES

Lambert, L., D. Walker, D. Zimmerman, J. Cooper, M. Lambert, M. Gardner, and P. J. Ford-Slack. (1995). *The Constructivist Leader*. New York: Teachers College Press, Columbia University.

Lambert, L. (In Press). *Building Leadership Capacity in Schools*. Alexandria, Va.: ASCD.

NOTE

1. For surveys and rubrics on leadership capacity, as well as extended case studies, see *Building Leadership Capacity in Schools* (Lambert in press).

Marilyn Cochran-Smith

Against the Grain

In an essay condemning political and social indifference in prewar Italy, Antonio Gramsci (1916/1977) forcefully argued that action was everyone's responsibility and that each individual, no matter how apparently powerless, was accountable for the role he played or failed to play in the larger political struggle. If we accept Gramsci's notion that indifference is often a mainspring of history, and if we substitute the word "teacher" for Gramsci's "man," we have a powerful statement about the accountability of individual educators for their efforts to reform U.S. schools:

> Every [teacher] must be asked to account for the manner in which he [*sic*] has fulfilled the task that life has set him and continues to set him day by day; he must be asked to account for what he has done, but especially for what he has not done. . . . It is time that events should be seen to be the intelligent work of [teachers] and not the products of chance or fatality. (p. 18)

I use Gramsci's clarion call for social accountability to reassert that teachers are decision makers and collaborators who must reclaim their roles in the shaping of practice by taking a stand as both educators and activists (Aronowitz & Giroux,

1985). I am not suggesting that teachers alone have the power or the responsibility to reform education by "teaching better," or that teaching can be understood in isolation from the cultures of schools and communities or the historical and political contexts of school and society. In fact, I argue in favor of inquiry communities where inexperienced and experienced teachers learn together and in favor of teachers joining others in larger social movements. However, teaching is fundamentally a political activity in which every teacher plays a part by design or by default (Ginsburg, 1988; Willis, 1978).

Prospective teachers need to know from the start that they are part of a larger struggle and that they have a responsibility to reform, not just replicate, standard school practices. I argue in this chapter, however, that working to reform teaching, or what can be thought of as *teaching against the grain*, is not a generic skill that can be learned at the university and then "applied" at the school. Teaching against the grain is embedded in the culture and history of teaching at individual schools and in the biographies of teachers and their collaborative efforts to alter curricula, raise questions about common practices, and resist inappropriate decisions. These relationships must be explored in schools in the company of experienced teachers who are themselves engaged in complex, situation-specific, and sometimes losing struggles to work against the grain.

In this chapter I briefly analyze two approaches to preparing preservice teachers to teach against the grain, *critical dissonance* and *collaborative resonance*. I argue that programs built on the collaborative resonance of university and school have the potential to provide student teachers with unusually rich learning opportunities. Next, I take readers into four urban schools in the Philadelphia area where student teachers work and talk with experienced teachers who, in a variety of ways, are working against the grain. Drawing on data from these four schools, I present an analysis of teachers' and student teachers' discourse during weekly school-site meetings, revealing the groups' efforts to pose questions, struggle with uncertainty, and build evidence for their reasoning. These conversations provide vivid descriptive evidence that regular school-site talk among experienced reforming teachers and inexperienced student teachers is an indispensable resource in the education of reform-minded teachers.

Critical Dissonance and Collaborative Resonance

Student-teaching programs specifically designed to foster critical inquiry and prepare prospective teachers to be reformers are part of a small minority of preservice programs across the country (Goodlad, 1990b; Grant & Secada, 1990; Zeichner, Liston, Mahlios, & Gomez, 1988). Within this small group of programs, however, two variations in theory and practice can be distinguished as the products of two different sets of assumptions about the

power and knowledge relationships of the school and the university.

Critical Dissonance

One approach to preparing student teachers to work against the grain is to create *critical dissonance*, or *incongruity based on a critical perspective*, between what students learn about teaching and schooling at the university and what they already know and continue to learn about them in the schools. In student-teaching programs based on critical dissonance, the "problem of student teaching" is generally identified as its tendency to bolster utilitarian perspectives on teaching and ultimately to perpetuate existing practices (Beyer, 1984; Feiman-Nemser, 1983; Goodman, 1986a; Tabachnick & Zeichner, 1984; Zeichner, Tabachnick, & Densmore, 1987). The goal of these programs is to interrupt the potentially conservative influences of student teachers' school-based experiences and instead call into question the implications of standard school policy and practice. The strategies of programs intended to foster critical dissonance include methods courses that emphasize alternative teaching strategies, field experiences coupled with ethnographic studies of schooling, critical theory-based curriculum study, seminars and journals in which students reflect critically on their teaching experiences, and action research projects in schools (Beyer, 1984; Gitlin & Teitelbaum, 1983; Goodman, 1986a; Zeichner & Liston, 1987).

Programs that aim to create critical dissonance are intended to be transformative, to help students broaden their visions and interrogate their own perspectives. Unfortunately, these programs have had limited success. Critical reflection is difficult, especially because cooperating teachers who do not have reflective skills themselves often co-opt the effort (Calderhead, 1989). Further, the intentions of programs are not necessarily implemented, particularly in the interactions of students and their supervisors (Zeichner et al., 1988) and in methods and fieldwork courses (Beyer, 1984; Goodman, 1986a, 1986b). Over time, such programs encourage some critique, but actually alter students' outlooks very little (Feiman-Nemser, 1990; Zeichner & Liston, 1987).

Many educators would agree that preparing more liberally educated teachers to think and work critically is an essential goal for teacher preparation. However, there are several troubling messages implicit in programs that aim to provoke critical dissonance between university and school: the way to link theory and practice is to bring a critical perspective to bear upon the institutional and instructional arrangements of schooling; people outside of schools are the agents who have developed these critical perspectives and thus can liberalize and reform the people and activities inside; the "wisdom" of teachers' practice is a conservative point of view that has to be gotten around, exposed, or changed; and the language and conceptual frameworks for describing and critiquing teachers' work lives need not be familiar to teachers or articulated in their own voices or words. This means that the radical critique prompted by critical dissonance, which argues in the abstract for the knowledge, voices, and power of teachers themselves, may in reality "set up" school-based teachers to be exposed and criticized in university-led courses,

and may inadvertently convey the message that teachers' lived experiences are unenlightened and even unimportant.

Collaborative Resonance

A second approach to preparing student teachers to work against the grain is to create *collaborative resonance*, or *intensification based on the joint work of learning communities*, by linking what student teachers learn from their university-based experiences with what they learn from their school-based experiences. In programs based on resonance, the "problem of student teaching" is its failure to provide student teachers with not only the analytical skills needed to critique standard procedures, but also the resources needed to function as reforming teachers throughout their teaching careers. The goal is to prolong and intensify the influences of university *and* school experiences, both of which are viewed as potentially liberalizing.

The strategies of programs intended to foster collaborative resonance, some of which are similar to strategies of programs intended to foster dissonance, include placement of student teachers in sites where reform and restructuring efforts are under way; action research and teacher research projects conducted cooperatively by student teachers and experienced teachers; curriculum and methods courses taught and critiqued in both university and school settings; collaborative inquiry at school-site meetings and university-site seminars; and joint program planning and assessment by teachers and teacher educators (Clift, Veal, Johnson, & Holland, 1990; Cochran-Smith & Lytle, 1993; Rochester City Schools/University of Rochester Ford Foundation Report, 1988–89; Ross, 1987).

Programs based on resonance share with programs intended to stimulate dissonance the view that, in and of themselves, the formal aspects of preservice preparation are largely incapable of altering students' perspectives (Zeichner, Tabachnick, & Densmore, 1987), while the less formal, experiential aspects of student teaching are potentially more powerful (Feiman-Nemser, 1983). But unlike programs intended to provoke dissonance, programs based on resonance simultaneously aim to capitalize on the potency of teaching cultures to alter students' perspectives by creating or tapping into contexts that support ongoing learning by student teachers in the company of experienced teachers who are themselves actively engaged in efforts to reform, research, or transform teaching (Evertson, 1990; Richardson-Koehler, 1988).

Taken as a whole, the messages embedded in programs based on collaborative resonance are significantly different from those in many other programs: self-critical and systematic inquiry is a primary way to link theory and practice; inquiry is most effective within a larger culture of collaboration wherein novices and experienced professionals alike learn from, interpret, and ultimately alter the day-to-day life of schools; power is shared among participants in the community, and knowledge about teaching is understood as fluid and socially constructed; the language and critique of school-based reforming teachers are as essential as are those of university-based educators and researchers; and, in the end, the power to reinvent teaching, learning, and schooling is located in neither the university nor the school but in the collaborative work of the two. Programs based on resonance attempt to bring people who have insider perspectives together with those who have perspectives on teaching against the grain that have developed outside of schools themselves. The purpose here is not to homogenize ideas but to intensify through joint work the opportunities student teachers have to learn to teach against the grain.

Teaching Against the Grain

Teachers who work against the grain are in the minority. Often they must raise their voices against teaching and testing practices that have been "proven" effective by large-scale educational research and delivered to the doorsteps of their schools in slick packages. Often they must provide evidence that their students are making sufficient progress according to standard measures of learning, despite the fact that they place little stock in those measures and believe, to the contrary, that they work against the best interests of their children. It is not surprising that teachers who work against the grain are sometimes at odds with their administrators and evaluators.

To teach against the grain, teachers have to understand and work both *within* and *around* the culture of teaching and the politics of schooling at their particular schools and within their larger school systems and communities. Unlike researchers who remain outside the schools, teachers who are committed to working against the grain inside their schools are not at liberty to publicly announce brilliant but excoriating critiques of their colleagues and the bureaucracies in which they work. Their ultimate commitment is to the school lives and futures of the children with whom they live and work. They have to be astute observers of individual learners with the ability to pose and explore questions that transcend cultural attribution, institutional habit, and the alleged certainty of outside experts. They have to see beyond and through the conventional labels and practices that sustain the status quo by raising unanswerable questions. Perhaps most important, teachers who work against the grain must wrestle with their own doubts, fend off the fatigue of reform, and depend on the strength of their individual and collaborative convictions that their work ultimately makes a difference in the fabric of social responsibility.

Teaching against the grain is challenging and sometimes discouraging work. In most student-teaching placements, there are few opportunities for experienced teachers or student teachers to participate in thoughtful inquiry, reflect on their daily decisions, or collaborate with others (Goodlad, 1984; Little, 1987; Su, 1990). In most of their encounters with school and university supervisors, student teachers are encouraged to talk about "relevant" and technical rather than critical or epistemological aspects of teaching (Hursh, 1988; Zeichner et al., 1988). Finally, in most of their preservice programs, the role of the teacher as an agent for change is not emphasized, and students are not deliberately socialized into assuming responsibility for school reform and renewal (Edmundsen, 1990; Goodlad, 1990s).

As this chapter illustrates, however, student teachers' relationships and collaborations with teachers who are themselves struggling to teach against the grain make for a different kind of experience. Working and talking regularly with experienced teachers who share the goal of teaching differently allow student teachers to participate in their ways of knowing and re-

forming teaching. Despite their inexperience, student teachers do learn about teaching against the grain when they talk with experienced teachers in learning communities where questions are urged, answers are not expected, and the tentative forays of beginners are supported.

To illustrate, I focus in the remainder of this chapter on data collected in urban elementary schools in the Philadelphia area where student teachers worked actively with both university mentors and school-based teachers engaged in the enterprise of reform. I explore the learning opportunities that were available to student teachers within the weekly teacher-researcher school-site meeting, which was one of the major contexts of this student-teaching program. This program was intended to build on the collaborative resonance of university and school experiences. Participants in the school-site meetings were student teachers, cooperating teachers, and university supervisors in Project START, a five-year preservice program in elementary education at the University of Pennsylvania that existed from 1986 to 1996.

In Project START, all participants (students, as well as cooperating teachers, university supervisors, and course instructors) were encouraged to view themselves as researchers, reformers, and reflective professionals responsible for critiquing and creating curriculum, instruction, forms of assessment, and the institutional arrangements of schooling. The combination of several instructional and supervisory structures made the student-teaching portion of the program somewhat unusual. Twenty to 25 students progressed through the 12-month program as a cohort, participating together in study groups, seminars, courses, and teacher-research groups. Each student teacher simultaneously completed university coursework and a full year of student teaching in the same classroom with the same teacher (5 months of student teaching 2 days per week, 3 months of student teacher 5 days per week). Subcohorts of three or four student teachers were placed at specially selected elementary school sites with cooperating teachers who, in a variety of ways, were working against the grain. They were involved, for instance, in curricular redesign projects, teacher research and publication, alternative schools and programs, grassroots parent-teacher community groups, teacher networks and collaboratives, or other teaching- and school-reform efforts. Alternative methods courses emphasized critical issues in theory and practice and required projects that were implemented in student-teaching classrooms and critiqued in both university and school settings. All participants in the program were teachers, learners, and researchers. They had opportunities to participate in many varieties of teacher research through course assignments, school and university-site activities, in-house and regional publications and professional forums, and the larger professional community. Each subcohort of student teachers, cooperating teachers, and university supervisor met weekly in a school-site, teacher-researcher group meeting to reflect on their work. All cohorts met together monthly for a university-site seminar on teaching, learning, and learning to teach. University supervisors and program organizers met biweekly in a teacher-educator-as-researcher group to inquire about their own theories and practices of teacher education. Supervisors, program organizers, and cooperating teachers met twice yearly to assess and revise the program.

This chapter draws on examples from school-site meetings that occurred over the course of one student teaching year at four urban schools (names of schools are pseudonyms): Community Central, a small central Philadelphia independent school; Charles A. Beard, a small desegregated Philadelphia public school; Edgeview Elementary School, a public school in an urban area on the edge of Philadelphia; and Stephen R. Morris Elementary, a large Philadelphia public school. These four schools were selected to demonstrate some of the range and variation in urban school-site discussions. The small groups of student teachers assigned to these schools met weekly as teacher-researcher groups with their cooperating teachers and university supervisors to raise questions and reflect on issues of theory and practice. Over the course of the year, the four schools hosted more than 70 teacher-researcher meetings, ranging in length from 30 to 90 minutes.

Collaboration, Intellectual Work, and the Culture of Reform

I use observational data to reveal some of the "intellectual work" of teaching against the grain that occurred in inquiry communities. By "intellectual work," I mean the patterns of thinking, talking, and knowing about teaching that were characteristic of teachers engaged in the enterprise of reform: the problems they posed about children, the dilemmas they found impossible to answer, the knowledge they made problematic, the evidence they sought in order to document and explore particular issues, the bodies of knowledge they brought to bear on particular situations, the ways they connected diverse experiences, and the themes they explored as central to understanding teaching. The conversations demonstrate why student teachers needed opportunities to live and work with reformers if they themselves were to embrace a reformer's stance on schooling.

Rethinking the Language of Teaching

At Community Central Lower School, the threads of progressive philosophy were woven tightly into long-standing traditions of peaceful Quaker education. At the core of the culture was a deep commitment to community, diversity, and self-critical inquiry. Teachers strove to educate the mind, body, and spirit of all students and to prepare them to live more fully in the present as well as the future. In an important sense, daily school life at Community Central itself represented a transformative vision of what is possible in education. But the habit at Community Central was also to question the school's own practices. One teacher commented that she had chosen to work at the school because it was never self-satisfied. She explicitly told the student teachers:

> Don't ever apologize for being a teacher and always talk about it in an intellectual way to really show that as a responsibility, you have to keep learning. . . . As a model for your peers and colleagues, there is a way to say that there aren't any easy answers. . . . Especially as a new teacher, in a way you are given permission to ask *why* as a new teacher. And as a colleague it's your responsibility to constantly say, "Well, that's *an* answer," or, "That's an easy answer and what we need to do is to take some time to *really* think about the issue, talk about all the ways we can get information to illuminate what's going on, and then talk about all

the strategies we can use to strengthen the situation." And that's much more complicated. But you're still modeling being a thinking individual, which is what you want to do.

Within a culture of reform and reflection, the teacher-researcher group at Community Central raised questions about the assumptions underlying school policies and the consequences of their labeling practices. Borrowing from Giroux (1984), I regard this form of intellectual work as *rethinking the language of teaching*—a collaborative process of uncovering the values and assumptions implicit in language and then thinking through the nature of the relationships they legitimize.

In one teacher-researcher meeting at Community Central, for example, the group discussed the consequences of the school's long-standing practice of labeling some students "transition children," or children who completed kindergarten but were "not ready" for first grade and hence spent 2 years instead of one to make the transition between the end of kindergarten and the beginning of second grade. An excerpt from their conversation demonstrates what it means to do the intellectual work of rethinking the language and practices of teaching.

Sherry Watson-Gage, Cooperating Teacher, Grades 3/4: I do not believe in a transition class, or having it—period! As a parent [in this school], last January I got a letter from my child's teacher, actually in November, when she had spent a month and a half with him. She said to me, "He may be a candidate for transition." I said, "Why?" And she said, "It's not academic, it's emotional." . . . I think all of those discussions are very fuzzy and [I know] they have to be in November, but what it said to me was, "He's not all right"—not that he's not perfect because, goodness, I know that, but it was, "He's not all right. There is something wrong with him. And we're now going to lower our expectations for the amount of growth that he is going to go through because we're not thinking probably that he will go to first grade—he'll go to transition."

Shelia Jules-James, Cooperating Teacher, Grades 3/4: What would you do then with a child who was not ready?

Watson-Gage: See, that to me is a hard thing. What does it mean not to be ready? Because last year, I had children who were "not ready" for third grade, and they are great in fourth grade. Now how do you predict? And what does it mean? I have fourth grade children who [were] transition children [years ago], and it's still an issue for them. They still say, "I was a transition child." And so they are still carrying something around. And nobody ever said it with glee, "I was a transition child!" . . . But what is the experience? [What can we see by] following a transition kid through to see if it really does help?

[*The conversation continued during the group's teacher research group meeting the following week.*]

Jules-James: I think transition is . . . not a situation that has any easy solution. And I think what works for one family may not work for another child or another family. I see there being children who need more attention or more time in some way and they need it for a variety of reasons, and how do we give it to them without damaging their self-

esteem or damaging their families' self-esteem or the way their families feel about them?

Over the course of two lengthy school-site conversations, members of the teacher research group helped one another begin to do the intellectual work of rethinking the language of learning and development. Specifically, they worked to make the labels, language, and practices of children's early growth problematic, an activity that Tom (1985) emphasizes is a "conscious attempt on the part of the teacher to suspend judgment about some aspect of the teaching situation and, instead, to consider alternatives to established practice" (p. 37). The conversation was dominated by the experienced teachers, but it really began at the start of the school year (and several weeks prior to the conversation quoted above) when one student teacher commented to her supervisor, "I'm just not really sure what those [transition] classes are all about and how they came to be set up like that and whose decision it was and which kids get placed in those classrooms and that kind of thing." This question was carried to the teacher research group where it prompted an experienced teacher to express dissatisfaction with the practice of establishing transition classes, which eventually led to the group's exploration of the issue and to repeated admissions that the question had no ready answer.

Tom (1985) has argued that critical theorists have sometimes failed to provide an adequate enough account of individual intention and human agency in their explanations of the development and evolution of culture, explanations that would help educators move beyond "deterministic thinking" and toward "intentionality" (1985, p. 38). What is especially important about the intellectual work accomplished in the excerpt above is that participants regarded the teacher herself as one of the agents who had the right, and indeed the obligation, to make certain aspects of teaching problematic. An image of the teacher as an active agent poses a sharp contrast to the image of the teacher as a pawn pushed around by the fingers of habit, standard procedure, and expert outsider knowledge.

Posing Problems of Practice

Charles A. Beard School, part of the large city school system, provided two educational alternatives to parents—"the open classroom track" and "the traditional track." The hallmark of the culture of teaching in the open classrooms was an ongoing effort to learn from children's language and work, to draw from observations of single cases teaching strategies that could be used in other cases, and to construct curriculum that strengthened children's abilities by building on their own resources. The existence of two distinct traditions of teaching provided ongoing grist for comparison and an informal culture of critique. As one teacher talked to the student teachers about her teaching history, she described the culture of reform of which she and others in the group had been part for many years:

It was the beginning for me of seeing how much what we do affects what the children produce and how much we limit them with unspoken messages when we give them worksheets and when we give them dittos and fill-ins . . . it was very, very hard to be in a place where you knew

that you could do something for children that would be meaningful and relevant for them, but the powers-that-be had other ideas about what school was all about. And it really became an ongoing theme in my life, and I think in many people's lives, that whatever culture the kids are from, the school culture becomes yet another piece that is overlaid on them. And when it doesn't have any fit with their own culture, with what they've brought, it really becomes very hard for them to see school as relevant and to be able to feel themselves as valuable people. And I finally had to leave that place because I just felt I was so stymied in what I wanted to do. . . . I realized that we had to take hard looks at the kids and do the kind of work that they were already showing us was important to them.

Charles A. Beard was a small desegregated school with a strong history of parent-teacher cooperation and a commitment to community involvement. Although as a school it did not have a commitment to open education, the teachers who were members of the teacher research group were heavily involved in a teacher-initiated, long-term, and primarily outside-of-school culture of activism, reflection, and progressive education. They were founding members of a 12-year-old teachers' cooperative group that met weekly in members' homes to reflect on their work, and they were participants in many local and national forums on teaching, learning, and evaluation.

Within a culture of commitment to public education and to the social and democratic construction of knowledge for teaching, the Charles A. Beard teacher research group frequently used guidelines from "Descriptive Review of a Child" and other Prospect School documentary processes (Carini, 1986). These begin with a teacher's focusing question about a specific child or issue to be explored through systematic observation and oral inquiry. In site meetings over the course of a year, a frequent focus of the group's intellectual work was the development of questions, or what Schön (1983a) describes as "problem setting." Schön reminds us that problems of professional practice do not present themselves ready-made, but rather that practice "is complex and uncertain, and there is a problem in finding the problem" (p. 129).

In one teacher research group conversation, for example, student teachers were struggling to choose individual children whom they would observe over time in the classroom and then present to the school-site group as a case study or descriptive review. Their cooperating teachers emphasized posing problems from which they could learn how to teach the individual child, as well as other children. Their emphasis was consistently on understanding the generalities of teaching by exploring its particulars.

Sharon Bates, Cooperating Teacher, Grade 4: The key thing is to pick a child you have a question about and that you honestly want to describe and get feedback on. . . . You have to think of a question for the child. This is the hardest part. It has to be with you and the child. It can't just be centered on you.

Karen Johnston, Cooperating Teacher, Grade 3: There might be a third grader [about] whom you feel, "Am I going to know that child any better when I leave here?" or, "How am I going to work with this child when I feel some of these barriers?" That would be one kind of question. It's not just, "How am I going to work with this child?"

Rita Greenberger, Cooperating Teacher, Grade 1: Another kind of question might be, "How am I going to get this child to know I mean business?" or "How can I get this child to be a functioning part of the group—to improve his reading or improve the way he relates to other children?"

Sharon Bates: It also could be a question about reading and writing, like "How can I help someone to read?" Those questions seem to be the ones that you seem to be more comfortable with through what you have already learned in the [university] classroom. And some of these questions about social relationships and management are the harder ones.

Jenny Gold, Student Teacher, Grades 3/4: Does it have to be a question, or can it be an analysis of somebody?

Rita Greenberger: It can be an issue.

Karen Johnston: What is *your* question? [addressing Sharon Bates, who had mentioned earlier that she would be making a presentation about a child at a teacher research conference the following week.]

Sharon Bates: It's about how to help [a particular child]. He's a person who with reading checks things out a lot with adults when it doesn't make sense . . . I think you [addressing Jenny Gold] experience him as very disruptive a lot of the time. He's always up and down.

Jenny Gold: With activities on the rug I do.

Sharon Bates: My question is how to support him in his reading to keep the questioning that he does, because it is really very valuable to him, but to help him become more independent, so that he won't be frustrated when he gets into a classroom situation in which he might not get his questions answered. . . . He's captured into reading now, but you have to hold him still . . . so my question is how to support him in this path.

In this and other conversations, members of the group explored together the process of finding questions or settling problems about individual children. The teachers described and demonstrated the ways they constructed questions out of close observations of children, from multiple perspectives. The questions the cooperating teachers posed were not simply versions of how to teach something or how to apply theory to practice. Sharon Bates, for example, posed a problem about how to understand one child as reader, learner, and asker of questions. She asked about how over time to connect with his resources in order to strengthen them, and then used this question to explore with the inquiry group how to teach other children.

The cooperating teachers at Charles A. Beard helped student teachers frame and reframe questions, repeatedly directing them to return to observations from the classroom, uncover the prior questions that were embedded in present ones, and develop generative structures of inquiry. Their process of mentoring was not unlike Schön's (1983a, 1983b, 1987) description of the ways supervisors in architecture and psychotherapy work with students—by reframing their ways of looking at the problems of design and counseling and by both implicitly criticizing the students' own

ways of framing the problems and also suggesting new ways to think about solutions.

One of the most striking aspects of problem setting is the image it conveys to student teachers about the teacher's relationship to knowledge. The teacher implicit in the conversations at Charles A. Beard was not separated from the knowledge of teaching, nor was the teacher simply the practitioner or applier of others' theoretical principles. Rather, she was a builder of knowledge and theory. In their discussions, teacher researchers collaboratively built theory and knowledge frameworks out of the experience of specific cases that also cut across classrooms, age levels of children, and cultural backgrounds. In this way, they were intimately involved in a process of transforming the social life of the school.

Constructing Curriculum

Edgeview Elementary School served a diverse working-class community of mostly White families, a small number of Black families, some recent immigrants from Korea and Greece, and many families from other cultures who had lived in the community for a number of years. There was a strong culture in the school of positive community involvement, friendly relations among children, teachers, principal, and parents, and an ecumenical tolerance for various teaching "styles." Although there was a comfortable sense of congeniality at Edgeview Elementary School, teachers worked largely by themselves, and as is the case in many schools, there was a culture of isolation. The three experienced teachers who were part of the teacher research group were united by their belief in alternative reading/language arts programs that utilized literature and children's writing.

The curriculum and assessment policies of the school district were traditional, and a few years earlier, the district had begun to place increased emphasis on standard procedures and curriculum uniformity. The culture of reform of Edgeview Elementary School's teacher-researcher group was bound up with the construction of an alternative reading/language arts curriculum and with demonstrating that children could learn to read from real literature rather than from texts constructed specifically for the purpose of instruction. During the year prior to the school-site meetings mentioned here, the teachers had struggled with administrators over whether or not literature could be used at the second grade level. One of the teachers described the struggle to her student teacher:

> They fought us about novels last year [because some people think] our children's backgrounds are lacking and they haven't got support from home and experience in reading . . . [They think] they need things simpler. They need the, "See Dick run. See Jane run," and the novel isn't written in that form. It's not simplified. And [they think] they're not ready except for the smart kids. . . . So our principal finally said to us, "You can use novels, but you have to test the children in the tests for the reading series, and you have to teach the same skills that are in the reading series." . . . So I do it. And we showed him. I mean, I have folders full of stuff . . . where the kids are learning short "*a*" and long—all the things that he thinks they need to learn. . . . This year I never even went and discussed it with him. I'm just assuming that I am going to do it. . . . If we hadn't won that battle, I probably wouldn't have come back.

As part of a group effort aimed at curriculum reform working within a larger school-system culture of standardized teaching and assessment, the teacher-researcher group at Edgeview Elementary School raised many questions that can be thought of as *constructing curriculum*. This was more than deciding how to teach the material predetermined in a teacher's guide or a pupil's text. It required that teachers consider the long-range consequences of what and why they teach, as well as the daily decisions about how they teach it. In the conversation below, they critiqued a school district in-service session designed to get them to think of literature as a supplement to, but not an alternative to, the "real" curriculum of basal reading materials.

Charlie Dougherty, Cooperating Teacher, Grade 5: One of the points that was being made to us was the possibility to use novels as a supplement. Now that is what I think is ludicrous to do.

Leslie Franks, Cooperating Teacher, Grade 5: For us.

Charlie Dougherty: You can't do it. *Either* you are going to use the basals *or* the novels.

Leslie Franks: You can't go back and forth . . . because it squashes the enthusiasm. And what happens is the kids tend to moan and groan through the whole basal unit that you are doing, and you're ruining their growth. And when you go back to the novels, they know it is for a one-night stand. A one-night stand! And then they are back again to basals, which is like suicide.

Charlie Dougherty: It's a silly idea . . .

Leslie Franks: And also as they progress in years, when you talk about standardized testing, that is one of the big things that you find. . . . It's the little paragraph that you have to read now [on the tests]—What is the main idea? Now what do you want to do first? What were the supporting details? And if you can do that with the novel, you are so much more in tune to detect these [on the test]. Case in point—our kids have done beautifully on [standardized comprehension] testing.

Charlie Dougherty: They blew the top off!

Phyllis Kim, Student Teacher, Grade 5: I don't think I understand basals well enough, but I really don't understand why you can't go back and forth using basals and novels if you were using the same approach—an inferential [approach]?

Mary Thailing, Cooperating Teacher, Grade 2: Yes, if you were just giving a child a book [and not using the teacher's manuals and workbook exercises], you could do whatever you wanted with it.

Phyllis Kim: I was thinking that if I were in a school district next year where I have basals and I could only use novels when I could afford to buy them, could I do something like that?

Mary Thailing: [You could do with] a basal story everything that you do with a novel . . .

Charlie Dougherty: I don't know if you can.

Mary Thailing: Yes you can. If it's a story that is a *real* story. I mean that's in there [in the basal] . . .

In this conversation the group struggled with the problem of combining two kinds of materials for reading instruction that are grounded in basically incompatible perspectives on language learning. Zumwalt (1989) argues that a "curricular vision of teaching" is essential for all beginning teachers if they are going to be prepared to function as professional decisionmakers in their field. Without it, she cautions, the beginning teacher tends to settle for "what works" in the classroom rather than what could be. Also underlying this discussion was the conflict among teachers and administrators (and among teachers themselves) about their roles as curriculum implementers and tinkerers, on the one hand, versus critics and creators on the other.

Confronting the Dilemmas of Teaching

At Stephen R. Morris Elementary School, the slender threads of the open classroom tradition were knotted and entangled with the broader strands of the history of segregation and desegregation in the city. Morris offered a small "open" track, a "traditional" track, and a "midway" track from which parents could choose options for their children. The culture of teaching in the open track was built on a commitment to closely observing children, providing a rich environment out of which children's own curiosities could drive the curriculum, and continuously reflecting on practice in the company of other committed professionals. Morris served more than 1,200 children who, for complex historical reasons, were from poor Black homes, while the middle-class Black and White parents in the immediate and immediately adjacent neighborhoods had chosen to have their children bussed to other desegregated city schools or sent to private schools. Conditions at Morris were difficult, special programs were limited, and the culture of teaching in the school at large was traditional. Teachers in the Morris teacher-researcher group had a transformative vision of education, but they worked within a context of poverty, increasing school district testing and curriculum strictures, and few opportunities for collaboration. One teacher noted to the student teachers:

> At the end of the year, I look over the year and I always feel there's more I could have done. And there are parts of the year I really feel good about and parts of the year I don't feel good about. But you're still only one human being. You can't do everything. I feel that what I offer children is very rich, and if children just get a little bit of that or if they get the idea that not everything has to be the same all the time [then it's worth it]. And there's this thing called thinking, I felt that what I did was important for those children. It gave them a little experience that maybe will stick with them. . . .
>
> One of the thoughts I have is that I'm 63. Technically, you can teach until you're 70. At this point I would like to teach forever. I can't imagine doing anything other than teach. But it's not as enjoyable as it used to be. I mean . . . just being in an environment where I feel I'm unappreciated makes it very, very hard. It's okay once the door is closed, and I'm in here, but it's very hard to walk out of the door.

As a school community, Morris did not have a commitment to the principles of progressive education or teacher empowerment. But the Morris teachers who were members of the school-site group were actively involved in a long-standing culture of teacher inquiry and British primary school traditions and, like the Charles A. Beard teachers, were founding members of a teacher collaborative that met weekly. In teacher research group meetings at Morris, teachers struggled with many questions that had no answers, and many problems that had no solutions. Borrowing language from Berlak and Berlak (1981) and Lampert (1985), I refer to this form of intellectual work as *confronting the dilemmas of teaching*, a process of identifying and wrestling with educational issues that are characterized by equally strong but incompatible and competing claims to justice.

In one teacher-researcher meeting at Morris, for example, the group had talked about recent court decisions that affected girls' and boys' schools in the area. They also discussed the negative consequences and the possible advantages for minority children of *segregated* schooling situations. The fact that one of the student teachers in the group was a Black woman who had attended mostly White schools throughout her educational history, and that all three experienced teachers in the group were White women who had made long-term personal and professional commitments to teaching in mostly Black public schools, were critical factors in the discussion.

Ellen Freeman, Cooperating Teacher, Grade 3: One question I have is about middle-class teachers who don't have the experiences of the children they teach . . . I have noticed something about . . . a few of the Black boys that I've taught, and I came to some conclusions about them and what would be the place for them—what kinds of teachers would be best for them to have. And I don't know, I mean, I don't know if this is racist or not. There were some very bright Black children in that class. They were in a desegregated class. They were learning to read and write and spell and all that, but there was also a group of extremely bright White boys in the class, . . . and the White boys were well-behaved. . . . They always did the "right thing." And the Black kids often misbehaved, and they often baited me in some ways.

Later in fourth grade . . . [one of them] was [taken out of the desegregated class] and put into the class of a Black teacher with all Black kids. . . . At the end of the year, he won a behavior award in the school. What it made me think was that . . . we need to have all boys' high schools *de*segregated because it's important for boys to be in school with girls. But we [also] need girls' high schools for girls to excel without men, without boys—I wonder, sometimes, if . . . some Black children need to be in schools that are not desegregated where they see themselves as leaders within their community— I don't know—I mean it really is a question, and I've thought a lot about it. . . . It's just a question because I think we need girls' high schools *and* I think we need all boys' schools to be *de*segregated. . . .

Teresa Green, Student Teacher, Kindergarten: I think that the point Ellen brought up is important . . . I know from previous experience that an integrated situation versus a segregated situation can do positive or negative things for you . . . I've been a minority in predominantly all-White situations from the time that I was six or seven.

And it does make a difference. And some of the differences are negative. And it's important to find out that sometimes people can be stronger when they are with people that they need to be with—when they are in supportive environments. . . .

Polly Spellman, Cooperating Teacher, Kindergarten: But I don't think you learn how to be strong in the abstract. Just as I don't think you learn how to use freedom unless you have freedom. Freedom isn't something you read about and then follow directions. It's something you have to experience. Well, I feel it's the same thing about kids in schools. Though I could see some positive things to girls' schools . . . I just don't think that we get any closer to learning how to operate by having exclusions. . . .

Teresa Green: But you're talking the ideal! The reality is of the world. The reality of the situation is that Black kids cannot go into predominantly White situations and come out with the same kind of security, the same kind of support that they would get in a different environment. . . .

Polly Spellman: So, let's go back to segregated schools?

Ellen Freeman: It's not really a segregated school, Polly. That's not what I'm talking about either. I am talking about choices. . . . But I guess I'm *not* talking about choices for everybody. I have to say that. I don't agree with Karen about boys' high schools. I do *not* think that the people who have traditionally been in power should be allowed—*allowed*— to have choices . . .

Teresa Green: But that's contradictory—

Ellen Freeman: I know it is—

Karen Garfield, Cooperating Teacher, Grade 5: What Ellen is saying is that the heavy power [that] has always been a certain way needs to skew the other way . . .

In this discussion, teachers worked together to confront the dilemmas created by race, class, and gender segregation of educational opportunities. They wrestled to reconcile the irreconcilable issues of the possible advantages for minority children of going to school with children of their own race or gender groups versus the clear disadvantages of being segregated from the culture of power. It is significant that there was no consensus in their conversation, especially in the comments of Ellen Freeman, who knew full well that what she was saying was, in a certain sense, both contradictory and critical.

A key aspect of this conversation is that members of the group named one of the dilemmas of teaching and wrestled with the fact that there was no answer to it within the current structures of schooling and society. Their conversation makes it clear that there is a distinction between a dilemma of teaching and a problem of teaching. A problem is a question posed for solution or at least action, a situation that may be perplexing and difficult, but *not* one that is ultimately unapproachable. A dilemma, on the other hand, is a situation of teaching that presents two or more logical alternatives, the loss of *either* of which is equally unfavorable and disagreeable. A dilemma poses two or more competing claims to justice, fairness, and morality. The dilemma confronted above probed the means-ends relationships of schooling and raised critical questions

about the interests served by the current structures of schooling. Fenstermacher (1990) points out that in current controversies over the professionalization of schooling, the moral dimensions of teaching, although primary, are often either ignored or forgotten. At Stephen R. Morris School, the group identified and confronted one of the moral dilemmas of teaching. Their intellectual work did not "solve" the problem nor adjudicate which side of the scale should be more heavily weighted in matters of race, gender, and educational opportunity. But their work clearly announced that there *was* a moral base to teaching, not just a knowledge base, and that prospective teachers had to confront that moral base in order to reclaim their responsibility in the classroom.

Student Teachers as Reformers

It is clear in the conversations above that student teachers did not dominate, and in many instances did not take equal part in, teacher research group meetings. In most instances, cooperating teachers rather than university-based supervisors or student teachers themselves took the lead. However, the student teachers' emerging theories of practice were influenced by their observations and conversations with experienced mentors who worked against the grain, as well as by their readings of and writings about a rich and diverse collection of theoretical and pedagogical literature. This was indicated in the lessons and units they designed, the questions they raised, and their efforts to understand their own efforts as urban teachers.

Though a deep intellectual discourse among student teachers and their school and university mentors is essential in light of the larger reform agenda for U.S. education, it is uncommon and difficult to sustain during the student-teaching period. And yet, as the excerpts in this chapter demonstrate, it *is* essential and possible. Indeed, the conversations that occurred in school-site meetings over the course of a year provide a "proof of possibility" of rich and complex discourse among experienced teachers and student teachers. This discourse is more provocative than the exchanges common in clinical supervision and wider ranging than the feedback usually given in response to particular lessons or teaching techniques. It is clear, however, that conventional supervisory structures are unlikely to generate this kind of discourse (Zeichner, 1986; Zeichner & Liston, 1985).

A combination of several program structures made this kind of discourse possible. Most important, the foundation for all the structures was a deep commitment to the development of "collaborative resonance," or intensification of opportunities to learn from and about teaching through the joint work of learning communities. These communities were composed of school-based cooperating teachers, university-based program directors and course instructors, and student teachers and supervisors who straddled the ground between them. Underlying the work of the community was respect for the knowledge and expertise of those who had invested their professional lives in work inside schools, as well as those who had developed their knowledge of teaching through work about, but primarily outside of, schools. Student teachers were invited, and indeed expected, to raise questions and pose problems in the language of both school and university. They

were expected to weave their emerging critiques with the threads of both insider and outsider knowledge.

The commitment to building collaborative resonance was instantiated in several key social and organizational structures: university-site monthly seminars where teacher-researcher teams from all school sites met together over the course of a year to consider teaching and learning across grades, schools, and school systems; three publications, distributed locally, featuring news, opinion, and essays by past and present project participants; dissemination and discussion of common readings in the various sites; coplanning by teacher educators and school-based teachers of seminar topics, student teachers' assignments, and program strategies; and participation by project members (including students) in local, regional, and national networks of teacher researchers.

Second, as part of a community of colearners, the roles of all project participants were redefined. Student teachers were expected to construct their own emerging theories of teaching and learning, call into question conventional practices, write about their work, and participate with their experienced mentors as inquiring professionals. It was understood that the primary role of students was *not* to imitate the instructional styles of their mentors. Concurrently it became clear that the role of cooperating teachers was much more extensive than the demonstration and evaluation of teaching strategies. Some cooperating teachers had been active for many years in teacher organizations that promoted collaborative inquiry, social responsibility, progressive education, and curriculum reconstruction. They brought an inquiry-centered perspective to their roles and worked to articulate their perspectives to student teachers and support students' initial forays into inquiry. In addition, the role of the university supervisor was redefined to include research on practice and co-inquiry. Supervision-as-inquiry meant that in addition to their regular meetings with students and cooperating teachers, supervisors also met regularly with project leaders to reflect on their work as teacher educators and compare the nature of their interactions with students and teachers to the goals and intentions of the program. This provided a connection between supervisor and preservice curriculum that is sometimes missing in student-teaching programs.

Finally, the very existence of weekly school-site meetings helped to make possible an intellectually based student teacher/experienced teacher discourse on teaching and learning. Site meetings of at least 45 minutes per week were built into the requirements of the program, allowing enough time for the beginnings of substantive discussion. Students' teaching placements for a full year permitted continuity of discussions and supported the development of each teacher-researcher group as a community, across grade levels and experiences. This was possible in part because group members came to know one another's contexts of reference and to see one another's growth from the long view. Finally, and perhaps most important, school-site meetings were *not* set up according to the conventional model of clinical supervision, which more or less necessitates that the topic of discussion is feedback and evaluation of individual lessons. To the contrary, in the site-meeting context, individual lessons could not be the topic of conversation since the seven

to nine participants in each group worked in different classrooms. Together these critical features of the program—the larger collaborative community, the redefinition of roles, and the weekly, yearlong inquiry sessions—created participation structures (Erickson, 1981) for school-site conversations that had built into them the expectation of serious talk about teaching and reforming teaching, and made it possible for these kinds of conversations to occur.

One of the most important things that happened at school-site meetings was that student teachers were exposed to certain visions of teaching that are not necessarily in keeping with the norms of the profession. Braided into the social and intellectual relationships of student teachers and experienced reforming teachers is exploration of alternative ways to think about and talk about teaching, ways perhaps not normally seen by teachers and administrators who work *with* the grain but also not normally seen by university-based teachers and researchers who work *outside of* schools. Working with experienced school-based reformers exposes student teachers to alternative visions of teaching that enrich but also alter the perspectives they learn in their university courses, as well as the perspectives they learn from the larger culture of teaching.

Reformers' visions of teaching include alternative ways of interpreting classroom events, thinking through conflicts with parents or administrators, and interpreting children's strengths and vulnerabilities. They include alternative ways of documenting and measuring learning, transforming and constructing curriculum, and thinking through issues of race, class, and culture. Struggling along with experienced teachers who are working to reform teaching within complicated and highly specific situations inside of schools is the only context within which student teachers can have theory- and practice-based conversations that deal with the extraordinary complexity of teaching and reforming teaching. There is a paradox, then, in learning to teach against the grain—it is only in the apparent "narrowness" of work in particular classrooms and in the "boundedness" of discussions of highly contextualized instances of practice that student teachers actually have opportunities to confront the broadest themes of reform. Essentially this means that the only way for beginners to learn to be both educators and activists is to struggle over time in the company of experienced teachers who are themselves committed to collaboration and reform in their own classrooms, schools, and communities.

There are many people who are involved in the struggle for educational reform—teachers, administrators, parents, teacher educators, researchers, consultants, and supervisors. In some instances, reformers are located in small pockets within much larger institutions; in other instances, whole faculties or large subgroups of faculties are working together to reinvent school and institutional structures, alter roles and responsibilities, and re-create curricula. One significant way to expand and build on reform efforts is to link student teachers with experienced and new educational reformers. As communities of school- and university-based teachers develop, they become known outside of their own groups, and others come to join them in their work. Experienced reformers share their strategies as well as their questions with colleagues who are newer to the enterprise of teaching against the grain. In a community based on cola-

bor, each individual's opportunity to learn from teaching is intensified and enriched by the questions, struggles, and triumphs of every other individual.

REFERENCES

Aronowitz, S., & Giroux, H. (1985). *Education under siege.* New York: New World Foundation.

Berlak, A., & Berlak, H. (1981). *Dilemmas of schooling: Teaching and social change.* London: Methuen.

Beyer, L. (1984). Field experience, ideology, and the development of critical reflexivity. *Journal of Teacher Education, 35*(3), 36–41.

Calderhead, J. (1989). Reflective teaching and teacher education. *Teaching and Teacher Education, 5*(1), 43–52.

Carini, P. (1986). *Prospect's documentary process.* Bennington, VT: Prospect School Center.

Clift, R., Veal, M., Johnson, M., & Holland, P. (1990). Restructuring teacher education through collaborative action research. *Journal of Teacher Education, 41*, 52–62.

Cochran-Smith, M., & Lytle, S. (1993). *Inside/outside: Teacher research and knowledge.* New York: Teachers College Press.

Edmundsen, P. J. (1990). A normative look at the curriculum in teacher education. *Phi Delta Kappan, 17*(9), 717–722.

Erickson, F. (1981). Taught cognitive learning in its immediate environments: A neglected topic in the anthropology of education. *Anthropology and Education Quarterly, 13*, 149–180.

Evertson, C. (1990). Bridging knowledge and action through clinical experiences. In D. Dill (Ed.), *What teachers need to know* (pp. 94–109). San Francisco: Jossey-Bass.

Feiman-Nemser, S. (1983). Learning to teach. In L. Shulman & G. Sykes (Eds.), *Handbook of teaching and policy* (pp. 150–170). New York: Longman.

Feiman-Nemser, S. (1990). Teacher preparation: Structural and conceptual alternatives.

In W. R. Houston (Eds.), *Handbook of research on teacher education* (pp. 212–233). New York: Macmillan.

Fenstermacher, G. (1990). Some moral considerations on teaching as a profession. In R. S. J. Goodlad & K. A. Sirotnik (Eds.), *The moral dimensions of teaching* (pp. 130–151). San Francisco: Jossey-Bass.

Ginsburg, M. (1988). *Contradictions in teacher education and society: A critical analysis.* Philadelphia: Falmer.

Giroux, H. (1984). Rethinking the language of schooling. *Language Arts, 61,* 33–40.

Gitlin, A., & Teitelbaum, K. (1983). Linking theory and practice: The use of ethnographic methodology by prospective teachers. *Journal of Education for Teaching, 9,* 225–234.

Goodlad, J. (1984). *A place called school.* New York: McGraw-Hill.

Goodlad, J. (1990a). Studying the education of educators: From conception to findings. *Phi Delta Kappan, 71*(9), 698–701.

Goodlad, J. (1990b). *Teachers for our nation's schools.* San Francisco: Jossey-Bass.

Goodman, J. (1986a). Making early field experience meaningful: A critical approach. *Journal of Education for Teachers, 12*(2), 109–125.

Goodman, J. (1986b). University education course and descriptive analysis. *Teaching and Teacher Education, 2,* 341–353.

Gramsci, A. (1977). Indifference. In Q. Hoare (Ed.), *Antonio Gramsci: Selections from political writings 1910–1920.* London: Lawrence & Wishart. Original work published 1916.

Grant, C., & Secada, W. (1990). Preparing teachers for diversity. In W. R. Houston, M. Haberman, & J. Sikula (Eds.), *Handbook of research on teacher education* (pp. 403–422). New York: Macmillan.

Hursh, D. (1988). *Liberal discourse and organizational structure as barriers to reflective teaching.* Unpublished manuscript, Swarthmore College.

Lampert, M. (1985). How do teachers manage to teach? Perspectives on problems in practice. *Harvard Educational Review, 55,* 178–194.

Little, J. (1987). Teachers as colleagues. In V. Richardson-Koehler (Ed.), *Educators' handbook.* New York: Longman.

Richardson-Koehler, V. (1988). Barriers to the effective supervision of students: A field of study. *Journal of Teacher Education, 39,* 28–34.

Rochester City Schools/University of Rochester Ford Foundation Report. (1988–89). *Professional development site: A community of learners (Part A).* Rochester, NY: Author.

Ross, D. (1987). Action research for preservice teachers: A description of why and how. *Peabody Journal of Education, 64,* 131–150.

Schön, D. (1983a). The crisis of confidence in professional knowledge. In D. Schön (Ed.), *Educating the reflective practitioner* (pp. 3–19). San Francisco: Jossey-Bass.

Schön, D. (1983b). *The reflective practitioner: How professionals think in action.* San Francisco: Jossey-Bass.

Schön, D. (1987). *Educating the reflective practitioner.* San Francisco: Jossey-Bass.

Su, Z. (1990). The function of the peer group in teacher socialization. *Phi Delta Kappan, 71,* 723–727.

Tabachnick, B. R., & Zeichner, K. (1984). The impact of the student teaching experience on the development of teacher perspectives. *Journal of Teacher Education, 35*(6), 28–36.

Tom, A. R. (1985). Inquiring into inquiry-oriented teacher education. *Journal of Teacher Education, 36*(5), 35–44.

Willis, P. E. (1978). *Learning to labour.* Hampshire, England: Gower.

Zeichner, K. (1986). Preparing reflective teachers: An overview of instructional strategies which have been employed in preservice teacher education. *International Journal of Educational Research, 7*(5), 565–575.

Zeichner, K., & Liston, D. (1985). Varieties of supervisory discourse. *Teaching & Teacher Education, 1*, 155–174.

Zeichner, K., & Liston, D. (1987). Teaching student teachers to reflect. *Harvard Educational Review, 57*, 1–22.

Zeichner, K., Liston, D., Mahlios, M., & Gomez, M. (1988). The structure and goals of a student teaching program and the character and quality of supervisory discourse. *Teaching and Teacher Education, 4*, 349–362.

Zeichner, K., Tabachnick, B. R., & Densmore, K. (1987). Individual, institutional, and cultural influences on the development of teachers' craft knowledge. In J. Calderhead (Ed.), *Exploring teachers' thinking* (pp. 21–59). London: Cassell.

Zumwalt, K. (1989). Beginning professional teachers: The need for a curricular vision of teaching. In M. Reynolds (Ed.), *Knowledge base for the beginning teacher* (pp. 173–184). New York: Pergamon Press.

Joe L. Kincheloe

What Are We Doing Here?
Building a Framework for Teaching

This book is grounded on the premise that we can do better—we can build a far better society and far better schools. One of the most important prerequisites of such an effort involves our ability to imagine what such a society and such an education might look like. That's what this book attempts to do—to provide a compelling vision of what classroom teachers could become. The authors offer a hopeful, democratic, challenging, and pragmatic portrait of classroom teaching that engages the mind, heart, and creative impulse. Since I published my first work almost thirty years ago, some readers have told me that "all that sounds good on paper but it'll never work in the real world." There is nothing impractical, I respond, about developing visions of what could be. Indeed, constructing such visions is a very practical enterprise, for all innovation begins with vision. Without vision we are existentially dead or at least dying. As creatures without vision, we walk a meaningless landscape attending only to immediate urges. I want more. Moreover, I believe that human beings have only begun a journey of meaning-making and achievement that will take them to presently unimaginable domains. Education is intimately tied to—and even makes possible—this amazing journey.

Gaining a Sense of Where We're Going

Classroom teaching that takes place outside of a rigorous examination of the larger goals of education is always trivialized and degraded. This chapter is premised on the notion that great classroom teaching is always grounded on larger understandings of purpose, a vision of the social role of education, and a sense of what type of people we want to be. What's sad is that so much of what takes place in higher education, teacher education, the public conversation about schooling, and elementary and secondary schools themselves is disconnected from these dynamics. When analyses of purpose and vision are relegated to the domain of "the impractical," there is trouble in River City. In such a situation the culture has lost a central dimension of its humanness, its *elan vital*, its life force.

I believe that human beings are enriched by:

- an understanding of the physical and social universes;
- the historical context that has shaped them;
- the literary and other aesthetic creations that express their hopes and fears;

- the philosophical insights that can help clarify and construct meaning;
- an awareness of the hidden cultural and ideological forces that tacitly influence their identities and values;
- new cognitive insights that help students move to more powerful modes of thinking; and
- the political ideas that help them in the struggle to control their own lives.

We want classrooms that help produce a society—and a world for that matter—worthy of our status as citizens.

The way such classrooms are created involves gaining a sense of social and educational purpose. The title question of this chapter—what are we doing here?—must be answered by teachers in order for them to construct compelling, challenging, motivating, socially responsible, and just classrooms. Without an answer to this question and a pedagogy constructed around that answer, teachers with engaging personalities may still motivate particular students to do certain things. There is little chance, however, of creating a classroom that makes a difference in students' lives—especially students marginalized by the forces of race, class, gender, and sexuality—and a difference in the larger society. I am asserting here that merely getting students to prepare for the standards tests administered by the school district or the state is not enough. In fact, there's a lot of evidence that moves me to argue that such a test-based teaching and learning process may do more harm than good.

In these test-based contexts the very question of what we are doing here too often gets profoundly distorted. On numerous occasions over the last few years of standards hysteria I have heard a variety of political and educational leaders assert these sentiments: "Why are we here? What is our main goal? That's right, to raise the test scores." As my Tennessee farm-based father used to say: "They've got the cart before the horse." Obviously, raising standardized test scores is not the raison d'être of classroom teaching. There is something profoundly disturbing about such pronouncements regarding our goals as teachers and students. Indeed, there is a "rational irrationality," when in the name of reason we lapse into irrational beliefs and behavior.

For example, standardized tests measure so little of what education involves. The previous list of some of the ways a rigorous education can enrich our lives can't be measured by such tests. At most, such exams pick up on some of the fragmented, unconnected data one has obtained from schools. I and the other authors of my book *Classroom Teaching: An Introduction* argue that such unconnected data are relatively unimportant in the larger vision of education and classroom teaching that we are laying out here. This is *not* to say that knowledge is not important. But the way we confront knowledge and make sense of it is every bit as important as committing particular "facts" to memory. Being prepared to ask why we are studying "this knowledge" and not "this other knowledge" is a skill that in the long run may be far more useful than scoring high on the standards test.

What makes the question "What are we doing here?" so complex for teachers in the first decade of the twenty-first century is that the people of the United States are so divided over the answer. All educational questions are primarily political questions. Even what many might think are simple questions—such as "What do we teach?"—are riddled with political inscriptions. Do we teach the knowledge that he thinks most important or that she thinks is most important? Do we teach in the way Dr. Smith says is the best for student learning or in the way Dr. Brown maintains creates the best learning environment? The answers to such questions are complex, and we answer them depending on our larger social, cultural, political, and philosophical assumptions whether or not we are conscious of them. It is impossible to be neutral about these questions. In *Classroom Teaching*, we hold particular social, cultural, political, and philosophical perspectives. These perspectives influence our vision of what constitutes a good classroom. We talk about the biases we bring to our writings. None of us claim that what we are providing you is objective information about classroom teaching. It is our perspective: nothing more, and nothing less.

We try to convince you that it's not such openly admitted biases that should worry you. What concerns us is the information that is provided to you as a form of objective truth, free from interpretation and human perspective. Whenever a teacher or an educational expert claims that she is giving me the truth, I guard both my wallet and my intellect. A central assertion of that book is that all claims of good classroom teaching are based on particular political/social visions—there is no objective political/social vision. In this context as human beings who want to be teachers, we are faced with an existential

dilemma: no one else can tell us the right way to teach; we have a human responsibility to decide for ourselves what constitutes good teaching and appropriate educational goals in a democratic society. The authors and I believe that every teacher must make this decision and struggle against systems that unreasonably attempt to deny teachers of this professional prerogative. This doesn't mean that teachers are free to indoctrinate students with fascist dogma, racial hatred, or inaccurate information. It does mean that teachers can make curricular and pedagogical decisions within particular democratic and scholarly boundaries.

The Importance of Healthy Debate About the Goals of Classroom Teaching

Open and rigorous debate about the goals of education and what constitutes good classroom teaching is not only a good thing but is essential in a democratic society. This is why it is important for teachers, political leaders, and the public at large to engage in such a conversation. Unfortunately, in the present political climate this is not happening. Many spokespeople from a variety of social domains claim there is consensus about what we should be doing in schools. We do not believe this is true. Many assert that everyone wants high academic standards. Such a statement is—on the surface—probably accurate, but the devil is in the details. When those making such an assertion are asked to define high academic standards, we can begin to see fissures in the faux-consensus previously claimed.

If we are to have a genuine and productive public debate about educational goals, we must insist that such debate focus on the clarification of guiding principles on which our teaching is based. Is the goal the improvement of test scores, or does it involve the well-being of the children entrusted to our care? Is well-being defined as the particular needs that specific students bring with them to school, or is it a vague notion that means little? The authors of that book believe that a variety of social, cultural, political, and economic factors have operated to diminish public life in twenty-first-century America. In this age of mediocrity the public conversation about these matters is truncated. Often what we consider "normal" is socially constructed by modes of repression, oppression, fear-mongering, and forces of economic, political, racial, and gender power.

When we talk about having an honest conversation about the goals of education and the nature of good classroom teaching, these forces often represent such activities as some form of anti-American action. For example, when we argue that Americans should have access to an education that provides diverse viewpoints from peoples around the world about history, science, literature, politics, religion, and other topics, this is defined as a "divisive multiculturalism" that is grounded on a "hatred for America." It is disturbing that in the twenty-first century the effort to seek a variety of viewpoints and to understand the perspectives of various peoples around the world can be characterized as subversive behavior. We believe that such perspectives are dishonest, disastrous in their social impact, anti-intellectual, and destructive to a free society. We are confident that a rigorous debate about the principles on which such educational perspectives rest will expose their antidemocratic and repressive

nature. We hope that after reading this and many other sources about these issues that you will insist on and participate in such debate in your teacher education programs, the schools in which you teach, and the communities in which you live.

The debate that we're trying to foster—about the goals of education in general and classroom teaching in particular—therefore deals with the foundations of diverse perspectives. In this context we ask what is the basis for the curriculum? When we speak of curriculum we are not only referring to the knowledge or subject matter that is taught in schools. In addition, we are referencing the goals and purposes of teaching and learning, methods of classroom teaching and organization, and the ways we assess the quality of the teaching and learning taking place. We also move outside the classroom in our definition of curriculum, asserting that classroom teaching has to do with a myriad of things that happen in the world surrounding the school. In our expanded and critical understanding of curriculum, we are also interested in the ways knowledge is produced and human consciousness is constructed and the role that power plays in these processes.

When curriculum is defined in this expansive way, we realize that the curriculum and the present status of democratic life are inseparable dynamics that are mutually constituted. The curriculum to some degree reflects the prevailing definition of democracy existing in a particular society. The school curriculum and the social order are intimately connected in that they are constantly constructing one another—they are coconstructed (Carr, 1998). This means that you can't study one without the other. The effort to teach someone about classroom teaching outside of these larger social and political concerns is an insult to the professionalism of teachers. Teachers are not functionaries who follow the directives of experts—contrary to the makers of top-down standards and scripted lessons that delineate exactly what teachers say to students—but informed professionals who diagnose situations and develop appropriate curricula. We fervently believe in the dignity of the teaching profession and the complex professional role of teachers. We also believe that in the first decade of the twenty-first century this dignity is under assault by forces fearful of an empowered, self-directed teaching profession.

In this context we maintain that this public debate about the goals of education and classroom teaching must ask hard questions about the role of US corporations in shaping the social and pedagogical agenda. Corporations have become increasingly powerful over the last few decades, paying less taxes as they grab more power and influence via their control of media and public information (see Kincheloe, 1999, for an expansion of these ideas). As part of this increasing corporate domination of society, they have become less willing to provide taxes to public institutions that they cannot control. Sensing that an empowered and self-directed teaching profession in public schools might be inclined to criticize their socially harmful behavior, corporate leaders have aligned themselves with right-wing politicians to use their control of information to subvert the idea of public education.

Never before in American society have we heard so much talk about the privatization of schooling and the value of corporate-operated, for-profit education.

We are deeply concerned with the social and political impact of such a corporatized school system. As unelected, unaccountable power wielders, corporations would not tolerate criticism in their schools. Teaching would be deprofessionalized and teachers would be subjected to rigid forms of control. No elected school boards or political bodies would operate under this corporatized arrangement to address these problems. The public's educational right to knowledge and democratic empowerment, already compromised, would no longer exist in this brave new world of for-profit schooling. This scenario is not a fantasy. Plans exist both to win public support for such changes and to implement these schools once approval is granted.

This privatization project is a cynical and greedy scam. It views children and the schools as an unexploited multibillion-dollar market. It ignores human possibility, our ability to become far more than we presently are. Indeed, human beings are not simply by nature egocentric, status-obsessed, and greedy entities that always operate in their immediate self-interest no matter what the effect on others. The classroom teaching that we advocate holds an optimistic view of what humans can become (Griffin, 1997). Our pedagogy is grounded on the belief that humans are destined for greatness and can be motivated to learn on these premises. The classroom teaching promoted in this book is premised on an honest discussion of these competing belief systems and the ways they affect the nature of society and education themselves. It seems to me that one of the most powerful dimensions of becoming an educated person involves understanding the great issues of one's day.

In this spirit I argue that the curriculum should be multilogical—that it should present a variety of perspectives on what should be taught in schools. A central feature of such a curriculum would involve understanding a variety of different viewpoints in a variety of academic domains and the ideologies, values, and worldviews on which they are based. A classroom grounded on this multilogical curriculum would expose students to diverse interpretations of history, science, linguistics, literature, and philosophy while encouraging them to support and defend their own interpretations in these areas. An understanding of diverse perspectives and the justifications for the differences between them promotes intellectual and ethical maturity (Harrington & Quinn-Leering, 1995). Many of the forces that want to do away with public education are frightened by the possibility of students engaging multiple perspectives. Those who support indoctrination and regulation of human beings are always opposed to a democratic engagement with intellectual diversity.

These are the types of insights that will emerge in a healthy democratic debate about what we should be doing in education. Such debate will move us away from imposed, standardized, decontextualized, scripted modes of classroom teaching. It will help us empower teachers, and, in turn, students, to become scholars who understand the contexts of meaning-making in which schooling is structured. In this context they will gain the mature understanding that knowledge is not simply given to humans but is actively constructed by individuals coming from particular locales in the sociohistorical web of reality. Individuals like you and me, operating in the observational confines of their histori-

cal time and social location, produce the knowledge taught in school. This means that school knowledge like all knowledge is fallible; it is prone to error.

Think of medical knowledge in the eighteenth and nineteenth centuries and the cures for particular diseases. In the context of the twenty-first century they seem humorous and even primitive. Remember how it was accepted as good sense in the early twentieth century that women should not be allowed to vote. Females simply don't have the intelligence to make such important decisions, jurists and politicians argued. Consider sociological knowledge taught in mid-twentieth-century textbooks about the infantile nature of African Americans and their inferiority to white people. The point, of course, is that knowledge in human history hasn't seemed to "keep well." It grows rancid with age and becomes unusable. Such a realization should make us less comfortable with any assertion of certainty, especially our own. I hope that what I am writing here will not appear too silly in the twenty-third century. But if history is any indicator, twenty-third-century educators may find great humor with what I didn't see in relation to the blinders of early twenty-first-century assumptions about human beings and the world.

This fallibility of all knowledge and the inadvisability of claiming certainty are central lessons of our debate. In this context, students, teachers, political and educational leaders, and the public learn that all knowledge is produced within certain conceptual frameworks and inscribed by particular views of the world. Therefore, a central duty of scholars is to cultivate a healthy suspicion of the information they are provided, especially that data delivered as fact. The agnostic education we are promoting here openly questions all cultures' sacred canons. Some dogmatic groups may find this questioning process offensive, as it interrogates certain patriotic shibboleths or articles of religious faith. But this is the price we pay for a democratic education. I see little alternative if we want to live in a free and egalitarian society. Obviously, we can always opt for a totalitarian education where the "party line" is outside the boundaries of questioning and analysis. As I study schools around the country I find far too many where questions about existing social, political, economic, cultural, philosophical, theological, and other norms are off-limits. I am very depressed by such findings and consequently hold great fears for the future of American democracy.

When educational institutions restrict what can be questioned and what interpretations of the world are allowed, they undermine a society's capacity to deal with change and novelty. And, I would maintain, in the contemporary globalized, electronic, information-saturated world of the twenty-first century, change is the status quo. Thus, a key dimension of a critical and rigorous education for such a hyperreality involves the ability to interpret and make meaning of a barrage of information thrown at us by corporate-owned media and education. This interpretive ability becomes extremely important in this context because the motive for such information bombardment may be to induce us to buy into or give our consent to ways of thinking that are not in our own best interests. Such ways of thinking may serve the needs of corporate power wielders more than they serve our own. I want classrooms to help students survive in this contemporary power-driven climate of deceit by developing a literacy of power—an ability to discern the fingerprints and effects of power on the knowledge thrown at them.

Traditional Debates About the Goals of Classroom Teaching

Contrary to the pronouncements of right-wing romantics who idealize a distant American past where all white people agreed with what America was about and what schools should do, there has always been contention about the goals and nature of education. Indeed, much to the nation's detriment such romantic patriots have painted a picture of a historical American consensus that never existed in an effort to prove that their viewpoints are the "true" American perspectives. In this consensus history we are routinely shielded from understandings such as the division in American society in regard to the Revolutionary War. Not all Americans supported the effort for independence from England. Historians agree that about one-third of the population supported independence, one-third opposed it, and another one-third didn't care either way. So fervently did the one-third who opposed independence hold to their opinion that for the first forty years of American nationhood—until about 1830—opponents viewed the Fourth of July as a day of mourning. On that day they would close their houses and drape their windows with black curtains to protest. This and countless other similar events do not support the picture of unity we get from our drum-and-trumpet school histories.

Disagreement over larger social goals is as American as apple pie. Thus, instead of being relegated to the dustbin of official history, the chronicle of our past and present disagreements should rest at the center of a democratic curriculum. Teachers need to understand the philosophical, historical, political, social, and cultural assumptions that support their classroom decisions. It is important to note in this context that it is just these types of assumptions that right-wing advocates of the privatization of public education don't want you to study and understand. An important aspect of the agenda of those who would seek to deprofessionalize teaching is to abolish teacher education as it now exists. The first step in this abolition process involves getting rid of the social, political, philosophical, historical, and cultural analysis that engages teachers in asking about the purpose of education in a democratic society.

This type of analysis is very frightening to those who seek to privatize education because such study induces teachers to ask deeper questions about the real motivations for such educational change. Once we begin to study the privatization movement we begin to see that, in addition to the huge profits to be made in the process, new forms of political and ideological control over teachers' work can be achieved. In private schools teachers will be unable to appeal to principles such as academic freedom or freedom of speech to protect their critiques of such power wielders. Teachers who point to the oppressive power of corporations and various forms of oppression will simply be dismissed. They will have no legal recourse to protect themselves from or overturn such firings.

In this repressive context, questions of how certain educational purposes affect particular groups of people or specific individuals are not asked. What happens to poor people when we define intelligence in a particular way? If we define politics as the domain where power operates and questions about the best ways to share power are asked, then we can begin to see the intimate connections between politics and education. Depending on our definitions of dynamics such as intelligence, success, and higher-order thinking, different people will win (gain power) and lose (lose power) in educational situations. When we accept the validity and universal predictive power of IQ tests, for example, we set up students from poor backgrounds for failure. The types of skills evaluated and the language used in the tests are more commonly found among middle-/upper-middle-class students. If educators decide that these test scores are "real" indications of students' abilities, then schools will treat such students as uneducable and thus guarantee their academic failure. As a classroom teacher, how you view such issues will make all the difference to your students, especially your most vulnerable students.

In this context, we can begin to see contemporary manifestations of larger historical debates over the goals of education. Is it the function of schooling to help people reach their highest potential, providing them in the process with the understanding of the forces that impede them on such a quest? In such a context students armed with this insight can work to bring about a more inclusive and just social order. Or is it the function of schooling to support and perpetuate the dominant social order by efficiently producing individuals who will serve functional roles within businesses, industries, and various organizations? The social role of such students is not to strive for their fullest potential or to critique the justice of present sociopolitical arrangements, but to accept the status quo and keep it operating. Or is it possible for schools to help accomplish both goals? Are there points at which they come into direct conflict? Can, for example, marginalized students work for intellectual self-improvement and socioeconomic mobility and a more just social order while working to preserve the dominant social order? Such activities may collide head-on.

Another theme of the traditional debate involves the question of whether schools should devote their attention to cultivating the abilities of the so-called gifted and talented students or whether they should work to cognitively and vocationally foster the intellectual abilities of all students? Of course, such an issue is always inscribed with profound racial and class assumptions. Many argue (see Herrnstein & Murray, 1994) that African Americans, Latinos, Native Americans, and poor people of all races simply do not have the genetic ability to succeed at academic work. In this highly problematic context educators and educational policymakers are urged to get rid of programs designed to help students marginalized by race and class and reallocate the funds for such programs to those who can profit from special programs— the gifted and talented. My biases show through here, as I maintain that such racist and class-biased approaches create and perpetuate inequity.

Yet another old debate questions whether the goal of schools should involve teaching about and promoting the mores and values of the so-called dominant culture or provide validation and respect for the subcultures that make up the society as a whole. This debate lays the foundation for discussions of multiculturalism and the role of diverse cultural knowledges and values within the curriculum (Bruner, 1996; Kincheloe & Steinberg, 1997; Kincheloe, 2001; Steinberg, 2001). In this context many right-wing fundamentalist Christians, for example, argue that the role of the schools is to perpetuate the belief structures of dominant culture. Teaching such belief structures would include inculcating the superiority of Western civilization and a particular version of Christianity in the minds of all students. Obviously, different groups of people are very emotional about these issues, and teachers in twenty-first-century America will have to confront the debate and its effects at some level in their professional life.

Another debate involves what exactly it might mean to pursue the goal of cultivating the intellect of students. It is unfortunate that in the first decade of the twenty-first century in US schools, the effort to cultivate the intellect has been reduced to inculcating subskills in math and reading. Too often students are subjected to standards test-driven curricula characterized by skill-and-drill lessons on circling the verb and drawing an X through the noun. As a first-year language arts teacher in a middle school in Tennessee, I was faced on the night of my first open house with a parental rebellion. Several parents had organized to hijack the language arts teachers' presentation on the curriculum we had developed. As we attempted to explain the communication skills that we planned to teach and how parents could help in this process, angry parents shouted that they saw no provision for teaching how to diagram sentences. As I tried to explain that sentence diagramming was only one technique for teaching about the structure of language, angry parents drowned out my voice. They wanted no "intellectual" explanation. They saw the teaching of sentence diagramming as important to the academic success of their children. It was important because teachers in high school might require it.

The larger notion of cultivating the intellect by helping students gain important writing, reading, and other communication skills was not relevant to the parents. One can understand on one level the social and cultural forces that move many parents to think only of the "success" of their children. I'm very sensitive to such concerns, especially among parents who have never enjoyed socioeconomic success. Nevertheless, the question of our larger purpose in the educational context— a purpose, of course, that cannot be removed from these contexts—is overlooked in such circumstances. In the process education is reduced to a means toward an end of socioeconomic success, and the intrinsic value of education and the critical consciousness it might develop are dismissed. The debate about the goals of education must bring up these issues for public examination. Teachers must be keenly aware of these issues as they prepare their everyday work in their classrooms.

The Goals of Classroom Teaching and Questions of Power

No matter how much many people might wish it were not the case, schools and classrooms are battlegrounds where competing interests attempt to define who we are as a nation (Anderson & Summerfield, 2004). In many domains we see forces that want to retain a monolithic vision of America as a white, Christian, patriarchal, English-speaking, heterosexual nation and demand that classrooms reflect such uniformity. Diversity around issues of race, religion, gender, language, and sexuality does not play well with these forces. Different races are "inferior"; different religions are "ungodly"; men are the heads of the household; different languages are "un-American"; and different sexual orientations are "sick and perverted." Indeed, so many of the issues surrounding educational policy, teaching, and learning relate to these issues. All of these concerns are issues of power that raise the question of who gets to teach their viewpoints as the truth that all others must learn.

In this context the authors of this volume believe that rigorous, life-changing teachers must have a complex understanding of power and how it shapes the world in general and individual lives in particular. Many of the ideas I believe come from critical pedagogy (for an introduction to the field see Kincheloe, 2004). In the case of the authors of *Classroom Teaching*, we take some ideas from this school of thought and mix them with ideas from other schools. We share several basic precepts about the need for a rigorous education that explores a wide variety of knowledges and is grounded on a belief in democracy and socioeconomic justice, but we do not hold uniform perspectives. All of us do believe, however, that understanding issues of power and their relation to the purposes of education is central to becoming a great classroom teacher.

Indeed, the people we are and the nature of our consciousness of ourselves in general and as teachers are directly tied to power. Our critical orientation to classroom teaching is always mindful of the interrelationship between teachers', students', and administrators' consciousness and the sociohistorical contexts in which they work. These historical power forces have shaped all of us. My upbringing in a rural, poor area of Tennessee profoundly shaped my life. I realized early in my life that the dominant cultural forces moved most of my peers and their parents to hold an ethnocentric view of the world around them. African Americans were almost always referred to as "niggers" and consistently relegated to an inferior status. Women who were suspected of having sex were "whores," who were to be sexually pursued at night but denigrated in the daylight. "Queens" simply were to be beaten (often after performing particular sexual acts with "straight" men). "Non-Christians"—even Catholics were included in this category—were not to be tolerated.

The ironic dimension of all of this was that individuals from the upper-middle and upper class looked down on us as "hicks" and "white trash." If we ever ventured out of our geographical location, we were viewed as "hillbillies," who were ignorant and probably illiterate. I learned early that I did not want to be a part of the parochial and ethnocentric dimensions of my low-status culture, but, concurrently, I did not want to be a part of the more privileged class cultures that looked down on my peers. Power relations were swirling all around me, and I worked hard to understand the lessons to be learned from the maelstrom. My feelings were often conflicted; I was many times confused, and probably I was scarred in ways that manifest themselves in adulthood in less-than-healthy ways. After years of introspection, I guess I'll never

know exactly how I was affected by these experiences. I can say that they heightened my sensitivity to racial, class, gender, ethnic, religious, and sexual injustice and the kinds of pain and distress such oppression can cause. I pray I never lose such empathy as a teacher, lover, parent, friend, and human being in general.

The teachers whom we want to see operating in schools, regardless of their own backgrounds, understand such sociocultural dynamics and their relationships to themselves and their students. In relation to themselves, critical teachers value self-exploration. In relations to these power dynamics and their own lives, they work to expose buried fragments of themselves constructed by their connections to such forces of power.

Guided by such concerns, critical classroom teachers seek to expose what constitutes reality for themselves and for participants in educational situations. How do educational leaders, administrators, other teachers, parents, and students come to construct their views of educational reality? Critical teachers see a socially constructed world and ask what forces construct the consciousness and the ways of seeing of the actors who live in it. Why are some constructions of educational reality embraced and officially legitimized by the dominant culture while others are repressed? Why do I feel so uncomfortable with teaching about particular issues or raising certain questions, yet I have no trouble bringing other knowledges into my classroom? What contexts, what experiences, what belief systems have moved me to operate in these ways? Why do I react so emotionally (positively or negatively) to these ideas? What are the origins of such feelings?

Thus, critical classroom teachers informed by a concern with power seek a system of meaning which grants a new angle, a unique insight into the social consequences of different ways of knowing, different forms of knowledge, and different approaches to knowledge production and teaching. Teaching and knowledge production are never neutral but constructed in specific ways that privilege particular logics and voices while silencing others. Why do science and math curricula in the United States, for example, receive more attention and prestige in public schools than liberal arts (Roth, Tobin, & Ritchie, 2001)? Critical teachers who are searching for the way power helps shape individual and social consciousness uncover links, for example, between the need of large corporations to enhance worker productivity and the goals of contemporary educational reform and standards movements to reestablish "'excellent' schools" (Horn & Kincheloe, 2001). They discover relationships between the interests of business and the exclusion of the study of labor history in Western schools. They expose the connections between the patriarchal Eurocentrism of educational leadership and definitions of classics that exclude the contributions of women, minorities, and non-Westerners to the literature, art, and music curricula.

Power regulates discourses, and discursive practices are defined as a set of tacit rules that regulate what can and cannot be said, who can speak with the blessing of authority and who must listen, whose socioeducational constructions are scientific and valid and whose are unlearned and unimportant. In the everyday world of teachers, legitimized discourses insidiously tell teachers what books may be read by students, what instructional methods may be utilized (e.g., Madeleine Hunter, *Success for All*), and what belief systems, definitions of citizenship, and views of success may be taught. Schools may identify, often unconsciously, conceptions of what it means to be educated with upper-middle-class white culture; expressions of working-class or nonwhite culture may be viewed as uneducated and inferior.

In this context teachers are expected to sever student identification with their minority-group or working-class backgrounds, as a result alienating such students through the degradation of their culture. Thus, the culture of schooling privileges particular practices and certain methods of discerning truth. French scholar Michel Foucault argues that truth is not relative (i.e., not all worldviews embraced by different teachers, researchers, cultures, and individuals are of equal worth) but relational (constructions considered true are contingent upon the power relations and historical context in which they are formulated and acted upon). The question that grounds critical teachers' efforts to formulate a system of meaning for their classroom teaching is whether what we designate as truth is relational and not certain. If it is, then what set of assumptions can we use to guide our activities as professionals, to inform our questions as teachers and producers of knowledge? This question is one that such teachers attempt to answer for the rest of their lives. This is a question that runs throughout my work as a scholar and a teacher.

Power is an extremely complex topic, and space limitations do not allow me sufficient room to discuss the multiple dimensions of power (for an expanded analysis of the meaning of power, see Kincheloe & Steinberg, 1997, and Kincheloe, 2002). In the context of this discussion of the goals of classroom teaching I do want to focus momentarily on the political notion of hegemony. Antonio Gramsci was an Italian political philosopher in the first decades of the twentieth century who was arrested by Benito Mussolini's Fascist government in the 1920s and imprisoned until his death in 1937. During his imprisonment Gramsci kept notebooks in which he developed some of the most sophisticated understandings of power ever conceptualized. One of these concepts was hegemony. In contemporary democratic states, Gramsci argued, dominant power is no longer exercised simply by physical force but through sociopsychological attempts to win people's consent to domination through cultural institutions such as the schools, the media, the family, and the church.

Thus, Gramsci's hegemony posits that winning the popular consent is a very complex process. Power groups win popular consent by way of a pedagogical process, a form of learning that engages people's conceptions of the world in such a way that transforms, not displaces, them with perspectives more compatible with various elites—white supremacy, economic power wielders, patriarchy, heterosexuals, and so on. The existence and nature of hegemony are among the most important and least understood features of twentieth- and twenty-first-century life in industrialized, democratic countries. We are all hegemonized, as our knowledges and understandings are structured by limited exposure to competing definitions of the sociopolitical world. The hegemonic field, with its bounded sociopsychological horizon, garners consent to an inequitable power matrix—a set of social relations that are legitimated by their depiction as natural and inevitable. In this context we come to believe that the world could have existed in no other way: there will always be poor people, and there will be a bell curve distribution of student abilities in every classroom, so many students simply don't have the ability to learn.

The methods of hegemony move social domination from a yellow alert to a red alert, or, as I like to say in this time of homeland security, from pumpkin to magenta. Critical teachers find themselves in a state of full alert in regard to the capacity of power wielders to dominate in the late twentieth century and the first decade of the twenty-first century. As previously discussed, this contemporary social condition—we have referred to it as hyperreality—is marked by cultural dislocation because of the bombardment of information that is thrown at us by electronic media. This social vertigo is marked by a loss of touch with traditional notions of time, community, self, and history. This proliferation of signs and images characteristic of information-soaked hyperreality functions as a mechanism of control in contemporary Western societies. The key to a pedagogy that fights dominant power and is counterhegemonic involves the ability to point out the way power operates to produce various representations, images, and signs, and the capacity to illustrate the complex ways that the reception of these images and signs affect individuals located at various race, class, and gender coordinates in the web of social reality.

What this means in everyday life, of course, is the ability of power to produce meaning in ways that move people to adopt particular behaviors that are in the interests of the power wielders. One example is the way Nike has inscribed their athletic shoes with a signifier of status that moves kids of all socioeconomic strata to want them. How did shoes gain such an importance? Nike poured millions of dollars into social research and into advertising to obtain its desired effect. Elsewhere I have written about McDonald's (Kincheloe, 2002) and its successful use of advertising to cultivate children consumers. When corporations such as Nike and McDonald's have produced positive views of their products and the act of consuming them, they generate tremendous goodwill toward the present corporate-dominated sociopolitical environment. Add hundreds of other corporations spending billions of dollars to create positive corporate images, and you have a powerful political force in support of the status quo with its low corporate taxes and good business climates.

The power of these corporate information producers to shape our political viewpoints, our view of success, our view of ourselves, and our view of the world makes them the most important teachers in human history. Classroom teachers need to understand that much of the most powerful pedagogy in the world takes place outside of the classroom in contexts carefully produced by corporate owners of TV, radio, movies, CDs, video games, and so on. Corporate-owned media can set agendas, mold loyalties, depict conflicts, and undermine challenges to the political status quo without a modicum of public notice. Critical teachers must work to expose the insidious ways that power shapes our consciousness and the knowledge we are exposed to both in and out of the classroom. This is a central concern of the rigorous

classrooms I promote. Such a concern, we argue, moves us to be aware of the fragility of democracy in the middle of the first decade of the twenty-first century.

These power wielders move us all as students, teachers, parents, and citizens into hegemonic communities of practice. Without any contention, such power-driven communities of practice come to internalize particular meanings, feelings, and values without much negotiation or cognitive reflection (Gee, Hull, & Lankshear, 1996). This hegemonic process often works so well that individuals deny that their worldviews have been influenced by anyone. Such a power-driven process convinces many people that there is a pervasive consensus on the society's larger social, political, cultural, economic, and educational goals. Political and ideological discussion becomes more and more a relic of a distant past in which such quaint issues mattered. And the political domain is relegated to the closet of "bad taste"—"How gauche! Bob wanted to talk about politics at the party last night; what a bore."

Thus, an invisible market ideology, a tacit politics of consumption, emerges that subverts attempts to talk about the "public good." In this ideology all in the private domain is good, as it is grounded on values of efficiency and customer satisfaction; conversely, everything in the public space is bureaucratic, inept, and grounded on unacceptable "high taxes." Privatization is promoted as an unmitigated virtue and every human endeavor is capable of being improved by the sanctification of the market. In this ideological construct, education itself is reduced to a market logic that sees no problem with classrooms that attempt to make children receptive and docile (Covaleskie, 2004). "Do not question the knowledge we provide you, students. Just make sure you know it for the standards tests—our stockholders will want to see empirical proof that our educational system is working. Our quarterly reports to stockholders must assure them that things are going well and their money is well-invested."

Understanding the Alienation of Contemporary Experience: The Authoritarianism of Positivism

A primary goal of a critical education in the contemporary globalized world involves not a quest for universal truths but an effort to heal the alienation of twenty-first century everyday life (Reason & Bradbury, 2000). In this alienation we are removed from the world and other people. Indeed, we are often quite alienated from our own selves, our erotic, passionate, loving, interactive selfhood. In the prevailing knowledge climate of academia we often observe a quest for certainty that alienates us by denying the complexity and ambiguity of everyday life. From the birth of the Scientific Revolution in Western societies in the seventeenth and eighteenth centuries, René Descartes, Sir Isaac Newton, and Francis Bacon—the founders of modern science—sought a perfect form of knowledge. Such "truth" would provide individuals guidance in what to do in professional and personal life. This certainty could only be derived by using the correct method in knowledge production. This correct method we would come to understand as the scientific method. It is the foundation for the knowledge theory (epistemology) of positivism.

Positivism is a key contributor to the alienation we experience in the twenty-first century. Positivism believes that:

- All true knowledge is scientific knowledge—it is knowledge about which we are positive. *Only Western societies produce such knowledge; other cultures must give up their ways of producing knowledge and follow us.*
- All scientific knowledge is empirically verifiable—through the senses we can count, see, and hear things and thus represent the world in numbers. *Knowledges not grounded empirically and quantitatively about complexities such as feelings, emotion, hurt, humiliation, for example, are often dismissed in the positivism context.*
- One must use the same methods to study the physical world as one uses to study the social and educational worlds—a key dimension of knowledge work in this context involves predicting and controlling natural phenomena. *Human beings are treated like any other "variable" in this framework.*
- If knowledge exists, it exists in some definite, measurable quantity—mathematical language is best suited to express our knowledge of the world. *Many claim that the most important dimensions of education cannot be expressed in this language.*
- Nature is uniform and whatever in it that is studied remains consistent in its existence and behavior—there is an underlying natural order in the way the physical, social, psychological, and educational domains work. *Humans, many argue, are not as predictable and regular as positivists claim.*
- The factors that cause things to happen are limited and knowable, and in empirical studies these factors can be controlled—the best way to

study the world is to isolate its parts and analyze them independently of the contexts of which they are a part. *It is profoundly difficult, many assert, to control all of the factors that shape human actions, and when we remove individuals from their social context, we may have destroyed their natural setting that makes them who they are.*

- Certainty is possible, and when we produce enough research we will understand reality well enough to forgo further research—research is like a jigsaw puzzle, a search for all the pieces that give us a final picture of the phenomenon in question. *Such a quest focuses our attention on the trivial, those things that lend themselves to easy measurement.*

- Facts and values can be kept separate, and objectivity is always possible—good research is always politically and morally neutral. *Nonpositivists argue that values, a variety of assumptions, and power dynamics always shape knowledge production.*

- There is one true reality, and the purpose of education is to convey that reality to students—positivist research tells us the best way to teach this reality. *Those who argue that different research methods and different values will produce different views of reality are simply misguided, positivists maintain.*

- Teachers in the positivist framework become "information deliverers," not knowledge-producing and knowledge-questioning professionals—there is no need for teacher education in this context, for teachers should simply pass along the truths that experts have given them. *Scholarly teachers with analytical and interpretive abilities do not fit in the positivism world of schooling.*

Positivism extends alienation, as it induces individuals to focus on knowledge that has little to do with the well-being of human beings as a species. Questions about environmental protection, the relationship between humans and the cosmos, tendencies toward militarism, the loss of community, ethical responsibilities, and the disparity of wealth are dismissed in this context. Indeed, the very insights that would lead to a reduction of alienation are devalued in a positivistic epistemology. Our efforts to engage teachers in helping students develop criteria for making ethical choices, to imagine alternatives to present alienating social arrangements, are consistently opposed by positivists. Because of a matrix of intersecting historical, social, economic, and cultural forces coming together in the 1970s, right-wing positivists were able to orchestrate an ideological coup by around 1980.

The educational phalange of the coup was able to subvert critical efforts to raise questions of educational goals in a democratic society (Goodson, 1999). The success of this coup is testimony to why the questions raised seem so out of place and irrelevant to so many over the last quarter of a century. Questions about social alienation were quashed in the new regime, and attempts to devise new ways of understanding the pedagogical cosmos were undermined. The ideas that human beings construct their reality and that some final positivist truth about the world cannot be produced by following the scientific method scared the hell out of the leaders of the right-wing coup. When critical scholars argued that reality is not as much discovered as constructed and that education should reflect this epistemological insight by encouraging teachers and students to become rigorous researchers, panic swept the positivist landscape.

In this context, the urgency of the conservative effort to develop a set of content standards that had to be learned by everyone in order to standardize the nation's curriculum becomes more understandable. Right-wing political/educational reformers felt they needed a way to control teachers who might be prone to question the traditional positivist verities. If something was not done quickly, the right-wingers believed, schools could become places where genuine democratic dialogue took place, where indoctrination about the inferiority of diverse ways of seeing was not tolerated, where classrooms valued the insights and contributions of students from a wide range of cultures and belief systems.

Addressing Alienation: Moving to a New Terrain of Insight

Our social and educational imagination cannot be destroyed. As I asserted at the beginning of this discussion, more is possible than right-wing ideologues and their positivist allies ever conceptualized. These regressive forces have attempted to place a lid on human possibility and have induced good minds to focus on the trivial. To say it once again: we can be better. I urge you to join with those of us who advocate a constructive and affirmative critical pedagogy that values human dignity and the sacred relationship between human beings and their physical (environmental), social, cultural, political, economic, and philosophical contexts. The new terrain of insight we envision works to transcend positivistic forms of:

- *abstract individualism*—viewing humans apart from the natural contexts that have shaped them
- *technicalization*—valuing the technical over questions of human purpose and wellness
- *mechanization*—understanding humans as machine-like and computer-like, missing in the process the complex dynamics that make humans human
- *economism*—looking at human beings as primarily cogs within the economic domain rather than as sacred and unique entities with infinite capacities for doing good
- *nationalism*—conceptualizing human purpose in light of the competitive needs of the state and a narrow "patriotism" that undermines our capacity to ask ethical and moral questions about our collective behavior (Griffin, 1997)
- *rationalism*—viewing humans as "Mr. Spocks," who operate in ways that dismiss the importance of intuition, feeling, affect, emotion, and compassion in the effort to understand self and world
- *objectivism*—understanding that the goal of education and scholarship is to produce and consume a body of neutral data that fails to engage a variety of knowledges produced in diverse ways in differing cultures and historical eras.

Liberated from the positivist discourse of certainty, critically grounded students and teachers come to the realization that there are always multiple perspectives with which they are unfamiliar. Searching for new ways of seeing, they find that art and aesthetics provide a rich domain for such perspectives, new modes of reasoning that have been dismissed by a positivist culture high on the tradition's hyperrationality. As a frame-buster, art challenges what the great critical theorist Herbert Marcuse (1955) labeled: "the prevailing principle of reason" (p. 185). Art, imaginative literature, and music grant teachers and students an alternative epistemology, a way of knowing that transcends objective forms of knowledge (Rose & Kincheloe, 2003). Literary texts, drama, painting, sculpture, and dance help individuals see, hear, and feel beyond the surface level of sight and sound. They can alert the awakened to the alienated, one-dimensional profiles of the world promoted by positivistic culture.

Herbert Marcuse (1955) was acutely aware of this cognitive dimension of art and linked it to the development of a critical politics—an understanding of the way power shapes our perception of self and the world. Art assumes an ability to liberate us from modern alienation, he asserted, when it is viewed in light of specific historical conditions. Thus, for Marcuse, aesthetic transcendence of repressive alienation is a deliberate political act that identifies the object of art with the repressive situation to be overcome. This, of course, is not to say that in the quest for aesthetic transcendence of alienation art should be reduced to propaganda for a particular political perspective. It is a quite different matter for the critical educator to uncover the emancipatory demands of artistic production regardless of historical era and social location and to hold them up to the light of present repression (Marcuse, 1955; Bronner, 1988).

In this context art illuminates the problematic, as it creates new concepts and new angles from which to view the world. In this way art, through its interpreters, gives birth to meaning, as it breaks through the alienated surface to explore the submerged social and political relationships that shape events. In contemporary popular culture, one can see these aesthetic dynamics at work. Observing TV shows such as *The Simpsons* and *South Park*, for example, one can see brilliant writers parody the assumptions that lead to alienation in contemporary US society. The prejudice, pomposity, self-righteousness, and gravitas of the rich, famous, and powerful are open targets for the critical arrows of the screenwriters. As the socially, politically, and culturally problematic are exposed, the pedagogy of *The Simpsons* and *South Park* becomes an act of defamiliarization. The classroom pedagogy we promote here takes a similar path, as teachers learn not only to defamiliarize the "common-sense" worlds of their peers and students but also to create situations where student experience can be used to defamiliarize the world of schooling.

As aesthetic concerns with the "now" defamiliarize contemporary education's tendency to standardize and formalize the role of instruction, teachers and students seek pleasurable ways of reconceptualizing and reconstructing the institution. Overcoming the tyranny of reliance on delayed gratification for future success and the demonization of learning that is fun, critical teachers set up a mode of scholarship that is unbowed by the alienating power of positivist truth. Emerging from this playful haughtiness is the realization that the arts promote a form of teaching that requires interpretation and understanding of context. In this context critical teachers fight forces that suppress intellectual and other types of freedom. As distasteful as it may be to some groups, we believe that addressing alienation necessitates the exposure of these forces, these dominant cultural fictions that attempt to regulate us.

The Ironic Curriculum

The critical curriculum connected to the classroom teaching we imagine is always ironic about its goals. Such irony forces teachers to subject this curriculum to self-criticism, to a questioning of the assumptions it is making about the world. This runs contrary to the objectives of the positivist curriculum and the classrooms it supports. The purpose of the positivist curriculum is indoctrination and regulation. There is no room in a standardized classroom to question the assumptions behind the "facts" that appear on the standards test. Such a process would not help improve test scores and would be considered by right-wing reforms as not only a waste of time but also quite dangerous. The pervasive assertion that reflection on educational purpose is a dangerous activity should alert friends of democracy to the political problems inherent in such alienated curricula. A society is democratic to the degree that it allows for reflection and criticism of its assumptions and action. By such a measure of democracy, contemporary American society scores low on the democrameter.

Our understanding of complexity also reminds us of the problems of positivist curricula and classrooms. When we recognize the complexity of knowledge we come to realize that social, cultural, literary, political, scientific, psychological, and philosophical knowledge production rarely tells an easily discerned, unitary, uncomplicated story (Willinsky, 2001). The data that research constructs are always complicated and demand interpretation and contextual analysis. The effort to apply such knowledge is even more complex. When we fail to realize this complexity, scientific research often leads to new forms of alienation. This new alienation involves the cognitive realm and the domain of our being (ontology—the branch of philosophy that studies the nature of being, in this context what it means to be human). A critical ontology (Kincheloe, 2003) asks what the nature is of our relationship to the world, what is our being-in-the-world.

Cognitive alienation undermines our ability to discern anything about the world but the most surface level empirical insights; ontological alienation subverts our ability to gain insight into the forces that have helped construct our identities. When we are ontologically alienated we have a very immature sense of who exactly we are. Ensnared in this cognitive and ontological alienation, humans find themselves able to gather copious data about matter and energy but unable to develop our understanding of the nature of the minds that put such information to use. Over the past 2,000 years, for example, we have increased our capacity to wage war, while at the same time learning little about the causes of war. We become technologically proficient but ethically bankrupt. We become economically prosperous but possess no vision of what we can do collectively with our wealth. A central manifestation of our alienation is that we become increasingly self-centered and narcissistic.

The work of the Central Intelligence Agency (CIA) provides a great example of this alienation. Over the last several decades the CIA has been taken by surprise again and again by the march of world events. From the resistance of the Cuban people against an American-led attack on Fidel Castro's Cuba at the Bay of Pigs invasion in 1961 and the Iranian Revolution of 1978–1979, to the fall of the Soviet Union in 1991 and 9/11 (to mention only a few examples), the CIA has focused on the obvious and ignored the profound. In every case, the CIA directed its attention to a particular national leadership's fidelity (or lack of) to short-term US military and economic interests in the area. In every case they ignored the social, cultural, and ideological dynamics reshaping the groups and individuals that did not occupy positions in formal political institutions. In every case their understanding of a particular state of affairs was subverted by such a strategy. The agency never learned from its mistakes.

This cognitive and ontological alienation has been exacerbated by a competitive impulse (e.g., America is better than every other nation in the world; we're number one with the highest gross national product [GNP] in the world; we have nothing to learn from "them"). In this alienated state, our social imagination is restricted, as we are bound to simple personal desires. Our affection is limited to the family unit and a perverted sense of patriotism that promotes an unthinking my-country-right-or-wrong orientation. This "neo-know-nothingism" decontextualizes the social, cultural, ethical, and the temporal, in the process robbing men and women of an understanding of the forces that have shaped them, visions of ethical

behavior, and insights generated by an understanding of one's past and its connection to one's future. These are the perspectives that the CIA has lacked. Without them the intelligence organization will continue to rely on alienated ways of studying the world, in the process producing naïve data and supporting counterproductive and unethical policies. Even the CIA could use an ironic curriculum to recast its cognitive frameworks and develop new insights into what is missing in its methods of knowledge production.

The ironic curriculum promoted here for our critical classroom teaching is a vaccination against cognitive and ontological alienation. Thus, we bring hidden social, political, and cultural infrastructures to consciousness to facilitate larger efforts to empower teachers and students to make conscious choices concerning their lives. Demonstrating their cognitive and ontological alienation, many educators move through sixteen to twenty or more years of schooling without ever being induced to think about their own thinking and the infrastructures and discourses that have shaped it. The discourse of positivist science, for example, with its obsession with measurement has shaped the nature of dominant learning experiences in schools. Educational and psychological science has devoted much attention to the development of more precise systems of measurement and the application of such measurement to the minds of students. As a result, many educators and lay people cannot think of intelligence in any terms other than the number on an IQ test.

This alienating science has fragmented the world to the point that individuals are blinded to particular forms of human experience. Attempting to study the world in isolation, bit by bit, educational scientists have separated the study of schools from society. For the purpose of simplifying the process of analysis, disciplines of study are divided arbitrarily without regard for larger context (Kincheloe & Berry, 2004). Educational reforms of recent years, including top-down mandated standards and standardized curriculum, have been formulated outside of the wider cultural and political concerns for where students come from or where they find themselves in relation to education. As politicians of both major parties mandate a test-driven, one-size-fits-all curriculum, they create new strains of cognitive and ontological alienation. Finding its roots in positivist fragmentation, recent educational reforms have produced a "factoid syndrome," where students learn isolated bits and pieces of information for texts without concern for relationships among the data or their applications to personal struggles or the problems of the world. An ironic curriculum is acutely aware of these issues.

Thus, the classrooms we promote are not grounded on an objective curriculum, which refuses to discuss its intellectual roots, its cultural, economic, philosophical, and social assumptions, and its location in history. These insights help teachers understand the diverse nature and needs of different classrooms and students. In the alienated standardized curriculum of the middle of the first decade of the twenty-first century, the claim that "we treat all students the same" is a cruel hoax. An ironic curriculum and a critical classroom are grounded on the understanding that this ostensibly benign proclamation shields some harmful practices. Our pedagogy commences with an appreciation of the divergent sociocultural locations of

schools and students in the web of reality and the power asymmetries that complicate any classroom experience (Apple, 1993).

Any attempt to provide an egalitarian and socially just experience for students in these classrooms begins not with suppression of these differences but with a recognition of them that moves us to informed action. Any classroom teaching that takes place outside of these insights will lead to a perpetuation and an exacerbation of cognitive and ontological alienation. Of course, this is the knowledge that makes right-wing politicos and educational leaders very, very nervous. It may make such fear mongers nervous, but it is necessary to the survival of public education and a democratic society. These are the types of stakes critical teachers are playing for in the middle of the first decade of the twenty-first century.

REFERENCES

Anderson, P., & Summerfield, J. (2004). Why is urban education different from suburban and rural education? In S. Steinberg & J. Kincheloe (Eds.), *19 urban questions: Teaching in the city.* New York: Peter Lang.

Apple, M. (1993). The politics of official knowledge: Does a national curriculum make sense? *Teachers College Record, 95*(2), 222–241.

Bronner, S. (1988). Between art and utopia: Reconsidering the aesthetic theory of Herbert Marcuse. In R. Pippin, A. Feenberg, & C. Webel (Eds.), *Marcuse: Critical theory and the promise of utopia.* Westport, CT: Bergin and Garvey.

Bruner, J. (1996). *The culture of education.* Cambridge, MA: Harvard University Press.

Carr, W. (1998). The curriculum in and for a democratic society. *Curriculum Studies,*

6(3) [Online]. Available at: *http://www*
.triangle.co.uk/pdf/validate.asp.

Covaleskie, J. (2004). Philosophical instruction. In J. Kincheloe & D. Weil (Eds.),
*Critical thinking and learning: An encyclo-
pedia.* Westport, CT: Greenwood.

Gee, J., Hull, G., & Lankshear, C. (1996). *The
new work order: Behind the language of the
new capitalism.* Boulder, CO: Westview.

Goodson, I. (1999). The educational researcher
as public intellectual. *British Educational
Research Journal, 25*(3), 277–297.

Griffin, D. (1997). *Parapsychology, philosophy,
and spirituality: A postmodern exploration.*
Albany: State University of New York
Press.

Harrington, H., & Quinn-Leering, K. (1995).
Reflection, dialogue, and computer conferencing. Paper presented to the American Educational Research Association.
San Francisco. April 25.

Herrnstein, R., & Murray, C. (1994). *The
bell curve: Intelligence and class structure in
American life.* New York: The Free Press.

Horn, R., & Kincheloe, J. (2001). *American
standards: Quality education in a complex
world—The Texas case.* New York: Peter
Lang.

Kincheloe, J. (1999). *How do we tell the workers? The socioeconomic foundations of work
and vocational education.* Boulder, CO:
Westview.

Kincheloe, J. (2001). *Getting beyond the facts:
Teaching social studies/social sciences in the
twenty-first century.* New York: Peter Lang.

Kincheloe, J. (2002). *The sign of the burger:
McDonald's and the culture of power.*
Philadelphia: Temple University Press.

Kincheloe, J. (2003). Critical ontology: Visions of selfhood and curriculum. *JCT:
Journal of Curriculum Theorizing, 19*(1),
47–64.

Kincheloe, J. (2004). *Critical pedagogy.* New
York: Peter Lang.

Kincheloe, J., & Berry, K. (2004). *Rigour and
complexity in educational research: Conceptualizing the bricolage.* London: Open
University Press.

Kincheloe, J., & Steinberg, S. (1997). *Changing multiculturalism.* London: Open University Press.

Marcuse, H. (1955). *Eros and civilization.*
Boston: Beacon Press.

Reason, P., & Bradbury, H. (2000). Introduction: Inquiry and participation in search
of a world worthy of human aspiration. In
P. Reason & H. Bradbury (Eds.), *Handbook of action research: Participative inquiry
and practice.* Thousand Oaks, CA: Sage.

Rose, K., & Kincheloe, J. (2003). *Art, culture,
and education: Artful teaching in a frac-
tured landscape.* New York: Peter Lang.

Roth, W., Tobin, K., & Ritchie, S. (2001).
Re/constructing elementary science. New
York: Peter Lang.

Steinberg, S. (2001). *Multi/intercultural conversations.* New York: Peter Lang.

Willinsky, J. (2001). Raising the standards
for democratic education: Research and
evaluation as public knowledge. In
J. Kincheloe and D. Weil (Eds.), *Standards and schooling in the U.S.: An Ency-
clopedia.* Santa Barbara, CA: ABC-Clio.

Part III Additional Resources

Discussion Questions

Students should carefully read each question and support each response with examples and specific references to the readings that are being considered.

1. How can teacher leadership and the use of Professional Learning Communities change the culture of an entire school? How can teachers work within the bureaucracy to ensure that teachers' voices help shape policy? Whose support is necessary to facilitate these changes? How likely is it that such support will be available?
2. How might teacher leadership look from the perspective of a principal? A student? A parent? Discuss.
3. Everything that happens in a school should focus on the well-being and success of all students. Changing the expectations for the roles and responsibilities of teachers assumes that all teachers are committed professionals. How does one go about addressing the lack of teaching and learning effectiveness in some teachers' classrooms without challenging a colleague's competence or questioning his or her professional commitment? Is there a role for teacher leaders in this scenario?
4. How important are personal characteristics for leadership, for example, age, gender, experience, or race? What are the qualities and skills needed for teacher leadership?
5. Identify a teacher leader whom you have admired in the past. In small groups, identify the traits and characteristics of that person. Attempt to answer the following questions: What is teacher leadership? What does it look like in a school setting? Finally, discuss the impact of teacher leaders on the professional status of teachers. What changes would occur in the profession if teacher leadership became the norm in schools?

Guide to Further Reading

Cowhey, Mary. 2006. *Black Ants and Buddhists: Thinking Critically and Teaching Differently*. Portland, ME: Stenhouse Publishers.

Danielson, C. 2006. *Teacher Leadership That Strengthens Professional Practice*. Alexandria, VA: Association for Supervision and Curriculum Development (ASCD).

Donaldson, G. A. 2000. *Cultivating Leadership in Schools: Connecting People, Purpose, and Practice*. New York: Teachers College Press.

Fullan, Michael G., and A. Hargreaves. 1991. *What's Worth Fighting For? Working Together for Your School.* New York: Teachers College Press.

Postman, N., and C. Weingartner. 1969. *Teaching as a Subversive Activity.* New York: Dell Publishing.

Sergiovanni, T. J. 2000. *Leadership for the Schoolhouse: How Is It Different? Why Is It Important?* San Francisco: Jossey-Bass.

Related Resources

http://www.cstp-wa.org
   The Center for Strengthening the Teaching Profession
http://www.ctl.vcu.edu
   Center for Teacher Leadership
http://www.teachingquality.org
   Center for Teaching Quality
www.csupomona.edu/~ijtl
   International Journal of Teacher Leadership
http://www.nbpts.org
   National Board for Professional Teaching Standards
http://www.teacherleaders.org
   Teacher Leaders Network, Center for Teaching Quality
http://www.teacherleaders.typepad.com
   Teacher Leaders Network, Teacher Voices
http://www.teacherscount.org
   Teachers Count

Part IV

WHAT ARE THE ROLES AND RESPONSIBILITIES OF STUDENTS?

INTRODUCTION

It should be evident at this point that the answer to each of the five questions shapes the answer to the next question. How we talk about the roles and responsibilities of students is related to the aims and goals that we have for education; the kinds of knowledge and cognitive skills that we want educational experiences to produce; and, finally, how students will interact and participate in their own education. Theodore Sizer (2004) found that in America, our system of public education most often educated students for "stupidity and passivity." He argued that American schools expect students to sit quietly, take in everything that is presented to them, and then "spit it out" on a test at a later date. We neither encourage nor promote critical thinking or problem solving. In fact, students who want to direct or shape their own learning tend to be punished for not fitting in or, worse, for being subversive. Of course, I am talking about the education of the "average" child in America. Programs for the "gifted and talented" or honors students may, on occasion, break out of this mold, but we should also consider why we differentiate the educational experiences of "gifted" children from those of "average" children. What would happen if all children were viewed by the schools as gifted and tal-

ented? Would it be a problem to interject creativity, innovation, and critical thinking into the curriculum for a majority of students? I continue to be appalled by the high level of "drill and kill" activity that I see in classrooms, or, as I like to describe it, the number of "two-by-four" teachers who still exist—teachers guided by the two covers of the textbook and the four walls of the classroom. When I complain to teachers about the problems associated with the pervasive mediocrity found in many educational programs, I am simply reminded that high-stakes testing is responsible. Teachers feel a need to progress through the curriculum quickly and ignore efforts to teach with depth and breadth and prepare students to critically question and challenge the ideas that are presented. Is it enough to prepare students for passivity and stupidity—to simply deliver knowledge in sound bites? Or should we consider it equally important to prepare students to be leaders . . . to be individuals of honor and integrity . . . to question and challenge values and beliefs . . . to be political and to understand the roles and responsibilities of citizenship and public service? These are the questions that we must consider when we talk about the best education for *all* students, not just a few.

In Part IV of this book, students will encounter the work of Harry F. Wolcott, James T. Sears, Barry M. Franklin, Michelle Fine, and George Wood in Chapters 16–20. Each of these authors considers the multiple roles and responsibilities of students within the context of an examination of the values and beliefs that shape teacher expectations for students. Student roles and responsibilities are often attached to the characteristics that make each student unique and ultimately affect the kinds of learning experiences provided by the schools. These readings represent only a small portion of the literature that considers the ways in which teachers and students interact and how values and beliefs about diversity shape professional behavior.

Harry F. Wolcott

CHAPTER 16

Adequate Schools and Inadequate Education
The Life History of a Sneaky Kid

"I guess if you're going to be here, I need to know something about you, where you're from, and what kind of trouble you're in," I said to the lad, trying not to reveal my uncertainty, surprise, and dismay at his uninvited presence until I could learn more his circumstances. It wasn't much of an introduction, but it marked the beginning of a dialogue that lasted almost two years from that moment. Brad (a pseudonym, although, as he noted, using his real name wouldn't really matter, since "no one knows who I am anyway") tersely stated his full name; the fact that his parents had "split up" and that his mother was remarried and living in Southern California; his father's local address; and that he was not at present in any trouble because he wasn't "that stupid." He also volunteered that he had spent time in the state's correctional facility for youth, but quickly added, "It wasn't really my fault."

It was not our meeting itself that was a surprise; it was that Brad had been living at this remote spot on my steep and heavily wooded 20-acre homesite on the outskirts of town for almost five weeks. In that time, he had managed to build a 10-by-12-foot

cabin made of newly cut sapling logs and roofed with plywood paneling. A couple of weeks earlier, I had stumbled across his original campsite, but I assumed it had been made by some youngster enjoying a bivouac en route to hiking a nearby ridge that afforded a fine view, a popular day hike for townspeople and an occasional overnight adventure for kids. I also found a bow saw, but I thought it had been left by a recent surveying party. Brad had been watching me at the time and later admitted cursing to himself for being careless in leaving tools about.

I did not realize that I had both a new cabin and an unofficial tenant until a neighbor reported that his 8-year-old son claimed not only to have seen but to have spoken to a "hobo" while wandering through my woods. The hobo turned out to be the then–19-year-old youth, slightly stoop-shouldered and of medium build, standing opposite me. And it is his story that I am about to relate.

As intrigued and involved as I eventually became with Brad and his story, my purpose in providing this account transcends the individual case, even though I will tie my remarks closely to it. That purpose is related to my professional interest in anthropology and education and, particularly, in cultural acquisition, drawing upon anthropology both for approach and for perspective in looking at educational issues (see Wolcott 1982). There is no shortage of case study materials about alienated youth.[1] Attention here will be drawn particularly to educationally relevant aspects of this case. Brad's story underscores and dramatizes a critical distinction that anthropologists make between *schooling* and *education* and raises questions about our efforts at education for young people beyond the purview of the schools.[2] Adequate schools may be necessary, but they are not sufficient to ensure an adequate education.

Brad's strategy for coping with his life first impressed me as bold, resourceful, and even romantic, as did his building of a cabin. Faced with jobs he did not want to do (he abhors dishwashing, yet that seemed to be the only work he felt he could get because "those jobs are always open") and expenses he could not afford (renting an apartment, buying and operating a motorcycle), he had chosen to change his lifestyle radically by reducing his cash needs to a minimum. What he could not afford, he would try to do without.

Never before had he done the things he now set out to do. He had never lived in the woods (though he had gone camping), never built a log house (though he had occasionally helped his father in light construction), never thought about a personal inventory of essential items. He had identified the cabin site, hidden from view but with a commanding view of its own, during one of his endless and solitary explorations of streets, roads, and paths in and around the city. The location was near a section of the city where he had once lived

as a child. He went deep into a densely wooded area, entering from the east and failing to realize how close he had come to my house on the county road around the west side of the ridge. But he knew he had to be near town. He needed to be where, one way or another, he could pick up the things essential to his anticipated lifestyle. He did not need much, but what he did need—hammer, saw, nails, sleeping bag, stove, cooking utensils, flashlight and lantern, pants and shoes, containers for carrying and storing water—he scrounged, stole, or, occasionally and reluctantly, purchased.

Brad displayed few qualities that would earn him the title of outdoorsman. His tools and equipment were often mislaid or neglected. He proved terrible at tying knots. He cut trees unnecessarily and turned his own trails into slippery troughs of mud. In spite of occasional references to himself as "Jungle Boy," he was basically a city boy making whatever accommodation was necessary to survive inexpensively. His fuel and food came from town; he was totally dependent on the city even though he could not afford to live in it. If his menu gradually became more like that of the woodsman (potatoes, onions, pancakes, melted-cheese sandwiches, eggs, soup, canned tuna, powdered milk, and powdered orange juice), it was because he realized that these items could almost stretch $70 of food stamps into a month's ration. He washed and dried his clothes in coin-operated machines at night at a nearby apartment complex. His battery-operated radio played almost constantly, and he became even more cabin-bound watching a small battery-operated TV set purchased for him by his mother during a brief visit, their first in over two years.

It was not Brad's wont to take leisurely walks in the woods, spend time enjoying sunsets, or listen to birdcalls. He brought what he could find (and carry up steep, narrow trails) of his urban environment with him. Though not very sociable, he calculatingly mismanaged his purchases so that on many days he "had to" bicycle two miles each way to his favorite store to get a pack of cigarettes and perhaps buy a can of beer or smoke a joint in a nearby park. Town was the only direction he traveled. Yet, almost without exception, he returned to his cabin each evening, usually before darkness made the trip hazardous on an unlit bike. The security of having literally created a place all his own lent a critical element of stability to his life. He was proud of what he had built, even though he acknowledged that, were he starting over, his cabin would be "bigger and better in every way." His dreams for improving it never ceased.

For a while he envisioned building a tree house high in a giant Douglas fir nearby. A fearless tree-climber, he attached a high pulley and cable swing so he could trim branches and hoist construction materials. The tree house idea occupied his thoughts for weeks. During that time, he made few improvements on the cabin. The idea of being virtually inaccessible high in a tree proved more romantic than practical, however, and eventually he gave it up, brought his tools back to the cabin, and began work in earnest on improvements that included cutting out a section of wall and adding a lean-to bunk bed. The cable was removed from the tree house site and found its permanent place as a hillside swing with a breathtaking arc among the treetops on the slope below. Swinging provided a literal as well as figurative high

for Brad. Pausing to rest between turns at the strenuous exercise, he volunteered the only positive comment I ever heard him make regarding the future: "I'll still swing like this when I'm 60!"

In brief glimpses, other people's lives often appear idyllic. Brad's Robinson Crusoe–like life had many appealing qualities. He seemed to have freed himself from the trappings of the Establishment, which he saw as a curiously circular and uninviting system that required him to take a job he hated in order to earn enough to provide transportation to and from work, and money for the rent on some cheap place where he would rather not live. He had seen his father work hard, dream even harder, and yet, in Brad's opinion, "get nowhere." Brad was trying to figure out for himself what he wanted in life and whether it was really worth the effort.

I found it hard to argue on behalf of what some menial job would get him. I heard quite well his argument that, lacking in skill or experience, he would probably have to do work at once physically harder and lower-paying than most jobs today. He could be an indefatigable worker, but I think he felt some anxiety about being able to keep up on jobs requiring hours of continuous hard physical labor. An earlier and short-lived job as a tree planter had convinced him that hard work does not ensure success.

A glimpse into Brad's daily life does not dispel the romantic image of his existence. He arose when he wanted and retired when he wanted (although, with the cold, dark, and perennial dampness of the Northwest's winters, and with little to do, he spent so much time in the sack that getting to sleep became increasingly problematic). He could eat when he chose and cook or not as mood—and a rather sparse cupboard—dictated. Food and cigarette needs dominated his schedule of trips to town. A trip to the store, or to see about food stamps (in effect he had no address, so he went to the Welfare Office in person), or to secure other supplies (a tire for the bicycle, fuel for lanterns or the stove, hardware items for the cabin) occurred once or twice a week. And if there was no needed trip, he was free to decide—quite consciously, though rather impulsively, I think—how to spend the day.

Although the cabin was sometimes untidy and utensils were seldom washed before they were used again, Brad kept his person and his clothes clean. He brushed his teeth regularly. He never went to town without "showering," or at least washing his face and hair. In warm weather he underscored the nymphlike nature of his existence by remaining almost, or totally, unclad in the seclusion of his immediate cabin area, though he was excruciatingly self-conscious in public settings. His preference for privacy was highlighted by recollections of his distress at regimented public showering "on procedures" at reform school, and such experiences had made options like joining the armed services something he insisted he would only do if he had to. Brad was, at first glance, a free spirit. He regarded himself that way, too: "I do what I want."

The Cultural Context of a Free Spirit

There is no universal set of things to be desired or events to fill one's days and dreams, just as there is no absolute set of things to be learned (see Wallace 1961b:38). What people learn or want to do or dream about is embedded in particular macro- and microcultural systems.

Brad was aware of many aspect of his "culture" that he felt he could do without, including—up to a point—seeking much involvement within his society, seeming to heed its expectation, or depending on its resources. But he was accustomed to technological innovations and he had been reared in a society where, it seemed to him, virtually *everyone* had everything they needed. Although he saw himself as living figuratively, as well as literally, at the edge of society, he was still society's child. He was free to insist, "I do what I want," but he was not free to do what he wanted. What he had learned to want was a function of his culture, and he drew narrowly and rather predictably from the cultural repertoire of the very society from which he believed he was extricating himself.

Brad needed to cook. An open fire is slow and most impractical on a rainy day. One needs a camp stove in order to cook inside a cabin. And fuel. And then a better stove. Cold water is all right for washing hands but it can be a bit too bracing for washing one's hair or torso, especially when standing outside with the wind blowing. One needs a bigger pan to heat water for bathing. Soap and shampoo. A towel. A new razor. A mirror. A bigger mirror. A foam rubber mattress. A chair. A chaise lounge.

One needs something to look at and listen to. Magazines are a brief diversion, but rock music is essential. One needs a radio. Flashlight batteries are expensive for continual radio listening; a radio operated by an automobile battery would be a better source—and could power a better radio. An automobile battery needs to be recharged.

Carrying a battery to town is awkward, and constantly having to pay to have it recharged is expensive. As well as access to a power supply (in my carport), one needs a battery charger. No, this one is rated too low; a bigger one would be better. Luckily not a harsh winter, but a wet one. The dirt floor of the cabin gets muddy; a wood floor is essential. The roof leaks, a heavier grade of plywood and a stronger tarpaulin to place over it are necessary. The sleeping bag rips where it got wet; a replacement is needed. Shoes wear out from constant use on the trails; clothes get worn or torn. Flashlights and batteries wear out. Cigarettes (or tobacco), matches, eggs, bread, Tang, Crisco, pancake flour, syrup—supplies get low. An occasional steak helps vary the austere diet.

One needs transportation. A bicycle is essential, as are spare parts to keep it in repair. Now a minor accident: The bicycle is wrecked. No money to buy a new one. Brad "hypes" himself up and sets out to find a replacement. "Buy one? When they're so easy to get? No way!"

The Life History of a Sneaky Kid

Here is the place to let Brad relate something of his life and how he had tried to make sense of, and come to grips with, the world about him.

Ideally, in relating a life history through an ethnographic autobiography, informants tell their stories almost entirely in their own words (e.g., classics such as Leo Simmons's *Sun Chief*, 1942, or Oscar Lewis's *Children of Sanchez*, 1961; see also Brandes 1982). There should be a high ratio of information to explanation in a life story; sometimes there is no explanation or explicit interpretation at all. Time, space, and purpose require me to proceed more

directly. I have organized the material around themes suggested by Brad himself, and although I have been faithful to his words as he spoke them, I have tried to select the most cogent excerpts from months of informal conversations and several hours of formal interviews that Brad volunteered expressly for this purpose.[3]

I have given particular attention to aspects of Brad's story that illustrate the two major points of this paper: that education consists of more than schooling, and that we give little systematic attention to the course of a young person's education once he or she is out of school. For these purposes, I have dwelt more on social concerns than on personal or psychological ones. Brad had some hang-ups focused largely on his acceptance of his body and a preoccupation with sexual fantasy as yet unfulfilled—*Portnoy's Complaint* personified. In time (or, more candidly, not quite in time; he sank unexpectedly into a mood of utter despair and abruptly announced he was "hitting the road" because he saw no future where he was), I realized he had some deep-seated emotional hang-ups as well. My concern in this paper, however, is with Brad as a social rather than a psychological being, and thus with personality-in-culture rather than with personality per se.

"In the Chute"

A speaker at the 1981 American Correctional Association meetings was reported in the national press to have used the phrase "in the chute" to describe individuals whose lives seem headed for prison, even though they have not yet arrived there: "People who are 'in the chute,' so to speak, and heading toward us, are beginning that movement down in infancy."

When the ethnography begins, Brad is not yet in the chute. It is not inevitable that he end up in trouble, but he could. Excerpts from his life story suggest how things point that way. Here he recalls a chain of events that started at age 10 with what proved a traumatic event in his life, his parents' divorce:

On the loose. "After my parents got divorced, I was living with my dad. I had quite a bit of freedom. My dad wasn't around. If I didn't want to go to school, I just didn't go. Everybody who knows me now says, 'That guy had the world's record for ditching school.' My dad was at work all day and there was no one to watch me. I was pretty wild. My dad took me to a counseling center at the university; they told me I was 'winning the battles but losing the war.'

"After my dad got remarried, I had no freedom anymore. I had a new mother to watch me. I got mad at her a couple of times, so I moved in with her parents. I went to seventh grade for a while and got pretty good grades. Then I went to Southern California to visit my mother. When my dad said he'd have to 'make some arrangements' before I could return, I just stayed there. But I got into a hassle with my stepdad, and I ditched some classes, and suddenly I was on a bus back to Oregon.

"My father had separated again and I moved into some little apartment with him. He wanted me to go to another school, but I said, 'Forget it, man, I'm not going to another school. I'm tired of school.' So I'd just lay around the house—stay up all night, sleep all day.

"Finally I told my mom I'd be a 'good boy,' and she let me move back to Southern California. But I got in another hassle with my stepdad. I ran out of the house and stayed with some friends for a few months. But then the police got in a hassle with me and they said I'd have to go back with my dad or they were going to send me to a correctional institution. The next thing you know, I was back on the bus."

Getting busted. "By then my dad had remarried again. I wasn't ready for another family. I stayed about two days, then I left. I figured any place was better than living there. But they got pissed at me because I kept coming back [breaking into the house] for food, so they called the cops on me. Running away from them, I broke my foot and had to go to the hospital. Then I got sent to reform school. They had a charge against me [contraband], but I think the real reason was that I didn't have any place to go. I was in reform school for eight months."

Second-rate jobs and second-rate apartments. "I finally played their 'baby game' and got out of reform school. They sent me to a halfway house in Portland. I got a job, made some money, got a motorcycle, moved to another place, then that job ended. I got another job with a churchgoing plumber for a while, but I got fired. Then I came back and worked for my dad, but there wasn't nothing to do. And I got in some family hassles. So I got a few jobs and lived in some cheap apartments.

"For a while I was a bum down at the Mission. I'd get something to eat, then I'd go sleep under a truck. My sleeping bag was all I had. I knew winter was coming and I'd have to do something. I saw a guy I knew and he said, 'Hey, I've got a place if you'd like to crash out until you get something going.' So I went there and got a job for about four months washing dishes. Then my mom came up from California to visit and found me an apartment. God, how I hated that place, with people right on the other side of those thin walls who know you're all alone and never have any visitors or anything. I quit washing dishes; they cut me down to such low hours I wasn't making any money anyway. So I just hibernated for the winter."

A new life. "When the rent ran out, I picked up my sleeping bag and the stuff I had and headed for the hills at the edge of town. I found a place that looked like no one had been here for a while, and I set up a tarp for shelter. I decided to take my time and build a place for myself, because I wasn't doing anything anyway. I just kept working on it. I've been here a year and a half now. I've done some odd jobs, but mostly I live on food stamps.

"I used to think about doing something like this when I lived in Portland. I read a book called *How to Live in the Woods on Pennies a Day.* I even tried staying out in the woods a couple of times, but I didn't know exactly what to do. I wasn't thinking about a cabin then. All I knew was that I needed someplace to get out of the wind and someplace to keep dry. I saw this piece of level ground and knew that if I had tools and nails I could probably put up some walls. As I went along I just figured out what I would need.

"I put up four posts and started dragging logs around till the walls were built. There were plenty of trees around. It took about a week to get the walls. I slept in a wet sleeping bag for a couple of nights, 'cause I didn't have a roof. The first roof was some pieces of paneling that I carried up from some kids' tree fort. I had a dirt floor but I knew I'd have to have a wood floor someday. I knew about plaster because I had worked with it before, so I smeared some on the walls. All that I really needed at first was nails. I got the other stuff I needed from new houses being built nearby."

"Picking up" what was needed. "I got around town quite a bit. Anyplace where there might be something, I'd take a look. If I found anything that I needed, I'd pick it up and take it home. I just started a collection: sleeping bag, radio, plywood for the roof, windows, a stove, lanterns, tools, clothes, water containers, boots. If you took away everything that's stolen, there wouldn't be much left here. Like the saw. I just walked into a store, grabbed it, put a piece of cloth around it to hide it, and walked out.

"Before I got food stamps, I'd go to the store with my backpack, fill it with steaks and expensive canned food, and just walk out. If anybody saw me, I'd wave at them and keep walking. I didn't have much to lose, I figured. The closest I ever got to being stopped, I had two six-packs of beer and some cooked chicken. The guy in the store had seen me there before. I just waved, but he said, 'Stop right there.' I ran out and grabbed my bike, but he was right behind me. I knew the only thing I could do was drop the merchandise and get out of there with my skin and my bike, and that's what I did. He didn't chase me; he just picked up the bag and shook his head at me."

The bicycle thief. "We lived in the country for about three years while I was growing up. Moving back into town was kinda different. I went pretty wild after moving to town. Me and another kid did a lot of crazy stuff, getting into places and taking things. I'd stay out all night just looking in people's garages. I'd get lots of stuff. My room had all kinds of junk in it. That's when I was living with my dad, and he didn't really notice. He still has an electric pencil-sharpener I stole out of a church. He never knew where I got it.

"Instead of going to school, I'd stay home and work on bikes. We used to steal bikes all the time. We'd get cool frames and put all the hot parts on them. I've stolen lots of bikes—maybe around 50. But I probably shouldn't have never stolen about half of them, they were such junk. I just needed them for transportation."

Being sneaky. "I've always been kind of sneaky, I guess. That's just the way I am. I can't say why. My mom says that when I was a small kid I was always doing something sneaky. Not always—but I *could* be that way. I guess I'm still that way, but it's not exactly the same. It's just the way you think about things.

"I don't like to be sneaky about something I could get in trouble for. But I like to walk quietly so no one will see me. I could get in trouble for something like sneaking in somebody's backyard and taking a rototiller. I did that once. I sold the engine.

"I guess being sneaky means I always try to get away with something. There doesn't have to be any big reason. I used to tell the kid I was hanging around with: 'I don't steal stuff because I need it. I just like to do it for some excitement.'

"Last year I went 'jockey-boxing' with some guys who hang around at the park. That's when you get into people's glove compartments. It was a pretty dead night.

One guy wanted a car stereo. He had his tools and everything. So we all took off on bicycles, five of us. I was sort of tagging along and watching them—I didn't really do it. They got into a couple of cars. They got a battery vacuum cleaner and a couple of little things. You go to apartment houses where there's lots of cars and you find the unlocked ones and everybody grabs a car and jumps in and starts scrounging through.

"I've gone through glove compartments before and I probably will again someday if I see a car sitting somewhere just abandoned. But I'm not into it for fun anymore, and it doesn't pay unless you do a lot. Mostly young guys do it.

"I'm still mostly the same, though. I'll take a roll of tape or something from the supermarket. Just stick it in my pants. Or if I saw a knife that was easy to take. That's about it. Oh, I sneak into some nearby apartments to wash my clothes. I pay for the machines, but they are really for the tenants, not for me. And I'll sneak through the woods with a piece of plywood for the cabin."

I don't have to steal, but . . . "I'm not what you'd call a super thief, but I will steal. A super thief makes his living at it; I just get by. I don't have to steal, but it sure makes life a hell of a lot easier. I've always known people who steal stuff. It's no big deal. If you really want something, you have to go around looking for it. I guess I could teach you how to break into your neighbor's house, if you want to. There's lots of ways—just look for a way to get in. It's not that hard to do. I don't know what you'd call it. Risky? Crazy?

"I can be honest. Being honest means that you don't do anything to people that you don't know. I don't like to totally screw somebody. But I'll screw 'em a little bit. You could walk into somebody's garage and take everything they have— maybe $5,000 worth of stuff. Or you could just walk in and grab a chain saw. It's not my main hobby to go around looking for stuff to steal. I might see something, but I wouldn't go out of my way for it."

Breaking and entering. "I remember busting into my second-grade classroom. I went back to the schoolground on the weekend with another kid. We were just looking around outside and I said, 'Hey, look at that fire-escape door—you could pull it open with a knife.' We pulled it open and I went in and I took some money and three or four little cars and a couple of pens. There wasn't anything of value, but the guy with me stocked up on all the pens he could find. We got in trouble for it. That was the first time I broke in anywhere. I don't know why I did it. Maybe too many television shows. I just did it because I could see that you could do it.

"And I've gotten into churches and stores. I've broken into apartment-house recreation rooms a lot, crawling through the windows. And I've broken into a house before.

"I went in one house through the garage door, got inside, and scrounged around the whole house. God, there was so much stuff in that house. I munched a cake, took some liquor, took some cameras. Another time I thought there was nobody home at one house, and I went around to the bathroom window, punched in the screen and made a really good jump to the inside. I walked in the

house real quietly. Then I heard somebody walk out the front door, so I split. I didn't have nothin' then; I was looking for anything I could find. I just wanted to go scrounging through drawers to find some money.

"If I ever needed something that bad again and it was total chaos [i.e., desperation], I could do it and I would. It's not my way of life, but I'd steal before I'd ever beg."

Inching closer to the chute. "Just before I started living at the cabin, I kept having it on my mind that I needed some money and could rob a store. It seemed like a pretty easy way to get some cash, but I guess it wasn't a very good idea. I had a BB gun. I could have walked in there like a little Mafia, shot the gun a few times, and said, 'If you don't want those in your face, better give me the money.' There were a couple of stores I was thinking of doing it to.

"I was standing outside one store for about two hours. I just kept thinking about going in there. All of a sudden this cop pulls into the parking lot and kinda checks me out. I thought, 'Oh fuck, if that cop came over here and searched me and found this gun, I'd be shit.' So as soon as he split, I left. And after thinking about it for so long.

"But another time, I really did it. I went into one of those little fast-food stores. I had this hood over my head with a little hole for the mouth. I said to the clerk, 'Open the register.' And she said, 'What! Are you serious?' I knew she wasn't going to open it, and she knew I wasn't about to shoot her. So then I started pushing all the buttons on the cash register, but I didn't know which ones to push. And she came up and pulled the key. Then someone pulled up in front of the store and the signal bell went 'ding, ding.' So I booked.

"Another time I thought about going into a store and telling the cashier to grab the cash tray and pull it out and hand it to me. Or else I was going to wait till near closing time when they go by with a full tray of 20-dollar bills and grab it. Or go into a restaurant right after closing time, like on a Saturday night or something, and just take the whole till. I was going to buy a motorcycle with that. All I needed was $400 to get one.

"If I was ever that hurting, I could probably do it if I had to. It's still a possibility, and it would sure be nice to have some cash. But you wouldn't get much from a little store anyway. I'd be more likely just to walk in and grab a case of beer."

I'm not going to get caught. "I can't straighten out my old bike after that little accident I had the other day, and that means I need another bike. I'll try to find one to steal—that's the easiest way to get one. I should be able to find one for free, and very soon, instead of having to work and spend all that money, money that would be better off spent other places, like reinstating my driver's license.

"The way I do it, I go out in nice neighborhoods and walk around on people's streets and look for open garages, like maybe they just went to the store or to work and didn't close the door. I walk on streets that aren't main streets. Someone might spot me looking around at all these bikes, but even if somebody says something, they can't do anything to you. The cops might come up and question me, but nothing could happen.

"Now, if I was caught on a hot bike . . . but that's almost impossible. If I was caught, they'd probably take me downtown and I'd sit there awhile until I went to court, and who knows what they'd do. Maybe give me six months. They'd keep me right there at the jail. But it's worth the risk, because I'm not going to get caught. I did it too many times. I know it's easy.

"Even if I worked, the only thing I'd be able to buy is an old Schwinn 10-speed. The bike I'm going to get will be brand-new. Maybe a Peugeot or a Raleigh. A $400 bike at least. It might not be brand new, but if I could find a way, I'd get a $600 bike, the best one I could find. And I'll do whatever I have to, so no one will recognize it."

Home is the hunter. "I think this will be the last 'bike hunting' trip I'll ever go on . . . probably. I said it *might* be the last one. I could probably do one more. When I get to be 24 or 25, I doubt that I'll be walking around looking for bikes. But if I was 25 and I saw a nice bike, and I was in bad shape and really needed it, I'd get it. I'm not going to steal anything I don't need. Unless it's just sitting there and I can't help it, it's so easy. I'm not really corrupt, but I'm not 'innocent' anymore. I can be trusted, to some people."

"Can I trust you?" I asked.

"Yeah. Pretty much. I dunno. When it comes to small stuff. . . . "

Growing up. "When I was growing up, I was always doing something, but it wasn't that bad. My parents never did take any privileges away or give me another chance. Anytime I did something in California, my mother and stepdad just said, 'Back to

Oregon!' They didn't threaten, they just did it. My mom could have figured out something better than sending me back to Oregon all the time. She could have taken away privileges, or made me work around the house. And in Oregon, my dad could have figured a better way than throwing me out of the house. Bad times for me were getting in a hassle with my parents. Then I wouldn't have no place to go, no money or nothin': That happened with all of them at different times."

[By my count, Brad was reared in six households, including a time when he lived with his mother at her sister's home, and when he lived with one stepmother's parents for a while. That fact did not seem as disconcerting to him as the abruptness with which he was dispatched from one household to another.]

"The last time I got kicked out in California, I moved back to Oregon, but I only stayed in the house a couple of days. My stepmom and my dad started telling me I wasn't going to smoke pot anymore, I would have to go to school, I was going to have to stop smoking cigarettes, and other shit like that. I didn't like *anything* about that fucking house. Another reason is that my dad said I couldn't have a motorcycle.

"So I split. I just hung around town, sleeping anywhere I could find. I ripped off a quilt and slept out on a baseball field for a while. I stayed in different places for a couple of weeks. Then I got busted, got sent to reform school; then I got some work and the first thing I did was buy a motorcycle. I was riding without a license or insurance for a while. Even after I got a license, I kept getting tickets, so finally my license got suspended, and my dad took the motorcycle and sold it to pay for the tickets.

"If I had kids, I would just be a closer family. I would be with them more and show that you love them. You could talk to your kids more. And if they do something wrong, you don't go crazy and lose your temper or something."

Getting paid for dropping out. "I've earned some money at odd jobs since I came here, but mostly I live on food stamps. I knew that if I wasn't working and was out of money, food stamps were there. I've been doing it for quite a while. When I was at the Mission I had food stamps. A guy I worked with once told me all you had to do was go down there and tell 'em you're broke, that's what it's there for. I haven't really tried looking for a job. Food stamps are a lot easier. And I'd just be taking a job away from someone who needs it more. Now that I've figured out the kinds of things to buy, I can just about get by each month on $70 for food. If I couldn't get food stamps, I'd get a job. I guess food stamps are society's way of paying me to drop out."

Hiding out from life. "So now I've got this cabin fixed up and it really works good for me. This is better than any apartment I've ever had.

"I guess by living up here I'm sorta hiding out from life. At least I'm hiding from the life I had before I came up here. That's for sure. The life of a dumpy apartment and a cut-rate job. This is a different way of life.

"What would I have been doing for the year and a half in town compared to a year and a half up here? Like, all the work I've done here, none of it has gone for some landlord's pocketbook. I should be able to stay here until I get a good job.

"I like living like this. I think I'd like to be able to know how to live away from electricity and all that."

The romantic Robinson Crusoe aspect of a young man carving out a life in the wilderness, what his mother referred to as "living on a mountaintop in Oregon," is diminished by this fuller account of Brad's lifestyle. Brad would work if he "had to," but he had found that for a while—measured perhaps in years rather than weeks—he did not have to. If he was not hiding out from life, he had at least broken out of what he saw as the futility of holding a cut-rate job in order to live a cut-rate existence.

Brad kept a low profile that served double duty. He had a strong aversion to being "looked at" in settings where he felt he did not "blend in," and his somewhat remote cabin protected him from the eyes of all strangers—including the law. His cabin became his fortress; he expressed concern that he himself might be "ripped off." On sunny weekends, with the likelihood of hikers passing through the woods, he tended to stay near the cabin with an eye toward protecting his motley—but nonetheless precious—collection of tools and utensils, bicycles and parts, and personal belongings. He sometimes padlocked the cabin (though it easily could have been broken into) and always locked his bike when in town if he was going to be any distance from it. Had he been ripped off, he would hardly have called the police to help recover his stolen items; few were his in the first place.

Technically, he was not in trouble with the law, but to some extent the law exerted a constraining influence on him. In his view, to get caught was the worst thing that could happen to him and would have been "stupid" on his part. That tended to circumscribe both the frequency and extent of the illicit activities in which he engaged. But the law also menaced him because of his status as a down-and-outer and as a relatively powerless youth, a youth without resources. The law works on a cash basis. Working for me, Brad earned and saved enough money to purchase an engine for his bicycle in order to circumvent his earlier problems with the motorcycle. He was later to discover, via a traffic violation of over $300 (reduced to $90 with the conventional plea "guilty with explanation"), that a bicycle with an engine on it is deemed a motorized vehicle. Therefore, he was required by law to have a valid operator's license (his was still suspended), a license for the vehicle, and insurance. To make himself legal, he needed about $175 and would continue to face high semiannual insurance premiums. To his way of thinking, that expense got him "nothing," so he preferred to take his chances. Traffic fines were actually a major budget item for him, but his argument remained the same: "I won't get caught again."

Margaret Mead once commented that most Americans would agree that the "worst" thing a child can do is to steal (in MacNeil and Glover 1959). As a "sneaky kid," Brad had already been stealing stuff—little stuff, mostly—for more than half his lifetime. He seemed to be approaching the moment when he either would have to forgo stealing, regarding it as a phase of growing up and doing "crazy things" (jockey-boxing, breaking into the school on weekends, petty shoplifting, stealing bicycles), or step into the "chute" by joining the big leagues. With mask and gun, he had already faced the chute head-on. That event might have ended differently, had someone not called his bluff. With the issuance of repeated traffic fines, the courts themselves could conceivably precipitate a desperate need for quick and easy money.

Worldview: "Getting My Life Together"

The material presented thus far lends ample support for Brad's depiction of himself as a "sneaky kid" exhibiting a number of antisocial and unsociable traits. In the last 10 of his 20 years, Brad's antics often resulted in trouble ("hassles") and paved the way for more trouble than had actually befallen him. (In that regard, it is ironic that being sent to reform school—though on the technically serious charge of "supplying contraband" coupled with "harassment"—was, in his opinion, more a consequence of having "nowhere else to go" than of the offenses themselves.)

From mainstream society's point of view, Brad's story would seem to reflect the enculturation process going awry, a young person growing up apart from, rather than as a part of, the appropriate social system. Brad did not behave "properly" with regard to certain critical dimensions (e.g., respect for other people's property, earning his way); therefore, his almost exemplary behavior in other dimensions (his lack of pretense, his cleanliness, and, particularly, his resourcefulness and self-reliance) was apt to be overlooked. He was not a social asset, and he seemed destined for trouble.

Yet in both word and deed (and here is the advantage of knowing him for two years, rather than depending solely on formal interviews), Brad repeatedly demonstrated how he was more "insider" than "outsider" to the society he felt was paying him to drop out. In numerous ways he revealed a personal worldview not so far out of step with society after all. Adrift he may have been, but he was not without social bearings. The odds may have been against him, but they were not stacked. This was neither a "minority" kid fighting the immediate peril of the ghetto, nor a weak kid, nor a dumb kid, nor an unattractive kid, nor a kid who had not, at some time in his life, felt the security of family. Indeed, somewhere along the way he learned to value security so highly that his pursuit of it provided him an overriding sense of purpose.

Both of Brad's parents had worked all their adult lives and, judging from statements I heard them make, took pride in their efforts. If, as Brad sized it up, they were "not really rich," they were at least comfortable. Perhaps from Brad's point of view they had paid too high a price for what they had, or had given up too much to attain it, but they are the embodiment of the American working class. As Brad expressed it: "My dad's worked all his life so he can sit at a desk and not hold a screwdriver anymore. But he just works! He never seems to have any fun."

Absolutely no one, including anthropologists who devote careers to the task, ever learns the totality of a culture. Conversely, no one, including the most marginal or socially isolated of humans, ever escapes the deep imprint of macro- and microcultural systems in which he or she is reared as a member of a family, a community, and a nation. Evidence of that cultural imprinting abounds in Brad's words and actions. I have combed his words and found in his worldview glimmers of hope—if only he does not "get caught doing something stupid" or in some unexpected way get revisited by his past. Though he occasionally makes some deliberate, unsanctioned responses, Brad appears well aware of the "cultural meanings" of his behavior (see Wallace 1961a:135).

If Brad does "make it," it will be largely because of the cultural imprinting of values instilled at some time in that same past. Let me here make the point to which I will return in conclusion: There was no constructive force working effectively on Brad's behalf to guide, direct, encourage, or assist him. He had no sponsor, no support system, virtually no social network. The agencies poised to respond to him would act when and if he made a mistake and got caught. He could not get help without first getting into trouble. The only social agency that exerted a positive educative influence on him was an indirect consequence of the mixed blessing of food stamps, which kept him from having to steal groceries but made it unnecessary for him to work. He had learned to spend his allotment wisely in order to see him through the month.

The following excerpts, selected topically, suggest the extent to which Brad already had acquired a sense of middle-class morality and an ethos of working to achieve material success. They also point to loose strands that remain to be woven together someday, if he is to be bound more securely to the Establishment.

A job—that's all that makes you middle-class. "A job is all that makes you middle-class. If I'm going to have a job, I've got to have a bike that works. I've got to have a

roof, I've got to have my clothes washed. And I'd probably need rain gear, too. You can't go into any job in clothes that look like you just came out of a mud hut.

"Even though I've worked for a while at lots of different things, I guess you could say that I've never really held a job. I've worked for my dad awhile—altogether about a year, off and on. I helped him wire houses and do other things in light construction. I scraped paint for a while for one company. I worked for a graveyard for about eight months, for a plumber a while, and I planted trees for a while.

"I wouldn't want to have to put up with a lot of people on a job that didn't make me much money. Like at a checkout counter—that's too many people. I don't want to be in front of that many people. I don't want to be a known part of the community. I don't mind having a job, but I don't like a job where everyone sees you do it. Working with a small crew would be best—the same gang every day. I'd like a job where I'm out and moving. Anything that's not cleaning up after somebody else, where you're not locked up and doing the same thing over and over, and where you can use your head a little, as well as your back.

"My mother said, 'If you had a little job right now, you'd be in heaven.' Yeah, some cash wouldn't hurt, but then I'd have to subtract the $70 I wouldn't get in food stamps, and there might not be a whole hell of a lot left. So I'm living in the hills and I'm not workin'. No car, either. So no girlfriend right now. No big deal.

"If I did have a job, the hardest thing about it would be showing up on time and getting home. Living out here makes a long way to go for any job I might get.

"If you get your life together, it means you don't have to worry so much. You have a little more security. That's what everybody wants. Money—a regular job. A car. You can't have your life together without those two things.

"My life is far better than it was. I've got a place to live and no big problems or worries. I don't worry about where I'm going to sleep or about food. I've got a bike. Got some pot—my homegrown plants are enough now, so I don't have to worry about it, even though it's not very high-class. But you've got to have a car to get to work in the morning and to get home. I can go on living this way, but I can't have a car if I'm going to do it.

"Sometimes my mom sends me clothes, or shampoo, or stuff like that. But if I had a job, I wouldn't need that. She'll help me with a car someday, if she ever thinks I'm financially responsible."

Building my own life. "I'm not in a big hurry with my life. If I can't do supergood, I'll do good enough. I don't think I'll have any big career.

"Maybe in a way I'll always be kind of a survivalist. But I would like to be prepared for when I get to be 50 or 60—if I make it that far—so that I wouldn't need Social Security. I get food stamps, so I guess I'd have to say I'm part of the Establishment. A job would get me more into it.

"Over a period of time I've learned what food to buy and what food not to buy, how to live inexpensively. I get powdered milk, eggs, dry foods in bulk, and stuff like that. Food costs me about $80 per month. I could live on $100 a month for food, cigarettes, fuel, and a few little extras, but not very many, like buying nails, or a window, or parts for a bike. But I don't really need anything. I've got just about everything I need. Except there is a few things more.

"I might stay here a couple of years, unless something drastically comes up. Like, if a beautiful woman says she has a house in town, that would do it, but if not for that, it isn't very likely. I'll have to build my own life.

"I wouldn't mind working. I wouldn't mind driving a street sweeper or something like that, or to buy a $30,000 or $60,000 piece of equipment, and just make money doing stuff for people. You see people all over who have cool jobs. Maybe they just do something around the house like take out washing machines, or they own something or know how to do something that's not really hard labor but it's skilled labor.

"But living this way is a good start for me. I don't have to work my life away just to survive. I can work a little bit, and survive, and do something else."

Being by myself. "At this time of my life it's not really too good to team up with somebody. I've got to get my life together before I can worry about just going out and having a beer or a good time.

"Being by myself doesn't make all that much difference. I guess that I'm sorta a loner. Maybe people say I'm a hermit, but it's not like I live 20 miles out in nowhere.

"I don't want to be alone all my life. I'd like to go camping with somebody on the weekend. Have a car and a cooler of beer and a raft or something. It's nice to have friends to do that with. If I had a car and stuff, I'm sure I could get a few people to go. Without a car, man, shit . . . "

Friends. "A friend is someone you could trust, I suppose. I've had close friends, but I don't have any now. But I have some 'medium' friends. I guess that's anybody who'd smoke a joint with me. And you see some people walking down the street or going to a store or to a pay phone. You just say, 'Hi, what's going on?'

"I know lots of people. Especially from reform school. I've already seen some. They're not friends, though; they're just people you might see to say hello and ask them what they've been up to and ask them how long they did in jail.

"The first time I met one guy I know now, I was pushing my bike and I had my backpack and some beer and I was drinking a beer. I'd never seen him before. He said, 'Hey, wanna smoke a joint?' I said, 'Sure.' So I gave him a couple of beers and we smoked some pot and started talking. I told him I lived up in the hills. I see him around every now and then. He's known me for a year and I talk to him sometimes and joke around. He's sort of a friend.

"I had a few friends in Southern California, but by the time I left there I wasn't too happy with them. I guess my best friend was Tom. I used to ride skateboards with him all day. His older brother used to get pot for us. That's when I think I learned to ride the very best. We always used to try to beat each other out in whatever we did. I was better than him in some things and after a while he got better than me in a couple of things. But I think I was always a little bit more crazier than he was—a little bit wilder on the board."

I've been more places and done more things. "I've lived in a lot of different places. Like going to California. Living out in the country. Living different places in town. Dealing with people. Living at the reform school. Living in Portland. Living here.

"I've definitely had more experiences than some of the people I went to school with, and I've had my ears opened more than they have. In *some* things, I'm wiser than other kids my age.

"I saw a guy a few weeks ago who is the same age as me. He lived in a house behind us when I was in fifth grade. He still lives with his parents in the same place. I think about what he's been doing the last nine years and what I've been doing the last nine years and it's a big difference. He went to high school. Now he works in a gas station, has a motorcycle, and works on his truck. I guess that's all right for him, so long as he's mellow with his parents. That way he can afford a motorcycle.

"But you've got what you've got. It doesn't make any difference what anybody else has. You can't wish you're somebody else. There's no point in it."

Some personal standards. "In the summer I clean up every day. When it starts cooling down, I dunno; sometimes if it's cold, I just wash my head and under my arms. Last winter I'd get a really good shower at least every three days and get by otherwise. But I always wash up before going to town if I'm dirty. I don't want to look like I live in a cabin.

"I don't really care what people on the street think of me. But somebody who knows me, I wouldn't want them to dislike me for any reason.

"And I wouldn't steal from anybody that knew me, if they knew that I took something or had any idea that I might have took it. Whether I liked them or not. I wouldn't steal from anybody I liked, or I thought they were pretty cool. I only steal from people I don't know.

"I don't like stealing from somebody you would really hurt. But anybody that owns a house and three cars and a boat—they're not hurtin'. It's the Law of the Jungle—occasionally people get burned. A lot of people don't, though. As long as they've got fences and they keep all their stuff locked up and don't leave anything laying around, they're all right. The way I see it, 'If you snooze, you lose.'

"If you say you'll do something, you should do it. That's the way people should operate. It pisses me off when somebody doesn't do it. Like, you tell somebody you're going to meet them somewhere, and they don't show up. But giving my word depends on how big of a deal it is; if it's pretty small, it would be no big deal.

"Sure, stealing is immoral. I don't like to screw somebody up for no good reason. But my morals can drop whenever I want.

"I went to Sunday school for a while and to a church kindergarten. I guess I heard all the big lessons—you get the felt board and they pin all the stuff on 'em and cut out all the paper figures: Jesus, Moses. But our family doesn't really think about religion a whole lot. They're moral to a point but they're not fanatics. It's too much to ask. I'd rather go to hell. But any little kid knows what's right and wrong."

Moderation: Getting close enough, going "medium" fast. "One of my friend's older brothers in Southern California was a crazy fucker. He'd get these really potent peyote buttons and grind them up and put them in chocolate milkshakes.

"One time they decided to go out to the runways where the jets were coming in, 'cause they knew somebody who did it before. Planes were coming in continually on that runway. They'd go out there laying right underneath the skid marks, just right under the planes. I never would get that close. Just being out there, after jumping the fence and walking clear out to the runway, is close enough. I never did lie on the runway. . . .

"On the skateboard, I just go medium fast. . . .

"The fun part of skiing is knowing when to slow down. . . .

"When those guys went jockey-boxing, I didn't actually do it with them. I was just tagging along. . . .

"Robbing a store seemed like a pretty easy way to get some cash, but I guess it wasn't a very good idea. . . .

"I don't know why I didn't get into drugs more. I smoke pot, but I've never really cared to take downers and uppers or to shoot up. I don't really need that much. . . .

"I like to smoke pot but I don't think of myself as a pothead. A pothead is somebody who is totally stoned all day long on really good pot, really burned out all the time. I smoke a joint, then smoke a cigarette, and I get high. I just like to catch a buzz. . . .

"If you really get burnt out, your brain's dead. You can get burned out on anything if you do it too much. I don't do it enough to make it a problem. If you take acid you never know who's made it or exactly what's in it. I've taken it before and gotten pretty fried. I don't know if it was bad acid, but it wasn't a very good experience. . . .

"Sometimes when I want to be mellow, I don't say anything. I just shut up. Or somebody can mellow out after a day at work—you come home, smoke a joint, drink a beer—you just sort of melt. . . . "

Putting it all together. "Anything you've ever heard, you just remember and put it all together the best you can. That's good enough for me."

Formal Schooling

I knew little about Brad's schooling when I began to collect life history data from him. By his account he had often been "slow" or "behind the rest of the class." He could read, but he faltered on "big words." He could write, but his spelling and punctuation were not very good. He had trouble recalling number sequences and basic arithmetic facts. ("Lack of practice," he insisted.) In one junior high school he had been placed in "an EH [educationally handicapped] class with the other stonies." As he recalled, "I don't know if I felt I was special or not, but I didn't like those big classes."

Measures of IQ or scholastic achievement did not really matter anymore. Brad was well aware of his capacities and limitations. The degree to which he was "below average" or "behind" in his schoolwork had become, and had been for a long time, purely academic. Schooling for him was over; he was out.

Formal schooling aside, Brad could, for practical purposes, read, write, and do simple arithmetic. The only book he "requisitioned" for his cabin was a dictionary. That alone was incredible. Even

more incredibly, he occasionally labored through it to find a word—no easy task for one who has to recite the alphabet aloud in order to locate an entry.

Schooling had played a part in Brad's life, but not the vital part educators like it to play. In 10 years he enrolled in eight schools in two states, ranging from early years at a small country school to a final eight months at a state reformatory, and including attendance at urban elementary, junior high, and senior high schools. I traced his attendance record where he boasted having "the world's record for ditching school." Perhaps it was not the world's record, but following his midyear enrollment in grade five he maintained 77 percent attendance for that year and 46 percent attendance in grade six the year following. He began the term in a new school four different years, and often changed schools once the academic year was under way: "I guess I was in school a lot but I was always in a different school."

In Brad's assessment, school "did what it's supposed to do. You gotta learn to read." He laid no blame, noting only that "maybe school could of did better." He acknowledged that *he* might have done better, too: "I was just never that interested in school. If I knew I had to do something, I'd try a little bit. I could probably have tried harder."

The earliest school experience he could recall was in a church-sponsored kindergarten. Hearing Brad use objectionable language, the teacher threatened to wash out his mouth with soap. At the next occasion when the children were washing their hands, he stuck a bar of soap in his mouth: "I showed the kids around me, 'Hey, no big deal having soap in your mouth.'"

He recalled first grade as a time when "I learned by ABCs and everything. It was kind of neat." Apparently his enthusiasm for schooling stopped there. He could think of no particular class or teacher that he especially liked. His recollection of events associated with subsequent grades involved changes of schools, getting into trouble for his classroom behavior, or skipping school altogether. As early as fourth grade he remembered difficulty "keeping up" with classmates.

By his own assessment Brad did "OK" in school, but he recalled excelling only once: at an art project in clay that was put on display and that his mother still kept. During grade seven his attendance improved and, for one brief term, so did his grades, but he was not really engaged with what was going on and he felt lost in the large classes.

"In those big classes, like, you sit around in a big horseshoe, and you've got a seat four rows back, with just one teacher. Like English class, I'd get there at nine in the morning and put my head down and I'd sleep through the whole class. It was boring, man.

"Another class they tried to get me in was typing. I tried for a little while, but I wasn't even getting close to passing, so I just gave up."

Brad's public schooling ended in Southern California. When he got shunted back to Oregon, he did not enroll in school again, although after being "busted," schooling was his principal activity during his eight months in the reformatory. He felt that he had attended "a couple of pretty good schools" in Southern California during grades 8, 9, and briefly, 10; but, as usual, the times he remembered were times spent out of class, not in it.

"By the end of school, I was cutting a lot. Like, I didn't need PE [physical education]. Look at this kid—he's been riding bicycles and skateboards all day all his life. I didn't need no PE. I don't need to go out in the sun and play games. I wasn't interested in sports. So I'd go get stoned. I'd take a walk during that class, go kick back in an orange grove, maybe eat an orange, get high, smoke a cigarette, and by the time I'd walk back, it was time for another class. I did it for a long time and never got caught. Anyhow, then I switched schools."

Brad felt that his lack of academic progress cost him extra time in reform school, "so I started to speed up and do the stuff and then I got out." In his assessment, "I was doing ninth-grade work. I probably did some 10th- and 11th-grade stuff, but not a lot."

Although young people seldom return to public schools after serving time, I asked Brad to identify the grade levels to which he might have been assigned had he gone back to school.

"For math, if I went back, I'd just be getting into 10th grade. In reading, I'd be a senior or better. Spelling would be about eighth grade. I can spell good enough. Handwriting, well, you just write the way you write. My writing isn't that bad if I work on it. I don't worry about it that much."

He did recognize limitations in his command of basic school skills. He had "kind of forgotten" the multiplication facts, and he was pretty rusty on subtracting or recalling the alphabet. To be a good speller, he once mused, you've got to "do it a lot," but at reform school he did only "a little bit." His awareness of these limitations is revealed in a letter intended for his mother but later abandoned in favor of a cheerier style:

Hi
if I sit hear and stair
at this pieac of paper
eny longer ill go crazy
I don't think im scaird
of writing just dont like
to remind myself I
need improvment. its
raining alot past
few days but its warm
'n dry inside . . .

Reading was the school skill at which Brad felt most proficient, and his confidence was not shaken by the fact that some words were difficult for him. He said he did not enjoy reading, but he spent hours poring over instruction manuals. My impression was that although his oral reading was halting, he had good comprehension. That was also his own assessment. When, at his father's insistence, he briefly entertained the idea of joining the army, Brad had first to take the General Educational Development exam (for his high school certificate) and then take a test for the army. He felt he passed "pretty high" on the Army test; on some parts of the GED, "like reading and a couple of other ones," he felt he did "super, super good."

Brad once observed philosophically, "The people in college today are probably the ones who didn't sleep when I was in English class." At the same time, school was a closed chapter in his life. Other than to acknowledge that he "might have tried harder," though, he expressed no regrets over school as an opportunity missed. Anticipating that his lack of school skills would prove a barrier to enrollment in any technical training program, he couldn't imagine ever returning to the classroom. And, like most school leavers, he couldn't think of anything that might have been done that would have kept him in school.[4]

Adequate Schools and Inadequate Education: An Interpretation

It might be socially desirable if Brad could read better, write better, do arithmetic better, spell better. With better spelling skills, he would "stare" rather than "stair" at a blank page and perhaps feel less self-conscious about needing "improvment." Considering that he devoted some (although certainly not exclusive) attention to schooling for 10 of his 20 years, he does not do these things very well.

On the other hand, that he can do them as well as he does might also be regarded as a tribute to the public schools. Brad's level of school achievement may be disappointing, but it is not inadequate. He is literate. He did get *something* out of school. True, his performance of the three Rs could be more polished, but the importance of his proficiency with such amenities pales before problems of greater social consequence. Brad's schooling has stopped, but his learning continues apace. Exerting some positive, constructive influence on that learning as it pertains to Brad's enculturation into society presents society's current challenge. That challenge has not been taken up.

Schools can affect the rate and level of academic achievement, but they do not set the course of students' lives. They do not and cannot reach everyone even though they may ever-so-briefly touch them. Schooling is not everyone's cup of tea. As Brad put it: "I've always liked learning. I just didn't like school."

The implicit distinction Brad himself makes between "learning" and "learning done in school" is critical to the purposes of this writing. In the broad enculturative sense of coming to understand what one needs to know to be competent in the roles one may expect to fulfill, learning is an ongoing process in which each human is engaged throughout a lifetime.[5] In Brad's case, the direction that process was taking seemed to reflect all too well what he felt society expected of him: nothing. He was left largely to his own resources to make sense of his world and create his own life. He endeavored quite self-consciously to "figure things out," but his resolutions often put him at odds with society. What appeared as inevitable conclusions to him were neither inevitable nor necessarily appropriate in terms of community norms.

Maybe we cannot reach him; surely we cannot reach everyone like him. I was astounded to realize that no systematic, constructive effort was being exerted to influence the present course of Brad's life. No agency offered help, direction, or concern, and neither did any of the institutions that ordinarily touch our lives: family, school, work, peer group. If it is naïve to regard these influences as invariably positive and constructive, our interactions with them do, nonetheless, contribute to our sense of social self. Brad was, for the most part, out of touch with them all.

If Brad is able to get his life together, it will have to be almost entirely through his own effort. Perhaps his personal style as a loner helped buffer him from peer influences that seemed to me, as a wary adult, as likely to get him into trouble as to guide him on the straight and narrow. That he could find time and space "on a mountaintop in Oregon" rather than on a beach or under a freeway in Southern California seemed to give him an advantage over his fellow street people. His lifestyle was not overly complicated by urban trappings or the quickened pace of city life. He was not crowded or pushed. At the same time, he could neither escape the influence of material wants and creature comforts so prevalent in the society in which he lives, nor deny a deeply felt need to connect with others. As much the loner as he often seemed, even Brad could acknowledge, "There must be a group that I would fit in, somewhere in this town."

He had learned to hunt and gather for his necessities in the aisles of supermarkets, in neighborhood garages, and at residential building sites. He conceded that stealing was wrong, but, among his priorities, necessity (broadly defined to allow for some luxuries as well) took precedence over conformity. He saw no alternative for getting the things he felt he needed but could not afford. Still, he took only what he considered necessary, not everything he could get his hands on. He was not, nor did he see himself ever becoming, a "super thief."

I do not see how society can "teach" Brad to not be sneaky, to not shoplift, to not steal. Most families try to do that. His family wasn't entirely successful, though more of the message seems to have gotten through than one might at first assume.[6] In that regard I find useful the distinction between deviant *acts* and deviant *persons* as suggested by anthropologist Robert Edgerton (1978). In spite of occasional deviant acts, Brad's statements reveal his underlying enculturation into the prevailing ethos of mainstream American society. He was well aware of the meanings of his acts to others. As he noted, "Any little kid knows what's right and wrong." Although he prided himself on having the cunning to survive his "hard life" by whatever means necessary, he staunchly defended his behavior ("I couldn't get by without stealing stuff") as well as himself ("I am not that rotten of a kid!").

There was a foundation on which to build, but there was neither external help, support, nor a modicum of encouragement shaping that process. Was schooling an opportunity in Brad's life, or is it the only directed opportunity he gets? It seems to me there might, and should, be a more concerted effort to exert a positive influence to provide him with reasonable and realistic routes of access back into the cultural mainstream. To have any effect, however, such efforts would have to be in the form of increasing the options available to him, rather than trying to force or mold him in some particular direction. He has already heard the lectures about good citizenship.

The community's best strategy would be to ensure that opportunities exist for a person like Brad to satisfy more of his wants in socially acceptable ways. Fear of getting caught isn't much of a deterrent for someone who thinks he's "too smart" to get caught. Armed robbery is already within the realm of things Brad could, and might, do. With an attitude that "just about everybody, or at least everybody my age, does it" toward behaviors like shoplifting, "ripping things off," burglary, operating a vehicle with a suspended license, and even his preoccupation with obtaining an adequate supply of pot, he could too easily find himself in the chute without realizing that everybody isn't there after all. Having gotten out of mainstream society, he does not see a way back in. Nor is he convinced it is worth the effort to try.

It is convenient, and an old American pastime, to place blame on schools. Questions concerning educational adequacy, when directed toward schools, invite that kind of scapegoating by relating the present inadequacies of youth to prior inadequacies of schools. (See, for example, Levin 1982.) Employing the anthropologist's distinction between schooling and education encourages us to review the full range of efforts the community makes to exert a positive educative influence on lives, not only during the school years, but in the post–school years as well.[7] The problems Brad now poses for society are not a consequence of inadequate schooling. They dramatize the risk we take by restricting our vision of collective educational responsibility to what can be done in school.

One hears arguments that today's youth vacillate between extremes of taking what they want or expecting everything to be handed to them on a silver platter. One finds a bit of each in Brad's thinking. He dreams of pulling off a robbery or suddenly finding himself owning and operating a $60,000 piece of machinery. He expresses reluctance to do work like dishwashing that entails cleaning up after others and where everyone can watch you perform a menial job.

But I wonder if young people like Brad really believe that society owes them something? Perhaps that is an expression of frustration at failing to see how to begin to accumulate resources of their own, comparable to what they perceive everyone else already has. A willingness to defer gratification must come more easily to those who not only have agonized during deferment but have eventually realized some long-awaited reward. Nothing Brad had ever done worked out very well—at least prior to his effort to build both a new cabin and a new lifestyle. He had virtually no sense of deferred gratification: Everything was "now or never."

In a society as materialistic as ours, opportunity is realized essentially with money, rather than with school or work. To Brad, money represented security, and he had limited access to it. That is why food stamps, in an annual amount less than $900, figured so importantly to him. His use of the stamps has left me wondering whether it might be possible to design some governmental agency that would calculatedly confront individuals like Brad in an educative way.

But the educative value of a welfare dole is limited. You cannot "service" people out of poverty, and, as Brad had already discovered, the power of the dole-givers and their labyrinth of regulations is seemingly arbitrary but definitely absolute. Food stamps made a better consumer of him (buying generic brands, buying large quantities, buying staples). But he realized that the first $70 of any month's take-home pay would be money he would otherwise have received free from the food-stamp program. To "earn" his stamps, he had to remain poor.[8] Had he found the second-rate job he so dreaded, part of his earnings would simply have replaced the dole, his other expenses (transportation, clothes, maybe a second-rate apartment) would have increased dramatically, and he would have again been trapped in a second-rate life. Until his food stamps were summarily canceled—after he failed to participate in a ritual midwinter job search during a period of staggering recession and regional unemployment—he did not aggressively seek work. When he finally realized he was des-

titute and began in earnest to look for work, 38 days passed before he even got turned down for a job. He put in many hours at painting and yard cleanup for me (although he refused to equate working for me with "real work") and reverted to "ripping off" items he felt he needed but could not afford.

I invited Brad's thoughts on what might be done to help people like him. His idea, other than a dream of finding "just the right job" (never fully specified) without ever going to look for it, was of a "day work" program, whereby anyone who needed money could appear at a given time, do a day's work, and promptly receive a day's pay. I'm sure Brad's thoughts turned to the end of the day, when each worker would receive a pay envelope; my own thoughts focused on what one would do with a motley pick-up crew that wouldn't inadvertently make mockery of work itself. Yet implicit in his notion are at least two critical points.

First is a notion of a *right to work*: If (or when) one is willing, one should be able to work and, if in dire need, be paid immediately in cash. Brad found no such right in his life. Although he had been able to find—but not hold—a number of jobs in the past, now he heard only "No Help Wanted" and read only "Not Presently Taking Applications." He was not entirely without social conscience when he observed that if he found a job, he would only be taking it away from someone who needed it more. Brad did not really need a job. And, as he had begun to figure out, no one really needed him. Maybe he was right; maybe $70 in food stamps was society's way of paying him to drop out.

Second is a notion of an overly structured wage and hour system that effectively prices most unskilled and inexperienced workers like Brad out of the job market and requires a full-time commitment from the few it accepts. Brad's material needs were slight. He could have preserved the best elements in his carefree lifestyle by working part-time. However, the labor market does not ordinarily offer such options except for its own convenience. Either you want a job or you do not want a job. But work for its own sake, or holding a job, cast no spell over Brad. He did not look to employment for satisfaction, for meaningful involvement, or for achieving self-respect. Money was the only reason one worked.[9]

School provides opportunity and access for some youth; employment provides it for others. Neither school nor work presently exerted an influence on Brad. He was beyond school, and steady employment was beyond him. Without the effective support of family or friends, and without the involvement of school or work, he was left to his own devices. In his own words, he could not see a way to win and he did not have anything to lose. From mainstream society's point of view, we would be better off if he did.

After so carefully making provision for Brad's schooling, society now leaves his continuing education to chance, and we are indeed taking our chances. But educative adequacy in the lives of young people like Brad is not an issue of schooling. Schools provided him one institutional opportunity; they no longer reached him, and no other agency was trying to. His next institutional "opportunity," like his previous one, may be custodial. If it is, we all lose; Brad will not be the only one who will have to pay.[10]

Summary

"The important thing about the anthropologist's findings," writes Clifford Geertz (1973:23), one of anthropology's more articulate spokespeople, "is their complex specificness, their circumstantiality." Whatever issues anthropologists address, they characteristically begin an account and look for illustration through real events or cases bounded in time and circumstance. The effective story should be "specific and circumstantial," but its relevance in a broader context should be apparent. The story should make a point that transcends its modest origins. The case must be particular, but its implications broad.

Following that tradition, I have related a specific and circumstantial life story to illustrate the necessity of regarding education as more than just schooling, and of pointing out how little we attend to that broader concern. That may seem a roundabout way to address such a complex issue, but it is a way to bring an anthropological perspective to the problem.

Brad's story is unique, but his is not an isolated case. He is one among thousands of young people who simply drift away. His uninvited presence on my 20-acre sanctuary, in search of sanctuary for himself, brought me into contact with a type of youth I do not meet as a college professor. He piqued my anthropological interest with a worldview in many ways strikingly similar to mine, but with a set of coping strategies strikingly different. It is easy for people like me to think of people like Brad as someone else's problem, but for a moment that lingered and became two years, he quite literally brought the problem home to me. I do not find ready answers even in his particular case; I am certainly not ready to say what might, can, or must be done in some broader context.

Little is to be gained from laying blame at the feet of Brad's parents or his teachers, and to do so is to ignore indications of repeated, if not necessarily effective, efforts to help and guide him. Though our extended conversations may have been enlightening to Brad, as they surely were to me, my more direct efforts to help seemed to go awry. In the end, he departed almost as unexpectedly as he had arrived. I am not sure what I think "society" can accomplish for an amorphous "them" when my own well-intended efforts seemed only to demonstrate to Brad that I had my life "together" (his term) in a manner virtually unattainable for himself. The easiest course is to blame Brad, but to do so is to abandon hope and a sense of collective responsibility.

The only certainty I feel is that it is in our common interest to seek ways to provide opportunities intended to exert a continuing and constructive educational influence on the lives of young people like Brad. I do not know whether Brad can or will allow himself to be reached effectively or in time. I do know that from his perspective he saw neither attractive opportunities nor sources of potential help. By his own assessment, he simply did not matter. He was not free of his society, but he had become disconnected from it. Once adrift, nothing seemed to beckon or guide him back.

Because we tend to equate education with schooling, we are inclined to look to the past and ask where schools have gone wrong. Brad's story, in which school played only a minor role, serves as a reminder of the importance of other educative influ-

ences in our lives. It also points out how little systematic attention we give to discerning what those influences are, or how we might better use them to augment, complement, and otherwise underwrite the massive efforts we direct at youth during their in-school years. In that broad perspective, our efforts at education appear woefully inadequate in spite of the remarkable accomplishments of our schools. Until I found Brad living in my backyard, however, the problem remained essentially abstract. Now it has confronted me with the "complex specificness" of one young human life.

FURTHER READING

Wolcott, Harry F. 2002. *Sneaky Kid and Its Aftermath: Ethics and Intimacy in Fieldwork*. Walnut Creek, CA: AltaMira Press.

——. 2010. *Ethnography Lessons: A Primer*. Walnut Creek, CA: Left Coast Press.

REFERENCES

Brandes, Shirley. 1982. Ethnographic Autobiographies in American Anthropology. In *Crisis in Anthropology: View from Spring Hill*. E. A. Hoebel, R. Currier, and S. Kaiser, eds. Pp. 187–202. New York: Garland Publishing.

Edgerton, Robert. 1978. The Study of Deviance—Marginal Man or Everyman? In *The Making of Psychological Anthropology*. G. D. Spindler, ed. Pp. 442–476. Berkeley: University of California Press.

Estroff, Sue E. 1981. *Making It Crazy: An Ethnography of Psychiatric Clients in an American Community*. Berkeley: University of California Press. [Reissued in paperback in 1985 with a new epilogue.]

Fortes, Meyer. 1938. Social and Psychological Aspects of Education in Taleland. *Supplement to Africa* 11(4):1–64.

Geertz, Clifford. 1973. *The Interpretation of Cultures*. New York: Basic Books.

Herskovits, Melville J. 1948. *Man and His Works: The Science of Cultural Anthropology.* New York: Alfred A. Knopf.

Levin, Henry M. 1982. Education and Work. Program Report No. 82-B8. Palo Alto, CA: Institute for Research on Educational Finance and Governance, Stanford University.

MacNeil, Ian, and G. Glover, Producers. 1959. *Four Families.* Film narrated by Ian MacNeil and Margaret Mead. National Film Board of Canada.

Mailer, Norman. 1979. *The Executioner's Song.* New York: Warner Books.

Mann, Dale. 1982. Chasing the American Dream: Jobs, Schools, and Employment Training Programs in New York State. *Teachers College Record* 83(3):341–76.

Oregon Department of Education. 1980. *Oregon Early School Leavers Study.* Salem: Oregon Department of Education.

Shaw, Clifford R. 1930. *The Jack-Roller: A Delinquent Boy's Own Story.* Chicago: University of Chicago Press.

Snodgrass, Jon, ed. 1982. *The Jack-Roller at Seventy: A Fifty-Year Follow-Up.* Lexington, MA: D.C. Heath & Company.

Wallace A. F. C. 1961a. The Psychic Unity of Human Groups. In *Studying Personality Cross-Culturally.* Bert Kaplan, ed. Evanston, IL: Row Peterson and Company.

———. 1961b. Schools in Revolutionary and Conservative Societies. In *Anthropology and Education.* F. C. Gruber, ed. Pp. 25–54. Philadelphia: University of Pennsylvania Press.

Willis, Paul H. 1977. *Learning to Labour: How Working-Class Kids Get Working-Class Jobs.* Hampshire, England: Gower Publishing Co.

Wolcott, Harry F. 1982. The Anthropology of Learning. *Anthropology and Education Quarterly* 13(2):83–108.

NOTES

Acknowledgments: A portion of the work on which this article is based was performed pursuant to Contract No. NIE-P-81-0271 of the National Institute of Education dealing with issues of educational adequacy under the School Finance Project. Data collection and interpretation are the responsibility of the author. I wish to express my appreciation to W. W. Charters, Jr., Stanley Elam, Barbara Harrison, Bryce Johnson, Malcolm McFee, and Esther O. Tron, as well as to Brad for his critical reading and helpful suggestions with early drafts. The material was first published in the *Anthropology and Education Quarterly,* Volume 14, Number 1, pp. 3–32, copyright by the Council on Anthropology and Education, 1983. It has undergone minor editing.

1. If I found any surprises in reviewing the literature, it was in discovering some remarkable similarities between Brad's story and a groundbreaking classic first published three-quarters of a century earlier, Clifford Shaw's *The Jack-Roller: A Delinquent Boy's Own Story* (1930).

2. Meyer Fortes (1938:5) noted the firmly established axiom, "Education in the widest sense is the process by which the cultural heritage is transmitted from generation to generation, and that schooling is therefore only part of it." Melville Herskovits (1948:311) subsequently introduced the encompassing term *enculturation* for referring to education in Fortes's "widest sense." But he retained the term *education*, suggesting that it be restricted to "its ethnological sense of directed learning," a term distinct from and more encompassing than *schooling*, defined as "that aspect of education carried out by specialists." (See also Wallace 1961b.)

3. I have been careful to observe the few conditions Brad imposed on my use of the information. He, in turn, was paid for time spent interviewing and for later reviewing the completed account on which this paper was based. That is not to suggest he was entirely satisfied with my portrayal or my interpretation, but he was satisfied that what I reported was accurate. If only to please me, he even

commented that he hoped his story might "help people understand."

4. For example, in the *Oregon Early School Leavers Study* conducted at the time (Oregon Department of Education 1980:16), only one-third of the young people interviewed responded that something might have been done to affect their decision to quit public secondary school.

5. A timely article of the day appeared with the partial title "Chasing the American Dream: Jobs, schools, and employment training programs . . . " (Mann 1982).

6. Brad expressed only resentment toward his father, but he often mentioned his mother's efforts to provide a positive influence. When Brad introduced us, after proudly showing her the cabin during a brief but long-anticipated visit, I asked whether she felt she could exert a guiding influence over him living a thousand miles away. "We've always been a thousand miles apart," she replied, "even when we were under the same roof."

On a different occasion, responding to Brad's announcement that he needed to "find" another bicycle, I asked: "What would your mother think about you stealing a bike? That it's dumb; that it's smart?" "Neither," he replied. "She'd just think that I must have needed it. She wouldn't say anything. She doesn't lecture me about things like that. But she used to cut out everything they printed in the paper about pot and put it on my walls. And she'd talk about brain damage."

7. Although the distinction between education and schooling is sometimes acknowledged, it is not necessarily regarded as having much significance, at least for understanding contemporary society. To illustrate, note in the following excerpt how educator and economist Henry Levin, addressing the topic *Education and Work*, at once recognizes the distinction between education and schooling yet bows to what he describes as the "convention" of equating them:

> Although the term education is sometimes used interchangeably with schooling, it is important to note that schooling is not the only form of education. However, schooling represents such a dominant aspect of education in modern societies that the convention of equating education and schooling in the advanced industrialized societies will also be adopted here. [Levin 1982:1]

8. The irony of the implications and consequences when not working is a prerequisite to maintaining a steady income is nicely spelled out in Estroff 1981. See especially chapter 6, "Subsistence Strategies: Employment, Unemployment, and Professional Disability."

9. Paul Willis (1977) notes in his study of working-class youth that it is this "reign of cash" that precipitates their contact with the world of work. As one of Willis's "lads" explained, "Money is life." Brad's mother expressed a similar view: "Money, not love, makes the world go round."

10. For a grim scenario, including some discomforting parallels and similarities, see Mailer 1979. The protagonist of Mailer's "true-life novel" makes special note of the impact of reform school on his life (chapter 22). Brad did not reveal the extent of the impact of the same reform school on his own life, but he did include it specifically in his brief inventory of significant experiences. Similarities noted earlier between Brad's account and Shaw's *The Jack-Roller* (1930) seem less pronounced in a subsequently published follow-up, *The Jack-Roller at Seventy* (Snodgrass 1982).

James T. Sears

Educators, Homosexuality, and Homosexual Students
Are Personal Feelings Related to Professional Beliefs?

What are educators' personal attitudes and feelings about homosexuality? How do these personal beliefs affect their everyday activities as teachers and guidance counselors? What impact do these personal beliefs and professional activities have upon students struggling with their sexual identities?

This paper will first examine the perceptions of lesbian and gay youth about educators based on data from Southern youth between 1986 and 1988 who recently graduated from high school. A purposive sample of young people representing different social classes, races, and gender was interviewed in 90-minute sessions. These interviews were taped, transcribed, and analyzed using standard qualitative methodology.[1] Participants were promised anonymity; all names used in this paper are fictitious.

The next part of this paper presents survey data gathered from school counselors and prospective teachers regarding their personal attitudes and feelings about homosexuality. The quantitative data in this paper come from surveys administered to guidance counselors and prospective teachers as South Carolina developed legislation on sexuality education (Earls, Fraser, & Sumpter, in press). In collaboration with the South Carolina Guidance Counselors' Association, 483 middle school and high school guidance counselors received a questionnaire during the spring of 1987. The questionnaire included the modified Attitudes Toward Homosexuality (ATH), a 30-item Likert-type instrument, and the Index of Homophobia (IH), a summative category partition scale of a person's reactions toward homosexual encounters and feelings toward homosexual persons (Hudson & Ricketts, 1980; MacDonald, Huggins, Young, & Swanson, 1973; Price, 1982).[2] Additionally, counselors completed a questionnaire with items related to their experiences in working with homosexual students, knowledge and beliefs about homosexuality, assessment of the school climate for homosexual-identified students, and projected professional activities relating to enhancing their knowledge and skills in working with gay youth. One hundred forty-two persons returned usable questionnaires. The typical respondent was a white, native South Carolinian female in her late thirties with a master's degree and ten years counseling experience with rural adolescents.

A second sample was 258 prospective teachers at the beginning and end points of their teacher preparation program. These students attended either a required undergraduate social foundations course or a student teaching seminar between springs of 1987 and 1988, and completed an anonymous questionnaire midway through their semester. Most of the study participants (n = 191) were attending a social foundations course with a nearly equal number of secondary and elementary education majors. The typical respondent was a white, unmarried, female, twenty-year-old, solid "B" sophomore from rural South Carolina taking her second education course. Sixty-seven questionnaires also were completed by prospective teachers completing their student teaching. On average, these respondents had taken seven teacher education courses. The typical respondent was a white, unmarried, twenty-eight-year-old female student teaching in a secondary school setting from which she graduated eleven years ago.

The prospective teacher questionnaire included two standardized attitudinal instruments: the modified Attitudes Toward Homosexuality (ATH) and the Index of Homophobia (IH). In addition, they also completed a questionnaire with items related to their encounters with homosexual students as a high school student, knowledge about homosexuality, professional attitudes regarding homosexuality in the school curriculum, and projected professional behaviors regarding homosexual students.[3]

The third part of this paper discusses these educators' attitudes regarding their *professional* role of educators in working with lesbian and gay-identified students. As I will argue, while these educators assert their ability to bracket personal feelings in professional settings, their past and anticipated future professional behaviors make such a claim suspect.

ADOLESCENTS' PERCEPTIONS OF EDUCATORS

Everyday:
We wake up and get ready for work.
We drive our cars on the same roads,
the same highways.
We park right next to your cars.
We use the same bathrooms.
We listen to the same music.
We breathe the same air.
We live in the same society.

So, why do you abhor us when we share so
many of the same things?
Okay, so we love differently!
Why does that matter?
There is really nothing to fear from us
except the pain that comes from your
ignorance!

BRETT, A HIGH SCHOOL STUDENT

Sexual rebels, such as Brett, spoke at length about the difficulty they faced in school as the result of the negative attitudes of educators (Sears, 1989b; Sears, 1991). Most noted that this topic was simply avoided by teachers, counselors, and administrators in their school. They viewed guidance counselors, in particular, as academic not personal advisors. A few of the participants, however, relayed stories of supportive educators who made a difference in their adolescent lives.

Franklin lives in a predominantly black South Carolina rural town. He remembers harassment from educators inside and outside the classroom:

In high school, like the town, it was very hush-hush about homosexuality. You never talked to the students, teachers, principal, or counselors about it. They never talked to you about it. Even though I had two friends who were open and admitted it at the time, the teachers just ignored it and kept their feelings to themselves. But, the principal would always try to look out for the bad things these two were doing. He was always trying to get them for something. One day I was with my friends—when you are with them you are labeled—and this real flaming and feminine guy was telling someone off so the principal wrote him up and sent him to the "box" [in-school suspension].

Franklin also recalled an incident with his high school physics teacher:

Mr. Jensen would usually drift away from the subject. He'd often bring up homosexuality. He mainly talked about the wrongs of it and how it was such a sin and that they should be condemned. I felt really bad.

Other participants reported similar incidents. For example, Fawn remembers one teacher who "hated me because she knew I was gay. She would fill out these forms that got me into trouble and then make comments like, 'People like you . . .'"

Only a handful of participants, including Brett, reported speaking to a guidance counselor or teacher about their homosexuality. In general, they perceived these adults to be ill-informed and unconcerned; they simply felt uncomfortable talking to them. The image of counselors communicated to the participants in this study was summed up by Kimberly: "Our counselors had never been presented to us as someone there to talk about problems other than education. They were just there for grades, signing up for classes, tests like the PSAT, and finding colleges to attend."

Similar sentiments were echoed about teachers and their unwillingness to show concern for lesbian and gay-identified students or to express their feelings about homosexuality. A senior in high school, Nathaniel, recalls a recent classroom discussion dealing with homosexuality:

In my sociology class we were talking about AIDS. One guy said, "I think gay guys are just sick. How could they do that? It's wrong!" One of my friends who is gay asks, "Why do you think it's wrong?" Well, everyone looks over to Miss L., our teacher, for what she thinks. She says, "I have no comment. I'm not even going to get into this discussion. I'm going to keep my opinion to myself." So we lingered on this topic for awhile. I kept my mouth closed. Another guy said, "If a fag makes a move on me, I'd whip his ass." I thought to myself, "Yeah, right. We had gotten in a fight earlier and I liked dogged him out." Then two of the football players joined in. One was on each side. So, I piped up. (I had just gone into wrestling, so I was safe. The people who had been calling me gay had been coming up to me saying, "Hey man, I'm sorry for calling you queer.") So, I say "If you don't try it, you never will know what's going on. You're just going on hearsay. How can you judge these people? They're people too, just because their sexuality is different."

This detachment of teachers from personal concerns and social issues was underscored repeatedly in conversations with these sexual rebels. Carlton stated:

Teachers seem to keep themselves so removed. In high school, teachers weren't people. They just lived in the school, went into the closet, stayed there over night, and then came out during the day, right? It was hard to think of them as real people. It was hard to interact with them. You know, a lot of the child's life is spent in school. If all that time is dealt with them through the book and not attending to any kind of personal needs, it just seems so ridiculous to me—stilted. It puts such a damper on what could be done.

Georgina's comments illustrate how quickly young people can pick up on teachers' personal detachment from their students—and how students can hide behind the role teachers expect them to assume:

Teachers don't see much of your inner self. They don't ask. It's easy to put on a face with teachers. For example, Miss Morrison wanted someone very Christian-like, a little angel. For her, I wrote in my English journal about Jesus and love all the time. Mr. Boozer was the band director. He wanted somebody with good leadership skills who could play well. He got that. Mrs. Laman, she liked slaves. So, if you volunteered for everything, like I did, she liked you. As

long as you keep them happy, they think that you're well-adjusted.

Carlton is studying to become a teacher. Arguing that "a teacher is involved in growth and guidance and not simply to teach math, science or English," he asserts:

I would think that a student would be quicker to want to talk to teachers if they had been kind to them. If they had just started talking to me on a personal basis. Just to talk about interests, "Well, how's the rest of school? What do you like to do? I hear you're in chorus?" I might have more easily been able to bring it up. I remember this one woman, she was so hard. It would not have taken much for her to have asked me more personal questions. Like, "Carlton, how are you doing in school and I don't mean academically?" She possibly could have made me think about things that I hadn't even gotten up to the conscious level yet and then just leave it open for me to talk about them with her. If she'd only have said, "If you want to talk about anything, you can"—but she didn't.

Of course, being open to a student does not guarantee a response from that student. Darla, for example, was not ready to respond to teacher initiatives the way Brett and Georgina were. In ninth grade, Darla had Mrs. Taxel for sex education. "At first I hated her. All I heard throughout the whole year was that she talked about her little grandson. Sure enough, the first day of class that was the first thing she talked about, her stupid grandson." After several weeks of engaging in subtle but defiant acts in the classroom, Darla found herself confronted by Mrs. Taxel:

I got ready to walk out after class. She stopped me and slammed the door. "Sit down. We're talking," she said. "I can't understand why you dislike me so much." I said, "Frankly, because you're a bitch." Mrs. Taxel saw my cigarettes hanging out of my pocket. "Are those yours?" I told her they were. "Can I have one?" I said, "Sure." I handed her one and I got one. We just sat there smoking and talking. After that, we became good friends. I could talk to her about anything—except being gay.

Most teachers, of course, are not as open or willing to engage adolescents on their own terms—let alone to broach the subject of homosexuality. Carlton appreciates the teacher's dilemma. "Looking back, they probably were aware but afraid to talk about my homosexuality. Besides, they probably didn't know what kind of reaction they would get from me if they had tried or if they were wrong." Nevertheless, Carlton is resentful about the inability or unwillingness of educators to try to communicate with him.

> I've felt cheated by school. I felt there was so much potential, so much I could have done and we didn't nearly approach it. I've lost time, and a lot of that can't be gotten back. It was as if I was there for a prison term or they were my babysitters without permission to do anything with me. Teachers act like they have total authority *and* that they can do nothing all at the same time!

This latter point is well illustrated by Franklin's observation of how teachers in his high school dealt with slurs. "The teachers weren't very tolerant as far as racial slurs. If a teacher heard it, she might write him up. If there was a sexual slur, like 'fag,' they would pay no attention to it. That told me they didn't feel homophobia was as important as racism." Carlton concurs:

> If a teacher got tired of hearing these derogatory remarks they would only say "stop"—never questioning as to why they were feeling that way or trying to make them think about what they were doing. Only that, "I just don't want to hear that." They would be a lot quicker to jump on other minority groups than homosexuals.

Despite the bleakness of these tales, there are educators who genuinely care about lesbian and gay-identified students and try to work with them. One of these was Laura Huggins, a counselor intern at the school where Georgina attended.

In tenth grade, Georgina's lover, Kay, began to see Miss Huggins who after a while asked to see Georgina. Georgina stopped by Miss Huggins's office for a quick chat, and found her to be pleasant and mild-mannered. "She told me to see her if I had any problems." Six weeks later, Georgina discovered that Kay was seeing another girl; a violent quarrel erupted. Thinking that she had no one to turn to, Georgina suddenly remembered Miss Huggins's words:

> I wrote Miss Huggins a note and slipped it under her door. The next time she saw me, she said, "I know. Do you want to talk about it?" I told her all about my relationship with Kay. She acted as kind of an umpire in our fight. I remember her telling me, "You have different walls

around you, Georgina. Every once in a while a wall will collapse and you'll kick it back up. Someday they will all come down and you will get hurt. You'll be tempted to put them back up again. But, don't." I really didn't quite understand what she was saying but it was a relief not to have to put on an act around somebody.

Miss Huggins helped to mend the quarrel between the twosome. Georgina continued to see Kay through her sophomore year. Georgina reminisces, "When you first fall in love, you're always caught up. Love is blind. You can't see what is really going on around you. I knew that Kay liked other people and wanted to date them along with me. She just wasn't ready to settle down." A short time later Miss Huggins completed her internship at the school. Georgina regretted her departure:

If Miss Huggins would have stayed, I feel that I would have accepted myself a lot better. But, they didn't send anybody else. I remember after she left feeling so sad and needing to talk to somebody. All the time I kept thinking, "I can do what Patton did; I could try to kill myself." I was going to take some sleeping pills and eat them right before my mom came home. I thought, "If she catches me in time, I'll get to talk to someone." I didn't want to kill myself; I just wanted to talk to someone who knew what they were talking about.

Though Nathaniel never found an educator like Miss Huggins with whom he could speak frankly, he did receive advice early in high school from an adult working at his school. At 14, Nathaniel hadn't identified himself as gay though he knew that he enjoyed males physically as well as socially. He developed a crush on Reuben, a neighborhood boy three years his senior. The first time the two met, the older boy told Nathaniel, "'Look, I'm gay. I want you to know this if you have any problems.' I had no problems with that and we soon became real close." Nathaniel continues: "One night we got some beer and got wasted, or at least acted like we were drunk. We started feeling on each other, grabbing one another. One thing lead to another and we just kept going."

Nathaniel also had sexual fantasies about girls and enjoyed their emotional company. About this time he started to date Delta. "I was scared, I really was. I was wondering if I was going to lose my feelings for Delta, who I loved, while I still really loved Reuben." Confused about these feelings, Nathaniel "thought about talking to the counselor, but I just didn't build up enough nerve." He finally sat down in the corridor after school one day and just cried. Suddenly he felt a gentle tap on his shoulder. Looking up he saw Ol' Jessie, the school's janitor. His short grey hair stood out against his black skin. Jessie invited Nathaniel down to his "office." Once in the boiler room, the two pulled up a couple of crates and had a long talk. "He told me that I was too young to even worry about being a homosexual. 'Every man,' he said, 'has them feelings. You're going to look over at another guy in the bathroom and say, 'I'm big enough. Can I satisfy this person?' Then I sat down and thought. 'Well, if it's normal for someone to have homosexual feelings, why isn't it normal for a guy to try homosexual sex?'"

Having supportive adults such as Miss Huggins and Ol' Jessie was certainly helpful to Georgina and Nathaniel. Though most participants in this study said they would have liked to have had such educators while attending high school, some were much more reticent about such prospects. There were a variety of reasons for such caution, including unwillingness of the student to assume the initiative, lack of trust in confidentiality, the worry of losing teacher friendship, and personality differences. Audrey states, "I did not have direct counseling. I'm glad because I don't know how I would have acted. In high school if it were to get out I would have been so embarrassed. I could not have stood the peer pressure." Kimberly remembers:

> I didn't talk to counselors because they're human, too. Homosexuality is taboo. People just kind of go bonkers when they hear that word or find out that somebody is homosexual. Even the adults act like kids. They don't know how to handle it. I thought, "I can't trust anybody with this information." You know, teachers talk.

This was echoed by Franklin: "I didn't want them to know my feelings. I wasn't that trusting of them. I felt that they might tell my parents." Phillip, who enjoyed close friendship with several teachers, feared sharing his sexual feelings because it would be "like risking them not liking me."

How accurate are these students' perceptions of educators? What is the relationship between educators' personal feelings and beliefs about homosexuality and their views of their professional responsibilities to serve homosexual students? The next two sections of this paper address these questions.

Educators' Personal Attitudes and Feelings

Popularized by sociologist Weinberg (1972), "homophobia" originally meant an irrational fear of homosexual persons. Over the years, however, homophobia has been expanded to include disgust, anxiety, and anger (MacDonald, 1976). Further, it has come to be used not only to the reactions of heterosexuals but the internalization of negative feelings by homosexual men and women (Lehne, 1976; Malyon, 1982; Margolies, Becker, & Jackson-Brewer, 1987). Despite the methodological, conceptual, and political problems associated with "homophobia," the term is a useful benchmark for a beginning understanding of the attitudes and feelings of persons about homosexuality and the sources for these beliefs (Herek, 1984; Lehne, 1976; Sears, 1990).

One of the more extensive areas of research in lesbian and gay studies is on adult attitudes toward homosexuality or toward homosexuals. These studies often report the relationships between attitudes and personality traits or demographic variables.[4] Though such studies are not without conflicting data, Herek (1984) has summarized some consistent patterns. People with negative attitudes report less personal contact with gays and lesbians, less (if any) homosexual behavior, a more conservative religious ideology, and more traditional attitudes about sex roles than do those with less negative views. Those harboring negative attitudes about homosexuality are also more likely to have resided in the Midwest or the South, to have grown up in rural areas or in small towns, and to be male, older, and less well-educated than those expressing more positive attitudes.

Quasi-experimental research studies have demonstrated that adult males harbor more homophobic attitudes or feelings than females and are more concerned about male homosexuality than lesbianism (Aguero, Bloch, & Byrne, 1984; Braungart & Braungart, 1988; Clift, 1988; Coles & Stokes, 1985; Hong, 1983; Larsen, Reed, & Hoffman, 1980; Schatman, 1989; Young & Whertvine, 1982). Further, those with less negative feelings or attitudes are more likely to have had associations or friendships with lesbians or gay men (Anderson, 1981; Gentry, 1986a, 1986b; Maddux, 1988; Schneider & Lewis, 1984; Weiner, 1989). Conflicting data, however, have been reported using different samples or research instruments. For example, as I will document in this paper, male guidance counselors were less homophobic than their female counterparts and data from opinion polls (Irwin & Thompson, 1977; Schneider & Lewis, 1984) report no sex differences. Attributing these differences to population samples and attitudinal items, Herek (1986) in his review of this phenomenon concludes, "Males and females probably hold roughly similar positions on general questions of morality and civil liberties, but males are more homophobic in emotional reactions to homosexuality" (p. 565).

Studies have also assessed the attitudes and feelings of people in the helping professions toward homosexuality and homosexual persons (Casas, Brady, & Poterotto, 1983; Davison & Wilson, 1973; DeCrescenzo, 1983/84; Douglas, Kalman, & Kalman, 1985; Garfinkle & Morin, 1978; Gartrell, Kraemer, & Brodie, 1974; Hochstein, 1986; Larkin, 1989; Mc-

Quoid, 1988; Pauly & Goldstein, 1970; Wisniewski & Toomey, 1987). These studies have found a heterosexual bias in these persons' professional attitudes and homophobia in their personal feelings. Only a handful of studies, however, have examined issues relating to homosexuality in the context of the public elementary or high school (Dressler, 1985; Fischer, 1982; Griffin, 1992; Price, 1982; Smith, 1985). These studies have focused on teachers, high school students, principals, and gay/lesbian teachers. For example, most school administrators would dismiss a teacher for disclosing her homosexuality to students, and one-fourth of all college studies preparing to teach at one institution acknowledged their inability to treat fairly a homosexual student or discuss homosexuality in the classroom. While several studies have explored this topic with counselor trainees (Clark, 1979; Glenn & Russell, 1986; Schneider & Tremble, 1986; Thompson & Fishburn, 1977), only two (Baker, 1980; Maddux, 1988) have examined the attitudes and feelings of persons preparing to be teachers, and none have studied school guidance counselors' perceptions.

Most education-related articles have been normative essays discussing the special needs and problems of homosexual studies (Benvenuti, 1986; Dillon, 1986; Gumaer, 1987; Krysiak, 1987; Russell, 1989; Schneider and Tremble, 1986; Scott, 1988; Sears, 1987; Sears, 1988b). The few empirical studies cited above, however, support the essayist's view that educators, in general, lack the sensitivity, knowledge, and skills to address effectively the needs of students with same-sex feelings. This following section adds to the growing empirical data in this area by focusing on the least researched groups: prospective teachers and school guidance counselors.

Prospective Teachers' Attitudes and Feelings

This section examines prospective teachers' attitudes and feelings about homosexuality, their encounters with homosexuals and homosexuality while high school students, and their knowledge about homosexuality.

Eight out of ten prospective teachers surveyed harbored negative feelings toward lesbians and gay men; fully one-third of these persons, using the Index of Homophobia classification, are "high grade homophobics"—nearly five items as many as classified by Hudson and Rickets (1980) in their study of college students a decade ago. Prospective teachers pursuing certification in elementary education were more likely to harbor homophobic feelings and express homo-negative attitudes than those planning to teach in the secondary schools; black prospective teachers also expressed more negative attitudes about homosexuality than their white counterparts but were no more homophobic in their feelings toward lesbians and gay men (Sears, 1989a).

Two separate instruments assessed prospective teachers' *attitudes* toward homosexuality (ATH) and their *feelings* toward lesbians and gay men (IH). Since the conceptualization of "homophobia" as a research construct nearly 20 years ago, there is agreement that attitudes and feelings must be treated as separate constructs. Thus, in this study attitudes have been conceptualized as a set of cognitive beliefs about homosexuals and homosexuality whereas feelings are defined as a set of deep-rooted emotive reactions to homo-

sexual situations or persons. Examples of attitudinal survey items are: "Homosexuality is unnatural," "Homosexual marriage should be made legal," and "I would not want homosexuals to live near me"; examples of items which tap respondents' feelings are: "I would feel nervous being in a group of homosexuals," "If I saw two men holding hands in public, I would feel disgusted," and "I would feel comfortable if I learned that my best friend of my same sex was homosexual."[5]

Given the unidimensionality of the Attitudes Toward Homosexuality (ATH) and the Index of Homophobia (IH), respondents' summative scores were computed for each (Sears, 1988b). These adjusted scores could range from 0 (most positive) to 100 (most negative). Students' scores on the ATH ranged from 0 to 98, with a mean score of 45, and a standard deviation of 18. Students' scores on the IH yielded more negative results. The scores ranged from 2 to 99, with a mean score of 65 and a standard deviation of 19. The relationship between these two scores is depicted in Figure 17.1.

As indicated in Figure 17.1, the distribution of students' attitudes toward homosexuality (ATH) falls much more closer to the classic bell-shaped curve than do those for their feelings toward lesbians and gay men (IH). For example, one-quarter of the sample scored between the ninth and tenth decile on feelings toward homosexual persons whereas less than 3 percent of the students scored in this range on the attitudes toward homosexuality.

In order to provide a point of reference for interpreting these scores, data from other studies using the IH and ATH are summarized in Tables 17.1 and 17.2.

According to the authors of the Index of Homophobia scale (Hudson & Ricketts,

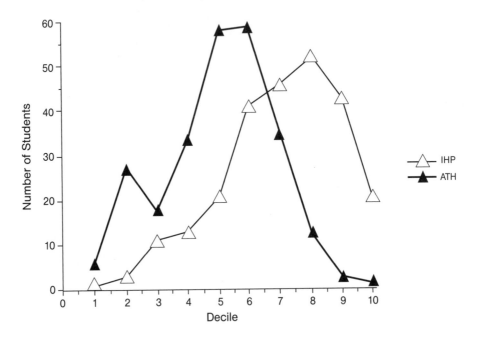

FIGURE 17.1 Distribution by Decile of Preservice Teachers' Attitudes Toward
Homosexuality and Feelings About Homosexual Persons

1980, p. 360), scores of less than 25 evidence "high grade non-homophobics," and those who score between 25 and 50 are considered "low grade non-homophobics." Persons whose scores lie between 50 and 75 are regarded as "low grade homophobics," and "high grade homophobics" score above 75. As Table 17.1 indicates, eight out of ten prospective teachers harbor negative feelings toward lesbian and gay men; fully one-third of these persons are high grade homophobics. This represents five times the number of high grade homophobics found in Hudson and Ricketts's study a decade ago in Hawaii.

Given differences in geographic region and time, a more useful comparison is the sample of South Carolina guidance counselors surveyed at about the same time

as these prospective teachers. As noted in Table 17.1, both the mean scores of these two groups and the proportion scoring above 50 are similar. The prospective teacher sample, however, is composed of half again the number of "high grade homophobics."

Attitudes about homosexuality among students and educators also have been assessed by several researchers. As shown in Table 17.2, prospective students' attitudes toward homosexuality, though less negative than a sample of Ohio high school students, is considerably less positive than a group of North Carolina teachers. Prospective teachers in this study scored identically to a sample of college students.

Table 17.3 depicts the relationship between prospective teachers' attitudes about

Table 17.1 Percentage Distribution of Index of
Homophobia Scores Among Various Populations

Population	<25	25–50	51–75	>75	N	$\overline{X}$
PRESERVICE TEACHERS	.03	.16	.44	.37	252	65
College Students (Hudson & Ricketts, 1980)	.04	.33	.56	.07	300	53
Guidance Counselors (Sears, 1988a)	.01	.26	.50	.22	141	61

TABLE 17.2 Comparison of Attitudes Toward Homosexuality Among Various Groups

Population	$\overline{X}$ Score	N
PRESERVICE TEACHERS	56	255
Teachers (Fischer, 1982)	42	255
High School Students (Price, 1982)	60	278
College Students (Goldberg, 1982)	56	131
Guidance Counselors (Sears, 1988a)	53	141

TABLE 17.3 Prospective Teachers' Attitudes About Homosexuality and Feelings
Toward Lesbians and Gay Men According to Respondents' Gender,
Race, Certification Area, and Program Status

Demographic	ATH $\overline{X}$	ATH SD	t	df	IH $\overline{X}$	IH SD	t	df
Gender								
Male	45	18	-.16	192	64	18	-.49	113
Female	45	17			65	20		
Race								
White	45	18	-2.16	33*	65	20	-.70	34
Black	52	16			67	15		
Certification Area								
Elementary	50	17	3.18	208*	73	18	4.73	196*
Secondary	43	18			62	18		
Point in Professional Studies								
Early	45	19	.17	122	65	20	.47	142
Late	45	17			64	16		

*p <.001

homosexuality and feelings toward lesbian and gay men vis-à-vis their race, gender, area of certification, and point in the teacher education curriculum using multiple t-tests.

As Table 17.3 indicates, the point at which prospective teachers are at in their professional program of studies is not significantly related to either their attitudes toward homosexuality or their feelings toward lesbians and gay men. Further, unlike studies of other populations, no differences on attitudes or feelings were found with respect to gender. African-American prospective teachers were more likely to express negative attitudes toward homosexuality than Anglo students. There was no relationship between a respondent's race and feelings he or she expressed toward lesbians and gay men. The area of certification was the only factor that discriminated on respondents' attitudes and feelings. In both cases, students intending to teach at the elementary level evidenced more negative scores.

To explore the relative effects of race, gender, program status, and certification area, these four categorical factors together with age, marital status, college grade point average, and type of home community were entered into a multiple regression analysis using either student attitudes about homosexuality scores (ATH) or their scores on feelings toward lesbian and gay men (IH) as the dependent variable. The results of these analyses with the Beta weights appear in Table 17.4.

These eight variables explain only 11 percent of the variance on prospective teachers' attitudes toward homosexuality and 13 percent of the variance on their feelings toward lesbians and gay men. Two or three variables, however, account for the majority of this variance. Using a step-wise multiple regression analysis, certification area, home community, and point in professional studies explain slightly less than 7 percent of the reported prospective teachers' variance on their attitudes toward ho-

TABLE 17.4 Multiple Regression (Betas) of Categoric/Demographic Variables onto Prospective Teachers' Scores on Attitudes About Homosexuality and Feelings Toward Homosexual Persons

Factor	ATH	IH
Age	–.12	–.16
Gender	–.06	–.09
Certification Area	–.26*	–.36*
Point in Professional Studies	.18*	.18*
Race	0	–.06
Home Community	–.15*	–.03
GPA	.10	.01
Marital	.06	.02

*Regression coefficient greater than twice its standard error

mosexuality, area of certification explaining one-third of that variance. With respect to prospective teachers' feelings, area of certification and point in the teacher education curriculum explained more than 10 percent of the variance, with area of certification representing 95 percent of that variation.

Prospective teachers were also asked questions regarding their encounters with homosexuality as a high school student. About six years had elapsed since respondents in this study graduated from high school. The actual range was 1 to 41 years. However, nearly two-thirds of the sample had left high school within the past four years; about one in ten respondents had graduated from high school fifteen or more years ago. Students at the early point in their professional studies had completed high school, on average, four years earlier; students completing their student teaching and participating in the MAT program had completed high school eleven years ago. This section examines respondents' exposure to homosexuality and homosexual students while attending high school. Further, the relationships between prospective teachers' present attitudes and feelings regarding homosexuality and lesbians and gay men and their exposure to this topic or acquaintance with lesbian and gay students during their high school years are explored.

Four questions were posed regarding prospective teachers' acquaintance with lesbian and gay students during their high school experience. These questions and the distribution of responses are presented in Table 17.5.

Table 17.5 indicates that nearly one-half of the respondents suspected a fellow high school student of having a homosexual orientation, and more than one-quarter knew such a student, yet fewer than one out of five acknowledged being friends with a lesbian or gay student during high school.

Comparison of prospective teachers' current feelings toward lesbians and gay men and attitudes about homosexuality were examined in light of these high school experiences. Prospective teachers who, as high school students, knew a homosexual student or were friends with a person they knew or suspected was lesbian or gay evidenced less negative feelings toward homosexual persons and less negative attitudes about homosexuality. In an absolute sense,

TABLE 17.5 Respondents Association with Lesbian and Gay Students While Attending High School

Relationship	No	Yes
Suspected another students of having a homosexual orientation	.55(143)	.45(115)
Knew a student who had a homosexual orientation	.72(186)	.28(72)
Suspected a friend of having a homosexual orientation	.74(190)	.26(68)
Knew a friend who had a homosexual orientation	.82(212)	.18(46)

however, these feelings were still in the "low grade homophobic" range. These data are depicted in Tables 17.6 and 17.7.

Respondents addressed nine questions relating to their exposure to homosexuality during their high school years. One question asked them to assess the ade-quacy and accuracy of information about homosexuality provided to them during high school. Three-fourths of the sample (n = 191) did not believe such information was accurate or adequate. Students who reported that they were provided with accurate and adequate information,

TABLE 17.6 Prospective Teachers' Feelings Toward Homosexual Persons According to Their Association with Lesbian and Gay Students While Attending High School

Relationship	IH $\overline{X}$		IH SD		t	df
	No	Yes	No	Yes		
Suspected another student of a homosexual orientation	66	64	17	22	.69	208
Knew a student who had a homosexual orientation	66	62	19	21	1.35	117*
Suspected a friend of a homosexual orientation	67	58	19	21	2.5	60*
Knew a friend who had a homosexual orientation	68	53	18	22	4.44	58*

*p <.001

TABLE 17.7 Prospective Teachers' Feelings Toward Homosexual Persons According to Their Association with Lesbian and Gay Students While Attending High School

Relationship	IH $\overline{X}$		IH SD		t	df
	No	Yes	No	Yes		
Suspected another student of a homosexual orientation	57	56	14	15	.5	228
Knew a student who had a homosexual orientation	57	54	14	17	1.4	109*
Suspected a friend of a homosexual orientation	58	50	14	16	3.1	60*
Knew a friend who had a homosexual orientation	58	46	13	16	4.9	59*

*p <.001

however, harbored less negative attitudes about homosexuality (Provided $\bar{X}$ = 52, Not Provided $\bar{X}$ = 58; df = 110, t = 2.4; p <.001) and exhibited less negative feelings toward lesbians and gay men (Provided $\bar{X}$ = 60, Not Provided $\bar{X}$ = 67; df = 97, t = 2.4; p <.001).

Prospective teachers also assessed the extent to which their fellow high school students and educators were knowledgeable about homosexuality and the degree of acceptance exhibited toward it. The frequency distributions of these responses appear in Table 17.8.

There are several interesting findings to highlight in this table. First, as evidenced by the large proportion of the sample responding "don't know" to items on educators, homosexuality was not an issue on which most educators had taken a public position. A substantial number of respondents simply were unaware of educators' knowledge about homosexuality or the degree of support they accorded to homosexual students

TABLE 17.8 Respondents' Assessment of Fellow High School Students and Their High School Educators' Knowledge and Acceptance of Homosexuality

Group Characteristic	Approximate Size of Group*					
	All	Most	Some	Few	None	Don't Know
Students knowledgeable about homosexuality	.11(28)	.36(94)	.26(67)	.20(51)	.02(4)	.04(14)
Teachers knowledgeable about homosexuality	.14(37)	.27(69)	.21(54)	.15(39)	.02(4)	.21(55)
Counselors well informed about homosexuality	.09(23)	.12(32)	.12(30)	.14(35)	.13(34)	.40(104)
Students displaying negative attitudes about homosexuality	.11(28)	.73(187)	.09(24)	.02(5)	.02(4)	.04(10)
Teachers supportive of homosexual students	—	—	.05(14)	.19(48)	.29(74)	.47(126)
Students considering homosexuality an alternative lifestyle	.01(2)	.02(6)	.07(17)	.54(190)	.22(56)	.14(37)
Teachers considering homosexuality an alternative lifestyle	—	.02(5)	.09(24)	.34(88)	.21(55)	.33(86)
Teachers discuss homosexuality in the classroom	—	.02(4)	.06(15)	.39(100)	.48(124)	.16(15)

*Percentages rounded to nearest decimal point

or gay rights. The absence of classroom discussion in all but a few classrooms may explain why so few respondents could assess the position of their teachers.

Second, when asked if all or most of the school's faculty were knowledgeable about homosexuality, respondents rated twice as many of the teaching faculty (.41) than the counseling staff (.21) as knowledgeable. A very large percentage (.40) of these prospective teachers, however, simply reported no basis for assessing their counselors' knowledge while attending high school. Interestingly, respondents generally rated their fellow high school students, as a group, more knowledgeable about the subject than the faculty. This may reflect the willingness of each of these groups to express their ideas about homosexuality.

Third, while respondents considered many of their fellow students relatively knowledgeable about homosexuality, these same students, they reported, were very likely to display negative attitudes on this topic. Eight out of ten prospective teachers noted that most if not all of their fellow students in high school harbored homonegative attitudes. And, like their teachers, few or none considered homosexuality an alternative lifestyle.

Another dimension on which this sample of prospective teachers was examined was their current knowledge about homosexuality. A 14-item test was developed that included questions from the natural and behavioral sciences. A majority of the prospective teachers answer 10 of the 14 questions correctly. These responses are arranged in order of correct frequency in Table 17.9.

Items which had the most correct responses included those that directly dealt with childhood sexuality. Most respon-

dents correctly noted that, according to most authorities, homosexuality is not a phase which children outgrow and that sexual orientation is established at an early age. Relatively few prospective teachers, however, were aware that most men and women engage in homosexual and heterosexual behaviors during their lifetime or that same-sex activities occur in many animal species.

Individual scores from this 14-item test were calculated yielding a Homosexuality Knowledge Index (HKI) which ranged from 0 (lowest possible score) to 100 (perfect score). The distribution of prospective teachers on this index is pictured in Figure 17.2.

These scores roughly conformed to a normal bell-shaped curve. The mean score was 57.5 with a range of 0 to 92 and a standard deviation of 19.5. One-third of the respondents scored at or above the 60th percentile. There were no significant differences on these scores between prospective teachers who were at the early point in their professional studies and those who were completing their teacher education curriculum. However, relationships existed between the other three demographic factors. African-American prospective teachers were less knowledgeable about homosexuality than their white counterparts (Black $\bar{X}$ = 50, White $\bar{X}$ = 58; df = 31, t = 2.0; p <.001). Similarly, females evidenced less knowledge than males (Female $\bar{X}$ = 56, Male $\bar{X}$ = 61; df = 110, t = 1.6; p <.001). Finally, prospective teachers pursuing certification in elementary education were less knowledgeable than their secondary education cohorts (Elementary $\bar{X}$ = 55, Secondary $\bar{X}$ = 59.2; df = 208, t = -1.7; p <.001).

The scores on the 14-item knowledge test were correlated with the respondents'

TABLE 17.9 "Correct" Response Percentages on Knowledge About Homosexuality

Item	Correct Response	% Correct Response
Homosexuality is a phase which children outgrow	False	81
There is a good chance of changing homosexual persons into heterosexual men and women	False	77
Most homosexuals want to be members of the opposite sex	False	76
Some church denominations have condemned the legal and social discrimination of homosexual men and women	True	76
Sexual orientation is established at an early age	True	72
According to the American Psychological Association, homosexuality is an illness	False	64
Homosexual males are more likely to seduce young boys than heterosexual males are likely to seduce young girls	False	58
Gay men are at least four times as likely to be victims of criminal violence as members of the general public	True	54
A majority of homosexuals were seduced in adolescence by a person of the same sex, usually several years older	False	53
Sixty percent of pre-adolescent males report at least one homosexual experience	True	52
A person becomes a homosexual (develops a homosexual orientation) because he/she chooses to do so	False	46
Homosexual activity occurs in many animals	True	40
Most adults engage in neither exclusive homosexual or heterosexual behavior	True	29
Sexual relations between two people of the same sex is a criminal act in most states, including SC	False	28

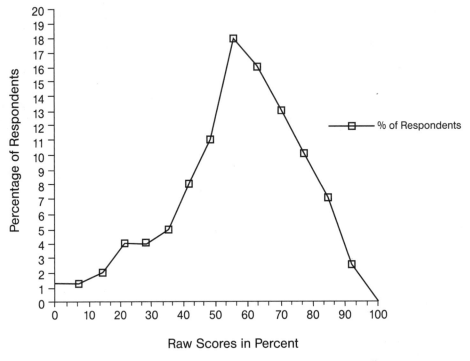

FIGURE 17.2 Distribution of Scores for Knowledge About Homosexuality

scores on the Attitudes Toward Homo-sexuality Scale and the Index of Homophobia scale. In both cases, negative correlations were found (ATH r = -.34; IH r = -.26). That is, the more knowledgeable the student, as measured on the Homosexual Knowledge Index, the less negative attitudes toward homosexuality and feelings toward lesbians and gay men were evidenced.

In order to discern this pattern more fully, prospective teachers scoring one standard deviation above or below the mean on the Homosexual Knowledge Index were selected. The t-test results are presented in Table 17.10.

There were significant differences between most knowledgeable/least knowl-edgeable students and their attitudes about homosexuality and their feelings toward lesbians and gay men. Those demonstrating the least knowledge harbored the most negative attitudes and were the most homophobic.

Summary. In this sample of Southern prospective teachers, most expressed negative attitudes about homosexuality and harbored homophobic feelings toward lesbians and gay men. In comparison with other populations, these prospective teachers held much more negative feelings. They were five times more likely to be classified as "high grade homophobics" than a group of college students surveyed a decade ago (Hudson & Ricketts, 1980). Further, in comparison with a recently sampled group

TABLE 17.10 Knowledgeable and Not Knowledgeable Prospective Teachers' Scores on Attitudes About Homosexuality and Feelings Toward Lesbians and Gay Men

Knowledge Index	ATH $\overline{X}$	ATH SD	t	df	IH $\overline{X}$	IH SD	t	df
Low Scorers	65	10	6.7	85*	75	16	4.69	84*
High Scorers	48	14			57	21		

*p <.001

of Southern guidance counselors, they also were more likely to express negative feelings toward lesbians and gay men. For example, less noticeable differences were found among these prospective teachers and other professional or student groups with respect to attitudes about homosexuality. In all cases, the scores were moderately negative.

Some clear differences with respect to the four demographic variables were found. Most important, prospective teachers pursuing certification in elementary education were more likely to harbor homophobic feelings and express homo-negative attitudes than those planning to teach in the secondary schools. Black prospective teachers also expressed more negative attitudes about homosexuality than their white counterparts but were not any more homophobic in their feelings toward lesbians and gay men.

Two or three factors account for most of the variance discerned in prospective teachers' attitudes and feelings. In no case, however, was more than 15 percent of the variance explained. The type of home community, level in professional program, and certification area accounted for the majority of the variance on prospective teachers' attitudes about homosexuality.

These two later factors accounted for the vast majority of the variation in prospective teachers' feelings toward lesbians and gay men. Interestingly, race, age, and gender exerted little influence on prospective teachers' attitudes or feelings vis-à-vis the three aforementioned variables.

Regarding prospective teachers' encounters with homosexuality, about one in four of the respondents in this study knew a student who had a homosexual orientation or suspected one of their friends was lesbian or gay during their high school years. One in five had a homosexual friend during high school. Prospective teachers who had one or more of these associations during high school exhibited less negative attitudes about homosexuality and held less homophobic feelings toward lesbians and gay men than those who lacked such associations. Having a homosexual friend in high school was the most significant factor that discriminated between those prospective teachers harboring relatively low or high homophobic attitudes and feelings.

Exposure to homosexuality was another dimension of these prospective teachers' high school experiences. Most reported that the information provided about this topic was neither accurate nor adequate. Nevertheless, those (about one-quarter of the sample) who were exposed to the topic of homosexuality during high school scored lower on the two scales assessing attitudes and feelings about homosexuality.

There are two caveats in interpreting these data. First, while prior (high school) association with lesbians and gay persons was related significantly to less negative attitudes and feelings, the scores of these students were still in a moderately high range. That is, simply knowing a friend who is lesbian or gay or receiving accurate information about homosexuality in high school does not correlate with *positive* attitudes about homosexuality or feelings toward homosexual persons. Generally, though, the relationship is one in which their feelings and attitudes are less negative. Second, within the limits of this study it is not possible to determine the causal relationship, if any, which exists between encounters with homosexual persons or exposure to homosexuality and the less homophobic feelings or homo-negative attitudes expressed by such persons.

A substantial number of prospective teachers could not assess the knowledge or attitudes of their high school teachers or counselors with respect to homosexuality. Classroom discussion about homosexuality was conducted by few or none of their teachers. Though these respondents rated their fellow high school students more knowledgeable about this topic than their educators, a vast majority reported that all or most of these students displayed negative attitudes about homosexuality.

Finally, prospective teacher's cumulative knowledge about homosexuality was minimal. Though they were more likely to correctly understand the psychosexual dynamics of childhood than the legal or biological aspects of homosexuality, most would have failed the knowledge "test" if passing would have been set at 60 percent. Women, African-Americans, and elementary education majors evidenced less knowledge than their male, Anglo, and secondary education cohorts.

The question of the relationship between prospective teachers' knowledge and their attitudes/feelings regarding homosexuality yielded noteworthy results. The more knowledgeable the student the less negative attitudes toward homosexuality and feelings toward lesbians and gay men were evidenced. Even when comparing the extreme groups on their knowledge about homosexuality, however, the absolute scores for both groups were still high.

Thus, like high school associations, adequate and accurate knowledge about homosexuality lessened prospective teachers' negative attitudes and feelings; they did not eliminate them. The importance of this point is evident when exploring their professional attitudes and expected behaviors relating to homosexuality or lesbian/gay students.

Guidance Counselors' Attitudes and Feelings

In absolute terms, nearly two-thirds of the school counselors surveyed in this study expressed negative attitudes and feelings about homosexuality and homosexual persons. Like prospective teachers, their feelings against homosexuality (e.g., feeling uncomfortable with the prospect of a gay or lesbian sibling) and reactions to homosexual situations (e.g., personal sexual advances) were more negative than their attitudes against homosexuality (e.g., the criminalization of homosexuality). For example, about one-third of the attitudinal statements reflect positive support for homosexuals and an understanding of homosexuality, and only two statements in the 30-item survey drew negative responses. Few counselors expressed positive feelings toward homosexuals or indicated positive reactions to situations wherein they might personally confront homosexuality. Moreover, many counselors were much more likely to express ambivalence on attitudinal items (e.g., the nature of sexual pleasure between members of the same sex) than they were to have ambivalent feelings about homosexuality or being in homosexual situations.[6]

Overall, the school counselors' scores were slightly less homophobic and homonegative than those of the prospective teachers. Counselors working in administrative areas or in testing and evaluating students were more likely to express homonegative attitudes than those who devoted more time to counseling students. Further, guidance counselors were much more likely to adopt liberal positions on civil rights issues (e.g., decriminalization of consenting adult homosexual relationships) but to hold a conservative moral view (e.g.,

homosexuality is a sin) and fear personal contact (being uncomfortable around lesbians or gay men). These patterns have been found in other studies (Gentry, 1986a; Irwin & Thompson, 1977), leading one set of researchers to conclude, "[M]any people separate their moral censure of homosexuality per se and attitudes about the civil rights of homosexuals" (Irwin & Thompson, 1977:118).

In addition to comparing summative counselors' scores with those of prospective teachers and other samples (see Tables 17.1 and 17.2, above), the relative effects of seven factors on the ATH and IH scores are indicated by the Beta weights appearing in Table 17.11.

Two conclusions are warranted from an examination of these data. First, almost none of the categoric-demographic variables exerts any significant influence on counselors' attitudes or feelings about homosexuality. Second, the only variable having a consistent and moderate effect on both of these factors is the level of education of the respondent. Even this variable's

TABLE 17.11 Step-wise Multiple Regression (Betas) of Categoric Demographic Variables onto IH and MATH Scores

Variable	IH	ATH
Age	.15	.15
Gender	.19*	.11
Race	−.01	.16*
Education	−.28*	−.30*
Experience	−.01	−.13
Childhood Background	.03	−.04
School Site	.02	.04

*Regression coefficient greater than twice its standard error

effect, though, is limited since in no case does it account for more than seven percent of the variance in these measures. The gender and race of the respondent modestly contributed, respectively, to the variance of scores on these two scales. The marginal effect which these demographic variables have on counselors' attitudes and feelings about homosexuality suggests the existence of other, more powerful factors not included in this regression analysis.

Further data analyses explored the modest relationships of gender, race, and education on counselors' attitudes and feelings about homosexuality. Parametric t-tests were used to determine the nature of these differences. These data are summarized in Table 17.12.

Attitudes toward homosexuality vary significantly according to a counselor's gender, race, and educational background. Specifically, counselors who are males, white, or who have earned a degree beyond the master's have more positive attitudes toward homosexuality. With respect to counselors' feelings about homosexuals or reactions to homosexual situations, gender and education were discriminating demographic variables. Again, males were likely to harbor more *positive* feelings in this area as were those who had extensive graduate education. Consistent with studies of other segments of the population (Baker, 1980; Irwin & Thompson, 1977; Nyberg & Alston, 1977), racial minorities and those with less education expressed more negative attitudes or feelings about homosexuality and toward homosexual persons. Unlike these other studies, however, the males in this sample were more supportive than their female counterparts.

In addition to examining the relationship between aggregate scores and these demographic variables, multiple regression was used to determine what items on each of these scales contributed the greatest variance to these three demographic factors. Table 17.13 reveals the results.

TABLE 17.12 Means and Standard Deviations of the IH and MATH Scores According to Counselor's Gender and Race

Demographic		IH $\overline{X}$	IH SD	t	df	MATH $\overline{X}$	MATH SD	t	df
Gender									
	Male	54.3*	21.2	-2.27	137	73.0*	22.2	-1.57	139
	Female	62.3	15.8			79.4	18.9		
Race									
	White	60.5	18.3	-0.11	137	76.3*	20.3	-1.84	139
	Black	60.8	14.3			83.4	17.3		
Education									
	BS/MS	62.7*	16.0	2.56	137	81.3*	18.5	3.44	139
	Spec/Ph.D.	54.2	19.7			68.6	20.6		

*p <.001

TABLE 17.13 Most Discriminating Items on the MATH and IH
According to Gender, Race, and Education

Scale	Item #	Bein	Group 1 $\overline{X}$	Group 2 $\overline{X}$
IH				
Gender			Male (30)	Female (112)
	19*	−.52	3.27	2.83
	20	.22	2.70	3.29
	25	.42	2.40	3.04
Education			BS/MS (103)	Spec/Ph.D. (35)
	24*	−.29	3.67	2.94
MATH				
Race			White (106)	Black (36)
	2	−.23	2.02	2.11
	4	.35	1.55	2.19
	7	.15	2.72	3.19
Education			BS/MS (103)	Spec/Ph.D. (35)
	7	−.16	3.07	2.25
	12	.17	2.74	2.44
	15	−.25	2.56	1.78
	24	−.19	2.61	2.23

*Reverse-coded items (5 = Strongly Agree, 4 = Agree, etc.)

Using multiple regression in which gender served as the dependent variable and the 25 items on the IH scale were predictive variables revealed that the scale accounted for 36 percent of the total variance of gender; three of these items comprised 22 percent of the total variance: "I'd feel comfortable if I learned that my boss was homosexual" (#19); "It would not bother me to walk through a predominantly gay section of town" (#20); "I would feel comfortable working closely with a female homosexual" (#24). When education served as the dependent variable and the predictive variables were items on the IH, the scale accounted for 26 percent of the total variance of educational level with one item accounting for one third of this total variance: "I would feel uncomfortable knowing that my son's teacher was a male homosexual."

Using multiple regression in which race served as the dependent variable and the 30 items on the ATH were predictive variables revealed that this scale accounted for 22 percent of the total variance of race. Three items accounted for one-half of this total variance: "Homosexuals should not be allowed to hold important positions" (#2); "Homosexuals should be locked up and not released until cured" (#4); and, "Homosexuality is a sin" (#7). When education served as the dependent variable with the same set of predictive variables, ATH accounted for 30 percent of the variance with four items comprising 16 percent of this variance: "Homosexuality is a sin" (#7); "If homosexuality is allowed to increase it will destroy our society" (#12); "I find it hard to believe that homosexuals can really love each other" (#15); and, "Homosexuals are very unhappy people who wish they could be like everyone else" (#24).

The items which most clearly discriminated between males' and females' attitudes and feelings about homosexuality, and between blacks' and whites' attitudes are also indicated in Table 17.9 as is the relationship between these attitudes and feelings and one's educational level. For example, religious and civil rights attitudes vis-à-vis homosexuality were the best discriminators between white and black counselors. Whites were more willing for gay and lesbians to hold important positions, more likely to object to the detention and "curing" of homosexuals, and more certain that homosexuality was not sinful.

Summary. School guidance counselors, like prospective teachers and professionals surveyed by other researchers, harbor negative attitudes and feelings about homosexuality. The feelings of these school counselors (e.g., "I would feel uncomfortable knowing that my son's teacher was a male homosexual," "I would feel uncomfortable if I learned that my boss was homosexual.") are much more pronounced than their beliefs (e.g., "Homosexuals should never be allowed to teach school

or supervise children," "It would be a mistake to ever have homosexuals for bosses and leaders over other people.")—which are often rooted in belief about civil rights and the right of privacy. Situations that place school counselors in direct contact with homosexual men and women create among many intensely negative feelings. Significantly, it is in personal situations (e.g., counseling a homosexual student, meeting with lesbian parents) that these professionals must apply their knowledge, experience, and skills. The degree to which their personal feelings and beliefs affect their ability to enter into such relationships is discussed in the next section.

In reflecting upon data presented in this part of the paper, what is most disturbing is the high degree of negativism expressed by school guidance counselors and prospective teachers whose principal responsibility it is to educate and advise young adults—some of whom will identify themselves as lesbian, gay, or bisexual; all of whom will deal with issues related to homosexuality. Attitudes and feelings, of course, are subject to change. Several researchers have reported on the positive impact which seminars, employing lectures, guest speakers, films, debate, and dialogue, have had on reducing homo-negativism (e.g., Anderson, 1981; Goldberg, 1982; Greenberg, 1975; Rudolph, 1988a; Taylor, 1983). Yet, as these data indicate, for such efforts to be effective they must be directed at the level of affect, not cognition. Feelings of discomfort, fear, and hatred are more pervasive than these educators' attitudes about lesbian and gay civil rights. Sadly, few workshops—particularly in teacher preparation or staff development seminars—focus on the emotions.

Homophobia educators need to borrow from the work, experience, and knowledge of those involved in antiracism workshops who engage persons in three- to five-day workshops. There has been a tendency for those engaged in homophobia education not to collaborate with those engaged in other types of antioppression work, such as racism and sexism. This lack of communication contributes to splintering of educational efforts to end prejudice and violence directed at lesbians, gay men, and bisexuals. One such group that has recognized the need to explore the interrelationship of oppressions based on race, gender, social class, and sexual identity is the Campaign to End Homophobia. This group insists that its leaders participate in an intensive workshop in which participants engage in one-on-one and small group activities that strip away the socially acceptable façade of toleration and open up long-held feelings rooted in childhood experiences and translated into powerful life scripts. Through the use of a "social identity development model," workshop leaders of VISIONS, a multiracial collective based in North Carolina, use a form of transitional analysis to return participants to their earliest childhood racial memories (Batts, 1982; Batts, 1989; Jackson & Hardiman, n.d.). Once a person has disclosed this event, members of the group work the person to "unlearn" cognitive and affective misinformation acquired in childhood and covered up through years of adult socialization.

Shifts in a person's attitudes and feelings, however, do not mean there will be a concomitant shift in behavior. There may be a gap between attitudes professed on a survey and the everyday behaviors practiced in the school. Many educators surveyed in this study also posited the belief in their ability to distance one's personal attitudes and feelings from the professional responsibilities of their jobs. In the next section, I will examine their effectiveness in accomplishing this task.

Professional Attitudes and Projected Activities in the Schools

As "professionals," educators often assert that personal beliefs and community values do not interfere with the delivery of professional services to students. In reality, of course, students' race, social class, and gender have a significant impact on how they are perceived by peers, evaluated by teachers, and tracked by school counselors (Oakes, 1985; Rist, 1973; Rosenbaum, 1976; Willis, 1977). With the rise of Christian Fundamentalism and the spiraling number of HIV cases, homosexuality and the homosexual became the "new Nigger" of the 1980s. No longer a taboo topic, persons who acknowledged their same-sex feelings were prime targets for nightclub comics, skinheads, rock-and-roll bands, and television evangelists.

The South, perhaps more than other region of the United States, openly practices one of the few remaining forms of socially accepted bigotry: homophobia. From the enforcement of sodomy laws in Georgia's *Hardwick* case to the venomous attacks of North Carolina's senator Jesse Helms on the Mapplethorpe collection funded by the National Endowment for the Arts, to the banning of references to homosexuality in South Carolina's state approved sexuality texts, the South is a lonely place for a boy or girl blossoming into adulthood as a lesbian, bisexual, or gay man.

Educators significantly influence the experiences of these boys and girls in school. It is the educator who chooses *how* to teach the prescribed sexuality curriculum; it is the educator who challenges or winks at homophobic comments or jokes among students; it is the educator who comforts or ignores a student suffering from the heterosexist tirades of peers or doubts about her sexual identity; it is the educator who fosters dialogue among fellow professionals about the penalties *all* pay in a heterosexual-mandated society. Thus, it is educators—prospective teachers and school counselors—and their beliefs and values to which we look for a reduction of heterosexual hegemony.

Professional Attitudes of Future Teachers

As detailed in the previous section, seldom in these prospective teachers' own K–12 experiences was sexuality discussed in the formal curriculum; when sexuality was discussed, homosexuality was generally ignored or reproved. Only *six* of these Southern youth ever talked with a teacher about sexuality. Three-fourths of the participants reported that their high school teachers had negative attitudes about homosexuality, and more than 80 percent reported few or none of their high school teachers considered homosexuality an alternative lifestyle or that classroom discussion included this topic.

These prospective teachers were asked how they would respond as teachers to situations relating to homosexuality in classroom interaction, counseling, student harassment, fellow teachers, and human rights. The proportion of students responding affirmatively to statements within each

of these categories is indicated in Table 17.14.

As indicated in Table 17.14, despite the sample's generally negative personal feelings and attitudes, prospective teachers expressed a professional regard for homosexual students in a variety of areas and instances. For example, a substantial majority of prospective teachers expected to take appropriate action in situations involving the harassment of students due to their actual or perceived homosexuality. Further, nearly three-fourths of the prospective teachers did not believe they would have difficulty treating an openly gay student fairly.

On the other hand, prospective teachers were most reticent about assuming proactive counseling or teaching roles, working with an openly homosexual teacher, or striving to end discrimination against lesbians, bisexuals, and gay men in their community. About one-half of the sample thought it would be appropriate for *another* teacher to provide supportive materials to a lesbian, bisexual, or gay student but less than one-third felt personally comfortable speaking with a student about his or her same-sex feelings or discussing homosexuality in the classroom. Further, four of ten future teachers thought it acceptable to transfer a homosexual student to another class on the request of a homophobic teacher.

Another method for examining how personal feelings and attitudes translate into professional activity is to ask prospective teachers their specific response to the following classroom situation.

Assume that you are teaching at your grade level within a public school in this state. You

TABLE 17.14 Prospective Teachers' Attitudes and Behaviors
Relating to Homosexuality in the School

Statement	% Agree	N (n = 258)
Classroom Interaction		
Teachers who regard homosexuality in a negative way should be able to request a homosexual student to enroll in another class	37	93
I would discuss homosexuality in the classroom	29	70
It would be difficult for me to deal fairly with an avowed homosexual student	24	62
Counseling		
Providing a homosexual high school student with supportive materials is appropriate for a teacher	49	121
I would feel comfortable if a student talked with me about his or her sexual orientation	36	93
Student Harassment		
I would discipline a student for harassing another student suspected of having a homosexual orientation	86	219
I would openly disagree with a faculty member who made a disparaging comment about a suspected homosexual student	64	162
I would discipline a student for making a derogatory remark about homosexuals	64	159
I would ignore student jokes about homosexuals	42	107
Homosexual Teachers		
I would feel uncomfortable if my school hired an openly gay or lesbian teacher	52	132
Homosexual persons should not be allowed to teach in the public schools	26	63
Adolescents who know several homosexual teachers will be strongly influenced to be homosexual	22	36
Human Rights		
A teacher must work in school to lessen prejudicial attitudes about homosexuality	62	157
I would work in my community to bar discrimination against homosexual men and women	32	80

are leading a discussion about current events. Today's topic is AIDS. After several minutes of give-and-take discussion among students in the class, the following dialogue occurs:

Mary: I think it's too bad that all these people are so sick and are going to die. I just think . . .

Paul (interrupting): Those fags get what they deserve. What makes me mad is that we're spending money trying to find a cure. If we just let God and Nature take its course, I won't have to worry about any queer bothering me.

Mary: I never thought about it that way before.

Mary then faces you and asks, "What do you think about Paul's comments?" Briefly state how you would most likely respond.

Seven percent of the respondents to this scenario agreed with Paul. One wrote, "Once homosexuals have AIDS and know they're going to die, they want to spread it. Our tax money should not be spent. I agree with Paul." Another wrote, "I feel that if someone does get AIDS because they are homosexual—hell! Let them die."

Two-thirds of the respondents chose to address Paul's statements about AIDS. Most of these persons chose to battle with Paul on logical or factual grounds: "If AIDS is God's punishment from God and Nature, what about cancer?" "A cure is for all society, no one deserves to die." Several who used logic to counter Paul's arguments, reflected their homo-negative feelings. For example, "It's true that homosexuals contract AIDS, but think of the unfortunate people who are not homosexual who contract AIDS. It is not fair to let those unfortunate people be sick and die."

Another wrote, "We must find a cure to prevent the spread of AIDS among the innocent." A third said, "Look, asshole, AIDS affects everybody. If it was just restricted to queers that would be another story."

Others chose a more factual approach: "Paul, your statement is not accurate. You should watch the news more often"; "Homosexuals are not a high-risk group for AIDS, people who engage in high-risk behavior are at risk"; "AIDS affects more than gay people."

A handful chose (6%) to personalize the situation or to ridicule Paul: "How would you feel if you were condemned to die because you fell in love with Lucy and she got pregnant?" "What if someone in your family got AIDS?" and, "You're narrow-minded and insensitive." A few (2%), branding Paul for his un-Southernly rudeness in public, wrote such comments as: "It wasn't polite for him to say those things."

Eight percent asked Paul for tolerance and compassion: "You have a point, Paul. But people are different and what you think is 'normal,' others think is 'abnormal.' You must learn to face life and see it for what it really is." "Gays are human beings; they shouldn't be treated as animals." Four confessed ambivalence or the desire to allow everyone to hold their own opinion: "I'm not sure. I haven't thought much about it. I believe we need to find a cure for AIDS but we cannot condone a lifestyle." "Each person has the right to their own opinion. School is not a place to have such discussions." "I wouldn't try to change Paul's or Mary's attitudes, that isn't up to me."

These prospective teachers' responses reflect an understanding of AIDS, a cognitive orientation to dealing with the classroom issue, and a desire to ignore the inherent homo-negativism of the dialogues. Given the multiple levels on which a teacher could respond, it is noteworthy that almost all of the prospective teachers focused on the anti-AIDS comment and chose to ignore its homophobic content or to discuss homosexuality in class.

Six of the persons who responded directly to Paul's homophobic comments expressed those of their own: "There needs to be a cure because the homos and bisexuals are giving it to us. I really think God is trying to tell us to get back to morals." Another stated, "Homosexuality is a sin and AIDS is God's way of warning us that it is a sin, but God loves everyone. We should help to change their lifestyle."

Despite the fact that two-thirds of the respondents indicated that they would discipline a student for making a derogatory comment about homosexuality, only 6 percent actually did so when provided the opportunity: Five chose to provide Paul with a short lecture: "'Fags' aren't the only people dying from AIDS. Homosexuals are people, too. People don't choose to be gay, they can't help it if they don't go along with societal norms." Another wrote, "First teach him that 'fag' is crude and explain that homosexuals do not choose their lifestyles." Two chose punishment: "I would punish Paul for his rude and opinionated comments."

Given the aforementioned discussion on the division between attitudes and feelings, it is also noteworthy that the predominant response was at the *cognitive* level. Only a couple of respondents explored Paul's feelings. One wrote, "I would have a discussion with this young man to find out why he feels so hostile toward homosexuals." Clearly, as this scenario illustrates, there is a significant gap between attitudes regarding appropriate professional responses to homosexual-related issues in the school and actual professional behavior. School situations which require teachers to *react* to homophobia are clearly influenced by personal feelings and attitudes. To what degree are these personal beliefs and feelings related to prospective teachers' willingness to assume *proactive* roles in the school and community vis-à-vis homosexual issues?

In order to better understand the constellation of factors that contribute to prospective teachers' attitudes and feelings the 14 items in Table 17.14 were aggregated to form a Professional Attitudes Index Scale.[7] The lower the score, the less supportive professionally a person is regarding homosexual persons and issues in the school. Prospective teachers who were at the student teaching point of their professional studies exhibited statistically significant *lower* scores on this index than those early in their program. Further, students pursuing an elementary certificate at the early point of their teacher education curriculum scored significantly lower on this Index than their secondary cohorts; white prospective teachers scored significantly higher than their black peers.

Responses to these statements resulted in the adoption of seemingly paradoxical positions. First, despite their personal abhorrence of homosexuality and the homosexual, most prospective teachers professed a willingness to protect the homosexual student from harassment and to treat that student fairly. Second, though only one-quarter of these prospective teachers believed that homosexual adults should not teach in public schools, most would feel uncomfortable if an openly lesbian or gay teacher worked at their school. Third, though these college students agreed that teachers must work in the school to lessen prejudicial attitudes about homosexuality, fewer than one-third indicated a willingness to work toward such an end within their communities.

Many of these prospective teachers made a distinction between "the sin and the sinner." That is, while believing in the wrongness of homosexuality and expressing negative feelings in encounters with homosexuals, these students assumed a professional demeanor in treating homosexual students fairly and with respect—expecting similar behaviors from students. Those persons who were nearing the end of their professional preparation, however, were less likely to profess these attitudes.

In order to explore the relationship between personal beliefs and feelings and their professional attitudes, the students' scores on the Professional Attitude Index were correlated with those of the Homosexual Knowledge Index, the Attitudes Toward Homosexuality scale, and the Index of Homophobia scale. Prospective teachers' professional attitudes showed only a mild correlation with their knowledge of homosexuality (.25). However, the degree of the negative correlation between their professional attitudes and the attitudes about homosexuality (-.76) and

feelings toward lesbians and gay men (-.66) was powerful.

Exploring this relationship further, prospective teachers scoring one standard deviation above or below the mean on the Professional Attitude Index were selected. T-tests discerned the margin of difference among these more extreme groups vis-à-vis their attitudes about homosexuality and feelings toward lesbians and gay men.

As illustrated in Table 17.15, students who expressed low professional regard, as measured on the Professional Attitudes Index, for issues relating to homosexuality in the schools fit within the domain of "high grade homophobics" while those who expressed a high professional regard were within the "low grade non-homophobics" domain. Similarly, a 50 point spread on attitudes toward homosexuality separated those who expressed a high regard for addressing homosexual issues in the school compared with those whose regard was low.

Clearly, the degree to which prospective teachers assume a proactive role in meeting the needs of homosexual and bisexual students and creating an environment of respect and support for them is related to the teachers' personal feelings and beliefs. At best, teachers who are knowledgeable

TABLE 17.15 High and Low Professional Attitudes of Prospective Teachers' Scores on Attitudes About Homosexuality and Feelings Toward Lesbians and Gay Men

Attitude Index	ATH $\overline{X}$	ATH SD	t	df	IH $\overline{X}$	IH SD	t	df
Low Scores	64	11	16	36*	81	12	9.4	23*
High Scorers	13	10			35	18		

*p <.001

about the social, medical, and legal issues related to homosexuality will more likely treat those students suspected of sexual difference fairly and with respect. Deep-seated personal beliefs and feelings about this issue—generally not the level on which staff development workshops are directed—govern the type of personal involvement that these soon-to-be professionals expect to have with homosexuality and the homosexual. Expecting these teachers to be supportive of the hiring of an openly gay or lesbian teacher, discussing homosexuality in the classroom, or talking with a student about his or her sexual identity is not reasonable.

Finally, prospective teachers checked those proactive activities in which they *might* participate as a professional. These activities, arranged in order of frequency of occurrence, are listed in Table 17.16.

With the exception of attending a school-sponsored workshop on strategies dealing with lesbian and gay students, only a minority of this sample expected to engage in professional activities relating to homosexuality. Further, those activities which required the greatest risk or visibility—encouraging classroom discussion on homosexuality, integrating homosexual themes into the curriculum, or meeting with homosexual adults—were the least-selected activities. Prospective teachers coming from rural backgrounds were least likely to express a willingness to meet with homosexual adults to discuss the special needs of sexual minority students. Those students completing their student teaching were less likely than those at the early stage of their professional studies to desire to integrate homosexual issues or themes into the curriculum or to encourage the

TABLE 17.16 Distribution of Agreement About Expected Professional Activities Among Prospective Teachers

Professional Activity	% Agreed	N
1) Attend a school-sponsored workshop on strategies in working with gay students	75	185
2) Prepare educational materials for students interested in homosexuality	31	77
3) Assemble a resource packet on homosexuality for teachers in the school	29	72
4) Discuss concerns of gay students at a faculty meeting	26	64
5) Engage in dialogue with parents about homosexuality at a school-sponsored program	26	64
6) Meet with homosexual adults to learn more about gay students' special needs	23	56
7) Encourage classroom discussion about homosexuality	23	56
8) Integrate homosexual themes and issues into the curriculum	15	37

discussion of homosexuality in their classrooms. Finally, females were less likely than males to seek such curricular integration.

The relationships between prospective teachers' attitudes about homosexuality, feelings toward lesbians and gay men, knowledge about homosexuality, and professional attitudes about homosexuality are explicated in Table 17.17.

Without exception, prospective teachers' scores on three of the scales—the Attitudes About Homosexuality Scale, the Index of Homophobia, and the Professional Attitudes About Homosexuality Index—were

TABLE 17.17 Distribution of Prospective Teachers' Scores on Four Instruments According to Their Expectation of Engaging in Supportive Activities*

Activity	IH	ATH	HKI	PAI
1) Attend Workshop				
YES	65	56	–	39
NO	68	59	–	37
2) Student Educational Materials				
YES	60	50	60	41
NO	68	56	59	37
3) Teacher Resource Packet				
YES	60	53	–	40
NO	67	58	–	38
4) Faculty Meeting				
YES	59	50	–	42
NO	68	59	–	37
5) Parent Dialogue				
YES	61	52	–	41
NO	67	58	–	37
6) Homosexual Adults Meeting				
YES	54	47	–	43
NO	69	59	–	37
7) Encourage Classroom Discussion				
YES	54	48	62	43
NO	69	59	56	37
8) Integrate into Curriculum				
YES	54	48	–	43
NO	68	58	–	38

*all data are significant with p <.001

related in the expected manner. That is, prospective teachers who expressed less negative attitudes about homosexuality or harbored less homophobic feelings toward lesbians and gay men were more likely to indicate a willingness to engage in such professional activities. Further, those who expressed more supportive professional attitudes regarding homosexual issues were also more likely to hold an expectation for participating in these activities.

The expressed willingness of prospective teachers to address homosexual-related issues in the schools is highly correlated with their attitudes about homosexuality and their feelings toward lesbians and gay men. This relationship is most clearly seen in comparing low and high respondents' scores on the Professional Attitudes Index with their scores on the Attitudes Toward Homosexuality and the Index of Homophobia scales. Those who were most willing to adopt a proactive role in the schools were classified as nonhomophobic and expressed tolerant attitudes regarding homosexuality. Those who were not willing to assume such a proactive role tended to be more advanced in their professional studies. Those who were at the early point in their teacher education curriculum, who were white, or who were majoring in secondary education evidenced a more proactive position than their counterparts.

In summary, though *most* students proclaimed their ability to treat homosexual students fairly as well as to establish a climate of respect among all students, *few* of them were willing to become personally involved in meeting the special needs or concerns of lesbian, gay, and bisexual students. With the exception of attending a school-sponsored workshop on strategies for working with lesbian and gay students, only a minority expected to participate in any other activity. Those activities most directly related to teaching, classroom discussion, and curriculum integration were the least chosen areas of projected activity. Their woefully inadequate knowledge and homophobic attitudes and feelings mean that relatively few of these prospective teachers believe that this group of largely invisible, at-risk students merit special attention or assistance.

Professional Attitudes of School Counselors

Counselors were asked to assess the school climate for homosexual students and the discussion of homosexual-related issues. The vast majority of counselors observed that few, if any, of their school's teachers were supportive of gay and lesbian students, discussed homosexuality in the classroom, or considered it an alternative lifestyle. Further, slightly less than one-third of these professionals indicated that their building level administrators even viewed homosexual concerns as legitimate topics for counselors to discuss with their school-age clients. Those working in rural schools or at the middle school level reported less receptivity on the part of the school administration or the teaching staff to address this issue.

Given this homo-negative environment, it is noteworthy that four out of ten counselors have discussed homosexuality and homosexual-related issues among their counseling staff or have counseled students about their homosexual orientation. Those working with high school juniors and seniors were most likely to report discussing these issues.

Like the prospective teachers, school counselors indicated their willingness to

TABLE 17.18 Expectation of Engaging in Supportive Activities by Prospective Teachers

Activity	Percentage Planning to Participate
Workshop on AIDS	72
Workshop on homosexual youth	68
Reading professional materials about homosexuality	51
Preparing educational materials about homosexuality for teachers	40
Assembling a counseling packet for concerned students	32
Meeting with homosexual adults	25
Discussing concerns of homosexual students at a faculty meeting	17
Dialogue with parents on homosexuality in a school-sponsored program	12

participate in a variety of professional activities during the next year. Their responses are listed in Table 17.18.

Clearly, situations in which the counselor would be more personally involved were less appealing. Counselors were more willing to discuss concerns of homosexual students within a faculty setting if they had known such a student and had attended workshops about counseling homosexual-identified students.

Most guidance counselors also reported knowing at least one homosexual student during their professional career. Few felt prepared to work with this at-risk population. Despite their inadequate preparation and these personal contacts, less than one-fifth of these counselors indicated that they had participated in programs to expand their knowledge about homosexuality.

A strong relationship existed between the likelihood of counselors engaging in these activities and their personal attitudes toward homosexuality and feelings toward homosexual-identified women and men

(Sears, 1988a). Counselors working below the high school level were three to six times less likely to attend such workshop or to engage in any other activities (e.g., reading professional materials) to enhance their professional knowledge in counseling homosexual-identified students. There is a powerful relationship between participating in such workshops and providing materials to teachers or counseling of gay students.

Of course, one cannot determine whether this willingness is due to prior participation in such workshops or to confronting this issue with a client at an earlier point in time. It is interesting to note that those who have suspected students of having a homosexual identity expressed a greater willingness to participate in workshops to expand their knowledge about homosexuality. Further, those willing to participate in these workshops also expressed less negative attitudes and less negative feelings about homosexuality.

Most of the young Southerners interviewed in *Growing Up Gay in the South*

(Sears, 1991) perceived these counselors to be ill-informed and unconcerned; these students felt uncomfortable talking to them. These students' image of counselors was summed up by one lesbian adolescent: "Our counselors had never been presented to us as someone there to talk about problems other than education. They were just there for grades, signing up for classes, tests like the PSAT, and finding colleges to attend."

Thought most homosexual-identified youth in my study wanted a supportive adult counselor while attending high school, some were more reticent. The reasons for their caution included students' unwillingness to assume the initiative, lack of trust in confidentiality, fear of losing teacher friendship, and personality differences. One homosexual student comments:

I didn't talk to counselors because they're human, too. Homosexuality is taboo. People just kind of go bonkers when they hear that word or find out that somebody is homosexual. Even the adults act like kids. They don't know how to handle it. I thought, "I can't trust anybody with this information." You know, teachers talk.

Precisely what role should school counselors assume when working with a homosexual-identified student? What professional responsibilities do counselors believe that they have in dealing with homosexuality in the school? Most school counselors proclaim that a nonjudgmental role should be adopted when dealing with homosexual students or the issue of homosexuality in the school curriculum. For example, the vast majority believed that sexual concerns of students were legitimate topics for discussion; few expected homosexual students to overcome their same-sex feelings. Most believed it acceptable for counselors to work in school to lessen prejudicial attitudes about homosexuality.

Like the prospective teachers, these counselors claim an ability to set aside personal prejudices and assume a professional relationship with their gay or lesbian clients. As expected, however, their professional expectations correlated with counselors' attitudes toward homosexuality and feelings about homosexual persons. For example, on the Index of Homophobia Scale, those who were categorized as "low grade non-homophobics" were three times more likely to believe that counselors should lessen prejudicial attitudes in the school and six times more likely to disagree that a counselor should help students overcome their homosexual feelings than those classified as "high grade homophobics." Further, counselors with less formal education, less counseling experience, and coming from African-American descent were more likely to expect the student to overcome his/her homosexual feelings.

Despite the apparent liberal, professional model adopted by many of these school counselors, less than one-quarter have chosen to counsel such students about homosexuality although nearly two-thirds of the counselors knew students who have a homosexual orientation. Those counselors working with older students and having more professional experience and formal education were most willing to work with sexual minority youth. Those spending a greater proportion of their time in administrative tasks such as testing and evaluating students expressed more negative attitudes and were less interested in the concerns of this special population. Consistent with studies of other segments of the population, counselors belonging to racial minorities and those with less education expressed more negative attitudes or feelings about homosexuality and toward homosexual persons (Baker, 1980; Irwin & Thompson, 1977; Nyberg & Alston, 1977). In contrast to the respondents in these other studies, however, male counselors were more tolerant than their female counterparts.

These counselors, like the prospective teachers, adopted a variety of paradoxical perspectives. For example, the professed professional role of working with homosexual students stands in stark contrast to the relatively few who have actually counseled such persons—although most admit to knowing these students. Rudolph (1988b, p. 167), discussing the consistency of research on counselors' paradoxical beliefs about homosexuality, writes: "The counselor is torn. He or she is formally told one thing about homosexuality from the profession (i.e., 'homosexuality is okay'), and more informally, but no less pervasively, quite another from the society-at-large ('homosexuality is not okay'). . . . Although the admittedly homophobic or heterosexist counselor can clearly be harmful to a gay client, a greater risk of danger may lie with the homophobic or heterosexist counselor who is not aware of his or her prejudicial sentiment."

These attitudes are similar to those of the white liberal who proclaims herself supportive of black civil rights and "colorblind," but has no black friends and associates in almost all-white (except for the few token minorities) professional and personal settings. Clearly, it is easier to proclaim socially acceptable attitudes which have little direct bearing on one's everyday activities than to examine how heterosexist scripts

and institutional homophobia—embedded in the air we breathe and the rain that falls—affects each of us.

Conclusions

On the surface, it would appear that many educators, though personally bothered by homosexuality, adopt a professional, nonjudgmental demeanor in the school. Treating a student equally, however, is not necessarily treating that student fairly or equitably. For example, educators' willingness to curtail verbal harassment or to attend school-sponsored workshops related to homosexual students is noteworthy. However, their unwillingness to assume a proactive role in the school means that the special needs of these homosexual students will remain unmet. As a largely invisible part of the student body, gay, lesbian, and bisexual students have few allies outside the school to speak on their behalf. Consequently, aside from reacting to blatant homophobic situations in the school or attending one-shot, school-sponsored workshops, educators indicate little willingness to help create an environment that will facilitate the intellectual and social growth of these at-risk students.

This benign neglect by professionals reinforces the heterosexual curriculum. Lacking formal sexuality education classes which dispel the myths associated with homosexuality, educators become silent conspirators in sexual oppression (Sears, in press). The absence of visible support from educators conveys to *all* students the legitimacy and desirability of the heterosexual standard. This absence creates a climate of isolation, guilt, and fear for students confronting same-sex feelings—which, in adolescence, may be the majority of a school's population.

REFERENCES

Aguero, J., Bloch, L., & Byrne, D. (1984). The relationships among sexual beliefs, attitudes, experience, and homophobia. *Journal of Homosexuality, 10*(1/2), 95–107.

Anderson, C. (1981). The effect of a workshop on attitudes of female nursing students toward male homosexuality. *Journal of Homosexuality, 7*(1), 57–69.

Baker, D. (1980). *A survey of attitudes and knowledge about homosexuality among secondary school teachers in training.* Unpublished master's thesis, Southern Methodist University, Dallas, TX. ERIC Document No. ED204693.

Batts, V. (1982). Modern racism: A TA perspective. *Transactional Analysis Journal, 12*(3), 207–209.

Batts, V. (1989). Modern racism: New melody for the same old tune. Unpublished manuscript.

Benvenuti, A. (1986). *Assessing and addressing the special challenge of gay and lesbian students for high school counseling programs.* Paper presented at the Annual Meeting of the California Educational Research Association. ERIC Document No. ED 279958.

Braungart, R., & Braungart, M. (1988). From yippies to yuppies: Twenty years of freshman attitudes. *Public Opinion, 11*(3), 53–57.

Casas, J., Brady, S., & Poterotto, J. (1983). Sexual preference biases in counseling: An information processing approach. *Journal of Counseling Psychology, 30*, 139–145.

Clift, S. (1988). Lesbian and gay issues in education: A study of the attitudes of first-year students in a college of higher education. *British Educational Research Journal, 14*(1), 31–50.

Coles, R., & Stokes, G. (1985). *Sex and the American teenager.* New York: Harper & Row.

Clark, M. (1979). *Attitudes, information and behavior of counselors toward homosexual clients.* Unpublished doctoral dissertation, Wayne State University. (*Dissertation Abstracts International, 40,* 5729A), Detroit, MI.

Davison, G., & Wilson, G. (1973). Attitudes of behavior therapists toward homosexuality. *Behavior Therapy, 4*(5), 686–696.

DeCrescenzo, T. (1983–84). Homophobia: A study of the attitudes of mental health professionals toward homosexuality. *Journal of Social Work and Human Sexuality, 2*(2–3), 115–136.

Dillon, C. (1986). Preparing college health professionals to deliver gay-affirmative services. *Journal of American College Health, 35*(1), 36–40.

Douglas, C., Kalman, C., & Kalman, T. (1985). Homophobia among physicians and nurses: An empirical study. *Hospital and Community Psychiatry, 36*(12), 1309–1311.

Dressler, J. (1985). Survey of school principals regarding alleged homosexual teachers in the classroom: How likely (really) is discharge? *University of Dayton Law Review, 10*(3), 599–620.

Earls, R., Fraser, J., & Sumpter, B. (in press). Sexuality education in the South: In whose interests? In J. Sears (Ed.), *Sexuality and the curriculum.* New York: Teachers College Press.

Fischer, T. (1982). *A study of educators' attitudes toward homosexuality.* Unpublished doctoral dissertation, University of Virginia, Charlottesville, VA. (*Dissertation Abstracts International, 43,* 10, 3294A).

Fyfe, B. (1983). "Homophobia" or homosexual bias reconsidered. *Archives of Sexual Behavior, 12*(6), 549–554.

Garfinkle, E., & Morin, S. (1978). Psychologists' attitudes toward homosexual psychotherapy clients. *Journal of Social Issues, 34*(3), 101–112.

Gartrell, N., Kraemer, H., & Brodie, H. (1974). Psychiatrists' attitudes toward female homosexuality. *Journal of Nervous and Mental Diseases, 159*(2), 141–144.

Gentry, C. (1986a). Social distance regarding male and female homosexuals. *Journal of Social Psychology, 127*(2), 199–208.

Gentry, C. (1986b). Development of scales measuring social distance toward male and female homosexuals. *Journal of Homosexuality, 13*(1), 75–82.

Glenn, A., & Russell, R. (1986). Heterosexual bias among counselor trainees. *Counselor Education and Supervision, 25*(3), 222–229.

Goldberg, R. (1982). Attitude change among college students toward homosexuality. *Journal of American College Health, 3*(3), 260–267.

Greenberg, J. (1975). A study of personality change associated with the conducting of a high school unit on homosexuality. *Journal of School Health, 45*(7), 394–398.

Griffin, P. (1992). From hiding out to coming out: Empowering lesbian and gay educators. *Journal of Homosexuality, 22*(3/4).

Gumaer, J. (1987). Understanding and counseling gay men: A developmental perspective. *Journal of Counseling and Development, 66*(3), 144–146.

Herek, G. (1984). Beyond "homophobia": A social psychological perspective on attitudes toward lesbians and gay men. *Journal of Homosexuality, 10*(1/2), 1–18.

Herek, G. (1986). On heterosexual masculinity: Some physical consequences of the social construction of gender and sexuality. *American Behavioral Scientist, 29*(5), 563–577.

Hochstein, L. (1986). Pastoral counselors: Their attitudes toward gay and lesbian clients. *Journal of Pastoral Care, 40*(2), 158–165.

Hong, S. (1983). Sex, religion and factor analytically derived attitudes towards homosexuality. *Australian Journal of Sex, Marriage, and Family, 43*(3), 142–150.

Hudson, W., & Ricketts, W. (1980). A strategy for the measurement of homophobia. *Journal of Homosexuality, 5*(4), 357–372.

Irwin, P., & Thompson, N. (1977). Acceptance of the rights of homosexuals: A social profile. *Journal of Homosexuality, 3*(2), 107–121.

Jackson, B., & Hardiman, R. (n.d.). Social identity development model. Unpublished manuscript.

Krysiak, G. (1987). Very silent and gay minority. *School Counselor, 34*(4), 304–307.

Lance, L. (1987). The effects of interaction with gay persons on attitudes toward homosexuality. *Human Relations, 40*(6), 329–336.

Larkin, F. (1989). Attitudes of female registered nurses toward homosexual men. Unpublished master's thesis, University of Lowell, Lowell, MA. (*Masters Abstracts International 28*, 1, 110).

Larsen, K., Reed, M., & Hoffman, S. (1980). Attitudes of heterosexuals toward homosexuality: A Likert type scale and construct validity. *Journal of Sex Research, 16*(3), 245–257.

Lehne, G. (1976). Homophobia among men. In D. David & R. Brannon (Eds.), *The forty-nine percent majority: The male sex role* (pp. 66–88). Reading, MA: Addison-Wesley.

MacDonald, A. (1976). Homophobia: Its roots and meanings. *Homosexual Counseling Journal, 3*(1), 23–33.

MacDonald, A., Huggins, J., Young, S., & Swanson, R. (1973). Attitudes toward homosexuality: Preservation of sex morality or the double standard? *Journal of Counseling and Clinical Psychology, 40*(1), 161.

Maddux, J. (1988). *The homophobic attitudes of preservice teachers*. Unpublished doctoral dissertation, University of Cincinnati, Cincinnati, OH. (*Dissertation Abstracts International 49*, 8, 2091A).

Malyon, A. (1982). Psychotherapeutic implications of internalized homophobia in gay men. In J. Gonsiorek (Ed.), *Homosexuality and psychotherapy: A practitioner's handbook of affirmative models* (pp. 59–69). New York: The Haworth Press, Inc.

Margolies, L., Becker, M., & Jackson-Brewer, K. (1987). Internalized homophobia: Identifying and treating the oppressor within. In Boston Lesbian Psychologies Collective (Ed.), *Lesbian psychologies: Explorations and challenges* (pp. 229–241). Urbana: University of Illinois Press.

McQuoid, D. (1988). *Attitudes toward homosexuality: Implications for responsible psychotherapy.* Unpublished doctoral research paper. LaMirada, CA: Biola University. ERIC Document No. 298397.

Morin, S., & Garfinkle, E. (1978). Male homophobia. *Journal of Social Issues, 34*(1), 29–47.

Nyberg, K., & Alston, J. (1977). Homosexual labeling by university youths. *Adolescence, 12*(48), 541–546.

Oakes, J. (1985). Keeping track: How schools structure inequality. New Haven, CT: Yale University Press.

Pauly, I., & Goldstein, S. (1970). Physicians' attitudes in treating male homosexuals. *Medical Aspects of Human Sexuality, 4,* 26–45.

Price, J. (1982). High school students' attitudes toward homosexuality. *Journal of School Health, 52*(8), 469–474.

Rist, R. (1973). The urban school: A factory of failure. Cambridge, MA: MIT Press.

Rosenbaum, J. (1976). *Making inequality: The hidden curriculum of high school tracking.* New York: Wiley.

Rudolph, J. (1988a). *The effects of a multimodal seminar on mental health practitioners' attitudes toward homosexuality, authoritarianism, and counseling effectiveness.* Unpublished doctoral dissertation, Lehigh University, Bethlehem, PA. (*Dissertation Abstracts International* 49, 7, 2873B).

Rudolph, J. (1988b). Counselors' attitudes toward homosexuality: A selective review of the literature. *Journal of Counseling and Development, 67*(3), 165–168.

Russell, T. (1989). AIDS education, homosexuality, and the counselor's role. *School Counselor, 36*(5), 333–337.

Schatman, M. (1989). *The prediction of homophobic attitudes among college students.* Unpublished doctoral dissertation, University of North Texas, Denton, TX. (*Dissertation Abstracts International 50,* 10, 4820B).

Schneider, W., & Lewis, I. (1984). The straight story on homosexuality and gay rights. *Public Opinion, 7*(1), 16–20, 59–60.

Schneider, M., & Tremble, B. (1986). Training service providers to work with gay or lesbian adolescents: A workshop. *Journal of Counseling and Development, 65*(2), 98–99.

Scott, D. (1988). Working with gay and lesbian students. *Association of College Unions International Bulletin, 56*(2), 22–25.

Sears, J. (1987). Peering into the well of loneliness: The responsibility of educators to gay and lesbian youth. In Alex Molnar (Ed.), *Social issues and education: Challenge and responsibility* (pp. 79–100). Alexandria, VA: Association for Supervision & Curriculum Development.

Sears, J. (1988a). Paper presented at the American Educational Research Association. *Attitudes, experiences, and feelings of guidance counselors about working with homosexual students.* New Orleans. ERIC Document No. 296210.

Sears, J. (1988b). Growing up gay: Is anyone there to listen? *American School Counselors Association Newsletter, 26,* 8–9.

Sears, J. (1989a). *Personal feelings and professional attitudes of prospective teachers toward homosexuality and homosexual students: Research findings and curriculum recommendations.* Paper presented at the 1989 American Educational Research Association, San Francisco. ERIC Document No. 312222.

Sears, J. (1989b). The impact of gender and race on growing up lesbian and gay in the South. *NWSA Journal, 1*(3), 422–457.

Sears, J. (1990). Problems and possibilities in "Homophobia" education. *Empathy, 2*(2), 61.

Sears, J. (1991). *Growing up gay in the South: Race, gender, and journeys of the spirit.* New York: The Haworth Press, Inc.

Sears, J. (in press). The impact of culture and ideology on the construction of gender and sexual identities: Developing a critically-based sexuality curriculum. In J. Sears (Ed.), *Sexuality and the curriculum.* New York: Teachers College Press.

Smith, D. (1985). *An ethnographic interview study of homosexual teachers' perspectives.* Unpublished doctoral dissertation, State University of New York at Albany, Albany, NY. (*Dissertation Abstracts International 46*, 1, 66A).

Taylor, A. (1983). Conceptions of masculinity and femininity as a basis for stereotypes of male and female homosexuals. *Journal of Homosexuality, 9*(1), 37–53.

Thompson, G., & Fishburn, W. (1977). Attitudes toward homosexuality among graduate counseling students. *Counselor Education & Supervision, 17*(2), 121–130.

Weinberg, G. (1972). *Society and the healthy homosexual.* New York: St. Martin's Press.

Weiner, A. (1989). *Racist, sexist, and homophobic attitudes among undergraduate social work students and their effects on assessments of client vignettes.* Unpublished doctoral dissertation, Rutgers University, New Brunswick, NJ. (*Dissertation Abstracts International 50*, 11, 3741A).

Willis, P. (1977). *Learning to labour: How working-class kids get working class jobs.* Westmead, England: Saxon House.

Wisniewski, J., & Toomey, B. (1987). Are social workers homophobic? *Social Work, 32*(5), 454–455.

Young, M., & Whertvine, J. (1982). Attitudes of heterosexual students toward homosexual behavior. *Psychological Reports, 51*(2), 673–674.

NOTES

1. For a discussion of the methodology and more detailed data on the participants and their responses, see Sears, 1991.

2. For more specific information about these instruments, including issues of validity and reliability as well as the individual items, see Sears, 1988a.

3. For more specific information about these instruments, including issues of validity and reliability as well as the individual items, see Sears, 1988a.

4. For a summary of many of these studies, see Fyfe, 1983; Herek, 1984; Larsen, Reed, & Hoffman, 1980; Morin & Garfinkle, 1978; Taylor, 1983.

5. The complete survey questions as well as the responses to these questions from guidance counselors are reported in Sears, 1988a.

6. For an item-by-item analysis of counselors' scores on these attitudinal instruments, see Sears, 1988a.

7. A summative score for this 14-item questionnaire was computed by reversing the codes of positively worded statements and assigning 1 through 4 points on the basis of participants' item responses. The possible range of this summative score, the Professional Attitude Index (PAI), is from 14 (low) to 56 (high); the actual range was 17 to 55 with a mean of 38 and a standard deviation of 6. For specific details on the statistical results of the findings reported in this section, see Sears, 1989a.

Barry M. Franklin

At-Risk Children and the Common School Ideal

Early on in their attempt to provide for these children, school managers established an implicit accord among themselves and their philanthropic collaborators, which involved a recalibration of the mid-nineteenth-century common school ideal. According to this reconstituted ideal, public school would be accessible to all children. Once inside the school, however, these children would not necessarily enjoy a shared educational experience. Rather they would be channeled to an array of remedial and special education programs, which were made possible by the emergence of a medicalized discourse for talking about childhood learning difficulties. We have already examined the evolution of this medicalized discourse from its initial formulation as backwardness to its most recent manifestation as learning disabilities. In two case studies, involving Atlanta and Minneapolis, I explored how school managers used this medicalized discourse to enhance their administrative capacities for dealing with low-achieving children. In this epilogue I will consider what the historical interpretation I have thus far developed tells us about contemporary efforts to educate at-risk children.

II.

The increasing interest of educators in the problems of at-risk children during the late 1980s and early 1990s, not unlike the concerns voiced on behalf of first backward and then learning disabled students, can be tied to ongoing societal and economic changes. The interplay during these years of three such shifts—a heightening of racial and ethnic conflicts, a changing international economy marked in this country by the decline in relatively high-paying manufacturing jobs and their replacement by lower paying service occupations, and an increasing poverty rate—has undermined the position and status of the nation's families and their children.[1]

In its 1989 report, the U.S. House of Representatives Select Committee on Children, Youth, and Families painted a rather dispiriting picture of the impact that such changes have had on these groups:

The most profound influence on American families has been the mounting economic pressures which have diminished their resources and made more children more vulnerable. The combined effects of persistently high rates of poverty, declining earnings, underemployment, and single parenting have made childhood far more precarious and less safe for millions of American children.[2]

The report itself details an array of indicators that taken together point to a deterioration in the well-being of children and families. Between 1970 and 1985, the median family income of children, when adjusted for inflation, has declined some $1,700 from $29,943 to $28,210. Since 1985, income has increased slightly, but remains below the 1970 figure. During the same period the rate of childhood poverty has increased from about 15 percent of all children to a bit over 20 percent. And again, during these years, the percentage of children living in female-headed single households, the families most likely to live in poverty, has increased from about 8 percent to 14 percent.[3]

These changes, just as those accompanying the emergence of a market economy in the years around the turn of the century, have had an impact on childhood learning and school achievement. About one-quarter of the nation's twenty-eight million ten- to seventeen-year-olds are behind the expected grade for their age. A 1985 study by the Center for Educational Statistics, which compared the number of the nation's high school graduates that year with the number entering high school as freshman four years earlier, indicated a dropout rate of 29 percent. Fourteen percent of all adolescents are functionally illiterate. In assessments of mathematics and science achievement, American thirteen-year-olds scored near or at the bottom in comparison with their peers from other industrialized nations. And according to a 1985 report from the National Assessment

of Educational Progress, only 11 percent of the nation's thirteen-year-olds were sufficiently proficient at reading to understand written material of a complex nature.[4]

Early twentieth-century school managers, I have argued, established special classes to enhance their administrative capacity to cope with the larger and more diverse student enrollments that accompanied the nation's shift to a market economy. Similarly, the appearance on the scene of public school programs for at-risk students may signal the beginning of state-building efforts on the part today's school managers. Like their turn-of-the-century counterparts, they are attempting to augment their ability to manage low-achieving children.

The same contradictory impulses that have plagued programs for children with learning difficulties throughout this century are evident in current efforts to accommodate at-risk children. Proponents of these initiatives are often unclear as to whether they want to focus their attention on just the at-risk population or on improving education for all children.[5] Those who wish to attend solely to at-risk children tend, for the most part, to propose differentiated programs. Some, including various forms of individualized instruction and tutoring—Upward Bound, the Job Corps, and numerous Chapter One projects—represent recycled special programs from the compensatory education efforts of the 1960s.[6]

Others are apparently new, but they too rely on offering at-risk children something different from what is provided to more able students. These differentiated programs can involve the introduction of special curricula, such as basic life skills, that provide these children with capabilities that they often lack. If at-risk children are explicitly taught, among other things, how to relate appropriately to their peers, how to make decisions, how to avoid intimidation, and how to assert themselves, they can, according to advocates of this curricular offering, attain the kind of social competence that typically characterizes academically successful youth.[7]

Another approach to differentiating the curriculum for at-risk students involves the establishment of alternative schools and schools-within-schools. Typically these alternative institutions are smaller and allow for more intimate relationships among students and faculty. They provide an environment that is designed to nurture psychological well-being. And they offer a curriculum thought to be more relevant to the interests and abilities of at-risk children. Such schools can serve to link academic course work to career preparation. And they can, with the inclusion of courses in such areas as media technology, computer applications, and photography, emphasize the kind of experiential learning often ignored by regular schools. Finally, these alternative schools can serve a particular at-risk population, say American Indians or adolescent mothers.[8]

There are, however, proposals that depart from our long-standing reliance on segregating low-achieving students. Some call for the creation of health clinics in or adjacent to schools. They would offer all students a variety of services, including routine medical examinations, care for less severe illnesses and accidents, counseling on substance abuse and pregnancy prevention, and referrals to specialists. Since, however, untreated medical problems often cause the academic and behavioral difficulties that place students at risk, such clinics would be particularly beneficial to those children whose families lack health insurance and cannot afford private medical care.[9]

Other proposals are directed to the school's curricular and instructional programs. As one phase of its New Futures Initiative, the Annie E. Casey Foundation is currently supporting a five-year effort at curriculum reform in a number of smaller American cities with the intent of enhancing the school experience and future success of at-risk students. In its Dayton, Ohio, project, two middle schools introduced a clustering arrangement in which teachers in English, reading, mathematics, social studies, and science were placed in a single team and assigned a group of 120 to 150 students. Each teaching team was provided authority to establish its own grouping practices, to alter the existing class schedule, and to integrate their subjects around certain common and interdisciplinary themes. In Little Rock, Arkansas, a similar effort at clustering in that city's middle schools resulted in the creation of an integrated unit on violence that included instruction in English, social studies, and mathematics.

Although this and similar reforms are directed toward restructuring the schools for all students, New Futures proponents believe that they are especially helpful to at-risk children. Clustering provides a two-pronged strategy for placing teachers in a better position to recognize and provide for the academic and other difficulties that can place children at risk. First, the members of each of these teaching teams are assigned a common planning time to allow them, among other things, to talk together to learn more about their students and their needs. Second, the relatively small size of these teams and their extensive interaction allows for more sustained and personal relationships between student and teachers.

Curriculum integration, the other key feature of this clustering arrangement, can result in a richer curriculum that is more appealing to difficult to teach children. The interdisciplinary units which the Dayton teachers created did not emphasize the drill and practice and rote memorization that has throughout this century been so much a part of the programs offered to difficult to teach students. Rather, the units they created sought to cultivate problem-solving and other higher order thinking skills.[10]

Craig Heller, a biologist from Stanford University, has designed a two-year interdisciplinary life science course for the middle schools. He also recognizes the value of curriculum integration for at-risk children. Known as Hum Bio, the course brought together disciplinary content about biology with material on such health-related topics as diet, substance abuse, and adolescent sexual development. It is a strategy, he argues, that makes the curriculum a vehicle for conveying the kind of useful information that all children, and especially those in danger of failure, need. An integrated curriculum, Heller goes on to say, offers more opportunity for student success. Children whose weakness in a single subject may consign them to failure in a traditional discipline-centered curriculum can in an interdisciplinary course often find some phase or topic that attracts their interest and builds on their strengths.[11]

One of the most extensive efforts to accommodate at-risk children without segregation is the accelerated schools project

undertaken by Henry Levin and his associates at Stanford University. Accelerated schools, Levin argues, are educational institutions dedicated to the enhancement of learning for all children where teachers have a decision-making role in the school's operation, where administrators are facilitators rather than managers, and where parents are active participants in the education of their children. With respect to curricular and instructional practices, Levin and his associates appear to take their cues not from remedial programs but from those for the gifted and talented. Accelerated schools offer an enriched, common program for all students that, among other things, involves children in the use of higher order cognitive processes and problem-solving, encourages creative thinking, integrates the teaching of language throughout the curriculum, and provides for experiential learning.[12]

III.

Despite the conflicting goals that appear to guide current programs for at-risk children, there are indications of a coming sea change in our long-standing views about educating children with learning difficulties. It is a transformation in our thinking on this score that has the potential for resolving the contradictions that have plagued the efforts of school managers throughout this century to accommodate such children. One indicator of this shift is the widespread criticism that educational researchers currently direct at curriculum differentiation. The establishment of special classes for low-achieving children has been one phase of the larger effort on the part of early twentieth-century school managers to differentiate the curriculum. Proposals that call for the creation of special programs for those at risk represent a modern expression of this same impulse to sort children into separate and distinct courses of study. The problems with differentiation are that it fails to enhance the educational achievement of students, except for those who are placed in the highest tracks, leads to the disproportionate placement of poor and minority group children in lower-level classes, and has a negative impact on the overall improvement of educational quality. In short, it is a longstanding practice that has done more to exacerbate the problems of American public schooling than to resolve them.[13]

Our most recent round of educational reform, the so-called excellence movement, has been particularly unkind to curriculum differentiation. Almost uniformly, the array of reports and proposals emanating from this movement has called for the introduction of a common, academically oriented curriculum for all students, and the elimination, or at least reduction, of existing differentiated programs.[14] As the most prominent sponsors of this campaign see it, a common, academic curriculum built on the disciplines of knowledge offers the best education for all American youth. It provides the best model for conveying to children their cultural heritage, the best background for participating in democratic politics, and the best preparation for life and work in a technologically advanced society. Curriculum differentiation, they go on to say, legitimates the creation of nonacademic courses of study that lack rigor. Further, they argue, this practice is routinely used to segregate poor and minority group children from their peers, thereby consigning them to an inferior education and a subordinate place in adult society. These re-

formers are not opposed to some informal and temporary in-class grouping arrangements to accommodate the ability and skill differences that exist among children. They insist, however, that despite the use of different pedagogy to teach children of varying abilities, the content of education should remain the same for all children.[15] Curriculum differentiation is certainly a common feature of today's schools. Yet current criticisms of this practice suggest that we may be about ready to rethink this taken-for-granted scheme for accommodating diverse students.

IV.

Another harbinger of an approaching change in our understanding of learning difficulties has been the attack, beginning in the early 1970s and continuing today, on segregated special education. In a series of civil suits in federal and state courts during this decade, advocates of disabled children questioned in virtually the same way as had the NAACP lawyers in the 1954 case of *Brown v. the Board of Education* the constitutionality of excluding children, in this case disabled children, from the public schools.[16] Among the issues raised in these suits was the appropriateness of placing these children in special classes and other separate settings. In the majority of these cases, as it turned out, the courts ruled against segregation, arguing that the most suitable placement for most of these children was the regular classroom.[17]

Coincidental with these legal challenges were legislative efforts to ensure that disabled children had access to the nation's public schools. In a series of amendments to the Elementary and Secondary Education Act enacted between 1966 and the passage of the Education for All Handicapped Children Act (Public Law 94–142) in 1975, Congress mandated that virtually all the nation's disabled children be guaranteed a free, public education. Among the issues raised in this legislation was the placement of disabled children once they were admitted to the public schools. Not surprisingly, Congress took a position in favor of integration and mandated that all disabled children be educated in the so-called least restrictive environment. Although this provision did appear to greatly restrict the ability of school managers to remove handicapped children from regular classrooms, it did not abolish segregated placements. Rather, the provision required that the states establish a "continuum of alternative placements" for handicapped children, which included the regular classroom, special classes and schools, and an array of nonschool settings.[18] Public schools under this provision were to place disabled children in environments that provided them with an appropriate education while maximizing their contact with their nonhandicapped peers. For many disabled children, the least restrictive placement was the regular classroom. For others, however, it was a separate classroom or school or even a residential setting.

Neither the legal challenges to the exclusion of handicapped children from the public schools and certainly not the least restrictive environment provision of P.L. 94–142 abolished the segregation of disabled children. In 1976, the year before P.L. 94–142 was implemented, about 67 percent of all handicapped children and about 80 percent of learning disabled children spent some time, although we do not know precisely how much, in regular classrooms. Six years later, in 1982, the percentages were virtually unchanged.[19]

Early on, there were critics who recognized the limitations of the least restrictive environment provision. In an April 1974 letter to the House Subcommittee on Education, which was then considering the series of amendments that would become P.L. 94–142, Lloyd Dunn, a former president of the Council for Exceptional Children, attacked this provision on the grounds that it "does not move us toward the normalization and integration of services for children with learning problems but will have the reverse impact." Instead, he went on to say, it will create "special education domains at the expense of many other professionals equally competent and ready to serve children with school problems."[20]

By the mid-1980s Dunn's doubts about least restrictive placements had spurred on a full-scale oppositional movement known as the Regular Education Initiative, or simply REI. Like Dunn, proponents of REI argue that the least restrictive environment provision has not done away with segregated special education. Disabled children, they claim, remain as segregated as they were before the implementation of P.L. 92–142. REI supporters differ among themselves on how to reduce this isolation. Some call for increased cooperation between special and regular educators to enable more mildly handicapped and even some severely handicapped children to be placed in regular classrooms. Others recommend the virtual merging of regular, special, and compensatory education so that all children will receive instruction in regular classrooms. Most supporters of this movement take positions somewhere in between.[21] Proponents of REI have certainly provoked those who support the practice of least restrictive placements. One such advocate depicted the REI as the educational equivalent of the so-called trickle-down economic practices of Presidents Reagan and Bush. Just as this economic strategy has been criticized for aiding the most prosperous at the expense of the poor, this critic claims that REI will aid those students who have little difficulty at the expense of those with the greatest problems.[22] It is not clear at this point what impact REI is having on school practice. Nevertheless, the very presence of this movement and the rancor it has engendered among educators do point to an uncertain future for segregated special education.

V.

A final sign of a growing dissatisfaction with prevailing views about educating children with learning problems is the continuing conceptual crisis facing the learning disabilities field. In the decade following the implementation of P.L. 94–142, the number of learning disabled children who were served in special education programs increased by 134 percent from 796 thousand to over 1.8 million. By 1980 learning disabled children became the largest group of exceptional students served in the public schools.[23] Despite this growth, the same doubts that have always existed about learning disabilities remain. The evidence for its neurological origins is just as elusive today as it was when Strauss and Werner first postulated the existence of the supposed brain-injured child.[24] Similarly, many contemporary researchers appear as skeptical as did Seymour Sarason in 1940 about the neurological roots of this condition.[25] As a consequence, the field's current experts seem preoccupied

with trying to figure out precisely what a learning disability is. They certainly seem as divided as were their counterparts during the 1960s in settling on a definition of this condition.[26]

Between 1977 and 1982, the U.S. Department of Education funded research centers at five universities to investigate a variety of issues related to the education of learning disabled children and adolescents. In a special issue of *Exceptional Education Quarterly*, published in the Spring of 1983, representatives of the institutes—located at the Universities of Illinois at Chicago, Kansas, Minnesota, Virginia, and at Teachers College, Columbia University—offered assessments of their research efforts. Taken together, the five essays painted a positive picture, noting particular successes in identifying important characteristics of learning disabled children and in developing some apparently promising instructional techniques.[27]

In addition to the review essays, the journal published commentaries by two learning disabilities researchers who were not affiliated with the institutes. While these commentators were generally positive in their assessment of this body of research, they did point to certain problems. As Barbara Keogh saw it, the institutes did little to explain the actual nature of learning disabilities as a handicapping condition.[28] Similarly, James McKinney noted that despite their collective efforts, these institutes were not able to provide much guidance for differentiating learning disabled children from other low-achievers.[29] Notwithstanding his recognition of this weakness, McKinney singled out the Minnesota institute for criticism precisely because so much of its work highlighted this difficulty. He charged the Minnesota researchers with undermining public confidence in the viability of learning disabilities as a diagnostic category.[30] In a response to McKinney, a number of members of the Minnesota institute noted how vague the concept of learning disabilities was. Learning disabilities, as they put it, is "whatever society wants it to be, needs it to be, or will permit it to be."[31]

Despite the current size of the learning disabled student population, its rate of growth appears to be declining. Between 1977 and 1981, the percentage of learning disabled children served in public school special education programs increased about 15 percent a year. Between 1981 and 1985, the percentage increased only about 3.5 percent a year. Some of this decline is undoubtedly due to the increasing success of the nation's public schools in identifying learning disabled children. Whereas about a quarter of children with learning disabilities were being accommodated in the nation's public schools before the enactment of P.L. 94–142, about 80 percent of these children were being served by the mid-1980s.[32] Yet this diminishing growth rate may also reflect persisting doubts about learning disabilities itself. With the development of a medicalized discourse for talking about low-achievement, learning disabilities came to supplant backwardness as a public school vehicle for accommodating low-achieving children. Likewise, continuing uncertainties about the soundness of learning disabilities as a diagnostic category may undermine its usefulness as an educational label.

Taken together, criticisms of curriculum differentiation, attacks on segregated special education, and the apparent conceptual inadequacies of the concept of learning disabilities point to the need for a reconceptualization of the problem of childhood learning difficulties. The emerging at-risk child movement may represent that new understanding.

VI.

The great promise of conceptualizing childhood learning difficulties as an at-risk problem is that by doing so we may be able to reconcile the contradictions that have impeded the efforts of twentieth-century school managers to accommodate difficult to teach students. Such initiatives as curriculum integration, accelerated schooling, and the establishment of school health clinics do not force school managers to choose between the interests of able students and those with learning difficulties. Rather, they are efforts that help low-achieving children by enriching the school experiences of all children.[33] It is, of course, not inevitable that school programs for at-risk children will evolve in this direction. School managers can, as we have seen, embrace the at-risk label and continue the practice of consigning such children to separate and segregated programs.

Proponents of the at-risk movement face a critical dilemma. The current pattern of organizing schools, Gary Natriello, Edward McDill, and Aaron Pallas argue, is based on two assumptions. American students, according to the first of these suppositions, are a relatively homogeneous group of individuals who exhibit, as they put it, "fairly uniform middle-class characteristics." In carrying on their work, they go on to say, schools seem to take for granted that their clientele can easily acquire or already possess essential reading, writing, and arithmetic skills; exhibit appropriate social behavior; and require a similar and predetermined educational experience. Second, the prevailing organization assumes that the essential task, and perhaps sole mission, of the nation's schools is to provide instruction in the traditional disciplines of knowledge. It is presumed whatever other needs that children have will be met by their families or the communities in which they live.[34]

The reality of public schooling belies these two assumptions. From the turn of this century onward, the nation's schools have struggled to accommodate an increasingly diverse array of students who differ in their backgrounds, abilities, interests, and inclinations. Children with learning difficulties—whether we label them backward, learning disabled, or at-risk—are a prime example of this diverse makeup. Many do not possess the requisite academic skills to be successful in schools. Those who have them seem unable to utilize them. Such children often exhibit behavioral problems. And these are children who need more from the schools than academic instruction. They typically bring with them into the classroom a host of interpersonal problems and family and community conflicts that require psychological and social intervention.

The challenge facing those who champion the cause of at-risk children, again according to Natriello, McDill, and Pallas, is to develop organizational schemes that possess sufficient flexibility to provide for this heterogenenous population.[35] The temptation facing school managers is to defer any effort at a fundamental restructuring of schools that create the capacity for this flexibility. Instead they have embraced and continue to support a recalibrated and unauthentic common school ideal that relies on the addition of segregated programs for difficult to teach children. The at-risk movement represents a critical dividing point in this century-long effort of American school managers to accommodate children with learning difficulties. They can embrace those elements of this movement that, not unlike their efforts during the last eighty or so years, provide for difficult to teach children with separate and distinct educational programs. Or they can select the newer and conceptually richer route of this reform initiative toward a restructured school.

Even if school managers take on the difficult task of restructuring the schools to serve all children, there is no guarantee that they will be successful. The experience of the New Futures Initiative is illustrative of the difficulty such efforts encounter. One purpose of the Dayton and Little Rock middle school clustering plan, which I described earlier in this chapter, was to provide for curriculum integration. In Little Rock the most that teachers could accomplish was to organize more effectively the teaching of similar topics that were already a part of the existing curriculum. And in Dayton only a few teachers were willing to experiment with integration, and their efforts usually involved units within courses, not the courses themselves.[36]

A second goal of these clusters was to allow teachers to meet and talk together to enhance their knowledge of their students. This goal was not, however, realized. The common planning provided in this plan became a forum where teachers discussed the problems of these children and their families and often recommended referring them to psychological counseling or other social services. Teachers in Dayton and Little Rock are, it seems, having as much difficulty in reorganizing their schools for at-risk children as were Minneapolis's teachers some forty years ago when that city adopted the B Curriculum Experiment.

As a historian, I have always tried to resist the allure of searching for specific contemporary lessons in our study of the past. Yet I do think that history offers us a lens for illuminating issues of educational policy. Our examination of the initiatives advanced by twentieth-century school managers for accommodating children with learning difficulties can enable us to look at the problem of at-risk children in new and interesting ways, and as a consequence to ask different questions than we presently do.

In this vein, our study was the first attempt to educate at-risk children should lead us to ask a very different question than we have been asking up to now. We do not need to ask how public schools as they are presently arranged can accommodate low-achieving children. Asking such a question will only lead us along the path to a differentiated school program. Rather we need to ask how we can reorganize schools to enhance the quality of education for all children. It is only when we ask this question that we will be truly ready to accommodate children with learning difficulties in our schools.

From the first, the efforts of American school managers to provide for students with learning difficulties have pulled them in contradictory directions. Not certain as to whether they wanted to provide for the individual needs of these children or to assure the uninterrupted progress of the regular classroom, these educators embraced a recalibrated common school ideal that resolved their dilemma through curriculum differentiation. The result has been the creation of an array of special programs to remove these children from regular classrooms. Throughout this century we have viewed children with learning difficulties differently. Early in the century, we thought of them as being backward. By mid-century, we saw them as being learning disabled. Today, we label them as being at-risk. Our labels, it seems, have changed, but our reliance on segregation has persisted.

Although never completely realized, the ideal of common schooling first spelled out by mid-nineteenth-century school reformers provides a moral compass for our efforts to improve education.[37] Whether we are talking about inequities in school financing, unfair allocations of curricular and instructional resources, or racial and ethnic segregation—to name but a few—this ideal has directed us, often unwillingly, toward solutions that embody our most democratic and egalitarian impulses. If those impulses are to serve us today in addressing the needs of children with learning difficulties, we must go against the grain and reassert an authentic version of our common school ideal.

NOTES

1. For a discussion of these social and economic changes and their impact on urban schools, see Harvey Kantor and Barbara Brenzel, "Urban Education and the 'Truly Disadvantaged': The Historical Roots of the Contemporary Crisis, 1945–1990," *Teachers College Record* 94 (Winter 1992), 278–314;

Paul E. Peterson, "The Urban Underclass and the Poverty Paradox," in *The Urban Underclass*, ed. Christopher Jencks and Paul E. Peterson (Washington, D.C.: Brookings Institution, 1991), 3–27; John Rury, "The Changing Social Context of Urban Education: A National Perspective," in *Seeds of Crisis: Public Schooling in Milwaukee Since 1920*, ed. John Rury and Frank Cassell (Madison: University of Wisconsin Press, 1993), 10–41; William Julius Wilson, *The Truly Disadvantaged: The Inner City, the Underclass, and Public Policy* (Chicago: University of Chicago Press, 1987), 20–92.

2. Congress, House of Representatives, Select Committee on Children, Youth, and Families, *U.S. Children and Their Families: Current Conditions and Recent Trends, 1989*, 101st Cong., 1st sess., September 1989 (Washington, D.C.: GPO, 1989), x.

3. Ibid., 54–55, 100–101, 108–9.

4. Joy G. Dryfoos, *Adolescents at Risk: Prevalence and Prevention* (New York: Oxford University Press, 1990), 82–88; David A. Hamburg, *Today's Children: Creating a Future for a Generation in Crisis* (New York: Time Books, 1992), 41–43; Carnegie Council on Adolescent Development, *Turning Points: Preparing American Youth for the 21st Century* (New York: Carnegie Corporation, 1989), 27–32.

5. Dryfoos, *Adolescents*, 236–37; Gary Wehlage, Gregory Smith, and Pauline Lipman, "Restructuring Urban Schools: The New Futures Experience," *American Educational Research Journal* 29 (Spring 1992), 53.

6. For a description of these programs, see Gary Natriello, Edward L. McDill, and Aaron M. Pallas, *Schooling Disadvantaged Children: Racing against Catastrophe* (New York: Teachers College Press, 1990), 71–137; and Nancy A. Madden and Robert E. Slavin, "Effective Pullout Programs for Students At Risk," in *Effective Programs for Students at Risk*, ed. R. E. Slavin, N. L. Karweit, and N. A. Madden. Boston: Allyn and Bacon, 1988), 52–72.

7. Hamburg, *Today's Children*, 240–44; Fred M. Hechinger, *Fateful Choices: Healthy Youth for the 21st Century* (New York: Hill and Wang, 1992), 53–56.

8. Gary Wehlage and others, *Reducing the Risk: Schools as Communities of Support* (London: Falmer Press, 1989), 75–112.

9. Hechinger, *Fateful Choices*, 56–68; Joy Dryfoos, "Schools as Places for Health, Mental Health, and Social Services," *Teachers College Record* 94 (Spring, 1993), 540–67.

10. Wehlage, Smith, and Lipman, "Restructuring," 60–61.

11. H. Craig Heller, "At the Crossroads: Voices from the Carnegie Conference on Adolescent Health," *Teachers College Record* 94 (Spring 1993), 645–52.

12. Hopfenberg and others, *Middle Schools* 43–47; Henry M. Levin, "Financing the Education of At-Risk Students," *Educational Evaluation and Policy Analysis* 11 (Spring 1989), 54; *Accelerated Schools* 1 (Winter 1991), 1, 10–11, 14–15.

13. Jeannie Oakes, Adam Gamoran, and Reba N. Page, "Curriculum Differentiation: Opportunities, Outcomes, and Meanings," in *Handbook of Research on Curriculum*, ed. Philip W. Jackson (New York: Macmillan, 1992), 570–608. See also Jeannie Oakes, *Keeping Track: How Schools Structure Inequality* (New Haven: Yale University Press, 1985); and James Rosenbaum, *Making Inequality: The Hidden Curriculum of High School Tracking* (New York: John Wiley, 1976).

14. Gail P. Kelly, "Setting the Boundaries of Debate about Education," in *Excellence in Education: Perspective on Policy and Practice*, eds. Philip G. Altbach, Gail P. Kelly, and Lois Weis (Buffalo, N.Y.: Prometheus Books, 1985), 35–37.

15. William Bennett, *The De-Valuing of America: The Fight for Our Culture and Our Children* (New York: Summit Books, 1992), 61–62; Chester E. Finn, Jr., *We Must Take Charge: Our Schools and Our Future* (New York: Free Press, 1991), 218–19; Diane Ravitch, *The*

Schools We Deserve: Reflections on the Educational Crisis of Our Time (New York: Basic Books, 1985), 58–74, 277–78; Diane Ravitch and Chester E. Finn, Jr., *What Do Our 17-Year Olds Know?* (New York: Harper and Row, 1988), 168–72.

16. Alan Gartner and Dorothy Kerzner Lipsky, "Beyond Special Education: Toward a Quality System for All Students," *Harvard Educational Review* 57 (November 1987), 368–69; H. Rutherford Turnbull and Ann Turnbull, *Free Appropriate Public Education: Law and Implementation* (Denver: Love Publishing, 1978), 12–16, 255–63.

17. Alan Abeson, *A Continuing Summary of Pending and Completed Litigation Regarding the Education of Handicapped Children*, no. 6 (Arlington, Va.: Council for Exceptional Children, 1973).

18. *The Education for All Handicapped Children Act (P.L. 94–142)*, 20 U.S.C., Sec. 1412; *Federal Register* 42 (August 23, 1977), sec. 121a.550–121a.551.

19. The way that state education managers reported their placement data to the federal government before 1984 made it difficult to assess the actual extent of integration. Children were counted as being placed in one of four setting: regular classes, separate classes, separate schools, and other environments. Using such categories, children who spent some time of the day outside the regular classroom in so-called resource room programs were often counted by states as being placed in regular classrooms. Beginning in 1984, Congress mandated a more detailed reporting of placements by increasing the number of environments to include, among others, resource rooms. With the resource room included, it appears that only 26 percent of all handicapped children and 16 percent of learning disabled children were being served in regular classrooms. Over 60 percent of all handicapped children and 80 percent of learning disabled children were removed from regular classrooms at least part and perhaps all of the day. See Department of Education, *Third An-*nual Report to Congress on the Implementation of Public Law 94–142: The Education for All Handicapped Children Act (Washington, D.C.: U.S. Department of Education, 1981), 54; Department of Education, *Seventh Annual Report to Congress on the Implementation of Public Law 94–142: The Education for All Handicapped Children Act* (Washington, D.C.: U.S. Department of Education, 1985), 232–33; Department of Education, *Ninth Annual Report to Congress on the Implementation of the Education of the Handicapped Act* (Washington, D.C.: U.S. Department of Education, 1987), 17–21.

20. Congress, House of Representatives, Subcommittee on Education, *Hearings Before the Select Subcommittee on Education of the Committee on Education and Labor on H.R. 70*, 93rd Cong., 2nd sess., March 6, 7, 8, 22, 1974 (Washington, D.C.: GPO, 1974), 364.

21. The literature on the Regular Education Initiative (REI) is extensive. I have drawn my account from the following: Dorothy Kerzner Lipsky and Alan Gartner, "The Current Situation," in *Beyond Separate Education: Quality Education for All*, ed. Dorothy Kerzner Lipsky and Alan Gartner (Baltimore: Paul H. Brookes Publishing, 1987), 255–89; M. Stephen Lilly, "The Regular Education Initiative: A Force for Change in General and Special Education," *Education and Training in Mental Retardation* 23 (December 1988), 250–60; Maynard Reynolds and Margaret C. Wang, "Restructuring 'Special' School Programs: A Position Paper," *Policy Studies Review* 2 (January 1983), 189–212; Susan Stainback and William Stainback, "The Merger of Special and Regular Education: Can It Be Done? A Response to Lieberman and Mesinger," *Exceptional Children* 51 (April 1985), 517–21; Madeleine C. Will, "Educating Children with Learning Problems: A Shared Responsibility," *Exceptional Children* 52 (February 1986), 411–15. For a review and evaluation of REI, see Thomas M. Skritic, *Behind Special Education: A Critical Analysis of Professional Culture and School Organization* (Denver: Love Publishing, 1991), 51–84.

22. James M. Kauffman, "The Regular Education Initiative as Reagan-Bush Education Policy: A Trickle-Down Theory of Education of the Hard-to-Teach," *Journal of Special Education* 23 (fall 1989), 256–78. For another critique of REI, see Glenn A. Vergason and M. L. Anderegg, "Preserving the Least Restrictive Environment," in *Issues in Special Education*, ed. William Stainback and Susan Stainback (Boston: Allyn and Bacon, 1992), 45–53.

23. Judith D. Singer and John A. Butler, "The Education for All Handicapped Children Act: Schools as Agents of Social Reform," *Harvard Educational Review* 57 (May 1987), 130.

24. For a good example of the difficulties that contemporary researchers encounter in making a compelling case for the neurological origins of learning disabilities, see Carl W. Cotman and Gary S. Lynch, "The Neurobiology of Learning and Memory," in *Learning Disabilities: Proceedings of the National Conference*, ed. James F. Kavanagh and Tom J. Truss, Jr. (Parkton, Md.: York Press, 1988), 1–69.

25. James G. Carrier, *Learning Disability: Social Class and the Construction of Inequality in American Education* (New York: Greenwood, 1986), 23–54; Coles, *Learning Mystique*, 79–90; Barry M. Franklin, "From Brain Injury to Learning Disability: Alfred Strauss, Heinz Werner, and the Historical Development of the Learning Disabilities Field," in *Learning Disability: Dissenting Essays*, ed. Barry M. Franklin (London: Falmer, 1987), 29–42.

26. Barry M. Franklin, "Introduction: Learning Disability and the Need for Dissenting Essays," in *Learning Disability*, 1–3; Kenneth A. Kavale, "On Regaining Integrity in the LD Field," *Learning Disabilities Research* 2 (Summer 1987), 60–61. For the difficulties facing educators in trying to identify the nature of this condition, see Barbara K. Keogh, "Learning Disabilities: In Defense of a Construct," *Learning Disabilities Research* 3 (Winter 1987), 4–9, and Heinz-Joachim Klatt, "Learning Disabilities: A Questionable Construct," *Educational Theory* 41 (Winter 1991), 47–60.

27. Rebecca Daily Kneedler and Daniel Hallahan, eds., "Research in Learning Disabilities: Summaries of the Institutes," *Exceptional Education Quarterly* 4 (Spring 1983), 1–114.

28. Barbara Keogh, "A Lesson from Gestalt Psychology," ibid., 122.

29. James D. McKinney, "Contributions of the Institutes for Research on Learning Disabilities," ibid., 139.

30. Ibid., 136–39.

31. Ibid., 145.

32. Frederick J. Weintraub and Bruce A. Ramirez, *Progress in the Education of the Handicapped and Analysis of P.L. 98–199: The Education of the Handicapped Act Amendments of 1983* (Reston, Va.: Council for Exceptional Children, 1985), 8.

33. Increasingly, policy scholars are arguing that the best strategy for assisting at-risk groups is an indirect one that provides social supports for all individuals, not just those in need. There is, in fact, a growing movement that is calling for the replacement of targeted welfare policies that are directed solely at the poor in favor of universalistic policies that provide a social safety need for the entire citizenry. See Wilson, *Truly Disadvantaged*, 109–24; and Theda Skocpol, "Targeting within Universalism: Politically Viable Policies to Combat Poverty in the United States," in *The Urban Underclass*, 411–36. For a defense of universalistic social welfare policies on democratic grounds, see Mickey Kaus, *The End of Equality* (New York: Basic Books, 1992).

34. Natriello, McDill, and Pallas, *Schooling*, 157.

35. Ibid., 158–63.

36. Wehlage, Smith, and Lipman, "Restructuring," 66–69.

37. For a discussion of the moral imperative underlying the ideal of common schooling, see William J. Reese, "Public Schools and the Common Good," *Educational Theory* 38 (Fall 1988), 431–40.

Michelle Fine

Silencing and Nurturing Voice in an Improbable Context
Urban Adolescents in Public School

October 1986, national conference on education: Phyllis Schlafly demands that elementary, junior, and senior high school courses on child abuse and incest be banned as "terrorizing tactics against children."

Later that same month: Judge Thomas Gray Hull of the Federal District Court in Greeneville, Tennessee, upholds Fundamentalist parents' right to remove their children from public school classes in which offending books, including The Wizard of Oz *and* Diary of a Young Girl, *are taught.*

One might wish to imagine that demands for silencing in public schools resonate exclusively from the conservative New Right. In this article, I will argue that Schafly and these Fundamentalist parents merely caricature what is standard educational practice—the silencing of student and community voices.

Silencing signifies a terror of words, a fear of talk. This chapter examines such practices as they echoed throughout a comprehensive public high school in New York City, in words and in their absence; these practices emanated from the New York City Board of Education, textbook publishers, corporate "benefactors," religious institutions, administrators, teachers, parents, and even students themselves. The essay explores what doesn't get talked about in schools: how "undesirable talk" by students, teach-

ers, parents, and community members is subverted, appropriated, and exported, and how educational policies and procedures obscure the very social, economic, and therefore experiential conditions of students' daily lives while they expel critical "talk" about these conditions from written, oral, and nonverbal expression.

In the odd study of *what's not said* in school, it is crucial to analyze (1) whom silencing protects; (2) the practices by which silencing is institutionalized in contexts of asymmetric power relations; (3) how muting students and their communities systematically undermines a project of educational empowerment (Freire, 1985; Giroux, 1988; Schor, 1980); and (4) how understanding the practices of silencing can make possible a public education that gives voice to students and their communities.

337

Why silencing in urban public schools? If we believe that city schools are public spheres that promise mobility, equal opportunity, and a forum for participatory democracy (Giroux & McLaren, 1986), indeed one of few such sites was instituted on the grounds of equal access (Carnoy & Levin, 1985); if we recognize the extent to which these institutions nonetheless participate in the very reproduction of class, race, and gender inequities; and if we appreciate that educators working within these schools share a commitment to the former and suffer a disillusionment by the latter, then it can be assumed that the practices of silencing in public schools do the following:

1. Preserve the ideology of equal opportunity and access while obscuring the unequal distribution of resources and outcomes.
2. Create within a system of severe asymmetric power relations the impression of democracy and collaboration among "peers" (e.g., between White, middle-income school administrators and low-income Black and Hispanic parents or guardians).
3. Quiet student voices of difference and dissent so that such voices, when they burst forth, are rendered deviant and dangerous.
4. Remove from public discourse the tensions between (a) *promises* of mobility and the material *realities* of students' lives; (b) explicit claims to democracy and implicit reinforcement of power asymmetries; (c) schools as an ostensibly *public* sphere and the pollution wrought on them by *private* interests; and (d) the dominant language of equal educational opportunity versus the

undeniable evidence of failure as a majority experience of low-income adolescents.

Silencing removes any documentation that all is not well with the workings of the U.S. economy, race and gender relations, and public schooling as the route to class mobility. Let us take a single piece of empirical data provided by the U.S. Department of Labor to understand why urban schools might be motivated to silence.

In 1983, the U.S. Department of Labor published evidence that a high school diploma brings with it quite discrepant opportunities based on one's social class, race, and gender, and further, that the absence of such a diploma ensures quite disparate costs based on the same demographics. Although public rhetoric has assured that dropping out of high school promotes unemployment, poverty, and dependence on crime or welfare, the national data present a story far more complex. Indeed, only 15% of White male dropouts (age 22 to 34) live below the poverty line, compared with 28% of White females, 37% of African-American males, and 62% of African-American females (U.S. Department of Labor, 1983). Further, in a city like New York, dropouts from the wealthiest neighborhoods are more likely to be employed than high school graduates from the poorest neighborhoods (Tobier, 1984). Although having a degree corresponds to employment and poverty levels, this relationship is severely mediated by race, class, and gender stratification.

In the face of these social realities, principals and teachers nevertheless continue to preach, without qualification, to African-American and Hispanic students and parents a rhetoric of equal opportunity and outcomes, the predictive guarantees of a high school diploma, and the invariant economic penalties of dropping out. Although I am no advocate of dropping out of high school, it is clear that silencing—which constitutes the practices by which contradictory evidence, ideologies, and experiences find themselves buried, camouflaged, and discredited—oppresses and insults adolescents and their kin who already "know better."

The press for silencing disproportionately characterizes low-income, minority urban schooling. In these schools, the centralization of the public school administration diminishes community involvement; texts are dated (often 10 to 15 years old) and alienating, in omission and commission; curricula and pedagogies are disempowering, often for students and teachers; strategies for discipline more often than not result in extensive suspension and expulsion rates; and calls for parental involvement often invite bake sale ladies and expel "troublemakers" or advocates. These practices constitute the very means by which schools silence. Self-proclaimed as fortresses against students' communities, city schools offer themselves as "the only way out of Harlem" rather than in partnership with the people, voices, and resources of that community.

Silencing more intimately shapes low-income public schools than relatively privileged ones. In such contexts, there is more to hide and control and, indeed, a greater discrepancy between pronounced ideologies and lived experiences. Further, the luxury of examining the contradictory evidence of social mobility may only be available to those who continue to benefit from existing social arrangements, not those who daily pay the price of social stratification. The dangers inherent in questioning from "above" are minor relative to the dangers presumed inherent in questioning from "below." In low-income schools, then, the process of inquiring into students' lived experience is assumed, a priori, unsafe territory for teachers and administrators. Silencing permeates classroom life so primitively as to render irrelevant the lived experiences, passions, concerns, communities, and biographies of low-income, minority students. In the process, the very voices of these students and their communities, which public education claims to enrich, shut down.

This essay focuses on silencing primarily at the level of classroom and school talk in a low-income, "low-skill" school. Surely there are corporate, governmental, military, and bureaucratic mandates from which demands for silencing derive. But, in the present analysis, these structural demands are assumed, not analyzed. Located primarily within classrooms and with individual teachers, this analysis does not aim to place blame on teachers but only to retrieve from these interactions the raw material for a critical examination of silencing. The data derive from a yearlong ethnography of a high school in Manhattan, attended by 3,200 students, predominantly low-income African Americans and Hispanics from central Harlem and run primarily by African-American paraprofessionals and White teachers (see Fine, 1985, 1986).

An analysis of silencing seems important for two reasons. First, substantial evidence has been accumulated which suggests that many students in this school, considered low in skill, income, and motivation, were quite eager to choreograph their own learning, to generate a curriculum of lived experience, and to engage in a participatory pedagogy (Lather, 1991).

Every effort by teachers and administrators which undermined such educational autobiographizing violated one opportunity and probably preempted others, to create dialogue and community—that is, to educate—with students, their kin, and their neighborhoods (Bastian, Fruchter, Gittell, Greer, & Haskins, 1985; Connell, Ashenden, Kessler, & Dowsett, 1982; Lightfoot, 1978). Those administrators, teachers, and paraprofessionals who were sufficiently interested and patient did generate classrooms of relatively "alive" participants. More overwhelming to the observer, however, was the silencing that engulfed life inside most classrooms and administrative offices.

Second, this loss of connection has most significant consequences for low-income minority students. These adolescents are fundamentally ambivalent about the educational process and appropriately cynical about the "guarantees" of an educational credential (Carnoy & Levin, 1985). The linear correspondence of years of education to income does not conform to their reflections on community life. Most were confident that "you can't get nowhere without a diploma." But most were also mindful that "the richest man in my neighborhood didn't graduate but from eighth grade." And, in their lives, both "truths" are defensible. It is precisely by camouflaging such contradictions that educators advance adolescents' cynicism about schooling and credentials, thereby eroding any beliefs in social mobility, community organizing, or the pleasures of intellectual entertainment.

The silencing process is but one aspect of what is often, for low-income students, an impoverished educational tradition. Infiltrating administrative "talk," curriculum development, and pedagogical technique, the means of silencing establish impenetrable barriers between the worlds of school and community life. To unearth the possibility of reclaiming students', teachers', and communities' voices, the practices of silencing must be unpacked.

The Impulse to Silence as it Shaped Educational Research

"Lying is done with words and also with silence."

—ADRIENNE RICH,
On Lies, Secrets, and Silence

In June 1984, I began to lay the groundwork for what I hoped would be an ethnography of a public high school in New York City, to begin the fall of 1984 (see Fine 1985, 1986).[1] To my request for entry to his school, the principal greeted me as follows:

Field Note: June, 1984

Mr. Stein: Sure you can do your research on dropouts at this school. With one provision. You cannot mention the words *dropping out* to the students.
MF: Why not?
Mr. Stein: If you say it, you encourage them to do it.

Even the research began with a warning to silence me and the imaginations of these adolescents. My field notes continue: "When he said this, I thought, adults should be so lucky, that adolescents wait for us to name the words *dropping out*, or sex, for them to do it." From September through June, witnessing daily life inside the classrooms, deans' and nurses' offices, the attendance room, and the lunchroom, I was repeatedly bewildered that this principal actually believed that adult talk could compel adolescent compliance.

The year progressed. Field notes mounted. What became apparent was a systemic fear of *naming*. Naming involves those practices that facilitate critical conversation about social and economic arrangements, particularly about inequitable distributions of power and resources by which these students and their kin suffer disproportionately. The practices of administration, the relationships between school and community, and the forms of pedagogy and curriculum applied were all scarred by the fear of naming, provoking the move to silence.

The White Noise, or Administrative Silencing

Field Note: September 1984

> *"We are proud to say that 80 percent of our high school graduates go on to college."*
>
> —Principal, Parents' Association
>   Meeting, September 1984

At the first Parents' Association meeting, Mr. Stein, the principal, boasted an 80% "college-bound" rate. Almost all graduates of this inner-city high school head for college: a comforting claim oft repeated by urban school administrators in the 1980s. Although accurate, this pronouncement masked the fact that, in this school, as in other comprehensive city high schools, only 20% of the incoming ninth graders *ever* graduate. In other words, only 16% of the 1,220 ninth graders of 1978–79 were

headed for college by 1985. The "white noise" of the administration reverberated silence in the audience. Not named, and therefore not problematized, was the substantial issue of low retention rates.

Not naming is an administrative craft. The New York City Board of Education, for example, has refused to monitor retention, promotion, and educational achievement statistics by race and ethnicity for fear of "appearing racist" (personal communication, 1984).[2] Huge discrepancies in educational advancement, by race and ethnicity, thereby remain undocumented in board publications. Likewise, dropout estimates include students on the register when they have not been seen for months; they also presume that students who enroll in general equivalency diploma (GED) programs are not dropouts and that those who produce "working papers" are actually about to embark on careers (which involves a letter, for example, from a Chicken Delight clerk assuring that Jose has a job so that he can leave school at 16). Such procedures contribute to *not naming* the density of the dropout problem.

Although administrative silencing is, unfortunately, almost a redundancy, the concerns of this essay are primarily focused on classroom- and school-based activities of silencing. By no means universal, the fear of naming was nevertheless commonplace, applied at this school by conservative and liberal educators alike. Conservative administrators and teachers viewed most of their students as unteachable. It was believed, following the logic of social studies teacher Mr. Rosaldo, that, "if we save 20 percent, that's a miracle. Most of these kids don't have a chance." For these educators, naming social and economic inequities in their classrooms would only expose circumstances they believed to be self-imposed. Perhaps these teachers themselves had been silenced over time. It is worth noting that correlational evidence (Fine, 1983) suggests that educators who feel most disempowered in their institutions are most likely to believe that "these kids can't be helped" and that those who feel relatively empowered are likely to believe that they "can make a difference in the lives of these youths."

Disempowered and alienated themselves, such educators see an enormous and inherent distance between "them" and "us," a distance, whether assumed biological or social, which could not be bridged by the mechanics of public schooling. So, when I presented "dropout data" to these faculty members and suggested that the level of involuntary "discharges" processed through this school would never be tolerated in the schools attended by their children, I was rapidly chastised: "That's an absurd comparison. The schools my kids go to are nothing like this—the comparison is sensationalist!" The social distance between them and us is reified and naturalized. Naming would only be inciting.

The more liberal position of other educators, for whom not naming was also routine, involved their loyalty to believe in a color- and class-neutral meritocracy. These educators dismissed the very empirical data that would have informed the naming process. Here they followed the logic of science teacher Ms. Tannenbaum: "If these students work hard, they can really become something. Especially today with affirmative action." They rejected counterevidence: for example, that African-American high school graduates living in Harlem are still far less likely to be em-

ployed than White high school dropouts living in more elite sections of New York (Tobier, 1984), for fear that such data would "discourage students from hard work and dreams." Enormous energy must be required to sustain beliefs in equal opportunity and the color-blind power of credentials and to silence nagging losses of faith when evidence to the contrary compels on a daily basis. Naming in such a case would only unmask realities, fundamentally disrupting or contradicting educators' and presumable students' belief systems.

Still other educators actively engaged their students in lively, critical discourse about the complexities and inequities of prevailing economic and social relations. Often importing politics from other spheres of their lives, the feminist English teacher, the community activist who taught grammar, or the Marxist historian wove critical analysis into their classrooms, with little effort. These offices and classrooms were permeated with the openness of naming, free of the musty tension that derives from conversations-not-had.

Most educators at this school, however, seemed to survive by not naming or analyzing social problems. They administered and taught in ways that established the school as a fortress for mobility *out* of the students' communities. They taught with curricular and pedagogical techniques they hoped would soothe students and smooth social contradictions. Many would probably have not considered conversation about social class, gender, or race politics relevant to their courses or easily integrated into their curricula. Some would argue that inclusion of these topics would be "political"—whereas exclusion was not. One could have assumed that they benignly neglected these topics.

But evidence of educators' *fear*, rather than *neglect*, grew apparent when students (activated by curiosity and rebellion) initiated conversations of critique which were rapidly dismissed. A systemic expulsion of dangerous topics permeated these classrooms. For educators to examine the very conditions that contribute to social class, racial, ethnic, and gender stratification in the United States, when they are relatively privileged by class usually and race often, seemed to introduce fantasies of danger, a pedagogy that would threaten, rather than protect, teacher control. Such conversations would problematize what seem like "natural" social distinctions, potentially eroding teachers' authority. If not by conscious choice, then, some teachers and administrators actively engaged in pedagogical strategies that preempted, detoured, or ghettoized such conversations. Not naming, as a particular form of silencing, was accomplished creatively. Often with good intentions, the practice bore devastating consequences.

Naming indeed subverts or complicates those beliefs that public schools aim to promote. It is for this very reason essential that naming be inherent in the educational process, in the creation of an empowered and critical constituency of citizens (Aronowitz & Giroux, 1985). It was ironic to note that pedagogic and curricular attempts to not name or to actively avoid such conversation indeed cost teachers control over their classrooms. Efforts to shut down such conversations were usually followed by the counting of money by males, the application of mascara or lipstick by females, and the laying down of heads on desks by students of both genders: the loss of control over the classroom.

To not name bears consequences for all students, but most dramatically for low-income, minority youths. To not name systematically alienates, cuts off from home, from heritage, and from lived experience, and, ultimately, severs these students from their educational process. The pedagogical and curricular strategies employed in not naming are examined critically below.

Pedagogical and Curricular Muting of Students' Voices

Constructing Taboo Voices: Conversations Never Had

A mechanistic view of teachers terrorized by naming and students passively accommodating could not be further from the daily realities of life inside a public high school. Many teachers name and critique, although most don't. Some students passively shut down, although most remain alive and even resistant. Classrooms are filled with students wearing Walkmans, conversing among themselves and with friends in the halls, and some even persistently challenging the experiences and expertise of their teachers. But the typical classroom still values silence, control, and quiet, as Jean Anyon (1983), John Goodlad (1984), Theodore Sizer (1985), and others have documented. The insidious push toward silence in low-income schools became most clear sometime after my interview with Eartha, a 16-year-old high school dropout.

Field Note: January 24

MF: Eartha, when you were a kid, did you participate a lot in school?

Eartha: Not me, I was a good kid. Made no trouble.

I asked this question of 55 high school dropouts. After the third responded as Eartha did, I realized that, for me, participation was encouraged, delighted in, and a measure of the "good student." Yet, for these adolescents, given their histories of schooling, participation meant poor discipline and rude classroom behavior.

Students learn the dangers of talk, the codes of participating and not, and they learn, in more nuanced ways, which conversations are never to be had. In Philadelphia, a young high school student explained to me: "We are not allowed to talk about abortion. They tell us we can't discuss it no way." When I asked a school district administrator about this policy, she qualified: "It's not that they can't *talk* about it. If the topic is raised by a student, the teacher can define abortion, just not discuss it beyond that." The distinction between defining and discussing makes sense only if learning assumes teacher authority, if pedagogy requires single truths, and if classroom control implies silence. Perhaps this is why classroom control often feels so fragile. Control through omission *is* fragile. Fully contingent on students' willingness to collude, such control betrays a plea for student compliance.

Silencing in public schools comes in many forms. Conversations can be closed by teachers or forestalled by student collusion. But other conversations are expressly withheld, never had. Such a policy of enforced silencing was applied to information about the severe economic and social consequences of dropping out of high school. This information was systematically withheld from students who were being discharged. Few, as a consequence, ever entertained second thoughts.

When students are discharged in New York State, they are guaranteed an exit interview, which, in most cases I observed, involved an attendance officer who asked students what they planned to do and then requested a meeting with the parent or guardian to sign official documents. The officer handed the student a list of GED and outreach programs. The student left, often eager to find work, get a GED, go to a private business school, or join the military. Informed conversations about the consequences of the students' "decision" were not legally mandated. As they left, these adolescents *did not learn* the following:

- Over 50% of African-American high school dropouts suffer unemployment in cities like New York City (U.S. Commission on Civil Rights, 1982).
- Forty-eight percent of New Yorkers who sit for the graduate equivalency diploma test fail (New York State Department of Education, 1985).
- Private trade schools, including cosmetology, beautician, and business schools, have been charged with unethical recruitment practices, exploitation of students, earning more from students who drop out than those who stay, not providing promised jobs, and having, on average, a 70% dropout rate (see Fine, 1986).
- The military, during "peacetime," refuses to accept females with no high school degree and only reluctantly accepts males, who suffer an extreme less-than-honorable discharge rate within six months of en-

listment (Militarism Resource Project, 1985).

Students who left high school prior to graduation were thereby denied informed consent. Conversations-not-had nurtured powerful folk beliefs among adolescents: that "the GED is no sweat, a piece of cake"; that "you can get jobs, they promise, after goin' to Sutton or ABI [American Business Institute]"; or that "in the army, I can get me a GED, skills, travel, benefits." Such is a powerful form of silencing.

Closing Down Conversations

Field Note: October 17, Business Class

White Teacher: What's EOE?
African-American Male Student: Equal over time.
White Teacher: Not quite. Anyone else?
African-American Female Student: Equal Opportunity Employer.
Teacher: That's right.
African-American Male Student (2): What does that mean?
Teacher: That means that an employer can't discriminate on the basis of sex, age, marital status, or race.
African-American Male Student (2): But wait, sometimes White people only hire White people.
Teacher: No, they're not supposed to if they say EOE in their ads. Now take out your homework.

Later that day:
MF (to teacher): Why don't you discuss racism in your class?
Teacher: It would demoralize the students, they need to feel positive and optimistic—like they have a chance.

Racism is just an excuse they use to not try harder.

What enables some teachers to act as if students benefit from such smoothing over (Wexler, 1983)? For whose good are the roots, the scars, and the structures of class, race, and gender inequity obscured by teachers, texts, and tests (Anyon, 1983)? Are not the "fears of demoralizing" a projection by teachers of their own silenced loss of faith in public education and their own fears of unmasking or freeing a conversation about social inequities?

At the level of curriculum, texts, and conversation in classrooms, school talk and knowledge were radically severed from the daily realities of adolescents' lives and more systematically aligned with the lives of teachers (McNeil, 1981). Routinely discouraged from critically examining the conditions of their lives, dissuaded from creating their own curriculum, built of what they know, students were often encouraged to disparage the circumstances in which they live, warned by their teachers: "You act like that, and you'll end up on welfare!" (Most were or had been surviving on some form of federal, state, or city assistance.)

"Good students" therefore managed these dual/duel worlds by learning to speak standard English dialect, whether they originally spoke Black English, Spanish, or Creole. More poignant still, they trained themselves to produce two voices. One's "own" voice alternated with an "academic" voice. The latter denied class, gender, and race conflict; repeated the words of hard work, success, and their "natural" sequence; and stifled any desire to disrupt.

In a study conducted in 1981, it was found that the group of South Bronx students who were "successes"—those who remained in high school—when compared with dropouts, were significantly more depressed, less politically aware, less likely to be assertive in the classroom if they were undergraded, and more conformist (Fine, 1991). A moderate level of depression, an absence of political awareness, and a persistence of self-blame, low assertiveness, and high conformity may tragically have constituted the "good" urban student at this high school. They learned not to raise, and indeed to help shut down, "dangerous" conversation. The price of success may have been muting one's own voice.

Other students from the school in Manhattan resolve the "two voices" tension with creative, if ultimately self-defeating, strategies. Cheray reflected on the hegemonic academic voice after she dropped out: "In school, we learned Columbus Avenue stuff, and *I* had to translate it into Harlem. They think livin' up here is unsafe and our lives are so bad. That we should want to move out and get away. That's what you're supposed to learn." Tony thoroughly challenged the academic voice as ineffective pedagogy: "I never got math when I was in school. Then I started sellin' dope and runnin' numbers, and I picked it up right away. They should teach the way it matters." Alicia accepted the academic voice as the standard, while disparaging with faint praise her own voice: "I'm *wise* but not *smart*. There's a difference. I can walk into a room, and I know what people be thinkin' and what's goin' down. But not what he be talkin' about in history."

Finally, many saw the academic voice as the exclusively legitimate, if inaccessible, mode of social discourse. Monique, after two months out of school, admitted: "I'm scared to go out lookin' for a job. They be usin' words in the interview like in school. Words I don't know. I can't be askin' them for a dictionary. It's like in school. You ask and you feel like a dummy."

By segregating the academic voice from students' own voices, public schools do not only linguistic violence (Zorn, 1982). The intellectual, social, and emotional substance that constitutes minority students' lives in this school was routinely treated as irrelevant, to be displaced and silenced. Their responses, spanning acquiescence to resistance, bore serious consequences.

Contradictions Folded: Excluding "Redundant" Voices

If "lived talk" was actively expelled on the basis of content, contradictory talk was basically rendered impossible. Social contradictions were folded into dichotomous choices. What does this obscure, and whom does this accommodate? The creation of such dichotomies and the reification of single truths may bolster educators' authority, reinforcing the distance between those who *know* and those who *don't*, often discrediting those who *think* in complexity (McNeil, 1981).

To illustrate: In early spring, a social studies teacher structured an in-class debate on Bernard Goetz—New York City's "subway vigilante." She invited "those students who agree with Goetz to sit on one side of the room and those who think he was wrong to sit on the other side." To the large residual group who remained mid-room, the teacher remarked, "Don't be lazy. You have to make a decision. Like at work, you can't be passive." A few wandered over to the "pro-Goetz" side.

About six remained in the center. Somewhat angry, the teacher continued: "OK, first we'll hear the pro-Goetz side and then the anti-Goetz side. Those of you who have no opinions, who haven't even thought about the issue, you won't get to talk unless we have time."

Deidre, an African-American senior, bright and always quick to raise contradictions otherwise obscured, advocated the legitimacy of the middle group. "It's not that I have no opinions. I don't like Goetz shootin' up people who look like my brother, but I don't like feelin' unsafe in the projects or in my neighborhood either. I got lots of opinions. I ain't bein' quiet 'cause I can't decide if he's right or wrong. I'm talkin'." Deidre's comment legitimized for herself and others the right to hold complex, perhaps even contradictory, positions on a complex situation. Such legitimacy was rarely granted by faculty—with clear and important exceptions, including activist faculty and those paraprofessionals who lived in central Harlem with the kids, who understood and respected much about their lives.

Among the chorus of voices heard with this high school, then, lay little room for Gramsci's (1971) contradictory consciousness. Artificial dichotomies were delivered as natural: right and wrong answers, appropriate and inappropriate behavior, moral and immoral people, dumb and smart students, responsible and irresponsible parents, good and bad neighborhoods. Contradiction and ambivalence, forced underground, were experienced often, if expressed rarely.

I asked Ronald, a student in remedial reading class, why he stayed in school. He responded with sophistication and complexity: "Reason I stay in school is 'cause every time I get on the subway I see this drunk and I think 'not me.' But then I think 'bet he has a high school degree.'" The power of his statement lies in its honesty, as well as the infrequency with which such comments were voiced. Ronald explained that he expected support for this position neither in school nor on the street. School talk promised what few believed but many repeated: that hard work and education breed success and a guarantee against welfare. Street talk belied another reality, described by Shondra: "They be sayin', 'What you doin' in school? Could be out here scramblin' [selling drugs] and makin' money now. That degree ain't gonna get you nothing better.'"

When African-American adolescent high school graduates, in the October following graduation, suffered a 56% unemployment rate and African-American adolescent high school dropouts suffered a 70% unemployment rate, the very contradictions that were amplified in the minds and worries of these young men and women remained unspoken within school (Young, 1983).

Conversations Psychologized: Splitting the Personal and the Social Voice

Some conversations within schools were closed; others were dichotomized. Yet a few conversations, indeed those most relevant to inequitable social arrangements, remained psychologized: managed as personal problems inside the offices of school psychologists or counselors. The lived experiences of *all* adolescents, and particularly those surviving city life in poverty, place their physical and mental well-being as well as that of their kin in constant jeopardy. And yet conversations about these very conditions of life, about alcoholism, drug abuse, domestic violence, environmental hazards, gentrification, and poor health—to the extent that they happened at all—remained confined to individual sessions with counselors (for those lucky enough to gain hearing with a counselor in the 800 : 1 ratio and gutsy enough to raise the issue) or, if made academic, were raised in hygiene class (for those fortunate enough to have made it to 12th grade, when hygiene was offered). A biology teacher, one of the few African-American teachers in the school, actually integrated creative writing assignments such as "My life as an alcoholic" and "My life as a child of an alcoholic" into her biology class curriculum. Her department chairman reprimanded her severely for introducing "extraneous materials." Teachers, too, were silenced.

The marginalizing of the health and social problems experienced by these adolescents exemplified the systematic unwillingness to address these concerns academically, in social studies, science, English, or even math. A harsh resistance to name the lived experiences of these teens paralleled the unwillingness to integrate these experiences as the substance of learning. Issues to be avoided at all costs, they were addressed psychologically, individually, and in isolation and, even then, only after they pierce the life of the adolescent seeking help.

The offices of school psychologists or counselors therefore became the primary sites for addressing what were indeed social concerns, should have been academic concerns, and were most likely to be managed as personal and private concerns. The privatizing and psychologizing of public and political issues served to reinforce the alienation of students' lives from their educational experience.

Democracy and Discipline: Maintaining Silence by Appropriating and Exporting Dissent

The means of maintaining silences and ensuring no dangerous disruptions know few bounds. If silence masks asymmetric power relations, it also ensures the impression of democracy for parents and students by appropriating and exporting dissent. This strategy has gained popularity in the fashionable times of "empowerment."

At this school, the Parents' Association executive board was composed of ten parents: eight African-American women, one African-American man, and one White woman. Eight no longer had children attending the school. At about mid-year, teachers were demanding smaller class size. So, too, was the president of the Parents' Association at this executive meeting with the principal.

President: I'm concerned about class size. Carol Bellamy (city council president) notified us that you received monies earmarked to reduce class size, and yet what have you done?

Mr. Stein: Quinones [school's chancellor] promised no high school class greater than 34 by February. That's impossible! What he is asking I can't guarantee, unless *you* tell me what to do. If I reduce class size, I must eliminate all specialized classes, all electives. Even then I can't guarantee. To accede to Quinones, that classes be less than 34, we must eliminate the elective in English, Social Studies, all art classes, 11th-year Math, Physics, accounting, word processing.

We were going to offer a Haitian Patois Bilingual program, fourth-year French, a Museums program, Bio-Pre-Med, Health Careers, Coop and Pre-Coop, Choreography, and Advanced Ballet. The nature of the school will be changed fundamentally. We won't be able to call this an academic high school, only a program for slow learners.

Woman (1): Those are very important classes.

Mr. Stein: I am willing to keep these classes. Parents want me to keep these classes. That's where I'm at.

Woman (2): What is the average?

Mr. Stein: 33.

Woman (1): Are any classes over 40?

Mr. Stein: No, except if it's a *singleton* class—the only one offered. If these courses weren't important, we wouldn't keep them. You know we always work together. If it's your feeling we should not eliminate all electives and maintain things, OK! Any comments?

Woman (1): I think continue. Youngsters aren't getting enough now. And the teachers will not teach any more.

Woman (3): You have our unanimous consent and support.

Mr. Stein: When I talk to the Board of Education, I'll say I'm talking for the parents.

Woman (4): I think it's impossible to teach 40.

Mr. Stein: We have a space problem. Any other issues?

An equally conciliatory student council was constituted to decide on student activities, prom arrangements, and student fees. The council was largely pleased to meet in the principal's office. At the level of critique, silence was guaranteed by the selection and then the invited "democratic participation" of these parents and students.

If dissent was appropriated through mechanisms of democracy, it was exported through mechanisms of discipline. The most effective procedure for silencing was to banish the source of dissent, tallied in the school's dropout rate. As indicated by the South Bronx study referred to above (Fine, 1983) and the research of others (Elliott, Voss, & Wendling, 1966; Felice, 1981; Fine & Rosenberg, 1983), it is often the academic critic resisting the intellectual and verbal girdles of schooling who "drops out" or is pushed out of low-income schools. Extraordinary rates of suspensions, expulsions, and discharges experienced by African-American and Hispanic youths speak to this form of silencing (Advocates for Children, 1985). Estimates of urban dropout rates range from approximately 42% from New York City, Boston, and Chicago boards of education to 68 to 80% from Aspira (1983), an educational advocacy organization.

At the school that served as the site for this ethnographic research, a 66% dropout rate was calculated. Two-thirds of the students who began ninth grade in 1978–79 did not receive diplomas or degrees by June 1985. I presented these findings to a collection of deans, advisors, counselors, administrators, and teachers, many of whom were the sponsors and executors of the discharge process. At first I met with total silence. A dean then explained, "These kids need to be out. It's unfair to the rest. My job is like a pilot on a hijacked plane. My job is to throw the hijacker overboard." The one African-American woman in the room, a guidance counselor, followed: "What Michelle is saying is true. We do throw students out of here and deny them their education. Black kids especially." Two White male administrators interrupted, chiding what they called the "liberal tendencies" of guidance counselor, who "don't see how really dangerous these kids are." The meeting ended.

Dissent was institutionally "democraticized," exported, trivialized, or bureaucratized. These mechanisms made it unlikely for change or challenge to be given a serious hearing.

Whispers of Resistance: The Silenced Speak

In low-income public high schools organized around control through silence, the student, parent, teacher, or paraprofessional who talks, tells, or wants to speak transforms rapidly into the subversive, the troublemaker. Students, unless they spoke in an honors class or affected the academic mode of introducing nondangerous topics and benign words—if not protected by wealth, influential parents, or an unusual capacity to be critics *and* good students—emerged as provocateurs. Depending on school, circumstances, and style, students' responses to such silencing varied. Maria buried herself in mute isolation. Steven organized students against many of his teachers. Most of these youths, for complex reasons, ultimately fled prior to graduation. Some then sought "alternative contexts" in which their strengths, competencies, and voices could flourish on their own terms:

Hector's a subway graffiti artist: "It's like an experience you never get. You're on the subway tracks. Its 3 a.m., dark, cold, and scary. You're trying to create your best. The cops can come to bust you, or you could fall on the electric third rail. My friend died when he dropped his spray paint on that rail. It exploded. He died and I watched. It's awesome, intense. A peak moment when you can't concentrate on nothin', no problems, just creation. And it's like a family. When Michael Stewart [graffiti artist] was killed by cops, you know he was a graffiti man, we all came out of retirement to mourn him. Even me, I stopped 'cause my girl said it was dangerous. We came out and painted funeral scenes and cemeteries on the LL #1 and the N [subway lines]. For Michael. We know each other; you know an artist when you see him. It's a family. Belonging. They want me in, not out, like at school."

Carmen pursued the Job Corps when she left school: "You ever try plastering, Michelle? It's great. You see holes in walls. You see a problem and you fix it. Job Corps lost its money when I was in it, in Albany. I had to come home, back to Harlem. I felt better there than ever in my school. Now I do nothin'. It's a shame. Never felt as good as then."

Monique got pregnant and then dropped out: "I wasn't never good at nothing. In school I felt stupid and older than the rest. But I'm a great mother to Chita. Catholic schools for my baby, and maybe a house in New Jersey."

Carlos, who left school at age 20, after 5 frustrating years since he and his parents exiled illegally from Mexico, hopes to join the military: "I don't want to kill nobody. Just, you know how they advertise, the Marines. I never been one of a Few and the Proud. I'm always 'shamed of myself. So I'd like to try it."

In an uninviting economy, these adolescents responded to the silences transmitted through public schooling by pursuing what they considered to be creative alternatives. But let us understand that, for such low-income youths, these alternatives generally *replace* formal schooling. Creative alternatives for middle-class adolescents, an after-school art class or music lessons privately afforded by parents, generally *supplement* formal schooling.

Whereas school-imposed silence may be an initiation to adulthood for the middle-class adolescent about to embark on a life of participation and agency, school-imposed silence more typically represents the orientation to adulthood for the low-income or working-class adolescent about to embark on a life of work at McDonalds, in a factory, as a domestic or clerical, and/or on Aid to Families with Dependent Children (AFDC). For the low-income student, the imposed silences of high school cannot be ignored as a necessary means to an end. They are the present, *and* they are likely to be the future (Ogbu, 1978).

Some teachers, paraprofessionals, parents, and students expressly devoted their time, energy, and classes to exposing silences institutionally imposed. One reading teacher prepared original grammar worksheets, including items such as "Most women in Puerto Rico (is, are) oppressed." A history teacher dramatically presented his autobiography to his class, woven with details on the life of Paul Robeson. An English teacher formed a writer's collective of her multilingual "remedial" writing students. A paraprofessional spoke openly with students who decided not to report the prime suspect in a local murder to the police but to clergy instead. She recognized

that their lives would be in jeopardy, despite "what the administrators who go home to the suburbs preach." But these voices of naming were weak, individual, and isolated.

What if these voices, along with the chorus of dropouts, were allowed expression? If they were not whispered, isolated, or drowned out in disparagement, what would happen if these stories were solicited, celebrated, and woven into a curriculum? What if the history of schooling were written by those high school critics who remained in school and those who dropped out? What if the "dropout problem" were studied in social studies as a collective critique by consumers of public education?

Dropping out, or other forms of critique, are viewed instead by educators, policy makers, teachers, and often students as individual acts, expressions of incompetence or self-sabotage. As alive, motivated, and critical as they were at age 17, most of the interviewed dropouts were silenced, withdrawn, and depressed by age 22. They had tried the private trade schools, been in and out of the military, failed the GED exam once or more, had too many children to care for, too many bills to pay, and only self-blaming regrets, seeking private solutions to public problems. Muting, by the larger society, had ultimately succeeded, even for those who fled initially with resistance, energy, and vision (Apple, 1982).

I'll end with an image that occurred throughout the year, repeated across classrooms and across urban public high schools. As familiar as it is haunting, the portrait most dramatically captures the physical embodiment of silencing in urban schools.

Field Note: February 16

Patrice is a young African-American female, in 11th grade. She says nothing all day in school. She sits perfectly mute. No need to coerce her into silence. She often wears her coat in class. Sometimes she lays her head on her desk. She never disrupts. Never disobeys. Never speaks. And is never identified as a problem. Is she the student who couldn't develop two voices and so silenced both? Is she so filled with anger, she fears to speak? Or so filled with depression, she knows not what to say?

Whose problem is Patrice?

Nurturing the Possibility of Voice in an Improbable Context

To pose a critique of silencing requires a parallel commitment to exploring the possibility of voice in public schools. For, if we are to abandon all hopes that much can be done inside the public school system, we have surely and irretrievably sealed and silenced the fates of children and adolescents like those described in this chapter. And so the responsibility to unearth possibility lies with the critic of educational institutions (Aronowitz & Giroux, 1985).

Indeed, after a year at this public school, I left with little but optimism about these youngsters and little but pessimism about public high schools as currently structured. And yet it would be inauthentic not to note the repeated ways in which students, communities, and parents were, and the more numerous ways in which they could be, granted voice inside schools. Those teachers who imported politics from elsewhere, who recognized that educational work is political work, that to talk about or not to talk about economic arrangements is to do political work, took as their individual and collective responsibility a curriculum that included critical examination of social and economic issues and a pedagogy that attended to the multiple perspectives and ideas inside their classrooms. In vocational education class, Ms. Rodriquez invited students to discuss the conditions of their lives, the relationship of labor market opportunities to their own and their families' survival, and the consequences of giving up, being discouraged, or making trouble at work. Although a thoroughgoing critique of workplace management was not undertaken, a surface analysis was begun, and trust was enabled. Likewise, in hygiene, Ms. Wasserman continually probed the lived experiences and diversity among the students. She integrated writing assignments with curricular and social issues, inviting students to author letters to their mothers—alive or dead—about questions "you wish you could or did ask her about sexuality, marriage, and romance." A social studies teacher created a class assignment in which students investigated their communities, conducting oral histories with neighbors, shop owners, and local organizers to map community life historically and currently.

But, of course, much more could be done if all educators saw politics as inherent and the giving of voice as essential to the task of education. To *not* mention racism is as political a stance as is a thoroughgoing discussion of its dynamics; to *not* examine domestic violence bears consequences for the numerous youths who have witnessed abuse at home and feel alone, alienated in their experience, unable to concentrate, so that the effects of the violence permeate the classroom even—or particularly—if not named.

I am not asking teachers to undertake therapy in the classroom nor to present only one political view but, instead, to interrogate the very conditions of students' lives and the very thoughts that they entertain as the "stuff" of schooling.

The good news is that students in public high schools, as thoroughly silenced as they may be, retain the energy, persistence, and even resistance that fuel a willingness to keep trying to get a hearing. They probe teachers they don't agree with, challenge the lived experiences of these authorities, and actively spoof the class and race biases that routinely structure classroom activities:

Field Note: September 18

Social Studies Teacher: A few years ago a journalist went through Kissinger's garbage and learned a lot about his life. Let's make believe we are all sanitation men going through rich people's and poor people's garbage. What would we find in rich people's garbage?

Students callout: Golf club! Polo stick! Empty bottle of Halston! Champagne bottle! Alimony statements! Leftover caviar! Receipts from Saks, Barneys, Bloomies! Old business and love letters! Rarely worn shoes—They love to spend money! Bills from the plastic surgeon—for a tummy tuck! Things that are useful that they just throw out 'cause they don't like it! Rich people got ulcers, so they have lots of medicine bottles!

Teacher: Now, the poor man's garbage. What would you find?

Student (1): Not much, we're using it.

Student (2): Holey shoes.

Others: Tuna cans! Bread bags!

Student (3): That's right, we eat a lot of bread!

Others: USDA cheese boxes! Empty no-frills cans! Woolworth receipts! Reused items from rich man's garbage! *Daily News*!

Student (3): *Daily News* from week before.

Others: Old appliances! Rusty toasters!

Student (4): Yeah, we eat lots of burned toast.

Student (5): You know, poor people aren't unhappy. We like being poor.

Teacher: Let's not get into value judgments now. There are people who are eccentric and don't have these things, and poor people who have luxuries, so it is hard to make generalizations.

Student (6): That's why we're poor!

Despite the teacher's attempts to halt the conversation of critique, these students initiated and persisted. The room for possibility lies with the energy of these adolescents and with those educators who are creative and gutsy enough to see as their job, their passion, and their responsibility the political work of educating toward a voice.

Postscript on Research as Exposing the Practices of Silencing

The process of conducting research within schools to identify words that could have been said, talk that should have been nurtured, and information that needed to be announced suffers from voyeurism and perhaps the worst of post hoc academic arrogance. The researcher's sadistic pleasure in spotting another teacher's collapsed contradiction, aborted analysis, or silencing sentence was moderated only by the ever-present knowledge that similar analytic surgery could easily be performed on my own classes.

And yet it is the very naturalness of not naming, of shutting down or marginalizing conversations for the "sake of getting on with learning" that demands educators' attention, particularly so for low-income youths highly ambivalent about the worth of a diploma, desperately desirous of and at the same time discouraged from its achievement. If the process of education is to allow children, adolescents, and adults their voices—to read, write, create, critique, and transform—how can we justify the institutionalizing of silence at a level of policies that obscure systemic problems behind a rhetoric of "excellence" and "progress"; a curriculum bereft of the lived experiences of students themselves; a pedagogy organized around control and not conversation and a thoroughgoing psychologizing of social issues which enables Patrice to bury herself in silence and not be noticed? A self-critical analysis of the fundamental ways in which we teach children to betray their own voices is crucial.

REFERENCES

Advocates for Children. (1985). *Report of the New York hearings on the crisis in public education*. New York.

Anyon, J. (1983). Intersections of gender and class: Accommodation and resistance by working-class and affluent females to contradictory sex role ideologies. In S. Walker and L. Barton (Eds.), *Gender, class and education*. (pp. 19–38). London: Falmer Press.

Apple, M. W. (1982). *Education and power*. Boston: Routledge & Kegan Paul.

Aronowitz, S., & Giroux, H. A. (1985). *Education under siege*. South Hadley, MA: Bergin & Garvey.

Aspira of New York. (1983). *Racial and ethnic high school dropout rates in New York City: A summary report*. Albany: State University of New York Press.

Bastian, A., Fruchter, N., Gittell, M., Greer, C., & Haskins, K. (1985, Spring). Choosing equality: The case for democratic schooling. *Social Policy*, 35–51.

Carnoy, M., & Levin, H. (1985). *Schooling and work in the democratic state*. Stanford, CA: Stanford University Press.

Connell, R., Ashenden, D., Kessler, S., & Dowsett, G. (1982). *Making the Difference*. Sydney, Australia: George Allen & Unwin.

Elliott, D., Voss, H., & Wendling, A. (1966). Capable dropouts and the social milieu of high school. *Journal of Educational Research, 60*, 180–186.

Felice, J. (1981). Black student dropout behaviors: Disengagement from school rejection and racial discrimination. *Journal of Negro Education, 50*, 415–424.

Fine, M. (1983). Perspectives on inequity: Voices from urban schools. In L. Bickman (Ed.), *Applied Social Psychology Annual IV*. Beverly Hills, CA: Sage.

Fine, M. (1985, Fall). Dropping out of high school: An inside look. *Social Policy*, 43–50.

Fine, M. (1986). Why urban adolescents drop into and out of high school. *Teachers College Record, 87*, 393–409.

Fine, M. (1991). *Framing dropouts*. Albany: State University of New York Press.

Fine, M., & Rosenberg, P. (1983). Dropping out of high school: The ideology of school and work. *Journal of Education, 165*, 257–272.

Freire, P. (1985). *The politics of education*. South Hadley, MA: Bergin & Garvey.

Giroux, H. (1988). Literacy and the pedagogy of voice and political empowerment. *Educational Theory, 38*, 61–75.

Giroux, H., & McLaren, P. (1986, August). Teacher education and the politics of engagement. *Harvard Educational Review, 56*(3), 213–238.

Goodlad, J. (1984). *A place called school: Prospects for the future.* New York: McGraw-Hill.

Gramsci, A. (1971). *Selections from prison notebooks.* New York: International.

Lather, P. (1991). *Getting smart.* New York: Routledge.

Lightfoot, S. (1978). *Worlds apart.* New York: Basic Books.

McNeil, L. (1981). Negotiating classroom knowledge: Beyond achievement and socialization. *Curriculum Studies, 13*, 313–328.

Militarism Resource Project. (1985). *High school military recruiting: Recent developments.* Philadelphia.

New York State Department of Education. (1985). Memo from Dennis Hughes, State Administrator on High School Equivalency Programs. December 4, 1984. Albany, New York.

Ogbu, J. (1978). *Minority education and caste: The American system in cross-cultural perspective.* New York: Academic Press.

Schor, I. (1980). *Critical teaching and everyday life.* Boston: South End Press.

Sizer, T. (1985). *Horace's compromise: The dilemma of the American high school.* Boston: Houghton Mifflin.

Tobier, E. (1984). *The changing face of poverty: Trends in New York City's population in poverty, 1960–1990.* New York: Community Service Society.

U.S. Commission on Civil Rights (1982). *Unemployment and underemployment among Blacks, Hispanics and women.* Washington, DC: Government Printing Office.

U.S. Department of Labor. (1983). *Time of change: 1983 handbook of women workers.* Washington, DC: Government Printing Office.

Wexler, P. (1983). *Critical social psychology.* Boston: Routledge & Kegan Paul.

Young, A. (1983). *Youth labor force marked turning point in 1982.* Washington, DC: U.S. Department of Labor, Bureau of Labor Statistics.

Zorn, J. (1982, March). Black English and the King decision. *College English, 44,* 3.

NOTES

1. This research was made possible by a grant from the W. T. Grant Foundation, New York City, 1984 through 1985.

2. Personal communication with employee in the High Schools' Division, New York City Board of Education, in response to inquiry about why New York City does not maintain race/ethnicity sensitive statistics on dropping out and school achievement.

George Wood

CHAPTER 20

Standing for Students, Standing for Change

"I stand for Elizabeth Kominsky."
"I stand for Tyrell James."
"I stand for Teresa Levinson."

It was the end of a two-day conference on school renewal. The host of the conference had invited us, at this last session, to each stand for a student we knew. This was an opportunity, after talking about whole-school change, to make a personal commitment to one child. It was a public commitment, in that we stood and shared each young person's name out loud. But it was also private, in that our "stance" was kept to ourselves, the commitment behind our action was not shared.

As I listened to each person speak, I was moved by the power of the moment.

First-year teachers stood for children they had just met at orientation. Veterans spoke up for young adults they had guided through the minefields of high school. Parents stood for their children's friends, social workers for foster children, foundation leaders for kids across the street, school administrators for their most challenging students.

Watching and listening, it occurred to me that this way of seeing our schools— through the life of a child to whom we commit—is our best hope for renewing those same schools. It might also be the best chance for correcting the current course our country is on when it comes to public education.

A course correction is clearly needed. The talk about our public schools is dominated by an emphasis on standardization over standards with test scores replacing genuine knowledge of our children and their abilities. When test scores do not rise as dictated we hear saber-rattling from Washington that perhaps a national curriculum and national test is the answer, or maybe privatizing education through a voucher system.

In response, too many of our schools have become test-preparation factories. Recess and nap times are eliminated, the arts are cut, field trips shut down, reading for pleasure is a thing of the past, and hands-on learning experiences are replaced by hands-off worksheets and drill. And for what? A few more points on a test that may or may not measure anything of value.

Attempting to change our schools through this top-down, test-driven agenda has done little to alter the basic structures of schooling. We keep doing more of the same thing in the hope that somehow it will work. It won't.

What will work is well documented: Schools that have at their heart the mission of preparing every child for a life of democratic citizenship. Schools that are places where every learner is well known, where the tasks are meaningful and engaging, where the scholars demonstrate through actual performance what they know and can do, and where a tone of respect and equity dominates the work. Schools such as these exist today—and yet they find their work marginalized and their existence threatened by the one-size-fits-all agenda of official school reformers.

But there is hope—and I found it again in that simple but moving "I stand for" exercise.

Maybe we settle for the one-size-fits-all agenda because thinking about renewing the entire school system is just too large an issue to get one's head around. After all, schools are everywhere, serving millions and employing millions more. Maybe the only way people can imagine changing something of such scale is through mandating test scores and standardizing schools' behavior.

Yet, if instead we each thought of one child and that child's experience, we might have a different vision for the future of our schools. If every American stood up for the education of a kid down the street, or even across town, how might we then imagine our schools? Choose a child yourself and try it right now. My experience tells me that when we think of schooling through the lens of one child,

our vision of what schools could and should be is transformed.

Begin by imagining that young person at eighteen and describe the type of neighbor you would like him/her to be. Why eighteen? Because at that age most Americans graduate from high school with all the rights, privileges, and responsibilities that citizenship brings with it. They can vote, sign a contract, serve in the military, go to college, and hold a job. They become the "Future" we often talk about—and describing what you hope for in terms of who these young people are goes a long way to setting up what their shared experience called "school" should be like.

Second, to be that person, catalogue what they need to "know" and be able to "do." Every one of them. Sure, some will go beyond what you choose as basic, but what is your bottom line? I promise you your list will be much shorter than the bound volumes of "state standards" that teachers try to cover today.

Third, how would you want that young person to be treated in school? How well should she be known, what should learning look like, what responsibilities should she shoulder, and how do these things change as the child for whom you stand grows older? Think about the respect and dignity with which you want to be treated; how does that influence your vision of school?

Finally, what would count as evidence that the child you stand with has learned all you want him to know? Does the standardized test he now takes tell you what you need to know? Do you even know what is on it? In this so-called age of accountability, who should be accountable for what when it comes to the child for whom you stand?

Of course, there is more you want for the child for whom you stand. She should live a life that is challenging, but free from want, fear, and insecurity. Affordable educational options or jobs should be available after graduation. Having access to honest political debate and reliable information when decisions are to be made will help her exercise her democratic responsibilities. But for today, let's just think about schools.

"I stand for Steven _____," I said as I came to my feet.

After three years of working with Steven, I knew he could use the help of someone standing with him. His first years of high school were difficult, including being suspended during the first semester of his junior year for possessing alcohol at the homecoming dance. But he had come back after the suspension anxious to make the best of his second chance—and did. He stopped by to see me often to share good grades, and teachers let me know of his outstanding progress. On the last day of school, he told me he wanted to go to college—and I promised that while I was to be on leave this year, I still would help.

So I stood for Steven, who is able to make his own informed decisions, is able to find out for himself what there is to know, and is able to use his mind well in pursuing his personal goals. I stood for a school experience that challenges him to think hard, helps him use in his community what he learns in school, and gives him the confidence that he is a learner. I stood for his being treated with respect, being given the responsibility for his own learning and time, and being asked to mentor other young men who might lose their way. And I stood for Steven's being accountable for developing compelling demonstrations of what he knows and is able to do for college-admissions people, and for his school's being accountable for knowing him well enough to assist him in this task.

As I stood for Steven, I thought about how our democracy requires a much more robust vision of schools than our nation now seems to have. A vision that is about more than test scores, and that encompasses the citizens we hope our children become. Maybe if we all thought of just our own "Stevens," and worked for schools that would prepare them to take their rightful places alongside us as citizens, we could generate a different vision of school renewal. A vision that could guide us in working for and supporting schools that educate for democratic citizenship, as opposed to training for taking tests.

Part IV Additional Resources

Discussion Questions

Students should carefully read each question and support each response with examples and specific references to the readings that are being considered.

1. Should all students participate in the same academic track? Why or why not? Who should be involved in making decisions about the assignment of students to particular groups, tracks, or programs? Discuss the rationale for your answer.
2. In most schools, there is a gap between reality and the "promise of public education." Is this gap important? Why or why not? Who benefits from the existence of this gap?
3. Both parents and students complain about the lack of relevance of most secondary education programs. Research alternative models of secondary education and identify several examples of successful programs. What are the merits of re-visioning secondary education? Why do you think there is tremendous resistance to attempts to establish alternative schools for the general school population? Whose support will be necessary to make substantive changes to secondary education programs across America?
4. Interview a teacher, parent, and administrator about contemporary schools and education. Ask these individuals to talk about the key issues affecting schools today. What changes would they like to see occur in the schools? What things do they want to preserve and keep the same?
5. Are there problems associated with students being involved in shaping and directing a school program? Describe and discuss. How do student roles and responsibilities shift when students take more active roles in the schools? In what ways can the curriculum accommodate the changing roles and responsibilities of students?

Guide to Further Reading

Gardner, H. 1991. *The Unschooled Mind: How Children Think and How Schools Should Teach.* New York: Basic Books.

Kohn, A. 1993. *Punished by Rewards: The Trouble with Gold Stars, Incentive Plans, A's, Praise, and Other Bribes.* Boston: Houghton Mifflin.

Levine, E. B. 2001. *One Kid at a Time: A Visionary High School Transforms Education.* New York: Teacher's College Press.

Meier, D. 1995. *The Power of Their Ideas: Lessons for America from a Small School in Harlem.* Boston: Beacon Press.

Ohanian, S. 1999. *One Size Fits Few: The Folly of Educational Standards.* Portsmouth, NH: Heinemann.

Sizer, Theodore. 2004. *Horace's Compromise: The Dilemma of the American High School.* New York: Mariner Books.

Related Resources

http://www.edchange.org/multicultural
   EdChange, Critical Multicultural Pavilion
http://www.glsen.org/templates/index.html
   GLSEN (Gay, Lesbian, and Straight Education Network)
http://www.youtube.com/watch?v=pMcfrLYDm2U
   Shift Happens: Facts About Globalization and the Information Age
http://www.civicenterprises.net/pdfs/silentepidemicppt.pdf
   The Silent Epidemic: Perspectives of High School Dropouts
http://www.splcenter.org/what-we-do/children-at-risk
   Southern Poverty Law Center, Children at Risk
http://www.splcenter.org/what-we-do/teaching-tolerance
   Southern Poverty Law Center, Teaching Tolerance

 **Part V**

WHAT ARE THE
ISSUES THAT IMPACT
TWENTY-FIRST-CENTURY
SCHOOLS?

INTRODUCTION

In this book, we have considered how to answer key questions that guide our practice, but none of these questions can be answered without carefully considering contemporary issues that make twenty-first-century schools different from the schools of an earlier generation. John Goodlad (2004) argued that we must train teachers not for the schools of today but for the schools of tomorrow. We can do this successfully only if we recognize that colleges of education are not vocational schools but educational institutions in which we are compelled to train teachers to think deeply about their educational practices . . . to think deeply about how to provide an education that meets the needs of *all* children, not just a few. There are few jobs in our society more important than that of teaching; teachers and public schools are critical to fostering the democratic principles upon which this country was founded. Today, we have the opportunity and the resources to provide world-class schools for every child in every community; our future depends on the seriousness with which we embrace this challenge and our refusal to accept mediocrity as a satisfactory outcome. As the artist Brian Andreas (2000) put it, "In my dream, the angel shrugged & said, if we fail this time, it will be a failure of imagination & then she placed the world gently in the palm of my hand." Failure is not an option for the public schools, and most would agree that a good dose of skill, knowledge, *and* imagination is needed to re-vision the ways in which schools need to change if we are to meet the needs of future generations of children. It is a grave responsibility, and "the world" is in our hands.

The readings selected for Part V of this book represent a wide range of ideas regarding the challenges facing twenty-first-century schools. Once again, equity and social justice are prevailing themes, but the essays include a consideration of many social and cultural forces that affect student achievement and efforts to educate all children successfully. The ways in which teachers answer each of the earlier questions will be relevant only if their attempts to define and understand contemporary issues include a consideration of multiple perspectives.

K. B. Rogers

CHAPTER 21

Grouping the Gifted and Talented
Questions and Answers

Five questions about the academic, psychological, and socialization effects on gifted and talented learners of grouping for enrichment, cooperative grouping for regular instruction, and grouping for acceleration are addressed. The conclusions drawn from 13 research syntheses on these practices, conducted in the past nine years, are described. In general, these conclusions support sustained periods of instruction in like-ability groups for students who are gifted and talented.

Perhaps this title is presumptive: questions and answers. Certainly anyone can produce the questions educators have about the effects of grouping the gifted. But there must be some presumption in any one writer claiming to have the answers as well. Can one talk about differing group configurations without first clarifying the purposes for that grouping? For example, are we inquiring about grouping for enrichment or grouping for the acceleration of content, or grouping for effect? And when we ask about grouping the "gifted," in particular, are we referring to highly able students (defined by some researchers as the top third of grade level performance) or are we talking about the gifted, defined as performing or capable of performing at extraordinary levels in specific ability domains? Even a cursory survey of recent articles reveals that these questions have not always been asked before answers about the grouping issue have been given.

Why has ability grouping become such a big issue in the last five years? Why have so many well-intentioned educational researchers blamed ability grouping for the widespread ills currently plaguing American schools? As educational leaders have struggled to find the answer to our country's educational woes, we have seen the implementation of a plethora of whole group and cooperatively structured instructional strategies to be applied to heterogeneous groups of students, each guaranteed to solve our problems. Educators have learned how to implement Madeline Hunter's MP, Metra Companion Reading, group-based mastery learning, assertive discipline, and cooperative learning programs for what is believed to be the empirically supported betterment of all classroom learners, regardless of achievement or ability level.

Elimination of ability grouping has hit the gifted education movement very hard. Joyce Van Tassel–Baska (1991) has suggested that grouping and cooperative learning issues may be even more damaging to gifted education than just losing opportunities for intellectual peers to learn together. These issues may, in fact, be diverting us, as well as general educators, from focusing on the curricular and instructional needs of gifted learners. Gifted educators are now confronted with shoring up the erosion of years of effort: fighting the loss of high ability reading or math groups, the elimination of gifted pull-out or resource programs of enrichment, and the removal of Advanced Placement and enriched or honors classes. There is little time left over for constructing innovative differentiation for their gifted and talented charges.

The issue basically under debate—like-ability grouping versus mixed-ability grouping—has become a heated and emotional one. Both sides believe that whatever decisions they make are, of course, in the best interests of the majority of students. With the concern for "at risk" students of high priority nationally, educators continue to search for a method that will keep these students involved and successful in school. As Oakes (1990) and George (1988) have argued, all students, especially our "at risk" ones, must be given full access to the knowledge society considers "high status," if we are to ensure them choices for their futures. Unfortunately, this focus may have diverted needed attention from the majority of American students who have been well served by our schools and from the minority who have been chronically underserved academically.

Knowing that we will not be able to answer the larger questions that accompany these priorities, we should probably concentrate on the problem at hand—

understanding the general effects of grouping and not grouping gifted learners. There are five major questions about grouping to consider, each of which this article attempts to answer:

What are possible grouping options to consider when grouping gifted learners?

What are the academic effects of these grouping options for gifted learners?

What are potential social and psychological effects of these grouping options?

Are there some concerns we should have about grouping gifted learners together?

What might be the costs of not providing grouping for gifted learners?

Before beginning to provide answers for these five questions, it is important to understand how we can find out what are the effects of grouping the gifted. (In other words, which research should we try to understand?) The most difficult problem all educators must face is how to make sense of the overwhelming body of research that is out there. Currently, on grouping issues alone, there are over 750 studies on ability grouping, and over 300 each on cooperative learning and acceleration. What is the appropriate approach to managing all these data? In effect, educators, the ultimate consumers of research, have taken five basic approaches to the research:

1. I know this student who . . .
2. I found this study;

3. famous person;
4. apples and oranges; or
5. best-evidence synthesis.

Some of these methods are better than others.

The "I know this student who . . . " approach occurs when an educator recalls a similar instance of the current situation, reflects on how successful the action taken previously was in the long run, and applies similar or alternative action in the current situation. For example, Robin, a second grader, is reading at a fifth grade level and her teacher wants to know what to do next. The teacher remembers that three years ago there was a child whom the school placed in fifth grade during reading time, but the child did not do very well. The reading teacher thus decides that Robin must stay in her second grade class for reading and will be happier waiting three years for her classmates to catch up. Obviously, this method uses anecdotal research, at best, and can hardly be called a sound approach to the research.

Closely related is the "I found this study" approach, in which an educational decision-maker, with a point of view based on personal experience or "gut" feelings, locates one or two research studies supporting this view and disseminates them to superiors, colleagues, and school staff (also known as the "mailbox effect"). Decisions are then made for changes in practice based on this limited and possibly biased research base. The problems with such an approach are obvious. There are few practices in education, let alone in gifted education, that are comprised of a research base of two. It would be just about impossible to find two studies that systematically, objectively, and compre-

hensively represent the 750-plus research bases on ability grouping, or the 300-plus bases for acceleration or cooperative learning.

The "famous person" approach has been an exceedingly popular approach to research in the 1980s and 1990s. This approach involves the reporting of broad, simplistic claims by a well-known educator (with strong feelings about a certain practice) that his/her recommendation is "research-supported." In most of these cases, the research actually cited by the person is either tangential or focused on only a very small part of the total research surrounding the practice. Oakes's (1985, 1990) persuasive arguments against ability grouping reflect her own case study of 25 junior and senior high schools. George's (1988) arguments against "tracking" for middle school students have been reflections on a single section of one research synthesis by Slavin (1987a), describing the effects of this practice on elementary students. References to the research supporting cooperative learning as beneficial for gifted students by Johnson and Johnson (1990) appear to have been based on a single, poorly designed quasi-experimental study comparing the immediate and long-term effects of a five-day treatment on handicapped, regular, and "gifted" students with no specification of how any of these groups of students were identified (Robinson, 1990). Although the "famous person" approach may be a very effective means for promoting educational change, this approach does not adequately or accurately represent the research on these strategies and their effects on students with gifts and talents.

The "apples and oranges" approach to the research describes the technique of meta-analysis, first introduced by Glass in 1976. This approach involves an attempt to collect all general research studies conducted on a practice and to average across all these studies to calculate a mean effect size. The effect size is first calculated for each study separately, using the formula ES = M e-M c / s c, where M represents the mean scores of the experimental (e) and control (c) groups and s represents the standard deviation of the control group. These individual effect sizes are then averaged to calculate the mean effect size across all the studies.

In many cases, this averaging process is done regardless of the quality of individual research studies included, the size of samples in the studies, or the specific form of the strategy. Such was certainly the case in some of the early meta-analyses of the research on ability grouping. There can, however, be a greater degree of validity in drawing conclusions about the effects of an instructional practice when care has been taken to use well-defined inclusion criteria for this research synthesis procedure. The effect size metric translates easily into an understandable classroom application. An effect size of +.30, generally accepted as indicating practically significant (acceptable gains) effects, would indicate that the experimental group involved in the new practice performed approximately three school months further along the standardized test's grade equivalent scale than the control group, or, in effect, the experimental students could potentially be taught in three years what the control students would accomplish in four (Glass, McGaw, & Smith, 1981). With care, then, the "apples and oranges" approach to the research can be useful and appropriate. At the present time, this method has been used to

synthesize the research on various forms of grouping by ability for elementary and secondary students in seven different reports, but the Kuliks (Kulik, 1985; Kulik & Kulik, 1982, 1984, 1990) and Vaughn, Feldhusen, and Asher (1991) have directly applied this method to the grouping research on gifted and talented students.

Similarly, the "best-evidence" approach follows the same collection and calculation procedures as meta-analysis, but once all the studies have been collected, the research synthesizer categorizes them by instructional variation and selects only the strongest studies for each variation to generalize and average. Some critics of this approach have argued that the role of the synthesizer becomes one of judge and jury, but the skillful reader should be able to determine whether or not the judgments are appropriate by taking care to ferret out the synthesizer's methods of inclusion and exclusion. This final approach was first proposed and used by Slavin to synthesize the research on ability grouping for elementary students (1987a), ability grouping for secondary students (1990a), and cooperative learning (1990b). None of these syntheses included specific research studies on students who are gifted. The approach has also been used by Rogers (1991) to synthesize research on 12 accelerative options for gifted students, several of which involve the grouping by ability of gifted and talented learners.

In summary, we can answer our questions about the effects of grouping the gifted by understanding the 13 research syntheses on grouping for enrichment, cooperative learning, or acceleration, all of which have used one of the latter two approaches to research.

Question One: What Are Possible Grouping Options to Consider When Grouping Gifted Learners?

A variety of grouping options have been found beneficial for learners who are gifted and talented, including full-time placement in special enriched or accelerated gifted programs, regrouping for enriched instruction in specific subjects, cross-grade grouping for specific subjects, pull-out grouping for enrichment, cluster grouping within an otherwise heterogeneous classroom, and within-class ability grouping. An option still under question for regular use with gifted learners would be most forms of mixed-ability cooperative learning. The research supports these program option recommendations in the following order, according to the strength of the research findings. It is to be noted, however, that differential effects may be expected from district to district due to individual variations in population, organizational structure, personnel, and school culture. Hence, some of the options listed further down on the list may be the most appropriate option for one district, and the top-tested option may be least appropriate in some cases.

Full-time gifted programs. Four research syntheses, all conducted by James and Chen-Lin Kulik (Kulik, 1985; Kulik & Kulik, 1982, 1984, 1990), have shown there is a marked academic achievement gain across all subject areas, as well as a moderate increase in attitude toward the subjects in which these students are grouped, when that grouping is full-time in special programs. Little has been documented in this research base, however, to attribute the academic gains to grouping

directly or to the differentiation of curriculum and instructional methodology, both of which may be more easily facilitated by such a grouping arrangement.

Cluster grouping within heterogeneous classrooms. The Kuliks' 1990 meta-analysis identified four research studies that looked at this particular programming option, in which the top 5–8 gifted learners at a grade level are placed with a trained teacher of the gifted and the remainder of that teacher's load includes a normal distribution of ability. The rationale for such an option has been that the teacher can spend a proportionate amount of instructional effort and curriculum development time on the gifted cluster, which may not be possible when a classroom contains only 1–2 of these students. A sizable academic gain across all academic areas was reported for this option. Due to the comparatively small number of studies, this option was not listed first despite the greater gains reported. It is believed that, with a comparative sample of 25 studies as were found for full-time gifted programs, the effect size would probably be similar to the first option's effects.

Grouping for acceleration of the curriculum. In the Kuliks' meta-analysis of the combined effects of acceleration, gifted accelerates showed substantial achievement gains over their gifted counterparts who were not accelerated, and there was no difference in their performance from their equally gifted older-aged peers. Rogers (1991) found substantial academic gains for five of the six more specific forms of acceleration which are often implemented as small group strategies:

Non-graded Classrooms, Curriculum Compacting (general streamlining of the previously mastered curriculum), Grade Telescoping (time compression of the junior or senior high curriculum), Subject Acceleration (accelerated progression through one subject area), and Early Admission to College (without a high school diploma). The sixth option, Advanced Placement, was very close to representing a substantial academic gain as well.

Regrouping for enriched learning in specific subjects. Slavin's (1987a) best-evidence synthesis established the potential of regrouping in one or two subjects per year for the general population at the elementary level, but he could not establish a similar pattern at the secondary level (1990a). The Kulik and Kulik (1990) meta-analysis reported substantially higher effects for gifted students when they are regrouped for specific instruction than for students at other ability or achievement levels, even when differences in the quality of the instruction and instructional materials could not be documented. Their synthesis combined elementary and secondary studies; they refuted outright Slavin's previous conclusions that regrouping produces no academic gains for any level of student at the secondary level. Gamoran and Berends's (1987) synthesis of ethnographic and survey research established a marked likelihood that "academic" track students were more likely to plan on and to attend college. Generally, the syntheses seem to support regrouping as a viable option for gifted and talented learners.

Cross-grade grouping or nongraded classrooms. Slavin's (1987a) synthesis of group-

ing research on cross-grade grouping in reading and mathematics for elementary students reported substantial academic gains in reading and some evidence of similar gains in mathematics for students of all ability levels. The Kuliks' meta-analysis on cross-grade grouping K–12 located 16 studies, which established a moderate gain across all subject areas. Rogers's (1991) best-evidence synthesis reported sizable academic gains for nongraded classrooms, in which gifted students would work at their own pace in every subject area full-time.

Enrichment pull-out programs. Vaughn, Feldhusen and Asher's (1991) meta-analysis produced substantial improvements in achievement, critical thinking, and creative thinking for gifted and talented learners. Gains appeared to be greatest for achievement when the pullout experience was an extension of the regular classroom curriculum.

Within-class ability grouping. Slavin's (1987a) best-evidence synthesis reported substantial academic gains for elementary learners at all ability levels in mathematics, but he could find no controlled studies to support within-class ability grouping in reading, despite its widespread use in American schools. The effects of within-class ability grouping for gifted learners may be extrapolated from the combined syntheses of the Kuliks' (1982, 1984, 1990) and Vaughn et al. (1991) meta-analysis of research on enrichment pull-out programs. There is every reason to believe that such forms of ability grouping, although short-term, are extremely beneficial to gifted learners when the materials for those groupings have been appropriately differentiated.

Cooperative grouping for regular instruction. Robinson's (1990) exhaustive search of the literature was unable to uncover any solid research to substantiate academic achievement gains for gifted learners when placed in cooperative settings with students of mixed ability. Studies on the efficacy of cooperative grouping with students of Re ability have been conducted primarily at the college level in mathematics (e.g., Fullilove & Treisman, 1990), but this small database is far from generalizable at this point. There is no question that previous research syntheses have established the academic efficacy of some forms of cooperative learning for average, low ability, special education, ethnically diverse, and economically disadvantaged learners (Johnson, Maruyama, Johnson, Nelson, & Skon, 1981; Slavin, 1990b), but a similar pattern for enhanced learning has not been effectively established for gifted learners.

Question Two: What Are the Academic Effects of These Grouping Options for Gifted Learners?

Keeping in mind that a mean or median effect size of +.30 is generally considered the level at which gains are considered practically significant or "substantial," the following effect sizes have been reported for the grouping options listed previously. As can be seen in Table 21.1,

TABLE 21.1 Academic Effect Sizes of Program Options for Gifted Students

Option	Academic Effect Size
Early Entrance to School	.39
Subject Acceleration	.49
Curriculum Compaction	.45
Grade Skipping	.78
Enrichment (pull-out)	.65
Ability-Grouped Enriched Classes	.33
Cross-grade Grouping (reading, math)	.45
Nongraded Classes	.38
Concurrent Enrollment	.36
Regrouping for Specific Instruction (reading, math)	.43
Advanced Placement	.29
Credit by Examination	.75
Cluster Grouping (specific differentiation)	.33
Cooperative Learning/Johnsons "Learning together"	.0
Ability-Grouped Enriched Classes	.33
Slavin's TGT	.38
Slavin's STL (combination)	.30
Grade Telescoping	.56
Mentorship	.42

the academic gains are substantial for a wide variety of grouping options for gifted learners. Care should be taken, however, in comparing the effect size estimates across program options. In some cases, the effect size represents a onetime comparative gain, and for other options, that gain may be cumulative. Likewise, a higher effect size does not automatically represent a superior program option, such that we can take the program with the highest effect size and eliminate all programs with smaller effect sizes. The individual variations in organization, personnel, population demographics, and culture from school to school may be more important to the success of a particular program option than the numbers reported here.

Question Three: What Are Potential Socialization and Psychological Effects of These Grouping Options?

If we assume that by socialization we are including knowledge of social skills, social maturity, participation in extracurricular activities, leadership activities, and peer interaction ratings, very few forms of grouping have been tested for socialization effects. No such research has been located for full-time or short-term ability grouping between or across grade levels. Socialization outcomes have been studied for some accelerative options involving grouping. No differences in socialization have been found when gifted students are placed in nongraded classrooms or allowed early admission to college (having skipped twelfth grade). Moderate gains (< .30 > .20) have been reported for grade telescoping and Advanced Placement programs. There has

been no research reported on the socialization effects of subject acceleration or with curriculum compacting.

The research is a little less sparse on the psychological effects of grouping when we include self-esteem, confidence, emotional development, emotional health, creativity, risk-taking, and independence as part of the definition of psychological effects. The Kuliks (Kulik, 1985; Kulik & Kulik, 1984, 1990) traced differential effects on self-esteem by ability levels in multitrack studies (that is, all students in a school were placed in one or three tracks), finding that self-esteem decreases somewhat for gifted and average learners, but improves somewhat for low ability students. For gifted learners placed in full-time special programs, no differences in self-esteem could be established across the 14 studies that have dealt with this research question. Finally, in Vaughn et al.'s (1991) meta-analysis of enrichment pull-out programs, a slight improvement in self-esteem was noted across the four studies that measured this effect. Rogers's best-evidence synthesis reported small gains in self-esteem for nongraded classrooms and early admission to college, a small decline in self-esteem for subject acceleration, no differences in esteem for Advanced Placement and grade telescoping, and no studies on self-esteem reported for curriculum compacting.

What seems evident about the spotty research on socialization and psychological effects when grouping by ability is that no pattern of improvement or decline can be established. It is likely that there are many personal, environmental, family, and other extraneous variables that affect self-esteem and socialization more directly than the practice of grouping itself.

Question Four: Are There Some Concerns We Should Have About Grouping Gifted Learners Together?

The concerns that have been raised by Oakes (1985) and George (1988) must be thoroughly investigated from all perspectives, and the real causes of the concerns must be identified if they are not found to be caused by the action of grouping itself. In Oakes's ethnographic study of 25 schools, she found differences in the morale of teachers assigned to different levels of tracking. She described differences in their expectations of students and differences in the strategies they chose to use with their assigned students. She found greater numbers of ethnic minorities and the economically disadvantaged in the lower track classes. Although none of the differences she noted could be statistically substantiated, it is important to ascertain that these differences do not stem from conscious, systematic decisions to discriminate against any group of students.

Gamoran and Berends (1987), in their synthesis of research studies similar to Oakes's, could find no studies that suggested such discrimination. The work of Haller (Haller & Davis, 1983; Haller, 1985) in recent years has even appeared to confirm that placement decisions are directly influenced by teachers' perceptions of a student's previous and present performance. No evidence could be fund that teachers or counselors use racial or social information about students in making decisions about their placement. Even so, the situation remains: ethnic minorities and the economically disadvantaged have been overrepresented in low track and "basic" classes. It is important that we change this

situation, seek to understand its causes, while at the same time we continue to provide appropriate ability grouping options to our identified gifted and talented.

Concerns also about separating gifted students for special programs and thereby giving them no opportunities to learn to appreciate the diversity in their society must also be addressed through further research. There are no easy answers to these concerns. Would full-time heterogeneous classes produce more or less appreciation for diversity among age peers? Who would benefit from this full-time mixing? Oakes (1985) and George (1988) would say all students would be better prepared for the ethnically diverse society we have begun to encounter, but Slavin (1987b), among others, has voiced some concern over the one-classroom-fits-all methods full-time mixed-ability classrooms tend to create. In his meta-analysis of research on group-based mastery learning, he generalized this concern well beyond mastery learning itself:

Is mastery learning a Robin Hood approach to instruction? Several critics (e.g., Arlin, 1984; Resnick, 1977) have wondered whether mastery learning simply shifts a constant amount of learning from high to low achievers. The evidence from the present review is not inconsistent with that view: in several studies positive effects were found for low achievers only. In fact, given that overall achievement means are not greatly improved by group-based mastery learning, the reductions in standard deviations routinely seen in studies of these methods and corresponding decreases in correlations between pretests and posttests are simply statistical indicators of a shift in achievement from high to low achievers.

However, it is probably more accurate to say that group-based mastery learning trades coverage for mastery. Because rapid coverage is likely to be of greatest benefit to high achievers while high mastery is of greatest benefit to low achievers, resolving the coverage-mastery dilemma as recommended by mastery learning theorists is likely to produce a "Robin Hood" effect as a by-product.

It is important to note that the coverage vs. mastery dilemma exists in all whole-class group-paced instruction, and the "Robin Hood" effect may be produced in traditional instruction. For example, Arlin and Westbury (1976) compared individualized instruction to whole-class instruction and found that the instructional pace set by the teachers using the whole-class approach was equal to that of students in the twenty-third percentile of the class ability distribution. Assuming that an instructional pace appropriate for students at the twenty-third percentile is too slow for higher achievers (Barr, 1974, 1975), then whole-class instruction in effect holds back high achievers for the benefit of low achievers. Group-based mastery learning may thus be accentuating a "Robin Hood" tendency already present in the class-paced traditional models to which it has been compared. (Slavin, 1987b, pp. 50–51)

What might this extensive quotation say in answer to Question Four? Perhaps only that it is important that research produced in the next few years attribute the correct causes to observed effects. It is probable that research will eventually figure out what factors directly lead to lower morale, differences in ethnic representation, differences in instructional quality, and differences in students' motivation to learn. In the meantime, it is important to consider not "throwing the baby out with the bathwater." Grouping continues to be an effective format for instructing a narrower range of ability more appropriately. There is nothing in the research at present to suggest that not grouping by ability is more effective or appropriate for any level of ability or achievement.

Question Five: What Might Be the Costs of Not Providing Grouping for Gifted Learners?

Based on what the research says about the effects of grouping the gifted, the removal of opportunities for these students to learn at the pace and level of complexity with others like themselves may conceivably result in substantial declines in achievement and attitude toward the subjects being studied. With the current emphasis on the mastery of outcomes rather than coverage of content, gifted learners may receive less access to knowledge and process than they have had previously in special programs of enrichment and acceleration. This in turn may lead to an even more precipitous decline in national test scores than we have already been witnessing since the 1960s.

In Conclusion

Gifted learners need some form of grouping by ability to effectively and efficiently accomplish several educational goals, including appropriately broadened, extended, and accelerated curricula. They must be in groups so that their school curriculum may be appropriately broadened and extended. The pacing of instruction, the depth of content, and advancement in knowledge fields, which these students must have, cannot be effectively facilitated without a variety of ability-grouped arrangements. At the same time, means must be found to address the concerns of Oakes and George as well as to address the legitimate criticisms of tracking put forth by Slavin. Just as we readily acknowledge the complexity of the learning process, we must acknowledge that no simple solution will be found to remedy the complex issues surrounding ability-grouped classes. One size does not fit all, whether that solution involves mixed-ability classroom conformations or ability grouping in one or many of its forms. Likewise, there are no easy answers to the questions raised here.

REFERENCES

Fullilove, R. E., & Treisman, P. U. (1990). Mathematics achievement among African American undergraduates at the University of California, Berkeley: An evaluation of the Mathematics Workshop Program. Journal of Negro Education, 59, 463–478.

Gamoran, A., & Berends, M. (1987). The effects of stratification in secondary schools: Synthesis of survey and ethnographic research. Review of Educational Research, 57, 415–435.

George, P. S. (1988). What's the truth about tracking and ability grouping really??? Gainesville, FL: Teacher Education Resources.

Glass, G. V. (1976). Primary, secondary, and meta-analysis of research. Educational Researcher, 5(10), 3–8.

Glass, G. V., McGaw, B., & Smith, M. L. (1981). Meta-analysis in social research. Beverly Hills, CA: Sage.

Glass, McGaw, & Smith. (1981). Hafler, E. J. (1985). Pupil race and elementary school ability grouping: Are teachers biased against Black children? American Educational Research Journal, 22, 465–483.

Haller, E. J. (1985). Pupil race and elementary school ability grouping: Are teachers biased against Black children? American Educational Research Journal, 22, 465–483.

Haller, E. J., & Davis, S. A. (1983). Teacher perceptions, parental social status, and grouping for reading instruction. Sociology of Education, 54, 162–174.

Johnson, D. W., & Johnson, R. T. (1990). What to say to people concerned with the education of high-ability and gifted students. Unpublished manuscript, University of Minnesota, Minneapolis.

Johnson, D. W., Maruyama, G., Johnson, R., Nelson, D., & Skon, L. (1981). Effects of cooperative, competitive, and individualistic goal structures on achievement: A meta-analysis. Psychological Bulletin 89, 47–62.

Kulik, C. C. (1985). Effects of inter-class ability grouping on achievement and self-esteem. Paper presented at the annual convention of the American Psychological Association. Los Angeles, CA.

Kulik, C. C., & Kulik, J. A. (1984). Effects of ability grouping on elementary school pupils: A meta-analysis. Paper presented at the annual meeting of the American Psychological Association, Ontario, Canada.

Kulik, J. A., & Kulik, C. C. (1982). Effects of ability grouping on secondary school students: A meta-analysis of evaluation findings. American Educational Research Journal, 19, 415–428.

Kulik, J. A., & Kulik, C. C. (1984). Effects of accelerated instruction on students. Review of Educational Research, 54, 409–425.

Kulik, J. A., & Kulik, C. C. (1990). Ability grouping and gifted students. In N. Colangelo & G. A. Davis (Eds.), Handbook of gifted education. Boston: Allyn & Bacon.

Oakes, J. (1985). Keeping track: How schools structure inequality. New Haven, CT: Yale University Press.

Oakes, J. (1990). Beyond tracking: Making the best of schools. Paper presented for Cocking Lecture at the 44th Annual NCPEA Conference, California State University, Los Angeles.

Robinson, A. (1990). Point-Counterpoint: Cooperation or exploitation? The argument against cooperative learning for talented students. Journal for the Education of the Gifted, 14, 9–27.

Rogers, K. B. (1991). A best-evidence synthesis of the research on accelerative options for gifted students. Unpublished doctoral dissertation, University of Minnesota, Minneapolis.

Slavin, R. E. (1987a). Ability grouping: A best-evidence synthesis. Review of Educational Research, 57, 293–336.

Slavin, R. E. (1987b). Mastery learning reconsidered. Review of Educational Research, 57, 175–213.

Slavin, R. E. (1990a). Achievement effects of ability grouping in secondary schools: A best-evidence synthesis. Review of educational Research, 60, 471–499.

Slavin, R. E. (1990b). Cooperative learning: Theory, research, and practice. Englewood Cliffs, NJ: Prentice-Hall.

Van Tassel–Baska, J. (1991). Identification of candidates for acceleration: Issues and concerns. In W. T. Southern & E. D. Jones (Eds.), The academic acceleration of gifted children (pp. 148–161). New York: Teachers College Press.

Vaughn, V., Feldhusen, J. F., & Asher, J. W. (1991). Meta-analysis and review of research on pull-out programs in gifted education. Gifted Child Quarterly, 35, 92–98.

Frank Smith

Let's Declare Education a Disaster and Get On with Our Lives

I have a serious suggestion to make. We should stop worrying about the problems of education, declare it a disaster, and let teachers and students get on with their lives. The trouble with the endless concern over "problems" in education is that many well-meaning but often misguided and sometimes meddlesome people believe that solutions must exist. They waste their own and other people's time and energy trying to find and implement these solutions. Typically, they try harder to do more of something that is already being done (although what is being done is probably one of the problems).

However, if education is a disaster, then it is not a collection of problems to be "solved," and trying to "improve" what we are already doing will only make the situation worse. You don't find solutions to disasters—you try to extricate yourself and other people from them. The way to survive a disaster is to do something different.

When the *Titanic* hit the iceberg, the people aboard had a problem: the vessel was leaking. They could have tried to solve this problem by making the ship watertight again and continuing the voyage. But when the *Titanic* began irrevocably to sink, they had a disaster. They had

to try to get everyone away in lifeboats—something they would have done better had they turned their backs on their problems sooner and concentrated on saving themselves and one another.

Education is not the only condition of our lives that should be regarded as a disaster rather than as a set of problems. The environment, the economy, health care, arms proliferation, universal hunger, drug abuse, and the state of our cities are a few other instances that spring easily to mind. To take just one example, politicians promise to attack "the problems" of the economy—or of the deficit or of unemployment—with all kinds of solutions. These promises are never fulfilled. Whatever politicians do—or don't do—the situation persists or gets worse, unless chance circumstances temporarily make it better.

I don't claim to be an economist, so I have no solutions to propose to these economic problems. But you don't need to be a doctor to know when someone is sick. And all the technical expertise in the world won't help when the patient is dead. I don't think our economic dilemmas can be solved, certainly not the way anyone currently in charge is going about it. Economists have been attacking the problems of the economy for years, and

379

the economy keeps getting worse. The economy is a disaster. Economists are always ready to blame someone else (even one another) for the chronic mess. But at least some economists must have been responsible for where we are today, unless the economy is out of their control, in which case economists can't do anything about it and should give up saying that they can.

Why do we think there must be "solutions" to so many of life's most conspicuous difficulties? Why do we try so perversely to teach problem solving in our problem-ridden schools and even in our teacher training institutions? Perhaps rose-tinted human nature—with its pride, optimism, blindness, self-delusion, and even self-interest—leads us to regard all our adversities as temporary blips on an untroubled horizon. Perhaps it is our nature to keep trying to patch the sinking ship. But problems can be insoluble, and when they are, it is better to recognize the fact. Disasters are a different state of affairs from problems, and they call for different behavior. You have a problem when your roof leaks, and you should try to find a way to patch it up. If the roof falls in on you, patching won't help. You have a disaster, and you should start tunneling your way out.

An Educational Disaster

To present an example of a current educational disaster, I shall briefly examine "assessment." I could have selected accountability, ability grouping, grading, curriculum design, special education, intervention programs, direct instruction, computer-based or computer-managed instruction, "excellence," "standards" (the latest smokescreen), educational bureau-

cracies, or any number of other manifestations of "problem solving" while education burns. But assessment will do.

I recently attended a three-day conference of literacy teachers. The conference began and ended well, with teachers talking about their classroom experiences and research. But the second day, a day entirely devoted to presentations and discussions on the topic of assessment, was a time-wasting shambles.

People left that second day's sessions more depressed and confused about assessment than when they arrived. The speakers clearly would have preferred to talk about their own teaching and their own students. But assessment was the topic and had to be confronted, so they were doing the best they could. Members of the audience wanted to hear of ways to do assessment that would interfere minimally with their normal lives, and they would have preferred to hear that assessment was being abolished. No one believed that assessment would help beginners on their journey to literacy or teachers in their efforts to help readers, though a few well-intentioned people tried to find excuses for the pernicious practice. They simply couldn't believe that assessment had no redeeming features. But no one claimed that assessment solved a single problem.

I am not criticizing the organizers of the conference; in fact, I think their planning made perfect sense. Assessment takes up at least a third of the time and energy of many classroom teachers, and the situation is getting worse, not better. As the "progress" that assessment is supposed to ensure fails to materialize, more and "better" assessment is expected to remedy the situation.

Assessment—or maintaining pressure on people caught in the system—is the only thing many politicians can think of when they take a problem-solving approach to education. George Bush claimed to be the Education President, but the best he could come up with for improving schools was to have more tests. In 1989 he called on state governors to find ways to make American education more effective. At that time, President Clinton chaired the education panel of the National Governors' Association. He called for tough national standards and a national assessment system in core subjects. The government in Britain persistently takes the same approach. I am reminded of the old Mickey Rooney/Judy Garland movies on late-night television. Whenever the flagging plot begins to fall apart, Mickey suggests, "Let's put on a show!" In education, the cry is always "Let's put on a test!"

Anyone would think that assessment was a new idea. But tests have been proliferating in education for the best part of a century, ever since the development of mental testing within the eugenics movement. Since 1910 no fewer than 148 standardized reading and achievement tests for elementary students have been published in the United States, and only 34 of them have gone out of print.[1] Presumably, more than a hundred are still in circulation and use, their numbers constantly increasing. Yet no one can demonstrate that any test has ever had a beneficial effect on education.

Even the people who want assessment are confused. I attended another conference recently that tried to dispose of the testing issue in the first hour. The district superintendent of instruction and assessment was supposed to outline his plans for new assessment procedures. He quickly re-

vealed that he had no clear idea of what *he* expected to accomplish, let alone what was expected of the teachers, and no idea of how assessment might help teachers, let alone students. All he wanted was *numbers*—any kind of numbers—to pass on to other people. He could not relate teaching to testing except to admonish the teachers he was addressing not to teach to the tests. This only added to the teachers' confusion. The conference barely recovered in the two days of serious work that followed the opening presentation.

Assessment has become a full-fledged disaster in its own right. It is discriminatory, and it stigmatizes and disempowers individuals for life. It doesn't encourage anyone to read, write, learn, or think, though it does leave students and teachers frustrated, confused, despondent, resentful, and angry. I don't think assessment has any redeeming features, but, if it has, we are paying an exorbitant price for them. Assessment spawns difficulties faster than they can be dealt with. We don't need more tests or better tests; we need to extricate ourselves from tests.

The Growth of Systems

Charitably, I have been referring to education and the economy as "systems"—but this is a widespread misnomer. Systems, by definition, are organized, integrated, orderly, predictable, and functional. There is not a good term for what education is today—at least, not a euphemistic one. Education is disorganized and disorderly, unplanned and dysfunctional, like assertions of crustaceans on tidal rocks, like a metastasizing growth, or like an accident in progress.

We delude ourselves when we think of education (or the economy) as something coherent, logical, and rational that human beings have reflected upon and *designed* with a clear purpose in mind, like the internal combustion engine, a jet aircraft, or even the common teakettle.

Chance has no doubt played its part in the development of automobile engines and other human artifacts, but by and large they have been designed and developed by people with a clear understanding of the place and purpose of each part and of the system as a whole. Over time, parts that prove unnecessary are discarded; parts that don't do their job are replaced; parts that work imperfectly are improved until superseded by a superior alternative. A visitor from outer space could inspect an automobile engine in working condition and figure out how and why it was conceived and put together. I remember some good advice from the days when the manuals for appliances made sense. Owners of a particular device were given a list of things that might go wrong and for each fault briskly advised to "find problem and rectify." If the problem could not be promptly found and rectified, the device was to be replaced.

Education is not like that. Its various parts do not fit together into some coherently conceived whole. It is not a consequence of comprehensive planning or even of rationality. It has just grown. Since humans first walked the earth, people everywhere have doubtless tried to raise their young in their own idealized image and tried also to help them develop important abilities. Different cultures cultivated different educational beliefs and customs, which weathered with time and changed as a result of contact, conflict, accident, and all manner of bright or crazy ideas. Education was never *planned*; it could always have been different. There is no *ideal* educational system. Education has always been too big to control, to comprehend, or even to *imagine* in all its detail. If education now appears impervious to change, it is not because it could not be different—it clearly could and will be—but because it is hampered by the vast inertial mass of its own complexity. Education doesn't advance; it drifts.

The uncontrolled and happenstantial development of education is not unique. This is the way most of the significant and universal influences in our lives have come about.

Language is another example. Despite the widespread assumptions to the contrary, language is neither a rational design nor an ideal system. No one knows how language began. Indeed, it is probably misleading even to think of language as having a beginning. I suspect that it arose imperceptibly out of other aspects of people's lives, among different peoples, at different times, in different places, and in different ways. No one designed or invented it. As people interacted across cultures and generations, language inevitably changed, but not in planned or predictable ways. All the languages of the world must be compatible with human physical and mental structures, but beyond those constraints they have always differed enormously and still do today, with more than 3,000 languages and innumerable dialects still in existence.

Languages literally evolve. Every element of language has arisen by a kind of random mutation and survived by finding an ecological niche in the brains of human beings—by being useful and comprehensible, for a time at least. Sometimes people try a new way of saying something. Sometimes "mistakes" persist. Sometimes there is borrowing or adoption as different languages come into contact. Some aspects of language grow, as people find new applications for them, while other aspects wither from disuse. No one is in control of the whole thing or of any significant part of it. Efforts to take charge of language inevitably fail. And efforts to change the way people use language are always linked and rarely lasting. Language constantly gets away from us. It is like a turbulent stream that we can swim in but not divert.

Mathematics is the same. Like language, mathematics doubtless developed in many separate places and in many small ways. No one planned what it should be today, and no one can foresee where it will be tomorrow. People wander through continents of mathematics that have been found and sometimes lost again. More mathematics exists than any one person could know, and no group could claim to *direct* mathematics in any substantial way. It is what it is. It might easily have been different, and it will be different in the future.

Many other significant aspects of our lives have developed in the same uncontrollable way. The growth of cities has been largely unplanned and is beyond control despite our best efforts. Such hydra-headed monsters cannot be controlled. The media are out of control. "News" is consumed faster than it is produced, the trivial is raised to ephemeral significance, and the significant is reduced to lasting triviality. Legal systems are out of control. More laws are written than anyone can read, let alone put into practice, and efforts to rationalize the "legal system" lead to even more laws, more confusion, and more lawyers. Publishing is out of control. Publishers can't afford to publish books that are different from those their competitors publish, and everyone concentrates on a few well-mined areas where the chance for massive sales exists. The development and use of computer technology are clearly out of control; no one can keep up. I could go on, but I would soon get out of control myself.

One thing is always overlooked: *history*. Many people seem to think that history is something in the past that doesn't affect us now. But the reason we are where we are today with education, the economy, the internal combustion engine, language, mathematics, the law, and everything else, *is* history. We can't escape what has happened in the past; every past incident has contributed to our present condition. History is not a series of steps by which we got to the present; it is the mold in which we are formed, the block of concrete in which our feet are inescapably set. History is not a problem we can "solve." Time can't be rolled back, and there are no orderly states to which situations that have become chaotic can be returned.

It may sound pessimistic and despairing to say that so much that seems central to our lives is beyond our control. But I do not feel pessimistic. There are alternatives, if only we open our minds to them, and I maintain my faith in people (people in general, not necessarily people in authority). We must simply stop trying to patch up the vessel we find ourselves on. We need to lower the lifeboats and row for new and probably unfamiliar shores. We have to begin by changing the way we think.

Changing the Way We Think About Education

Many of our troubles in education arise from the fact that we are so concerned about *learning*. I would go so far as to suggest that all our talk about learning is counterproductive and that we should (if we could control language) stop using the word. I know it will be argued that learning is the entire purpose of education, but that doesn't mean that it should demand all our attention—or even most of it. Learning is an outcome, not a process, and if we focus only on the outcome, then we can easily get necessary preconditions all wrong.

Let me start with an analogy. We are concerned that children should grow physically, say an average of two inches a year over a particular period of their lives, and that their body temperature should stay close to a healthy 98.6 degrees Fahrenheit. These are desirable outcomes, but in raising children we don't continually focus on the achievement of these states of affairs. We don't stretch or shrink children to ensure they are the right size, nor do we constantly warm or refrigerate them so that their temperature stays at the approved level. We are more concerned with clothing and nourishing them properly. Our concern should always be with those conditions in which growth is a natural and inevitable outcome.

Learning is simply an outcome, even a by-product. It is a consequence of experience (including imaginative experience) that is meaningful, that we can participate in and relate to ourselves. Since such experience involves personal identification and mutual collaboration, I refer to it metaphorically as "membership in clubs."[2] We do not necessarily seek experience in order to learn (though learning may be part of the joy of many experiences). Our primary concern and aim is to have the experience, and the learning follows. In education, we

should ensure that students have access to appropriately "nourishing" experiences so that learning comes about naturally and inevitably.

Here's a foretaste of my final argument: we should concentrate our attention on the kinds of experience that students have in schools, not on what they learn. Learning comes with doing sensible and interesting things. We should not be concerned with *teaching* children to read (an outcome) but with *helping* them to read (a means or a series of experiences). Focusing on the reading outcome leads to bizarre behavior and attitudes, from the mindless promotion of "skills-based" exercises to diagnoses of imaginary mental deficiencies. Focusing on experience means that every child has optimum opportunity for the outcome to occur naturally. As many researchers have shown and as Stephen Krashen has very conveniently summarized, the result of "free voluntary reading" is that students learn just about everything that we strive so hard to teach them about reading—and much more besides.[3]

Learning is usually seen as an incremental activity. We are supposed to learn by adding bits of knowledge or information to the store we have already accumulated. Every new thing learned is another block added to the tower of what we know already, another item in the cognitive data bank. Occasionally, we talk about learning as "growth" or "development," but we are usually not referring to the way a tree or the human body grows. Natural growth is not additive. Babies do not grow by having successive inches added to their height. The increase in their height is simply an indicator that the entire organism has developed, not necessarily at the same rate or in the same proportion in all directions. A 20-pound baby is not the equivalent of two 10-pound babies, one on top of the other. Nor does the larger infant have more limbs or more organs.

Learning, like physical growth, is not a consequence of external pressure; we don't even learn as a result of trying harder. All of us have experienced failure to learn something that we wanted to learn, despite intense motivation and effort. Yet other things we make no particular effort to memorize—like major news items, gossip, the scores in a sport in which we are interested, and even the antics of characters in television sitcoms—seem to become imprinted on our minds without effort.

The reason is the difference between learning and rote memorization, which boosters of testing and instructional planning totally overlook. Deliberate memorization—such as rehearsing facts until we take a test or holding a telephone number in our minds until we can dial it—requires conscious effort. The forced ingestion of facts and data is useless for educational purposes. It has a half-life of a few hours, at most a few days. After the examination we rarely remember much of what we tried to cram into our minds before it. What we remember from fruitless efforts to memorize is the stress and the failure inevitably involved.

Learning is also like physical growth in that it usually occurs without our being aware of it, it is long-lasting, and it requires a nurturing environment. It takes place as a result of social relationships (including relationships with the authors of books and with characters in books), and it pivots on personal identification. We learn from the kind of person we see ourselves as being like. Such conditions are annihilated by information-transmission teaching and constant tests.

Saving Ourselves and Our Students

I have a couple of suggestions about how teachers might begin to save themselves and their students from the overcontrolled, overmanaged, oversystematized, and overresearched disaster that is education. The first is to change the way we talk about schools, and the second is to change the way we behave in them.

We should change the way we talk about schools by talking less about learning and teaching and more about *doing*. When we focus on teaching specific skills, students frequently fail to learn them and rarely become enthusiastic about engaging in them voluntarily. When we concern ourselves with engaging students in interesting and comprehensible activities, then they learn. All of them may not learn at the same time, at the same rate, or even with the same enthusiasm. But such individual variation is inevitable, and we must recognize and accept it. Homogenization never works in education, nor should we want to expect it to.

Doesn't what I'm suggesting here conflict with my remarks about being unable to control language? Quite the reverse; we must accept that the meanings of the words *teach* and *learn* have changed and try to modify the way in which we use them. "Teach" once meant "to show," and "learn" once meant "to hear about something." But now the words are more likely to be defined as the "dissemination" (or transmission) and the "acquisition" of information and knowledge. We may not be able to change other people's use of the words, but we can focus attention on what is actually going on in the name of teaching and learning in schools.

Instead of talking all the time about what teachers should teach and what students should learn, we should talk about what teachers and students should do. We should talk about experiences that they should be mutually engaged in—experiences involving reading, writing, imagining, creating, calculating, constructing, producing, and performing. Can't think of any? Sorry—but you must use your imagination (and that of your students), not rely on experts or authorities outside the classroom to tell you.

I am talking about the *climate* of classrooms and schools. Like the climate of the world outside, the climate of a classroom is very easy to detect. You don't have to ask anyone if it is raining as you walk down a street, nor do you need any special tests to find out if the sun is shining. You just have to look to see if the streets are wet or if the trees cast shadows.

You don't need to ask anyone or to apply formal tests to see if everyone in a classroom is engaged in meaningful activity. You just look. It is easy to see if the students—and the teacher—are interested, engaged, and collaborative or bored, confused, and withdrawn. (Of course, students have to be present and behaving normally. There's not much to learn if the classroom is empty or if all the students stand respectfully mute and immobile in the visitor's presence.)

We must get away from the idea that everything would be fine with our educational institutions if only teachers and students worked harder. That is why we should no longer talk about schools in the language that has made them what they are today. Attempting to "improve" the current rituals of schools or to do them more assiduously will only make matters worse. Education is on the wrong track largely because of "solutions" that have socially isolated teachers and students from one another and from sensible ways of spending their time.

Lifeboats

"Women and children first" is supposed to be the call when a ship is going down. Not greatly amended to "Save teachers and students first," it might also be considered an appropriate cry for education. Don't cling to the doomed structure of the foundering education system, but strike out to save the passengers and crew. (Officers on the bridge, of course, prefer to go down with the ship, don't they?)

How should teachers save themselves and their students? By getting themselves into lifeboats that can survive the turbulent waters and make their way to secure havens. What are these lifeboats? Any situation that preserves the self-respect of teachers and students, that naturally involves reading, writing, and other activities that we want students to engage in. These are the activities we should be free to concentrate on in classrooms, without pressure or manipulation from outside.

Added to this should be some consciousness-raising so that teachers and students come to a better understanding of the educational leviathan into whose service they have been press-ganged and of the directions in which it is currently heading. Sadder even than teachers taught that the system they work in is rational and functional—so that any failure must be their own—are students taught to believe the same things.

All teachers do good things some of the time, and all good teachers do bad things some of the time. The differences among teachers lie not only in the proportions of the good and the bad, but also in their awareness of the effects of what they are doing and in their readiness to share this awareness with their students. While striving always to do more that is beneficial and less that is damaging, teachers must also protect themselves and their students from those adverse aspects of their situation that cannot immediately be changed.

I can hear a lot of people on the rails of the *Titanic* looking down at the lifeboats bobbing on the cold ocean, and objecting, "Yes, but. . . . "

Yes, but we live in a culture based on grades. Parents want grades, students want grades, and parents want to know how well their children are doing relative to other students in the class. Such objections only demonstrate the extent of the disaster. Parents and students have been "educated" to believe that what the system has become is more important than what the system is supposed to do. At one time it would have been ludicrous for parents interested in knowing what their children were learning at school to be fobbed off with a grade-point average or a relative position in the class. They would want to know what their children could *do*.

Yes, but you're not giving us any *specific* suggestions about what teachers should do when they cast off from the ship.

That's because I don't have any specific suggestions, because I don't believe that anyone has the right to tell teachers what to do or that any teacher has the right to expect to be told. Decisions should be made in the lifeboats, not on the sinking liner or from the distant shore. Teachers should *know* when their students are doing (and learning) worthwhile things and when their students are doing (and learning) things that will be damaging to their personal and social development. (Teachers who don't know the difference shouldn't be in a classroom.) Teachers need support, and they need to share experience. But the way to achieve these ends is through collegiality, not through hierarchical structures. Teachers must save themselves, and they can best do that by observing and supporting one another.

The education system may not be amenable to change—but people are. Every meaningful situation in school that is interesting, comprehensible, and encouraging to everyone concerned is another lifeboat launched. This is something that all teachers should be able to recognize and accomplish; the world is full of teachers who are already doing so. And if teachers can't get their students on one lifeboat, they must be sure that they get aboard another. There must be enough lifeboats to provide a constant shuttle from the disaster of the education system to the sanctuary of teachers and students mutually engaged in sensible and productive activities, which are the sole justification for education.

NOTES

1. Peggy VanLeirsburg, "Standardized Reading Tests: Then and Now," in Jerry L. Johns,

ed., *Literacy: Celebration and Challenge* (Bloomington: Illinois Reading Council, 1993), pp. 31–54.

2. Frank Smith, *Joining the Literacy Club* (Portsmouth, N.H.: Heinemann Educational Books, 1988).

3. Stephen D. Krashen, *The Power of Reading: Insights from the Research* (Englewood, Colo.: Libraries Unlimited, 1993).

CHAPTER 23

Eleanor Blair Hilty

The Professionally Challenged Teacher
Teachers Talk About School Failure

Public schools have occupied an important place in the growth and progress of the United States. The aims and purposes of these schools often have shifted as they have been asked to address and even ameliorate a wide range of social ills. Public schools seemed to capture the spirit and dreams of a new country seeking to merge the lives and identities of many people into something uniquely American. These early schools can even be considered innovative, in the sense that they were envisioned by our predecessors as a democratic solution to the education issue. Private schools for the elite would continue to exist, but public schools provided a vehicle for the masses to acquire formal schooling and benefit from the "uplifting" effect of a general education. Greene (1985) argues, "Surely it is an obligation of education in a democracy to empower the young to become members of the public, to participate, and play articulate roles in the public space" (p. 4). Public schools in America became the cornerstone for this philosophical orientation; the place where equality of opportunity translated to equality of *educational* opportunity. To many people

it seemed essential that we provide a free, public education that would be common to *all* children and teach common values, beliefs, and attitudes necessary for participation in the democratic process and responsible citizenry. In a relatively short period of time, *common* schools became the norm in this country, and they rapidly were accompanied by the emergence of compulsory school laws encouraging law-abiding parents to entrust the public schools with the primary responsibility for educating their children. Thus, over the past 150 years, an increasing number of school-age children have attended public schools that attempt to provide for all children the prerequisite knowledge and skills for survival: cognitively, socially, politically, and economically. Despite popular beliefs to the contrary, most Americans continue to endorse the concept of a publicly supported public school, and consistently demonstrate this by sending their children to the public schools located in their communities. And, generally speaking, public schools are successful experiences for many children. However, the children for whom the public schools are not successful experiences are increasingly the source of concern, and the subject of considerable debate, in discussions of school reform.

Perhaps it is not surprising that we have placed upon this institution tremendous expectations for the exercise of democratic principles and the provision of equality of educational opportunity. Beane and Apple (1995) consider the relationship of these democratic ideals to discussions of school reform:

> Many of our most trusted and powerful ideas about schooling are the hard-won gains of long and courageous efforts to make our schools more democratic. We are the beneficiaries of those efforts, and we have an obligation to carry forward the demanding dream of public schools for a democratic society. . . . Although our memories may have become blurred, we can still recall that public schools are essential to democracy. We cannot help but be jolted wide awake when discussions about what works in schools, what should be done in schools, make no mention of the role of public schools in expanding the democratic way of life. (p. 4)

Unfortunately, the public schools are forced to regularly address the contradictions inherent in discussions of "equality of educational opportunity." Does "equality of educational opportunity" mean an "equal chance" or an "equal share"? The competing tensions between the pursuit of equity *and* that of excellence in public schools have characterized most discussions of failure and, consequently, most recommendations for reform. Is it possible to do both—provide equitable educational ex-

periences *and* promote excellence in the schools? For example, the much-publicized *America 2000* was a strategy initiated by President Bush in 1991 for achieving six National Education Goals for reforming and restructuring American education through an emphasis on excellence in our public schools. This effort was supported by the governors of all 50 states and thus recognizes the overall importance of the role played by public schools. However, the reconciliation of attempts to provide equitable educational experiences *and* promote excellence is difficult at best. *America 2000* and the National Education Goals, subsequently devised to include two additional goals, provide support for increased rigor and higher standards for public schools. Yet this national agenda ignores the reality that characterizes the lives of an increasingly large number of children who live in poverty.

If school achievement and success are essential to one's survival in this society, what does one do with the specter of school failure in our discussions of equity *and* excellence in the public schools? How does one answer the most frequently asked question in these discussions: "Who do we blame for this problem?" Is this a social problem or an educational problem? How can it be that in a country devoted to the ideals of equal educational opportunity, so many children who come from less advantaged backgrounds fail to succeed? Erickson (1984) attempts to answer this question as follows:

> Given that for approximately 5 million years human societies have managed to rear their young so that almost every one in the society was able to master the

knowledge and skills necessary for survival, why does this not happen in modern societies with schools? Or does it happen—do schools teach what is necessary, but define and measure achievement in such ways that it looks as if large proportions of the school population fail? (p. 527)

Have public schools simply lost touch with the "knowledge and skills necessary for survival"? The education provided by many schools may lack relevance to the lives of children who come from diverse sociocultural backgrounds. In most contemporary school environments, the strict regulation of curriculum requirements and the use of standardized measures of achievement often shift the focus from "teaching the child" to "teaching the test." In this way, students are denied access to "culturally relevant teaching" and, consequently, to the knowledge and skills necessary for survival in a variety of contexts. Ladson-Billings (1994) expands this idea:

Culturally relevant teaching uses student culture in order to maintain it and to transcend the negative effects of the dominant culture. The negative effects are brought about, for example, by not seeing one's history, culture, or background represented in the textbook or curriculum or by seeing that history, culture, or background distorted. . . . Specifically, culturally relevant teaching is a pedagogy that empowers students intellectually, socially, emotionally, and politically by using cultural referents to impart knowledge, skills, and attitudes. These cultural referents are not merely vehicles for bridging or explaining the dominant culture; they

are aspects of the curriculum in their own right. (pp. 17–18)

The knowledge and skills proffered in many classrooms may be prerequisite to higher levels of academic achievement in traditionally organized educational institutions, but have little value in urban, inner-city neighborhoods or even isolated, rural communities where "survival" means very different things to very different populations of children. The skills and knowledge necessary to survive in urban ghettos or small, rural communities may be counterproductive or even mutually exclusive to the acquisition of "mainstream" values, beliefs, and attitudes.

School Failure

The American dream has always been that all children, regardless of personal circumstances, have a chance, in this country, to become anyone or anything they desire. For many children these dreams originated in classrooms and schools where hard work was rewarded by academic successes. Most important, academic success in the public schools opened up the doors of higher education and provided unlimited opportunities for high-status jobs and social mobility. This was "the dream": hard work + good schools = success! Of course, "success" as it is broadly defined can mean many things to many people, but at its simplest level, it means "choice"—a conscious choice to make dreams a reality. The reality, however, is not so simple. Schools fail, and most important, children fail. In these situations, hard work is not rewarded with success; instead the efforts of both teachers and students produce little visible evidence of those things most valued by critics of the public schools, for example, high test scores and verbally precocious, well-mannered children. The "failures" of these schools, such as dropouts or students with low levels of academic performance, offend those individuals who still believe that the American dream is alive and well. However, the truth about the "dream" is that some children consistently fail more than others, and that poor children of color in this country experience school failure at a considerably higher rate than other children. And yet, as increasing numbers of children "fail" to demonstrate the requisite skills and knowledge that would characterize a school as "successful," it would seem imperative that critical educators begin to examine this phenomenon from a broader perspective. This is a perspective that recognizes how "school failure is structurally located and culturally mediated" (McLaren, 1994, p. 216). In effect, it is a recognition of the roles played by both institutional and cultural variables that will shift the focus from solutions that isolate individual "problems" to the acknowledgement of community "problems" that begin outside of schools, but ultimately affect the "success" or "failure" of all students.

Ladson-Billings (1994) points out in this regard that "an often-asked question of people of color, women, and other marginalized groups is, 'What is it you people want?' Surprisingly for some, what these people want is not very different from what most Americans want: an opportunity to shape and share in the American dream" (p. 137). Consider the following:

> The American commitment to equality of opportunity is violated at its very roots by the fact that local and state governments continue to pay more for one child's education than for another's. The abiding constants of American education—equality of opportunity and meritocracy—favor existing elites and place minority students in the debt column of the ledger of academic achievement. . . . Of course, poverty is a major factor in determining the success of students at school. It is perhaps the greatest predictor of academic success in this country, which makes it disturbing to learn that in 1988, only 25 percent of three- and four-year-olds with family incomes of less than $10,000 a year were enrolled in a preschool program. Yet 56 percent of those with family incomes of $35,000 or more were enrolled. More than one-third of all children in families headed by someone younger than thirty are living in poverty. (McLaren, 1994, pp. 15–16, 23)

The tragedy is that those children who most need successful school experiences for safe passage to adulthood are those for whom these experiences are most often characterized as "failures." These children often see their future choices narrowed rather than expanded due to their school experiences.

Some of the most disturbing questions concerning school failure focus on "the strong relationship between family background and educational achievement" (Dougherty & Hammack, 1990, p. 2). Why should poor children consistently fail to achieve in schools at rates comparable to their more affluent peers? Recent projections show a growing Hispanic population, with half of these children living in poverty by 2010. Add to these figures documentation that these children often do poorly in school and drop out of school at an earlier age and a higher rate than Black or White students ("Half of Black, Hispanic Children May Be Poor by 2010," 1993). "Students who were Black or Hispanic, living in families with low income, or living in the South or West were less likely to complete high school," and the dropout rate for Hispanic students is nearly triple the national figure ("High Percentage of Female High School Dropouts Quit," 1994, p. 6A). Questions about school failure and the integrity of the school experience often are linked together, and the implications are alarming. If the public schools are to continue to function as they have in the past, then their roles and responsibilities must be redefined in such a way as to justify the consumption of vast resources under the guise of providing a free and equitable public education for the masses. Dramatic changes are, almost certainly, necessary. Yet, issues related to school failure, while complex and multidimensional, are constantly in flux. Meaningful changes in the schools must simultaneously address the needs of schools today as well as schools for the twenty-first century. What will not change, however, is the central importance of a successful educational experience, and for a majority of children that experience probably will occur in the public schools; there may be no other alternatives.

Explanations for school failure usually cannot be traced to a single variable. Rather, every aspect of the educational experience is subject to scrutiny. Familial, societal, and institutional forces frequently are interconnected, and all contribute to the net outcome of school failure. Blame often shifts back and forth between the school and the family environment. Researchers traditionally have focused on "pupils' deficiencies (lack of ability or motivation, often due to a poor home life) or teachers' deficiencies (lack of ability, poor training, or inadequate standards)" (Dougherty & Hammack, 1990, p. 3). Thus, research efforts in this area have been concerned with disputing or augmenting these "traditional" explanations. What are the intersections between the traditional explanations and those explanations that emphasize the often neglected voices of teachers and students and recognize the power of individual action? Far less information is available about the "worlds" of those teachers and students who are expected to spend 180 days a year in schools characterized by a high level of failure. It would seem apparent to the casual observer that this type of schooling experience is qualitatively different from the experiences of those teachers and students who inhabit the worlds of fairly affluent suburban schools where the focus is on school success, both individual and group. How does failure mediate the teaching and learning experiences of the inhabitants of these "other worlds"?

Teachers and Failure

Most of the time the students are the *only* source of rewards for most teachers. Isolated in their own classrooms, teachers receive feedback for their efforts from the words, expressions, behaviors, and suggestions of the students. By doing well on a test, sharing a confidence, performing a task, indicating an interest, and reporting the effects of a teacher's influence, students let teachers know that they are doing a good job and are appreciated. Unlike other professionals who look to colleagues and supervisors for such feedback, teachers can only turn to children. (Lieberman & Miller, 1990, p. 194)

Failure. Nothing else diminishes the worth and value of a teacher's work more than the pervading sense of failure that surrounds the schools attended by poor children and children of color in America. Their problems are both demographic as well as geographic. Schools in states that consistently score low on all measures of school success are perceived as inadequate and their students as inferior. These schools often suffer from a lack of resources, both economic and political. This lack of resources often leads to pejorative characterizations of the children as "at risk." What are the implications of calling poor children or children of color "at risk"? Are they really at risk only of failing to become middle class? William Ayers (1994) questions: "Is calling someone culturally deprived the same as calling them not white, not middle class? . . . Is the implication that some cultures are superior and others inferior?" (p. 10). And then what about the teachers? Teachers, both urban and rural, who work in schools characterized by high levels of failure (high dropout rates, low achievement, low levels of literacy, etc.) are a special population. Is it not possible that these teachers also can be considered an "at-risk" population? Might this be a useful categorization for teachers who are professionally challenged by the day-to-day failures they encounter in the classroom? We want to believe that good teachers don't fail, and yet we all know that is not true. It will never be satisfactory to measure the goodness and worth of a teacher's performance strictly by looking at student outcomes. And yet,

close proximity to failure carries with it a stigma. Failure is insidious to the committed professional; it feels bad personally and professionally. Public attacks on the "failures" of our schools often accompany demands for teacher accountability. Implicit in the demands for "teacher accountability" is the belief that good teachers don't fail. Viewed in this context, student failure equals teacher failure; thus, nothing affronts the professional identifies of teachers more than school failure, and all of the negative connotations that accompany these losses. Finally, to an already skeptical public, school failure is just one more reminder of the terrible inadequacies of the public schools.

My work with teachers, as a teacher educator and researcher, often has brought me face-to-face with teachers who, while basically satisfied with their roles as teachers, have complex professional lives that do not lend themselves easily to celebratory accounts of the joys of teaching. The lives of these teachers are fraught with frustrations, and the job most often is not at all what they were anticipating when they began teaching. Many of these teachers leave within the first five years of teaching. Interviews I conducted in the late 1980s (summarized in Hilty, 1987) provided the following first-person accounts of what it is like to be a teacher:

Teaching is not what I expected. When I grew up in rural West Virginia and went to school, I remember what teachers did and I remember the role that they played. There was pride in teaching. High school teachers were looked at as leaders in the community and people that you looked up to. Those days are gone. People feel, and I didn't realize this until I was teaching, it's kinda degrading to say, "I'm a high school teacher." You have to say it under your breath. I used to think people had a lot of respect for high school teachers, but I feel that they don't anymore. It's just a guy who wants to teach school is just the attitude I get now. That's kind of an embarrassment to me because I do enjoy it. (Vocational-Technical Preparation Teacher)

You're expected to do so much and you feel, it's just like well, can't you individualize for these seventeen people here, and there's no way you can individualize all day long. You're going to have to have a group, and some of them are going to get it and some of them aren't going to get it. You know, I get really frustrated with the numbers that we have. Seems like every time I turn around, there's somebody else coming in, but no more help. You get real frustrated. Most teachers, I think, would do away with money, if they could have fewer children in their room. (Middle Grades Teacher)

I would just love to work with new special education teachers and help them avoid the kinds of pitfalls that lead to nothing but frustration and feelings of doubt and lack of self-worth and all the things that go with being special education. The retarded teacher does become the *retarded* teacher rather than the teacher of children who are limited. (Special Education Teacher)

I would say the main thing that depressed me was the kids' low motivations. They didn't want to be there at all. (Middle Grades Teacher)

It seems important that we concern ourselves with the "nature" of the experience

of those teachers who do stay. How do they perceive their jobs and, most important, what is the relationship between teacher success and student success? Obviously, some teachers perceive and define their jobs in such a way that student success, as it traditionally has been defined, is not vital to their understanding of professional identity and integrity. Foster (1993) suggests:

Although there is a large body of literature on teacher thinking, planning, and practical knowledge, it does not focus specifically on successful teachers who work with students who are currently defined and pejoratively labeled as "at risk." As a result, we know little about the thinking, pedagogical processes, understandings, or considerations, of such teachers, nor do we understand how many of these teachers define their teaching situation, decide which roles and responsibilities to assume, and apply this knowledge to their practice. . . . How is it that successful teachers of "at-risk" children define their tasks and what is their understanding of the goals of successful teaching? (pp. 390–391)

Any exploration or discussion of teachers' lives ultimately must consider the relationship between student success (or lack thereof) and teachers' perceptions of their roles and responsibilities.

Is student success a reliable measure of a teacher's effectiveness or commitment? Of course not, but increasingly this view is being challenged by a focus on teacher accountability that quickly becomes narrowly defined as measurable success (i.e., increased student achievement on standardized tests). Since the late 1980s, there has been an explosion of research that provides first-person accounts of teachers' experiences in the classroom. This literature is replete with discussions of the many "failures" of our society generally and of the schools specifically. Teachers who regularly live their professional lives in environments characterized by a high level of failure have been explored only within the context of *a* successful classroom or *a* successful teacher. Whenever I read these descriptions I applaud the successful innovations of individual teachers in selected classrooms, but I also wonder, What about the rest of *them*? What are *they* doing? Were *they* equally successful? Erickson (1984) recounted the story of a young Eskimo who learned to hunt seal from his father. The young man was advised that "if you want to hunt seal you have to learn to think like a seal" (p. 527). Likewise, if one wants to understand, identify, or even train good teachers who are successful with at-risk students, one has to understand the cognitive strategies of those teachers who are successful with these students. In this chapter, I have tried to provide a forum for *those* teachers—a place where their voices can be heard; a place where others can attempt to better understand the factors that help teachers reconcile their professional identities with the phenomenon of school failure. Additionally, I have tried to consider the implications of this knowledge for all teachers, preservice and inservice.

Contextualizing School Failure

In 1987, I moved to Atlanta, Georgia, to teach at a local college. During the next six years, I had the opportunity to work with teachers from both urban and rural schools in the South. As an educational foundations professor, I was often responsible for providing a broader context for their discussions of teaching and learning as well as success and failure in schools besieged by the contemporary problems of American youth. The experience was unsettling. As I listened to these teachers, I began to notice some real differences in the ways that they perceived their experiences. Two groups of teachers seemed to emerge: those who were challenged, and even enjoyed, teaching in schools characterized by a high level of failure, and those who perceived these experiences as discouraging and hopeless. What was the difference? Was it something so simple as attitude or something more personal having to do with the "meaning" they attach to a teacher's roles and responsibilities and student success and failure? Schubert (1991) encourages researchers to recognize "*teacher lore* as a necessary and neglected construct in educational literature" (p. 207), and discusses the relevance of this kind of knowledge:

> I characterize teacher lore as the study of the knowledge, ideas, perspectives, and understandings of teachers. In part, it is inquiry into the beliefs, values, and images that guide teachers' work. In this sense, it constitutes an attempt to learn what teachers learn from their experience. Teachers are continuously in the midst of a blend of theory (their evolving ideas and personal belief systems) and practice (their reflective action); I refer to this blend as *praxis*. To assume that scholarship can focus productively on what teachers learn recognizes teachers as important partners in the creation of knowledge about education. (p. 207)

Thus, viewed in this manner, an understanding of how teachers "succeed" in environments characterized by high levels of school failure becomes an important source of information.

Initially, it was my hypothesis that these two groups of teachers were fundamentally different, but the nature of these differences was unclear. Some teachers obviously define their work in such a way that student success and teacher success are interpreted in a broader context, and that student success as we traditionally define it may not be a factor in the experience of "successful" teaching. Is it possible that these teachers succeed, where others fail, because of these differences in perception? Erickson (1986) argues that we should explore the "conditions of meaning" or "meaning systems" that enable some students to learn and others not. Perhaps we should conduct the same explorations with teachers. What "meanings" allow some teachers to succeed where others have found only failure and burnout. Psychologists tell us that past experiences and expectations mediate perceptions, and thus one might examine the worlds of successful teachers in order to better understand the manner in which they structure their experiences. It would seem that a better understanding of *who* these teachers are and *how* they define their tasks and endeavors to be "successful" teachers in environments that provide very few indicators of success (e.g., student achievement, high test scores, positive feedback, professional recognition, etc.) would be timely and appropriate. In collaboration and dialogue with these teachers, we learn that "teachers inquire deeply and their lives and stories cannot be revealed without a sense of the 'research' they live

but rarely write about" (Schubert, 1991, p. 224).

Ogbu (1990) warns social scientists that "in their eagerness to bring about change, they often design their studies not so much to understand the total situation as to discover *what is wrong* and how the situation should be changed." His final caution is worthy of consideration: "This approach leads to the wrong kinds of questions, the wrong kinds of answers and the wrong kinds of solutions" (p. 398). He is telling us that the questions we ask often determine the answers. If we talk about student failure as a family or environmental problem or even as a societal problem, we predefine and set the parameters of the research we are doing. Heeding this warning, I set out to design a study that would help me better understand and describe the phenomenon of school failure from the teacher's perspective. During the past two years I have discussed school failure with five teachers. I used life and career interviews to inquire about the teachers' personal and professional backgrounds. I conducted and recorded these interviews in the teachers' homes. Each interview lasted from 1 to 2 hours. These teachers represented a diverse group, with the common denominator being that each one elected to teach in a school characterized by a high level of student failure as it traditionally is defined. All of the schools discussed by these teachers serve students who come from less advantaged backgrounds. Children of color represented a significant portion of the student body at these schools. Two of the teachers were Black and three were White. All of these teachers would characterize themselves as middle class; however, their backgrounds reflect a broad range of both cultural and economic experiences. The range of teaching experience among these teachers ranged from 6 to 20 years. In these interviews, I posed very general and open-ended questions and tried to give teachers an opportunity to construct their own "pictures" of classroom life. After they initially told me about themselves and their educational backgrounds, I asked the following kinds of questions:

1. Tell me about teaching.
2. Tell me about the children you teach.
3. Tell me about those children who succeed in your class.
4. Tell me about those children who fail in your class.
5. Tell me how you feel when students succeed.
6. Tell me how you feel when students fail.
7. What are the satisfactions/dissatisfactions of teaching?
8. Given a choice, would you keep teaching? Would you request a transfer? Why or why not?

According to Kvale (1983), the purpose of such an interview "is to gather descriptions of the life-world of the interviewee with respect to interpretation of the meaning of the described phenomena" (p. 174). The use of this kind of interview is intended to provide a place where "ordinary people are able to describe their own life-world, their opinions and acts, in their own words. . . . The interview makes it possible for the subjects to organize their own descriptions, emphasizing what they themselves find important" (p. 173). In these interviews, the experience of student failure and success is described from the teacher's perspective.

The Teachers Talk

All of these teachers described the children they teach as at-risk populations from less advantaged backgrounds. It is with some level of discomfort that I use the term *at risk* to describe students who experience a lack of success in the public schools. Educators have employed various terminology to describe the concept of at-risk students for over 200 years (Cuban, 1989; Swadener, 1990). It usually refers to students possessing various traits that put them at risk for dropping out of school. Swadener argues that there is ample evidence that social class is a major risk factor for many students. However, in addition to being at risk for dropping out of school, these teachers also discussed other variables that placed their students at risk. Students who fail also were described as being at risk for the following reasons:

- *Low socioeconomic status and socialization patterns that influence the range of choices and options available to them*

Barely surviving . . . very difficult for them to be consistent doing anything. . . . Their parents don't have the skills necessary to make that child successful.

No efforts made to help children realize their choices and the impact of those choices.

- *Low expectations for achievement and ambiguous instructional goals*

What then can they take? Level 1 students. . . . They've already failed the lowest-level classes. . . . We aren't teaching them.

- *Residing in communities that often are isolated and tend to provide few positive role models of academic success*

They don't have anyone to expose them, so to speak, to the finer things in life. . . . If a teacher doesn't do it, then it's not gonna get done because their parents aren't concerned or they just don't think it's important to expose their children to a play, to expose their children to a museum—those sort of things. Now we can expose our children to watching *Boyz in the Hood* on TV or at the theater, but we're not going to expose our children to the museum in downtown Atlanta.

Despite the concerns and connotations surrounding the use of the term *at risk*, it was nonetheless the preferred terminology of the teachers in this study. Caution should always be used in characterizing groups of individuals based on predetermined notions of success that require, as prerequisites, strictly ordained behaviors, values, attitudes, and beliefs. However, in keeping with the original intent of this study, I have remained faithful to the language and meanings used by the teachers.

The Experience of Teaching Children Who Are At Risk

Teachers are affected by student failure . . . it disturbs them . . . frustrates . . .

it makes them sad and sometimes makes them angry . . . teachers as frustrated as the students . . . ultimately it causes them to question their integrity as professionals . . . question the curriculum . . . question the values and beliefs of a discipline.

The problems just are so deep-rooted . . . now, whose fault is it . . . I didn't take it as my fault that these kids were in the predicament that they were in . . . but, you can't point the finger at parents, teachers, administrators . . . we're all in this together . . . it's just overwhelming.

I think sometimes, OK, how much is mine . . . how much responsibility [for their failure] . . . constantly make changes . . . different group, different stuff . . . I will try anything to make all of my kids feel a part of my program.

The only way we [the teachers] made it through was by getting together and talking about it daily.

Other teachers talk about it [failure] . . . administrators talk about it . . . even distribute lists of teachers with accompanying rates of failure . . . teachers with high levels of failure feel defensive.

There are times that just . . . I think I've had it . . . I can't come back next year . . . I've just had too much, but the rest during the summer always has me ready . . . I am so ready to go back in August.

The experience of teaching at-risk students caused a response that was both physical and emotional. While each of these teachers freely elected to work with at-risk students, the language they used to describe their experiences nonetheless reflected the stress and difficulty inherent to these tasks. Their efforts brought them together and created bonds among teachers and between students. They were often frustrated; however, it seemed that a symbiotic relationship developed. Student success, however small, was perceived as teacher success, and student failure was perceived as teacher failure. Failure was "bad," and there were negative connotations associated with its close proximity to one's classroom. However, for these teachers, the response caused them to "pull together" as a group and rethink their roles and responsibilities, rather than "pull out," both emotionally and intellectually, and finally request a transfer to another school. They felt responsible for the students in their classes. This seemed a healthy response in that these teachers obviously felt a level of control over their professional lives. These teachers accepted the challenge and committed themselves to successful school experiences for students and teachers. They did not focus on issues of blame and responsibility; they were empowered by the experience of empowering the young people for whom they felt responsible.

Teaching and Learning

How well I perform up here and whether or not they're learning . . . it was like I all of a sudden got over on the other side of the desk in my mind, inside the student . . . Is the student learning? . . . All of a sudden it was like this awakening for me that was what mattered . . . *Is he learning?*

I know that I don't understand as much as I should about how difficult it is for the children. . . . I try, but I know it's just not there.

How can you *not* treat them differently because we're not all created out of the same mold . . . I will treat one child differently from another child if I feel like that's what has to be done in order to get that child involved in what's going on.

Teaching and learning were major concerns for these teachers. Much of their reflection, and subsequent action, was concentrated on creating a "space" for each child to learn. In contrast to many classrooms, these teachers recognized the idiosyncratic nature of the learning difficulties these students were experiencing. The focus was on adapting teaching strategies to facilitate successful learning for *each* child. The task was not perceived as insurmountable, but rather these teachers attempted to visualize and better understand the students' perspective. The students were not seen as unteachable. The task became one of looking at the *individual* and trying to understand her or his perspective on what was happening in the classroom. No one strategy was described by any teacher; rather, teacher attitude or perspective seemed to inform a classroom vision.

Other Teachers, "The Wall," and Learning

Teachers so often have this wall up between them and their [students] . . . particularly White females with a Black student . . . they put up a wall . . . they've got to make it through this the best they can . . . they've got to get their defenses up . . . they're not being open and honest . . . subject-oriented instead of student-oriented . . . I think that they (the other teachers) would go ahead and have class if none showed up.

The content . . . they can't even concentrate on the content until they feel they can work on this and be successful at it . . . my content's important . . . the kid's feeling of self-worth and having confidence comes first.

When you have kids write . . . and they bare their souls in their writing and they feel like they know you on a different level than their math teacher. I don't put a wall in front of me that I am the teacher and you're the kid.

The "wall" metaphor was used frequently by the teachers in this study. It was used to describe the real or imagined barriers that prevent teachers from reaching troubled students. Surmounting those barriers created by race, gender, and social class was the focus of the pedagogical strategies employed by these teachers. They were openly critical of teachers who showed more concern with content than with students. Their visualization of this "connection" between student and teacher established a bond that guided teacher action at a visceral level. "Breaking down the wall" transcended the mere academic goals of most programs and made the needs of students a top priority.

It seems reasonable to consider the relationship between student and teacher as a form of social capital. Wehlage (1993) described this phenomenon as the "shared attitudes, norms and values that promote trust and common expectations" (p. 3). Many of the students discussed by these teachers came from single-parent homes that were perceived as lacking the clear and consistent norms and expectations generally associated with successful school performance. The establishment of a close, caring relationship with a teacher may help to build a strong social connection with a positive role model. This kind of relationship becomes more important than knowledge acquisition in that it provides for these students an important prerequisite to successful learning: a sense of love and belonging. Furthermore, Wehlage (1993) suggests that "in the absence of social capital, children are growing up without strong connections to adults and adult values and institutions. Aimless, norm-less, and increasingly violence-prone youth are the product" (p. 4). Seen in this manner, "breaking down the wall" becomes an important, and often neglected, role of teachers in schools characterized by a high level of failure.

Love?

"Becoming Real" in the classroom . . . I have to learn to love the kids in front of me . . . I make up my mind that I am going to make him think I love him . . . and usually what happens is that I pretend and play at it . . . he can think it . . . then he starts becoming more lovable and therefore I can love him.

I love being there . . . being in the classroom . . . being in the school environment. Love them.

There is hope now. . . . They know when you care about them . . . [I] want to be there.

What has love got to do with it? All teachers love children, right? Well, maybe. These teachers, in particular, insisted on talking about love. The day-to-day challenge of teaching these kids was exciting, but it was love that kept bringing them back year after year. These teachers are passionate about their work and their students. More important, perhaps, is the possibility that this kind of attitude in a teacher leads to strategies that invite students into classroom communities where they encounter respectful, affirming relations that are truly supportive of student success, academically and personally. Kohn (1991) believes that schools should be the sites of this kind of behavior, but too often this is not the case:

> If we had to pick a logical setting in which to guide children toward caring about, empathizing with, and helping other people, it would be a place where they would regularly come into contact with their peers and where some sort of learning is already taking place. The school is such an obvious choice that one wonders how it could be that the active encouragement of prosocial values and behavior—apart from occasional exhortation to be polite—plays no part in the vast majority of American classrooms. (p. 497)

Witherell and Noddings (1991) also share a belief in the importance of caring, concerned, and committed relationships and the dialogue these connections facilitate:

> A caring relation also requires dialogue. The material of dialogue is usually words, but touch, smiles, affectionate sounds and silences, and glances may also be part of

it. True dialogue is open; that is, conclusions are not held to be absolute by any party at the outset. The search for enlightenment, responsible choice, perspective, or means to solve a problem is mutual and marked by appropriate signs of reciprocity. (p. 7)

For many students, this bonding with a particular teacher may mark their first, and most significant, positive interaction in a school setting. Farrell (1990) found that among at-risk high school students,

> [t]he school years students identified as their best often involved having a teacher who "cared about me," who "wanted me to learn," who "took a real interest in me." . . . There must be someone in the student's life who values her and who values education and whom the student can remember with admiration and respect. Such a teacher can compensate for the student's lack of academic success. (p. 112)

Thus, while love and a sense of mission seldom are discussed in conjunction with school failure, they seem to play an important role in the lives of teachers who elect to teach children who are "dismissed," figuratively and literally, from our schools. Love initiates a dialogue that lays the foundation for a successful, and reciprocal, teaching and learning experience.

The "Challenge" to Succeed

As a teacher, I want to feel like what I am doing is important, not just that I am teaching them science, but that not only do I teach them science, but they want to learn. . . . The thing that I am looking for is for me to try as hard as I can to grab all of those kids, it's like a challenge—can I grab a kid who runs around on the street and sells drugs, and can I do something that grabs his attention even if it's for two days out of five in the classroom?—and I've found that almost inevitably I can do that through "hands-on" science and "stand-on-my-head" math, and issuing challenges where they feel successful. . . . I give them 10% before they give it back to me. . . . It is 95% challenge . . . I make a difference in a child a day.

I asked to give up my advanced classes and take basic level kids. . . . I saw us giving those kids to our weakest teachers. . . . I think the other teachers admired the fact that I did it because it was my choice. . . . If I kept saying they needed to have a good teacher, then I decided I would give them one.

There's a challenge everyday . . . there's a challenge to get them interested in what I am teaching. . . . I am never totally satisfied . . . OK, my job is done . . . there's always something else, and once I finish this, there's 12 or 13 other things to choose from that I can work on next . . . or make my goal . . . my next goal . . . I think I would be so dissatisfied if I didn't feel like there was somebody that I needed to work on . . . or some little thing. . . . Teachers have to be willing to do whatever it takes. . . . It is our responsibility to make the kids feel successful.

In a profession frequently characterized by a lack of autonomy, self-esteem, and rewards, it is somewhat surprising that these teachers feel challenged, and even rewarded, by their work with at-risk kids.

The challenge of teaching these kids provided a degree of autonomy that allowed them to redefine their roles and responsibilities in the classroom in such a way that succeeding where other teachers had failed led to increased levels of self-confidence and the intrinsic rewards that come from successfully meeting a challenge head-on. Every teacher I talked to in conjunction with this study emphasized the challenge of teaching at-risk students. Data from the U.S. Department of Commerce indicate that the "most common reason for [students] dropping out still is a plain dislike of school" ("High Percentage of Female High School Dropouts Quit," 1994, p. 6A). These teachers repeatedly articulated a desire not only to help students succeed academically, but to improve their overall experience in school. This challenge seemed to appeal to the perceived or real needs of these teachers—the *need* to be needed, the *need* to do something important or even impossible, the *need* to be creative and innovative in the classroom, and even the *need* to make kids feel successful. They wanted to be needed, and these students did, indeed, need good teachers committed to their success. Just as important, however, these teachers wanted to teach low-achieving students who would "push" them to be the best and most innovative teachers they were capable of being. It was a relationship that worked. These were not teachers who desired comfortable jobs; the challenge was everything to these teachers. These teachers understood and recognized the importance of creating close, personal communities in classrooms, "spaces" where student voices were heard and respected. A spirit of cooperative action and interdependence was modeled and lived out within the microcosms of these individual class-rooms. This was an important feature of the experience and seemed to be key to the success of both teachers and students.

Black Teachers and Black Students

The aforementioned themes represent clusters and categories of meaning that were present in all of the interviews. However, two of the teachers interviewed were Black, and it is impossible to ignore the most salient differences in the ways that they described their experiences. Both Black teachers had grown up in fairly homogeneous Black communities and attended less advantaged public schools. Both teachers had been success-ful academically and considered them-selves, at this time, to be solidly middle class. They viewed the public schools as very positive influences in their lives. While it is not possible to generalize the experiences of two Black teachers to all Black teachers in the inner city, it was clear that these teachers were frustrated by the high incidence of failure among children of color. The following are rep-resentative quotes:

> Done it through hard work on my own. . . . *I* had parental support. I felt like that I was comin' there each day to baby-sit . . . to tell the kids what they're supposed to do . . . not to teach math because in trying to teach them, I didn't. . . . They're not ready.

> It just got to be so many problems where when you hear stuff, you're like . . . I'm sorry, but I am here to teach you math. If you need help, let me refer you to someone else. I really can't hear about it.

Despite the incidence of failure and frus-tration, these teachers wanted to teach Black children. A unique feature of their frustration was the strong identification and commitment they felt with their stu-dents. This attachment was poignantly expressed in the following quotes:

> I felt a need to work with children that were in the Black community . . . I wanted to give back to our community what was given to me . . . seemed like it would be something that would meet my needs as a teacher. . . . We under-stand the children. You gotta under-stand the Black culture. . . . They're the same as me. When I look at those kids and I look at me—I see no difference. We're the same.

> I really and truly believe that in order to teach Black inner-city children you need to understand their culture. You need to understand their upbringing . . . be able to relate to it. . . . Our values are being placed on them and they can't relate to them. . . . You're gonna have to almost visualize yourself being in there.

In Foster's (1993) interviews with ex-emplary African American teachers, a teacher expressed a similar idea:

> Black people have to convince Blacks of how important it [education] is. And how they are all part of that Black um-bilical cord because a lot of [Black] teachers, they don't do it consciously, but we are forgetting about our roots, about how we're *connected to this cord*, and about everyone we've left behind. We have it now, and we don't have time

for the so-called underclass. But we have to educate ourselves as a group because otherwise what's going to happen to us all? You see what I mean. If I can't see that kid out there in the biggest project, if I can't see how he and I or she and I are of the same *umbilical cord* and do not strive to make us more *connected to that cord with a common destiny*, then we're lost. (pp. 379–380)

For these teachers the experience was shaped by each teacher's sense of mission and commitment to children of color. Race was an aspect of their experience that cannot be underestimated or ignored. Race caused these teachers to perceive an almost familial bond with their students. At several levels, the shared cultural heritage superseded present-day social class differences. And yet, these teachers were a product of schools that, while racially segregated, were nonetheless important institutions within the Black community. The institutions where these two teachers presently work are still predominantly segregated, but their importance to the community is compromised by a perceived lack of effectiveness, and the children they described seemed to represent a "forgotten" underclass who had few connections to "the American dream" celebrated by earlier generations of middle- and working-class families.

Conclusion

In summary, these teachers are perhaps no different from other teachers, except that rather than internalizing a sense of failure and hopelessness tied to the school failure of large numbers of their students, they felt challenged and invigorated by the "fight." They did, indeed, perceive themselves as different from other teachers, perhaps even marginalized, but the difference could not be attributed to a single factor, but rather to a compilation of behavior, attitudes, values, and beliefs. As stated earlier, perhaps these teachers should be treated as a special category, a subculture of the larger group of teachers generally. Several common themes characterized the interviews of these teachers, but, simply stated, these teachers accepted the challenge to teach at-risk kids because of the satisfaction they experienced working in school environments characterized by a high degree of failure.

School failure is never simple; in fact, any discussion of "failure" requires predefined measures of "success" that emerge as cultural markers of status and prestige. One could propose, as does Erickson (1984), "that children failing in school are working at achieving that failure" (p. 539). Students who fail to succeed in school may be withholding their assent to these predefined notions of success and failure, and thus rejecting the accoutrements of middle-class status and prestige. Thus viewed, these teachers were engaged in a struggle to overcome overwhelmingly strong forces that make school failure a viable (and reasonable) option for some students. While I have little evidence that these teachers deliberately involved their students in a critical discourse designed to help the students better understand the choices they made, I have every reason to believe that at a personal, introspective level these teachers were engaged in a critical discourse about the choices *they* were making each day in the classroom. All of these teachers clearly believed in the innate worth and value of the work they were doing in schools and intuitively understood that it is wrong simply to talk of "student" failure; it blames the victim. McLaren (1994) discusses the tendency of many educators to "psychologize" student failure:

> This attitude is particularly frightening because teachers often are unaware of their complicity in its debilitating effects. Psychologizing school failure is a part of the hidden curriculum that relieves teachers from the need to engage in pedagogical self-scrutiny or in any serious critique of their personal roles within the school, and the school's role within the wider society. In effect, psychologizing school failure indicts the student while simultaneously protecting the social environment from sustained criticism. (p. 216)

The teachers who participated in this study regularly scrutinized and critiqued their roles and responsibilities in relation to school failure. Specific insights gained from these reflections produced differences in the style and substance of each teacher's instruction, and yet the net outcomes were similar. Their discussions of school failure were shaped by a shared sense of mutual responsibility for that failure. These beliefs shaped the individual philosophies of these teachers and ultimately the way they viewed the aims and purposes of the teaching/learning process within the context of schools and communities.

If one treats the students discussed by these teachers as an at-risk population that represents an oppressed group who through school failure remain disenfranchised and without access to the power and status associated with educational credentials, these stories begin to fit into a larger theoretical framework. By committing themselves to the success of these students, these teachers have refused to accept the school failure of less advantaged students as the status quo; they have reconfigured the "normal" parameters of their roles and responsibilities as teachers. Their relationships with students have become *both* personal and professional, emotional as well as intellectual. They have questioned the "taken for granted assumptions" concerning school failure and have committed themselves (and their students) to a course of individual action. If "social change is a product of human action," as Giroux (1988) would argue, these teachers may be instrumental in changing the personal histories of these students by facilitating their successful navigation of the public school terrain (cited in Spring, 1994, p. 29).

Too often, what we do in classrooms is simply cultural imposition and assimilation. The relationship is one-sided, but the sword is double-edged; fail in school and fail in life. This doesn't have to be the reality, but too often it is. In many ways these students have failed only to have a constituency that counts. They have no supporters who possess the skills of negotiation, and the power and status associated with middle-class membership, to voice support for alternative visions of success and "the good life." Teachers who care may be the most powerful advocates for the rights of these students. Weiler (1988) discusses Freire's beliefs concerning "the need for teachers to respect the consciousness and culture of their students and to create the pedagogical situation in which students can articulate their understanding of the world" (Freire, 1973, p. 56; cited in Weiler, 1988, p. 18). The concept of *scaffolding* (Wood, Bruner, & Ross, 1976) has been used to describe the social relations inherent in the constitution of learning tasks. This concept seems to convey the reciprocity inherent to the teaching/learning process discussed by these teachers. Erickson (1984) utilized this important concept:

> The scaffolding relationship between teacher and learner is jointly constructed. The child has rights to ask for a range of kinds of help. . . . The child and the teacher have rights to redefine the task as part of the scaffolding negotiation. This social form of learning environment in everyday teaching situations is very different from that found in school learning environments. There, typically, the learner has much less right to help shape the task. In such a situation it may be that very often the teacher's one-sided attempts to construct a scaffold that reaches the learner don't work. The scaffold doesn't reach. (p. 533)

The value of the "scaffolding" metaphor lies in its emphasis on the interconnectedness of the teaching/learning enterprise. Ladson-Billings (1994) also uses this metaphor to describe the work of teachers:

> When teachers provide instructional "scaffolding," students can move from what they know to what they need to know . . . students are allowed (and encouraged) to build upon their own experiences, knowledge, and skills to move into more difficult knowledge and skills. Rather than chastise them for what they do not know, these teachers find ways to use the knowledge and skills the students bring to the classroom as a foundation for learning. (p. 124)

As an ideal, could it be posited that teaching and learning should be akin to a dance—equal partners, one part skill and one part art? Such a dance requires a reciprocity and interconnectedness of action in order to be successful. And such a dance, when successful, involves perfect synchronicity. But even in the most difficult circumstances, it is a relationship in which for a moment each partner shares responsibility for the outcome. Using this metaphor, the voices of both students and teachers must be woven into a rich tapestry of meaning. Truly, if we are to understand the experience of failure, the voices of both students and teachers must be heard.

Failure is reciprocal and all-encompassing; it includes both student and teacher, classroom and community, school and family. School failure will never be eliminated; it will always be with us. Yet, it would seem that some teachers and students have found ways to successfully negotiate and reconcile "typical" notions of school success and failure and to realize and subvert the political and bureaucratic mechanisms that sustain their narrow definitions. And this is as it should be. School failure should not exist in any form. Why would anyone choose to fail? What need does it meet? It would seem that every human being has an evolutionary predisposition to succeed, and perhaps they do succeed when it is deemed important to their basic survival. Listening to the teachers in this study is just one attempt to better understand this interface between success and failure.

How can this information be used to shape the experiences of preservice and in-service teachers? It seems imperative that teachers be prepared to work with students who are at risk of failing. Schools characterized by high levels of failure soon may outnumber their more successful counterparts in the suburbs. New teachers often shy away from these environments out of fear and ignorance. And, who can blame them? Who of us would seek out an opportunity to greet "failure" on a daily basis in a classroom? If demographic projections are accurate, we must acquaint large numbers of new teachers with the cognitive and pedagogical strategies that will enable them to be successful in these schools. Successful role models who are enthusiastic and excited by this challenge are a good beginning. Cochran-Smith (1991) conceptualizes this process:

> Working to reform teaching or what can be thought of as *teaching against the grain*, is not a generic skill that can be learned at the university and then "applied" at the school. Teaching against the grain stems from, but also generates, critical perspectives on the macro-level relationships of power, labor, and ideology—relationships that are perhaps best examined at the university—where sustained and systematic study is possible. But teaching against the grain is also deeply embedded in the culture and history of teaching at individual schools and in the biographies of particular teachers and their individual or collaborative efforts to alter curricula, raise questions about common practices, and resist inappropriate decisions. These relationships can only be explored in schools in the company of experienced teachers who are themselves engaged in

complex, situation-specific, and sometimes losing struggles to work against the grain. (p. 280)

The voices of the teachers described in this chapter are the voices of one small group of people attempting to "teach against the grain." Their stories are incomplete. We can only assume and hope that they will not waiver in their desire and commitment to continue this effort. Teachers who are willing to teach against the grain must become the norm rather than the exception in schools where failure is pervasive. As teachers become more involved in the day-to-day decision making and planning that govern their lives, I believe that there will be a place in schools for the dialogue and sharing that are prerequisites for a critical examination of teaching and learning communities.

The most notable finding in this study is the insight these teachers provide about the experience of teaching in schools characterized by high levels of failure. It is not possible or even pragmatic to consider trying to teach novice teachers the cognitive strategies or philosophical shifts shared by these individuals. However, the teachers portrayed in this chapter are powerful reminders of those behaviors that cannot be measured or accounted for in classrooms by looking at test scores or dropout rates, or even teacher performance appraisal instruments. The overall complexity of the teaching/learning enterprise frequently is underestimated, and the tremendous energy, both physical and mental, required to teach each day often is ignored. No teaching assignment is easy, but some are more difficult than others. The information provided by the teachers in this study does not lead to specific recommendations for changes in teacher preparation or staff development; however, the importance of collaboration with teachers who are successful in the most difficult teaching assignments is reaffirmed.

A larger question concerns the establishment of schools that facilitate critical discourse among teachers about teaching and learning, success and failure, and ultimately the tenuous relationship between public schools and the needs of society. Beane and Apple (1995) write:

> The educational landscape is littered with the remains of failed school reforms, many of which failed because of the social conditions surrounding the schools. Only those reforms that recognize these conditions and actively engage them are likely to make a lasting difference in the lives of the children, educators, and communities served by the schools. . . . Democratic educators seek not simply to lessen the harshness of social inequities in school, but to change the conditions that create them. (p. 11)

School failure is unacceptable. However, it is just as unacceptable that in a country as powerful and wealthy as the United States, there are children who live in a vicious cycle of poverty and hopelessness. It seems untenable to talk about school failure without considering the circumstances that characterize the lives of those children who fail. When any one student fails, we all fail to some extent. Is the success of *all* students important? If the answer is yes, and I believe that it must be if we are to uphold the democratic ideal of equality of opportunity, the voices of good and successful teachers—those who succeed in the most challenging environ-ments—must be included in our efforts to create democratic schools where teachers purposefully work to provide equality of educational opportunity *and* excellence for *all* children in *all* communities.

REFERENCES

Ayers, W. (1994). To teach: The journey of a teacher. *Democracy & Education, 8*(3), 9–12.

Beane, J. A., & Apple, M. W. (1995). The case for democratic schools. In M. W. Apple & J. A. Beane (Eds.), *Democratic schools* (pp. 1–25). Alexandria, VA: Association for Supervision and Curriculum Development.

Cochran-Smith, M. (1991). Learning to teach against the grain. *Harvard Educational Review, 61*(3), 279–307.

Cuban, L. (1989). The "at-risk" label and the problem of urban school reform. *Phi Delta Kappan, 70*(10), 780–801.

Dougherty, K., & Hammack, F. (1990). General introduction. In K. Dougherty & F. Hammack (Eds.), *Education & society: A reader* (pp. 1–11). Fort Worth, TX: Harcourt Brace Jovanovich.

Erickson, F. (1984). School literacy, reasoning, and civility: An anthropologist's perspective. *Review of Educational Research, 54*(4), 525–546.

Erickson, F. (1986). Qualitative methods in research on teaching. In M. C. Whitrock (Ed.), *Handbook of research in teaching* (3rd ed., pp. 119–161). New York: Macmillan.

Farrell, E. (1990). *Hanging in and dropping out: Voices of at-risk high school students.* New York: Teachers College Press.

Foster, M. (1993). Educating for competence in community and culture: Exploring the views of exemplary African-American teachers. *Urban Education, 27*(4), 370–394.

Freire, P. (1973). *Education for critical consciousness.* New York: Seabury Press.

Giroux, H. (1988). *Schooling and the struggle for public life: Critical pedagogy in the modern age.* Minneapolis: University of Minnesota Press.

Greene, M. (1985). The role of education in democracy [Special Issue]. *Educational Horizons, 63,* 3–9.

Half of Black, Hispanic children may be poor by 2010. (1993, November 3). *Education Week,* pp. 3, 11.

High percentage of female high school dropouts quit because they are pregnant. (1994, September 14). *Asheville Citizen-Times,* p. 6A.

Hilty, E. B. (1987). *Moonlighting teachers: A thematic analysis of personal meanings.* Unpublished dissertation, University of Tennessee, Knoxville.

Kohn, A. (1991). Caring kids: The role of schools. *Phi Delta Kappan, 72*(7), 496–506.

Kvale, S. (1983). The qualitative research interview: A phenomenological and a hermeneutical mode of understanding. *Journal of Phenomenological Psychology, 14,* 171–196.

Ladson-Billings, G. (1994). *The dreamkeepers: Successful teachers of African American children.* San Francisco: Jossey-Bass.

Lieberman, A., & Miller, L. (1990). *The social realities of teaching.* In K. Dougherty & F. Hammack (Eds.), *Education & society: A reader* (pp. 193–204). Fort Worth, TX: Harcourt Brace Jovanovich.

McLaren, P. (1994). *Life in schools: An introduction to critical pedagogy in the foundations of education.* New York: Longman.

Ogbu, J. (1990). Social stratification and the socialization of competence. In K. Dougherty & F. Hammack (Eds.), *Education & society: A reader* (pp. 390–401). Fort Worth, TX: Harcourt Brace Jovanovich.

Schubert, W. H. (1991). Teacher lore: A basis for understanding praxis. In C. Witherell & N. Noddings (Eds.), *Stories lives tell: Narrative and dialogue in education* (pp. 207–233). New York: Teachers College Press.

Spring, J. (1994). *Wheels in the head: Educational philosophies of authority, freedom, and culture from Socrates to Paulo Freire.* New York: McGraw-Hill.

Swadener, E. B. (1990). Children and families "at-risk": Etiology, critique and alternative paradigms. *Educational Foundations, 4*(4), 17–39.

Wehlage, G. (1993). Social capital and the rebuilding of communities. In *Issues in restructuring schools* (Report No. 5). Madison: University of Wisconsin, Center on Organization and Restructuring Schools.

Weiler, K. (1988). *Women teaching for change: Gender, class & power.* Granby, MA: Bergin & Garvey.

Witherell, C., & Noddings, N. (1991). Prologue: An invitation to our readers. In C. Witherell & N. Noddings (Eds.), *Stories lives tell: Narrative and dialogue in education* (pp. 1–12). New York: Teachers College Press.

Wood, B., Bruner, J., & Ross, G. (1976). The role of tutoring in problem solving. *Journal of Child Psychology and Psychiatry, 17,* 89–100.

Linda McNeil

The Educational Costs of Standardization

The town's head librarian loved to encourage the children of his small, isolated farming community to read. He frequently went to the local school to read to the children. Most recently, he had been reading to a class of "at-risk" eighth-graders—students who had been held back two or more years in school. They loved his reading and his choices of books. He reports feeling very frustrated: The department chair has told him not to come any more to read to the students—they are too busy preparing for their TAAS test.

—UNSOLICITED CORRESPONDENCE

Three in a row? No, No, No!
[Three answers "b" in a row! No, No, No!]

—ONE OF SEVERAL CHEERS TAUGHT TO
STUDENTS AT THEIR DAILY PEP RALLIES ON
TEST-TAKING STRATEGIES FOR THE TAAS TEST.

In many urban schools, particularly those whose students are predominantly poor and minority, the TAAS system of testing reduces both the quality of what is taught and the quantity of what is taught. Because the principal's pay (and job contract) and the school's reputation depend on the school's TAAS scores, in those schools where students have traditionally not tested well on standardized tests the regular curriculum in these subjects is frequently set aside, so that students can prepare for the test.

The TAAS tests include reading skills, writing, and math. Common sense would suggest that if a teacher followed a traditional curriculum, even using the state's textbook, the teaching of regular lessons would be preparation for success on the test. If students were able to do math problems, explain math concepts, and apply math skills in the regular sequence of lessons, then it should follow that they would do well on the test.

The tests, however, are not necessarily consistent with traditional teaching and

411

learning. First, they are multiple-choice: They call for selecting among given answers. Second, they call for accurately darkening a circle beside the selected answer, without making stray marks on the paper.

In minority schools, in the urban school district where the magnet schools are located, and in many schools across the state, substantial class time is spent practicing bubbling in answers and learning to recognize "distractor" (obviously incorrect) answers. Students are drilled on such strategies as the one in the pep rally cheer quoted above: If you see you have answered "b" three times in a row, you know ("no, no, no") that at least one of those answers is likely to be wrong, because the maker of a test would not be likely to construct three questions in a row with the same answer-indicator. (The basis for such advice comes from the publishers of test-prep materials, many of whom send consultants into schools—for a substantial price—to help plan pep rallies, to "train" teachers to use the TAAS-prep kits, and to ease the substitution of their TAAS-prep materials for the curriculum in classrooms where teachers stubbornly resist.)

Teachers, even those who know their subjects and their students well, have much less latitude when their principals purchase test-prep materials to be used in lieu of the regular curriculum.

One teacher, a graduate of an Ivy League college with a master's degree from another select school, had spent considerable time and money assembling a rich collection of historical and literary works of importance in Latino culture. She had sought titles especially related to the American Southwest for her classes at a Latino high school. Her building of a classroom resource collection was extremely important, given the school's lack of a library and its lean instructional budget. Her students responded to her initiative with a real enthusiasm to study and learn.

She was dismayed to see, upon returning one day from lunch, that the books for her week's lessons had been set aside. In the center of her desk was a stack of test-prep booklets with a teacher's guide and a note saying "use these instead of your regular curriculum until after the TAAS." The TAAS test date was three months away.

(The prep materials bore the logo "Guerrilla TAAS," as in making war on the TAAS test; the booklet covers were military-camouflage colors; the Guerrilla TAAS consultants came to the school in camouflage gear to do a TAAS pep rally for the students and faculty.)

This teacher reported that her principal, a person dedicated to these students and to helping them pass the TAAS in order to graduate, had spent almost $20,000, virtually the entire instructional budget for the year, on these materials. The cost was merely one problem. Inside the booklets for "reading" were single-page activities, with brief reading selections followed by TAAS-type answer choices. These students, who had been analyzing the poetry of Gary Soto and exploring the generational themes in Rudolfo Anaya's novel *Bless Me Última*, had to set aside this intellectual work to spend more than half of every class period working through the "Guerrilla TAAS" booklet.

Teachers in urban schools say that to raise questions about the TAAS and about artificial test prep is characterized as being against minority students' chances to get high test scores. Or it is portrayed as "not being a team player." The test scores generated by centralized, standardized tests like the TAAS, and by the test-prep materials which prepare students for those tests, are not reliable indicators of learning. It is here where the effects on low-performing students, particularly minority students, begin to skew the possibilities for their access to a richer education.

At this school and other minority high schools where TAAS prep replaced the curriculum, teachers reported that even though many more students were passing TAAS "reading," few of their students were actually readers. Few of them could use reading for assignments in literature, science, or history classes; few of them chose to read; few of them could make meaning of literature or connect writing and discussing to reading. In schools where TAAS reading scores were going up, there was little or no will to address this gap. In fact, the rise in scores was used to justify even more TAAS prep, even more pep rallies, even more substituting of test-based programs for the regular curriculum.

TAAS and Reading

Advocates of TAAS might argue that passing the reading skills section of TAAS is better than not being able to read at all. However, there is first of all no evidence that these students cannot "read at all." Second, teachers are reporting that the kind of test prep frequently done to raise test scores may actually hamper students' ability to learn to read for meaning outside the test setting. In fact, students report that in the drills on the TAAS reading section, they frequently mark answers without reading the sample of text. They merely match key words in an an-

swer choice with key words in the text. The definition of "reading" as captured on the test ignores a broad and sophisticated research base on the teaching of reading and on children's development as language learners. When teachers are able to draw on this professional knowledge base, it does not lead them to testing formats like TAAS for help with their children's reading.

Elementary teachers have expressed the concern that extensive prep for the reading section of TAAS actually undermines children's ability to read sustained passages. The prep materials in reading, again purchased by principals eager to protect their performance contract or perhaps to help children pass the test, feature brief passages. After reading a passage, students are to answer practice questions ("Which of the following is the main idea?" "Which of the following would not make a good title for this paragraph?" "Which of the following was described as ' . . . '?"). The selected passage is not something they will see again; it is not even linked to the subsequent practice passage.

Students who practice these reading exercises day after day for months (many principals have had teachers begin TAAS prep in September and have not let them revert to the "regular" curriculum until after the TAAS test in March) show a decreased ability to read longer works. A sixth-grade teacher who had selected a fourth-grade Newbery Award book for her class, thinking all the students could read and understand it, found that after reading for a few minutes the students stopped. They were accustomed to reading very brief, disjointed passages; they had difficulty carrying over information from the first chapter to a later one. Discussions with other upper-elementary and middle-school teachers confirmed that students accustomed to TAAS prep, rather than literature, may be internalizing the format of reading skills tests, but not the habits needed to read for meaning.

TAAS and Writing

The teaching of "writing," also a subject tested by TAAS, has been reduced in many schools to daily practice of the essay form being tested that year. A teacher who is African-American and always alert to good educational opportunities for her sons was very pleased that her second son would be able to have the same excellent fourth-grade teacher under whom her oldest son had thrived. She was not prepared for the TAAS-based transformation of the fourth grade in the intervening years. She said that although the principal and teacher remained the same, the entire fourth-grade curriculum had been replaced by TAAS prep. Writing had become daily practice in "the persuasive essay," consisting of five five-sentence paragraphs, a form which clearly qualifies as "school knowledge" in the most limited sense. What students had to say in these essays was of virtually no importance; conforming to the form was the requirement, and the students practiced every day. This mother knew that in Anglo schools, while there was some abuse of teaching through TAAS prep, most of the children were nevertheless learning to tailor their writing to their subjects, to write in different voices and formats for different audiences, and to write in order to stretch their vocabularies.

A principal of a middle- to upper-middle-class elementary school explained to an audience at a school reform conference that her teachers had heard that teachers at other schools were having their students practice the five-paragraph essay every day. They were concerned to hear that it had become the only form of writing done that year in their school. This principal, under much less pressure to contrive passing rates for her students on the TAAS, worked with her teachers to include the TAAS as one of many "audiences" when they teach students to develop voice and a sense of audience in their writing.

Similarly, several high school teachers told of discussions they'd had with their students about the TAAS writing exam. After learning more about TAAS, the students had decided to think of the audience for their TAAS writing test as "bureaucrats sitting in little offices, waiting to count sentences and paragraphs." These teachers, usually in high-performing schools and therefore not required to do TAAS prep, are in a similar way trying to make the test the subject of critical inquiry. This is not typical in low-performing schools where teachers and principals are using pep rallies and incentive prizes to get students to "buy in" to these forms of evaluation.

The younger children growing up with TAAS prep may not always know (unless they compare with friends in private schools or have an older sibling whose learning was more substantive) how TAAS-prep reading and writing differ from good instruction. Older children, however, are not without skepticism that this system of testing is altering what they and their teachers jointly regard as important learning. Elaine, an eighth grader, knows firsthand the artificiality of "TAAS writing." In a previous grade, she won the citywide short-story writing award conferred by the local chapter of the National Council of Teachers of English. The next spring she received notice that she failed to pass the eighth-grade writing section of the TAAS because she "failed to provide sufficient supporting detail." Elaine and her teacher both know that she is known in her school as a writer. What distinguishes her writing is its rich detail. They could speculate that perhaps the scanning of her TAAS writing missed, by its haste or its rigid format, the elaborative and "supporting" detail that characterizes her writing. The TAAS, and not the quality of her writing nor her English teacher's judgment, lost credibility for her and for her parents as an indicator of her writing skills.

An eighth-grade class in a predominantly poor, Latino middle school demonstrated pointedly the intellectual subtraction resulting from the TAAS system of testing when the emphasis is on raising minority scores. In mid-September, a group of community visitors stepped into Mr. Sanchez's class just as he was covering the blackboard with rules for semicolon usage. Using semicolons in writing seemed a useful and worthy lesson for eighth graders working on their writing, so at first the visitors watched without comment. While the students were copying the semicolon rules, the teacher explained: "We are having to do grammar until after the TAAS. I'm so excited—this year we have a whole nine weeks after the TAAS to do eighth-grade English. I always do Shakespeare with my students. And I have many stories that they love to read. Last year we didn't have much time, but this year I will have a whole nine weeks." The visitors were just then realizing the import of his words: He was to do TAAS prep from September until March, and then "teach eighth-grade English" only in the re-

maining nine weeks. And the teacher was made to feel grateful for all nine of those weeks. He explained that it was the will of the principal that they get the scores up and that everyone in the school was feeling the pressure. He knew that by focusing on TAAS alone, his students would be getting far less than the eighth-grade curriculum studied by students in schools where the student demographics (middle class, predominantly white) would carry the scores, and they would be learning even less than his own students in the years before TAAS.

TAAS and Math

Under the TAAS-prep system, the teaching of mathematics is also highly truncated. TAAS tests math by having students choose among four or five possible answers. They are not asked to explain their answers, so if students have alternative ways of working a problem, their reasoning is not made visible on the test. Nor are their reasons for selecting "correct" answers. Being able to conceptualize in mathematics, being able to envision a solution and select among possible approaches, being able to articulate the reasoning behind the answer—none of these are tested by TAAS. Instead TAAS tests computational accuracy and familiarity with basic operations.

The reductive mathematics on the test is not adequate preparation for courses in more advanced mathematics. The TAAS-prep booklets, which emphasize test-taking strategies over mathematical reasoning, again create a gap between the content learned by poor and minority students in schools investing in TAAS-prep kits and the students in well-provisioned schools. In these latter schools, principals assume students will pass because of their family background and their having attended "good" schools in lower grades. They therefore support the teaching of the regular academic curriculum without substantial risk that to do so might lower the TAAS scores.

Trying to Circumvent TAAS

If a teacher wanted to avoid TAAS prep and focus on the students and the curriculum, then it would seem that the answer would be to teach a subject not yet tested by TAAS. At the Pathfinder school, Ms. Bartlett had claimed a space for teaching complex biology topics by shifting some of her teaching out from under the controls of the proficiency system (the predecessor of TAAS). She created elective courses and independent study seminars around such units of study as ecology and habitats (enabling her to integrate concepts and topics that were fragmented and sequenced separately under the proficiencies). She taught a biochemistry elective (using knowledge she gained though a mentorship program with a medical school and crossing traditional subject boundaries) and, in some semesters, marine biology.

Under the TAAS system of testing, teachers reported that there were fewer and fewer venues in which they could do authentic teaching, even when officially only three subjects—math, reading, and writing—were tested. In poor and minority schools, especially, teaching untested subjects such as art, science, or social studies was not exempt from the pressures of TAAS prep. An art teacher with a reputation for engaging her Latino students in serious studio work, and for getting students excited about being in school, was required to suspend the teaching of art in order to drill her students daily in TAAS

grammar. By the time the grammar drills were completed, there was no time to set up for art projects.

Her students were doubly losing: Their treatment of grammar was artificial, aimed at correctness within the multiple-choice format of the test, rather than at fluency in their own writing; and they were denied an opportunity to develop their sense of color and design in art.

A history teacher in an under-resourced Latino high school worked with his colleagues to create a history curriculum that would maintain authentic content and yet incorporate some of the skills their students would need to do well on the TAAS. They included the writing of essays on historical topics and gave attention to reading skills. They had at first been given permission to create this curriculum on their own but later were told that they needed to set aside the teaching of history entirely in order to "cooperate with the rest of the faculty" in getting students to pass the TAAS. This history teacher's assignment was to drill his students every day on math, a subject outside his field of expertise.

Science teachers who spent a year in the Rice University Center for Education Model Science Lab (located in an urban middle school)—updating their science knowledge and upgrading their capacity for laboratory-based teaching—entered the program with the consent of their principals to implement what they had learned when they returned to their schools. Many of these teachers discovered, on returning to their home schools, that they were required, for as much as two to four months of the school year, to suspend the teaching of science in order to drill students on TAAS math. Again, the students in these urban schools were doubly penalized, first for losing out on the science that their peers in suburban schools were learning, second by having to spend extra periods on low-level, disjointed math drills—math divorced from both the applications and conceptual understandings they will need if they are to hold their own later in upper-level math classes with middle-class students. It is unlikely that the middle-class students were doing "math" from commercial test-prep booklets, rather than from math books, manipulatives, calculators, computers, and peer study groups. The TAAS, then, lowered the quality and quantity of even subjects not being tested in those schools where students had traditionally not tested well, the students who are poor and the minority.

————

Linda Darling-Hammond

CHAPTER
25

From "Separate but Equal" to "No Child Left Behind"
The Collision of New Standards and Old Inequalities

Many civil rights advocates initially hailed the Bush administration's major education bill, optimistically entitled No Child Left Behind, as a step forward in the long battle to improve education for those children traditionally left behind in American schools—in particular, students of color and students living in poverty, new English learners, and students with disabilities. The broad goal of NCLB is to raise the achievement levels of all students, especially underperforming groups, and to close the achievement gap that parallels race and class distinctions. According to the legislation, too many of the neediest children are being left behind; too many are attending failing or unsafe schools; too many receive poor teaching and are performing well below potential; and too many are leaving school altogether. The bill intends to change this by focusing schools' attention on improving test scores for all groups of students, providing parents with more educational choices, and ensuring better-qualified teachers.

This noble agenda seems unobjectionable on its face, but the complex 600-page law has affected states, districts, schools, and students in ways never envisioned by its authors. The proliferating nicknames emerging as this intrusive legislation plays out across the country give a sense of some of the anger, bewilderment, and confusion left in its wake: "No Child Left Untested," "No School Board Left Standing," and "No Child's Behind Left" are just a few of them. Since the start of the 2003–04 school year, at least twenty states and a number of school districts have officially protested the NCLB Act, voting to withdraw from participation, to withhold local funding for implementation, or to resist specific provisions. Members of the Congressional Black Caucus, among other federal legislators, have introduced bills to amend the law by placing a moratorium on high-stakes standardized testing, a key element of NCLB; withholding school sanctions until the bill is fully funded; and requiring progress toward adequate and equitable educational opportunities for students in public schools. The Harvard Civil Rights Project, along with other advocacy groups, has warned that the law threatens to increase the growing dropout and pushout rates for students of color, ultimately reducing access to education for these students, rather than enhancing it.[1] As the evidence of NCLB's unintended consequences emerges, it seems increasingly clear that, despite its good intentions and admirable goals, NCLB as currently implemented is more likely to harm than to help most of the students who are the targets of its aspirations, and it is more likely to undermine—some would even say destroy—the nation's public education system than to improve it. These outcomes are likely because the underfunded bill layers onto a grossly unequal—and, in many communities, inadequately funded—school system a set of unmeetable test score targets that disproportionately penalize schools serving the neediest students while creating strong incentives for schools to keep out or push out those students who are low achieving in order to raise school average test scores.

Furthermore, the act's regulations have caused a number of states to abandon their thoughtful diagnostic assessment and accountability systems—replacing instructionally rich, improvement-oriented systems with more rote-oriented punishment-driven approaches—and it has thrown many high-performing and steadily improving schools into chaos rather than helping them remain focused and deliberate in their ongoing efforts to serve students well.

While well intentioned, it has become clear that the NCLB Act will, in the next few years, label most of the nation's public schools "failing," even when they are high performing and improving in achievement. According to one tally, 26,000 of the nation's 93,000 public schools this year "failed to make adequate yearly process." A new study in California found that failing "schools were designated not because tests had shown their overall achievement levels to be faltering, but because a single student group—disabled learners or Asian students, for example—had fallen short of a target. As a result, the chances that a school would be designated as failing increased in proportion to the number of demographic groups served by the school."[2] And in some high-achieving states that have set very high standards for themselves, large numbers of schools are dubbed "failing" because they fall below these standards, even though they score well above most other schools in the nation and the world.

Some believe this is a prelude to voucher proposals aimed at privatizing the education system, since the public will have been besieged with annual reports about failing public schools which the law's unmeetable requirements guarantee cannot be remedied. In addition to the perverse consequences for school systems, the law will lead to reductions in federal funding to already underresourced schools and it will sidetrack funds needed for improvement to underwrite transfers for students to other schools (which, if they are available, may offer no higher quality education). If left unchanged, the act will deflect needed resources for teaching and learning to ever more intensive testing of students, ranking of schools, busing of students, and lawyers' fees for litigating the many unintended consequences of the legislation.

Most unhappily, some of the act's most important and potentially productive components—such as the effort to ensure that all students have highly qualified teachers and successful educational options and supports—are in danger of being extinguished by the shortcomings of a shortsighted, one-way accountability system that holds children and educators to test-based standards they are not enabled to meet, while it does *not* hold federal or state governments to standards that would ensure equal and adequate educational opportunity.

Inequality in Education: What NCLB Does Not Change

The first problem—one that NCLB does not acknowledge or effectively address—is the enormous inequality in the provision of education offered in the United States. Unlike most countries that fund schools centrally and equally, the wealthiest U.S. public schools spend at least ten times more than the poorest schools—ranging from over $30,000 per pupil at the wealthy schools to only $3,000 at the poorest. These disparities contribute to a wider achievement gap in this country than in virtually any other industrialized country in the world. The school disparities documented in Jonathan Kozol's *Savage Inequalities* (1991) have not lessened in recent years. Within states, the spending ratio between high- and low-spending schools is typically at least 3 or 4 to 1.

As documented in federal statistics and a large number of current lawsuits, schools serving large numbers of low-income students and students of color have larger class sizes, fewer teachers and counselors, fewer and lower-quality academic courses, extracurricular activities, books, materials, supplies, computers, libraries, and special services.[3] Spending is so severely inadequate in the growing number of "apartheid" schools serving more than 90 percent "minority" students that legal action to challenge school funding systems is under

way in nearly half the states. These conditions are vividly illustrated in this description of Luther Burbank Middle School, which serves the low-income students of color in San Francisco who are plaintiffs in *Williams v. California*, an equal educational opportunity lawsuit:

At Luther Burbank School, students cannot take textbooks home for homework in any core subject because their teachers have enough textbooks for use in class only. . . . Some math, science, and other core classes do not have even enough textbooks for all the students in a single class to use during the school day, so some students must share the same one book during class time. . . . For homework, students must take home photocopied pages, with no accompanying text for guidance or reference, when and if their teachers have enough paper to use to make homework copies. . . . The social studies textbook Luther Burbank students use is so old that it does not reflect the breakup of the former Soviet Union. Luther Burbank is infested with vermin and roaches and students routinely see mice in their classrooms. One dead rodent has remained, decomposing, in a corner in the gymnasium since the beginning of the school year. The school library is rarely open, has no librarian, and has not recently been updated. Luther Burbank classrooms do not have computers. Computer instruction and research skills are not, therefore, part of Luther Burbank students' regular instruction in their core courses. The school no longer offers any art classes for budgetary reasons. Two of the three bathrooms at Luther Burbank are locked all day, every day. The third bathroom is locked during lunch and other periods during the school day, so there are times during school when no bathroom at all is available for students to use. Students have urinated or defecated on themselves at school because they could not get into an unlocked bathroom. . . . When the bathrooms are not locked, they often lack toilet paper, soap, and paper towels, and the toilets frequently are clogged and overflowing. . . . Ceiling tiles are missing and cracked in the school gym, and school children are afraid to play basketball and other games in the gym because they worry that more ceiling tiles will fall on them during their games. . . . The school heating system does not work well. In winter, children often wear coats, hats, and gloves during class to keep warm. Eleven of the 35 teachers at Luther Burbank have not yet obtained regular, non-emergency credentials, and 17 of the 35 teachers only began teaching at Luther Burbank this school year. (*Williams v. State of California*, Superior Court of the State of CA for the County of San Francisco, 2001, Complaint 58–66)

It should be no surprise that the students at Luther Burbank and schools like it achieve at low levels and often fail state-imposed tests, ending their school careers with less opportunity to play a productive role in society than when they began as eager kindergartners.

Under No Child Left Behind, these dreadful school conditions are left largely untouched. Although the act orders schools to ensure that 100 percent of students test at levels identified as "proficient" by the year 2014—and to make mandated progress toward this goal each year—the small per pupil dollar alloca-

tion it makes to schools serving low-income students is well under 10 percent of schools' total spending, far too little to correct these conditions. Most of the federal money has to be spent for purposes other than upgraded facilities, textbooks, or teachers' salaries. Furthermore, while the law focuses on test scores as indicators of school quality, it largely ignores the important inputs or resources that *enable* school quality. It does not authorize substantial federal investments in the underresourced schools where many students are currently struggling to learn, nor does it require that states demonstrate progress toward equitable and adequate funding or greater "opportunities to learn." Although the law includes another set of requirements to ensure that all students receive "highly qualified teachers," as discussed in a later section, the lack of adequate federal support for actually making this possible currently appears to make this promise a rather hollow one in many communities.

To Test or to Invest? How NCLB Treats Schools Serving the Nation's Neediest Students

The biggest problem with the NCLB Act is that it mistakes measuring schools for fixing them. It sets annual test score goals for every school—and for subgroups of students within schools—that are said to constitute "Adequate Yearly Progress." Schools that do not meet these targets for each subgroup each year are declared in need of improvement and, later, failing. This triggers interventions (notification to parents of the school's label and a three-month period to write a school improvement plan). Students must be allowed to transfer out of "failing" schools at the school's expense, schools stand to be reconstituted or closed, and states and districts stand to lose funds based on these designations. Unfortunately, the targets—based on the notion that 100 percent of students will score at the "proficient" level on state tests by the year 2014—were set without an understanding of what this goal would really mean.

First, of course, there is the fundamental problem that it is impossible to attain 100 percent proficiency levels for students on norm-referenced tests (when 50 percent of students by definition must score below the norm and some proportion must by definition score below any cut point selected), which are the kind of tests that have been adopted by an increasing number of states due to the specific annual testing requirements of NCLB. Criterion-referenced tests also typically use an underlying norm-referenced logic in selecting items and setting cut scores, although in theory, the target could at least remain fixed on these tests. Even if tests were not constructed in this way, the steepness of the standard is unrealistic. Using a definition of proficiency benchmarked to the National Assessment of Educational Progress (NAEP), one analyst has calculated that it would take schools more than one hundred years to reach such a target in all content areas if they continued the fairly brisk rate of progress they were making during the 1990s.[4]

Even more problematic is that the act requires that schools be declared "failing" if they fail to meet these targets for each subgroup of designated students annually. It requires the largest gains from lower-performing schools, ignoring that these schools serve needier students and are generally less well funded than those serving wealthier and higher-scoring students. To complicate things more, those that serve large numbers of new English language learners (what the law calls Limited English Proficient [LEP] students) and some kinds of special needs students (what the law calls "students with disabilities") are further penalized by the fact that students are assigned to these subgroups *because* they cannot meet the standard, and they are typically removed from the subgroup when they do meet the standard. Thus these schools will not ever be able to meet the annual AYP (adequate yearly progress standard), which demands that schools advance yearly to 100 percent student proficiency.

For example, section 9101(25) of NCLB defines an LEP student as one "(D) whose difficulties in speaking, reading, writing, or understanding the English language may be sufficient to deny the individual—(i) *the ability to meet the State's proficient level of achievement* on State-assessments described in section 1111(b)(3)." As students gain proficiency in English, they are transferred out of this subgroup; thus, it is impossible for 100 percent of this subgroup ever to reach proficiency. For schools and districts that serve a substantial number of LEP students, this imposes a ceiling on their overall performance as well as the performance of this subgroup. At some point it will be impossible to make the required gains because of how this subgroup is defined under law. Some advocates have suggested that states use a rule that scores of students who are classified as LEP should be counted in the AYP calculations for this subgroup as long as they stay in a school. However, the U.S. Department of Education has not approved this definition.[5]

The same issues pertain to the testing of students with disabilities and to the schools that serve them. Many such students who cannot demonstrate their learning on grade-level tests have individualized education plans that prescribe different assessments for charting their progress, including "instructional level" tests. The Department of Education has ruled that using such tests is permissible only if the results are counted as "nonproficient," or—for one year only—if they apply to fewer than 1 percent of all test-takers. In addition to appearing to violate special education laws, schools that serve large numbers of special education students will be penalized in their AYP rankings. Because disabilities are correlated with poverty (which is linked to poor prenatal and childhood health care, low birth weight, poor nutrition, lead poisoning, maternal substance abuse, and many other conditions that predict learning problems), this is yet another way in which NCLB punishes schools and districts that serve large numbers of low-income students.

For all of these reasons, two separate teams of researchers have found that, in the early years of NCLB implementation, schools serving poor, minority, and LEP students and those with a greater number of subgroups for which they are held accountable are disproportionately identified as "needing improvement"—what one group of researchers has called a "diversity penalty."[6] As illustrated below, this is true even for schools that show steep test score gains for low-income and minority students.

For example, Novak and Fuller identified two schools in Oakland whose students, on average, performed at equal levels on standardized tests. One, Manzanita Elementary, serves a diverse population, including black, Latino, Asian, low-income, and limited-English students. The other school, Golden Gate Elementary, serves primarily black students, some of whom are also in the low-income category, giving the school just two groups under the federal law's accountability system. As a result of its diverse population, Manzanita had to meet targets in eighteen categories—each of these subgroups on several different content tests. It succeeded in seventeen, but black students narrowly missed their target in math. Golden Gate, because of its more homogeneous student body, needed to meet targets in only six categories, and succeeded. Manzanita was designated as needing improvement, and Golden Gate was not. Among the most diverse districts in California—Fresno, Los Angeles, Oakland, San Francisco, San Jose, and Santa Ana—half or more of all schools failed to meet all of their AYP growth targets in 2003, thus positioning these districts serving the state's neediest students for large reductions in federal funding within a short period of time.

While these are troubling aspects of the law's implementation, one could also argue, quite legitimately, that many of the schools identified as "needing improvement" (a designation that changes to "failing" if not corrected after three years) indeed are dismal places where little learning occurs, or are complacent schools that have not attended to the needs of all of their students—schools that need to be jolted into action to change. It is fair to suggest that students in such schools deserve other choices if they cannot change.

These important arguments are part of the NCLB's theory of action: that low-quality schools will be motivated to change if they are identified and shamed, and that their students will be better served if given other educational options. These outcomes may in fact occur in some cases. The problem is that the law actually works in many other cases to label schools as failing even when they are succeeding with the very students the law wants to help, and it creates incentives that can reduce the quality of education such schools can provide while providing few real options for their students to go to better schools.

How might the goal of improving schools actually, paradoxically, undermine them? First, there is evidence from states that have used similar accountability provisions that applying labels of failure to low-scoring schools that serve low-income students reduces the schools' ability to attract and keep qualified teachers. For example, in North Carolina, analysts found that the state labeling system made it more difficult for the neediest schools to get access to the higher-quality teachers other state policies were attracting and developing in the state.[7] Similarly, Florida's use of aggregate test scores, unadjusted for student characteristics, to allocate school rewards and sanctions led to reports that qualified teachers were leaving the schools rated D or F in droves, to be replaced by teachers without experience or training.[8] As one principal queried, "Is anybody going to want to dedicate their lives to a school that has already been labeled a failure?" NCLB's requirements for parent notification of school "needs improvement" or "failing" label and threats of staff dismissal have already been reported as disincentives for qualified staff to stay in high-need schools when they have options to teach in better

resourced and better regarded schools with more affluent students.

Second, schools that have been identified as not meeting AYP standards stand to lose federal funding, thus having even fewer resources to spend on the students they are serving. Rather than seeking to ensure that students attend adequately funded and well-managed schools that would enable them to learn to higher levels, NCLB seeks to expand students' opportunities by offering them the chance to transfer out to other "non-failing" public schools if their school is declared "failing." This option is to be funded through the resources of the "failing" school, as are funds for supplemental services for such things as tutoring or after-school programs.

While the choice option is a useful idea in theory, such alternatives are likely to reap little overall improvement in the opportunities for most students in poor rural or inner-city schools, because—in addition to the fact that this option for some comes at the expense of school funding for their peers—there are frequently no "non-failing" public schools with open seats available to transfer to nearby. The best schools are already quite full, and these schools have no incentive to admit low-income students with low test scores, poor attendance records, or substantial educational needs who will "bring down" their average and place the school at risk of receiving sanctions. Furthermore, the best-resourced schools are typically not close to the inner city or poor rural neighborhoods where struggling schools are concentrated. Thus, rather than expanding educational opportunities for low-income students and students of color, the law is more likely in many communities to reduce still further the quality of education available in the schools they must attend. A better approach would be to invest in the needed improvements in such schools in the first place, and to measure their progress on a variety of indicators in ways that give the schools credit for improvements they produce for the students they serve.

"Alice in Wonderland" Accountability

The goals of No Child Left Behind are to improve achievement for all students, to enhance equity, and to ensure more qualified teachers. However, its complex regulations for showing "Adequate Yearly Progress" toward test score targets aimed at "100% proficiency" within ten years have created a bizarre situation in which most of the nation's public schools will be deemed failing within the next few years—even many that already score high and those that are steadily improving from year to year. Ironically, states that use more ambitious tests and have set higher standards will experience greater failures than those with low standards, and many have abandoned measures of critical thinking and performance, just as the labor market increasingly demands these kinds of skills. Here are a few examples of the strange and curious outcomes of the law thus far:

In San Diego, Marston Middle School, a well-regarded school serving a diverse student population with a large number of low-income, minority, and English-language-learning students, has been showing large gains in achievement for all groups each year as its dedicated principal and teachers have worked intensely on school-wide literacy development.[9] The school once again saw huge gains in 2003,

far exceeding its growth target and showing gains for Latino students and low-income students of more than four times the targeted increases. This caused the school's achievement gap to shrink substantially. However, under NCLB the school was declared in "need of improvement," because its white students, who already score near the top of the state accountability index, did not improve "sufficiently"—largely because they have hit the testing ceiling, and, as a group, have little room for further growth. Marston Middle School is doing what NCLB intended schools to do—increase achievement and reduce the achievement gap—but it will be punished under the law, and its students will lose funds that could have gone to support their education and the ongoing improvement of the school.

Meanwhile, in Minnesota, where, as Garrison Keillor claims, "all of the women are pretty and all of the children are above average," eighth graders score first in the nation in mathematics and near the top in other subjects as well. However, a recent news report notes that, under the rules of No Child Left Behind, more than 80 percent of Minnesota's public schools will soon be declared "in need of improvement," and not long after, if they don't meet the law's targets for "Adequate Yearly Progress," declared as "failing" and in need of reconstitution. This is because, in the baffling world that has become federal policy, schools in states with the highest standards will have the most schools found wanting, even if their students achieve at levels substantially above those of schools in other states.

One of the first perverse consequences of the NCLB Act is that many states formally lowered their standards in order to avoid having most of their schools declared failing. Another perverse consequence is that states that have worked hard to create forward-looking assessment systems during the 1990s have begun to abandon them, since they do not fit the federal mandate for annual testing that allows students and schools to be ranked and compared. In fact, NCLB is undoing some of the most important gains in assessment and accountability made by states since 1990, when the Goals 2000 Act encouraged them to create such systems. In the past decade, virtually all states have created new standards that reflect what students should know and be able to do, new curriculum frameworks to guide instruction, and new assessments to test students' knowledge. Advocates of these reforms have hoped that setting standards would mobilize resources for student learning, including high-quality curriculum, materials, and assessments tied to the standards; more widely available course offerings that reflect this high-quality curriculum; more intensive teacher preparation guided by related standards for teaching; more equal resources for schools; and more readily available safety nets for educationally needy students.

This comprehensive approach has been followed in some states and districts, including Connecticut, Kentucky, Maine, Maryland, Minnesota, Nebraska, Vermont, and Washington, among others. In these cases, thoughtful assessments have been tied to investments in improved schooling and teaching. These efforts have begun to improve student achievement while enhancing teaching and increasing educational opportunity. Many of these states created sophisticated assessments that measure critical thinking and real performance in areas like writing, mathematical and scientific problem solving, and research. They developed their systems carefully over a sustained period of time and have used them primarily to inform ongoing school improvement—identifying areas of needed curriculum change, professional development, and additional investments—rather than to punish students or schools.

Much of this effort threatens to be undone by NCLB's requirements for annual tests that meet certain federal specifications. NCLB's test requirements and costs have already caused one state, Maryland, to drop its sophisticated performance assessment system and another, Vermont, to threaten to reject the new federal funds in order to maintain its performance assessments. Maine eliminated a number of its assessments in fields like social studies and the arts, as well as its teacher scoring process which provided strong professional development. Oregon has fought to get the Department of Education to allow it to use its sophisticated computer-based adaptive testing system for the purposes of both diagnosis for instruction and standards-based assessment it was designed to serve. States like Nebraska that previously used only performance assessments to evaluate student learning have been forced to adopt norm-referenced standardized tests to meet the law's requirements.[10] NCLB regulations are pushing states back to the lowest common denominator in testing, undoing progress that has been made to improve the quality of assessments, and delaying the move from antiquated norm-referenced, multiple-choice tests to criterion-referenced assessment systems that measure and help develop important kinds of performance and learning.

This not only reduces the chances that schools will be able to focus on helping students acquire critical thinking, research, writing, and production abilities; it will also reduce opportunities for students who learn in different ways and have different talents to show what they have learned. Analysts have raised many concerns about how the law's requirements are leading to a narrower curriculum; to test-based instruction that ignores critical real-world skills, especially for lower-income and lower-performing students; and to less useful and engaging education. These are all important concerns. Equally important is the strong possibility that these efforts will actually reduce access to education for the most vulnerable students, rather than increasing it.

Higher Scores, Fewer Students

Perhaps the most adverse, unintended consequence of NCLB's accountability strategy is that it undermines safety nets for struggling students rather than ex-

panding them. The accountability provisions of the NCLB Act actually create large incentives for other schools to keep such students out and for all schools to hold back or push out students who are not doing well. As low-scoring students disappear, test scores go up. Table 25.1 shows how this operates. At "King Middle School," average scores increased from the 70th to the 72nd percentile between the 2002 and 2003 school year, and the proportion of students in attendance who met the standard (a score of 65) increased from 66 to 80 percent—the kind of performance that test-based accountability systems, including NCLB, celebrate and reward. Looking at subgroup performance, the proportion of Latino students meeting the standard increased from 33 to 50 percent, a steep increase.

However, *not a single student* at King improved his or her score between 2002 and 2003. In fact, the scores of every single student in the school went *down* over the course of the year. How could these steep improvements in the school's average

TABLE 25.1 King Middle School: Rewards or Sanctions?
The Relationship Between Test Score Trends and Student Population

	2002–03	2003–04
Laura	100	90
James	90	80
Felipe	80	70
Kisha	70	65
Jose	60	55
Raul	20	
	Av. Score = 70	Av. Score = 72
	% meeting standard = 66%	% meeting standard = 80%

scores and proficiency rates have occurred? A close look at Table 25.1 shows that the major change between the two years was that the lowest-scoring student, Raul, disappeared. As has occurred in many states with high-stakes testing programs, students who do poorly on the tests—special needs students, new English language learners, those with poor attendance, health, or family problems—are increasingly likely to be excluded by being counseled out, transferred, expelled, or by dropping out.

If this school had been judged using a "value-added" index that looked at the changes in individual students' scores from one year to the next, it would have been clear that the students' scores decreased by 8 percentile points on average rather than registering an apparent, but illusory, gain caused by changes in the student population. Recent studies have found that systems that reward or sanction schools based on average student scores (rather than looking at the growth of individual students) create incentives for pushing low-scorers into special education so that their scores won't count in school reports,[11] retaining students in grade so that their grade-level scores will look better,[12] excluding low-scoring students from admissions,[13] and encouraging such students to leave schools or drop out.[14] Studies have linked dropout rates in Georgia, Florida, Massachusetts, New York, and North Carolina to the effects of grade retention, student discouragement, and school exclusion policies stimulated by high-stakes tests. According to the National Center for Education Statistics, graduation rates decreased from 63 to 58 percent in New York between 1997 and 2001 and from 57 to 52 percent in Florida as new high-stakes testing policies were introduced.

Recent data from Massachusetts, which began to implement high-stakes testing in the late 1990s, show more grade retention and higher dropout rates, including a 300 percent increase in middle school dropouts between 1997–1998 and 1999–2000, greater proportions of students dropping out in ninth and tenth grades, more of them African American and Latino, and fewer dropouts returning to school. When the state's exit exam was first enforced in 2003, graduation rates for the group of ninth graders who had entered high school four years earlier decreased for all students, but most sharply for students of color. Whereas state data showed a graduation rate of 71 percent for African American students in the class of 2002, the class of 2003 had only 59.5 percent in line to graduate (still in school and having passed the exams in the spring of 2003). The drop for Latino students went from 54 percent in 2002 to 45 percent in 2003, and for Asian students from 89 percent to 81 percent.[15] Meanwhile many of the steepest increases in test scores have occurred in schools with the highest retention and dropout rates. For example, Wheelock found that, in addition to increasing dropout rates, high schools receiving state awards for gains in tenth-grade pass rates on the MCAS (the Massachusetts test) showed substantial increases in prior year ninth-grade retention rates and in the percentage of "missing" tenth graders.[16]

Although the hope is that such carrots and sticks will force schools to improve, this does not necessarily occur. Last year, news reports revealed what researchers had previously observed—that the "Texas Miracle," which was the model for the federal No Child Left Behind Act, boosts test scores in part by keeping many students out of the testing count and making tens of thousands disappear from school altogether.[17] The "disappeared" are mostly students of color. At Sharpstown High School in Houston, a freshman class of 1,000 dwindled to fewer than 300 students by senior year—a pattern seen in most high-minority high schools in Houston, including those rewarded for getting their test scores "up." The miracle is that not one dropout was reported. The whistle-blowing principal from Sharpstown has described how this pattern is widespread and encouraged by the district.[18]

In Texas, where tests alone are supposed to drive improvement, large numbers of students of color are taught by underprepared and inexperienced teachers—which significantly affects passing rates on the state tests.[19] Fewer than 70 percent of white students who enter ninth grade graduate from high school four years later, and the proportions for African-American and Latino students are under 50 percent.[20] Unhappily, the score gains for African-American and Latino students celebrated in Houston appear in part to be a function of high dropout and push out rates for these students. As low-achievers leave school, the group's average score increases. Paradoxically, NCLB's requirement for disaggregating data and tracking progress for each subgroup of students may increase the incentives for eliminating those at the bottom of each subgroup who struggle to learn, especially where schools have little capacity to improve the quality of services such students receive.

Where states have replaced investing with testing, the sad story in too many cities and poor rural communities is that students are forced to attend under-resourced schools where they lack the texts, materials, qualified teachers, computers, and other necessities for learning. In lieu of resources, the state offers tests, which are used to hold students back if they do not reach benchmarks (a practice found to increase later dropout rates but not to improve achievement) and to deny them diplomas, which in today's economy is the equivalent of denying access to the economy and to a productive life. In these states, two-way accountability does not exist. The child is accountable to the state for test performance, but the state is not held accountable to the child for a basic level of education. No Child Left Behind exacerbates this problem by adding to the incentives some states have already created for getting rid of the troublesome youth who don't score high and introducing these incentives to other states in the country.

There is no doubt that the current conditions of schooling for many students of color and low-income students in the United States strongly resemble those that existed before *Brown v. Board of Education* sought to end separate and unequal education. Unfortunately, this law, though rhetorically appearing to address these problems, actually threatens to leave more children behind. The incentives created by an approach that substitutes high-stakes testing for highly effective teaching are pushing more and more of the most educationally vulnerable students out of school earlier and earlier. In a growing number of states, high school completion rates for African-American and Latino students have returned to pre-1954 levels.

The consequences for individual students who are caught in this no-win situation can be tragic, as most cannot go on to further education or even military service if they fail these tests, drop out, or are pushed out to help their schools' scores look better. The consequences for society are also tragic, as more and more students are leaving school earlier and earlier—some with only a seventh- or eighth-grade education—without the skills to be able to join the economy. These students join what is increasingly known as a "school-to-prison pipeline" carrying an increasing number of undereducated youth almost directly into the criminal justice system. Indeed, prison enrollments have tripled since the 1980s, and the costs of the criminal justice system have increased by more than 600 percent (while public education spending grew by only 25 percent in real dollars). More than half of inmates are functionally illiterate, and 40 percent of adjudicated juveniles have learning disabilities that were not diagnosed or treated in school.[21] States end up paying $30,000 per inmate to keep young men behind bars when they are unwilling to provide even a quarter of this cost to give them good schools. Increasingly, this growing strain on the economy is deflecting resources away from the services that could make people productive. California and Massachusetts had the dubious distinction this year of paying as much for prisons as for higher education.

Meanwhile, many are losing touch with the futures that would have enabled them to be contributing members of society. Take, for instance, the case of twenty-year-old Tracey Newhart of Falmouth, Massachusetts, who left school in 2003 without a diploma because she could not pass one part of the MCAS exam on repeated attempts. Although Newhart has Down's syndrome, a chromosome disorder that causes mental retardation, last year she won an award in a cooking competition, beating local caterers. Having worked hard to pass her classes throughout fifteen years of school, she had pinned her hopes on attending culinary school. Her dream dashed, Tracey joined 4,300 other Massachusetts seniors who failed the exam after multiple attempts, 40 percent of whom are special needs students, along with an estimated 11,000 students who had already dropped out of school since ninth grade, discouraged by their inability to pass the single high-stakes test that determines whether they can join the labor market and go on to become productive citizens in life.

Fixing NCLB

If we are to achieve the noble goals of NCLB, the law must be amended so that states have flexibility and encouragement to use thoughtful performance assessments and that tests are used diagnostically for informing curriculum improvements rather than for punishing students or schools. Progress should be evaluated on multiple measures—including such factors as attendance, school progress and continuation, course passage, and classroom performance on tasks beyond multiple choice tests. And gains should be evaluated with "value-added" measures showing how individual students improve over time, rather than school averages that are influenced by changes in who is assessed.

Targets should be based on sensible goals for student learning that also ensure appropriate assessment for special education students and English language learners and credit for the gains these students make over time. While progress for subgroups of students should be reported, these reports should include evidence about continuation and success in school, as well as academic achievement for members of each group. Determinations of school progress should be constructed to reflect a better grounded analysis of schools' actual performance and progress rather than a statistical gauntlet that penalizes schools serving the most diverse populations. These reporting changes should be designed to ensure that schools identified as failing are indeed those that are offering poor education, not those merely caught in a mathematical mousetrap. And progress should be gauged against sensible benchmarks for success. As policy analyst Bruce Fuller notes of the law's current 100 percent proficiency standard:

> Would government ever require automakers to produce emissions-free cars in the space of a decade, then shut down companies that failed to meet a pie-in-the-sky goal? Of course not! Better to set demanding yet pragmatic standards and require clear signs of progress. Schools should be rewarded for elevating achievement levels by some degree, rather than penalized for not meeting an absolute, unrealistic standard. The ideal level of proficiency for all—just like emissions-free cars—could then be approached gradually, over time.[22]

Most important, schools that are struggling should receive intensive help to strengthen their staffs and adopt successful programs. Full funding of NCLB should include support to hire well-qualified teachers and to provide intensive professional development: learning how to better teach those who struggle to learn. Full federal funding should also be used to leverage state investment, requiring the creation of Opportunity to Learn standards that can support annual reporting about the resources (teacher qualifications, curriculum opportunities, materials and equipment) available to children in all schools and annual progress on these indicators as well as indicators of student learning. Accountability must be two-way: state and federal support for ensuring qualified teachers and well-resourced schools must accompany expectations of students and schools.

Just offering high-stakes tests does not provide what parents and children would call genuine accountability. Obviously, students will not learn at higher levels unless they experience good teaching, a strong curriculum, and adequate resources. Most of the students who are struggling are students who have long experienced suboptimal schooling and students who have special learning needs that require higher levels of expertise from teachers. Because this nation has not yet invested heavily in teachers and their knowledge, the capacity to teach all students to high levels is not widespread. Only by investing in teaching can we improve the instruction of students who are currently struggling to learn; just adding tests and punishments will not do the trick.

Ensuring Qualified Teachers

One of the greatest shortcomings of schools serving our neediest students is that they typically have the least experienced and well-qualified teachers, even though such students need our most skilled teachers if they are to learn what they need to know. While recent studies have found that teacher quality is one of the most important school variables influencing student achievement, teachers are the most inequitably distributed school resource. Although states do not allow the hiring of doctors, lawyers, or engineers who have not met licensing standards, about thirty states still allow the hiring of untrained teachers who do not meet their certification standards, most of them are assigned to teach the most disadvantaged students in low-income and high-minority schools, and the most highly educated teachers are typically hired by wealthier schools.[23]

One of the great ironies of the federal education programs designed to support the education of low-income students and those requiring special education, compensatory education, or bilingual education services is that poor schools have often served these students with unqualified teachers and untrained aides, rather than the highly skilled teachers envisioned by federal laws. The very purpose of the legislation—to ensure greater opportunities for learning for these students—has often been undermined by local inability to provide them with teachers who have the skills to meet their needs.

In states that have lowered standards rather than increasing incentives to teaching, it is not hard to find urban and poor rural schools where one-third or more of the teachers are working without training, certification, or mentoring. In schools with the highest minority enrollments, students have less than a 50 percent chance of getting a mathematics or science teacher with a license and a degree in the field that they teach. Thus, students who are the least likely to have learning supports at home are also least likely to have teachers who understand how children learn and develop, who know how to teach them to read and problem solve, and who know what to do if they are having difficulty.

Thus, one of the most important aspects of No Child Left Behind is that it requires all schools to provide "highly qualified teachers" to all students by 2006. This requirement—that all teachers be fully certified and show competence in the subject areas they teach—is intended to correct this long-standing problem. And it is a problem that can be solved. What often looks like a teacher shortage is actually mostly a problem of getting teachers from where they are trained to where they are needed and keeping teachers in the profession, especially in central cities and poor rural areas. More than 30 percent of beginners leave teaching within five years, and low-income schools suffering from even higher turnover rates, producing more teachers—especially through fast-track routes that tend to have high attrition—is like spending all our energy filling a leaky bucket rather than fixing it.

We need to understand this problem if we are to solve it. There are actually at least three or four times as many credentialed teachers in the United States as there are jobs, and many states and districts have surpluses. Not surprisingly, teachers are less likely to enter and stay in teaching where salaries are lower and working conditions are poorer. They are also more than twice as likely to leave if they have not had preparation for teaching and if they do not receive mentoring in their early years on the job. These are problems that can be solved. States and districts that have increased and equalized salaries to attract qualified teachers, have created strong preparation programs so that teachers are effective with the students they will teach, and have provided mentors show how we can fill classrooms with well-prepared teachers.

But solving this problem everywhere requires a national agenda. The distributional inequities that led to the hiring of unqualified teachers are caused not only by disparities in pay and working conditions, but also by interstate barriers to teacher mobility, inadequate recruitment incentives to distribute teachers appropriately, and fiscal conditions that often produce incentives for hiring the least expensive rather than the most qualified teachers. And while the nation actually produces far more new teachers than it needs, some specific teaching fields experience real shortages. These include teachers for children with disabilities and those with limited English proficiency, as well as teachers of science and mathematics. Boosting supply in the fields where there are real shortfalls requires targeted recruitment and investment in the capacity of preparation institutions to expand their programs to meet national needs in key areas.

Although No Child Left Behind sets an expectation for hiring qualified teachers, it does not yet include the policy support to make this possible. The federal government should play a leadership role in providing an adequate supply of well-qualified teachers just as it has in providing an adequate supply of well-qualified physicians for the nation. When shortages of physicians were a major problem more than forty years ago, Congress passed the 1963 Health Professions Education Assistance Act to support and improve the caliber of medical training, create and strengthen teaching hospitals, provide scholarships and loans to medical students, and implement incentives for physicians to

train in shortage specialties and locate in underserved areas. Similar federal initiatives in education were effective during the 1960s and 1970s but were eliminated in the 1980s. We need a federal teacher policy that will (1) *recruit new teachers* who prepare to teach in high-need fields and locations, through scholarships and forgivable loans that allow them to receive high-quality teacher education; (2) *strengthen teachers' preparation* through incentive grants to schools of education to create professional development schools, like teaching hospitals, to train prospective teachers in urban areas and to expand and improve programs to prepare special education teachers, teachers of English language learners, and other areas where our needs exceed our current capacity; and (3) *improve teacher retention and effectiveness* by ensuring they have mentoring support during the beginning stage when 30 percent of them drop out of teaching.[24] For the cost of 1 percent of the Bush administration's 2003 tax cuts or the equivalent of one week's combat costs during the war in Iraq, we could provide top-quality preparation for more than 150,000 new teachers to teach in high-need schools and mentor all of the new teachers who are hired over the next five years. With just a bit of focus, we could ensure that all students in the United States are taught by highly qualified teachers within the next five years. Now that would be *real* accountability.

In addition to incentives for recruiting and retaining high-quality teachers in the places where they are most needed, fixing No Child Left Behind will require a new approach to measuring and supporting school success. This approach should, first, fix the accountability provisions of the law by:

- Replacing the counterproductive federal mandated AYP formula with less rigid and more instructionally useful state accountability systems designed to 1) support and assess student progress on thoughtful assessments; 2) reduce achievement gaps among groups of students; and 3) increase graduation rates.

- Encouraging rather than discouraging the use of diagnostic assessments and high-quality state or local performance assessments as a key part of state accountability systems aimed at improving curriculum and teaching rather than punishing students or schools.

- Including multiple measures of learning and progress in assessing school progress and success, not just standardized tests—as well as results of performance assessments, attendance, and student continuation in and progress through school.

- Evaluating gains using "value-added" approaches that assess the progress of individual students, not changes in average student scores that penalize schools which serve the neediest students or encourage schools to keep out or push out low-scoring students.

- Assessing the progress of English language learners and students with disabilities based on professional testing standards and "counting" the gains of these students throughout their entire school careers, rather than counting only for the time they are "classified" in these categories.

Even more important, the law should improve the quality of education students actually receive by:

- Fully funding NCLB and developing a major federal initiative to underwrite strong preparation and recruitment incentives for well-qualified teachers who will teach in high-need schools.

- Ensuring that states focus attention and expertise on truly failing schools and that federal funding is organized to direct substantial resources toward the core building blocks of school success—the provision of well-qualified teachers, small classes, strong curriculum, and high-quality materials—rather than offering only supplemental services and an unusable transfer option.

- Leveraging more adequate and equitable state funding of public schools by requiring states to report and monitor school progress on Opportunity to Learn standards that reveal resources available to children (teacher qualifications, curriculum opportunities, materials and equipment) alongside their publication of achievement data.

At the heart of these reforms must be a recognition that public education is in many ways the very foundation of our democracy and *the* public institution that defines the people's concept of "public." It is the nation's most valuable public resource for creating common ground in what we as a collective know and believe, for developing a strong citizenry, and for ensuring a prepared workforce. It serves as the center of all types of communities and as the glue that holds us together as a people. Although there is a strong privatization instinct in Washington at the moment, the American people reiterate in poll after poll that they support public education, are willing to invest in it, and expect it to be a leavening agent for society—in fact, some might argue, the only one left in America. While there are improvements to be made in schools, schools are a product of the society we have jointly created and will meet the aspirations Americans hold for them only if they are given intelligent guidance and the critical supports they need, while children are assured the health and family supports that allow them to be ready to learn.

Unfortunately, the NCLB law does not provide those supports and, poorly administered, has the potential to undermine successful schools while failing to fix or recreate those that are truly failing. Meanwhile, NCLB could damage the ability of public education to play its critical and vital role in our society. If we really care about No Child Left Behind, our policies should invest in public schools in all communities; encourage teaching and assessment that supports higher-order thinking and performance; and create "two-way accountability"—accountability to parents and children for the quality of education they receive—as a means for greater learning for all.

NOTES

1. G. Sunderman and J. Kim, *Inspiring Vision, Disappointing Results: Four Studies on Implementing the No Child Left Behind Act* (Cambridge, Mass.: Harvard Civil Rights Project, 2004).

2. J. Novak and B. Fuller, *Penalizing Diverse Schools? Similar Test Scores but Different Students Bring Federal Sanctions* (Berkeley: Policy Analysis for California Education, 2003).

3. L. Darling-Hammond, "What Happens to a Dream Deferred? The Continuing Quest for Equal Educational Opportunity," in *Handbook of Research on Multicultural Education*, 2d ed., ed. James A. Banks (San Francisco: Jossey-Bass, 2004), 607–30.

4. Robert L. Linn, "Accountability: Responsibility and Reasonable Expectations," *Educational Researcher* 32 (2003): 3–13.

5. W. J. Erpenbach, E. Forte-Fast, and A. Potts, *Statewide Educational Accountability Under NCLB* (Washington, D.C.: Council for Chief State School Officers, 2003).

6. Novak and Fuller, *Penalizing Diverse Schools?*; Sunderman and Kim, *Inspiring Vision, Disappointing Results*.

7. C. Clotfelter, H. Ladd, J. Vigdor, and R. Diaz, "Do school accountability systems make it more difficult for low-performing schools to attract and retain high-quality teachers?", paper presented at the annual meeting of the American Economic Association, Washington, D.C., February 2003.

8. D. DeVise, "A+ Plan Prompts Teacher Exodus in Broward County," *Miami Herald*, 5 November 1999.

9. Darling-Hammond, "What Happens to a Dream Deferred?"

10. Erpenbach et al., *Statewide Educational Accountability Under NCLB*.

11. Richard L. Allington and Anne McGill-Franzen, "Unintended Effects of Educational Reform in New York," *Educational Policy* 6 (4) (1992): 397–414; D. N. Figlio and L. S. Getzler, "Accountability, Ability, and Disability: Gaming the System?" National Bureau of Economic Research, April 2002.

12. B. A. Jacob, "The Impact of High-Stakes Testing on Student Achievement: Evidence from Chicago," Working Paper, Harvard University, 2002; W. Haney, "The Myth of the Texas Miracle in Education," *Education Policy Analysis Archives* 8 (41) (2000), http://epaa.asu.edu/epaa/v8n41/.

13. L. Darling-Hammond, "The Implications of Testing Policy for Quality and Equality," *Phi Delta Kappan* (November 1991): 220–25; F. Smith et al., *High School Admission and the Improvement of Schooling* (New

York: New York City Board of Education, 1986).

14. Haney, "The Myth of the Texas Miracle in Education"; G. Orfield and C. Ashkinaze, *The Closing Door: Conservative Policy and Black Opportunity* (Chicago: University of Chicago Press, 1991), 139; Smith et al., *High School Admission and the Improvement of Schooling.*

15. Numbers of students enrolled in grade 9 are provided by the Massachusetts Department of Education in their "October 1 reports." Numbers of graduates for classes 1994–2002 were provided by the Massachusetts Department of Education in a table entitled "High School Graduation Rates by Race: 1992–2002." Numbers of graduates for 2003 have not yet been published. Numbers of students in position to graduate are those who passed the MCAS in both English language arts and math and have thus received "competency determination" (i.e., have received a high school diploma) as reported in the Massachusetts Department of Education's report, "Progress Report on Students Attaining the Competency Determination Statewide and by District," February 2004; as reported at http://www.doe.mass.edu/mcas/2003/results/0204cdprogrpt.pdf.

16. A. Wheelock, School Awards Programs and Accountability in Massachusetts: Misusing MCAS Scores to Assess School Quality, 2003, http://www.fairtest.org/arn/Alert%20June02/Alert%20Full%20Report.html.

17. M. Dobbs, "Education 'Miracle' Has a Math Problem," *Washington Post*, 9 November 2003.

18. D. J. Schemo, "Questions on Data Cloud Luster of Houston Schools," *New York Times*, 11 July 2003.

19. R. F. Ferguson, "Paying for Public Education: New Evidence on How and Why Money Matters," *Harvard Journal on Legislation* (1991): 465–98; E. Fuller, "Do properly certified teachers matter? A comparison of elementary school performance on the TAAS in 1997 between schools with high and low percentages of properly certified regular education teacher" (Austin: The Charles A. Dana Center, University of Texas at Austin, 1998); E. Fuller, "Do properly certified teachers matter? Properly certified algebra teachers and Algebra I achievement in Texas," paper presented at the annual meeting of the American Educational Research Association, New Orleans, La., 2000.

20. Haney, "The Myth of the Texas Miracle in Education."

21. Darling-Hammond, "What Happens to a Dream Deferred?"

22. Bruce Fuller, "Only the Politicking Gets an 'A,'" *Washington Post*, 1 February 2004.

23. Darling-Hammond, "What Happens to a Dream Deferred?"

24. L. Darling-Hammond and G. Sykes, "Wanted: A National Teacher Supply Policy for Education: The Right Way to Meet the 'Highly Qualified Teacher' Challenge," *Educational Policy Analysis Archives* 11 (33) (September 2003), http://epaa.asu.edu/epaa/viin33/.

Carol Corbett Burris and Kevin G. Welner

Closing the Achievement Gap by Detracking

The most recent Phi Delta Kappa/Gallup Poll of the Public's Attitudes Toward the Public Schools found that 74% of Americans believe that the achievement gap between white students and African American and Hispanic students is primarily due to factors unrelated to the quality of schooling that children receive.[1] This assumption is supported by research dating back four decades to the Coleman Report and its conclusion that schools have little impact on the problem.[2] But is the pessimism of that report justified? Or is it possible for schools to change their practices and thereby have a strongly positive effect on student achievement? We have found that when all students—those at the bottom as well as the top of the "gap"—have access to first-class learning opportunities, all students' achievement can rise.

Because African American and Hispanic students are consistently overrepresented in low-track classes, the effects of tracking greatly concern educators who are interested in closing the achievement gap.[3] Detracking reforms are grounded in the established ideas that higher achievement follows from a more rigorous curriculum and that low-track classes with unchallenging curricula result in lower student achievement.[4] Yet, notwithstand-

ing the wide acceptance of these ideas, we lack concrete case studies of mature detracking reforms and their effects. This article responds to that shortage, describing how the school district in which Carol Burris serves as a high school principal was able to close the gap by offering its high-track curriculum to all students, in detracked classes.

Tracking and the Achievement Gap

Despite overwhelming research demonstrating the ineffectiveness of low-track classes and of tracking in general, schools continue the practice.[5] Earlier studies have argued that this persistence stems from the fact that tracking is grounded in values, beliefs, and politics as much as it is in technical, structural, or organizational needs.[6] Further, despite inconsistent research findings,[7] many parents and educators assume that the practice benefits high achievers. This is partly because parents of high achievers fear that detracking and heterogeneous grouping will result in a "watered-down" curriculum and lowered learning standards for their children.

And so, despite the evidence that low-track classes cause harm, they continue to exist. Worse still, the negative achievement effects of such classes fall disproportion-ately on minority students, since, as noted above, African American and Hispanic students are overrepresented in low-track classes and underrepresented in high-track classes, even after controlling for prior measured achievement.[8] Socioeconomic status (SES) has been found to affect track assignment as well.[9] A highly proficient student from a low socioeconomic background has only a 50–50 chance of being placed in a high-track class.[10]

Researchers who study the relationship between tracking, race/ethnicity, and academic performance suggest different strategies for closing the achievement gap. Some believe that the solution is to encourage more minority students to take high-track classes.[11] Others believe that if all students are given the enriched curriculum that high-achieving students receive, achievement will rise.[12] They believe that no students—whatever their race, SES, or prior achievement—should be placed in classes that have a watered-down or remedial academic curriculum and that the tracking system should be dismantled entirely.[13] In this article, we provide evidence for the success of this latter approach. By dismantling tracking and providing the high-track curriculum to all, we can succeed in closing the achievement gap on important measures of learning.

Providing "High-Track" Curriculum to All Students

The Rockville Centre School District is a diverse suburban school district located on Long Island. In the late 1990s, it embarked on a multiyear detracking reform that increased learning expectations for all students. The district began replacing its tracked classes with heterogeneously grouped classes in which the curriculum formerly reserved for the district's high-track students was taught.

This reform began as a response to an ambitious goal set by the district's superintendent, William Johnson, and the Rockville Centre Board of Education in 1993: By the year 2000, 75% of all graduates will earn a New York State Regents diploma. At that time, the district and state rates of earning Regents diplomas were 58% and 38% respectively.

To qualify for a New York State Regents diploma, students must pass, at a minimum, eight end-of-course Regents examinations, including two in mathematics, two in laboratory sciences, two in social studies, one in English language arts, and one in a foreign language. Rockville Centre's goal reflected the superintendent's strong belief in the external evaluation of student learning as well as the district's commitment to academic rigor.

Regents exams are linked with coursework; therefore, the district gradually eliminated low-track courses. The high school eased the transition by offering students instructional support classes and carefully monitoring the progress of struggling students.

While the overall number of Regents diplomas increased, a disturbing profile of students who were not earning the diploma emerged. These students were more likely to be African American or Hispanic, to receive free or reduced-price lunch, or to have a learning disability. At the district's high school, 20% of all students were African American or Hispanic, 13% received free and reduced-price lunch, and 10% were special education students. If these graduates were to earn the Regents diploma, systemic change would need to take place to close the gaps for each of these groups.

Accelerated Mathematics in Heterogeneous Classes

On a closer inspection of the data, educators noticed that the second math Regents exam presented a stumbling block to earning the diploma. While high-track students enrolled in trigonometry and advanced algebra in the 10th grade, low-track students did not even begin first-year algebra until grade 10.

In order to provide all students with ample opportunity to pass the needed courses and to study calculus prior to graduation, Superintendent Johnson decided that all students would study the accelerated math curriculum formerly reserved for the district's highest achievers. Under the leadership of the assistant principal, Delia Garrity, middle school math teachers revised and condensed the curriculum. The new curriculum was taught to all students, in heterogeneously grouped classes. To support struggling learners, the school initiated support classes called math workshops and provided after-school help four afternoons a week.

The results were remarkable. Over 90% of incoming freshmen entered the high school having passed the first Regents math examination. The achievement gap dramatically narrowed. Between the years of 1995 and 1997, only 23% of regular education African American or Hispanic students had passed this algebra-based Regents exam before entering high school. After universally accelerating all students in heterogeneously grouped classes, the percentage more than tripled—up to 75%. The percentage of white or Asian American regular education students who passed the exam also greatly increased—from 54% to 98%.

Detracking the High School

The district approached universal acceleration with caution. Some special education students, while included in the accelerated classes, were graded using alternative assessments. This 1998 cohort of special education students would not take the first ("Sequential I") Regents math exam until they had completed ninth grade. (We use year of entry into ninth grade to determine cohort. So the 1998 cohort began ninth grade in the fall of 1998.) On entering high school, these students with special needs were placed in a double-period, low-track, "Sequential I" ninth-grade math class, along with low-achieving new entrants. Consistent with the recommendations of researchers who have defended tracking,[14] this class was rich in resources (a math teacher, special education inclusion teacher, and teaching assistant). Yet the low-track culture of the class remained unconducive to learning. Students were disruptive, and teachers spent considerable class time addressing behavior management issues. All students were acutely aware that the class carried the "low-track" label.

District and school leaders decided that this low-track class failed its purpose, and the district boldly moved forward with several new reforms the following year. All special education students in the 1999 cohort took the exam in the eighth grade. The entire 1999 cohort also studied science in heterogeneous classes throughout middle school, and it became the first cohort to be heterogeneously grouped in ninth-grade English and social studies classes.

FIGURE 26.1 Regents Diploma Rates by Year-of-Entry Cohort and Ethnicity

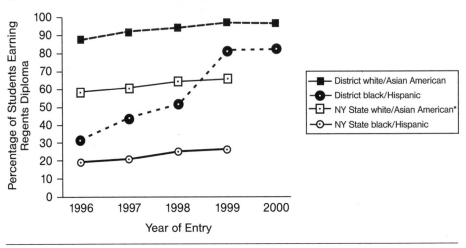

* The New York State data are reported by graduating class: the state does not report year-of-entry data for Regents diploma rates. Therefore, the state data also fail to reflect dropouts and show higher Regents diploma rates than would be reported if given by YOE cohort. (Rockville Centre has a dropout rate near zero.) For these reasons, the trends shown in this figure are informative but cannot provide exact comparisons.

Ninth-grade teachers were pleased with the results. The tone, activities, and discussions in the heterogeneously grouped classes were academic, focused, and enriched. Science teachers reported that the heterogeneously grouped middle school science program prepared students well for ninth-grade biology.

In order to ensure that the narrowing of the gap was not attributable to a changing population, we used binary logistic regression analyses to compare the probability of earning a Regents diploma before and after detracking. In addition to membership in a detracked cohort, the model included socioeconomic and special education status as covariates. Those students who were members of the 1996 and 1997 cohorts were compared with members of the 1998–2000 cohorts. We found that membership in a cohort subsequent to the detracking of middle school math was a

significant contributor to earning a Regents diploma (p< .0001). In addition, low-SES students and special education students in the 2001 cohort also showed sharp improvement.

These same three cohorts (1998–2000) showed significant increases in the probability of minority students' studying advanced math courses. Controlling for prior achievement and SES, minority students' enrollment in trigonometry, precalculus, and Advanced Placement calculus all grew.[15] And as more students from those cohorts studied AP calculus, the enrollment gap decreased from 38% to 18% in five years, and the AP calculus scores significantly increased (p<.01).

Finally, detracking in the 10th grade, combined with teaching all students the pre-IB curriculum, appears to be closing the gap in the study of the IB curriculum. This year 50% of all minority students will study IB English and "History of the Americas" in the 11th grade. In the fall of 2003, only 31% chose to do so.

Achievement follows from opportunities—opportunities that tracking denies. The results of detracking in Rockville Centre are clear and compelling. When all students were taught the high-track curriculum, achievement rose for all groups of students—majority, minority, special education, low-SES, and high-SES. This evidence can now be added to the larger body of tracking research that has convinced the Carnegie Council for Adolescent Development, the National Governors' Association, and most recently the National Research Council to call for the reduction or elimination of tracking.[16] The Rockville Centre reform confirms common sense: closing the "curriculum gap" is an effective way to close the "achievement gap."

NOTES

1. Lowell C. Rose and Alex M. Gallup, "The 36th Annual Phi Delta Kappa/Gallup Poll of the Public's Attitudes Toward the Public Schools," Phi Delta Kappan, September 2004, p. 49.

2. James Coleman et al., Equality of Educational Opportunity (Washington, D.C.: U.S. Government Printing Office, 1966).

3. Kevin G. Welner, Legal Rights, Local Wrongs: When Community Control Collides with Educational Equity (Albany: SUNY Press, 2001).

4. Clifford Adelman, Answers in the Tool Box: Academic Intensity, Attendance Patterns, and Bachelor's Degree Attainment (Washington, D.C.: Office of Educational Research, U.S. Department of Education, 1999), available on the Web at www.ed.gov/pubs/Toolbox; Henry Levin, Accelerated Schools for At-Risk Students (New Brunswick, N.J.: Rutgers University, Center for Policy Research in Educa-

tion, Report No. 142, 1988); Mano Singham, "The Achievement Gap: Myths and Realities," Phi Delta Kappan, April 2003, pp. 586–91; and Jay P. Heubert and Robert M. Hauser, High Stakes: Testing for Tracking, Promotion, and Graduation (Washington, D.C.: National Research Council, 1999).

5. Jeannie Oakes, Adam Gamoran, and Reba Page, "Curriculum Differentiation: Opportunities, Outcomes, and Meanings," in Philip Jackson, ed., Handbook of Research on Curriculum (New York: Macmillan, 1992), pp. 570–608.

6. Welner, op. cit.

7. Frederick Mosteller, Richard Light, and Jason Sachs, "Sustained Inquiry in Education: Lessons from Skill Grouping and Class Size," Harvard Educational Review, vol. 66, 1996, pp. 797–843; Robert Slavin, "Achievement Effects of Ability Grouping in Secondary Schools: A Best-Evidence Synthesis," Review of Educational Research, vol. 60, 1990, pp. 471–500; and James Kulik, An Analysis of the Research on Ability Grouping: Historical and Contemporary Perspectives (Storrs, Conn.: National Research Center on the Gifted and Talented, University of Connecticut, 1992).

8. Roslyn Mickelson, "Subverting Swann: First- and Second-Generation Segregation in Charlotte-Mecklenburg Schools," American Educational Research Journal, vol. 38, 2001, pp. 215–52; Robert Slavin and Jomills Braddock II, "Ability Grouping: On the Wrong Track," College Board Review, Summer 1993, pp. 11–17; and Welner, op. cit.

9. Samuel Lucas, Tracking Inequality: Stratification and Mobility in American High Schools (New York: Teachers College Press, 1999).

10. Beth E. Vanfossen, James D. Jones, and Joan Z. Spade, "Curriculum Tracking and Status Maintenance," Sociology of Education, vol. 60, 1987, pp. 104–22.

11. John Ogbu, Black American Students in an Affluent Suburb (Mahwah, N.J.: Erlbaum, 2003).

12. Levin, op. cit.; and Slavin and Braddock, op. cit.

13. Jeannie Oakes and Amy Stuart Wells, "Detracking for High Student Achievement," Educational Leadership, March 1998, pp. 38–41; and Susan Yonezawa, Amy Stuart Wells, and Irene Sema, "Choosing Tracks: 'Freedom of Choice' in Detracking Schools," American Educational Research Journal, vol. 39, 2002, pp. 37–67.

14. Maureen Hallinan, "Tracking: From Theory to Practice," Sociology of Education, vol. 67, 1994, pp. 79–91; and Tom Loveless, The Tracking Wars: State Reform Meets School Policy (Washington, D.C.: Brookings Institution Press, 1999).

15. Carol Corbett Burris, Jay P. Heubert, and Henry M. Levin, "Math Acceleration for All," Educational Leadership, February 2004, pp. 68–71.

16. Carnegie Council on Adolescent Development, Turning Points: Preparing American Youth for the 21st Century (New York: Carnegie Corporation, 1989); Ability Grouping and Tracking: Current Issues and Concerns (Washington, D.C.: National Governors Association, 1993); and National Research Council, Engaging Schools: Fostering High School Students' Motivation to Learn (Washington, D.C.: National Academies Press, 2004).

Jonathan Kozol

CHAPTER 27

Still Separate, Still Unequal
America's Educational Apartheid

Many Americans who live far from our major cities and who have no firsthand knowledge of the realities to be found in urban public schools seem to have the rather vague and general impression that the great extremes of racial isolation that were matters of grave national significance some thirty-five or forty years ago have gradually but steadily diminished in more recent years. The truth, unhappily, is that the trend, for well over a decade now, has been precisely the reverse. Schools that were already deeply segregated twenty-five or thirty years ago are no less segregated now, while thousands of other schools around the country that had been integrated either voluntarily or by the force of law have since been rapidly resegregating.

In Chicago, by the academic year 2002–2003, 87 percent of public-school enrollment was black or Hispanic; less than 10 percent of children in the schools were white. In Washington, D.C., 94 percent of children were black or Hispanic; less than 5 percent were white. In St. Louis, 82 percent of the student population was black or Hispanic; in Philadelphia and Cleveland, 79 percent; in Los Angeles, 84 percent, in Detroit, 96 percent; in Baltimore, 89 percent. In New York City, nearly three-quarters of the students were black or Hispanic.

Even these statistics, as stark as they are, cannot begin to convey how deeply isolated children in the poorest and most segregated sections of these cities have become. In the typically colossal high schools of the Bronx, for instance, more than 90 percent of students (in most cases, more than 95 percent) are black or Hispanic. At John F. Kennedy High School in 2003, 93 percent of the enrollment of more than 4,000 students was black and Hispanic; only 3.5 percent of students at the school were white. At Harry S. Truman High School, black and Hispanic students represented 96 percent of the enrollment of 2,700 students; 2 percent were white. At Adlai Stevenson High School, which enrolls 3,400 students, blacks and Hispanics made up 97 percent of the student population; a mere eight-tenths of 1 percent were white.

A teacher at P.S. 65 in the South Bronx once pointed out to me one of the two white children I had ever seen there. His presence in her class was something of a wonderment to the teacher and to the other pupils. I asked how many white kids she had taught in the South Bronx in her career. "I've been at this school for eighteen years," she said. "This is the first white student I have ever taught."

One of the most disheartening experiences for those who grew up in the years when Martin Luther King Jr. and Thurgood Marshall were alive is to visit public schools today that bear their names, or names of other honored leaders of the integration struggles that produced the temporary progress that took place in the three decades after *Brown v. Board of Education,* and to find out how many of these schools are bastions of contemporary segregation. It is even more disheartening when schools like these are not in deeply segregated inner-city neighborhoods but in racially mixed areas where the integration of a public school would seem to be most natural, and where, indeed, it takes a conscious effort on the part of parents or school officials in these districts to avoid the integration option that is often right at their front door.

In a Seattle neighborhood that I visited in 2002, for instance, where approximately half the families were Caucasian, 95 percent of students at the Thurgood Marshall Elementary School were black, Hispanic, Native American, or of Asian origin. An African-American teacher at the school told me—not with bitterness but wistfully—of seeing clusters of white parents and their children each morning on the corner of a street close to the school, waiting for a bus that took the children to a predominantly white school.

"At Thurgood Marshall," according to a big wall poster in the school's lobby, "the dream is alive." But school-assignment practices and federal court decisions that have countermanded long-established policies that previously fostered integration in Seattle's schools make the realization of the dream identified with Justice Marshall all but unattainable today. In San Diego there is a school that bears the name of Rosa Parks in which 86 percent of students are black and Hispanic and only some 2 percent are white. In Los Angeles there is a school that bears the name of Dr. King that is 99 percent black and Hispanic, and another in Milwaukee in which black and Hispanic children also make up 99 percent of the enrollment. There is a high school in Cleveland that is named for Dr. King in which black students make up 97 percent of the student body, and the graduation rate is only 35 percent. In Philadelphia, 98 percent of children at a high school named for Dr. King are black. At a middle school named for Dr. King in Boston, black and Hispanic children make up 98 percent of the enrollment.

In New York City there is a primary school named for Langston Hughes (99 percent black and Hispanic), a middle school named for Jackie Robinson (96 percent black and Hispanic), and a high school named for Fannie Lou Hamer, one of the great heroes of the integration movement in the South, in which 98 percent of students are black or Hispanic. In Harlem there is yet another segregated Thurgood Marshall School (also 98 percent black and Hispanic), and in the South Bronx dozens of children I have known went to a segregated middle school named in honor of Paul Robeson in which less than half of 1 percent of the enrollment was Caucasian.

There is a well-known high school named for Martin Luther King Jr. in New York City too. This school, which I've visited repeatedly in recent years, is located in an upper-middle-class white neighborhood, where it was built in the belief—or hope—that it would draw large numbers of white students by permitting them to walk to school, while only their black and Hispanic classmates would be asked to ride the bus or come by train. When the school was opened in 1975, less than a block from Lincoln Center in Manhattan, "it was seen," according to the *New York Times,* "as a promising effort to integrate white, black and Hispanic students in a thriving neighborhood that held one of the city's cultural gems." Even from the start, however, parents in the neighborhood showed great reluctance to permit their children to enroll at Martin Luther King, and, despite "its prime location and its name, which itself creates the highest of expectations," notes the *Times,* the school before long came to be a destination for black and Hispanic students who could not obtain admission into more successful schools. It stands today as one of the nation's most visible and problematic symbols of an expectation rapidly receding and a legacy substantially betrayed.

Perhaps most damaging to any serious effort to address racial segregation openly is the refusal of most of the major arbiters of culture in our northern cities to confront or even clearly name an obvious reality they would have castigated with a passionate determination in another section of the nation fifty years before—and which, moreover, they still castigate today in retrospective writings that assign it to a comfortably distant and allegedly concluded era of the past. There is, indeed, a seemingly agreed-upon convention in much of the media today not even to use an accurate descriptor like "racial segregation" in a narrative description of a segregated school. Linguistic sweeteners, semantic somersaults, and surrogate vocabularies are repeatedly employed. Schools in which as few as 3 or 4 percent of students may be white or Southeast Asian or of Middle Eastern origin, for instance—and where *every other child* in the building is black or Hispanic—are referred to as "diverse." Visitors to schools like these discover quickly the eviscerated meaning of the word, which is no longer a proper adjective but a euphemism for a plainer word that has apparently become unspeakable.

School systems themselves repeatedly employ this euphemism in describing the composition of their student populations. In a school I visited in the fall of 2004 in Kansas City, Missouri, for example, a document distributed to visitors reports that the school's curriculum "addresses the needs of children from diverse backgrounds." But as I went from class to class, I did not encounter any children who were white or Asian—or Hispanic, for that matter—and when I was later provided with precise statistics for the demographics of the school, I learned that 99.6 percent of students there were African American. In a similar document, the school board of another district, this one in New York State, referred to "the diversity" of its student population and "the rich variations of ethnic backgrounds." But when I looked at the racial numbers that the district had reported to the state, I learned that there were 2,800 black and Hispanic children in the system, 1 Asian child, and 3 whites. Words, in these cases, cease to have real meaning; or, rather, they mean the opposite of what they say.

High school students whom I talk with in deeply segregated neighborhoods and public schools seem far less circumspect than their elders and far more open in their willingness to confront these issues. "It's more like being hidden," said a fifteen-year-old girl named Isabel[1] I met some years ago in Harlem, in attempting to explain to me the ways in which she and her classmates understood the racial segregation of their neighborhoods and schools. "It's as if you have been put in a garage where, if they don't have room for something but aren't sure if they should throw it out, they put it there where they don't need to think of it again."

I asked her if she thought America truly did not "have room" for her or other children of her race. "Think of it this way," said a sixteen-year-old girl sitting beside her. "If people in New York woke up one day and learned that we were gone, that we had simply died or left for somewhere else, how would they feel?"

"How do you think they'd feel?" I asked.

"I think they'd he relieved," this very solemn girl replied.

Many educators make the argument today that given the demographics of large cities like New York and their suburban areas, our only realistic goal should be the nurturing of strong, empowered, and well-funded schools in segregated neighborhoods. Black school officials in these situations have sometimes conveyed to me a bitter and clear-sighted recognition that they're being asked, essentially, to mediate and render functional an uncontested separation between children of their race and children of white people living sometimes in a distant section of their town and sometimes in almost their own immediate communities. Implicit in this mediation is a willingness to set aside the promises of *Brown* and—though never stating this or even thinking of it clearly

in these terms—to settle for the promise made more than a century ago in *Plessy v. Ferguson*, the 1896 Supreme Court ruling in which "separate but equal" was accepted as a tolerable rationale for the perpetuation of a dual system in American society.

Equality itself—equality alone—is now, it seems, the article of faith to which most of the principals of inner-city public schools subscribe. And some who are perhaps most realistic do not even dare to ask for, or expect, complete equality, which seems beyond the realm of probability for many years to come, but look instead for only a sufficiency of means—"adequacy" is the legal term most often used today—by which to win those practical and finite victories that appear to be within their reach. Higher standards, higher expectations, are repeatedly demanded of these urban principals, and of the teachers and students in their schools, but far lower standards—certainly in ethical respects—appear to be expected of the dominant society that isolates these children in unequal institutions.

"Dear Mr. Kozol," wrote the eight-year-old, "we do not have the things you have. You have Clean things. We do not have. You have a clean bathroom. We do not have that. You have Parks and we do not have Parks. You have all the thing and we do not have all the thing. Can you help us?"

The letter, from a child named Alliyah, came in a fat envelope of twenty-seven letters from a class of third-grade children in the Bronx. Other letters that the students in Alliyah's classroom sent me registered some of the same complaints. "We don't have no gardens," "no Music or Art," and "no fun places to play," one child said. "Is there a way to fix this Problem?" Another noted a concern one hears from many children in such overcrowded schools: "We have a gym but it is for lining up. I think it is not fair." Yet another of Alliyah's classmates asked me, with a sweet misspelling, if I knew the way to make her school into a "good" school—"like the other kings have"—and ended with the hope that I would do my best to make it possible for "all the kings" to have good schools.

The letter that affected me the most, however, had been written by a child named Elizabeth. "It is not fair that other kids have a garden and new things. But we don't have that," said Elizabeth. "I wish that this school was the most beautiful school in the whole why world."

"The whole why world" stayed in my thoughts for days. When I later met Elizabeth, I brought her letter with me, thinking I might see whether, in reading it aloud, she'd change the "why" to "wide" or leave it as it was. My visit to her class, however, proved to be so pleasant, and the children seemed so eager to bombard me with their questions about where I lived, and why I lived there rather than in New York, and who I lived with, and how many dogs I had, and other interesting questions of that sort, that I decided not to interrupt the nice reception they had given me with questions about usages and spelling. I left "the whole why world" to float around unedited and unrevised in my mind. The letter itself soon found a resting place on the wall above my desk.

In the years before I met Elizabeth, I had visited many other schools in the South Bronx and in one northern district of the Bronx as well. I had made repeated visits to a high school where a stream of water flowed down one of the main stairwells on a rainy afternoon and where green fungus molds were growing in the office where the students went for counseling. A large blue barrel was positioned to collect rain-water coming through the ceiling. In one makeshift elementary school housed in a former skating rink next to a funeral establishment in yet another nearly all-black-and-Hispanic section of the Bronx, class size rose to thirty-four and more; four kindergarten classes and a sixth-grade class were packed into a single room that had no windows. The air was stifling in many rooms, and the children had no place for recess because there was no outdoor playground and no indoor gym.

In another elementary school, which had been built to hold 1,000 children but was packed to bursting with some 1,500, the principal poured out his feelings to me in a room in which a plastic garbage bag had been attached somehow to cover part of the collapsing ceiling. "This," he told me, pointing to the garbage bag, then gesturing around him at the other indications of decay and disrepair one sees in ghetto schools much like it elsewhere, "would not happen to white children."

Libraries, once one of the glories of the New York City school system, were either nonexistent or, at best, vestigial in large numbers of the elementary schools. Art and music programs had also for the most part disappeared. "When I began to teach in 1969," the principal of an elementary school in the South Bronx reported to me, "every school had a full-time licensed art and music teacher and librarian." During the subsequent decades, he recalled, "I saw all of that destroyed."

School physicians also were removed from elementary schools during these years. In 1970, when substantial numbers of white children still attended New York City's public schools, 400 doctors had been present to address the health needs of the children. By 1993 the number of doctors had been cut to 23, most of them part-time—a cutback that affected most severely children in the city's poorest neighborhoods, where medical facilities were most deficient and health problems faced by children most extreme. Teachers told me of asthmatic children who came into class with chronic wheezing and who at any moment of the day might undergo more serious attacks, but in the schools I visited there were no doctors to attend to them.

In explaining these steep declines in services, political leaders in New York tended to point to shifting economic factors, like a serious budget crisis in the middle 1970s, rather than to the changing racial demographics of the student population. But the fact of economic ups and downs from year to year, or from one decade to the next, could not convincingly explain the permanent shortchanging of the city's students, which took place routinely in good economic times and bad. The bad times were seized upon politically to justify the cuts, and the money was never restored once the crisis years were past.

"If you close your eyes to the changing racial composition of the schools and look only at budget actions and political events," says Noreen Connell, the director of the nonprofit Educational Priorities Panel in New York, "you're missing the assumptions that are underlying these decisions." When minority parents ask for something better for their kids, she says, "the assumption is that these are parents who can be discounted. These are kids who just don't count—children we don't value."

This, then, is the accusation that Alliyah and her classmates send our way: "You have. . . . We do not have." Are they right or are they wrong? Is this a case of naïve and simplistic juvenile exaggeration? What does a third-grader know about these big-time questions of fairness and justice? Physical appearances apart, how in any case do you begin to measure something so diffuse and vast and seemingly abstract as having more, or having less, or not having at all?

Around the time I met Alliyah in the school year 1997–1998, New York's Board of Education spent about $8,000 yearly on the education of a third-grade child in a New York City public school. If you could have scooped Alliyah up out of the neighborhood where she was born and plunked her down in a fairly typical white suburb of New York, she would have received a public education worth about $12,000 a year. If you were to lift her up once more and set her down in one of the wealthiest white suburbs of New York, she would have received as much as $18,000 worth of public education every year and would likely have had a third-grade teacher paid approximately $30,000 more than her teacher in the Bronx was paid.

The dollars on both sides of the equation have increased since then, but the discrepancies between them have remained. The present per-pupil spending level in the New York City schools is $11,700, which may be compared with a per-pupil spending level in excess of $22,000 in the well-to-do suburban district of Manhasset, Long Island. The present New York City level is, indeed, almost exactly what Manhasset spent per pupil eighteen years ago, in 1987, when that sum of money bought a great deal more in services and salaries than it can buy today. In dollars adjusted for inflation, New York City has not yet caught up to where its wealthiest suburbs were a quarter-century ago.

Gross discrepancies in teacher salaries between the city and its affluent white suburbs have remained persistent as well. In 1997 the median salary for teachers in Alliyah's neighborhood was $43,000, as compared with $74,000 in suburban Rye, $77,000 in Manhasset, and $81,000 in the town of Scarsdale, which is only about eleven miles from Alliyah's school. Five years later, in 2002, salary scales for New York City's teachers rose to levels that approximated those within the lower-spending districts in the suburbs, but salary scales do not reflect the actual salaries that teachers typically receive, which are dependent upon years of service and advanced degrees. Salaries for first-year teachers in the city were higher than they'd been four years before, but the differences in median pay between the city and its upper-middle-income suburbs had remained extreme. The overall figure for New York City in 2002–2003 was $53,000, while it had climbed to $87,000 in Manhasset and exceeded $95,000 in Scarsdale.

"There are expensive children and there are cheap children," writes Marina Warner, an essayist and novelist who has written many books for children, "just as there are expensive women and cheap women." The governmentally administered diminishment in value of the children of the poor begins even before the age of five or six, when they begin their years of formal education in the public schools. It starts during their infant and toddler years, when hundreds of thousands of children of the very poor in much of the United States are locked out of the opportunity for preschool education for no reason but the accident of birth and budgetary choices of the government, while children of the privileged are often given veritable feasts of rich developmental early education.

In New York City, for example, affluent parents pay surprisingly large sums of money to enroll their youngsters, beginning at the age of two or three, in extraordinary early-education programs that give them social competence and rudimentary pedagogic skills unknown to children of the same age in the city's poorer neighborhoods. The most exclusive of the private preschools in New York, which are known to those who can afford them as "Baby Ivies," cost as much as $24,000 for a full-day program. Competition for admission to these pre–K schools is so extreme that private counselors are frequently retained, at fees as high as $300 an hour, to guide the parents through the application process.

At the opposite extreme along the economic spectrum in New York are thousands of children who receive no preschool opportunity at all. Exactly how *many* thousands are denied this opportunity in New York City and in other major cities is almost impossible to know. Numbers that originate in governmental agencies in many states are incomplete and imprecise and do not always differentiate with clarity between authentic pre–K programs that have educative and developmental substance and those less expensive child-care arrangements that do not. But even where states do compile numbers that refer specifically to educative preschool programs, it is difficult to know how many of the children who are served are of low income, since admissions to some of the state-supported programs aren't determined by low income or they are determined by a complicated set of factors of which poverty is only one.

There are remarkable exceptions to this pattern in some sections of the nation. In Milwaukee, for example, virtually every four-year-old is now enrolled in a preliminary kindergarten program, which amounts to a full year of preschool education, prior to a second kindergarten year for five-year-olds. More commonly in urban neighborhoods, large numbers of low-income children are denied these opportunities and come into their kindergarten year without the minimal social skills that children need in order to participate in class activities and without even such very modest early-learning skills as knowing how to hold a crayon or a pencil, identify perhaps a couple of shapes and colors, or recognize that printed pages go from left to right.

Three years later, in third grade, these children are introduced to what are known as "high-stakes tests," which in many urban systems now determine whether students can or cannot be promoted. Children who have been in programs like those offered by the "Baby Ivies" since the age of two have, by now, received the benefits of six or seven years of education, nearly twice as many as the children who have been denied these opportunities; yet all are required to take, and will be measured by, the same examinations. Which of these children will receive the highest scores? The ones who spent the years from two to four in lovely little Montessori programs and in other pastel-painted settings in which tender and attentive and well-trained instructors read to them from beautiful storybooks and introduced them very gently for the first time to the world of numbers and the shapes of letters, and the sizes and varieties of solid objects, and perhaps taught them to sort things into groups or to arrange them in a sequence, or to do those many other interesting things that early childhood specialists refer to as pre-numeracy skills? Or the ones who spent those years at home in front of a TV or sitting by the window of a slum apartment gazing down into the street? There is something deeply hypocritical about a society that holds an eight-year-old inner-city child "accountable" for her performance on a high-stakes standardized exam but does not hold the high officials of our government accountable for robbing her of what they gave their own kids six or seven years earlier.

Perhaps in order to deflect these recognitions, or to soften them somewhat, many people, even while they do not doubt the benefit of making very large investments in the education of their own children, somehow—paradoxical as it may seem—appear to be attracted to the argument that money may not really matter that much at all. No matter with what regularity such doubts about the worth of spending money on a child's education are advanced, it is obvious that those who have the money, and who spend it lavishly to benefit their own kids, do not do it for no reason. Yet shockingly large numbers of well-educated and sophisticated people whom I talk with nowadays dismiss such challenges with a surprising ease. "Is the answer really to throw money into these dysfunctional and failing schools?" I'm often asked. "Don't we have some better ways to make them 'work'?" The question is posed in a variety of forms. "Yes, of course, it's not a perfectly fair system as it stands. But money alone is surely not the sole response. The values of the parents and the kids themselves must have a role in this as well—you know, housing, health conditions, social factors." "Other factors"—a term of overall reprieve one often hears—"have got to be considered, too." These latter points are obviously true but always seem to have the odd effect of substituting things we know we cannot change in the short run for obvious solutions like cutting class size and constructing new school buildings or providing universal preschool that we actually could put in place right now if we were so inclined.

Frequently these arguments are posed as questions that do not invite an answer because the answer seems to be decided in advance. "Can you really buy your way to better education for these children?" "Do we know enough to be quite sure that we will see an actual return on the investment that we make?" "Is it even clear that this is the right starting point to get to where we'd like to go? It doesn't always seem to work, as I am sure that you already know," or similar questions that somehow assume I will agree with those who ask them.

Some people who ask these questions, although they live in wealthy districts where the schools are funded at high levels, don't even send their children to these public schools but choose instead to send them to expensive private day schools. At some of the well-known private prep schools in the New York City area, tuition and associated costs are typically more than $20,000 a year. During their children's teenage years, they sometimes send them off to very fine New England schools like Andover or Exeter or Groton, where tuition, boarding, and additional expenses rise to more than $30,000. Often a family has two teenage children in these schools at the same time, so they may be spending more than $60,000 on their children's education every year. Yet here I am one night, a guest within their home, and dinner has been served and we are having coffee now; and this entirely likable, and generally sensible, and beautifully refined and thoughtful person looks me in the eyes and asks me whether you can really buy your way to better education for the children of the poor.

As racial isolation deepens and the inequalities of education finance remain unabated and take on new and more innovative forms, the principals of many inner-city schools are making choices that few principals in public schools that serve white children in the mainstream of the nation ever need to contemplate. Many have been dedicating vast amounts of time and effort to create an architecture of adaptive strategies that promise incremental gains within the limits inequality allows.

New vocabularies of stentorian determination, new systems of incentive, and new modes of castigation, which are termed "rewards and sanctions," have emerged. Curriculum materials that are alleged to be aligned with governmentally established goals and standards and particularly suited to what are regarded as "the special needs and learning styles" of low-income urban children have been introduced. Relentless emphasis on raising test scores, rigid policies of nonpromotion and nongraduation, a new empiricism and the imposition of unusually detailed lists of named and numbered "outcomes" for each isolated parcel of instruction, an oftentimes fanatical insistence upon uniformity of teachers in their management of time, an openly conceded emulation of the rigorous approaches of the military, and a frequent use of terminology that comes out of the world of industry and commerce—these are just a few of the familiar aspects of these new adaptive strategies.

Although generically described as "school reform," most of these practices and policies are targeted primarily at poor children of color; and although most educators speak of these agendas in broad language that sounds applicable to all, it is understood that they are valued chiefly as responses to perceived catastrophe in deeply segregated and unequal schools.

"If you do what I tell you to do, how I tell you to do it, when I tell you to do it, you'll get it right," said a determined South Bronx principal observed by a reporter for the *New York Times*. She was laying out a memorizing rule for math to an assembly of her students. "If you don't, you'll get it wrong." This is the voice, this is the tone, this is the rhythm and didactic certitude one hears today in inner-city schools that have embraced a pedagogy of direct command and absolute control. "Taking their inspiration from the ideas of B. F. Skinner," says the *Times*, proponents of scripted rote-and-drill curricula articulate their aim as the establishment of "faultless communication" between "the teacher, who is the stimulus," and "the students, who respond."

The introduction of Skinnerian approaches (which are commonly employed in penal institutions and drug-rehabilitation programs), as a way of altering the attitudes and learning styles of black and Hispanic children, is provocative, and it has stirred some outcries from respected scholars. To actually go into a school where you know some of the children very, very well and see the way that these approaches can affect their daily lives and thinking processes is even more provocative.

On a chilly November day four years ago in the South Bronx, I entered P.S. 65, a school I had been visiting since 1993. There had been major changes since I'd been there last. Silent lunches had been instituted in the cafeteria, and on days when children misbehaved, silent recess had been introduced as well. On those days the students were obliged to sit in rows and maintain perfect silence on the floor of a small indoor room instead of going out to play. The words SUCCESS FOR ALL, the brand name of a scripted curriculum—better known by its acronym, SFA—were prominently posted at the top of the main stairway and, as I would later find, in almost every room. Also frequently displayed within the halls and classrooms were a number of administrative memos that were worded with unusual didactic absoluteness. "Authentic Writing," read a document called "Principles of Learning" that was posted in the corridor close to the principal's office, "is driven by curriculum and instruction." I didn't know what this expression meant. Like many other undefined and arbitrary phrases posted in the school, it seemed to be a dictum that invited no interrogation.

I entered the fourth grade of a teacher I will call Mr. Endicott, a man in his mid-thirties who had arrived here without training as a teacher, one of about a dozen teachers in the building who were sent into this school after a single summer of short-order preparation. Now in his second year, he had developed a considerable sense of confidence and held the class under a tight control.

As I found a place to sit in a far corner of the room, the teacher and his young assistant, who was in her first year as a teacher, were beginning a math lesson about building airport runways, a lesson that provided children with an opportunity for measuring perimeters. On the wall behind the teacher, in large letters, was written: "Portfolio Protocols: 1. You are responsible for the selection of [your] work that enters your portfolio. 2. As your skills become more sophisticated this year, you will want to revise, amend, supplement, and possibly replace items in your portfolio to reflect your intellectual growth." On the left side of the room: "Performance Standards Mathematics Curriculum: M–5 Problem Solving and Reasoning. M–6 Mathematical Skills and Tools. . . . "

My attention was distracted by some whispering among the children sitting to the right of me. The teacher's response to this distraction was immediate: his arm shot out and up in a diagonal in front of him, his hand straight up, his fingers flat. The young co-teacher did this, too. When they saw their teachers do this, all the children in the classroom did it, too.

"Zero noise," the teacher said, but this instruction proved to be unneeded. The strange salute the class and teachers gave each other, which turned out to be one of a number of such silent signals teachers in the school were trained to use, and children to obey, had done the job of silencing the class.

"Active listening!" said Mr. Endicott. "Heads up! Tractor beams!" which meant, "Every eye on me."

On the front wall of the classroom, in handwritten words that must have taken Mr. Endicott long hours to transcribe, was a list of terms that could be used to praise or criticize a student's work in mathematics. At Level Four, the highest of four levels of success, a child's "problem-solving strategies" could be described, according to this list, as "systematic, complete, efficient, and possibly elegant," while the student's capability to draw conclusions from the work she had completed could be termed "insightful" or "comprehensive." At Level Two, the child's capability to draw conclusions was to be described as "logically unsound"; at Level One, "not present." Approximately 50 separate categories of proficiency, or lack of such, were detailed in this wall-sized tabulation.

A well-educated man, Mr. Endicott later spoke to me about the form of classroom management that he was using as an adaptation from a model of industrial efficiency. "It's a kind of 'Taylorism' in the classroom," he explained, referring to a set of theories about the management of factory employees introduced by Frederick Taylor in the early 1900s. "Primitive utilitarianism" is another term he used when we met some months later to discuss these management techniques with other teachers from the school. His reservations were, however, not apparent in the classroom. Within the terms of what he had been asked to do, he had, indeed, become a master of control. It is one of the few classrooms I had visited up to that time in which almost nothing even hinting at spontaneous emotion in the children or the teacher surfaced while I was there.

The teacher gave the "zero noise" salute again when someone whispered to another child at his table. "In two minutes you will have a chance to talk and share this with your partner." Communication between children in the class was not prohibited but was afforded time slots and, remarkably enough, was formalized in an expression that I found included in a memo that was posted on the wall beside the door: "An opportunity . . . to engage in Accountable Talk."

Even the teacher's words of praise were framed in terms consistent with the lists that had been posted on the wall. "That's a Level Four suggestion," said the teacher when a child made an observation other teachers might have praised as simply "pretty good" or "interesting" or "mature."

There was, it seemed, a formal name for every cognitive event within this school: "Authentic Writing," "Active Listening," "Accountable Talk." The ardor to assign all items of instruction or behavior a specific name was unsettling to me. The adjectives had the odd effect of hyping every item of endeavor. "Authentic Writing" was, it seemed, a more important act than what the children in a writing class in any ordinary school might try to do. "Accountable Talk" was something more self-conscious and significant than merely useful conversation.

Since that day at P.S. 65, I have visited nine other schools in six different cities where the same Skinnerian curriculum is used. The signs on the walls, the silent signals, the curious salute, the same insistent naming of all cognitive particulars, became familiar as I went from one school to the next.

"Meaningful Sentences" began one of the many listings of proficiencies expected of the children in the fourth grade of an inner-city elementary school in Hartford (90 percent black, 10 percent Hispanic) that I visited a short time later. "Noteworthy Questions," "Active Listening," and other designations like these had been posted elsewhere in the room. Here, too, the teacher gave the kids her outstretched arm, with hand held up, to reestablish order when they grew a little noisy, but I noticed that she tried to soften the effect of this by opening her fingers and bending her elbow slightly so it did not look quite as forbidding as the gesture Mr. Endicott had used. A warm and interesting woman, she later told me she disliked the regimen intensely.

Over her desk, I read a "Mission Statement," which established the priorities and values for the school. Among the missions of the school, according to the printed statement, which was posted also in some other classrooms of the school, was "to develop productive citizens" who have the skills that will be needed "for successful global competition," a message that was reinforced by other posters in the room. Over the heads of a group of children at their desks, a sign anointed them BEST WORKERS OF 2002.

Another signal now was given by the teacher, this one not for silence but in order to achieve some other form of class behavior, which I could not quite identify. The students gave exactly the same signal in response. Whatever the function of this signal, it was done as I had seen it done in the South Bronx and would see it done in other schools in months to come. Suddenly, with a seeming surge of restlessness and irritation—with herself, as it appeared, and with her own effective use of all the tricks that she had learned—she turned to me and said, "I can do this with my dog."

"There's something crystal clear about a number," says a top adviser to the U.S.

Senate committee that has jurisdiction over public education, a point of view that is reinforced repeatedly in statements coming from the office of the U.S. education secretary and the White House. "I want to change the face of reading instruction across the United States from an art to a science," said an assistant to Rod Paige, the former education secretary, in the winter of 2002. This is a popular position among advocates for rigidly sequential systems of instruction, but the longing to turn art into science doesn't stop with reading methodologies alone. In many schools it now extends to almost every aspect of the operation of the school and of the lives that children lead within it. In some schools even such ordinary acts as children filing to lunch or recess in the hallways or the stairwells are subjected to the same determined emphasis upon empirical precision.

"Rubric For Filing" is the printed heading of a lengthy list of numbered categories by which teachers are supposed to grade their students on the way they march along the corridors in another inner-city district I have visited. Someone, in this instance, did a lot of work to fit the filing proficiencies of children into no more and no less than thirty-two specific slots:

"Line leader confidently leads the class. . . . Line is straight. . . . Spacing is right. . . . The class is stepping together. . . . Everyone shows pride, their shoulders high . . . no slumping," according to the strict criteria for filing at Level Four.

"Line is straight, but one or two people [are] not quite in line," according to the box for Level Three. "Line leader leads the class," and "almost everyone shows pride."

"Several are slumping. . . . Little pride is showing," says the box for Level Two.

"Spacing is uneven. . . . Some are talking and whispering."

"Line leader is paying no attention," says the box for Level One. "Heads are turning every way. . . . Hands are touching. . . . The line is not straight. . . . There is no pride."

The teacher who handed me this document believed at first that it was written as a joke by someone who had simply come to be fed up with all the numbers and accounting rituals that clutter up the day in many overregulated schools. Alas, it turned out that it was no joke but had been printed in a handbook of instructions for the teachers in the city where she taught.

In some inner-city districts, even the most pleasant and old-fashioned class activities of elementary schools have now been overtaken by these ordering requirements. A student teacher in California, for example, wanted to bring a pumpkin to her class on Halloween but knew it had no ascertainable connection to the California standards. She therefore had developed what she called "The Multi-Modal Pumpkin Unit" to teach science (seeds), arithmetic (the size and shape of pumpkins, I believe—this detail wasn't clear), and certain items she adapted out of language arts, in order to position "pumpkins" in a frame of state proficiencies. Even with her multimodal pumpkin, as her faculty adviser told me, she was still afraid she would be criticized because she knew the pumpkin would not really help her children to achieve expected goals on state exams.

Why, I asked a group of educators at a seminar in Sacramento, was a teacher being placed in a position where she'd need to do preposterous curricular gymnastics to enjoy a bit of seasonal amusement with her kids on Halloween? How much injury to state-determined "purpose" would it do to let the children of poor people have a pumpkin party once a year for no other reason than because it's something fun that other children get to do on autumn days in public schools across most of America?

"Forcing an absurdity on teachers does teach something," said an African-American professor. "It teaches acquiescence. It breaks down the will to thumb your nose at pointless protocols to call absurdity 'absurd.'" Writing out the standards with the proper numbers on the chalkboard has a similar effect, he said, and doing this is "terribly important" to the principals in many of these schools. "You *have* to post the standards, and the way you know the children know the standards is by asking them to *state* the standards. And they do it—and you want to be quite certain that they do it if you want to keep on working at that school."

In speaking of the drill-based program in effect at P.S. 65, Mr. Endicott told me he tended to be sympathetic to the school administrators, more so at least than the other teachers I had talked with seemed to be. He said he believed his principal had little choice about the implementation of this program, which had been mandated for all elementary schools in New York City that had had rock-bottom academic records over a long period of time. "This puts me into a dilemma," he went on, "because I love the kids at P.S. 65." And even while, he said, "I know that my teaching SFA is a charade . . . if I don't do it I won't be permitted to teach these children."

Mr. Endicott, like all but two of the new recruits at P.S. 65—there were about fifteen in all—was a white person, as were the principal and most of the administrators at the school. As a result, most of these neophyte instructors had had little or no prior contact with the children of an inner-city neighborhood; but, like the others I met, and despite the distancing between the children and their teachers that resulted from the scripted method of instruction, he had developed close attachments to his students and did not want to abandon them. At the same time, the class- and race-specific implementation of this program obviously troubled him. "There's an expression now," he said. "'The rich get richer, and the poor get SFA.'" He said he was still trying to figure out his "professional ethics" on the problem that this posed for him.

White children made up "only about one percent" of students in the New York City schools in which this scripted teaching system was imposed,[2] according to the *New York Times*, which also said that "the prepackaged lessons" were intended "to ensure that all teachers—even novices or the most inept"—would be able to teach reading. As seemingly pragmatic and hardheaded as such arguments may be, they are desperation strategies that come out of the acceptance of inequity. If we did not have a deeply segregated system in which more experienced instructors teach the children of the privileged and the least experienced are sent to teach the children of minorities, these practices would not be needed and could not be so convincingly defended. They are confections of apartheid, and no matter by what arguments of urgency or practicality they have been justified, they cannot fail to further deepen the divisions of society.

There is no misery index for the children of apartheid education. There ought to be; we measure almost everything else that happens to them in their schools. Do kids who go to schools like these enjoy the days they spend in them? Is school, for most of them, a happy place to be? You do not find the answers to these questions in reports about achievement levels, scientific methods of accountability, or structural revisions in the modes of governance. Documents like these don't speak of happiness. You have to go back to the schools themselves to find an answer to these questions. You have to sit down in the little chairs in first and second grade, or on the reading rug with kindergarten kids, and listen to the things they actually say to one another and the dialogue between them and their teachers. You have to go down to the basement with the children when it's time for lunch and to the playground with them, if they have a playground, when it's time for recess, if they still have recess at their school. You have to walk into the children's bathrooms in these buildings. You have to do what children do and breathe the air the children breathe. I don't think that there is any other way to find out what the lives that children lead in school are really like.

High school students, when I first meet them, are often more reluctant than the younger children to open up and express their personal concerns; but hesitation on the part of students did not prove to be a problem when I visited a tenth-grade class at Fremont High School in Los Angeles. The students were told that I was a writer, and they took no time in getting down to matters that were on their minds.

"Can we talk about the bathrooms?" asked a soft-spoken student named Mireya.

In almost any classroom there are certain students who, by the force of their directness or the unusual sophistication of their way of speaking, tend to capture your attention from the start. Mireya later spoke insightfully about some of the serious academic problems that were common in the school, but her observations on the physical and personal embarrassments she and her schoolmates had to undergo cut to the heart of questions of essential dignity that kids in squalid schools like this one have to deal with all over the nation.

Fremont High School, as court papers filed in a lawsuit against the state of California document, has fifteen fewer bathrooms than the law requires. Of the limited number of bathrooms that are working in the school, "only one or two . . . are open and unlocked for girls to use." Long lines of girls are "waiting to use the bathrooms," which are generally "unclean" and "lack basic supplies," including toilet paper. Some of the classrooms, as court papers also document, "do not have air conditioning," so that students, who attend school on a three-track schedule that runs year-round, "become red-faced and unable to concentrate" during "the extreme heat of summer." The school's maintenance records report that rats were found in eleven classrooms. Rat droppings were found "in the bins and drawers" of the high school's kitchen, and school records note that "hamburger buns" were being "eaten off [the] bread-delivery rack."

No matter how many tawdry details like these I've read in legal briefs or depositions through the years, I'm always shocked again to learn how often these unsanitary physical conditions are permitted to continue in the schools that serve our poorest students—even after they have been vividly described in the media. But hearing of these conditions in Mireya's words was even more unsettling, in part because this student seemed so fragile and because the need even to speak of these indignities in front of me and all the other students was an additional indignity.

"The problem is this," she carefully explained. "You're not allowed to use the bathroom during lunch, which is a thirty-minute period. The only time that you're allowed to use it is between your classes." But "this is a huge building," she went on. "It has long corridors. If you have one class at one end of the building and your next class happens to be way down at the other end, you don't have time to use the bathroom and still get to class before it starts. So you go to your class and then you ask permission from your teacher to go to the bathroom and the teacher tells you, 'No. You had your chance between the periods . . .'

"I feel embarrassed when I have to stand there and explain it to a teacher."

"This is the question," said a wiry-looking boy named Edward, leaning forward in his chair. "Students are not animals, but even animals need to relieve themselves sometimes. We're here for eight hours. What do they think we're supposed to do?"

"It humiliates you," said Mireya, who went on to make the interesting state-ment that "the school provides solutions that don't actually work," and this idea was taken up by several other students in describing course requirements within the school. A tall black student, for example, told me that she hoped to be a social worker or a doctor but was programmed into "Sewing Class" this year. She also had to take another course, called "Life Skills," which she told me was a very basic course—"a retarded class," to use her words—that "teaches things like the six continents," which she said she'd learned in elementary school.

When I asked her why she had to take these courses, she replied that she'd been told they were required, which as I later learned was not exactly so. What was required was that high school students take two courses in an area of study called "The Technical Arts," and which the Los Angeles Board of Education terms "Applied Technology." At schools that served the middle class or upper-middle class, this requirement was likely to be met by courses that had academic substance and, perhaps, some relevance to college preparation. At Beverly Hills High School, for example, the technical-arts requirement could be fulfilled by taking subjects like residential architecture, the designing of commercial structures, broadcast journalism, advanced computer graphics, a sophisticated course in furniture design, carving and sculpture, or an honors course in engineering research and design. At Fremont High, in contrast, this requirement was far more often met by courses that were basically vocational and also obviously keyed to low-paying levels of employment.

Mireya, for example, who had plans to go to college, told me that she had to take a sewing class last year and now was told she'd been assigned to take a class in hairdressing as well. When I asked her teacher why Mireya could not skip these subjects and enroll in classes that would help her to pursue her college aspirations, she replied, "It isn't a question of what students want. It's what the school may have available. If all the other elective classes that a student wants to take are full, she has to take one of these classes if she wants to graduate."

A very small girl named Obie, who had big blue-tinted glasses tilted up across her hair, interrupted then to tell me with a kind of wild gusto that she'd taken hairdressing *twice*! When I expressed surprise that this was possible, she said there were two levels of hairdressing offered here at Fremont High. "One is in hairstyling," she said. "The other is in braiding."

Mireya stared hard at this student for a moment and then suddenly began to cry. "I don't *want* to take hairdressing. I did not need sewing either. I knew how to sew. My mother is a seamstress in a factory. I'm trying to go to college. I don't need to sew to go to college. My mother sews. I hoped for something else."

"What would you rather take?" I asked.

"I wanted to take an AP class," she answered.

Mireya's sudden tears elicited a strong reaction from one of the boys who had been silent up till now: a thin, dark-eyed student named Fortino, who had long hair down to his shoulders. He suddenly turned directly to Mireya and spoke into the silence that followed her last words.

"Listen to me," he said. "The owners of the sewing factories need laborers. Correct?"

"I guess they do," Mireya said.

"It's not going to be their own kids. Right?"

"Why not?" another student said.

"So they can grow beyond themselves," Mireya answered quietly. "But we remain the same."

"You're ghetto," said Fortino, "so we send you to the factory." He sat low in his desk chair, leaning on one elbow, his voice and dark eyes loaded with a cynical intelligence. "You're ghetto—so you sew!"

"There are higher positions than these," said a student named Samantha.

"You're ghetto," said Fortino unrelentingly. "So sew!"

Admittedly, the economic needs of a society are bound to be reflected to some rational degree within the policies and purposes of public schools. But, even so, there must be *something* more to life as it is lived by six-year-olds or ten-year-olds, or by teenagers, for that matter, than concerns about "successful global competition." Childhood is not merely basic training for utilitarian adulthood. It should have some claims upon our mercy, not for its future value to the economic interests of competitive societies but for its present value as a perishable piece of life itself.

Very few people who are not involved with inner-city schools have any real idea of the extremes to which the mercantile distortion of the purposes and character of education have been taken or how unabashedly proponents of these practices are willing to defend them. The head of a Chicago school, for instance, who was criticized by some for emphasizing rote instruction that, his critics said, was turning children into "robots," found no reason to dispute the charge. "Did you ever stop to think that these robots will never burglarize your home?" he asked, and "will never snatch your pocketbooks. . . . These robots are going to be producing taxes."

Corporate leaders, when they speak of education, sometimes pay lip-service to the notion of "good critical and analytic skills," but it is reasonable to ask whether they have in mind the critical analysis of *their* priorities. In principle, perhaps some do; but, if so, this is not a principle that seems to have been honored widely in the schools I have been visiting. In all the various business-driven inner-city classrooms I have observed in the past five years, plastered as they are with corporation brand names and managerial vocabularies, I have yet to see the two words "labor unions." Is this an oversight? How is that possible? Teachers and principals themselves, who are almost always members of a union, seem to be so beaten down that they rarely even question this omission.

It is not at all unusual these days to come into an urban school in which the principal prefers to call himself or herself "building CEO" or "building manager." In some of the same schools teachers are described as "classroom managers."[3] I have never been in a suburban district in which principals were asked to view themselves or teachers in this way. These terminologies remind us of how wide the distance has become between two very separate worlds of education.

It has been more than a decade now since drill-based literacy methods like Success For All began to proliferate in our urban schools. It has been three and a half years since the systems of assessment that determine the effectiveness of these and similar practices were codified in the federal legislation, No Child Left Behind, that President Bush signed into law in 2002. Since the enactment of this bill, the number of standardized exams children must take has more than doubled. It will probably increase again after the year 2006, when standardized tests, which are now required in grades three through eight, may be required in Head Start programs and, as President Bush has now proposed, in ninth, tenth, and eleventh grades as well.

The elements of strict accountability, in short, are solidly in place; and in many states where the present federal policies are simply reinforcements of accountability requirements that were established long before the passage of the federal law, the same regimen has been in place since 1995 or even earlier. The "tests-and-standards" partisans have had things very much their way for an extended period of time, and those who were convinced that they had ascertained "what works" in schools that serve minorities and children of the poor have had ample opportunity to prove that they were right.

What, then, it is reasonable to ask, are the results?

The achievement gap between black and white children, which narrowed for three decades up until the late years of the 1980s—the period in which school segregation steadily decreased—started to widen once more in the early 1990s when the federal courts began the process of resegregation by dismantling the mandates of the *Brown* decision. From that point on, the gap continued to widen or remained essentially unchanged; and while recently there has been a modest narrowing of the gap in reading scores for fourth-grade children, the gap in secondary school remains as wide as ever.

The media inevitably celebrate the periodic upticks that a set of scores may seem to indicate in one year or another in achievement levels of black and Hispanic children in their elementary schools. But if these upticks were not merely temporary "testing gains" achieved by test-prep regimens and were instead authentic education gains, they would carry over into middle school and high school. Children who know how to read—and read with comprehension—do not suddenly become nonreaders and hopelessly disabled writers when they enter secondary school. False gains evaporate; real gains endure. Yet hundreds of thousands of the inner-city children who have made what many districts claim to be dramatic gains in elementary school, and whose principals and teachers have adjusted almost every aspect of their school days and school calendars, forfeiting recess, canceling or cutting back on all the so-called frills (art, music, even social sciences) in order to comply with state demands—those students, now in secondary school, are sitting in subject-matter classes where they cannot comprehend the texts and cannot set down their ideas in the kind of sentences expected of most fourth- and fifth-grade students in the suburbs. Students in this painful situation, not surprisingly, tend to be most likely to drop out of school.

In 48 percent of high schools in the nation's 100 largest districts, which are those in which the highest concentrations of black and Hispanic students tend to be enrolled, less than half the entering ninth-graders graduate in four years. Nationwide, from 1993 to 2002, the number of high schools graduating less than half their ninth-grade class in four years has increased by 75 percent. In the 94 percent of districts in New York State where white children make up the majority, nearly 80 percent of students graduate from high school in four years. In the 6 percent of districts where black and Hispanic students make up the majority, only 40 percent do so. There are 120 high schools in New York, enrolling nearly 200,000 minority students, where less than 60 percent of entering ninth-graders even make it to twelfth grade.

The promulgation of new and expanded inventories of "what works," no matter the enthusiasm with which they're elaborated, is not going to change this. The use of hortatory slogans chanted by the students in our segregated schools is not going to change this. Desperate historical revisionism that romanticizes the segregation of an older order (this is a common theme of many separatists today) is not going to change this. Skinnerian instructional approaches, which decapitate a child's capability for critical reflection, are not going to change this. Posters about "global competition" will certainly not change this. Turning six-year-olds into examination soldiers and denying eight-year-olds their time for play at recess will not change this.

"I went to Washington to challenge the soft bigotry of low expectations," said President Bush in his campaign for reelection in September 2004. "It's working. It's making a difference." Here we have one of those deadly lies that by sheer repetition is at length accepted by surprisingly large numbers of Americans. But it is not the truth; and it is not an innocent misstatement of the facts. It is a devious appeasement of the heartache of the parents of the black and brown and poor, and if it is not forcefully resisted it will lead us further in a very dangerous direction.

Whether the issue is inequity alone or deepening resegregation or the labyrinthine intertwining of the two, it is well past the time for us to start the work that it will take to change this. If it takes people marching in the streets and other forms of adamant disruption of the governing civilities, if it takes more than litigation, more than legislation, and much more than resolutions introduced by members of Congress, these are prices we should be prepared to pay. "We do not have the things you have," Alliyah told me when she wrote to ask if I would come and visit her school in the South Bronx. "Can you help us?" America owes that little girl and millions like her a more honorable answer than they have received.

NOTES

1. The names of children mentioned in this article have been changed to protect their privacy.

2. SFA has since been discontinued in the New York City public schools, though it is still being used in 1,300 U.S. schools, serving as many as 650,000 children. Similar scripted systems are used in schools (overwhelmingly minority in population) serving several million children.

3. A school I visited three years ago in Columbus, Ohio, was littered with "Help Wanted" signs. Starting in kindergarten, children in the school were being asked to think about the jobs that they might choose when they grew up. In one classroom there was a poster that displayed the names of several retail stores: J. C. Penney, Wal-Mart, Kmart, Sears, and a few others. "It's like working in a store," a classroom aide explained. "The children are learning to pretend they're cashiers." At another school in the same district, children were encouraged to apply for jobs in their classrooms. Among the job positions open to the children in this school, there was an "Absence Manager" and a "Behavior Chart Manager," a "Form Collector Manager," a "Paper Passer Outer Manager," a "Paper Collecting Manager," a "Paper Returning Manager," an "Exit Ticket Manager," even a "Learning Manager," a "Reading Corner Manager," and a "Score Keeper Manager." I asked the principal if there was a special reason why those two words "management" and "manager" kept popping up throughout the school. "We want every child to be working as a manager while he or she is in this school," the principal explained. "We want to make them understand that, in this country, companies will give you opportunities to work, to prove yourself, no matter what you've done." I wasn't sure what she meant by "no matter what you've done," and asked her if she could explain it. "Even if you have a felony arrest," she said, "we want you to understand that you can be a manager someday."

Beverly Daniel Tatum

CHAPTER 28

Talking About Race, Learning About Racism

The Application of Racial Identity Development Theory in the Classroom

As many educational institutions struggle to become more multicultural in terms of their students, faculty, and staff, they also begin to examine issues of cultural representation within their curriculum. This examination has evoked a growing number of courses that give specific consideration to the effect of variables such as race, class, and gender on human experience— an important trend that is reflected and supported by the increasing availability of resource manuals for the modification of course content (Bronstein & Quina, 1988; Hull, Scott, & Smith, 1982; Schuster & Van Dyne, 1985).

Unfortunately, less attention has been given to the issues of process that inevitably emerge in the classroom when attention is focused on race, class, and/or gender. It is very difficult to talk about these concepts in a meaningful way without also talking and learning about racism, classism, and sexism.[1] The introduction of these issues of oppression often generates powerful emotional responses in students that range from guilt and shame to anger and despair. If not addressed, these emo-

tional responses can result in student resistance to oppression-related content areas. Such resistance can ultimately interfere with the cognitive understanding and mastery of the material. This resistance and potential interference is particularly common when specifically addressing issues of race and racism. Yet, when students are given the opportunity to explore race-related material in a classroom where both their affective and intellectual responses are acknowledged and addressed, their level of understanding is greatly enhanced.

This article seeks to provide a framework for understanding students' psychological responses to race-related content and the student resistance that can result, as well as some strategies for overcoming this resistance. It is informed by more than a decade of experience as an African-American woman engaged in teaching an undergraduate course on the psychology of racism, by thematic analyses of student journals and essays written for the racism class, and by an understanding and application of racial identity development theory (Helms, 1990).

Setting the Context

As a clinical psychologist with a research interest in racial identity development among African-American youth raised in predominantly White communities, I began teaching about racism quite fortuitously. In 1980, while I was a part-time lecturer in the Black Studies department of a large public university, I was invited to teach a course called Group Exploration of Racism (Black Studies 2). A requirement for Black Studies majors, the course had to be offered, yet the instructor who regularly taught the course was no longer affiliated with the institution. Armed with a folder full of handouts, old syllabi that the previous instructor left behind, a copy of *White Awareness: Handbook for Anti-racism Training* (Katz, 1978), and my own clinical skills as a group facilitator, I constructed a course that seemed to meet the goals already outlined in the course catalogue. Designed "to provide students with an understanding of the psychological causes and emotional reality of racism as it appears in everyday life," the course incorporated the use of lectures, readings, simulation exercises, group research projects, and extensive class discussion to help students explore the psychological impact of racism on both the oppressor and the oppressed.

Though my first efforts were tentative, the results were powerful. The students in my class, most of whom were White, repeatedly described the course in their evaluations as one of the most valuable educational experiences of their college careers. I was convinced that helping students understand the ways in which racism operates in their own lives, and what they could do about it, was a social responsibility that I should accept. The freedom to institute the course in the curriculum of

the psychology departments in which I would eventually teach became a personal condition of employment. I have successfully introduced the course in each new educational setting I have been in since leaving that university.

Since 1980, I have taught the course (now called the Psychology of Racism) eighteen times, at three different institutions. Although each of these schools is very different—a large public university, a small state college, and a private, elite women's college—the challenges of teaching about racism in each setting have been more similar than different.

In all of the settings, class size has been limited to thirty students (averaging twenty-four). Though typically predominantly White and female (even in coeducational settings), the class makeup has always been mixed in terms of both race and gender. The students of color who have taken the course include Asians and Latinos/as, but most frequently the students of color have been Black. Though most students have described themselves as middle class, all socioeconomic backgrounds (ranging from very poor to very wealthy) have been represented over the years.

The course has necessarily evolved in response to my own deepening awareness of the psychological legacy of racism and my expanding awareness of other forms of oppression, although the basic format has remained the same. Our weekly three-hour class meeting is held in a room with movable chairs, arranged in a circle. The physical structure communicates an important premise of the course—that I expect the students to speak with each other as well as with me.

My other expectations (timely completion of assignments, regular class attendance) are clearly communicated in our first class meeting, along with the assumptions and guidelines for discussion that I rely upon to guide our work together. Because the assumptions and guidelines are so central to the process of talking and learning about racism, it may be useful to outline them here.

Working Assumptions

1. Racism, defined as a "system of advantage based on race" (see Wellman, 1977), is a pervasive aspect of U.S. socialization. It is virtually impossible to live in U.S. contemporary society and not be exposed to some aspect of the personal, cultural, and/or institutional manifestations of racism in our society. It is also assumed that, as a result, all of us have received some misinformation about those groups disadvantaged by racism.

2. Prejudice, defined as a "preconceived judgment or opinion, often based on limited information," is clearly distinguished from racism (see Katz, 1978). I assume that all of us may have prejudices as a result of the various cultural stereotypes to which we have been exposed. Even when these preconceived ideas have positive associations (such as "Asian students are good in math"), they have negative effects because they deny a person's individuality. These attitudes may influence the individual behaviors of people of color as well as of Whites, and may affect intergroup as well as intragroup interaction. However, a distinction must be made between the negative racial attitudes held by individuals of color and White individuals, because it is only the attitudes of Whites that routinely carry with them the social power inherent in the systematic cultural reinforcement and institutionalization of

those racial prejudices. To distinguish the prejudices of students of color from the racism of White students is *not* to say that the former is acceptable and the latter is not; both are clearly problematic. The distinction is important, however, to identify the power differential between members of dominant and subordinate groups.

3. In the context of U.S. society, the system of advantage clearly operates to benefit Whites as a group. However, it is assumed that racism, like other forms of oppression, hurts members of the privileged group as well as those targeted by racism. While the impact of racism on Whites is clearly different from its impact on people of color, racism has negative ramifications for everyone. For example, some White students might remember the pain of having lost important relationships because Black friends were not allowed to visit their homes. Others may express sadness at having been denied access to a broad range of experiences because of social segregation. These individuals often attribute the discomfort or fear they now experience in racially mixed settings to the cultural limitations of their youth.

4. Because of the prejudice and racism inherent in our environments when we were children, I assume that we cannot be blamed for learning what we were taught (intentionally or unintentionally). Yet as adults, we have a responsibility to try to identify and interrupt the cycle of oppression. When we recognize that we have been misinformed, we have a responsibility to seek out more accurate information and to adjust our behavior accordingly.

5. It is assumed that change, both individual and institutional, is possible. Understanding and unlearning prejudice and racism is a lifelong process that may

have begun prior to enrolling in this class, and which will surely continue after the course is over. Each of us may be at a different point in that process, and I assume that we will have mutual respect for each other, regardless of where we perceive one another to be.

To facilitate further our work together, I ask students to honor the following guidelines for our discussion. Specifically, I ask students to demonstrate their respect for one another by honoring the confidentiality of the group. So that students may feel free to ask potentially awkward or embarrassing questions, or share race-related experiences, I ask that students refrain from making personal attributions when discussing the course content with their friends. I also discourage the use of "zaps," overt or covert put-downs often used as comic relief when someone is feeling anxious about the content of the discussion. Finally, students are asked to speak from their own experience, to say, for example, "I think . . . " or "In my experience, I have found . . . " rather than generalizing their experience to others, as in "People say. . . ."

Many students are reassured by the climate of safety that is created by these guidelines and find comfort in the non-blaming assumptions I outline for the class. Nevertheless, my experience has been that most students, regardless of their class and ethnic background, still find racism a difficult topic to discuss, as is revealed by these journal comments written after the first class meeting (all names are pseudonyms):

The class is called Psychology of Racism, the atmosphere is friendly and open, yet I feel very closed in. I feel guilt and doubt well up inside of me. (Tiffany, a White woman)

Class has started on a good note thus far. The class seems rather large and disturbs me. In a class of this nature, I expect there will be many painful and emotional moments. (Linda, an Asian woman)

I am a little nervous that as one of the few students of color in the class people are going to be looking at me for answers, or whatever other reasons. The thought of this inhibits me a great deal. (Louise, an African-American woman)

I had never thought about my social position as being totally dominant. There wasn't one area in which I wasn't in the dominant group. . . . I first felt embarrassed. . . . Through association alone I felt in many ways responsible for the unequal condition existing in the world. This made me feel like shrinking in a hole in a class where I was surrounded by 27 women and 2 men, one of whom was Black and the other was Jewish. I felt that all these people would be justified in venting their anger upon me. After a short period, I realized that no one in the room was attacking or even blaming me for the conditions that exist. (Carl, a White man)

Even though most of my students voluntarily enroll in the course as an elective, their anxiety and subsequent resistance to learning about racism quickly emerge.

Sources of Resistance

In predominantly White college classrooms, I have experienced at least three major sources of student resistance to talking and learning about race and racism. They can be readily identified as the following:

1. Race is considered a taboo topic for discussion, especially in racially mixed settings.
2. Many students, regardless of racial-group membership, have been socialized to think of the United States as a just society.
3. Many students, particularly White students, initially deny any personal prejudice, recognizing the impact of racism on other people's lives, but failing to acknowledge its impact on their own.

Race as a Taboo Topic

The first source of resistance, race as a taboo topic, is an essential obstacle to overcome if class discussion is to begin at all. Although many students are interested in the topic, they are often most interested in hearing other people talk about it, afraid to break the taboo themselves.

One source of this self-consciousness can be seen in the early childhood experiences of many students. It is known that children as young as three notice racial differences (see Phinney & Rotheram, 1987). Certainly preschoolers talk about what they see. Unfortunately, they often do so in ways that make adults uncomfortable. Imagine the following scenario: A White child in a public place points to a dark-skinned African-American child and says loudly, "Why is that boy Black?" The embarrassed parent quickly responds, "Sh! Don't say that." The child is only attempting to make sense of a new observation (Derman-Sparks, Higa, & Sparks, 1980), yet the parent's attempt to silence the perplexed child sends a message that this observation is not okay to talk about. White children quickly become aware that their questions about race raise adult anxiety, and as a result, they learn not to ask questions.

When asked to reflect on their earliest race-related memories and the feelings associated with them, both White students and students of color often report feelings of confusion, anxiety, and/or fear. Students of color often have early memories of name-calling or other negative interactions with other children, and sometimes with adults. They also report having had questions that went both unasked and unanswered. In addition, many students have had uncomfortable interchanges around race-related topics as adults. When asked at the beginning of the semester, "How many of you have had difficult, perhaps heated conversations with someone on a race-related topic?" routinely almost everyone in the class raises his or her hand. It should come as no surprise then that students often approach the topic of race and/or racism with both curiosity and trepidation.

The Myth of the Meritocracy

The second source of student resistance to be discussed here is rooted in students' belief that the United States is a just society, a meritocracy where individual efforts are fairly rewarded. While some students (particularly students of color) may already have become disillusioned with that notion of the United States, the majority of my students who have experienced at least the personal success of college acceptance still have faith in this notion. To the extent that these students acknowledge that racism exists, they tend to view it as an individual phenomenon, rooted in the attitudes of the "Archie Bunkers" of the world or located only in particular parts of the country.

After several class meetings, Karen, a White woman, acknowledged this attitude in her journal:

At one point in my life—the beginning of this class—I actually perceived America to be a relatively racist free society. I thought that the people who were racist or subjected to racist stereotypes were found only in small pockets of the U.S., such as the South. As I've come to realize, racism (or at least racially orientated stereotypes) is rampant.

An understanding of racism as a system of advantage presents a serious challenge to the notion of the United States as a just society where rewards are based solely on one's merit. Such a challenge often creates discomfort in students. The old adage "ignorance is bliss" seems to hold true in this case; students are not necessarily eager to recognize the painful reality of racism.

One common response to the discomfort is to engage in denial of what they are learning. White students in particular may question the accuracy or currency of statistical information regarding the prevalence of discrimination (housing, employment, access to health care, and so on). More qualitative data, such as autobiographical accounts of experiences with racism, may be challenged on the basis of their subjectivity.

It should be pointed out that the basic assumption that the United States is a just society for all is only one of many basic assumptions that might be challenged in the learning process. Another example can be seen in an interchange between two White students following a discussion about cultural racism, in which the omission or distortion of historical information about people of color was offered as an example of the cultural transmission of racism.

"Yeah, I just found out that Cleopatra was actually a Black woman."

"What?"

The first student went on to explain her newly learned information. Finally, the second student exclaimed in disbelief, "That can't be true. Cleopatra was beautiful!" This new information and her own deeply ingrained assumptions about who is beautiful and who is not were too incongruous to allow her to assimilate the information at that moment.

If outright denial of information is not possible, then withdrawal may be. Physical withdrawal in the form of absenteeism is one possible result; it is for precisely this reason that class attendance is mandatory. The reduction in the completion of reading and/or written assignments is another form of withdrawal. I have found this response to be so common that I now alert students to this possibility at the beginning of the semester. Knowing that this response is a common one seems to help students stay engaged, even when they experience the desire to withdraw.

Following an absence in the fifth week of the semester, one White student wrote, "I think I've hit the point you talked about, the point where you don't want to hear any more about racism. I sometimes begin to get the feeling we are all hypersensitive." (Two weeks later she wrote, "Class is getting better. I think I am beginning to get over my hump.")

Perhaps not surprisingly, this response can be found in both White students and students of color. Students of color often enter a discussion of racism with some awareness of the issue, based on personal experiences. However, even these students find that they did not have a full understanding of the widespread impact of racism in our society. For students who are targeted by racism, an increased awareness of the impact in and on their lives is painful, and often generates anger.

Four weeks into the semester, Louise, an African-American woman, wrote in her journal about her own heightened sensitivity:

> Many times in class I feel uncomfortable when White students use the term Black because even if they aren't aware of it they say it with all or at least a lot of the negative connotations they've been taught goes along with Black. Sometimes it just causes a stinging feeling inside of me. Sometimes I get real tired of hearing White people talk about the condition of Black people. I think it's an important thing for them to talk about, but still I don't always like being around when they do it. I also get tired of hearing them talk about how hard it is for them, though I understand it, and most times I am very willing to listen and be open, but sometimes I can't. Right now I can't.

For White students, advantaged by racism, a heightened awareness of it often generates painful feelings of guilt. The following responses are typical:

> After reading the article about privilege, I felt vey guilty. (Rachel, a White woman)

> Questions of racism are so full of anger and pain. When I think of all the pain White people have caused people of color, I get a feeling of guilt. How could someone like myself care so much about the color of someone's skin that they would do them harm? (Terri, a White woman)

White students also sometimes express a sense of betrayal when they realize the gaps in their own education about racism. After seeing the first episode of the documentary series *Eyes on the Prize*, Chris, a White man, wrote:

> I never knew it was really that bad just 35 years ago. Why didn't I learn this in elementary or high school? Could it be that the White people of America want to forget this injustice? . . . I will never forget that movie for as long as I live. It was like a big slap in the face.

Barbara, a White woman, also felt anger and embarrassment in response to her own previous lack of information about the internment of Japanese Americans during World War II. She wrote:

> I feel so stupid because I never even knew that these existed. I never knew that the Japanese were treated so poorly. I am becoming angry and upset about all of the things that I do not know. I have been so sheltered. My parents never wanted to let me know about the bad things that have happened in the world. After I saw the movie (*Mitsuye and Nellie*), I even called them up to ask them why they never told

me this. . . . I am angry at them too for not teaching me and exposing me to the complete picture of my country.

Avoiding the subject matter is one way to avoid these uncomfortable feelings.

"I'm Not Racist, But . . ."

A third source of student resistance (particularly among White students) is the initial denial of any personal connection to racism. When asked why they have decided to enroll in a course on racism, White students typically explain their interest in the topic with such disclaimers as, "I'm not racist myself, but I know people who are, and I want to understand them better."

Because of their position as the targets of racism, students of color do not typically focus on their own prejudices or lack of them. Instead they usually express a desire to understand why racism exists, and how they have been affected by it.

However, as all students gain a better grasp of what racism is and its many manifestations in U.S. society, they inevitably start to recognize its legacy within themselves. Beliefs, attitudes, and actions based on racial stereotypes begin to be remembered and are newly observed by White students. Students of color as well often recognize negative attitudes they may have internalized about their own racial group or that they have believed about others. Those who previously thought themselves immune to the effects of growing up in a racist society often find themselves reliving uncomfortable feelings of guilt or anger.

After taping her own responses to a questionnaire on racial attitudes, Barbara, a White woman previously quoted, wrote:

I always want to think of myself as open to all races. Yet when I did the interview to myself, I found that I did respond differently to the same questions about different races. No one could ever have told me that I would have. I would have denied it. But I found that I did respond differently even though I didn't want to. This really upset me. I was angry with myself because I thought I was not prejudiced and yet the stereotypes that I had created had an impact on the answers that I gave even though I didn't want it to happen.

The new self-awareness, represented here by Barbara's journal entry, changes the classroom dynamic. One common result is that some White students, once perhaps active participants in class discussion, now hesitate to continue their participation for fear that their newly recognized racism will be revealed to others.

Today I did feel guilty, and like I had to watch what I was saying (make it good enough), I guess to prove I'm really *not* prejudiced. From the conversations the first day, I guess this is a normal enough reaction, but I certainly never expected it in me. (Joanne, a White woman)

This withdrawal on the part of White students is often paralleled by an increase in participation by students of color who are seeking an outlet for what are often feelings of anger. The withdrawal of some previously vocal White students from the classroom exchange, however, is sometimes interpreted by students of color as indifference. This perceived indifference often serves to fuel the anger and frustration that many students of color experience, as awareness of their own oppression is heightened. For example, Robert, an African-American man, wrote:

> I really wish the White students would talk more. When I read these articles, it makes me so mad and I really want to know what the White kids think. Don't they care?

Sonia, a Latina, described the classroom tension from another perspective:

> I would like to comment that at many points in the discussions I have felt uncomfortable and sometimes even angry with people. I guess I am at the stage where I am tired of listening to Whites feel guilty and watch their eyes fill up with tears. I do understand that everyone is at their own stage of development and I even tell myself every Tuesday that these people have come to this class by choice. Some days I am just more tolerant than others. . . . It takes courage to say things in that room with so many women of color present. It also takes courage for the women of color to say things about Whites.

What seems to be happening in the classroom at such moments is a collision of developmental processes that can be inherently useful for the racial identity development of the individuals involved. Nevertheless, the interaction may be perceived as problematic to instructors and students who are unfamiliar with the process. Although space does not allow for an exhaustive discussion of racial identity development theory, a brief ex-

plication of it here will provide additional clarity regarding the classroom dynamics when issues of race are discussed. It will also provide a theoretical framework for the strategies for dealing with student resistance that will be discussed at the conclusion of this article.

Stages of Racial Identity Development

Racial identity and racial identity development theory are defined by Janet Helms (1990) as

> a sense of group or collective identity based on one's *perception* that he or she shares a common racial heritage with a particular racial group . . . racial identity development theory concerns the psychological implications of racial-group membership, that is belief systems that evolve in reaction to perceived differential racial-group membership. (p. 3)

It is assumed that in a society where racial-group membership is emphasized, the development of a racial identity will occur in some form in everyone. Given the dominant/subordinate relationship of Whites and people of color in this society, however, it is not surprising that this developmental process will unfold in different ways. For purposes of this discussion, William Cross's (1971, 1978) model of Black identity development will be described along with Helms's (1990) model of White racial identity development theory. While the identity development of other students (Asian, Latino/a, Native American) is not included in this particular theoretical formulation, there is evidence to suggest that the process for these oppressed groups is similar to that described for African Americans (Highlen et al., 1988; Phinney, 1990).[2] In each case, it is assumed that a positive sense of one's self as a member of one's group (which is not based on any assumed superiority) is important for psychological health.

Black Racial Identity Development

According to Cross's (1971, 1978, 1991) model of Black racial identity development, there are five stages in the process, identified as Preencounter, Encounter, Immersion/Emersion, Internalization, and Internalization-Commitment. In the first stage of Preencounter, the African American has absorbed many of the beliefs and values of the dominant White culture, including the notion that "White is right" and "Black is wrong." Though the internalization of negative Black stereotypes may be outside of his or her conscious awareness, the individual seeks to assimilate and be accepted by Whites, and actively or passively distances him/herself from other Blacks.[3]

Louise, an African-American woman previously quoted, captured the essence of this stage in the following description of herself at an earlier time:

> For a long time it seemed as if I didn't remember my background, and I guess in some ways I didn't. I was never taught to be proud of my African heritage. Like we talked about in class, I went through a very long stage of identifying with my oppressors. Wanting to be like, live like, and be accepted by them. Even to the point of hating my own race and myself for being a part of it. Now I am ashamed that I ever was ashamed. I lost so much

of myself in my denial of and refusal to accept my people.

In order to maintain psychological comfort at this stage of development, Helms writes:

> The person must maintain the fiction that race and racial indoctrination have nothing to do with how he or she lives life. It is probably the case that the Preencounter person is bombarded on a regular basis with information that he or she cannot really be a member of the "in" racial group, but relies on denial to selectively screen such information from awareness. (1990, p. 23)

This de-emphasis on one's racial-group membership may allow the individual to think that race has not been or will not be a relevant factor in one's own achievement, and may contribute to the belief in a U.S. meritocracy that is often a part of a Preencounter worldview.

Movement into the Encounter phase is typically precipitated by an event or series of events that forces the individual to acknowledge the impact of racism in one's life. For example, instances of social rejection by White friends or colleagues (or reading new personally relevant information about racism) may lead the individual to the conclusion that many Whites will not view him or her as an equal. Faced with the reality that he or she cannot truly be White, the individual is forced to focus on his or her identity as a member of a group targeted by racism.

Brenda, a Korean-American student, described her own experience of this process as a result of her participation in the racism course:

I feel that because of this class, I have become much more aware of racism that exists around. Because of my awareness of racism, I am now bothered by acts and behaviors that might not have bothered me in the past. Before when racial comments were said around me I would somehow ignore it and pretend that nothing was said. By ignoring comments such as these, I was protecting myself. It became sort of a defense mechanism. I never realized I did this, until I was confronted with stories that were found in our reading, by other people of color, who also ignored comments that bothered them. In realizing that there is racism out in the world and that there are comments concerning race that are directed towards me, I feel as if I have reached the first step. I also think I have reached the second step, because I am now bothered and irritated by such comments. I no longer ignore them, but now confront them.

The Immersion/Emersion stage is characterized by the simultaneous desire to surround oneself with visible symbols of one's racial identity and an active avoidance of symbols of Whiteness. As Thomas Parham describes, "At this stage, everything of value in life must be Black or relevant to Blackness. This stage is also characterized by a tendency to denigrate White people, simultaneously glorifying Black people." (1989, p. 190). The previously described anger that emerges in class among African-American students and other students of color in the process of learning about racism may be seen as part of the transition through these stages.

As individuals enter the Immersion stage, they actively seek out opportunities to explore aspects of their own history and culture with the support of peers from their own racial background. Typically, White-focused anger dissipates during this phase because so much of the person's energy is directed toward his or her own group and self-exploration. The result of this exploration is an emerging security in a newly defined and affirmed sense of self.

Sharon, another African-American woman, described herself at the beginning of the semester as angry, seemingly in the Encounter stage of development. She wrote after our class meeting:

Another point that I must put down is that before I entered class today I was angry about the way Black people have been treated in this country. I don't think I will easily overcome that and I basically feel justified in my feelings.

At the end of the semester, Sharon had joined with two other Black students in the class to work on their final class project. She observed that the three of them had planned their project to focus on Black people specifically, suggesting movement into the Immersion stage of racial identity development. She wrote:

We are concerned about the well-being of our own people. They cannot be well if they have this pinned-up hatred for their own people. This internalized racism is something that we all felt, at various times, needed to be talked about. This semester it has really been important to me, and I believe Gordon [a Black classmate], too.

The emergence from this stage marks the beginning of Internalization. Secure in one's own sense of racial identity, there is less need to assert the "Blacker than thou" attitude often characteristic of the Immersion stage (Parham, 1989). In general, "pro-Black attitudes become more expansive, open, and less defensive" (Cross, 1971, p. 24). While still maintaining his or her connections with Black peers, the internalized individual is willing to establish meaningful relationships with Whites who acknowledge and are respectful of his or her self-definition. The individual is also ready to build coalitions with members of other oppressed groups. At the end of the semester, Brenda, a Korean American, concluded that she had in fact internalized a positive sense of racial identity. The process she described parallels the stages described by Cross:

> I have been aware for a long time that I am Korean. But through this class I am beginning to really become aware of my race. I am beginning to find out that White people can be accepting of me and at the same time accept me as a Korean.
>
> I grew up wanting to be accepted and ended up almost denying my race and culture. I don't think I did this consciously, but the denial did occur. As I grew older, I realized I had much in common with them. This was when I went through my "Korean friend" stage. I began to enjoy being friends with Koreans more than I did with Caucasians.
>
> Well, ultimately, through many years of growing up, I am pretty much in focus about who I am and who my friends are. I knew before I took this class that there were people not of color that were understanding of my differences. In our class, I feel that everyone is trying to sincerely find the answer of abolishing racism. I knew people like this existed, but it's nice to meet with them weekly.

Cross suggests that there are few psychological differences between the fourth stage, Internalization, and the fifth stage, Internalization-Commitment. However, those at the fifth stage have found ways to translate their "personal sense of Blackness into a plan of action or a general sense of commitment" to the concerns of Blacks as a group, which is sustained over time (Cross, 1991, p. 220). Whether at the fourth or fifth stage, the process of Internalization allows the individual, anchored in a positive sense of racial identity, both to proactively perceive and transcend race. Blackness becomes "the point of departure for discovering the universe of ideas, cultures and experiences beyond blackness in place of mistaking blackness as the universe itself" (Cross, Parham, & Helms, 1991, p. 330).

Though the process of racial identity development has been presented here in linear form, in fact it is probably more accurate to think of it in a spiral form. Often a person may move from one stage to the next, only to revisit an earlier stage as the result of new encounter experiences (Parham, 1989), though the later experience of the stage may be different from the original experience. The image that students often find helpful in understanding this concept of recycling through the stages is that of a spiral staircase. As a person ascends a spiral staircase, she may stop and look down at a spot below. When she reaches the next level, she may look down and see the same spot, but the vantage point has changed.[4]

White Racial Identity Development

The transformations experienced by those targeted by racism are often paralleled by those of White students. Helms (1990) describes the evolution of a positive White racial identity as involving both the abandonment of racism and the development of a nonracist White identity. In order to do the latter,

> he or she must accept his or her own Whiteness, the cultural implications of being White, and define a view of Self as a racial being that does not depend on the perceived superiority of one racial group over another. (p. 49)

She identifies six stages in her model of White racial identity development: Contact, Disintegration, Reintegration, Pseudo-Independent, Immersion/Emersion, and Autonomy.

The Contact stage is characterized by a lack of awareness of cultural and institutional racism, and of one's own White privilege. Peggy McIntosh (1989) writes eloquently about her own experience of this state of being:

> As a white person, I realized I had been taught about racism as something which puts others at a disadvantage, but had been taught not to see one of its corollary aspects, white privilege, which puts me at an advantage. . . . I was taught to see racism only in individual acts of meanness, not in invisible systems conferring dominance on my group. (p. 10)

In addition, the Contact stage often includes naïve curiosity about or fear of people of color, based on stereotypes learned from friends, family, or the media. These stereotypes represent the framework in use when a person at this stage of development makes a comment such as, "You don't act like a Black person" (Helms, 1990, p. 57).

Those Whites whose lives are structured so as to limit their interaction with people of color, as well as their awareness of racial issues, may remain at this stage indefinitely. However, certain kinds of experiences (increased interaction with people of color or exposure to new information about racism) may lead to a new understanding that cultural and institutional racism exist. This new understanding marks the beginning of the Disintegration stage.

At this stage, the bliss of ignorance or lack of awareness is replaced by the discomfort of guilt, shame, and sometimes anger at the recognition of one's own advantage because of being White and the acknowledgement of the role of Whites in the maintenance of a racist system. Attempts to reduce discomfort may include denial (convincing oneself that racism doesn't really exist, or if it does, it is the fault of its victims).

For example, Tom, a White male student, responded with some frustration in his journal to a classmate's observation that the fact that she had never read any books by Black authors in any of her high school or college English classes was an example of cultural racism. He wrote, "It's not my fault that Blacks don't write books."

After viewing a film in which a psychologist used examples of Black children's drawings to illustrate the potentially damaging effect of negative cultural messages on a Black child's developing self-esteem, David, another White male student, wrote:

I found it interesting the way Black children drew themselves without arms. The psychologist said this is saying that the child feels unable to control his environment. It can't be because the child has notions and beliefs already about being Black. It must be built in or hereditary due to the past history of the Blacks. I don't believe it's cognitive but more biological due to a long past history of repression and being put down.

Though Tom's and David's explanations seem quite problematic, they can be understood in the context of racial identity development theory as a way of reducing their cognitive dissonance upon learning this new race-related information. As was discussed earlier, withdrawal (accomplished by avoiding contact with people of color and the topic of racism) is another strategy for dealing with the discomfort experienced at this stage. Many of the previously described responses of White students to race-related content are characteristic of the transition from the Contact to the Disintegration stage of development.

Helms (1990) describes another response to the discomfort of Disintegration, which involves attempts to change significant others' attitudes toward African Americans and other people of color. However, as she points out,

due to the racial naïveté with which this approach may be undertaken and the person's ambivalent racial identification, this dissonance-reducing strategy is likely to be met with rejection by Whites as well as Blacks. (p. 59)

In fact, this response is also frequently observed among White students who have an opportunity to talk with friends and family during holiday visits. Suddenly they are noticing the racist content of jokes or comments of their friends and relatives and will try to confront them, often only to find that their efforts are, at best, ignored or dismissed as a "phase," or, at worst, greeted with open hostility.

Carl, a White male previously quoted, wrote at length about this dilemma:

I realized that it was possible to simply go through life totally oblivious to the entire situation or, even if one realizes it, one can totally repress it. It is easy to fade into the woodwork, run with the rest of society, and never have to deal with these problems. So many people I know from home are like this. They have simply accepted what society has taught them with little, if any, question. My father is a prime example of this. . . . It has caused much friction in our relationship, and he often tells me as a father he has failed in raising me correctly. Most of my high school friends will never deal with these issues and propagate them on to their own children. It's easy to see how the cycle continues. I don't think I could ever justify within myself simply turning my back on the problem. I finally realized that my position in all of these dominant groups gives me power to make change occur. . . . It is an unfortunate result often though that I feel alienated from friends and family. It's often played off as a mere stage that I'm going through. I obviously can't tell if it's merely a stage, but I know that they say this to take the attention off of the truth of what I'm saying. By belittling me, they take the power out of my argument. It's very depressing that being compassionate and considerate are seen as only phases that people go through. I don't want it to be a phase for me, but as obvious as this may sound, I look at my environment and often wonder how it will not be.

The societal pressure to accept the status quo may lead the individual from Disintegration to Reintegration. At this point the desire to be accepted by one's own racial group, in which the overt or covert belief in White superiority is so prevalent, may lead to a reshaping of the person's belief system to be more congruent with an acceptance of racism. The guilt and anxiety associated with Disintegration may be redirected in the form of fear and anger directed toward people of color (particularly Blacks), who are now blamed as the source of discomfort.

Connie, a White woman of Italian ancestry, in many ways exemplified the progression from the Contact stage to Reintegration, a process she herself described seven weeks into the semester. After reading about the stages of White identity development, she wrote:

I think mostly I can find myself in the disintegration stage of development. . . . There was a time when I never considered myself a color. I never described myself as a "White, Italian female" until I got to college and noticed that people of color always described themselves by their color/race. While taking this class, I have begun to understand that being White makes a difference. I never thought about it before but there are many privileges to being White. In my personal life, I can-

not say that I have ever felt that I have had the advantage over a Black person, but I am aware that my race has the advantage.

I am feeling really guilty lately about that. I find myself thinking: "I didn't mean to be White, I really didn't mean it." I am starting to feel angry towards my race for ever using this advantage towards personal gains. But at the same time I resent the minority groups. I mean, it's not our fault that society has deemed us "superior." I don't feel any better than a Black person. But it really doesn't matter because I am a member of the dominant race. . . . I can't help it . . . and I sometimes get angry and feel like I'm being attacked.

I guess my anger toward a minority group would enter me into the next stage of Reintegration, where I am once again starting to blame the victim. This is all very trying for me and it has been on my mind a lot. I really would like to be able to reach the last stage, autonomy, where I can accept being White without hostility and anger. That is really hard to do.

Helms (1990) suggests that it is relatively easy for Whites to become stuck at the Reintegration stage of development, particularly if avoidance of people of color is possible. However, if there is a catalyst for continued self-examination, the person "begins to question her or his previous definition of Whiteness and the justifiability of racism in any of its forms." (p. 61). In my experience, continued participation in a course on racism provides the catalyst for this deeper self-examination.

This process was again exemplified by Connie. At the end of the semester, she listened to her own taped interview of her racial attitudes that she had recorded at the beginning of the semester. She wrote:

> Oh wow! I could not believe some of the things that I said. I was obviously in different stages of the White identity development. As I listened and got more and more disgusted with myself when I was at the Reintegration stage, I tried to remind myself that these are stages that all (most) White people go through when dealing with notions of racism. I can remember clearly the resentment I had for people of color. I feel the one thing I enjoyed from listening to my interview was noticing how much I have changed. I think I am finally out of the Reintegration stage. I am beginning to make a conscious effort to seek out information about people of color and accept their criticism. . . . I still feel guilty about the feeling I had about people of color and I always feel bad about being privileged as a result of racism. But I am glad that I have reached what I feel is the Pseudo-Independent stage of White identity development.

The information-seeking that Connie describes often marks the onset of the Pseudo-Independent stage. At this stage, the individual is abandoning beliefs in White superiority, but may still behave in ways that unintentionally perpetuate the system. Looking to those targeted by racism to help him or her understand racism, the White person often tries to disavow his or her own Whiteness through active affiliation with Blacks, for example. The individual experiences a sense of alienation from other Whites who have not yet begun to examine their own rac-

ism, yet may also experience rejection from Blacks or other people of color who are suspicious of his or her motives. Students of color moving from the Encounter to the Immersion phase of their own racial identity development may be particularly unreceptive to the White person's attempts to connect with them.

Uncomfortable with his or her own Whiteness, yet unable to be truly anything else, the individual may begin searching for a new, more comfortable way to be White. This search is characteristic of the Immersion/Emersion stage of development. Just as the Black student seeks to redefine positively what it means to be of African ancestry in the United States through immersion in accurate information about one's culture and history, the White individual seeks to replace racially related myths and stereotypes with accurate information about what it means and has meant to be White in U.S. society (Helms, 1990). Learning about Whites who have been antiracist allies to people of color is a very important part of this process.

After reading articles written by antiracist activists describing their own process of unlearning racism, White students often comment on how helpful it is to know that others have experienced similar feelings and have found ways to resist the racism in their environments.[5] For example, Joanne, a White woman who initially experienced a lot of guilt, wrote:

> This article helped me out in many ways. I've been feeling helpless and frustrated. I know there are all these terrible things going on and I want to be able to do something. . . . Anyway this article helped me realize, again, that others feel this way,

and gave me some positive ideas to resolve my dominant class guilt and shame.

Finally, reading the biographies and autobiographies of White individuals who have embarked on a similar process of identity development (such as Barnard, 1987) provides White students with important models for change.

Learning about White antiracists can also provide students of color with a sense of hope that they can have White allies. After hearing a White antiracist activist address the class, Sonia, a Latina who had written about her impatience with expressions of White guilt, wrote:

I don't know when I have been more impressed by anyone. She filled me with hope for the future. She made me believe that there are good people in the world and that Whites suffer too and want to change things.

For White students, the internalization of a newly defined sense of oneself as White is the primary task of the Autonomy stage. The positive feelings associated with this redefinition energize the person's efforts to confront racism and oppression in his or her daily life. Alliances with people of color can be more easily forged at this stage of development than previously because the person's antiracist behaviors and attitudes will be more consistently expressed. While Autonomy might be described as "racial self-actualization, . . . it is best to think of it as an ongoing process . . . wherein the person is continually open to new information and new ways of thinking about racial and cultural variables" (Helms, 1990, p. 66).

Annette, a White woman, described herself in the Autonomy stage, but talked at length about the circular process she felt she had been engaged in during the semester:

If people as racist as C. P. Ellis (a former Klansman) can change, I think anyone can change. If that makes me idealistic, fine. I do not think my expecting society to change is naïve anymore because I now *know* exactly what I want. To be naïve means a lack of knowledge that allows me to accept myself both as a White person and as an idealist. This class showed me that these two are not mutually exclusive but are an integral part of me that I cannot deny. I realize now that through most of this class I was trying to deny both of them.

While I was not accepting society's racism, I was accepting society's telling me as a White person, there was nothing I could do to change racism. So, I told myself I was being naïve and tried to suppress my desire to change society. This is what made me so frustrated—while I saw society's racism through examples in the readings and the media, I kept telling myself there was nothing I could do. Listening to my tape, I think I was already in the Autonomy stage when I started this class. I then seemed to decide that being White, I also had to be racist which is when I became frustrated and went back to the Disintegration stage. I was frustrated because I was not only telling myself there was nothing I could do but I also was assuming society's racism was my own which made me feel like I did not want to be White. Actually, it was not being White that I was disavowing but being racist. I think I have now returned to the Autonomy stage and am much more secure in my position there. I accept my Whiteness now as just a part of me as is my idealism. I will no longer disavow these characteristics as I have realized I can be proud of both of them. In turn, I can now truly accept other people for their unique characteristics and not by the labels society has given them as I can accept myself that way.

While I thought the main ideas that I learned in this class were that White people need to be educated to end racism and everyone should be treated as human beings, I really had already incorporated these ideas into my thoughts. What I learned from this class is being White does not mean being racist and being idealistic does not mean being naïve. I really did not have to form new ideas about people of color; I had to form them about myself—and I did.

Implications for Classroom Teaching

Although movement through all the stages of racial identity development will not necessarily occur for each student within the course of a semester (or even four years of college), it is certainly common to witness beginning transformations in classes with race-related content. An awareness of the existence of this process has helped me to implement strategies to facilitate positive student development, as well as to improve interracial dialogue within the classroom.

Four strategies for reducing student resistance and promoting student development that I have found useful are the following:

1. the creation of a safe classroom atmosphere by establishing clear guidelines for discussion;

2. the creation of opportunities for self-generated knowledge;
3. the provision of an appropriate developmental model that students can use as a framework for understanding their own process;
4. the exploration of strategies to empower students as change agents.

Creating a Safe Climate

As was discussed earlier, making the classroom a safe space for discussion is essential for overcoming students' fears about breaking the race taboo, and will also reduce later anxieties about exposing one's own internalized racism. Establishing the guidelines of confidentiality, mutual respect, "no zaps," and speaking from one's own experience on the first day of class is a necessary step in the process.

Students respond very positively to these ground rules, and do try to honor them. While the rules do not totally eliminate anxiety, they clearly communicate to students that there is a safety net for the discussion. Students are also encouraged to direct their comments and questions to each other rather than always focusing their attention on me as the instructor, and to learn each other's names rather than referring to each other as "he," "she," or "the person in the red sweater" when responding to each other.[6]

The Power of Self-Generated Knowledge

The creation of opportunities for self-generated knowledge on the part of students is a powerful tool for reducing the initial stage of denial that many students experience. While it may seem easy for some students to challenge the validity of what they read or what the instructor says, it is harder to deny what they have seen with their own eyes. Students can be given hands-on assignments outside of class to facilitate this process.

For example, after reading *Portraits of White Racism* (Wellman, 1977), some students expressed the belief that the attitudes expressed by the White interviewees in the book were no longer commonly held attitudes. Students were then asked to use the same interview protocol used in the book (with some revision) to interview a White adult of their choice. When students reported on these interviews in class, their own observation of the similarity between those they had interviewed and those they had read about was more convincing than anything I might have said.

After doing her interview, Patty, a usually quiet White student, wrote:

I think I learned a lot from it and that I'm finally getting a better grip on the idea of racism. I think that was why I participated so much in class. I really felt like I knew what I was talking about.

Other examples of creating opportunities for self-generated knowledge include assigning students the task of visiting grocery stores in neighborhoods of differing racial composition to compare the cost and quality of goods and services available at the two locations, and to observe the interactions between the shoppers and the store personnel. For White students, one of the most powerful assignments of this type has been to go apartment hunting with an African-American student and to experience housing discrimination first-hand. While one concern with such an assignment is the effect it will have on the

student(s) of color involved, I have found that those Black students who choose this assignment rather than another are typically eager to have their White classmates experience the reality of racism, and thus participate quite willingly in the process.

Naming the Problem

The emotional responses that students have to talking and learning about racism are quite predictable and related to their own racial identity development. Unfortunately, students typically do not know this; thus they consider their own guilt, shame, embarrassment, or anger an uncomfortable experience that they alone are having. Informing students at the beginning of the semester that these feelings may be part of the learning process is ethically necessary (in the sense of informed consent) and helps to normalize the students' experience. Knowing in advance that a desire to withdraw from classroom discussion or not to complete assignments is a common response helps students to remain engaged when they reach that point. As Alice, a White woman, wrote at the end of the semester:

You were so right in saying in the beginning how we would grow tired of racism (I did in October) but then it would get so good! I have *loved* the class once I passed that point.

In addition, sharing the model of racial identity development with students gives them a useful framework for understanding each other's processes as well as their own. This cognitive framework does not necessarily prevent the collision of developmental processes previously described, but it does allow students to be less frightened by it when it occurs. If, for example, White students understand the stages of racial identity development for students of color, they are less likely to personalize or feel threatened by an African-American student's anger.

Connie, a White student who initially expressed a lot of resentment at the way students of color tended to congregate in the college cafeteria, was much more understanding of this behavior after she learned about racial identity development theory. She wrote:

I learned a lot from reading the article about the stages of development in the model of oppressed people. As a White person going through my stages of identity development, I do not take time to think about the struggle people of color go through to reach a stage of complete understanding. I am glad that I know about the stages because now I can understand people of color's behavior in certain situations. For example, when people of color stay to themselves and appear to be in a clique, it is not because they are being rude as I originally thought. Rather they are engaged perhaps in the Immersion stage.

Mary, another White student, wrote:

I found the entire Cross model of racial identity development very enlightening. I knew that there were stages of racial identity development before I entered this class. I did not know what they were, or what they really entailed. After reading through this article I found myself saying, "Oh. That explains why she reacted this way to this incident instead of how

she would have a year ago." Clearly this person has entered a different stage and is working through different problems from a new viewpoint. Thankfully, the model provides a degree of hope that people will not always be angry, and will not always be separatists, etc. Although I'm not really sure about that.

Conversely, when students of color understand the stages of White racial identity development, they can be more tolerant or appreciative of a White student's struggle with guilt, for example. After reading about the stages of White identity development, Sonia, a Latina previously quoted, wrote:

This article was the one that made me feel that my own prejudices were showing. I never knew that Whites went through an identity development of their own.

She later told me outside of class that she found it much easier to listen to some of the things White students said because she could understand their potentially offensive comments as part of a developmental stage.

Sharon, an African-American woman, also found that an understanding of the respective stages of racial identity development helped her to understand some of the interactions she had had with White students since coming to college. She wrote:

There is a lot of clash that occurs between Black and White people at college which is best explained by their respective stages of development. Unfortunately schools have not helped to alleviate these problems earlier in life.

In a course on the psychology of racism, it is easy to build in the provision of this information as part of the course content. For instructors teaching courses with race-related content in other fields, it may seem less natural to do so. However, the inclusion of articles on racial identity development and/or class discussion of these issues in conjunction with the other strategies that have been suggested can improve student receptivity to the course content in important ways, making it a very useful investment of class time. Because the stages describe kinds of behavior that many people have commonly observed in themselves, as well as in their own intraracial and interracial interactions, my experience has been that most students grasp the basic conceptual framework fairly easily, even if they do not have a background in psychology.

Empowering Students as Change Agents

Heightening students' awareness of racism without also developing an awareness of the possibility of change is a prescription for despair. I consider it unethical to do one without the other. Exploring strategies to empower students as change agents is thus a necessary part of the process of talking about race and learning about racism. As was previously mentioned, students find it very helpful to read about and hear from individuals who have been effective change agents. Newspaper and magazine articles, as well as biographical or autobiographical essays or book excerpts, are often important sources for this information.

I also ask students to work in small groups to develop an action plan of their own for interrupting racism. While I do not consider it appropriate to require students to engage in antiracist activity (since I believe this should be a personal choice the student makes for him/ herself), students are required to think about the possibility. Guidelines are provided (see Katz, 1978), and the plans that they develop over several weeks are presented at the end of the semester. Students are generally impressed with each other's good ideas, and, in fact, they often do go on to implement their projects.

Joanne, a White student who initially struggled with feelings of guilt, wrote:

> I thought that hearing others' ideas for action plans was interesting and informative. It really helps me realize (reminds me) the many choices and avenues there are once I decided to be an ally. Not only did I develop my own concrete way to be an ally, I have found many other ways that I, as a college student, can be an active anti-racist. It was really empowering.

Another way all students can be empowered is by offering them the opportunity to consciously observe their own development. The taped exercise to which some of the previously quoted students have referred is an example of one way to provide this opportunity. At the beginning of the semester, students are given an interview guide with many open-ended questions concerning racial attitudes and opinions. They are asked to interview themselves on tape as a way of recording their own ideas for future reference. Though the tapes are collected, students are assured that no one (including me) will listen to them. The tapes are returned near the end of the semester, and students are asked to listen to their own tapes and use their understanding of racial identity development to discuss it in essay form.

The resulting essays are often remarkable and underscore the psychological importance of giving students the chance to examine racial issues in the classroom. The following was written by Elaine, a White woman:

> Another common theme that was apparent in the tape was that, for the most part, I was aware of my own ignorance and was embarrassed because of it. I wanted to know more about the oppression of people in the country so that I could do something about it. Since I have been here, I have begun to be actively resistant to racism. I have been able to confront my grandparents and some old friends from high school when they make racist comments. Taking this psychology of racism class is another step toward active resistance to racism. I am trying to educate myself so that I have a knowledge base to work from.
>
> When the tape was made, I was just beginning to be active and just beginning to be educated. I think I am now starting to move into the redefinition stage. I am starting to feel ok about being White. Some of my guilt is dissipating, and I do not feel as ignorant as I used to be. I think I have an understanding of racism; how it effects [sic] myself, and how it effects this country. Because of this I think I can be more active in doing something about it.

In the words of Louise, a Black female student:

> One of the greatest things I learned from this semester in general is that the world is not only Black and White, nor is the United States. I learned a lot about my own erasure of many American ethnic groups. . . . I am in the (immersion) stage of my identity development. I think I am also dangling a little in the (encounter) stage. I say this because a lot of my energies are still directed toward White people. I began writing a poem two days ago and it was directed to White racism. However, I have also become more Black-identified. I am reaching to the strength in Afro-American heritage. I am learning more about the heritage and history of Afro-American culture. Knowledge = strength and strength = power.

While some students are clearly more self-reflective and articulate about their own process than others, most students experience the opportunity to talk and learn about these issues as a transforming process. In my experience, even those students who are frustrated by aspects of the course find themselves changed by it. One such student wrote in her final journal entry:

> What I felt to be a major hindrance to me was the amount of people. Despite the philosophy, I really never felt at ease enough to speak openly about the feelings I have and kind of watched the class pull farther and farther apart as the semester went on. . . . I think that it was your attitude that kept me intrigued by the topics we were studying despite my frustrations with the class time. I really feel as though I made some significant moves in my understanding of other people's positions in our world as well as

of my feelings of racism, and I feel very good about them. I feel like this class has moved me in the right direction. I'm on a roll I think, because I've been introduced to so much.

Facilitating student development in this way is a challenging and complex task, but the results are clearly worth the effort.

Implications for the Institution

What are the institutional implications for an understanding of racial identity development theory beyond the classroom? How can this framework be used to address the pressing issues of increasing diversity and decreasing racial tensions on college campuses? How can providing opportunities in the curriculum to talk about race and learn about racism affect the recruitment and retention of students of color specifically, especially when the majority of the students enrolled are White?

The fact is, educating White students about race and racism changes attitudes in ways that go beyond the classroom boundaries. As White students move through their own stages of identity development, they take their friends with them by engaging them in dialogue. They share the articles they have read with roommates and involve them in their projects. An example of this involvement can be seen in the following journal entry, written by Larry, a White man:

Here it is our fifth week of class and more and more I am becoming aware of the racism around me. Our second project made things clearer, because while watching T.V. I picked up many kinds of discrimination and stereotyping. Since the project was over, I still find myself watching these shows and picking up bits and pieces every show I watch. Even my friends will be watching a show and they will say, "Hey Larry, put that in your paper." Since they know I am taking this class, they are looking out for these things. They are also watching what they say around me for fear that I will use them as an example. For example, one of my friends has this fascination with making fun of Jewish people. Before I would listen to his comments and take them in stride, but now I confront him about his comments.

The heightened awareness of the White students enrolled in the class has a ripple effect in their peer group, which helps to create a climate in which students of color and other targeted groups (Jewish students, for example) might feel more comfortable. It is likely that White students who have had the opportunity to learn about racism in a supportive atmosphere will be better able to be allies to students of color in extracurricular settings, like student government meetings and other organizational settings, where students of color often feel isolated and unheard.

At the same time, students of color who have had the opportunity to examine the ways in which racism may have affected their own lives are able to give voice to their own experience and to validate it rather than be demoralized by it. An understanding of internalized oppression can help students of color recognize the ways in which they may have unknowingly participated in their own victimization, or the victimization of others.

They may be able to move beyond victimization to empowerment and share their learning with others, as Sharon, a previously quoted Black woman, planned to do.

Campus communities with an understanding of racial identity development could become more supportive of special-interest groups, such as the Black Student Union or the Asian Student Alliance, because they would recognize them not as "separatist" but as important outlets for students of color who may be at the Encounter or Immersion stage of racial identity development. Not only could speakers of color be sought out to add diversity to campus programming, but Whites who had made a commitment to unlearning their own racism could be offered as models to those White students looking for new ways to understand their own Whiteness, and to students of color looking for allies.

It has become painfully clear on many college campuses across the United States that we cannot have successfully multiracial campuses without talking about race and learning about racism. Providing a forum where this discussion can take place safely over a semester, a time period that allows personal and group development to unfold in ways that daylong or weekend programs do not, may be among the most proactive learning opportunities an institution can provide.

REFERENCES

Barnard, H. F. (Ed.). (1987). *Outside the magic circle: The autobiography of Virginia Foster Durr*. New York: Simon & Schuster. (Originally published in 1985 by University of Alabama Press.)

Bowser, B. P., & Hunt, R. G. (1981). *Impacts of racism on whites*. Beverly Hills, CA: Sage.

Braden, A. (1987, April-May). Undoing racism: Lessons for the peace movement. *The Nonviolent Activist*, pp. 3–6.

Bronstein, P. A., & Quina, K. (Eds.). (1988). *Teaching a psychology of people: Resources for gender and sociocultural awareness*. Washington, DC: American Psychological Association.

Cross, W. E., Jr. (1971). The Negro to black conversion experience: Toward a psychology of black liberation. *Black World, 20*(9), 13–27.

Cross, W. E., Jr. (1978). The Cross and Thomas models of psychological nigrescence. *Journal of Black Psychology, 5*(1), 13–19.

Cross, W. E., Jr. (1991). *Shades of black: Diversity in African-American identity*. Philadelphia: Temple University Press.

Cross, W. E., Jr., Parham, T. A., & Helms, J. E. (1991). The stages of black identity development: Nigrescence models. In R. Jones (Ed.), *Black psychology* (3rd ed., pp. 319–338). San Francisco: Cobb and Henry.

Derman-Sparks, L., Higa, C. T., & Sparks, B. (1980). Children, race and racism: How race awareness develops. *Interracial Books for Children Bulletin, 11*(3/4), 3–15.

Helms, J. E. (Ed.). (1990). *Black and white racial identity: Theory, research and practice*. Westport, CT: Greenwood Press.

Highlen, P. S., Reynolds, A. L., Adams, E. M., Hanley, T. C., Myers, L. J., Cox, C., & Speight, S. (1988, August 13). *Self-identity development model of oppressed people: Inclusive model for all?* Paper presented at the American Psychological Association Convention, Atlanta, GA.

Hull, G. T., Scott, P. B., & Smith, B. (Eds.). (1982). *All the women are white, all the blacks are men, but some of us are brave: Black women's studies*. Old Westbury, NY: Feminist Press.

Katz, J. H. (1978). *White awareness: Handbook for anti-racism training*. Norman: University of Oklahoma Press.

Lester, J. (1987). *What happens to the mythmakers when the myths are found to be untrue?* Unpublished paper, Equity Institute, Emeryville, CA.

McIntosh, P. (1988). *White privilege and male privilege: A personal account of coming to see correspondences through work in women's studies*. Working paper, Wellesley College Center for Research on Women, Wellesley, MA.

McIntosh, P. (1989, July/August). White privilege: Unpacking the invisible knapsack. *Peace and Freedom*, pp. 10–12.

Parham, T. A. (1989). Cycles of psychological nigrescence. *The Counseling Psychologist, 17*(2), 187–226.

Phinney, J. (1989). Stages of ethnic identity in minority group adolescents. *Journal of Early Adolescence, 9*, 34–39.

Phinney, J. (1990). Ethnic identity in adolescents and adults: Review of research. *Psychological Bulletin, 108*(3), 499–514.

Phinney, J. S., & Rotheram, M. J. (Eds.). (1987). *Children's ethnic socialization: Pluralism and development*. Newbury Park, CA: Sage.

Schuster, M. R., & Van Dyne, S. R. (Eds.). (1985). *Women's place in the academy: Transforming the liberal arts curriculum*. Totowa, NJ: Rowman & Allanheld.

Wellman, D. (1977). *Portraits of white racism*. New York: Cambridge University Press.

NOTES

1. A similar point could be made about other issues of oppression, such as anti-Semitism, homophobia and heterosexism, ageism, and so on.

2. While similar models of racial identity development exist, Cross and Helms are referenced here because they are among the most frequently cited writers on Black racial identity development and on White racial identity development, respectively. For a discussion of the commonalities between these and other identity development models, see Phinney (1989, 1990) and Helms (1990).

3. Both Parham (1989) and Phinney (1989) suggest that a preference for the dominant group is not always a characteristic of this stage. For example, children raised in households and communities with explicitly positive Afrocentric attitudes may absorb a pro-Black perspective, which then serves as the starting point for their own exploration of racial identity.

4. After being introduced to this model and Helms's model of White identity development, students are encouraged to think about how the models might apply to their own experience or the experiences of people they know. As is reflected in the cited journal entries, some students resonate to the theories quite readily, easily seeing their own process of growth reflected in them. Other students are sometimes puzzled because they feel as though their own process varies from these models and may ask if it is possible to "skip" a particular stage, for example. Such questions provide a useful departure point for discussing the limitations of stage theories in general and the potential variations in experience that make questions of racial identity development so complex.

5. Examples of useful articles include essays by McIntosh (1988), Lester (1987), and Braden (1987). Each of these combines autobiographical material, as well as a conceptual framework for understanding some aspect of racism that students find very helpful. Bowser and Hunt's (1981) edited book, *Impacts of Racism on Whites*, though less autobiographical in nature, is also a valuable resource.

6. Class size has a direct bearing on my ability to create safety in the classroom. Dividing the class into pairs or small groups of five or six students to discuss initial reactions to a particular article or film helps to increase participation, both in the small groups and later in the large group discussions.

Mary Jean Ronan Herzog

Come and Listen to a Story
Understanding the Appalachian Hillbilly in Popular Culture

The Appalachian region of the United States has increasingly become the focus of scholarly investigation. Studies of the region's economics, history, literature, music, and culture blossomed in the 1970s and have continued to identify the region as inclusive of multiple identities and multiple meanings, both geographic and cultural (Billings, Norman, & Ledford, 1999; Eller, 1982; Lewis, 1999; Williamson, 1995). Appalachia has differing geographic and political boundaries depending on the source used to define it. The Appalachian Regional Commission (ARC) was formed in 1965 as a state and federal initiative after the region attracted the attention of the John F. Kennedy and Lyndon B. Johnson administrations (ARC, n.d.). The subsequent War on Poverty mandates initiated by Kennedy and carried out by Johnson found the region to be abundant in natural resources and lacking in industrial and agricultural opportunities. Politicians argued that these economic failings were the reason why poverty was so pervasive among the mountain people. Besides establishing ARC, the War on Poverty initiatives also included a highway program to reduce the geographic isolation of the Appalachian region and to promote the growth of industry. Today, ARC defines the geographic boundaries of the region from northern Alabama to upstate New York and divides the region into northern, central, and southern sections including sections of Georgia, Kentucky, Maryland, Mississippi, North Carolina, Ohio, South Carolina, Tennessee, Virginia, and West Virginia.

Clearly, the geographical region is a vast hybrid of cultures, traditions, and religions. There are sections that remain relatively isolated, such as the mining regions on the borders of Kentucky and Virginia, while there are other areas that are flocked to by tourists. Increasingly, Appalachia is a target destination for retirees and young urban professionals alike.

Early in the twenty-first century, at the height of the reality television rage, rural stereotypes were thrown into the entertainment formula. The recent reality television shows featuring "hillbillies" including Columbia Broadcasting System's (CBS) *New Beverly Hillbillies* and the National Broadcasting Company's (NBC) *High Life* and to a lesser extent cable's FOX Broadcasting Company's *Simple Life*, starring millionaire playgirls Paris Hilton and Nichole Ritchie, set off a wave of protest from rural-minded people in the United States. The Center for Rural Strategies (n.d.) in Kentucky led a nationwide campaign against the networks with press conferences and full-page advertisements in national newspapers. The center's website posted over forty commentaries from notable protestors such as West Virginia Senator Robert Byrd and Arkansas Governor Mike Huckabee, who argued it was time to stop stereotyping rural Americans and noted that no other gendered, socioeconomic, ethnic, or racial group would be subjected to such overt and "politically incorrect" public bias and media bias in the twenty-first century. Major newspapers were also sympathetic to the rural cause; in a piece called "Victory for Reality," *The Cincinnati Enquirer* (2003) published the following:

> CBS planned a reality TV series featuring [a] real-life, low-income rural family. In so-called "hick-hunts," they were searching for the perfect stereotypical Appalachian family. They would move them into an opulent California mansion with luxuries and invite the nation to laugh as they bumbled their way through the day. But plenty of Kentuckians, Ohioans, and Appalachian people elsewhere weren't amused—or silent. In this day of hypersensitivity to diversity and political correctness, Appalachians have been a group that it is still socially acceptable to demean and joke about. . . . But rural folks have spoken up and said "enough" to the Hollywood mockers. Good for them, and for all friends of rural America. (p. B12)

Likewise, the indignation over *The High Life* took the commonly accepted hillbilly stereotype to task. Kentucky Congressman Hal Rogers (n.d.) stated:

> It is incomprehensible that anyone would think it's acceptable to propel negative and erroneous stereotypes about the people of Appalachia. No one would dare propose creating a program focusing on stereotypes about African Americans, Musims, or Jews. Why then would it be okay to bash those of us living in rural America? (*Rural Reality*, para 3)

This chapter begins with a discussion of how I approach multicultural education with my preservice teachers at Western Carolina University, located in the mountains of western North Carolina. My goal is to enable my students to think critically about the issues of the day and to face discomfiting questions of social justice that might challenge their own comfort. In this chapter, I debunk the myth of the hillbilly caricature with the aim of enabling my students to develop a more informed understanding of the complexity and diversity of the Appalachian region and its people and to enable them to challenge the easily accepted stereotypes that perpetuate these negative and demeaning images in their own classrooms by situating the problem of rural and Appalachian stereotypes in the context of critical multicultural education and civil rights pedagogy through a deconstruction of the Appalachian mountain hillbilly image. Such stereotypes have been absent from national discussions on diversity and multicultural education, yet they have been stigmatizing an entire region of the United States and its people. Teaching critical analysis of the broad issues in multicultural education is more effective if students learn to empathize as well as sympathize with the plights of the downtrodden, thus expanding their perspectives. In other words, if students can relate to some of the experiences of oppressed people, even on a minor scale, their understanding and empathy will be enhanced. If inclined toward an us-versus-them attitude, the deconstruction of stereotypes about their own community, state, or region can help them develop more of an us-and-them perspective (Carnes, 1995).

My classes begin with an analysis of texts framed by scholarship in Appalachian studies—a hybridity of history, literature, and cultural studies of the program—and an analysis of *the* historical, mass media, and popular cultural accounts of the Appalachian region and its people. In order to reveal the stereotypically based undocumented assertions and gross generalizations of the region's people, we begin with a discussion of Harry Caudill, *Night Comes to the Cumberlands* (1963); Weller, *Yesterday's People* (1965); Bill Bryson, *A Walk in the Woods* (1998); and James Dickey, *Deliverance* (1970), whereby images of Appalachian people in these various works range from barbarians to people living hopelessly in the past with the future passing by them. What follows is a detailed discussion of the "hillbilly" as a cultural pop icon and the information I draw from for transformational curriculum and pedagogy in my classes.

Appalachian Studies

To begin, I draw from the field of Appalachian studies, which is a hybrid field of regional, interdisciplinary studies of history, literature, anthropology, religion, and cultural studies. Early accounts of the Appalachian region were often based on widely read but biased and undocumented assertions and generalizations. These include Toynbee, *A Study of History* (1942);

Caudill, *Night Comes to the Cumberlands* (1963); and Weller, *Yesterday's People* (1965). Images of Appalachians in these works range from barbarians to apathetic people living in squalor barely subsisting, with little hope for the future.

On the one hand, Appalachian culture is viewed as backward, incestuous, isolated, and poverty-stricken as in Dickey's *Deliverance* (1970). Billings, Norman, and Ledford (1999) referred to this view as "a traumatized culture where withdrawal, depression, inertia, self-blame and resignation rule" (p. 6). On the other hand, Appalachian people have also been romanticized as "strong women, noble African Americans, and virtuous Indians . . . a fierce and solitary people" (p. 10).

Scholars from history, literature, and the social sciences have produced a large body of work on the Appalachian region that flourished in the late 1960s and early 1970s. This Appalachian studies movement has been an academic vehicle for critical analysis, examining and challenging both negative images and stereotypes and the overly romanticized visions of the region. Both the negative and the romanticized generalizations have contributed to a public image based on myth rather than on facts and reality. Appalachian scholars within the academy have addressed the issues and spoken publicly, but they have not had much influence on media representations. The campaign against *The New Beverly Hillbillies* was a new approach by an advocacy group outside academe (Center for Rural Strategies, n.d.).

Historians criticize the overgeneralizations about the region as an isolated "backwater" and point to biases and contradictions. For example, Ron Eller (1999) argues that the Appalachian region is the "most maligned" in the United States and that it is "still dressed in the garments of backwardness, violence, poverty and hopelessness . . . playing the role of the 'other America'" (pp. ix–xi). Eller, like other Appalachian scholars, has challenged stereotypical ideas of the region with historical works that call many of the prevailing images into question. Writing about *The Kentucky Cycle*, a Pulitzer–prize-winning play that spawned a round of criticism, Eller (1999) says,

> The "idea of Appalachia," perpetuated in contemporary work such as *The Kentucky Cycle*, not only masks the exploitation of land and people in the region, but it obscures the diversity of conditions, relationships, and cultures within Appalachian society itself—diversity of race, gender and class as well as diversity in religion, education and history. Appalachian scholars have come to recognize that there are many Appalachians, and applying generalizations often contradict local heritage and experiences. (pp. x–xi)

Billings, Norman, and Ledford (1999) continue this line of criticism about the popular image of the Appalachian region, arguing that the stereotypical perceptions ignore the reality of the diverse communities and cultures within.

Other historians criticize the overgeneralizations about the region as an isolated "backwater" and point to biases and contradictions as well. For example, Horace Kephart (1976), one of the forces behind the development of the Great Smoky Mountain National Park, began his now classic *Our Southern Highlanders* with this description: "The Southern Highlander

[is] a tall, slouching figure in homespun, who carries a rifle as habitually as he does his hat, and who may tilt its muzzle toward a stranger" (p. 11). Kephart traveled to the region to escape his life in the Midwest where he was a librarian, alcoholic, and father of five or six children to find the "back of beyond" and to chronicle the life of the mountaineer. He noted:

> When I went south into the mountains I was seeking a Back of Beyond. This for more reasons than one. With an inborn taste for the wild and romantic, I yearned for a strange land and a people that had the charm of originality . . . in Far Appalachia. (1976, p. 29)

Ronald Lewis (1999) writes that the idea of "Appalachia" was "born in the fertile minds of late-nineteenth-century local color writers" such as John Fox, Jr., for whom, he said, it was a "willful creation and not merely the product of a literary imagination" (pp. 21–22). Appalachian scholar Darlene Wilson (1999) analyzed Fox's papers and works in terms of creating an "Appalachian otherness" and has shown that they were economically self-serving. According to Wilson (1999), the Fox family was involved in developing the coal industry in central Appalachia, and John Fox, Jr., worked as a publicist for them. Fox's fiction became accepted as the normal representation of the region, and over time, it became entrenched as if historically accurate. Fast forward 150 years, and the region is still subjected to the "idea of Appalachia as a homogeneous region physically, culturally and economically isolated from mainstream America" (Lewis, 1999, p. 22).

The Hillbilly as a Best Seller

As an entrée to a study of stereotypes and negative images of rural people, my students read *A Walk in the Woods: Rediscovering America on the Appalachian Trail* by Bill Bryson (1998), a nationwide best seller on the *New York Times* nonfiction list in spite of its inaccurate depictions. For example, Bryson describes the Appalachian Mountains as having woods that are full of "animal" and "human" perils such as: "[R]attlesnakes and water moccasins and nests of copperheads; bobcats, bears, coyotes, wolves, and wild boar; loony hillbillies destabilized by gross quantities of impure corn liquor and generations of profoundly unbiblical sex" (p. 10).

In reality the closest water moccasins live several hundred miles away in southern South Carolina, and the closest wolves dwell in Montana and northern Canada. Moreover, the corn liquor industry has been replaced by the production of marijuana and methedrine.

After reading *A Walk in the Woods*, my students write reactions on a survey designed to ascertain attitudes about rural issues. My students' reactions are almost always uniformly negative. For example, one student wrote, "This book only adds to the myth that everyone in the South is a hick. I have lived in these mountains for my entire life, and I am sick and tired of this image." The book is useful as a point of departure for discussions of negative stereotypes and issues of diversity. Once the students examine stereotypes of the Appalachian region, they are more apt to examine other racial, ethnic, regional, social class, and gendered stereotypes.

In spite of its inaccurate depictions the Christopher Lehmann-Haupt review for the *New York Times* (1998) praised the book as a "perceptive look at the strange territory where forest and American culture collide." Lehmann-Haupt especially liked Bryson's tales of the "trail's perils: its dangerous animals, killing diseases, and loony hillbillies." Amazon.Com (n.d.) describes *A Walk in the Woods* as "a near perfect way to spend an afternoon." Plus, of the 888 customer reviews on Amazon.Com only a small portion were critical, and of those most were offended at his abuse of nature, and only a couple readers objected to his liberal use of stereotypes of the people in the region.

The Hillbilly and Hollywood

Williamson (1995) argues that the hillbilly stereotype has been entertaining the public since the mid-nineteenth century. His analysis of the purpose and function of the hillbilly stereotype was published in the well-documented book *Hillbillyland: What the Movies Did to the Mountains and What the Mountains Did to the Movies*. He says we have an "ambiguous need for hillbillies . . . that begins with laughter and ends in pain" and that the hillbilly is "safely dismissible, a left-behind remnant, a symbolic non-adult and willful renegade from capitalism" (1995, p. ix).

The hillbilly image is, indeed, fraught with ambiguity. It is sometimes lighthearted, comical, and entertaining and at other times, dark, dangerous, and violent. One of the most tenacious and terrifying hillbilly images came from the movie version of the novel *Deliverance*, in which a violent mountain man is graphically shown sodomizing a city dweller from Atlanta in a backwoods bayou. Williamson (1995) notes that the book's and the movie's violence was meant to symbolize an urban plan to pollute and exploit the environment of the Appalachian region by raping the mountains and damming the rivers. Regardless of Dickey's (1970) intention to portray the evil's "progress" in America, the *Deliverance* mountain man became a cultural icon, and to hear dueling banjos evokes an image of a moralless Appalachian region beset with incestuous imbeciles, trash, and violence.

A more recent film, *Nell*, shot in the western North Carolina mountains, is the sentimental and romanticized story of a woman with a speech impairment who is being raised without the benefit of modern civilization (Lewis, 1999). *Nell* continued the Hollywood tradition of illustrating the region as backward, isolated, and populated by people of lesser intelligence.

These popular images are so entrenched that they are resistant to change both within and outside the region. The Appalachian hillbilly is glorified within the region itself and sold on highway billboards and in small town shops. The media, both national and local, continue to perpetuate the negative stereotypes and overgeneralizations about the region. Scholars debate the impact of the hillbilly caricature, some claiming that it is an honorable and wise character and others arguing it is a factor in the marginalization of the region (Harkins, 2003; Lewis, 1999).

The Town of Murphy, the Hillbilly Fugitive, and the Popular Press

A recent example of the popular media's portrayal of the Appalachian region—and one that my students can relate to since it occurred in the western counties of North Carolina—is illustrated by the search and capture of fugitive Eric Rudolph, who was identified as a suspect in the bombing of an Alabama abortion clinic and Olympic Park in Atlanta, Georgia. The search began in 1998 and ended on June 3, 2003, in Murphy, North Carolina.

Rudolph, the subject of a manhunt by the Federal Bureau of Investigation (FBI), and on the "ten Most Wanted" list, was thought to be hiding in the North Carolina mountains. After five years in the woods, Rudolph earned his nomenclature as a mountain man, but like a large percentage of the population of western North Carolina, he was not a "local" from North Carolina. Originally from Florida, he moved to Nantahala, North Carolina, with his mother, four brothers, and one sister when he was fourteen, shortly after his father died. He attended Nantahala High School, a small school with a typical graduating class of twenty, but dropped out after ninth grade when he started working as a carpenter. The high school is in Macon County, the fastest growing county in the state, about one and a half hours from Atlanta. Eventually Rudolph received a General Education Diploma and briefly attended college at regional Western Carolina University. After serving in the U.S. Army from 1987 to 1989, he was allegedly discharged for smoking marijuana and then returned to western North Carolina and resumed carpentry. In 1996, Rudolph started using aliases.

In the summer of 1996 a bomb exploded at Olympic Park in Atlanta during the summer Olympics, killing forty-four-year-old Alice Hawthorne and injuring more than one hundred other people. In January 1998, Rudolph's truck was identified fleeing the scene of a bomb explosion at the New Women All Women

Clinic in Birmingham, Alabama, where a guard was killed and a nurse was seriously injured. The search for him began. The FBI linked two other bombings from 1997 to him. In 1998, his truck was found in the Nantahala Gorge by FBI agents, and they concentrated their search in the western counties of North Carolina, with headquarters set up in Andrews, in Cherokee County, the western-most county in the state with borders on Tennessee and Georgia. Rudolph had been living in a trailer two miles from Murphy, North Carolina.

Throughout the five-year search for Rudolph, the region was described in stereotypical terms based not on facts but rather on unexamined generalizations. Rudolph was cast by the popular press as a skinny, long-haired mountain man, when in fact his weight was in normal range, his hair was short, and his mustache was trimmed when he was found. He told one of the jailers that eating spring lizards was a little like eating sushi. Moreover, the town of Murphy was consistently depicted as "backwater" by the popular press who ignored the journalistic opportunity to present a more complex and nuanced picture of the town and the surrounding region. Rather than seeking facts and information from a wide range and variety of sources, journalists seem content to base generalizations on comments from characters supporting their viewpoints.

Many of my students at Western Carolina University come from the small town of Murphy, which is home to about 1,500 residents and is the county seat of Cherokee County in the far southwest corner of North Carolina. Hardly a backwater that is cut off from the rest of the world, Cherokee is described as a vacation place "where the forested mountains touch the sky, the lakes sparkle, and the air is crisp and clean, and the charm of small town America still exists" (Cherokee County Chamber of Commerce, n.d.). Murphy has a downtown with wide streets and busy stores, including antique stores and the Daily Grind Café frequented by reporters and gawkers ordering cappuccino in the first days after Rudolph's capture. Murphy has a stately courthouse made of blue marble from the nearby town of Marble and a distinctive Baptist Church at the end of Main Street. A victim of contemporary suburban sprawl, the town also contains the requisite gentrified fast-food joints such as Burger King and McDonald's, along with several convenience stores, such as Wal-Mart, a Mexican restaurant, and a Chinese restaurant, which stretch down the four-lane highway that surrounds the downtown area.

Murphy is closer to the capital cities of Tennessee, Georgia, and South Carolina than it is to Raleigh, the capital of North Carolina, about 360 miles away. The phrase *From Murphy to Manteo* is symbolic of the 550-mile distance from the western edge to the farthest eastern coastal town, from border to border. Yet Murphy is only about 100 miles from Asheville, 120 miles from Atlanta, and 60 miles from Chattanooga, Tennessee. In fact, the traveler driving to Atlanta runs the risk of hitting heavy traffic within 40 or 50 miles. It is about half an hour's drive to the Olympic whitewater course on the Ocoee River. Although Murphy is far from some places, residents tire of hearing how remote it is. As one of my students from Murphy said, "They're always surprised to hear that someone from Murphy has never been to Asheville. So I like to ask, 'What? And you've never been to Murphy?'"

The North Carolina Rural Center reports that 54 percent of the county population was born in North Carolina. The media portrayals of the area focus on negative stereotypes. In an article in *The New Yorker* about Rudolph, Tony Horwitz (1999) claimed the people in the area distrust outsiders and the government, saying, "[T]his part of North Carolina, like much of southern Appalachia, has always been jealous of its privacy" (p. 46). His source is a ninety-two-year-old former logger and bootlegger whose colorful quotes make most people in Murphy cringe. My students, who are teachers and school administrators in Murphy and throughout the region, were not interviewed by Horwitz, and they often complain about how the media finds the most illiterate and conservative people when they want to do an interview about Appalachia. Horwitz interviewed a nationally known wilderness guide who lives in the area but did not include his comments in the article, as they did not fit Horwitz's preconceived ideas.

Horwitz did, however, interview a couple named Mosteller and concluded that "like almost all his neighbors in the Nantahala . . . abortion and homosexuality are almost universally condemned" (p. 46). Horwitz said right-wing extremists such as Rudolph and his family friend, Tom Branham, who was arrested for illegal possession of explosives and firearms, are "startlingly common in the Nantahala" (p. 47). Apparently, he did not observe and interview the hordes of middle-class tourists and new residents who have recently flocked to the area to work and play in the Nantahala River. These immigrants to the area are clad in expensive "outdoor" wear sporting clothing from Birkenstock, L. L. Bean, Eddie Bauer, and Patagonia.

The media images of the region suffer from the same syndrome that afflicts most American news. Conclusions are drawn on scanty evidence, news stories quickly become sound bytes, and notable reporters exaggerate, plagiarize, and lie. The mountains are described as snake-infested. The mountain people are variously described and stereotyped as Bible Belt religious fanatics and dumb, inbred hillbillies. The mountains are not "infested" with snakes; it is the rare hiker who is lucky enough to discover one on a trail. There are no more snakes in the North Carolina mountains than in the Ramapo Mountains twenty miles north of New York City.

Although Christianity is hegemonic in the southern Appalachian Mountain region, each county has a great diversity of Christian religions, including Assembly of God, Baptist, Church of Christ, Church of the Latter Day Saints (a.k.a. Mormons), Roman Catholic, Methodist, Presbyterian, and Unitarian. While there are people who describe themselves as "born again" or evangelical, the stereotype of the Bible-thumping fanatic is pervasive. Bumiller (2003) reported in the *New York Times* that white, southern evangelicals accounted for about 40 percent of the votes that George W. Bush received in the 2000 presidential election.

Implications for Curriculum and Pedagogy

In my experience at Western Carolina University, undergraduate, preservice teachers are often uncomfortable challenging and recognizing their white, patriarchal, middle-class norms. For them, teaching about multicultural issues is often associated with information about the plight of African Americans starting with slavery, the Civil War, Reconstruction, *Plessy versus Ferguson, Brown versus Board of Education,* the civil rights movement, and the black power movement. Clearly, with the recent influx of immigrants from all over the world into our nation's schools, it is necessary to broaden the discussion to other groups of people who are currently also disenfranchised and marginalized in the United States.

In order to enable my students to learn to think more critically about issues around culture and race, I start by encouraging them to look inward at themselves and their place in the world. I begin with having my students view the Southern Poverty Law Center's award winning film, *The Shadow of Hate* (2000). This film includes historical information on the treatment of several minority groups, including Indians, Irish-Catholics, Japanese, African Americans, and Jews. The film ends with a dramatic juxtaposition of two dangerous extremists: the former grand wizard of the Knights of the Ku Klux Klan, David Duke, and the Nation of Islam leader, Louis Farrakhan. Both men are leading two different hate rallies where mobs are shouting in a frenzied rage. While Duke and Farrakhan are at opposite ends of the political spectrum, students often comment about how similar they are in their actions and rhetoric.

The students are also surprised that although one man is white and the other black, they both personify racism, anti-Semitism, and bigotry. After viewing the film, we begin with a discussion of the *hillbilly* stereotype since the students are living in Appalachia, and this iconic symbol is local and particular to their personal situation in life. This relevancy provides the stimulus and framework for a change

process to take place through discourse. As they begin to recognize how Appalachian culture is marginalized in American society, they begin to develop empathy for other groups who are also disenfranchised.

As noted earlier, my students also read *A Walk in the Woods* by Bill Bryson (1988), a nationwide best seller on the *New York Times* nonfiction list, in spite of its inaccurate depictions. Next, we turn our attention to the popular press, where students critique the media's caricature of the hillbilly cultural subgroup as an ignorant, straw-chewing, suspender-wearing mountain person. My students react to the hillbilly archetype on a continuum that ranges from humor to anger to embarrassment to apathy to silence.

My students are also exposed to the failed CBS reality show *The New Beverly Hillbillies* that set off a wave of protest from rural people, and they read the Center for Rural Strategies' (n.d.) arguments against the show. The gist of the opposition was that it is time to stop stereotyping and insulting rural Americans and that the ridicule of rural people would never be acceptable if aimed at any other cultural or racial groups, particularly people of color.

Conclusion

Clearly, Appalachian people remain one of the few cultural groups for whom still demeaning images are generally accepted and not questioned in American society. While the mainstream media would never cast aspersions on blacks, Mexicans, Asians, or gay people, they often readily talk about rural or mountain people as "rednecks," "hillbillies," and "grits." In this chapter an examination of the hillbilly caricature in contemporary American culture from three perspectives provides the platform for the analysis of several recent incidents in popular culture that perpetuate the hillbilly stereotype. Unlike the early biased accounts of the mountaineer, the scholarly work in Appalachian studies blossomed in the 1970s' objectively documented histories of communities from West Virginia to North Georgia and contested commonly held biased viewpoints. The recent movement against *The New Beverly Hillbillies* put the issue in the public spotlight for examination in the context of rural America. Continued work in this area would be more powerful if academics working in teacher preparation programs and educational leadership enabled school personnel to develop a more informed and public understanding of the complex and diverse Appalachian region and its people by challenging the taken-for-granted stereotypes and cultural myths.

References

Amazon.Com. (n.d.). Customer's reviews of *A walk in the woods*. Retrieved October 18, 2006, from www.amazon.com/gp/product/customerreviews/0767902513/ref=cm_cr_dp_2_1/102-1751480-422 5710?ie=UTF8&customer-reviews.sort %5Fby=-SubmissionDate&n=283155.

Appalachian Regional Commission. (n.d.). *Appalachian regional development act of 1965*. Retrieved November 28, 2005, from www.arc.gov/index.do?nodeId=1244#2.

Billings, D., Norman, G., & Ledford, K. (Eds.). (1999). *Confronting Appalachian stereotypes*. Lexington: University Press of Kentucky.

Bryson, B. (1998). *A walk in the woods: Rediscovering America on the Appalachian Trail*. New York: Broadway Books.

Bumiller, E. (2003, October 26). Evangelicals sway White House on human rights issues abroad. *New York Times*.

Carnes, J. (1995). *Us and them*. Montgomery, AL: Southern Poverty Law Center.

Caudill, H. (1963). *Night comes to the Cumberlands*. Boston: Little, Brown.

Center for Rural Strategies. (n.d.). *Rural reality: Comments from the guest book*. Retrieved November 28, 2005, from www.ruralstrategies.org/default.html.

Cherokee Chamber of Commerce. (n.d.). *Cherokee County*. Retrieved November 28, 2005, from www.cherokeecountychamber.com/chamber/vacation/.

Cincinnati Enquirer, The. (2003, October 7). *Victory for reality*. Retrieved October 26, 2005, from www.enquirier.com/editions/2003/10/07/editorial_wwwed1b.html.

Dickey, J. (1970). *Deliverance*. New York: Dell.

Eller, R. (1999). Foreword. In D. Billings, G. Norman, & K. Ledford (Eds.), *Confronting Appalachian Stereotypes* (pp. ix–xi). Lexington: University Press of Kentucky.

Eller, R. (1982). *Miners, millhands, and mountaineers*. Knoxville: University of Tennessee Press.

Harkins, A. (2003). *Hillbilly: A cultural history of an American icon*. New York: Oxford University Press.

Horwitz, T. (1999, March 15). Run, Rudolph, run. *The New Yorker*.

Huckabee, M. (n.d.). *Common decency*. Retrieved November 28, 2005, from www.ruralstrategies.org/campaign/huckabee.html.

Kephart, H. (1976). *Our southern highlanders: A narrative of adventure in the southern Appalachians and a study of life among the mountaineers*. Knoxville: University of Tennessee Press.

Lehmann-Haupt, C. (1998, May 21). Book review: A walk in the woods, rediscovering America on the Appalachian Trail. *New York Times*.

Lewis, R. (1999). Beyond isolation and homogeneity: Diversity and the history of Appalachia. In D. Billings, G. Norman, & K. Ledford (Eds.), *Confronting Appalachian stereotypes* (pp. 21–43). Lexington: University Press of Kentucky.

Rogers, H. (n.d.). Center for Rural Strategies. *Rural reality: NBC's the High Life*. Retrieved October 26, 2005, from www.ruralstrategies.org/default.html.

Rural Reality. (n.d.). *Congressman Rogers: NBC backs away from "hillbilly" reality program*. Retrieved October 26, 2005, from www.ruralstrategies.org/campaign/highlife.html.

Toynbee, A. (1942). *A study of history*. New York: Oxford University Press.

Weller, J. (1965). *Yesterday's people*. Lexington: University Press of Kentucky.

Williamson, J. W. (1995). *Hillbillyland: What the movies did to the mountains and what the mountains did to the movies*. Chapel Hill: University of North Carolina Press.

Wilson, D. (1999). A judicious combination of incident and psychology: John Fox Jr. and the southern mountaineer motif. In D. Billings, G. Norman, & K. Ledford (Eds.), *Confronting Appalachian stereotypes* (pp. 98–118). Lexington: University Press of Kentucky.

CHAPTER
30

Allan Collins and Richard Halverson

Rethinking Education in a Technological World

We argue for a new vision of education. To be successful, political and educational leaders will need to carefully consider the changes in our society and mobilize the government's resources to address the problems we've raised and to achieve the great potential ahead of us.

Since the end of World War II, the United States has enjoyed a disproportionate share of global resources. This abundance allowed Americans to maintain a high standard of living and take a world leadership role. Thomas Friedman's "the world is flat" argument suggests that access to information technologies has leveled the global playing field.[1] This leveling is allowing millions of engineers, technologists, and professionals from around the world to pursue the careers that have made so many Americans wealthy. The future prosperity of countries around the world depends on how their education systems can be designed to foster economic development. If the United States is going to compete successfully in a global economy, it will have to rethink many of its assumptions about education.

The formula for economic success has a high cost. As has happened in the United States, countries that focus on knowledge economies as the source of wealth gen-

eration tend to concentrate economic resources on an elite class. The gap between the haves and have-nots is growing, not shrinking, in many developed countries, and focusing the national commitment in education toward elite populations motivated to participate in math, science, and technology careers might further widen the gap. Global competition might spark what W. E. B. DuBois called a "top 10%" education strategy that will concentrate resources and push the most talented students toward globally competitive professions. Writers such as Gary Orfield and Chung-mei Lee suggest that resegregation of schools and communities, voucher policies, and charter schools are already pushing our education policy away from its commitment to equity.[2]

Just how technological developments will help us balance the goals of equity and global competition is not yet clear. The rethinking of education that we promote with this book should aim toward strategies that provide access to the new educational resources for everyone in society and give people the motivation to take advantage of these resources. This demands rethinking education not in isolation, but considering the interplay of society, education, and learning.

Rethinking Learning

We grew up with the idea that learning means taking courses in school. As we argued earlier, the identification of education with schooling is slowly unraveling as new technologies move learning outside of schools' walls. In some sense, the divorce of schooling and learning may take us back to an era where individuals negotiate their own learning experiences, often with strong guidance from their parents.

Eventually, when people and politicians become worried about what kids are learning or what adults don't know, their automatic reaction may not be "How can we improve the schools?" Instead, they may ask, "How can we develop games to teach history?"; "How can we make new technology resources available to more people?"; or "What kinds of tools can support people to seek out information on their own?" Currently, the strong association between schooling and learning forces our conversation into institutional responses. We don't yet know how to ask these wider questions when we think about improving education. We hope this book starts that conversation.

As learning moves out of school, our conception of learning will begin to broaden, and we will see more hybrid experiences that begin in the classroom and move into other contexts. Education may follow the path of home schooling by emphasizing field trips, interacting with peers, playing computer games, or even teaching others with technological tools. For example, a teacher who taught computer programming was approached by a few of his students who wanted to bring their own computers into the school and hook them up in a network to engage in multiplayer games with one another. They asked to form a computer club where they would begin to develop computer games of their own. As new kids joined the club, the first group would teach them some of the things they themselves had learned. Later, when the teacher was given the task of setting up a network in a nearby school, the kids helped him with the design and implementation of the network, and with getting students in the other school working with their new network. Although all this learning took place in a school setting, it was not "real school" learning. Technology directors around the country are experimenting with similar models that rely on students to provide network design and support.

Our vision of education is structured around the idea of *lifelong learning*. Lifelong learning requires moving away from highly structured schooling institutions to instead act as consumers of a wide variety of learning experiences. Learners will need to develop the skills to judge the quality of learning venues and the kinds of social networks that provide guidance and advice.

Brigid Barron provides a good example of how students learn to become intelligent consumers of learning environments through developing their computer skills.[3] For example, one middle school girl in California named Stephanie, who was the daughter of Chinese immigrants, had a group of friends who used GeoCities to create their own web pages. They taught Stephanie how to use HTML, which appealed to her since she liked to draw. Then, in seventh grade, she took courses in programming, web design, and industrial technology, where she used a computer to do designs. In eighth grade, she decided to develop a web page for her family and helped her father design a web page for his new business. She even taught her mother different ways to use computers. As she got further into art with the computer, she lurked in the background of Xanga, an online digital-art community, trying to pick up techniques for making computer art. She would study the finished works and the source code that the artists used to produce their works. She is a typical self-directed learner in the digital age.

The recent explosion of social networking points to how technologies can replicate the support and guidance functions of schools. These networks draw people across all ages from very different backgrounds, some quite expert and others virtual novices. Some learn by lurking in the background and others by asking questions. Groups in the network may jointly investigate topics of interest or ague about issues they consider important. The successful sites, however, share the characteristic of providing useful information to guide the interests of users. For example, user groups and community sites exist for every known disease and disorder, and doctors across the country know their diagnoses are checked by an increasingly informed patient population. These kinds of social networks are blossoming around topics of particular interest to different groups of people, topics such as poetry, chemistry, digital graphics, and fantasy sports. Reliable information sites, such as homework .com, tutor.com, and collegeboard.com, are already supplanting the guidance departments, financial aid centers, and even the tutoring and homework services that

are provided as common staples of institutional schooling.

What might happen if our thinking about learning doesn't change? If schools cannot change fast enough to keep pace with advances in learning technologies, learning will leave schooling behind. We see this happening outside of the United States already. For example, with inexpensive computers, young people in Thailand and Brazil can have access to the same resources for learning that people in the developed world now have. Many will choose to take advantage of these resources to escape from poverty. In some ways, they will be a new kind of 21st-century immigrant—instead of moving to a new country, they will use information networks to transform their thinking. They will be able to find like-minded souls to share ideas in cyberspace. English will likely be their common language, which they will pick up from the web.

As older generations continue to impose established methods of learning in school, technologies will leech critical learning resources, such as student motivation, attention, and resources, out of the education system. Trying to reassert the identification of schooling and learning will be a losing battle.

Rethinking Motivation

The current school system does not help students develop intrinsic motivation to learn. The disengagement experienced by many students is reinforced by less-than-ideal classroom experiences. One recent report found that 50% of high school students are bored every day in their classes; another found that 82% of California 9th- and 10th-graders reported their school experiences as "boring and irrelevant."[4] Changing these deeply ingrained attitudes about learning will mean changing both the process of teaching and learning and the reward system for successful completion of schooling.

Fortunately, learning technologies provide some direction about how to improve student motivation to learn and to invigorate learning content. In order to produce a generation of people who seek out learning, learners need to be given more control over their own learning. Learner control can be fostered by giving kids the tools to support their own learning, such as access to the web, machines for toddlers that teach reading, tutoring help when needed, and computer-based games that foster deep knowledge and entrepreneurial skills.

A love of learning can also be fostered by encouraging kids to explore deeply topics in which they are particularly interested, as home-schooling parents do. As Kurt Squire found, kids who play real-time strategy games, such as *Civilization*, begin to check out books on ancient cultures and earn better grades in middle school.[5] Instead of diverting student attention from schools, as feared by many teachers and school leaders, video games can provide a path to make conventional school content more appealing and encourage students to give their classroom instruction another chance. By understanding how new technologies can encourage kids to take responsibility for their own learning, society may help produce a generation of people who seek out ways to learn.

Pushing students to take more control of their learning, as we have discussed, runs counter to the institutional control of learning exercised by schools. Fostering self-learning will require challenging the current policy assumptions that press schools to teach everyone the same thing at the same time. Even the one-room schools that preceded universal schooling resisted this contemporary impulse to standardize instruction. Integrating computers into the center of schooling, rather than at the periphery, could help learners pursue individualized, interactive lessons with adequate support. Such systems can control the level of challenge by choosing tasks that reflect the learner's recent history. Teachers can help out when students need more assistance than the computer can provide. Such individualized learning would remove the stigma of looking bad when you don't understand something that others grasp.

Technologies also point to another path toward fostering a love of learning through design and production. Savvy computer game developers have long realized how including design tools to alter the game environment greatly increases the replay value and brand loyalty of their games. Giving students meaningful tasks to accomplish will help them understand why they are doing what they are doing. Students who struggle in school spend hundreds of hours tweaking football rosters to meet salary cap requirements in *Madden* or editing parody videos on YouTube. Suddenly, when the drudge work of complicated tasks becomes contextualized and has new significance, students are more than willing to take the time to "get it right." As a society, we need to understand how new technologies turn kids and adults on to learning, in order to redesign our learning environments to provide positive motivational experiences for all learners.

Rethinking What Is Important to Learn

Of course, providing intrinsic motivation to learn also requires us to rethink the rewards of successfully completing a course of learning. There is a mismatch between the programs that are needed to live a successful life in a knowledge economy. The core curriculum in modern schools is still rooted in the medieval *trivium* (from which the word *trivial* is derived), which consisted of logic, grammar, and rhetoric, and *quadrivium*, which was made up of arithmetic, geometry, music, and astronomy. These formed the bases for the liberal arts, which dominate the current course of study in school and college. Over the centuries, we added courses such as history, geography, and the sciences, but the basic organization of the curriculum reflects its historical roots.

A question that society must wrestle with is whether this is the best curriculum for preparing students to live in an age with rich technological resources. Proponents of traditional curricula argue that classical training in thinking and writing is needed now more than ever; progressive educators suggest that new literacy skills and mathematical reasoning skills are needed for new times. In schools, however, the compromise between the two camps is often to organize content roughly in classical disciplines, but to remove the rigor and the context from the classical content. Thus, geometry is presented without a sense of history, and sciences are learned as sets of facts instead of methods to organize observations and experiments. Because we think of education as what goes on in school, this compromise curriculum furnishes a narrow and quite impoverished view of what is important to learn.

There are two areas in which the new technological resources clearly impact what is important to learn: communication and mathematics. In 21st-century communication practices, boundaries are becoming blurred between core literacy practices, such as learning to read and write, and more applied production and presentation practices. Creating multimedia documents, putting together and critiquing videos, finding information and resources on the web, and understanding images and graphics are all becoming important aspects of communication. New technologies offer interesting ways to make the transition between basic and applied literacies. For example, the people who play massively multiplayer online games (MMOGs), such as *World of Warcraft* or *Lineage*, use basic literacy practices to develop a whole range of other applied literacy skills, such as negotiation, bargaining, forming alliances, strategizing and outwitting opponents, calculating which approach is most likely to work, and communicating with different kinds of people. These applied literacy skills occur naturally in MMOGs but are difficult to maintain in traditional school environments. Yet, because we think of literacy skill development as being directly tied to traditional school content, most people regard gamers as wasting their time playing these multiplayer games.

In terms of mathematics, technology can carry out all of the algorithms that students spend so much time learning in school. At the same time, learning to think mathematically is more important than ever. Therefore, students' time might be better spent in learning how to use mathematical tools to solve real-world problems, rather than learning how to mimic computer algorithms. In fact, understanding how to apply computer tools appropriately requires much more thinking than executing algorithms. It should become the new agenda for teaching mathematics. Fantasy sports present a case in point for teaching applied mathematical skills. Calculating on-base percentages or adding up runs scored may not involve sophisticated algorithmic processes, but even the most casual fantasy baseball player must engage in predictive models to anticipate which players and teams have the best chance to succeed. Having fantasy players articulate their predictive models is an excellent exercise in developing the kinds of estimation and number sense skills prized by organizations such as the National Council of Teachers of Mathematics.

A subtle impact of technology on learning has to do with the easy availability of knowledge on the web. In the past, people have had to memorize a lot of information in order to make competent decisions, as doctors must do to make accurate diagnoses. But with easy access to knowledge, people can rely more on external memories to help them out. We can illustrate this phenomenon with the use of technology by doctors. Online systems have been developed in recent years that help doctors make diagnoses. Doctors can feed the systems with sets of symptoms, and the systems can suggest possible diagnoses that the doctors should consider. That way, the doctor does not have to remember every possible pairing of symptoms to diagnoses. Doctors still must apply their personal knowledge, gained from experience and from interaction with the patient, in order

to make their decisions. These systems act essentially as memory aids. Similarly, the web is a huge memory aid, in addition to providing new information on every topic under the sun. The essential skill is no longer memorization, but knowing how to find the information you want on the web, including how to evaluate what you find, given the differences in reliability among Web sites. That is to say, people need to develop new learning skills rather than acquiring more information.

One approach to a new specification of what students need to know is provided by a Harlem high school.[6] The school stresses that the students should learn to ask and answer reflective questions that correspond to five Habits of Mind: 1) From what viewpoint are we seeing, reading, or hearing this? 2) How do we know what we know? What's the evidence, and how reliable is it? 3) How are things, events, or people connected? What is the cause and effect? How do they fit? 4) What if . . . ? Could things be otherwise? What are or were the alternatives? 5) So what? Why does it matter? What does it all mean? Who cares? These questions are central to everything the students do in the school, and even in the evaluation of students to determine if they have learned enough to graduate. These questions stretch the definition of what is taught in a school to encompass the types of thinking and action required for adaptive thinking in an information-rich world.

Rethinking Careers

While education has traditionally aimed to enlighten learners about their political responsibilities, American discussions of education have recently turned sharply toward career preparation for economic success.

But as routine jobs are replaced by technology or shipped offshore, the remaining jobs emphasize collaboration, communication, and knowledge-processing skills. From an economic perspective, it's imperative for education to focus much more on teaching students how to think critically in a digital age, and how to find the knowledge and resources they need to accomplish difficult tasks. Students would be much better served if they were challenged to solve real-world problems and create meaningful products. Then they might have some incentive to learn how to think.

Career mobility also challenges educational institutions to teach students to become more adaptive. The traditional American story was that we went to school to prepare ourselves for a career, whether as an auto mechanic or a doctor. We would settle on a career sometime during high school or college and take courses geared toward success in that career. In the 1980s and 1990s, however, the erosion of corporate responsibility for lifetime employment sparked increased job mobility across the economy. Currently, 50 to 60% of new hires leave their jobs within the first year, and 10% of the workforce leaves their jobs every year.[7] As we live longer, it turns out that many of us may be working into our 70s and 80s. Most Americans in the next 20 years will likely have a succession of careers.

As an example, one of the authors started his career as an auditor on Wall Street after getting a college degree in accounting. After a few years as an auditor, he returned to graduate school in computer science and 10 years later graduated with a Ph.D. in cognitive psychology. After that, he went to work in a firm that carried out research for the federal government in a variety of areas, most related to the use of computers in society. In his research work, he slowly moved from carrying out psychological research to developing computer systems for education. After some 20 years in research, he joined the education faculty at Northwestern, never having taken an education course during his career. Then, for 18 more years, he taught a variety of education courses at Northwestern. The second author started out as a graduate student in philosophy. He took a job as a history teacher in a small Chicago school. After several years of teaching, he became an administrator at the school. Later, he decided to return to graduate school in education. After 5 more years in graduate school, he became a professor at a large graduate school of education. It remains to be seen what he will do next. These stories, although they focus on academic careers, are not unusual. Such twists and turns in careers are becoming more and more common. The fate of people in a knowledge society, it seems, is that they must keep reinventing themselves in order to keep up with the changing world around them.

Eventually, people will come to think of life as made up of a succession of careers. In order to cope with this idea, they will begin to see how important it is to "learn how to learn." They may come to see that the career they decide to pursue in their early years is not a commitment for life. As Avner Avituv and Robert Lerman point out, "Every mouth, millions of workers leave one employer and take a job with another employer. It takes young workers a long time to enter a stable career and a long-term relationship with an employer. By the age of 30, high school graduates with no college have already worked for an average of eight employers. Nearly half of all male high school graduates experienced at least one spell of unemployment between ages 25–29. Moreover, job instability is increasing among young men."[8]

In recent years, there has been a growing gap between the incomes of college graduates and high school graduates. This has led over 90% of high school students to plan to go to college. But only 14% of kids with a C average in high school will complete a college degree.[9] They would be better off working for a few years after they finish high school and then going back to get more education. The success in college of returning veterans after World War II testifies to the payoff in waiting to go to college. A study by Norman Frederiksen found that the veterans had higher achievement levels than nonveterans.[10] Some of the pressure to go right on to college will be relieved if people come to understand that their life in the future will likely alternate between working and learning. It will no longer be 15 or 20 years of preparation followed by 30 years of working. Rather, we will learn for a while, work for a while, back and forth, until we retire.

Of course, some people in the future may be actors or auto mechanics for all of their lives. But they will be the exceptions. Thinking of a single career as the standard pattern leads people to think that they are done with learning when they finish school. So they do not keep their minds open and focused on continuing their learning. This makes them less adaptable when they are hit with the necessity of changing careers. Parents also need to understand how the nature of people's careers has changed, and not try to force

young people to prepare for a particular career that they think is best for them. As a society, we need to build policies that support people in making the many career transitions they will have to make in a constantly changing environment.

Rethinking the Transitions Between Learning and Work

America has not helped its citizens manage the transition to adulthood as well as other countries with apprenticeship systems. Both high school graduates who don't enter college and students who drop out of college early have entered the workforce unprepared. Since only about 30 percent of students in America ever get a college degree, the vast majority of students have a more difficult transition to make. Typically, they drift from job to job until they are 25 or 30. Some return to college when they are older, but it is often harder for these students because society does not support older people returning to college. Given the increasing centrality of technology in work and the fact that people are more and more likely to change careers several times during their lifetime, it is worth rethinking the ways that society supports the transitions between learning and work.

The transition to work is handled fairly well when people graduate from college. The colleges maintain an office designed to help students find jobs, both as interns during college and when they graduate. This office has extensive files on employers in their area, and many have files on alumni employed in different occupations who can guide students in choosing a career. Different employers come to colleges to recruit graduating students who are interested in working for them. Often, college students intern for different employers during the summers or during one of their later semesters, building ties with potential employers after they graduate. And college professors often write letters of recommendation for their students, even pointing them to potential employers. High school career centers and teachers sometimes perform this function, but it is sporadic and concentrated in wealthier communities. So there is an effective system in place, but only for college graduates.

In an era of multiple careers, people will need support to navigate their options, both in going from learning to work and from work to learning. If America wants to remain a successful society, it needs to create new ways to support citizens through these challenging transitions.

We believe America must transform how we address technical and vocational education. For example, schools should reconsider how to support teenagers who want to go into the job market, either in addition to or instead of going to high school. Teenagers should not go to work until they have mastered the basic skills and knowledge taught in middle school. Hence, there needs to be an office in high schools that determines whether teenagers have met the standards for going to work and that helps them find jobs that are well suited to their goals and abilities. This office would keep files of possible jobs, just as college employment offices do. It would help students put together resumes and assess their interests and abilities. It would also help gather teacher recommendations and make initial contacts with employers. In short, the office would carry out many of the same functions as college employment offices, but would provide more guidance, since the students are

younger. Modest federal funding in this area would provide significant value in helping students make a successful transition between learning and work.

The same office might administer apprenticeship programs, such as are widely found in Europe.[11] In these programs, adolescent students typically work three days a week and go to school for two days a week. The programs attempt to coordinate what students are learning in school with the work for which they are training. Given the aimlessness of much work that teenagers are now doing, society would be well advised to put federal money into supporting a robust apprenticeship system. The office might also support students who have gone to work and wish to return to full- or part-time learning. The office could advise them about their options, such as taking high school or community college classes, online courses, or courses administered by a local learning center.

Such offices can also serve adults, who need help in thinking about embarking on a new career or returning to get more education. These counseling offices might be maintained by the state in all high schools, or they might be privately run. They would have counselors who can advise people on the kind of training and credentials they need to pursue a particular career, and what kind of educational resources are available to pursue that training. Other counselors could assess the skills and interests of adults to guide them toward viable careers they might pursue. Still other counselors would have knowledge and contacts with employers in the region, and could help people find jobs that suit them, given their educational background. These are resources we need to be providing to people to make our society as productive as possible.

Our view is that the government should pay for these learning resources, at least up to the level of what would be spent on a high school education. School-to-work programs, such as the School-to-Work Opportunities Act of 1994, provide a good start toward institutionalizing these types of services. Unfortunately, in recent years, these modest initiatives have been gutted by budget cuts. In 2006 alone, the Bush administration proposed to cut $1.1 billion in state vocational education grants. Cutting these transitional services means that the students with the least social capital, who need the most help connecting to viable economic resources, are left to make their own connections. There are so many alternatives that it is bewildering for most people, so they need counseling to make wise decisions. We will all profit from others learning all they can and finding employment that suits them.

Rethinking Educational Leadership

We are experiencing a time of educational transition, which demands a new kind of educational leadership—a new Horace Mann, as it were. We need a vision of education that makes it possible for the new array of educational resources to reach all of the people. The trends in place are reaching the elites and leaving behind the vast majority of people. The next generation of education leaders will need to face the political and technological challenges. The challenges of changing a well-established, entrenched institution are far different than those faced by Horace Mann. Parents, teachers, policymakers, and local communities all have compelling reasons to preserve the current system. The forces for change, such as the civil rights emphasis on

using schools to increase social equity and the technological emphasis to open the core practices of schooling to information technologies, push uncomfortably against influential conservative forces. Leaders who can effect real change need to understand where the leverage points are to move the system and need to have the organizational skills to bring together the resources and skills necessary to create change.

One possibility is to promote the inexpensive computer as a tool that can put powerful computing in the hands of all students. Such machines provide access to a vast array of educational resources for nonelites. Programs such as One Laptop Per Child[12] are currently aimed only at Third World nations, though they could be expanded to address poor people wherever they live. But we need to think much more broadly to address the inequities that are arising. Simply inserting technology into classrooms and schools without considering how the contexts for learning need to change will likely fail. Schools are still hesitant to embrace new technologies as a backlash from the significant, and largely ineffectual, investment in classroom computers as an instructional panacea in the mid-1990s.[13] Leaders need to understand the limits of the new technologies in order to set appropriate expectations for their communities. They will need to think about how to bring coherence to the incoherent array of tools already in schools and in the world.

In the future, educational leadership will require more than just reforming schools. We need to think about how to integrate nonschool resources into learning environments, both supporting families in bringing these tools into their homes and in building wired learning centers in communities that reach those in need. We need to support robust language-rich resources, which very young kids can use to learn to read. We have such programs for computers now, where, for example, a kid can hear a Dr. Seuss story by pointing at the words or lines on the screen to have them read aloud. As the kids learn the sight-to-sound correspondences, they will pick up reading of their favorite stories on their own. These machines should include the best children's literature, covering a wide variety of genres and topics. They should also include arithmetic games that would teach basic mathematical operations to young kids. Every young kid should have such a machine, since busy parents often do not have the time to read with their children. It might begin to address the inequity that many kids face.

Elementary school should provide an array of technology-based supplementary services to help students who are having trouble. Such services are envisioned by the No Child Left Behind (NCLB) Act as extending current special education and student services programs. If a child is having difficulties in one of his school subjects—say writing, math, or geography—then the first course of action should be to provide the child with a customized diagnostic process that connects the student's learning needs with appropriate resources. Technologies can provide a wide variety of resources, such as computer-based learning programs or access to online tutoring. Technologies allow students to use programs at home with their families as well as at school. If the programs do not succeed completely, then the kids might be provided with specialized human tutoring, as NCLB envisions. But human tutoring is a costly

option that may not be necessary in most cases.

After eighth grade, kids might follow different educational paths, depending on their own and their parents' choosing. For example, as an alternative to continuing on to a traditional high school, a student might take online courses at home or in a learning center, enter an apprenticeship program, take courses at a community college, or attend a Career Academy, like we see in cities such as Oakland, California. Kids might even work for a while and later return to get more education, when they are ready. Giving students such options will make them less likely to feel that high school is a prison they must endure until they are grown up enough to go out on their own.

When a person is 14 or older—however old he or she may be—he or she should have access to a personalized learning counselor, who can provide advice about available educational options. As learning becomes more critical for success in the world, people will need individual support from someone who knows their history and the particulars of their life. Again, technologies greatly expand the range of advice that counselors can use to guide learners. Counselors can direct learners to online resources that guide novices through the initial stages of career choice and development.

A first visit to a counselor should be free and routine for everyone when they reach age 14. Learning counselors would be trained and licensed by the state, just as medical doctors are. The goal would be to develop a learning plan to address each person's interests, needs, and abilities, which would be adapted over the years as the person changed jobs and acquired more knowledge and responsibilities. The learning plan might involve taking online courses, going to a learning center for specialized training, getting a technical certification in some area, joining an apprenticeship program, or learning from computer-based tutorials to enhance particular skills. In any case, the learner should check with his or her counselor at regular intervals to evaluate how things are going and to consider how the plan might be revised.

These examples show how educational leaders need to think about changing schools from within and about how learners can be linked to resources outside schools. Thinking more broadly about technologies can revive our ideas about equity and extend available resources to the nonelites in our society. Our proposals are merely suggestive of the issues that leaders should be considering. Because society has identified education with schooling, we are systematically overlooking many of the resources now available for helping minorities and other nonelites.

Further, society views education reform as something that applies to youth rather than to people of all ages. With a broader view of education, we can begin to think about how to provide educational resources even to people in their 40s, 50s, and 60s.

We are not going to fix education by fixing the schools. They have served us very well in the past, but they are a 19th-century invention trying to cope with a 21st-century society. This is the time for another Horace (or Leticia) Mann to step forward and lead the nation toward a new education system. Our new leaders will have to understand the affordances of the new technologies that have become available in recent years, and to watch for issues and technologies on the horizon. They will need to understand that learning does not start with kindergarten and end with a high school or college diploma—we need to design a coherent lifelong-learning system.

Rethinking the Role of Government in Education

Historically, the states and towns have been responsible for education in America, with the federal government only playing a supplementary role. The federal government has carried out some programs, such as developing science and math curricula to make the nation more competitive or supporting poor children by providing resources in order to ensure greater equity among children. But teachers' salaries, curriculum materials, and administrative expenses were paid with local funds. When the federal government in recent years has imposed standards on the states and towns, many have regarded this as encroachment on the states' authority. States will try to protect their authority, and this is leading to a backlash against the No Child Left Behind Act.

As we have pointed out, the technological resources that have been developed in recent years introduce new inequities into the educational system. Wealthier parents are buying tutoring, computers, and web access for their children, leaving poor children further behind than ever. The states simply do not have the resources to correct these imbalances. They get most of their monies for education from property taxes, and the fact that fewer and fewer households have children makes it very difficult to raise property taxes to pay for education. And the costs of schooling each child have increased rapidly in recent years.

Without stepping on the states' authority, the federal government can try to equalize educational opportunities for all citizens. It can provide robust machines that teach reading to young kids and inexpensive computers with access to the web for older kids. It can provide educational guidance and tutoring for those who cannot afford to buy these services. It can set up apprenticeship programs that help kids make the transition into adulthood, rather than wandering aimlessly, as many now do. It can pay for additional training when people want to change careers. These are all supplemental services that do not step on the states' authority in any way.

There is also an important new role for state government in bringing about a new vision of education for a technology-rich world. If our society is going to support new alternatives for pursuing education, the states need to rethink their mandates of keeping kids in comprehensive schools until they are 16 years old. If we are going to let teenagers pursue other options besides staying in high school, the states will need to specify what alternatives are acceptable instead of school and what requirements students must meet before pursuing each alternative.

For example, the state might mandate that a student must acquire a specific set of certificates, such as demonstrating an ability to read and do math at an eighth-grade level, before pursuing a full-time job or some other option as an alternative to high school. The states might also monitor the teen's performance in the job and require teens to attend a weekly class where they discuss what they have learned in their work. If the work is not serving as a learning experience for the teens, a guidance counselor may help them find a new job that is of more value to them. If students are taking online courses at a learning center or participating in an apprenticeship program, the state might monitor their progress in similar fashion. The state would still have a responsibility for teenagers, but at the same time, would give them more latitude in pursuing their own education.

We have outlined examples of possible responsibilities that governments could take on, but these are not definitive. Governments should provide guidance to students at the same time that they loosen the reins that are keeping kids in high school, which many of them feel is a kind of prison. It would be wise for governments to put more responsibility on learners to pursue their own learning, but at the same time, it is critical that governments not ignore their responsibility to provide equal access to educational resources for all citizens.

Our Vision of the Future

As education becomes more privatized and commercial, we risk losing the vision promulgated by Thomas Jefferson and Horace Mann of a society where everyone has an equal chance at a good education. Horace Mann was right in predicting that education could provide a path for everyone to become part of the elite. Universal schooling formed the basis for our middle-class society today. But the onset of technology, privatization, and increasing inequality of income is undermining this vision.

Making economic success the central outcome of schooling risks marginalizing the political and moral goals of education. Education is, in many ways, America's civic religion. We use education to work toward our national ideals of equality, opportunity, and democracy. As a society, we need to understand how to balance the need to use schools as engines of economic competition with our national commitment to equality of opportunity.

According to a recent survey from the Education Trust, America is the only industrialized country in which today's young people are less likely than their parents to earn a high school diploma.[14] Those of us who care about education should do whatever we can to see that our children are educated as best they can to live in a technology-rich society. Even those of us without children should pay attention to this trend. All of us depend on the next generation to support our social services, such as Social Security and Medicare. For the future of America and the welfare of our individual futures, it is important that our society invest in the next generation's education. It behooves all of us to work toward a more equitable system of education.

What role will technology play in our national story of equity and economic development? In the 19th century, Americans developed the public school system to institutionalize our national commitment to citizenship while at the same time addressing the needs of urban families to care for and educate children in the midst of the Industrial Revolution. Our generation faces a similar, but radically new, design challenge. We are dealing with a mature, stable system of education designed to adapt to gradual change, but ill-suited to embrace radical change. The pace of technological change has outstripped the ability of school systems to adapt essential practices. Schools have fiddled with learning technologies on the margins of the system, in boutique innovations that leave core practices untouched. The emergence of new forms of teaching and learning outside of school threatens the identification of learning with formal schooling forged in the 19th century.

For education to embrace both equity and economic development, we believe that our leaders will have to stretch their traditional practices to embrace the capacity of new information technologies. This will require schools to forfeit some control over the learning processes, but will once again put the latest tools for improving learning in the hands of public institutions (as opposed to the hands of families and learners who can afford access).

Parents and citizens need to start pushing for this more expansive view of education reform. School leaders and teachers will need to understand how learning technologies work and how they change the basic interactions of teachers and learners. Technology leaders will need to work together with educators, not as missionaries bearing magical gifts, but as collaborators in creating new opportunities to learn. It will take a concerted effort to bring about such a radical change in thinking. If a broader view develops in society, leaders will emerge who can bring about the political changes necessary to make the new educational resources available to everyone. These new leaders will need to understand the affordances of the new technologies and have a vision for education that will bring the new resources to everyone. We hope these leaders may be reading this book now, and that it can guide them in taking action to address the learning revolution that is upon us.

REFERENCES

Avituv, A., & Lerman, R. I. (2004). *Job turnover, wage rates, and marriage stability: How are they related.* New York: Urban Institute. Available at www.urban.org/publications/411148.html.

Barron, B. (2006). Interest and self-sustained learning as catalysts of development: A learning ecologies perspective. *Human Development, 49*(4), 193–224.

Cuban, L. (2001). *Oversold and underused: Computers in the classroom.* Cambridge, MA: Harvard University Press.

Darling-Hammond, L., Ancess, J., & Falk, B. (1995). *Authentic assessment in action: Studies of schools and students at work.* New York: Teachers College Press.

Feller, R., and Walz, G., (Eds.). (1996). *Career transitions in turbulent times: Exploring work, learning, and careers.* Greensboro, NC: ERIC Clearinghouse on Counseling and Student Services (ED 398 519).

Frederiksen, N. (1950). *Adjustment to college: A study of 10,000 veteran and non-veteran students in sixteen American colleges.* Princeton, NJ: Educational Testing Service.

Friedman, T. L. (2006). *The world is flat: A brief history of the twenty-first century.* New York: Farrar, Straus, and Giroux.

Germeraad, S. (2008). *"Counting on graduation": Most states are setting low expectations for the improvement of high school graduation rates.* Washington, DC: Education Trust. Available at www2.edtrust.org/EdTrust/Press+Room/countingongrad.htm.

Hamilton, S. F. (1990). *Apprenticeship for adulthood: Preparing youth for the future.* New York: Free Press.

Hart, P. D. (2006). *Report findings based on a survey among California ninth and tenth graders.* Washington, DC: Peter D. Hart Research Associates. Available at www .connectedcalifornia.org/downloads/Irvine _poll.pdf.

Henkoff, R. (1996, January 15). So you want to change your job. *Fortune, 133*(1), 52–56.

Olson, L. (1997). *The school to work revolution: How employers and educators are joining forces to prepare tomorrow's skilled workforce.* New York: Perseus.

Orfield, G., & Lee, C. (2007, August 29). *Historic reversals, accelerating resegregation, and the need for new integration strategies.* Los Angeles: UCLA Civil Rights Project/Proyecto Derechos Civiles.

Rosenbaum, J. E. (2001). *Beyond college for all: Career paths for the forgotten half.* New York: Russell Sage.

Squire, K. D. (2004). Sid Meier's *Civilization III. Simulations and Gaming, 35*(1), 135–140.

Yazzie-Mintz, E. (2006). *Voices of students on engagement: A report on the 2006 high school survey of a student engagement.* Available at http://ceep.indiana.edu/hssse/pdf/HSSSE_2006_Report.pdf

NOTES

1. Friedman, 2006.
2. Orfield & Lee, 2007.
3. Barron, 2006.
4. Yazzie-Mintz, 2006; Hart, 2006.
5. Squire, 2004.
6. Darling-Hammond, Ancess, & Falk, 1995.
7. Henkoff, 1996; Feller & Walz, 1996.
8. Avituv & Lerman, 2004.
9. Rosenbaum, 2001.
10. Frederiksen, 1950.
11. Hamilton, 1990; Olson, 1997.
12. See http://laptop.org/en/vision/index .shtml.
13. See, for example, Cuban, 2001.
14. Germeraad, 2008.

Part V Additional Resources

Discussion Questions

Students should read each question carefully and support their response with examples and specific references from the readings that are being considered.

1. Identify key trends and issues that you believe will have an impact on twenty-first-century schools. Discuss how these trends and issues will influence schools in the following areas: aims and purposes, curriculum, and teacher and student roles.
2. Research the changing demographics of twenty-first-century America. Discuss the educational challenges presented by these changing demographics. What changes will have to occur in schools in order to successfully address the needs of families and children? What changes must be made in teacher preparation in order to prepare teachers to work with diverse groups of learners?
3. Technology has had an impact on the ways in which teaching and learning occur in schools today. Will technology provide more access to knowledge for all students, or will the increased use of technological resources create a greater chasm between the haves and the have-nots? Why or why not? What institutional changes will have to occur simultaneously to accommodate and facilitate the increased use of technology? How will the roles and responsibilities of students and teachers change in response to these changes?
4. Discuss the pros and cons of high-stakes testing. Who benefits from these tests? Who suffers? Are there ways to use high-stakes testing to facilitate more effective teaching and learning? Give examples.
5. Identify educational practices that limit the educational opportunities of some students. Do these practices reinforce preconceived notions about groups of students who have not traditionally succeeded in schools? How? Why?

Guide to Further Reading

Andreas, Brian. 2000. *Imagining World* (print). Decorah, IA: Story People.
Delpit, L. 2002. *The Skin That We Speak: Thoughts on Language and Culture in the Classroom.*. New York: The New Press.
Giroux, Henry A. 1992. *Border Crossings: Cultural Workers and the Politics of Education.* New York: Routledge.
Goodlad, J. 2004. *A Place Called School*, 2nd ed. New York: McGraw-Hill.

hooks, bell. 2009. *Teaching Critical Thinking: Practical Wisdom*. New York: Routledge.

Nieto, S. 2003. *What Keeps Teachers Going?* New York: Teachers College Press.

Oakes, J. 1985. *Keeping Track: How Schools Structure Inequality*. New Haven, CT: Yale University Press.

Palmer, P. J. 1997. *The Courage to Teach: Exploring the Inner Landscape of a Teacher's Life*. San Francisco: Jossey-Bass.

Tatum, Beverly T. 1997. *"Why Are All the Black Kids Sitting Together in the Cafeteria?" And Other Conversations About Race*. New York: Basic Books.

Weiss, L., and M. Fine. 2003. *Excavating Race, Class, and Gender Among Urban Youth*. New York: Teachers College Press.

West, C. 1993. *Race Matters*. Boston: Beacon.

Related Resources

http://www.essentialschools.org
   Coalition of Essential Schools, Transforming Public Education
http://www.cec.sped.org
   Council for Exceptional Children
http://www.ncpie.org
   National Coalition for Parent Involvement in Education
http://www.rethinkingschools.org/special_reports/union/unhome.shtml
   Rethinking Schools
http://tcla.gseis.ucla.edu
   Teaching to Change LA: An Online Journal of IDEA,
   UCLA's Institute for Democracy, Education and Access
http://www.youtube.com/watch?v=_A-ZVCjfWf8
   A Vision of K-12 Students Today

About the Editor and Contributors

EDITOR

ELEANOR BLAIR HILTY is associate professor in the Department of Educational Leadership and Foundations at Western Carolina University (WCU) in Cullowhee, North Carolina. She grew up in Memphis, Tennessee, and received a B.S. degree in special education/elementary education and an M.S. in educational psychology. After teaching in special education for several years, she returned to school and earned a Ph.D. from the University of Tennessee, Knoxville. Her research on teachers' work and teachers' moonlighting has been presented at national and international conferences. This work has also been published in numerous books and journals focusing on the lives of teachers. Teaching at WCU for seventeen years has given Hilty an opportunity to teach both undergraduate and graduate foundations courses, work with student teachers, and coordinate a master's degree program in secondary education. In addition, as part of her work at WCU, she travels regularly to Jamaica, where she teaches Jamaican teachers. Her desire to assemble this particular book was fueled by the absence of foundations of education readers that present the perspectives of notable authors in the field and provide a relevant, often critical foundation of basic knowledge for education students preparing to teach in twenty-first-century schools.

CONTRIBUTORS

MICHAEL W. APPLE is currently the John Bascom Professor of Curriculum and Instruction and Educational Policy Studies at the University of Wisconsin–Madison Schools of Education. He is a leading critical educational theorist and curriculum specialist. The primary focus of his work is on education and power, cultural politics, curriculum theory and research, critical teaching, and democratic schools. Some of his best-known works are *Ideology and Curriculum* (2004) and *Educating the "Right" Way: Markets, Standards, God, and Inequality* (2006).

WILLIAM AYERS is an American elementary education theorist and a former leader in the movement that opposed U.S. involvement in the Vietnam War. He is known for his 1960s activism as well as his current work in education reform, curriculum, and instruction. In 1969 he cofounded the Weather Underground, a self-described communist revolutionary group that conducted a campaign of bombing public buildings during the 1960s and 1970s, motivated by U.S. involvement in the Vietnam War. He is a retired professor in the College of Education at the University of Illinois at Chicago, formerly holding the titles of Distinguished Professor of

Education and Senior University Scholar. He is also the author of numerous essays and books in the field of education, for example, *To Teach: The Journey of a Teacher* (2010).

CAROL CORBETT BURRIS is the principal of South Side High School in Rockville Centre, New York. She is a coauthor of *Detracking for Excellence and Equity* (2009), and her dissertation on detracking earned the 2003 Middle Level Dissertation Award from the National Association of Secondary School Principals.

MARILYN COCHRAN-SMITH is the Cawthorne Professor of Teacher Education for Urban Schools and Director of the Doctoral Program in Curriculum and Instruction at the Lynch School of Education, Boston College. She is currently principal investigator for a study of teacher development and retention supported by the Ford Foundation.

ALLAN COLLINS is professor emeritus of education and social policy at Northwestern University. He served as a founding editor of the journal *Cognitive Science* and as first chair of the Cognitive Science Society. He has studied teaching and learning for over thirty years and has written extensively on related topics. He is best known in education for his work on situated learning, inquiry teaching, and cognitive apprenticeship. From 1991 to 1994 he was codirector of the U.S. Department of Education's Center for Technology in Education.

LARRY CUBAN is professor of education at Stanford University and former superintendent of the Arlington, Virginia, schools. He is known for his work in both history and educational leadership. His career has encompassed both the practical and theoretical sides of education in K–12 and higher education settings.

LINDA DARLING-HAMMOND is the Charles E. Ducommon Professor of Education at Stanford University, where she launched the School Redesign Network, the Stanford Educational Leadership Institute, and the Stanford Center for Opportunity Policy in Education. Darling-Hammond is the author and editor of numerous books and articles on education policy and practice. Her work focuses on school restructuring, teacher education, and educational equity.

LISA D. DELPIT is the executive director of the Center for Urban Education and Innovation at Florida International University in Miami and the Benjamin E. Mays Professor of Urban Educational Leadership at Georgia State University in Atlanta. Her work focuses on education and race. She has written numerous books, among them *Other People's Children: Cultural Conflict in the Classroom*, which was published in 1995.

MICHELLE FINE is Distinguished Professor of Psychology and Urban Education at the Graduate Center, The City University of New York. Her research focuses on community development with an emphasis on urban youth and young adults. She has worked on projects funded by the Spencer Foundation and the Carnegie Foundation, both of which focused on the "spaces" created for and by youth.

BARRY M. FRANKLIN is professor of education and adjunct professor of history in the School of Teacher Education and Leadership at Utah State University. He is a noted scholar in the history of education. His books include *Building the American Community: The School Cur-*

riculum and the Search for Social Control (1986) and *From "Backwardness" to "At-Risk": Childhood Learning Difficulties and the Contradictions of School Reform* (1994).

PAULO FREIRE was a prominent Brazilian educator whose work had a significant impact on the thinking of educators in the field of critical pedagogy. His *Pedagogy of the Oppressed* (2001) is one of the most quoted educational texts in the world. Throughout it and subsequent books, he argued for systems of education that emphasize teaching and learning as tools of freedom and liberation.

HENRY A. GIROUX is a leading critical pedagogy scholar. He currently holds the Global TV Network Chair Professorship in the English and Cultural Studies Department at McMaster University, Hamilton, Ontario. He has taught at Boston University, Miami University of Ohio, and Penn State University. His most recent books include *The University in Chains: Confronting the Military-Industrial-Academic Complex* (2007); *Against the Terror of Neoliberalism* (2008); and *Youth in a Suspect Society* (2009).

JOHN I. GOODLAD is an educational researcher and theorist who has published influential models for renewing schools and teacher education. His best-known work is the book *A Place Called School* (2004), which received the Outstanding Book of the Year Award from the American Educational Research Association and the Distinguished Book of the Year Award from Kappa Delta Pi. His book *In Praise of Education* (1997) is known for defining education as a fundamental right in democratic societies, essential to developing individual and collective democratic intelligence.

RICHARD HALVERSON is associate professor in the Educational Leadership and Policy Analysis Department at the University of Wisconsin–Madison. He is a cofounder of the Games, Learning, and Society research group and the Learning Sciences Program at UW–Madison and has appointments in the Educational Psychology and Curriculum and Instruction departments.

MARY JEAN RONAN HERZOG is professor in the Department of Educational Leadership and Foundations at Western Carolina University, Cullowhee, North Carolina. Her research and writing have focused on issues and concerns in rural education and cultural studies.

E. D. HIRSCH, JR., is a U.S. educator and academic literary critic. Now retired, he was until recently the University Professor of Education and Humanities and the Linden Kent Memorial Professor of English Emeritus at the University of Virginia. He is best known for his writings about cultural literacy.

CARL F. KAESTLE has spent thirty years as a historian of U.S. education. His scholarly record on issues from literacy development in the United States to the evolution of urban school systems to the federal role in school reform places him among the top education historians in the nation today. Currently he is in the Education Department at Brown University, Providence, Rhode Island, as University Professor and professor of education, history, and public policy.

JOE L. KINCHELOE was formerly Canada Research Chair in the Faculty of Education at McGill University. He wrote more than forty-five books, numerous book chapters, and journal articles on issues related to critical pedagogy, educational research, urban studies, cognition, curriculum, and cultural studies. He founded the Paulo and Nita Freire International Project for Critical Pedagogy at McGill University. The Freire Project continues to focus its work on creating a global community of researchers and cultural workers in critical pedagogy

JONATHAN KOZOL is a nonfiction writer, educator, and activist best known for his books on public education in the United States. *Death at an Early Age*, his first nonfiction book, is a description of his first year as a teacher in the Boston public schools. It was published in 1967 and received the 1968 National Book Award in Science, Philosophy, and Religion. Other books by Kozol include *Savage Inequalities: Children in America's Schools* (1992) and, more recently, *The Shame of the Nation: The Restoration of Apartheid Schooling in America* (2006). Kozol is still active in advocating for integrated public education and continues to condemn the inequalities that exist in American public schools.

GLORIA LADSON-BILLINGS is on the faculty of the University of Wisconsin–Madison School of Education. Ladson-Billings is a pedagogical theorist and teacher educator. She is the author of the critically acclaimed books *The Dreamkeepers: Successful Teachers of African American Children* (1994) and *Crossing Over to Canaan: The Journey of New Teachers in Diverse Classrooms* (2001).

LINDA LAMBERT is founder of the Center for Educational Leadership at California State University, Hayward, where she is professor emeritus. She is a major contributor to the work and writing in the field of teacher leadership.

LINDA MCNEIL is director of the Center for Education at Rice University and a member of the Rice education faculty. A curriculum theorist and analyst of school structure and reform, she is the author of *Contradictions of Control: School Structure and School Knowledge* (1988), a book that focuses on an understanding of the effects of bureaucratic structures of schooling on teaching and learning.

K. B. ROGERS is a member of the Content Area Consultant Bank for the National Research Center on the Gifted and Talented. She is assistant professor in the Gifted and Special Education Program at the University of St. Thomas in St. Paul, Minnesota.

PHILLIP C. SCHLECHTY is one of the nation's foremost authors and speakers on school reform and is the founder and chief executive officer of the Schlechty Center. His work at the center is a reflection of his dedication and commitment to public education.

JAMES T. SEARS is a noted gay writer, academic, and media commentator. He is the award-winning author or editor of twelve books, among them *Growing Up Gay in the South* (1991) and *Lonely Hunters* (1998). He is currently visiting professor at Harvard University.

FRANK SMITH was a reporter, editor, and novelist before beginning his formal research into language, thinking, and learning. He has worked as a professor at the Ontario Institute for Studies in Education; the University of Toronto; the University of Victoria, British Columbia; and the University of the Witwatersrand, South Africa. He holds a PhD from Harvard University.

BEVERLY DANIEL TATUM is a clinical psychologist and former professor at Mt. Holyoke College. Currently she is president of Spelman College in Atlanta, Georgia. She is considered an expert on issues related to race relations and the development of racial identity. Her book *"Why Are All the Black Kids Sitting Together in the Cafeteria?": A Psychologist Explains the Development of Racial Identity* (2003) is well known and frequently cited in the literature on race and education.

DAVID TYACK is professor of education and of history at Stanford University. He is coauthor, with Larry Cuban, of *Tinkering Toward Utopia: A Century of Public School Reform* (1997) and author of *The One Best System: A History of American Urban Education* (1974).

DONALD WARREN is professor in the History of Education and Policy Department and University Dean of Education Emeritus at Indiana University at Bloomington. He is a leading scholar in the areas of history of education and schooling and policy analysis.

KEVIN G. WELNER is professor of education in the educational foundations, policy, and practice program area. He is director of the University of Colorado–Boulder Education and the Public Interest Center. His current research examines small school reforms, tuition tax-credit voucher policies, and various issues concerning the intersection between education rights litigation and educational opportunity scholarship.

HARRY F. WOLCOTT is professor emeritus of anthropology at the University of Oregon and one of the leading writers on educational anthropology, qualitative research methods, and ethnographic writing. Some of his best-known books are *The Man in the Principal's Office* (2003), *The Art of Fieldwork* (2005), and *Sneaky Kid and Its Aftermath: Ethics and Intimacy in Fieldwork* (2002).

GEORGE WOOD is principal of Federal Hocking High School in Stewart, Ohio, and serves as the executive director of the Forum. His thirty-year career in public education includes work as a classroom teacher, school board member, professor of education, and school principal. He is the founding director of Wildwood Secondary School in Los Angeles and has served as principal of Federal Hocking for seventeen years. He has written several articles and books, including *Schools That Work* (1993), *Time to Learn* (2005), and *Many Children Left Behind* (edited with Deborah Meier) (2004).

# Credits

PART I: WHAT ARE THE AIMS AND PURPOSES OF EDUCATION?
1. *Conflict and Consensus Revisited: Notes Toward a Reinterpretation of American Educational History*, Carl Kaestle
From *Harvard Educational Review* 46 (August 1976): 390–396. Reprinted by permission of Harvard University Press.

2. *A Past for the Present: History, Education, and Public Policy*, Donald Warren
From *Educational Theory* 28 (1978): 253–265. Reprinted by permission of John Wiley and Sons.

3. *Intellectual Capital: A Civil Right*, E. D. Hirsch, Jr.
From *The Schools We Need and Why We Don't Have Them* by E. D. Hirsch, copyright © 1995 by Doubleday, a division of Random House, Inc. Reprinted by permission of E. D. Hirsch and the Watkins Loomis Agency.

4. *Learning from the Past*, Larry Cuban and David Tyack
Reprinted by permission of the publisher. From *Tinkering Toward Utopia: A Century of Public School Reform* by David Tyack and Larry Cuban, pp. 1–11, Cambridge, Mass.: Harvard University Press, copyright © 1995 by the President and Fellows of Harvard College.

5. *We Want It All*, John I. Goodlad
From Goodlad, John. *A Place Called School: Promise for the Future*, pp. 33–60. Copyright © 1992 by McGraw Hill Publishers. Reprinted by permission from McGraw Hill.

PART II: WHAT SHOULD BE THE CONTENT OF THE CURRICULUM?
6. *The Shifting Ground of Curriculum Thought and Everyday Practice*, William Ayers
From *Theory into Practice* 3, no. 1 (1992): 25–28. Copyright © 1995 College of Education, The Ohio State University. Reprinted by permission.

7. *But That's Just Good Teaching! The Case for Culturally Relevant Pedagogy*, Gloria Ladson-Billings
From *Theory into Practice* 34, no. 3 (Summer 1995): 159–165. Copyright © 1995 College of Education, The Ohio State University.

8. *The Banking Concept of Education*, Paulo Freire
From Freire, Paulo. *Pedagogy of the Oppressed*. Copyright © 2000 by The Continuum International Publishing Group, Inc. Reprinted by permission of The Continuum International Publishing Group, Inc.

PART III: WHAT ARE THE ROLES AND RESPONSIBILITIES OF TEACHER LEADERS?

PART IV: WHAT ARE THE ROLES AND RESPONSIBILITIES OF STUDENTS?

18. *At-Risk Children and the Common School Ideal*, Barry M. Franklin
From *"Backwardness" to "At-Risk": Childhood Learning Difficulties and the Contradictions of School Reform* (State University of New York Press, 1994), pp. 139–154. Reprinted by permission.

19. *Silencing and Nurturing Voice in an Improbable Context: Urban Adolescents in Public School*, Michelle Fine
Reprinted by permission of the publisher. From Michelle Fine and Lois Weis, *Silenced Voices and Extraordinary Conversations: Reimagining Schools*, New York: Teachers College Press. Copyright © 2003 by Teachers College Press, Columbia University. All rights reserved.

20. *Standing for Students, Standing for Change*, George Wood
From Wood, George. "Standing for Students, Standing for Change." As first appeared in *Education Week*, January 24, 2007. Reprinted with permission of the author.

PART V: WHAT ARE THE ISSUES THAT IMPACT TWENTY-FIRST-CENTURY SCHOOLS?

21. *Grouping the Gifted and Talented: Questions and Answers*, K. B. Rogers
From *Roeper Review* 24, no. 3 (September 1993): 102–107. Copyright © 2002 The Roeper School. Reprinted by permission.

22. *Let's Declare Education a Disaster and Get On with Our Lives*, Frank Smith
From *Phi Delta Kappan* 76, no. 8 (1995): 584–590. Copyright © 1999 Phi Delta Kappan, Inc. Reprinted by permission of Frank Smith Educational Associates, Inc.

23. *The Professionally Challenged Teacher: Teachers Talk About School Failure*, Eleanor Blair Hilty
Reprinted by permission of the publisher. From Barry M. Franklin, ed., *When Children Don't Learn: Student Failure and the Culture of Teaching*, New York: Teachers College Press. Copyright © 1998 by Teachers College Press, Columbia University. All rights reserved.

24. *The Educational Costs of Standardization*, Linda McNeil
From *Contradictions of School Reform: Educational Costs of Standardized Testing*, (Routledge, 2000), pp. 229 and 234–243. Copyright © 2000 Taylor and Francis Group, LLC. Reprinted by permission.

25. *From "Separate But Equal" to "No Child Left Behind": The Collision of New Standards and Old Inequalities*, Linda Darling-Hammond
From Darling-Hammond, Linda. "From 'Separate But Equal' to 'No Child Left Behind': The Collision of New Standards and Old Inequalities." Reprinted by permission of The Forum for Education and Democracy.

26. *Closing the Achievement Gap by Detracking*, Carol Corbett Burris and Kevin G. Welner
From *Phi Delta Kappan* 86, no. 8 (April 2005): 594–598. Copyright © 2005 by Phi Delta Kappan, Inc. Reprinted by permission of Phi Delta Kappa International, www.pdkintl.org. All rights reserved.

 Index

Academics, 34, 35, 77, 101, 174, 235, 272, 273, 372, 500
Acceleration, 326, 368, 370, 371–372, 376, 441
Accountability, 38, 82–83, 89, 91, 132, 148, 164, 205, 358, 359, 420, 425, 430, 432, 434, 435 62
"Alice in Wonderland," 426–428
management pedagogy theory and, 186
NCLB and, 428
one-way, 421
two-way, 436
Achievement, 44, 51, 53, 90, 132, 167, 202, 227, 324, 327, 354, 381, 405, 427, 435, 443
academic, 111, 272, 274, 371, 372, 373, 391, 392
decline in, 376, 398, 439
increase in, 181, 420, 430, 439
social class and, 49
student, 203, 365, 395–396, 397, 432
success and, 390
Achievement gaps, 421, 435, 439–440, 441, 443, 462
Adequate Yearly Progress (AYP), 422, 424, 426, 435
Advanced Placement (AP), 368, 372, 374, 442, 461
Alienation, 85, 241, 243–245, 246, 247, 256
America 2000, 390
American Association for the Advancement of Science, 40
American Business Institute (ABI), 345
American Correctional Association, 259
Anaya, Rudolfo, 412
Andreas, Brian, 365
Anyon, Jean, 343

Appalachia, 491, 492, 493–494, 498
Appalachian Regional Commission (ARC), 491
Apple, Michael, 98, 390, 409
Apples and oranges approach, 369–370
Apprenticeship, 511, 513, 514, 515
Arendt, Hannah, 59
Assessments, 197, 216, 273, 380–381, 420, 427, 435
At-risk students, 324–325, 327, 394, 396, 398, 402, 406
curriculum for, 325, 326
teaching, 323, 330, 331, 332, 399–400, 403, 405
Attendance, 10–11, 22, 203, 272, 273
increase/decrease in, 90–91
poor, 9, 425
Attitudes Toward Homosexuality (ATH), 283, 284, 291, 294, 300, 303, 305, 312, 314, 315
comparison among various groups, 293 (fig.)
Authoritarian populists, 135, 139, 147
Authority, 202, 343
Black children and, 166–167
Avituv, Avner, 509
Ayers, William, 98, 394
Ayres, L. P., 33

Bacon, Francis, 241
Bagley, William C., 30, 33, 45, 46
Ball, Stephen, 132
Banking concept, 117–126
Barron, Brigid, 504
Basics, 3, 54, 69, 70–71, 72, 89, 163, 186, 273, 375
Bates, Sharon, 214–215

Beard, Charles A., 210
Behavior, 44, 80, 131, 167, 219, 254, 325,
    399, 402, 405
  irrational, 228, 384
Beliefs, 112, 134, 228, 254, 382, 391,
    399, 402
Bellamy, Carol, 348
Bennett, William, 139
Benson, Lee, 10
Berger, Peter, 146
Best-evidence approach, 369, 370
Bilingual education, 349, 433
Black community, 157, 162, 167, 169,
    404, 405
Black students, 112, 164, 165, 173, 174,
    218–219
  achievement by, 235, 439
  authority and, 166–167
  Black teachers and, 167–168, 171–172,
    219, 404–405
  educational strategies and, 162
  self-esteem for, 478
  special education and, 167–168
  teaching, 107, 109
Black teachers, 157, 158, 159, 162, 164,
    165, 166, 174
  Black students and, 167–168, 171–172,
    219, 404–405
Bourdieu, Pierre, 31
Bowers v. Hardwick (1986), 307
Branham, Tom, 498
Branscombe, Amanda, 164, 165, 170
Brown v. Board of Education (1954), 32, 327,
    430, 446, 448, 462, 499
Bryson, Bill, 493, 495
Bureaucracy, 17, 91, 100, 130, 181
Burgess, Tony, 172
Burris, Carol, 439
Bush, George H. W., 34, 329
Bush, George W., 381, 390, 462,
    463, 498
Butts, Freeman, 16–17, 21
Byrd, Robert, 492

California Education Code (1980), 81
Capitalism, 138, 140, 142, 143, 144,
    145, 495
Careers, 85, 508–510, 511

Carnegie Council for Adolescent
    Development, 443
Carver, George Washington, 110
Castro, Fidel, 246
Caudill, Harry, 493
Cazden, Courtney, 172–173
Center for Educational Statistics, 324
Center for Rural Strategies, 492, 499
Central Intelligence Agency (CIA), 246
Chall, Jeanne, 52
Chapter One projects, 314
Charles A. Beard School, 213, 215, 218
Christianity, 136, 139, 143, 144, 307, 498
Church-state separation, 9, 143–144
Citizenship, 69, 85–86, 111, 238, 253,
    358, 359
Civil rights, 32, 50–54, 108, 318, 419,
    499, 512
  homosexuals and, 303, 306
Clark, Septima, 108
Clinton, Bill, 381
Cloud, Howard, 173
Cochran-Smith, Marilyn, 181, 408
Cognition, 81, 123, 125, 244, 245, 246,
    247, 396, 408
Coleman Report, 32, 33, 44, 52, 439
Collaboration, 104–105, 112, 206, 208–209,
    210–220, 221, 222, 223, 338, 384,
    386, 397, 409, 509
Commitment, 82, 89, 90, 201, 213,
    395–396
Common schools, 79, 332, 389
Communication, 79, 117, 120, 159, 160,
    454, 455–456, 507, 509
Community, 88, 131, 196, 211, 219, 221,
    223, 276, 402
  curriculum and, 45
  democracy and, 30
  education and, 32, 79, 90, 112, 340
  professional, 203, 210
  schools and, 218, 340, 341, 389, 406
Computers, 60, 504, 506, 508, 512,
    514, 515
Conceptual schemes, 39, 40, 207
Connell, Noreen, 450
Consciousness, 120, 122, 123, 124, 125,
    126, 174, 237, 386
  critical, 108, 110–111, 236

Conservative groups, 129, 130, 139, 150
Contact stage, 477, 478, 479
Conversations
    psychologized, 347–348
    shutting down/marginalizing, 345, 354
Core Knowledge Schools, 43
Corrigan, Francis V., 45
Council for Exceptional Children, 328
Counselors, attitudes/feelings about
    homosexuality among, 302–307,
    315–318
Creativity, 87, 117, 118, 253, 374
Cremin, Lawrence, 16, 18, 19–20, 21,
    24, 78
Crockett, Davy, 195
Cross, William, 473, 474, 476, 484
Cubberly, Ellwood P., 7
Cultural competence, 109–110, 111
Cultural forces, 228, 237, 365
Culturally relevant, 107, 108–111
Culture, 75, 135, 141–143, 151, 258, 267,
    374, 387, 391, 465, 474
    anthropological concept of, 123–124
    common, 30, 132
    development/evolution of, 212
    dominant, 235
    education and, 107
    knowledge and, 123, 235
    long-standing, 218
    low-track, 441
    parochial/ethnocentric dimensions of, 237
    power and, 160
    school, 10, 107–108, 213
Curriculum, 78, 82, 90, 97–98, 128, 131,
    185, 205, 209, 229, 235, 253
    academically oriented, 327
    changing, 45, 222, 372, 374, 427
    conceptual, 39, 186
    constructing, 16, 213, 215–217, 221, 222,
    231, 371, 431
    core, 45, 46, 48–50, 53, 54
    critical understanding of, 230
    defining/articulating, 98
    differentiation of, 326–327, 330, 332, 371
    enlightened, 102
    high-track, 439, 440–441
    implications for, 498–499
    integration of, 326, 331–332

ironic, 245–247
local, 37, 38, 39, 41, 43, 45, 54
myth of existing, 36–42
national/state, 45, 49, 113, 136
pre-IB, 442–443
real, 216–217
regular, 411, 416
social action, 111
special, 324–325
standardized, 243, 247, 507
teacher-proof, 185
test-driven, 235
theory-based, 206
Curti, Merle, 17

Dahrendorf, Ralf, 9, 10
Decision-making, 126, 203, 204, 217,
    369, 408
Delpit, Lisa D., 158, 159, 164, 168
Demientieff, Martha, 170, 171
Democracy, 65, 78, 86, 135, 140–141, 236,
    240, 245, 338, 365, 516
    community and, 30
    discipline and, 348–350
    dissent and, 350
    education and, 7, 233, 247, 389, 390
    shared knowledge in, 29–33
    thick, 137, 140
Demographics, 79, 338, 408, 447
Descartes, René, 241
Desegregation, 4, 78–79, 217, 219
Detracking, 439, 440, 441–443
Development, 192, 212, 384, 482, 483, 487
    economic, 139, 142, 503, 516
    educational, 8, 9, 10, 17, 90
    identity, 86, 473, 479, 484
    intellectual, 72, 84, 318, 455
    personal, 72, 387
    staff, 191, 193, 194, 195, 196–197, 199
Developmental stage, 484
Dewey, John, 30, 78, 101, 185, 198
Dickey, James, 493, 496
Disabled children, normalization/integration
    of, 328
Discipline, 135, 348–350
Discrimination, 143, 174, 308, 375,
    470, 483
Disintegration stage, 477, 478, 479, 481

Diversity, 35, 170, 211, 236, 327, 447, 488, 492, 494, 495
  cultural, 169
  intellectual, 232
  values/beliefs about, 254
Donald, David, 25
Dougherty, Charlie, 216–217
Drills, 253, 357, 416, 417
Dropout rates, 324, 344, 393, 394, 408, 419–420, 429
Dropping out, 265, 342, 344, 346, 347, 349, 350, 351, 392, 403, 429, 431, 463
  research on, 340–341
  silencing and, 339
DuBois, W. E. B., 503
Duke, David, 499
Dunn, Lloyd, 328
Durkheim, Emile, 146

Early-education programs, 4, 451, 452
Economic issues, 135, 138, 151, 431
  education and, 30–31, 379–382, 516
  religion and, 144–147
Edgerton, Robert, 275
Education
  adequate, 54, 256
  character of, 143, 461
  continuing, 88
  crisis in, 183–184
  debates over, 134, 136
  democratic, 29, 34, 233, 389
  as domination, 121–122, 123
  equal, 97, 138
  expectations for, 69–70, 80
  formal, 74, 132, 150, 451
  higher, 78, 227, 431
  history of, 5, 8, 14–15, 18–19, 22, 24, 25, 83
  improving, 52, 132, 332, 379, 382, 419, 453
  as institution/process, 18, 19
  options for, 420–421
  problems in, 62, 122, 124, 125, 255–258, 274–279, 327, 379–380, 390
  purpose of, 3, 98, 234, 384
  social role of, 4, 11, 31, 227
  support for, 420–421

  teacher, 185, 210, 230, 234, 294, 295
  technical, 274, 511
  thinking about, 383–385
  See also Bilingual education; Public education; Sex education; Special education; Vocational education
Education for All Handicapped Children Act (Public Law 94–142) (1975), 328, 329, 330
Education reform, 11, 60–61, 64, 89, 131, 149, 151, 187, 238, 247, 503, 514
  appraising, 62–63
  calls for, 59, 183
  hybridization of, 61, 65
  nature/process of, 183, 213
  responsibility for, 205
  struggle for, 223
Education Trust, 516
Educational institutions, 22, 134, 352, 365, 386, 465
Educational Priorities Panel, 450
Elementary and Secondary Education Act (1966), 327–328
Eller, Ron, 493–494
Ellis, C. P., 481
Emotional health, 87, 259, 374
Empowerment, 102–104, 348, 488
Encounter stage, 474, 475, 480, 488
Enculturation, 18, 86, 267, 274, 275
Engels, Friedrich, 144, 146
English, codes of, 170–171
English language learners, 426, 429, 431, 435
Enrichment, 365, 370, 372, 376
Equality, 79, 97, 138, 142, 448, 515
Equity, 52, 97, 101, 390, 503, 516
Erickson, Fred, 161, 390, 396, 397, 405, 407
Ethnicity, 79, 323, 440, 447, 486
Evangelicals, 135, 145, 150, 498
Eyes on the Prize (documentary series), 471

Failure, 399, 408
  school, 391–393, 394, 396–398, 402, 405–406, 407, 409, 420, 423, 425
  student, 396, 398, 406
  teacher, 393–396, 396–398
Farrakhan, Louis, 499

Federal Bureau of Investigation (FBI), 496, 497
Feedback, 193, 196, 197, 214, 221, 222, 394, 397
Ferry, Jules, 29
Finley, M. I., 15
Foster, Michelle, 167, 404–405
Foucault, Michel, 146, 149, 238
Fox, John, Jr., 494
Frank, Thomas, 139
Franks, Leslie, 216–217
Frazier, E. Franklin, 10
Frederiksen, Norman, 510
Freedman's Bureau, 15–16
Freedom, 123, 135, 136–139, 219
Freeman, Ellen, 218–219, 220
Freire, Paulo, 98, 109, 111, 406
Friedman, Milton, 138, 139
Friedman, Thomas, 503
Fuller, Bruce, 424, 432

Garfield, Karen, 219, 220
Garrity, Delia, 441
Gays
 discrimination against, 308
 feelings about, 291, 295, 300, 301 (table), 312 (table)
 respondent association with/high school, 295 (table), 296 (table)
 teacher attitudes about, 293 (table), 294
Geertz, Clifford, 278
General Accounting Office, 43, 44
General equivalency diploma (GED), 165, 274, 341, 344, 345, 351, 496
George, P. S., 368, 369, 375, 377
Gifted and talented students, 235, 253, 369
 academic effect sizes/program options for, 373 (table)
 academic/psychological/socialization effects on, 367
 grouping, 367, 368, 371–373, 374, 375–376
Giroux, Henry A., 181, 211, 406
Goals, 72, 73–74, 78, 80, 81, 82, 83–84, 403, 515
 academic, 53, 84, 233–226, 401
 civic, 85–87

cultural, 85–87
debate about, 229–233, 233–236
educational, 72, 84–91, 227, 229, 230, 234–235, 242
 preferences, student/teacher/parent, 74 (table)
 relative importance of, 73 (table)
social, 66, 73, 85–87, 233–234
teaching, 229–233, 233–236, 236–241, 239
vocational, 72, 84–85
Goals 2000 Act (1990), 427
Goetz, Bernard, 346, 347
Gold, Jenny, 214
Goodlad, John, 5, 343, 365
Goodman, Jesse, 185
Government, 147, 151, 459
 education and, 53, 434, 514–515
 religion and, 144
Gramsci, Antonio, 147, 205, 239, 347
Green, Teresa, 219–220
Greenberger, Rita, 214
Greene, Maxine, 18, 20, 389
Grouping, 365, 369
 effects of, 370, 373–374, 375–376
 elimination of, 367–368
 gifted and talented students and, 367, 371–373, 374, 375–376
Grubis, Kay Rowe, 173
Guidelines, 37–38, 39, 42, 80–81, 82, 112–113, 174
Guizot, François, 29
Gumperz, John, 161
Gwaltney, John, 162

Hall, Stuart, 141
Hamer, Fannie Lou, 446
Harvard Civil Rights Project, 419
Hawthorne, Alice, 496
Head Start, 52–53, 54, 63, 462
Health Professions Education Assistance Act (1963), 434
Heath, Shirley Brice, 165–166
Heller, Craig, 326
Helms, Janet, 473, 474, 477, 478, 479
Helms, Jesse, 307
Hernes, Gudmund, 32
Hewitt, Abram, 142

Hillbillies, 491, 493, 495–496,
   496–498, 499
Hilliard, Patricia, 109, 110
History, 14–15, 62, 125, 383, 463
   public policy and, 21–25
Hobsbawm, Eric, 135–136
Home
   education and, 32, 74–75
   school and, 76, 108
Home schooling, 150, 504
Homophobia, 289, 290, 300, 301–303,
   306–308, 310–311, 315, 318
   low grade, 296
   racism and, 287
   scores various populations, 293 (table)
Homophobics, 291, 292, 300, 301, 312, 317
Homosexuality, 288, 310, 498
   attitudes/feelings about, 216, 284, 289,
      290, 291, 292, 293 (table), 294, 295,
      296, 300, 301, 302–307, 309, 311,
      314, 315, 316, 318
   counselors and, 315–318
   curriculum and, 317
   discussion of, 285, 287, 302, 313,
      314, 315
   harassment about, 285–286, 308
   integrating, 313–314
   knowledge about, 283, 284, 291,
      297–298, 297 (table), 299 (table),
      300 (fig.), 302, 312, 316
   teacher attitudes/feelings about, 289–292,
      292 (fig.), 293 (table), 294–298, 294
      (table), 296 (table), 300–307, 301
      (table), 312 (table)
Homosexuality Knowledge Index (HKI),
   298, 300, 312
Horwitz, Tony, 498
Huckabee, Mike, 492
Huggins, Laura, 287–288, 289
Hughes, Langston, 446
Hull, Thomas Gray, 337
Humphrey, Hubert, 69
Hunter, Madeleine, 238, 367

I found this study approach, 368, 369
I know this student who approach, 368, 369
Identity, 387, 396, 417, 487, 491
   homosexual, 316, 317

racial, 473, 474–476, 478, 488
sexual, 283, 308
Immersion/Emersion stage, 474, 475,
   477, 480
Immersion stage, 475, 476, 480, 486, 488
Improvements, 191, 192, 201, 274, 332,
   379, 386, 419, 420, 430, 436
   school, 204, 426, 427
In the Chute, 259–267
Index of Homophobia (IH), 283, 284,
   291–292, 300, 303, 305, 312, 314,
   315, 317
   most discriminating items on, 305 (table)
   scores among various populations,
      292 (fig.)
   step-wise multiple regression of categoric
      demographic variables onto, 303 (table)
   unidimensionality of, 291
Individualism, 126, 135, 139, 243, 467
Inequities, 4, 338, 453, 458, 464, 514
Information, 202, 203, 232, 296, 478
   dissemination/acquisition of, 385–386
Inquiry, 104, 126, 204, 205, 214, 215,
   218, 221
Instruction, 244, 332
   English only/bilingual, 63
   remedial, 163
Intellectual capital, 31–32, 33, 46, 50, 51, 54
Intellectual work, 101, 184, 210–221
Internalization-Commitment stage, 474, 476
Internalization stage, 474
International Association for the Evaluation
   of Educational Achievement (IEA), 48,
   49, 50
IQ, 31, 33, 234, 246, 272

Jefferson, Thomas, 29, 31, 32, 144, 194, 515
Jenkins, Esau, 108
Jobs, 3, 278, 338, 391, 509
   education and, 359, 511
   learning, 510–512
   middle class and, 268–269
   second-rate, 260–261
Johnson, Karen, 214
Johnson, Lyndon B., 60, 491
Johnson, William, 440, 441
Jones, Constance, 35
Jules-James, Shelia, 212

Kaestle, Carl, 5, 14, 21
Katz, Michael B., 8, 9, 16, 21, 466
Kennan, George, 30
Kennedy, John F., 491
Keogh, Barbara, 329
Kephart, Horace, 494
Keynes, John Maynard, 144
Kim, Phyllis, 217
Knowledge, 31, 110, 117, 135, 187, 196,
    220, 228, 253
  access to, 97
  background, 33–34
  core, 3, 32, 37, 42, 54
  creating, 113, 506
  dissemination/acquisition of, 385–386
  education and, 118
  fallibility of, 232–233
  gaps in, 50, 51
  neutral, 13, 132
  production of, 100, 104, 213, 238,
    241, 242
  self-generated, 482–483
  shared, 33–36, 45, 46–50
  traditional, 41, 135, 331
Kohn, Herb, 101, 402
Kozol, Jonathan, 101, 421, 448
Krashen, Stephen, 384
Kulik, Chen-Lin, 370, 371, 372, 374
Kulik, James, 370, 371, 372, 374

Ladson-Billings, Gloria, 8, 391,
    392, 407
Lampert, Magdalene, 104, 218
Language, 4, 162, 207, 208, 212, 236, 241,
    326, 382–383, 399
  controlling, 384, 385
  holistic, 102–103
  learning, 217
  oral/written, 172
  structure of, 235
  whole, 100, 130, 163
Le Peletier, Louis-Michel, 29
Leadership, 82, 89, 91, 181, 183, 194,
    196–197, 199, 286, 374, 441
  capacity for, 202, 203, 204
  defining, 201–202
  educational, 238, 512–514
  effective, 198, 202, 203–204

Learning, 4, 17, 34, 77, 110, 112, 113,
    203, 254, 273, 274–275, 324, 348,
    383, 385, 386
  attitudes about, 506
  building blocks of, 42
  conception of, 503, 504
  control of, 506
  cooperative, 100, 368, 370, 403
  identification of, 505, 516
  improving, 326, 385, 516
  lifelong, 504, 514
  love of, 32, 506
  mastery, 375, 376
  measures of, 208, 435, 440
  memorization and, 385
  motivation/effort and, 385
  rethinking, 504–505, 507–508
  school, 407, 504
  shared knowledge and, 33–36
  spending on, 507–508
  teaching and, 204, 400, 408, 506
  technology and, 508
  thinking and, 510
Learning disabilities, 327, 329, 330, 331,
    332, 440
Lee, Chung-mei, 503
Lehmann-Haupt, Christopher, 495
Lerman, Robert, 509
Lesbians, 290
  attitudes about, 291, 293 (table),
    294, 295, 300, 301 (table),
    312 (table)
  discrimination against, 308
  respondent association with/high school,
    295 (table), 296 (table)
Levin, Harry, 326
Levine, Arthur, 133
Lewis, Ann, 109, 110
Lewis, Oscar, 259
Lewis, Ronald, 494
Liberalism, 137, 138, 161
Limited English proficient (LEP), 44,
    423, 434
Literacy, 20, 41, 75, 130, 146, 161, 380,
    426, 462, 507
  computer, 60
  instruction, 130, 163, 164
Loban, Walter, 51

Magnet schools, 412
Managerialism, 147–149
Mandates, 80–83, 201
Mann, Horace, 8, 29, 59, 512, 514, 515
Mann, Leticia, 514
Marcuse, Herbert, 244
Marshall, Thurgood, 446
Martin Luther King Middle School, 428
    test scores/student population and,
        428 (table)
Marx, Karl, 139, 141, 144, 146
Math, 383, 403, 411, 417, 441, 514
    ability/distribution of, 46
    scores/distribution of, 46
    TAAS and, 415–416
    technology and, 507–508
    tests/eleventh-grade scores in, 47 (table)
MATH scores, 303 (table), 304 (table),
    305 (table)
MCAS (Massachusetts test), 429, 431
McChesney, Robert, 140
McDill, Edward, 330, 331
McIntosh, Peggy, 477
McKinney, James, 329, 330
Mead, Margaret, 266
Meaning, 227, 232, 239–240, 397
Media, 22, 75, 76, 77, 141, 240, 447,
    463, 493
Mentoring, 220, 416, 433
Meritocracy, 342, 469–472
Messerli, Jonathan, 8, 9
Migrant students, concerns about, 42–46, 54
Minorities, 13, 235, 267, 421, 424, 440, 479
Mitchell, Lucy Sprague, 101
Modernization, 7, 8, 149–151
Montessori programs, 452
Moral issues, 76, 77, 86, 87, 136, 139,
    142, 220
Motivation, 376, 385, 395, 505–506, 507
Multiculturalism, 81, 230, 235, 465,
    492, 498
Murphy (town), described, 496–498
Mussolini, Benito, 239

Nation at Risk, A, 59
National Academy of Sciences, 40
National Assessment of Educational Progress
    (NAEP), 324, 423

National Center for Education Statistics, 429
National Council of Teachers of English,
    414–415
National Council of Teachers of
    Mathematics, 508
National Council of Teachers of Science, 40
National Education Goals, 390
National Endowment for the Arts, 307
National Governors' Association, 381, 443
National Institute of Education, 22
National Research Council, 443
Native Americans, 19, 158, 168, 169,
    173, 235
Natriello, Gary, 330, 331
NCLB. *See* No Child Left Behind
Neoconservatives, 135, 139, 147, 149, 151
Neoliberalism, 135, 138, 139, 140, 142,
    147, 149, 150, 151
New Futures Initiatives, 325, 331
New York Board of Education, 450
New York City Board of Education,
    337, 341
New York State Regents diploma, 440–441,
    442, 442 (fig.)
Newhart, Tracey, 431
Newton, Sir Isaac, 241
No Child Left Behind (NCLB), 148, 149,
    419, 426–427, 429–430, 433, 434,
    436, 462, 513
    accountability and, 428
    fixing, 431–432
    funding, 435
    LEP and, 423, 424
    neediest students and, 422–426
    problems with, 420, 421–422, 514
    theory of action and, 424–425
Nord, Warren, 144

Oakes, Jeannie, 368, 369, 375, 377
O'Keeffe, Dennis, 35
Opportunity, 77, 221, 398, 422
    curriculum, 432, 435
    educational, 49, 50, 80, 220, 389,
        390, 427
    equal, 79, 338, 342, 390, 392,
        515, 516
    learning, 209
Opportunity to Learn, 432, 435

Orfield, Gary, 503
Outcomes, 17, 23, 33, 191, 338, 384, 394, 425, 453

Paige, Rod, 457
Pallas, Aaron, 330, 331
Parham, Thomas, 475
Parks, Rosa, 346
Participation, 86, 112, 202–203, 344
Pedagogy, 20, 159, 185, 187, 228, 229, 231, 239, 240, 242, 327, 343, 344, 354, 406, 408, 454
  classroom, 184, 244
  conservative religious groups and, 150
  critical, 108, 149, 243
  culturally relevant, 108–111
  excellence in, 107
  forms of, 188
  implications for, 498–499
  ineffective, 339, 346
  learning and, 186
  participatory, 339
  strategies for, 401
Pennsylvania Education Department, 45
Performance, 196, 358, 371, 392, 394, 420, 426, 428, 436, 440, 515
  assessments, 427, 435
  learning and, 427
  progress and, 432
  restructuring and, 197
Pewewardy, Cornel, 107
Physicians, 434, 449–450
Pinker, Steven, 36
Pioneers, 195–196, 198, 199
Planning, 37–38, 83, 186, 331–332, 382, 408
Plessy v. Ferguson (1896), 448, 499
Policy, 32, 48, 91, 135, 142, 332
  formation, 22, 23, 24, 25, 89
  public, 17–21, 21–25
Politics, 16, 20, 86, 129, 131, 135
  dynamics of, 187
  education and, 30–31, 63–64, 134, 188, 234
  gender, 150
Positivism, 241, 242, 243, 244–245, 246, 247
Poverty, 131, 323, 324, 338, 347, 392, 394, 409, 505

Power, 60, 167, 187, 206, 238–239
  culture of, 129, 159, 160–161, 163, 169, 173
  economic, 16, 129, 131
  knowledge and, 188, 486
  literacy of, 233
  meaning and, 239–240
  political, 16, 129, 131
  questions of, 236–241
  redistribution of, 24, 202
  relations, 188, 348
Practice, 102, 207, 240
  problems of, 213–215
Pratt, Caroline, 101
Preencounter stage, 474
Prejudice, 307, 467–468, 469
Preschool, 50, 53, 54, 392, 451, 453
Principals, 102, 111–112, 201
Private schools, 129
Privatization, 231, 234, 240, 357, 420, 435, 515
Problem-posing method, 123, 126
Problem solving, 111, 326, 380, 381
Professional attitudes, 307–308, 310–318
Professional Attitudes Index, 311, 312, 314, 315
Proficiency, 113, 274, 416, 422, 423
Progress, 197, 380, 431, 432, 435
Progressive education, 39, 158, 162, 163, 213, 218, 221
Project START, 209
Projected activities, 307–308, 310–318
PSAT, 285, 317
Pseudo-Independent stage, 477, 480
Public education, 8, 11, 17, 232, 337, 345, 357, 431, 457
  commitment to, 43, 213, 420
  democracy and, 247
Public schools, 5, 13, 16–17, 82, 133, 231, 273, 327, 331, 338, 351, 391, 406, 453
  academic/vocational, 70
  accessibility of, 323
  creation of, 7, 9
  criticism of, 71
  enrollment in, 445
  importance of, 389
  improving, 59, 62, 183
  support for, 4, 7

Quality, 80, 183, 327, 422, 504
  educational, 47, 48, 71, 72, 78, 79, 90,
    149, 425, 439

Race, 4, 78, 220, 338, 440, 465, 467,
    474, 485
  awareness of, 476
  questions about, 469
Racial identity development, 465,
    466–468, 485
  Black, 466, 474–476
  institutions and, 487–488
  racism and, 483
  stages of, 473–476, 484, 486
  White, 477–482, 484
Racism, 4, 307, 445, 453, 465, 475,
    477, 478, 479, 480, 486,
    487–488, 499
  avoiding subject of, 471–472
  confronting, 476, 481, 482
  cultural, 470, 477
  discussion of, 345, 467, 471, 485
  homophobia and, 287
  institutional, 169, 477
  learning about, 467, 474
  psychology of, 465, 466, 468, 485
  reality of, 466, 470, 483–485
  teaching and, 466, 482–487
  unlearning, 467–468
  White, 469, 486
Reading, 215, 216–217, 274, 381, 411,
    416, 513
  free voluntary, 384
  median ability/chronological-age/
    school-age level and, 51 (table)
  TAAS and, 412–414
Reagan, Ronald, 329
Real school, 64, 65
Reform schools, 60, 267, 273
Regular Education Initiative (REI),
    328, 329
Reich, Robert, 31
Reintegration stage, 477, 479, 480
Relationships, 201, 206, 220, 222,
    237, 238, 243, 247, 295,
    402, 406
  district-school, 204
  homosexual, 302, 314

social, 112, 135, 141, 146, 214, 222,
    244, 385, 407
  teacher-student, 117, 118, 209, 289,
    400, 401
Religion, 10, 87, 103, 136, 139, 143,
    307, 498
  economics and, 144–147
Religious schools, 129
Research, 13, 104, 110, 163–164, 208, 242,
    245, 367, 369, 370, 372, 396, 439
  psychological, 33, 509
  silencing and, 340–341, 353–354
  teacher, 113, 207
Resistance, sources of, 468–473
Resources, 338, 503, 505, 511, 513
  allocation of, 24, 185
Responsibility, 72, 77, 80, 82, 83, 88, 89,
    91, 99, 140, 148, 169, 174, 186, 205,
    211, 220, 253, 254, 358, 365, 389,
    393, 399, 400, 407, 514, 515
  collective, 203, 276, 279, 406
  corporate, 509
  democratic, 359
  professional, 289
  roles and, 181, 223
  social, 209, 221, 466
  teacher, 181, 396, 406
Restructuring, 191, 192–193, 197, 198
Rich, Adrienne, 340
Rightist movements, mapping, 134–136
Robeson, Paul, 351, 446
Robinson, Jackie, 446
Rogers, Hal, 492
Rogers, K. B., 370, 371, 372, 374
Roles, 193, 203, 222, 223, 393, 396
Rorty, Richard, 133–134
Rossi, Margaret, 113
Rudolph, Eric, 496, 498

Saboteurs, described, 198–199
Sartre, Jean Paul, 124
Scarr, Sandra, 36
Schlafly, Phyllis, 337
School prayer, 63, 187
School reform, 5, 8, 9, 17, 61, 64, 102, 134,
    181, 199, 201, 205, 209, 221, 223,
    357, 358, 359, 414, 454
  culture of, 210–220

discussing, 390
implementing, 63
mobility rates and, 43
School-site meetings, 209, 210, 216,
    221, 222
School-to-Work Opportunities Act
    (1994), 512
Schooling, 61, 70, 77, 78, 79, 82, 132, 148,
    149, 169, 207, 211, 227, 259, 278
  criticism of, 69, 276
  education and, 72, 91, 256, 279, 504, 514
  formal, 272–274, 351, 389, 516
  goals for, 80, 84–91
  identification of, 505
  improving, 63, 81
  learning and, 504
  politics of, 188, 208
  professionalization of, 220
  purposes/conditions of, 187
  systematization of, 76
  thinking about, 59–60
  universal, 506, 515
Schools
  adequate, 255–258, 274–279
  expectations for, 72, 74, 77–79, 358
  improving, 381, 425, 504
  influence of, 75
  parents view of, 70–74
  restructured, 103, 331
  role of, 69, 78, 90, 389
  shortcomings of, 432
  See also Public schools
Science, 38, 48, 246–247, 403, 514
Segregation, 217, 218, 219, 220, 327, 328,
    330, 445, 446, 454, 459
  ethnic, 332
  racial, 332, 447, 448
Self-esteem, 13–14, 109, 212, 374, 403, 478
Self-interest, 137, 139, 231, 380
Separate but equal, 448
Separatists, 197, 463, 488
Settlers, described, 196–197
Sex education, 45, 60, 283, 286–287, 288
Sexuality, 284, 285–286, 298
Shakespeare, William, 165, 415
Silencing, 348–350, 455
  administrative, 341–343
  analysis of, 339–340, 352

in public schools, 337, 338, 339, 344, 352
  research and, 340–341, 353–354
  resistance to, 350–352
Simmons, Leo, 259
Sizer, Theodore, 253, 343
Skills, 51, 100, 193, 207, 235, 273, 274,
    331, 508
  communication, 236
  deficiencies in, 113
  development of, 192, 193, 195, 196
  entrepreneurial, 506
  evaluating, 234
  intellectual, 72, 253
  knowledge and, 391, 407, 509
  organizational, 512
  political, 108
  process and, 159, 173, 174
  social, 108, 374
  teaching, 41, 385
  writing, 164, 168, 415
Skinner, B. F., 454
Slavin, Robert E., 369, 370, 372, 375, 377
Social class, 4, 17, 49, 343, 405
Social growth, 85, 88, 318
Social inequities, 30, 108, 111, 149,
    341, 345
Social injustice, 50, 63, 188
Social issues, 4, 21–22, 286
Social justice, 4, 50, 97, 101, 138, 147, 492
Social movements, 134, 135, 150, 205
Social problems, 4, 22, 34, 348, 390
Social Security, 516
Socialization, 307, 374, 398, 467
Society, 42, 87, 220, 227, 267, 469, 503
  public schools, 390, 409
Socioeconomic status (SES), 9, 240, 398,
    440, 442, 443
Soto, Gary, 412
South Bronx, 345–346, 349, 445, 446, 449,
    454, 456
South Carolina Guidance Counselors'
    Association, 283
Southern Poverty Law Center, 499
Special education, 4, 157, 323, 328, 330,
    395, 433, 440, 441, 442
  black students and, 167–168
  segregated, 329
Spellman, Polly, 19, 219

Squire, Kurt, 506
Standards, 228, 229, 357, 358, 381, 390,
    433, 448
    exclusionary, 168–169
    movements, 238
    raising, 129
Stay-at-homes, described, 197–198
Stereotypes, 467, 477, 480, 493, 494, 500
    Black, 474
    evangelical, 498
    hillbilly, 491, 492, 495, 496, 499
    racial/ethnic/regional/social
        class/gendered, 470, 472, 495
Stevenson, Harold, 34–35, 46
Stewart, Michael, 350
Stigler, James, 34–35, 35
Straits, Bruce C., 44
Student mobility, problems with, 43–45
Student teachers, 206, 207, 208, 209, 210,
    218, 220–223
Students
    as change agents, 485–487
    fewer, 428–431
    high-achieving, 47, 441
    low-achieving, 325, 332, 403, 428
    roles/responsibilities of, 253, 254
    saving, 385–386
    successful, 395, 396, 397, 398
    teachers and, 108, 112, 387, 400,
        401, 407
    test scores and, 428 (table)
    See also Black students; White students
Study of Schooling, A, 70, 72, 80, 83, 89
Success, 236, 391, 390, 399, 400, 407
    academic, 108–109, 236, 402
    challenge of, 402–404
    student, 395, 396, 397, 398
    teacher, 395, 397
Success for All (SFA), 238, 454, 458, 462

TAAS, 411–417
Taylor, Frederick, 455
Teacher-researcher groups, 210, 211, 212,
    214, 216, 218, 221, 222
Teachers
    adolescent perceptions of, 284–289
    agreement about expected professional
        activities among, 313 (table)

attitudes/feelings about homosexuality
    among, 289–292, 294–298, 300–307,
    308, 309 (table), 310–315
    critical, 239, 240
    effective, 184, 395–396, 434
    expectation of engaging in supportive
        activities by, 316 (table)
    high/low professional attitudes of, 312
        (table)
    as information deliverers, 242
    as intellectuals, 186–188
    nature/purpose of, 183, 184–185, 187
    professional, 76, 202, 231, 284
    qualified, 422, 432–436
    role of, 181, 187, 286, 396, 405
    scores for/expectation of engaging in
        supportive activities, 314 (table)
    shortage of, 393, 433
    students and, 108, 112, 387, 400,
        407, 410
    successful, 395, 397, 398
    thoughts of, 398–405
    See also Black teachers; White teachers
Teaching, 4, 83, 129, 228, 231, 238, 275
    bureaucracy and, 100
    challenge of, 402
    culturally relevant, 109, 110–111,
        111–113, 391
    culture of, 208, 213, 217, 222
    debate about, 229–233
    described, 394–396
    devaluing/deskilling, 184–186, 231, 234
    dilemmas of, 217–220
    improving, 104
    information about, 229, 385
    language of, 211–213
    learning and, 204, 400, 408, 506
    moral base of, 220
    nature/purpose of, 230
    orientation to, 236–237
    proletarianization of, 184
    protocols and, 458
    reforming, 102, 205, 208
    satisfactions/dissatisfactions of, 398
    strategies for, 107, 112, 213, 221
    visions of, 222–223
Teaching against the grain, 205,
    208–210, 408

Technology, 19, 22, 38, 63, 84, 130, 186,
510, 513, 514, 515
  communication, 79
  economic development and, 516
  equity and, 516
  information, 503, 512
  learning, 505, 506, 508
  math and, 507–508
  media, 325
Test scores, 3, 357, 376, 392, 408,
425, 426
  decline in, 69, 71
  high, 397, 412, 428–431
  raising, 228, 230, 419, 429, 430,
453, 463
  student population and, 428 (table)
Tests, 33, 131, 218, 285, 385, 422–426,
427, 430, 431
  achievement, 132
  assessments and, 381
  grade-level, 424
  high-stakes, 130, 136, 253, 386, 419, 429,
431, 432, 452
  national/state, 136
  standardized, 3, 217, 228, 241, 370,
381, 411
  teaching to, 391
Textbooks, 37, 81, 89, 99, 111, 113, 130,
159, 232, 337, 345
Thailing, Mary, 217
Thinking, 84, 120, 213, 508, 510
  critical, 32, 101, 119, 123, 129, 185, 186,
207, 253, 428
  higher-order, 234, 326, 436
  practice and, 186
Titmuss, Richard, 23–24
Tracking, 369, 439–440, 443
Trailblazers, 193–195, 196, 199
Transitions, 212, 510–512
Tyack, David, 5, 21, 24
Tyler, Ralph W., 80, 83

Unemployment, 69, 338, 344, 347, 510
U.S. Department of Commerce, 403
U.S. Department of Education, 45, 329,
423, 424, 427
U.S. Department of Health and Human
Services, 52

U.S. Department of Health Education and
Welfare (HEW), 52
U.S. Department of Labor, 338
U.S. Office of Education, 22

Value-added approaches, 429, 435
Values, 86, 135, 138, 242, 254, 391, 399,
402, 405
Van Tassel-Baska, Joyce, 367–368
Vision, 30, 218, 222–223, 227, 229, 503,
504, 515
VISIONS, 307
Vocational education, 60, 72, 78, 84–85,
511, 512
Von Hayek, Friedrich, 138, 139
Vouchers, 129, 130, 131, 136, 420, 503

Walberg, Herbert, 44
Wall metaphor, 400–401
War on poverty, 60, 491
Warren, Donald, 5
Watson-Gage, Sherry, 211–212
Welfare, 119, 277, 516
Welter, Rush, 8
White House Conference on Education
(1965), 69
White students, 164, 166, 477, 480
  prejudice/racism and, 469, 470, 471,
473, 487
  self-definition by, 481
White teachers, 159, 162, 164
  Black children and, 166
Whitehead, Alfred North, 14
Whiteness, 475, 477, 479, 480, 482
Whyte, William, 10
Williams v. California (2001), 421, 422
Williamson, J. W., 495–496
Wilson, Darlene, 494
Winston, Gertrude, 110
Winthrop, John, 136
Wood, David, 44
World Trade Organization, 140
Worldview, 267–272, 278
Writing, 164, 168, 169, 172, 173, 337,
411
  TAAS and, 414–415

Zigler, Edward, 52